CAPTAIN MARVEL

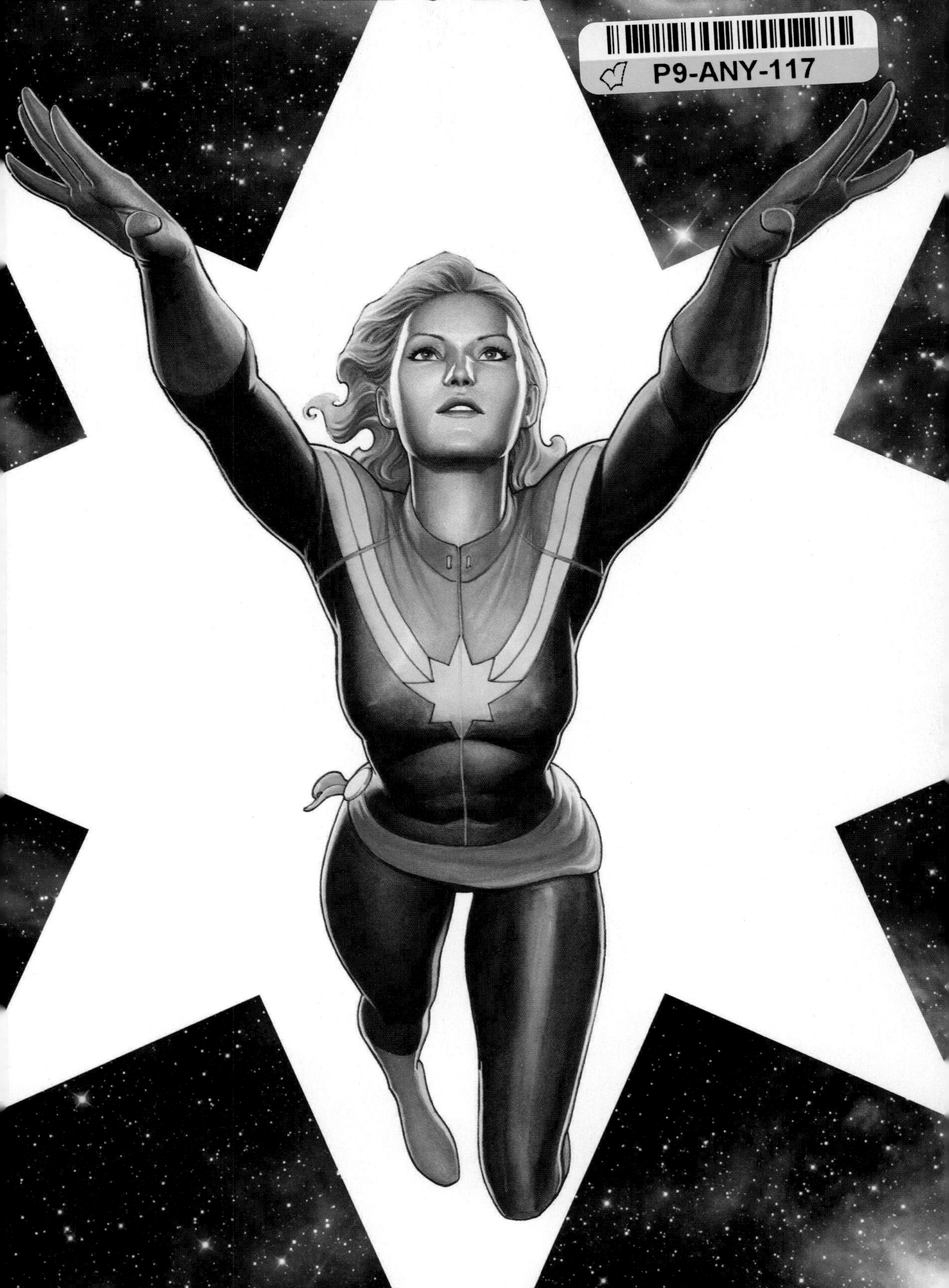

THE MANY LIVES OF CAROL DANVERS

COLLECTION EDITOR: MARK D. BEAZLEY
ASSISTANT MANAGING EDITOR: MAIA LOY
ASSISTANT MANAGING EDITOR: LISA MONTALBANO
ASSOCIATE MANAGER, DIGITAL ASSETS: JOE HOCHSTEIN
MASTERWORKS EDITOR: CORY SEDLMEIER
SENIOR EDITOR, SPECIAL PROJECTS: JENNIFER GRÜNWALD
VP PRODUCTION & SPECIAL PROJECTS: JEFF YOUNGQUIST
RESEARCH & LAYOUT: JEPH YORK
BOOK DESIGNER: RODOLFO MURAGUCHI
SVP PRINT, SALES & MARKETING: DAVID GABRIEL
EDITOR IN CHIEF: C.B. CEBULSKI

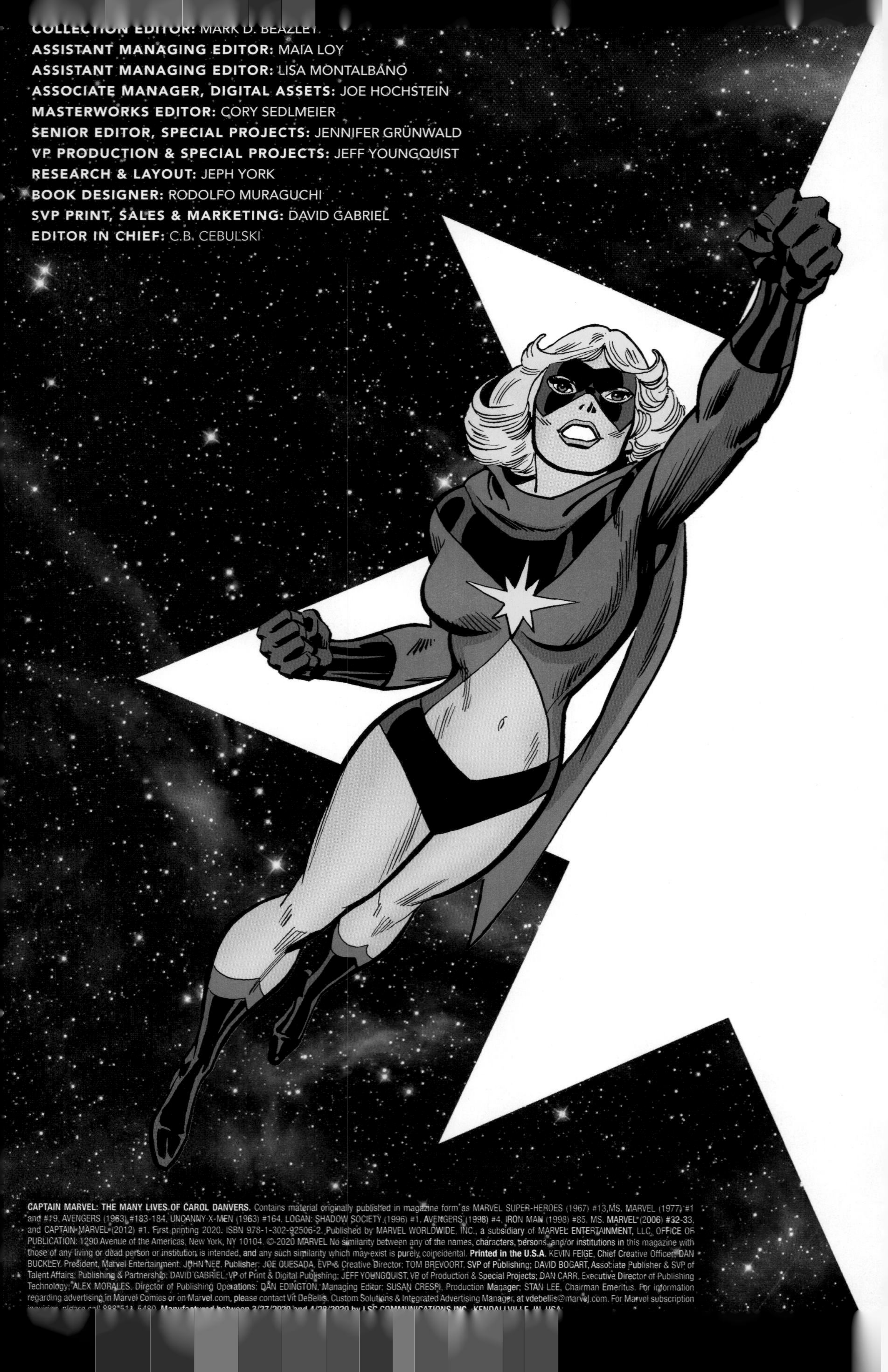

CAPTAIN MARVEL: THE MANY LIVES OF CAROL DANVERS. Contains material originally published in magazine form as MARVEL SUPER-HEROES (1967) #13,MS. MARVEL (1977) #1 and #19, AVENGERS (1963) #183-184, UNCANNY X-MEN (1963) #164, LOGAN: SHADOW SOCIETY (1996) #1, AVENGERS (1998) #4, IRON MAN (1998) #85, MS. MARVEL (2006) #32-33, and CAPTAIN MARVEL (2012) #1. First printing 2020. ISBN 978-1-302-92506-2. Published by MARVEL WORLDWIDE, INC., a subsidiary of MARVEL ENTERTAINMENT, LLC. OFFICE OF PUBLICATION: 1290 Avenue of the Americas, New York, NY 10104. **Printed in the U.S.A.** KEVIN FEIGE, Chief Creative Officer; DAN BUCKLEY, President, Marvel Entertainment; JOHN NEE, Publisher; JOE QUESADA, EVP & Creative Director; TOM BREVOORT, SVP of Publishing; DAVID BOGART, Associate Publisher & SVP of Talent Affairs; Publishing & Partnership; DAVID GABRIEL, VP of Print & Digital Publishing; JEFF YOUNGQUIST, VP of Production & Special Projects; DAN CARR, Executive Director of Publishing Technology; ALEX MORALES, Director of Publishing Operations; DAN EDINGTON, Managing Editor; SUSAN CRESPI, Production Manager; STAN LEE, Chairman Emeritus. For information regarding advertising in Marvel Comics or on Marvel.com, please contact Vit DeBellis, Custom Solutions & Integrated Advertising Manager, at vdebellis@marvel.com. For Marvel subscription inquiries, please call 888-511-5480. **Manufactured between 3/27/2020 and 4/28/2020 by LSC COMMUNICATIONS INC., KENDALLVILLE, IN, USA.**

CAPTAIN MARVEL
THE MANY LIVES OF CAROL DANVERS

MARVEL SUPER-HEROES #13, MARCH 1968
WRITER: Roy Thomas
PENCILER: Gene Colan
INKER: Paul Reinman
COLORIST: Stan Goldberg
LETTERER: Sam Rosen
COVER ART: Gene Colan
EDITOR: Stan Lee

MS. MARVEL #1, JANUARY 1977
WRITER: Gerry Conway
PENCILER: John Buscema
INKER: Joe Sinnott
COLORIST: Marie Severin
LETTERER: John Costanza
COVER ART: John Romita Sr. & Dick Giordano
EDITOR: Gerry Conway

MS. MARVEL #19, AUGUST 1978
WRITER: Chris Claremont
PENCILER: Carmine Infantino
INKER: Bob McLeod
COLORIST: Janice Cohen
LETTERER: Joe Rosen
COVER ART: John Romita Jr. & Josef Rubinstein
ASSISTANT EDITOR: Jim Salicrup
EDITOR: Roger Stern

AVENGERS #183-184, MAY-JUNE 1979
WRITER: David Michelinie
PENCILER: John Byrne
INKERS: Klaus Janson & more
COLORIST: Bob Sharen
LETTERERS: Jim Novak & Diana Albers
COVER ART: George Pérez & Terry Austin
ASSISTANT EDITOR: Jim Salicrup
EDITOR: Roger Stern

UNCANNY X-MEN #164, DECEMBER 1982
WRITER: Chris Claremont
PENCILER: Dave Cockrum
INKER: Bob Wiacek
COLORIST: Janine Casey
LETTERER: Joe Rosen
COVER ART: Dave Cockrum & Bob Wiacek
ASSISTANT EDITOR: Danny Fingeroth
EDITOR: Louise Jones

FRONT COVER ARTISTS: Dave Cockrum,
Bob Wiacek & Veronica Gandini

BACK COVER ARTISTS: John Romita Sr.,
Dick Giordano & Morry Hollowell

LOGAN: SHADOW SOCIETY, DECEMBER 1996
PLOTTER: Howard Mackie
SCRIPTER: Mark Jason
PENCILER: Tomm Coker
INKERS: Keith Aiken with Octavio Cariello
COLORIST: Christie Scheele
COLOR SEPARATIONS: Malibu
LETTERER: Richard Starkings &
Comicraft's Emerson Miranda
COVER ART: Tomm Coker & Keith Aiken
ASSISTANT EDITOR: Dan Hosek
EDITORS: Mark Bernardo & Mark Powers

AVENGERS #4, MAY 1998
WRITER: Kurt Busiek
PENCILER: George Pérez
INKERS: Al Vey & Bob Wiacek
COLORIST: Tom Smith
LETTERER: Richard Starkings &
Comicraft's Dave Lanphear
COVER ART: George Pérez & Tom Smith
ASSISTANT EDITOR: Gregg Schigiel
EDITOR: Tom Brevoort

IRON MAN #85, AUGUST 2004
WRITER: John Jackson Miller
ARTIST: Jorge Lucas
COLORIST: Studio F's Antonio Fabela
LETTERER: VC's Randy Gentile
COVER ART: Steve Epting & Laura Martin
ASSISTANT EDITORS: Andy Schmidt
& Nicole Wiley
EDITOR: Tom Brevoort

MS. MARVEL #32-33, DECEMBER 2008-JANUARY 2009
WRITER: Brian Reed
PENCILERS: Paulo Siqueira (#32) &
Adriana Melo (#33)
INKERS: Amilton Santos (#32) &
Mariah Benes (#33)
COLORIST: Chris Sotomayor
LETTERER: Dave Sharpe
COVER ART: David Yardin & Rain Beredo
ASSISTANT EDITOR: Thomas Brennan
EDITOR: Stephen Wacker

CAPTAIN MARVEL #1, SEPTEMBER 2012
WRITER: Kelly Sue DeConnick
ARTIST & COLORIST: Dexter Soy
LETTERER: VC's Joe Caramagna
COVER ART: Ed McGuinness, Dexter Vines &
Javier Rodríguez
ASSISTANT EDITOR: Ellie Pyle
ASSOCIATE EDITOR: Sana Amanat
EDITOR: Stephen Wacker

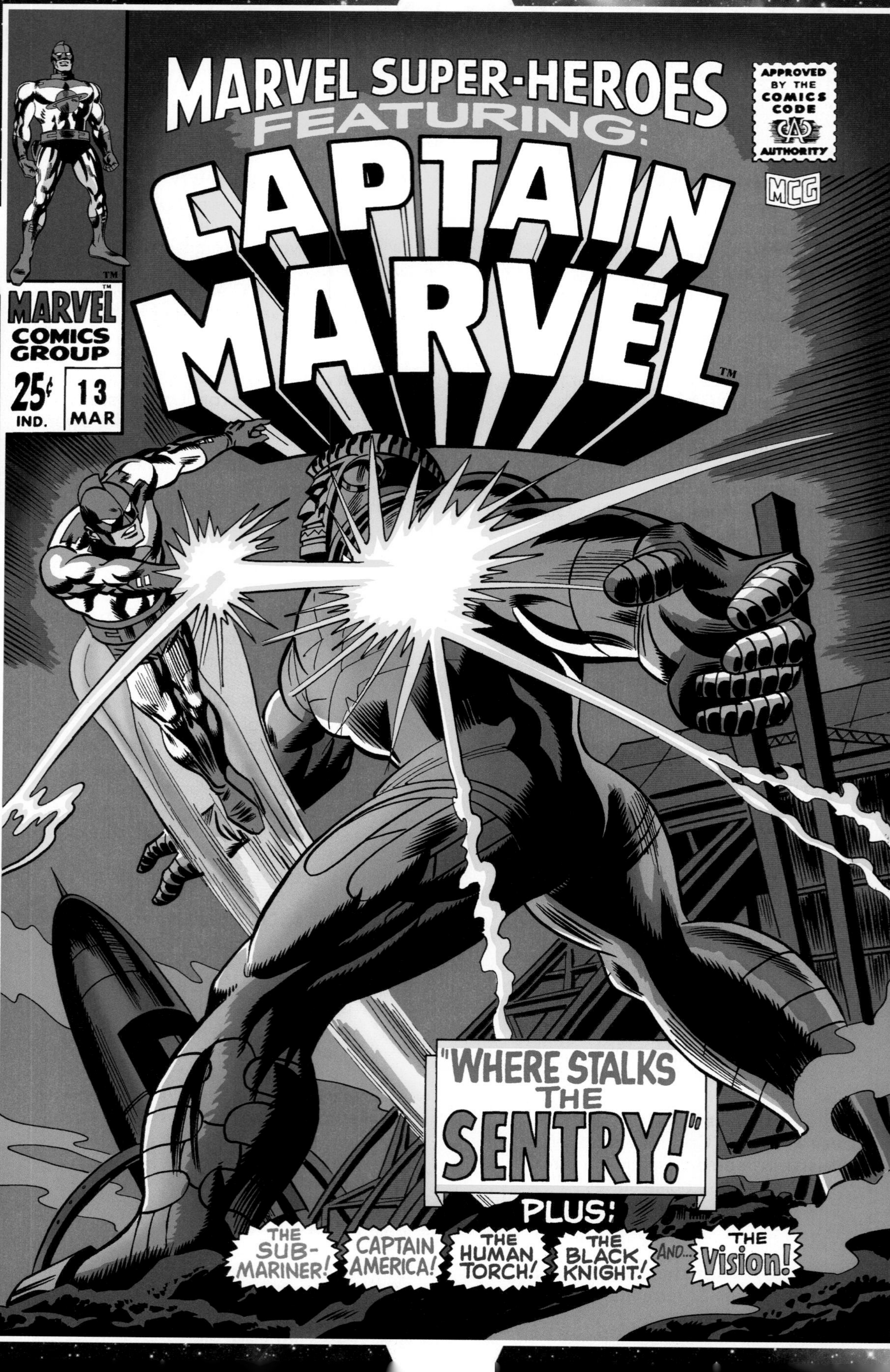

MARVEL SUPER-HEROES
FEATURING:
CAPTAIN MARVEL
APPROVED BY THE COMICS CODE AUTHORITY
MCG
MARVEL COMICS GROUP
25¢ IND.
13 MAR
"WHERE STALKS THE SENTRY!"
PLUS:
THE SUB-MARINER!
CAPTAIN AMERICA!
THE HUMAN TORCH!
THE BLACK KNIGHT!
AND... THE Vision!

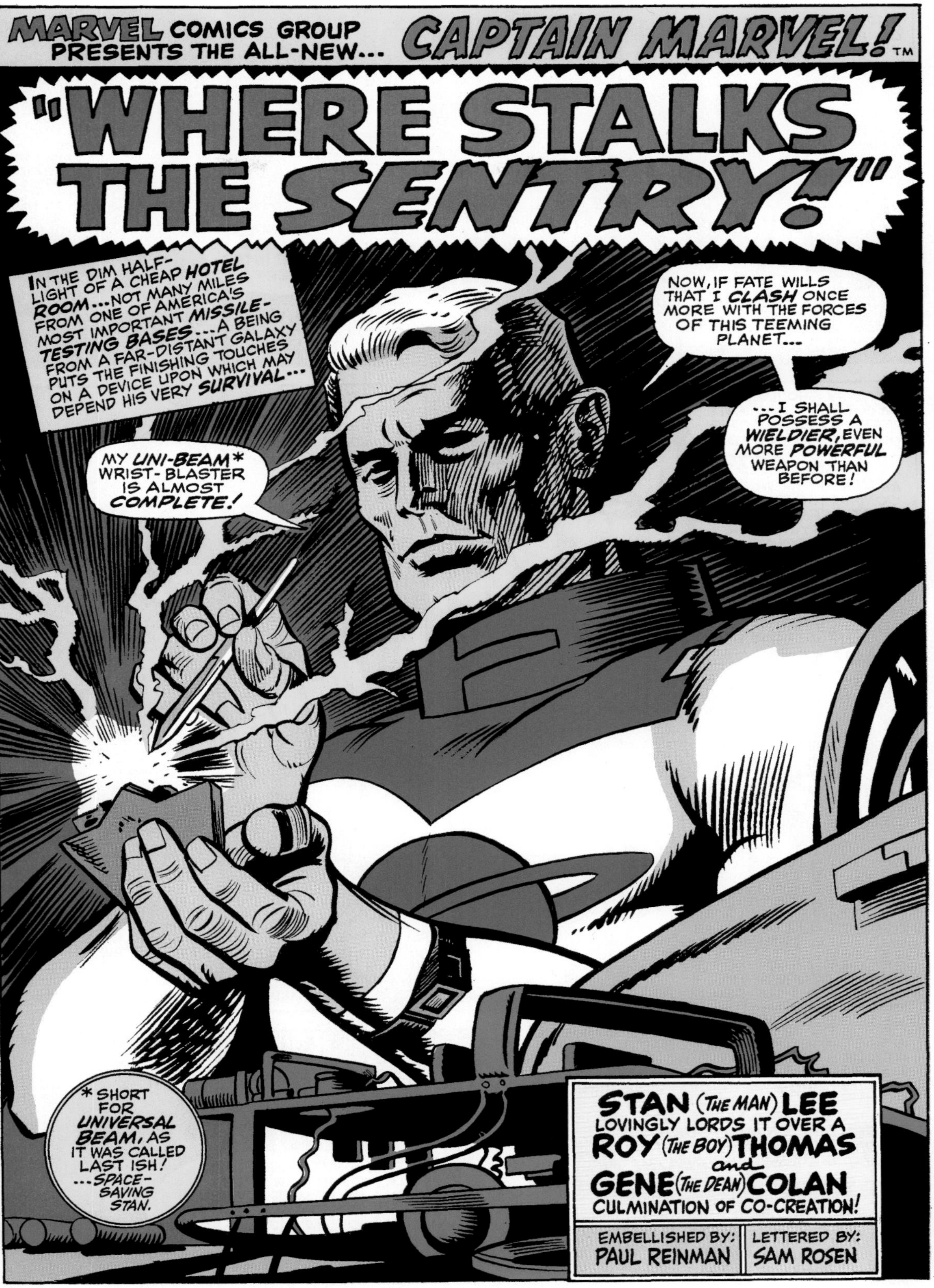
MARVEL COMICS GROUP PRESENTS THE ALL-NEW... CAPTAIN MARVEL! TM
"WHERE STALKS THE SENTRY!"
IN THE DIM HALF-LIGHT OF A CHEAP HOTEL ROOM... NOT MANY MILES FROM ONE OF AMERICA'S MOST IMPORTANT MISSILE-TESTING BASES... A BEING FROM A FAR-DISTANT GALAXY PUTS THE FINISHING TOUCHES ON A DEVICE UPON WHICH MAY DEPEND HIS VERY SURVIVAL...
MY UNI-BEAM* WRIST-BLASTER IS ALMOST COMPLETE!
NOW, IF FATE WILLS THAT I CLASH ONCE MORE WITH THE FORCES OF THIS TEEMING PLANET...
...I SHALL POSSESS A WIELDIER, EVEN MORE POWERFUL WEAPON THAN BEFORE!
* SHORT FOR UNIVERSAL BEAM, AS IT WAS CALLED LAST ISH! ...SPACE-SAVING STAN.
STAN (THE MAN) LEE LOVINGLY LORDS IT OVER A ROY (THE BOY) THOMAS and GENE (THE DEAN) COLAN CULMINATION OF CO-CREATION!
EMBELLISHED BY: PAUL REINMAN
LETTERED BY: SAM ROSEN

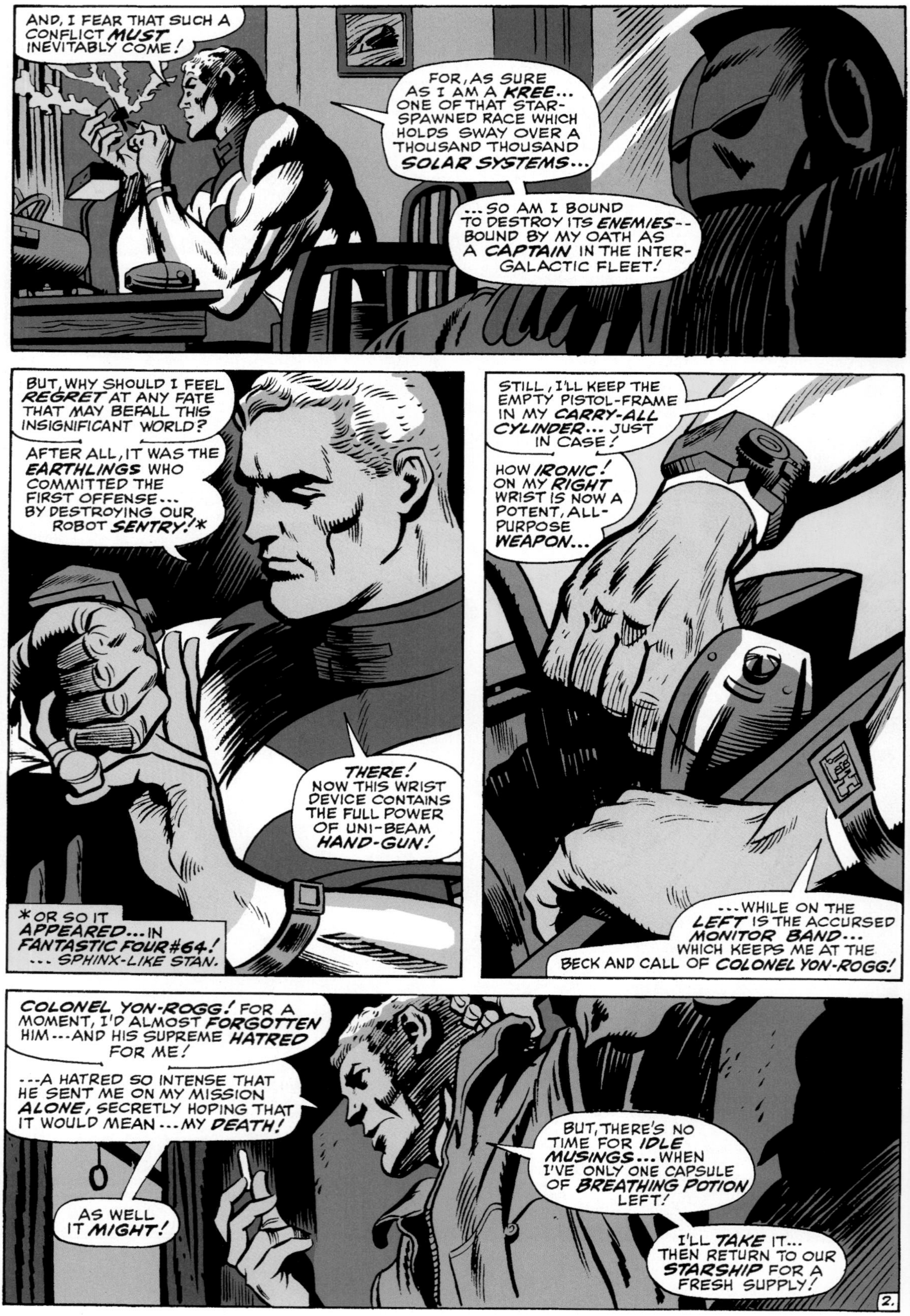
AND, I FEAR THAT SUCH A CONFLICT MUST INEVITABLY COME!
FOR, AS SURE AS I AM A KREE... ONE OF THAT STAR-SPAWNED RACE WHICH HOLDS SWAY OVER A THOUSAND THOUSAND SOLAR SYSTEMS...
...SO AM I BOUND TO DESTROY ITS ENEMIES-- BOUND BY MY OATH AS A CAPTAIN IN THE INTER-GALACTIC FLEET!
BUT, WHY SHOULD I FEEL REGRET AT ANY FATE THAT MAY BEFALL THIS INSIGNIFICANT WORLD?
AFTER ALL, IT WAS THE EARTHLINGS WHO COMMITTED THE FIRST OFFENSE... BY DESTROYING OUR ROBOT SENTRY!*
THERE! NOW THIS WRIST DEVICE CONTAINS THE FULL POWER OF UNI-BEAM HAND-GUN!
*OR SO IT APPEARED... IN FANTASTIC FOUR #64! ... SPHINX-LIKE STAN.
STILL, I'LL KEEP THE EMPTY PISTOL-FRAME IN MY CARRY-ALL CYLINDER... JUST IN CASE!
HOW IRONIC! ON MY RIGHT WRIST IS NOW A POTENT, ALL-PURPOSE WEAPON...
...WHILE ON THE LEFT IS THE ACCURSED MONITOR BAND... WHICH KEEPS ME AT THE BECK AND CALL OF COLONEL YON-ROGG!
COLONEL YON-ROGG! FOR A MOMENT, I'D ALMOST FORGOTTEN HIM---AND HIS SUPREME HATRED FOR ME!
---A HATRED SO INTENSE THAT HE SENT ME ON MY MISSION ALONE, SECRETLY HOPING THAT IT WOULD MEAN---MY DEATH!
AS WELL IT MIGHT!
BUT, THERE'S NO TIME FOR IDLE MUSINGS... WHEN I'VE ONLY ONE CAPSULE OF BREATHING POTION LEFT!
I'LL TAKE IT... THEN RETURN TO OUR STARSHIP FOR A FRESH SUPPLY!
2.

THUS, DOWNSTAIRS, A FEW MINUTES LATER...

LEAVIN' IN THE MIDDLE OF THE *NIGHT*, SON?

WELL, I *NEVER!* HE ACTS LIKE HE DIDN'T EVEN *HEAR* ME!

AND, HE'S TAKING THAT FUNNY-LOOKING *SUITCASE* OF HIS WITH HIM!

WHAT KIND OF BAG *IS* THAT, ANYWAY? IT SURE WON'T HOLD ANY FRESH-PRESSED *SUITS!*

YEP, HE'S A *STRANGE* ONE, ALL RIGHT! WONDER IF HE WORKS AT THE *CAPE!?*

LESSEE NOW, WHAT *NAME* DID HE SIGN IN THE REGISTER, ANYWAY?

OH YES... *HERE* IT IS! M·A·R·V·E·L... C. MARVEL! NOW WHAT KIND OF NAME IS *THAT* FOR AN HONEST MAN TO HAVE?

AND, I HOPE HE *IS* HONEST...'CAUSE I JUST REMEMBERED... I FORGOT TO ASK HIM ABOUT HIS *BILL!*

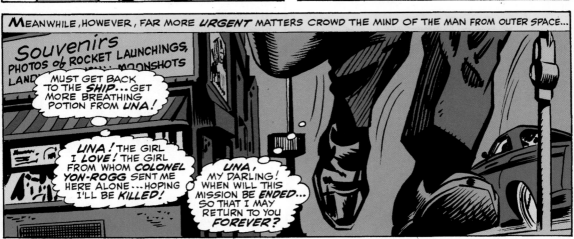

MEANWHILE, HOWEVER, FAR MORE *URGENT* MATTERS CROWD THE MIND OF THE MAN FROM OUTER SPACE...

Souvenirs
PHOTOS OF ROCKET LAUNCHINGS, LAND... MOONSHOTS

MUST GET BACK TO THE *SHIP*... GET MORE BREATHING POTION FROM *UNA!*

UNA! THE GIRL I *LOVE!* THE GIRL FROM WHOM *COLONEL YON-ROGG* SENT ME HERE ALONE...HOPING I'LL BE *KILLED!*

UNA, MY DARLING! WHEN WILL THIS MISSION BE *ENDED*... SO THAT I MAY RETURN TO YOU *FOREVER?*

SOON, JUST A SHORT *DISTANCE* FROM THE SLEEPING TOWN...

I'VE CONTACTED THE *STARSHIP*... WHICH SHOULD NOW BE LEAVING ITS ASSUMED *ORBIT* AROUND THE EARTH!

EVEN AT *REDUCED SPEED*, IT SHOULD BE HERE WITHIN *MINUTES!*

IN THE MEANTIME, I'D BETTER TEST MY NEW *WRIST LENS!*

FOR, ONE DAY SOON, MY *LIFE* MAY WELL DEPEND UPON IT!

3.

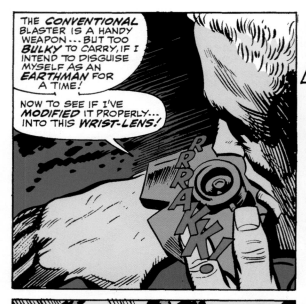

THE CONVENTIONAL BLASTER IS A HANDY WEAPON... BUT TOO BULKY TO CARRY, IF I INTEND TO DISGUISE MYSELF AS AN EARTHMAN FOR A TIME!

NOW TO SEE IF I'VE MODIFIED IT PROPERLY... INTO THIS WRIST-LENS!

RRRAKK!

BTAP

THAT TREE... WHICH HAS STOOD IN THIS DESOLATE SPOT FOR YEARS...

A MERE INSTANT OF EXPOSURE TO THE UNI-BEAM---AND IT'S BLASTED INTO NOTHINGNESS!

AND, THAT HUGE BOULDER... IT FLIES INTO A THOUSAND ROCKY FRAGMENTS!

SURELY, NO BEING ON THIS PUNY PLANET HAS EVER KNOWN SUCH SHEER, UNADULTERATED POWER!

SPTAK!

BUT NOW---THE MOST UNIQUE TEST OF ALL!

EVEN AS THE FRAGMENTS FLY OUTWARD, I'VE SET THE LENS FOR REVERSE EFFECT...

4

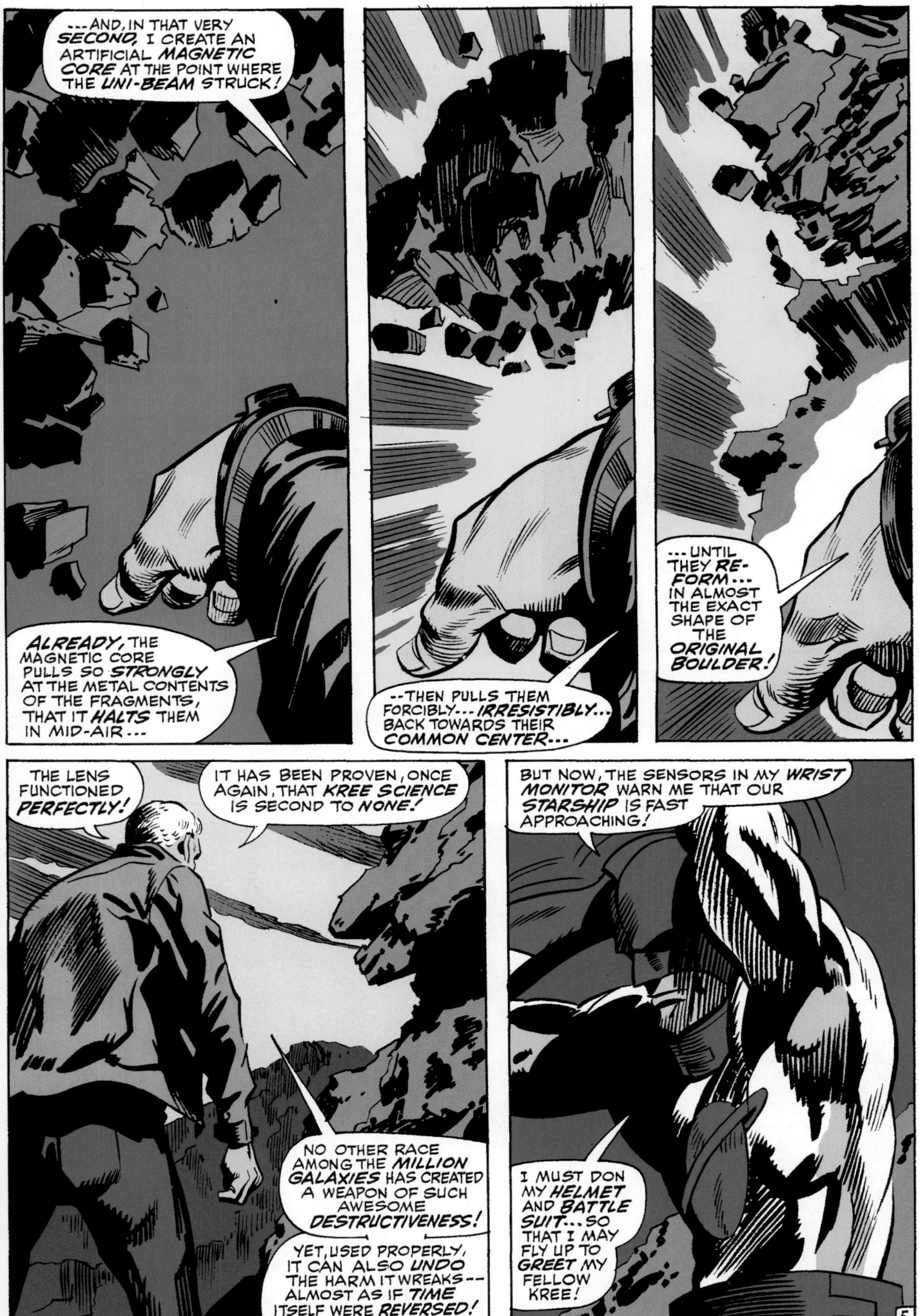
...AND, IN THAT VERY SECOND, I CREATE AN ARTIFICIAL MAGNETIC CORE AT THE POINT WHERE THE UNI-BEAM STRUCK!
ALREADY, THE MAGNETIC CORE PULLS SO STRONGLY AT THE METAL CONTENTS OF THE FRAGMENTS, THAT IT HALTS THEM IN MID-AIR...
--THEN PULLS THEM FORCIBLY... IRRESISTIBLY... BACK TOWARDS THEIR COMMON CENTER...
...UNTIL THEY RE-FORM... IN ALMOST THE EXACT SHAPE OF THE ORIGINAL BOULDER!
THE LENS FUNCTIONED PERFECTLY!
IT HAS BEEN PROVEN, ONCE AGAIN, THAT KREE SCIENCE IS SECOND TO NONE!
NO OTHER RACE AMONG THE MILLION GALAXIES HAS CREATED A WEAPON OF SUCH AWESOME DESTRUCTIVENESS!
YET, USED PROPERLY, IT CAN ALSO UNDO THE HARM IT WREAKS-- ALMOST AS IF TIME ITSELF WERE REVERSED!
BUT NOW, THE SENSORS IN MY WRIST MONITOR WARN ME THAT OUR STARSHIP IS FAST APPROACHING!
I MUST DON MY HELMET AND BATTLE SUIT... SO THAT I MAY FLY UP TO GREET MY FELLOW KREE!
5.

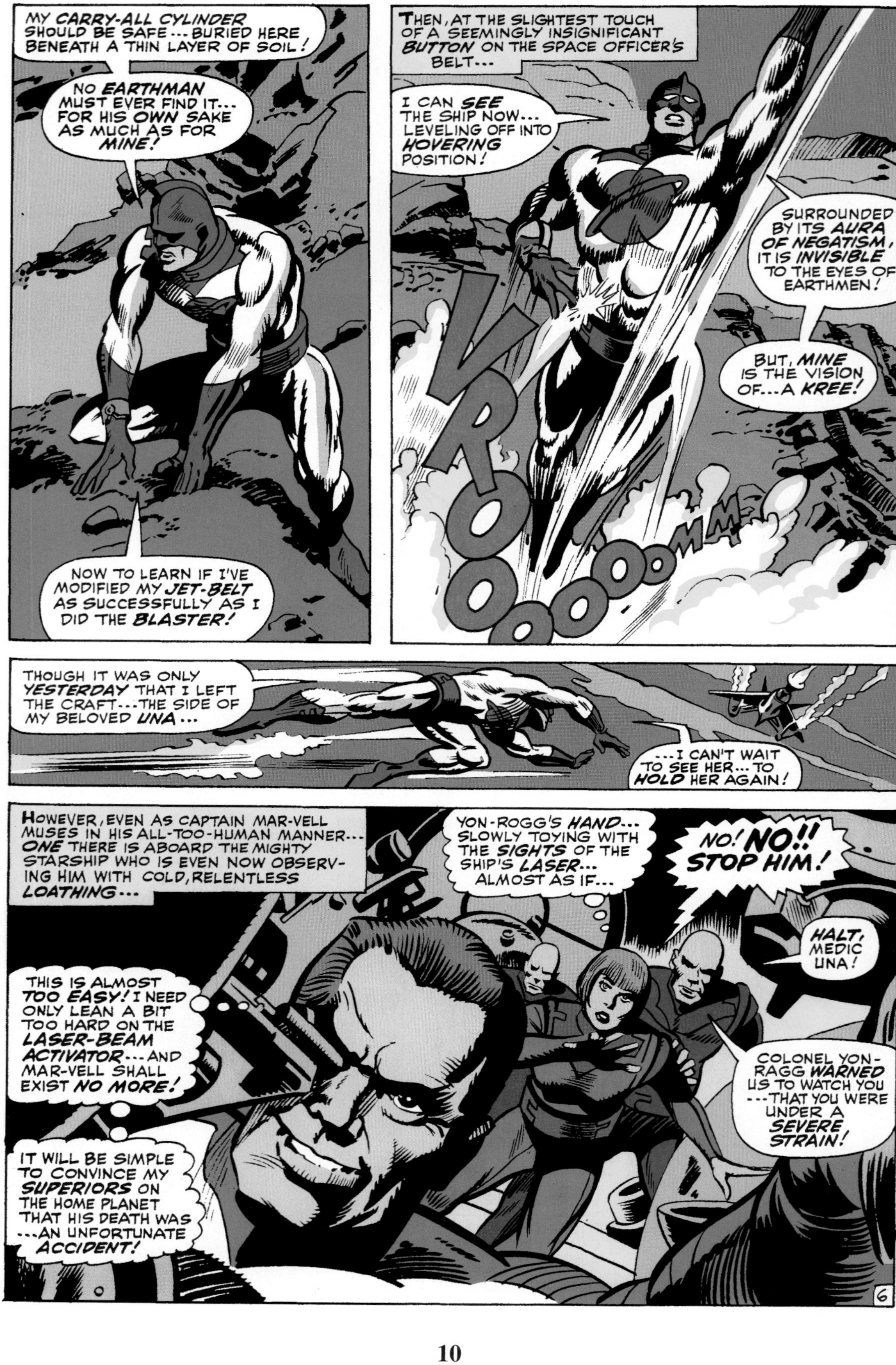
MY CARRY-ALL CYLINDER SHOULD BE SAFE... BURIED HERE BENEATH A THIN LAYER OF SOIL!
NO EARTHMAN MUST EVER FIND IT... FOR HIS OWN SAKE AS MUCH AS FOR MINE!
NOW TO LEARN IF I'VE MODIFIED MY JET-BELT AS SUCCESSFULLY AS I DID THE BLASTER!
THEN, AT THE SLIGHTEST TOUCH OF A SEEMINGLY INSIGNIFICANT BUTTON ON THE SPACE OFFICER'S BELT...
I CAN SEE THE SHIP NOW... LEVELING OFF INTO HOVERING POSITION!
SURROUNDED BY ITS AURA OF NEGATISM, IT IS INVISIBLE TO THE EYES OF EARTHMEN!
BUT, MINE IS THE VISION OF... A KREE!
VROOOOOOOMM
THOUGH IT WAS ONLY YESTERDAY THAT I LEFT THE CRAFT---THE SIDE OF MY BELOVED UNA...
...I CAN'T WAIT TO SEE HER... TO HOLD HER AGAIN!
HOWEVER, EVEN AS CAPTAIN MAR-VELL MUSES IN HIS ALL-TOO-HUMAN MANNER... ONE THERE IS ABOARD THE MIGHTY STARSHIP WHO IS EVEN NOW OBSERVING HIM WITH COLD, RELENTLESS LOATHING...
YON-ROGG'S HAND... SLOWLY TOYING WITH THE SIGHTS OF THE SHIP'S LASER... ALMOST AS IF...
NO! NO!! STOP HIM!
THIS IS ALMOST TOO EASY! I NEED ONLY LEAN A BIT TOO HARD ON THE LASER-BEAM ACTIVATOR---AND MAR-VELL SHALL EXIST NO MORE!
IT WILL BE SIMPLE TO CONVINCE MY SUPERIORS ON THE HOME PLANET THAT HIS DEATH WAS ---AN UNFORTUNATE ACCIDENT!
HALT, MEDIC UNA!
COLONEL YON-RAGG WARNED US TO WATCH YOU ---THAT YOU WERE UNDER A SEVERE STRAIN!
6

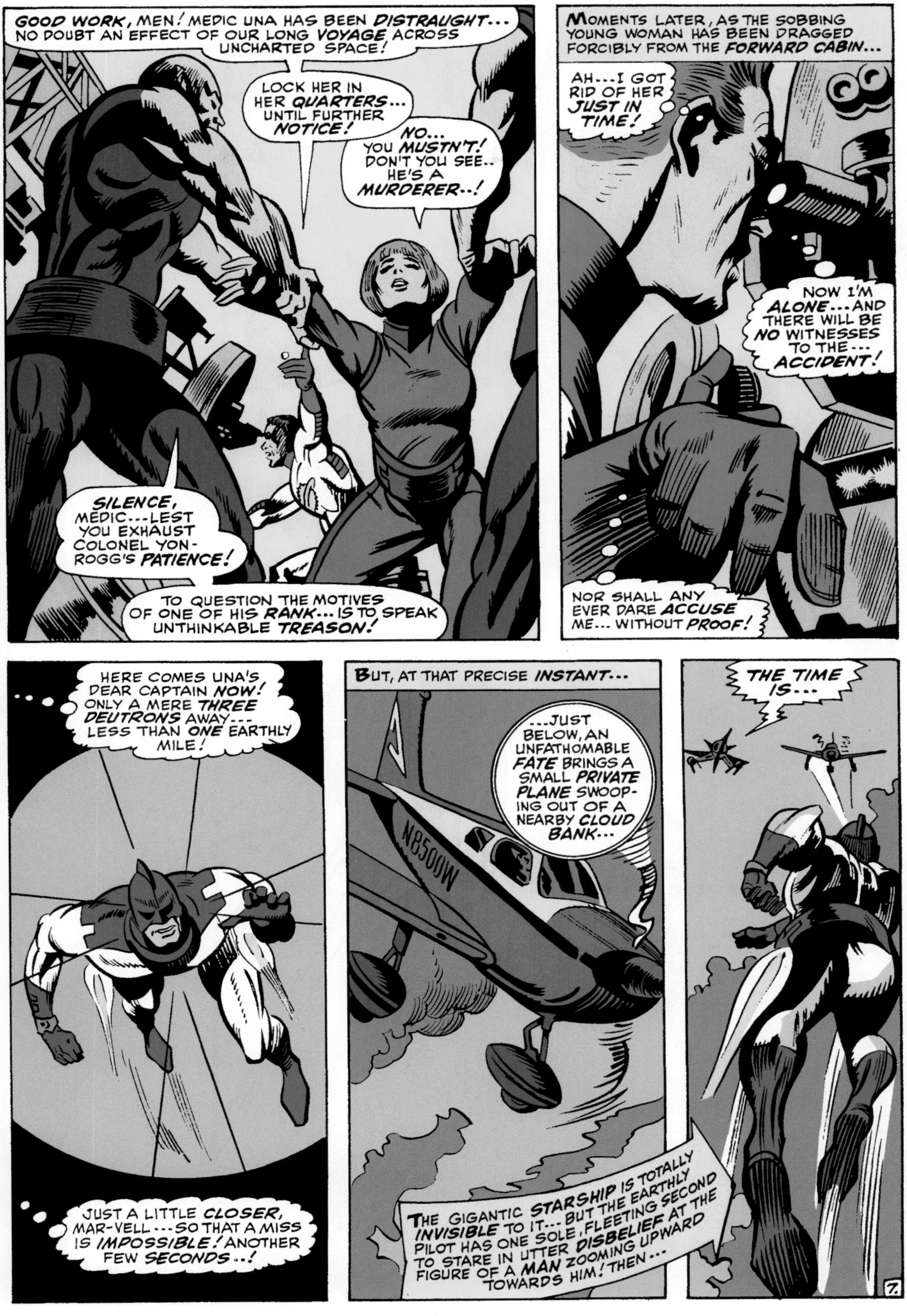
GOOD WORK, MEN! MEDIC UNA HAS BEEN DISTRAUGHT... NO DOUBT AN EFFECT OF OUR LONG VOYAGE ACROSS UNCHARTED SPACE!
LOCK HER IN HER QUARTERS... UNTIL FURTHER NOTICE!
NO... YOU MUSTN'T! DON'T YOU SEE.. HE'S A MURDERER..!
SILENCE, MEDIC...LEST YOU EXHAUST COLONEL YON-ROGG'S PATIENCE!
TO QUESTION THE MOTIVES OF ONE OF HIS RANK... IS TO SPEAK UNTHINKABLE TREASON!
MOMENTS LATER, AS THE SOBBING YOUNG WOMAN HAS BEEN DRAGGED FORCIBLY FROM THE FORWARD CABIN...
AH...I GOT RID OF HER JUST IN TIME!
NOW I'M ALONE...AND THERE WILL BE NO WITNESSES TO THE... ACCIDENT!
NOR SHALL ANY EVER DARE ACCUSE ME... WITHOUT PROOF!
HERE COMES UNA'S DEAR CAPTAIN NOW! ONLY A MERE THREE DEUTRONS AWAY... LESS THAN ONE EARTHLY MILE!
JUST A LITTLE CLOSER, MAR-VELL... SO THAT A MISS IS IMPOSSIBLE! ANOTHER FEW SECONDS..!
BUT, AT THAT PRECISE INSTANT...
...JUST BELOW, AN UNFATHOMABLE FATE BRINGS A SMALL PRIVATE PLANE SWOOPING OUT OF A NEARBY CLOUD BANK...
N8500W
THE GIGANTIC STARSHIP IS TOTALLY INVISIBLE TO IT... BUT THE EARTHLY PILOT HAS ONE SOLE, FLEETING SECOND TO STARE IN UTTER DISBELIEF AT THE FIGURE OF A MAN ZOOMING UPWARD TOWARDS HIM! THEN...
THE TIME IS...
7.

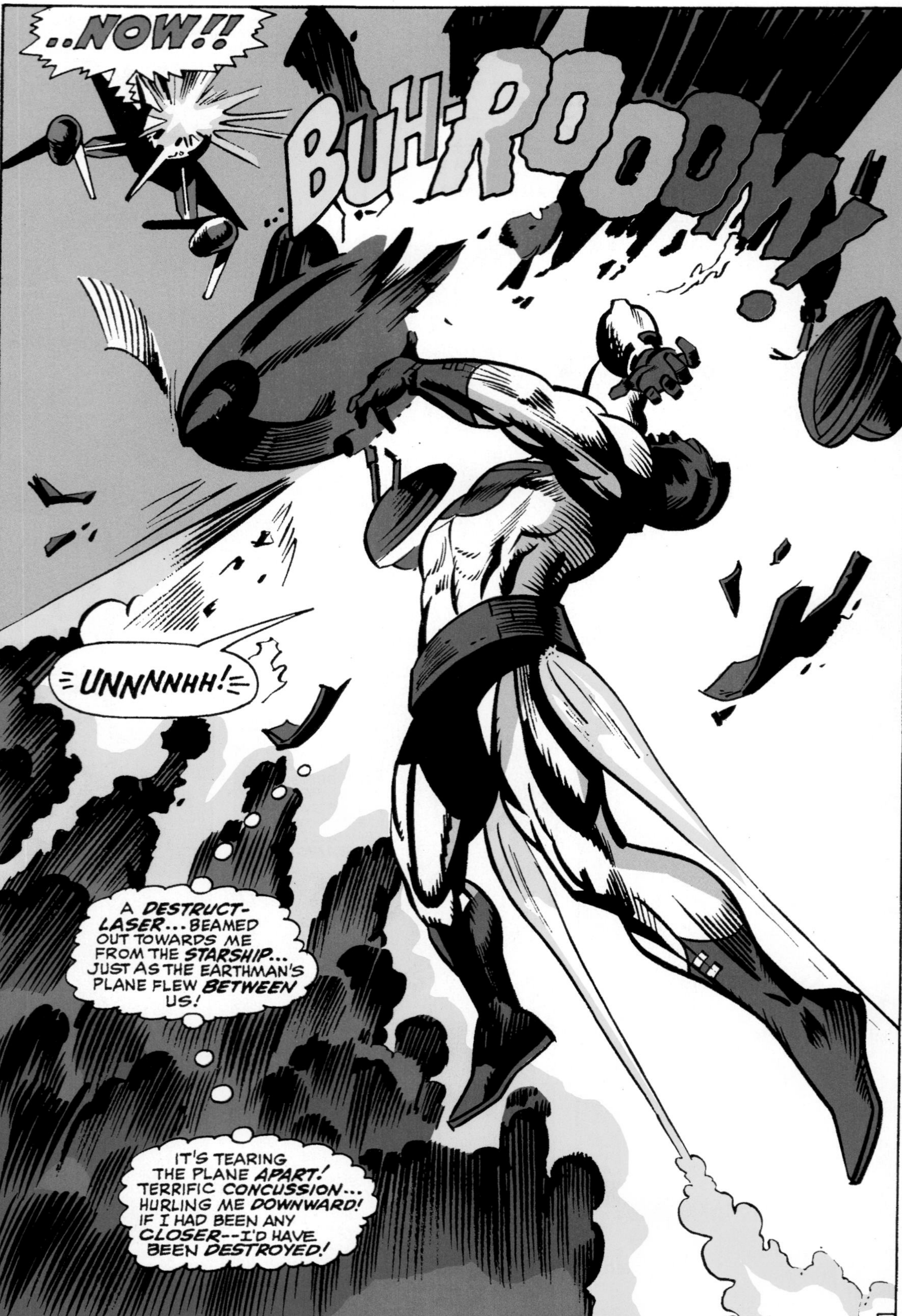
..NOW!!
BUH-ROOOM!
UNNNNHH!
A DESTRUCT-LASER... BEAMED OUT TOWARDS ME FROM THE STARSHIP... JUST AS THE EARTHMAN'S PLANE FLEW BETWEEN US!
IT'S TEARING THE PLANE APART! TERRIFIC CONCUSSION... HURLING ME DOWNWARD! IF I HAD BEEN ANY CLOSER--I'D HAVE BEEN DESTROYED!
8

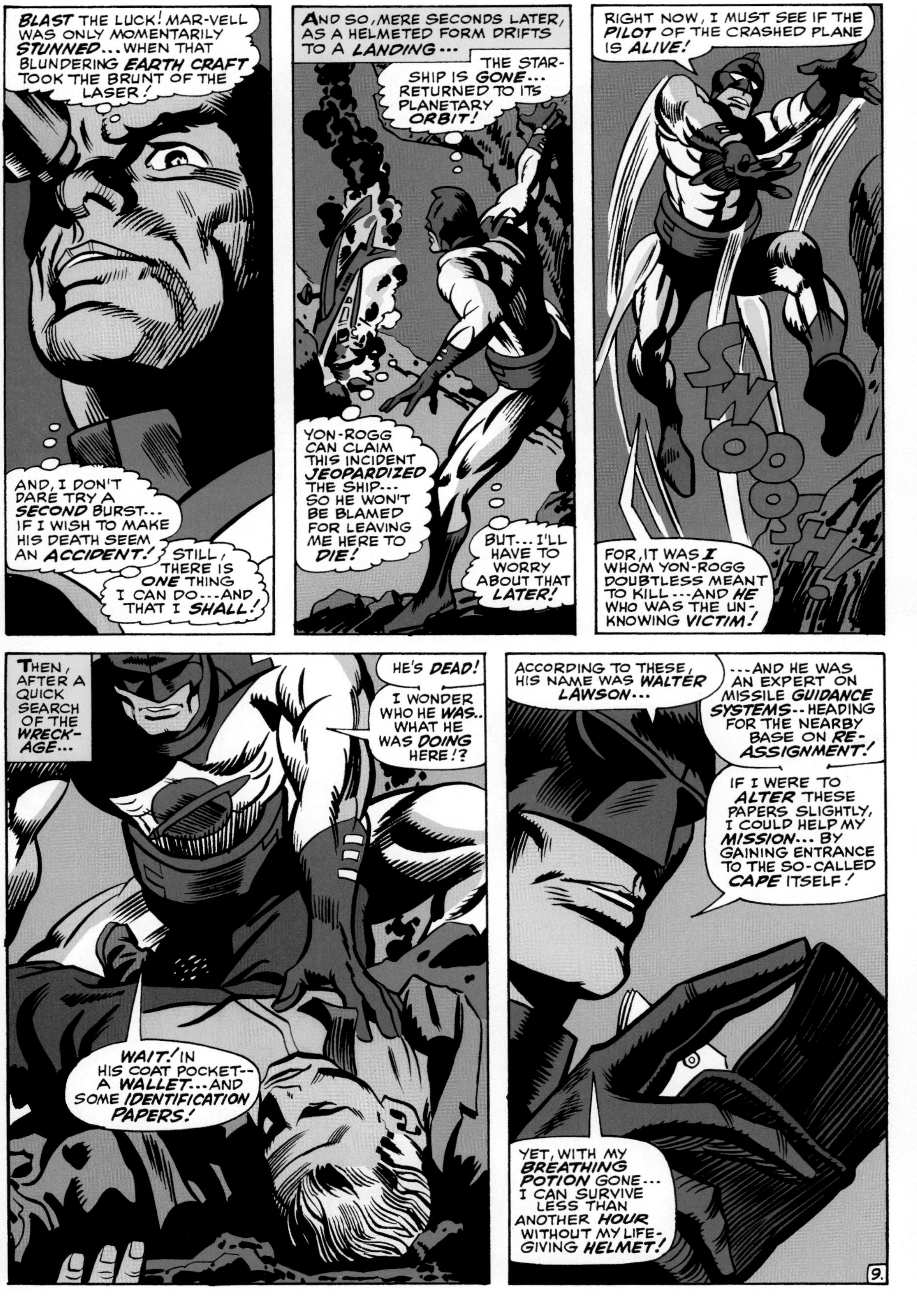
BLAST THE LUCK! MAR-VELL WAS ONLY MOMENTARILY STUNNED... WHEN THAT BLUNDERING EARTH CRAFT TOOK THE BRUNT OF THE LASER!
AND, I DON'T DARE TRY A SECOND BURST... IF I WISH TO MAKE HIS DEATH SEEM AN ACCIDENT!
STILL, THERE IS ONE THING I CAN DO...AND THAT I SHALL!
AND SO, MERE SECONDS LATER, AS A HELMETED FORM DRIFTS TO A LANDING...
THE STAR-SHIP IS GONE... RETURNED TO ITS PLANETARY ORBIT!
YON-ROGG CAN CLAIM THIS INCIDENT JEOPARDIZED THE SHIP... SO HE WON'T BE BLAMED FOR LEAVING ME HERE TO DIE!
BUT... I'LL HAVE TO WORRY ABOUT THAT LATER!
RIGHT NOW, I MUST SEE IF THE PILOT OF THE CRASHED PLANE IS ALIVE!
SWOOOSH!
FOR, IT WAS I WHOM YON-ROGG DOUBTLESS MEANT TO KILL---AND HE WHO WAS THE UN-KNOWING VICTIM!
THEN, AFTER A QUICK SEARCH OF THE WRECK-AGE...
HE'S DEAD!
I WONDER WHO HE WAS.. WHAT HE WAS DOING HERE!?
WAIT! IN HIS COAT POCKET-- A WALLET...AND SOME IDENTIFICATION PAPERS!
ACCORDING TO THESE, HIS NAME WAS WALTER LAWSON...
...AND HE WAS AN EXPERT ON MISSILE GUIDANCE SYSTEMS--HEADING FOR THE NEARBY BASE ON RE-ASSIGNMENT!
IF I WERE TO ALTER THESE PAPERS SLIGHTLY, I COULD HELP MY MISSION... BY GAINING ENTRANCE TO THE SO-CALLED CAPE ITSELF!
YET, WITH MY BREATHING POTION GONE... I CAN SURVIVE LESS THAN ANOTHER HOUR WITHOUT MY LIFE-GIVING HELMET!
9.

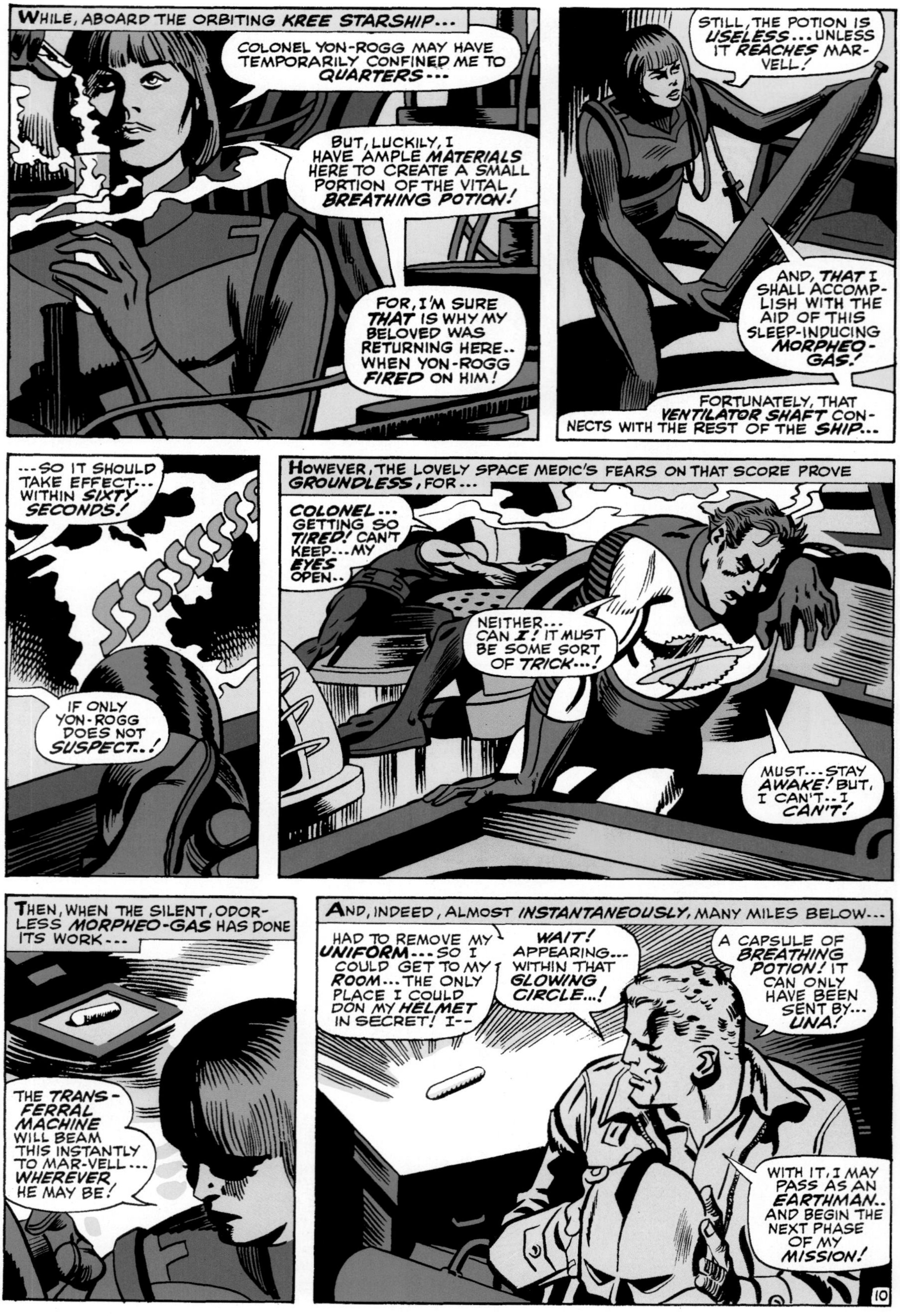
WHILE, ABOARD THE ORBITING KREE STARSHIP...
COLONEL YON-ROGG MAY HAVE TEMPORARILY CONFINED ME TO QUARTERS---
BUT, LUCKILY, I HAVE AMPLE MATERIALS HERE TO CREATE A SMALL PORTION OF THE VITAL BREATHING POTION!
FOR, I'M SURE THAT IS WHY MY BELOVED WAS RETURNING HERE.. WHEN YON-ROGG FIRED ON HIM!
STILL, THE POTION IS USELESS... UNLESS IT REACHES MAR-VELL!
AND, THAT I SHALL ACCOMPLISH WITH THE AID OF THIS SLEEP-INDUCING MORPHEO-GAS!
FORTUNATELY, THAT VENTILATOR SHAFT CONNECTS WITH THE REST OF THE SHIP...
---SO IT SHOULD TAKE EFFECT--- WITHIN SIXTY SECONDS!
SSSSSSSSSS
IF ONLY YON-ROGG DOES NOT SUSPECT..!
HOWEVER, THE LOVELY SPACE MEDIC'S FEARS ON THAT SCORE PROVE GROUNDLESS, FOR...
COLONEL... GETTING SO TIRED! CAN'T KEEP... MY EYES OPEN..
NEITHER... CAN I! IT MUST BE SOME SORT OF TRICK...!
MUST... STAY AWAKE! BUT, I CAN'T.. I CAN'T!
THEN, WHEN THE SILENT, ODORLESS MORPHEO-GAS HAS DONE ITS WORK---
THE TRANSFERRAL MACHINE WILL BEAM THIS INSTANTLY TO MAR-VELL... WHEREVER HE MAY BE!
AND, INDEED, ALMOST INSTANTANEOUSLY, MANY MILES BELOW...
HAD TO REMOVE MY UNIFORM--- SO I COULD GET TO MY ROOM... THE ONLY PLACE I COULD DON MY HELMET IN SECRET! I--
WAIT! APPEARING... WITHIN THAT GLOWING CIRCLE...!
A CAPSULE OF BREATHING POTION! IT CAN ONLY HAVE BEEN SENT BY... UNA!
WITH IT, I MAY PASS AS AN EARTHMAN.. AND BEGIN THE NEXT PHASE OF MY MISSION!
10

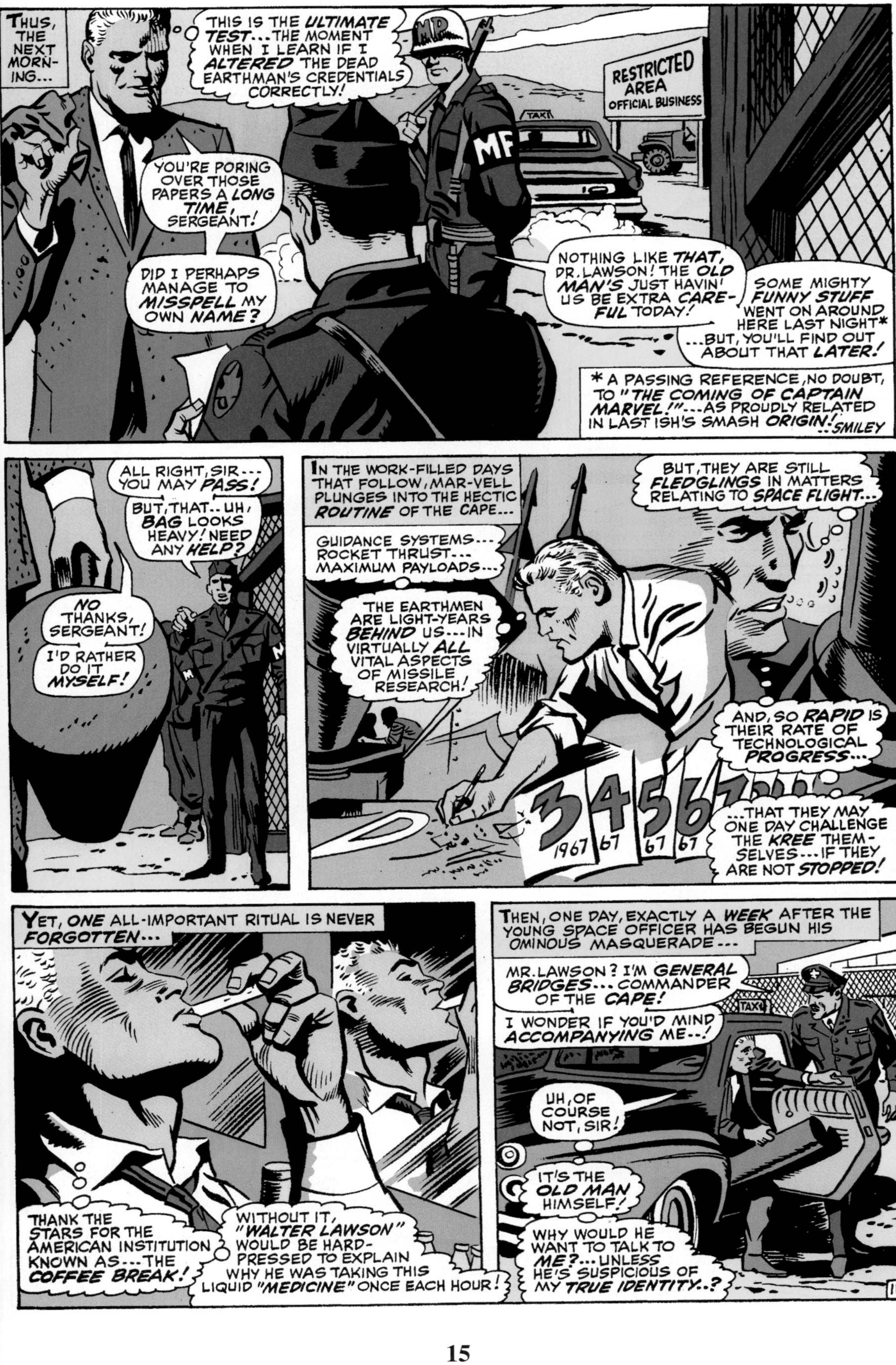
THUS, THE NEXT MORNING...
THIS IS THE ULTIMATE TEST... THE MOMENT WHEN I LEARN IF I ALTERED THE DEAD EARTHMAN'S CREDENTIALS CORRECTLY!
RESTRICTED AREA OFFICIAL BUSINESS
TAXI
MP
YOU'RE PORING OVER THOSE PAPERS A LONG TIME, SERGEANT!
DID I PERHAPS MANAGE TO MISSPELL MY OWN NAME?
NOTHING LIKE THAT, DR. LAWSON! THE OLD MAN'S JUST HAVIN' US BE EXTRA CAREFUL TODAY!
SOME MIGHTY FUNNY STUFF WENT ON AROUND HERE LAST NIGHT* ...BUT, YOU'LL FIND OUT ABOUT THAT LATER!
* A PASSING REFERENCE, NO DOUBT, TO "THE COMING OF CAPTAIN MARVEL!"...AS PROUDLY RELATED IN LAST ISH'S SMASH ORIGIN! ..SMILEY
ALL RIGHT, SIR... YOU MAY PASS!
BUT, THAT.. UH, BAG LOOKS HEAVY! NEED ANY HELP?
NO THANKS, SERGEANT!
I'D RATHER DO IT MYSELF!
IN THE WORK-FILLED DAYS THAT FOLLOW, MAR-VELL PLUNGES INTO THE HECTIC ROUTINE OF THE CAPE...
GUIDANCE SYSTEMS... ROCKET THRUST... MAXIMUM PAYLOADS...
THE EARTHMEN ARE LIGHT-YEARS BEHIND US... IN VIRTUALLY ALL VITAL ASPECTS OF MISSILE RESEARCH!
BUT, THEY ARE STILL FLEDGLINGS IN MATTERS RELATING TO SPACE FLIGHT...
AND, SO RAPID IS THEIR RATE OF TECHNOLOGICAL PROGRESS...
3 4 5 6
1967 67 67 67
...THAT THEY MAY ONE DAY CHALLENGE THE KREE THEMSELVES... IF THEY ARE NOT STOPPED!
YET, ONE ALL-IMPORTANT RITUAL IS NEVER FORGOTTEN...
THANK THE STARS FOR THE AMERICAN INSTITUTION KNOWN AS... THE COFFEE BREAK!
WITHOUT IT, "WALTER LAWSON" WOULD BE HARD-PRESSED TO EXPLAIN WHY HE WAS TAKING THIS LIQUID "MEDICINE" ONCE EACH HOUR!
THEN, ONE DAY, EXACTLY A WEEK AFTER THE YOUNG SPACE OFFICER HAS BEGUN HIS OMINOUS MASQUERADE...
MR. LAWSON? I'M GENERAL BRIDGES... COMMANDER OF THE CAPE!
I WONDER IF YOU'D MIND ACCOMPANYING ME..!
TAXI
UH, OF COURSE NOT, SIR!
IT'S THE OLD MAN HIMSELF!
WHY WOULD HE WANT TO TALK TO ME?... UNLESS HE'S SUSPICIOUS OF MY TRUE IDENTITY..?
11.

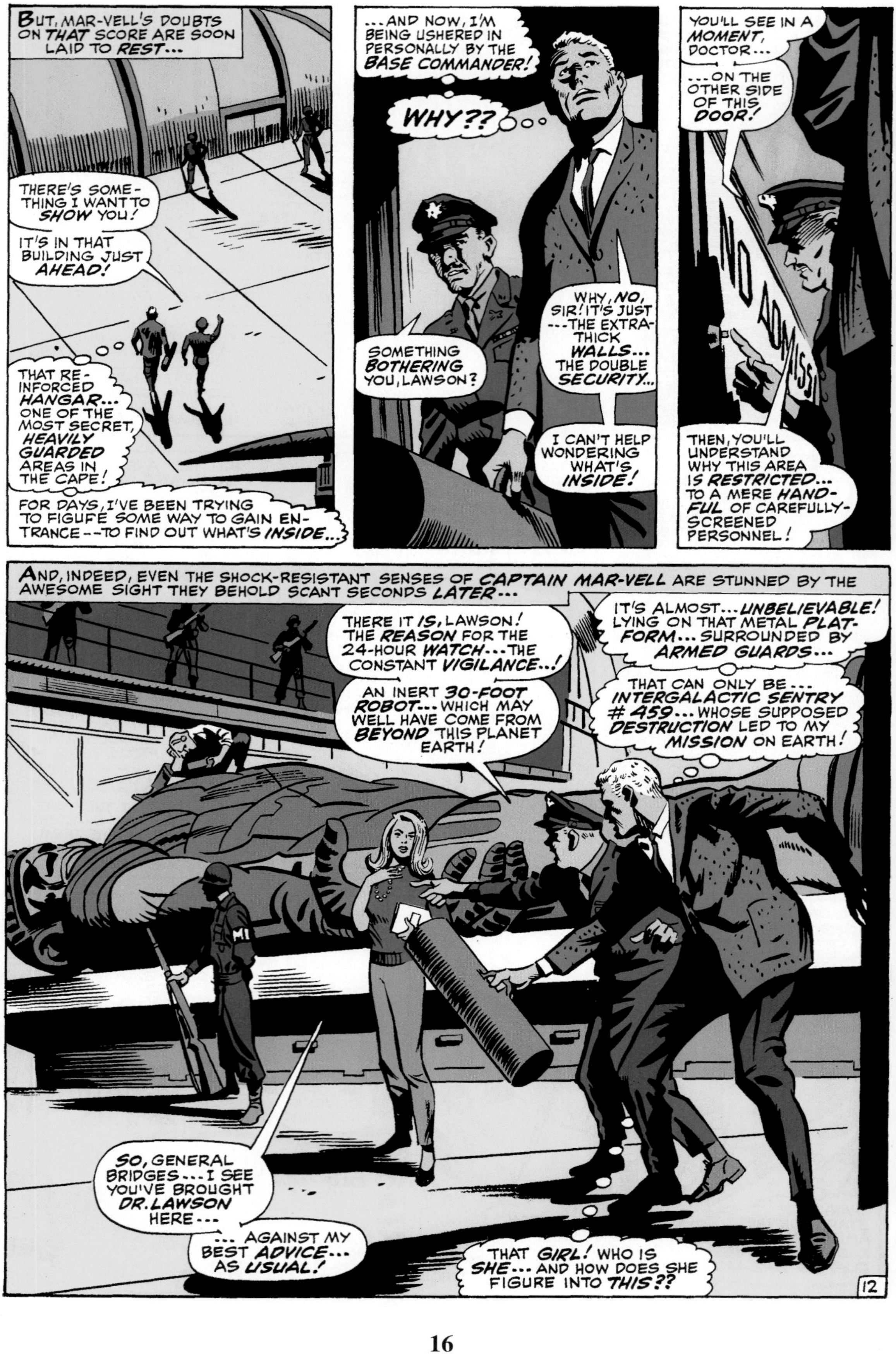
BUT, MAR-VELL'S DOUBTS ON THAT SCORE ARE SOON LAID TO REST...
THERE'S SOMETHING I WANT TO SHOW YOU!
IT'S IN THAT BUILDING JUST AHEAD!
THAT REINFORCED HANGAR... ONE OF THE MOST SECRET, HEAVILY GUARDED AREAS IN THE CAPE!
FOR DAYS, I'VE BEEN TRYING TO FIGUFE SOME WAY TO GAIN ENTRANCE--TO FIND OUT WHAT'S INSIDE...
...AND NOW, I'M BEING USHERED IN PERSONALLY BY THE BASE COMMANDER!
WHY??
SOMETHING BOTHERING YOU, LAWSON?
WHY, NO, SIR! IT'S JUST---THE EXTRA-THICK WALLS... THE DOUBLE SECURITY...
I CAN'T HELP WONDERING WHAT'S INSIDE!
YOU'LL SEE IN A MOMENT, DOCTOR...
...ON THE OTHER SIDE OF THIS DOOR!
NO ADMISSI
THEN, YOU'LL UNDERSTAND WHY THIS AREA IS RESTRICTED... TO A MERE HANDFUL OF CAREFULLY-SCREENED PERSONNEL!
AND, INDEED, EVEN THE SHOCK-RESISTANT SENSES OF CAPTAIN MAR-VELL ARE STUNNED BY THE AWESOME SIGHT THEY BEHOLD SCANT SECONDS LATER...
THERE IT IS, LAWSON! THE REASON FOR THE 24-HOUR WATCH---THE CONSTANT VIGILANCE..!
AN INERT 30-FOOT ROBOT... WHICH MAY WELL HAVE COME FROM BEYOND THIS PLANET EARTH!
IT'S ALMOST... UNBELIEVABLE! LYING ON THAT METAL PLATFORM... SURROUNDED BY ARMED GUARDS...
THAT CAN ONLY BE... INTERGALACTIC SENTRY # 459... WHOSE SUPPOSED DESTRUCTION LED TO MY MISSION ON EARTH!
MI
SO, GENERAL BRIDGES... I SEE YOU'VE BROUGHT DR. LAWSON HERE---
... AGAINST MY BEST ADVICE... AS USUAL!
THAT GIRL! WHO IS SHE... AND HOW DOES SHE FIGURE INTO THIS??
12

DR. LAWSON, THIS IS *MISS DANVERS!* MAN OR WOMAN, SHE'S THE FINEST *HEAD OF SECURITY* A MISSILE BASE COULD WANT!

THANK YOU FOR *THAT* ANYWAY, GENERAL!

I'M REALLY QUITE PLEASED TO *MEET* YOU, DOCTOR...

..THOUGH I'D RATHER TALK TO YOUR *FACE* THAN TO YOUR *BACK!*

SORRY, MISS DANVERS...

IT'S JUST THAT I CAN'T TAKE MY EYES OFF THAT, UH, *ROBOT!*

WHERE WAS IT *FOUND,* IF I MAY ASK?

YOU *MAY...*NOW! IT WAS SPOTTED BY *PEARL DIVERS...* IN AN ISLAND CHAIN IN THE *SOUTH PACIFIC!*

I SEE!

I JUST REALIZED.. WHY THE OLD MAN MUST HAVE *BROUGHT* ME HERE!

THE *REAL* WALTER LAWSON WAS LISTED AS AN EXPERT NOT ONLY IN *GUIDANCE SYSTEMS...*BUT ALSO IN *ROBOTICS!*

YOU...UP THERE ON THE ROBOT! WHAT *METAL* IS HE COMPOSED OF?

THAT'S WHAT WE'VE BEEN TRYIN' TO *LEARN,* MAC!

HACKSAWS OR ACETYLENE TORCHES---*NOTHIN'* GETS THROUGH THIS BABY'S HIDE!

I MUST STUDY IT MORE *CLOSELY..* AS SOON AS I FINISH A RUSH PROJECT TO DEVELOP AN IMPROVED *SPACE-GYROSCOPE!*

BY THE WAY, MISS DANVERS... JUST *WHY* DID YOU OPPOSE MY SEEING THE ROBOT?

NOTHING *PERSONAL,* DR. LAWSON...

BUT, YOUR DOSSIER IS STILL BEING EXAMINED BY MY *SECURITY* DIVISION!

IF YOU MUST KNOW, YOU'VE ALWAYS HAD A REPUTATION AS A *RECLUSE...* EVEN AN *ECCENTRIC!*

AND FRANKLY, AFTER SEEING THAT STRANGE *BRIEF-CASE* OF YOURS...! WELL...

THAT'S *ENOUGH,* MISS DANVERS!

YES, SIR!

COMING, LAWSON?

AN *ECCENTRIC!* IF ONLY THATS *ALL* SHE SUSPECTS!

I'LL SEE YOU BOTH *LATER!*

SOMEHOW, I CAN'T HELP FEELING... THAT WALTER LAWSON IS *HIDING* SOMETHING!

IF HE *IS,* I WON'T REST TILL I FIND OUT *WHAT...*AND *WHY!*

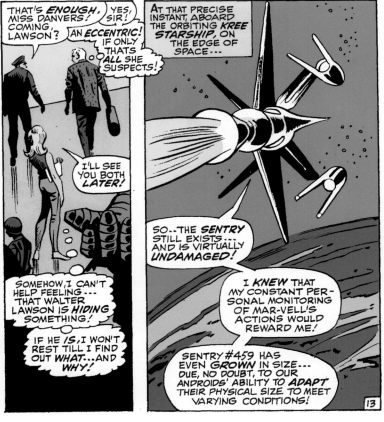

AT THAT PRECISE INSTANT, ABOARD THE ORBITING *KREE STARSHIP,* ON THE EDGE OF SPACE...

SO--THE *SENTRY* STILL EXISTS... AND IS VIRTUALLY *UNDAMAGED!*

I *KNEW* THAT MY CONSTANT PERSONAL MONITORING OF MAR-VELL'S ACTIONS WOULD *REWARD* ME!

SENTRY #459 HAS EVEN *GROWN* IN SIZE... DUE, NO DOUBT, TO OUR *ANDROIDS'* ABILITY TO *ADAPT* THEIR PHYSICAL SIZE TO MEET VARYING CONDITIONS!

13

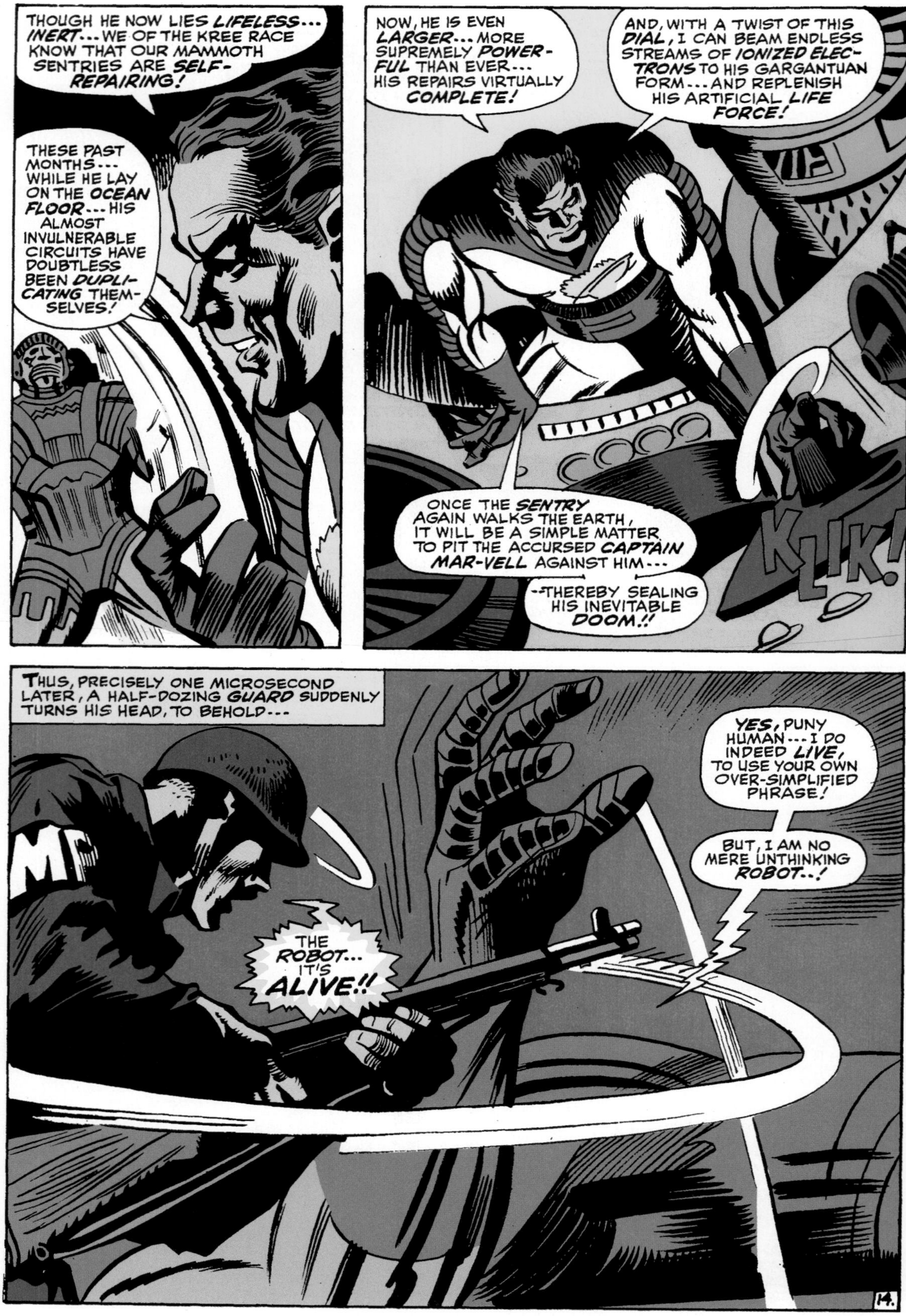
THOUGH HE NOW LIES LIFELESS... INERT... WE OF THE KREE RACE KNOW THAT OUR MAMMOTH SENTRIES ARE SELF-REPAIRING!
THESE PAST MONTHS... WHILE HE LAY ON THE OCEAN FLOOR... HIS ALMOST INVULNERABLE CIRCUITS HAVE DOUBTLESS BEEN DUPLICATING THEMSELVES!
NOW, HE IS EVEN LARGER... MORE SUPREMELY POWERFUL THAN EVER... HIS REPAIRS VIRTUALLY COMPLETE!
AND, WITH A TWIST OF THIS DIAL, I CAN BEAM ENDLESS STREAMS OF IONIZED ELECTRONS TO HIS GARGANTUAN FORM... AND REPLENISH HIS ARTIFICIAL LIFE FORCE!
ONCE THE SENTRY AGAIN WALKS THE EARTH, IT WILL BE A SIMPLE MATTER TO PIT THE ACCURSED CAPTAIN MAR-VELL AGAINST HIM---
--THEREBY SEALING HIS INEVITABLE DOOM!!
KLIK!
THUS, PRECISELY ONE MICROSECOND LATER, A HALF-DOZING GUARD SUDDENLY TURNS HIS HEAD, TO BEHOLD---
THE ROBOT... IT'S ALIVE!!
YES, PUNY HUMAN... I DO INDEED LIVE, TO USE YOUR OWN OVER-SIMPLIFIED PHRASE!
BUT, I AM NO MERE UNTHINKING ROBOT..!
MP
14.

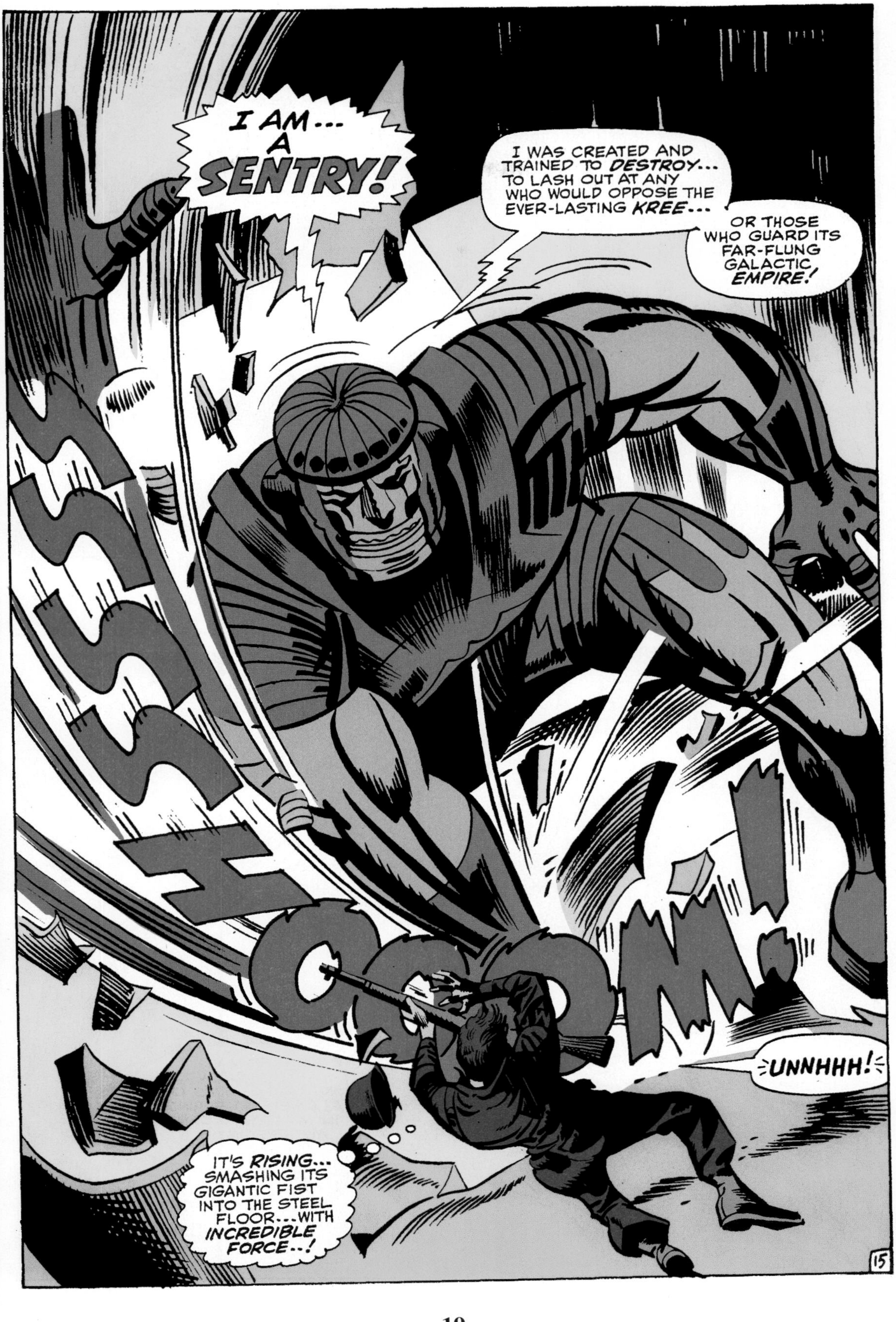
I AM... A SENTRY!
I WAS CREATED AND TRAINED TO DESTROY... TO LASH OUT AT ANY WHO WOULD OPPOSE THE EVER-LASTING KREE...
OR THOSE WHO GUARD ITS FAR-FLUNG GALACTIC EMPIRE!
SSSHHOOOOM!
UNNHHH!
IT'S RISING... SMASHING ITS GIGANTIC FIST INTO THE STEEL FLOOR... WITH INCREDIBLE FORCE..!
15

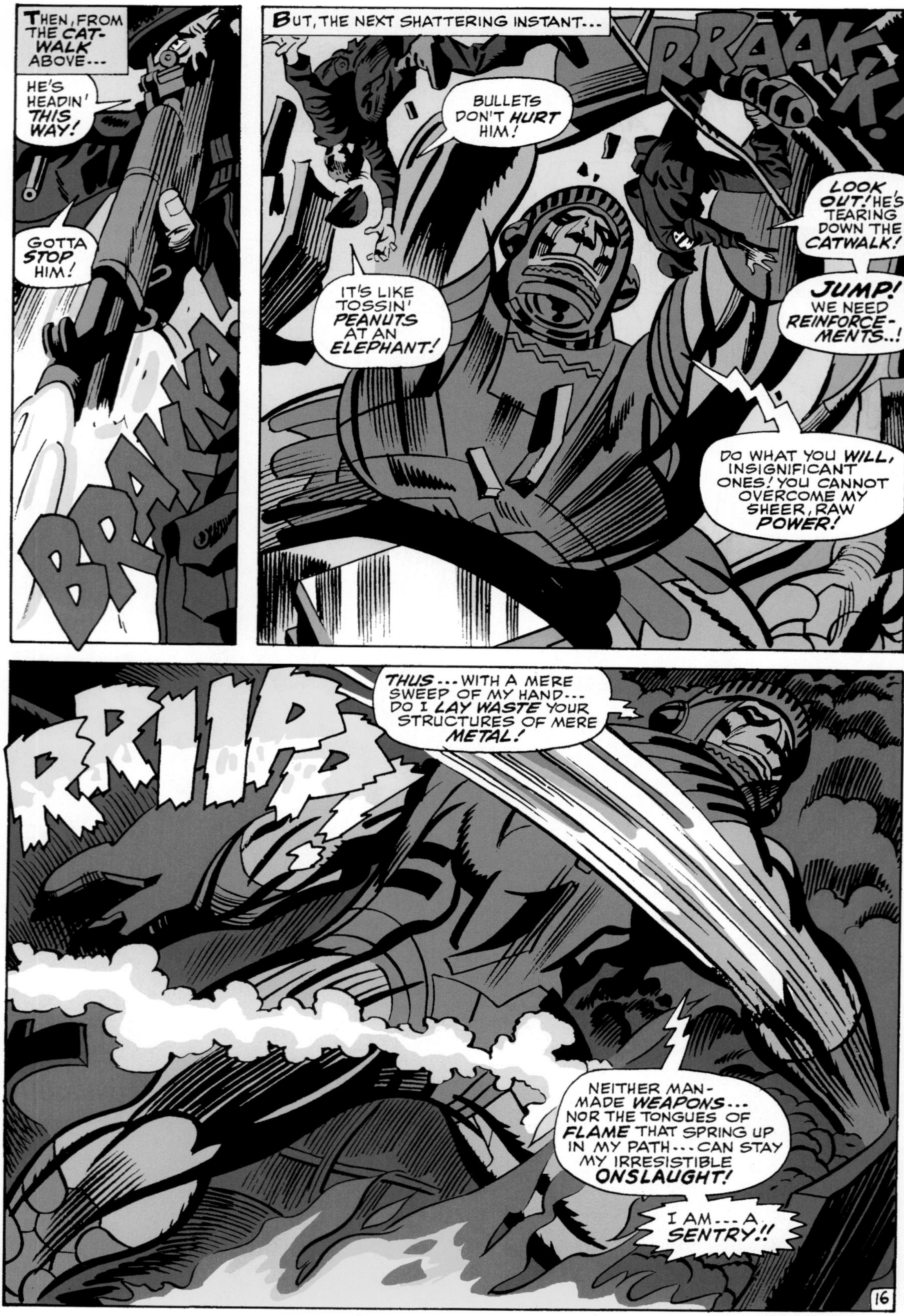
THEN, FROM THE CAT-WALK ABOVE...
HE'S HEADIN' THIS WAY!
GOTTA STOP HIM!
BRAKKA!
BUT, THE NEXT SHATTERING INSTANT...
RRAAK!
BULLETS DON'T HURT HIM!
IT'S LIKE TOSSIN' PEANUTS AT AN ELEPHANT!
LOOK OUT! HE'S TEARING DOWN THE CATWALK!
JUMP! WE NEED REINFORCE-MENTS..!
DO WHAT YOU WILL, INSIGNIFICANT ONES! YOU CANNOT OVERCOME MY SHEER, RAW POWER!
RRIIP
THUS... WITH A MERE SWEEP OF MY HAND... DO I LAY WASTE YOUR STRUCTURES OF MERE METAL!
NEITHER MAN-MADE WEAPONS... NOR THE TONGUES OF FLAME THAT SPRING UP IN MY PATH... CAN STAY MY IRRESISTIBLE ONSLAUGHT!
I AM... A SENTRY!!
16

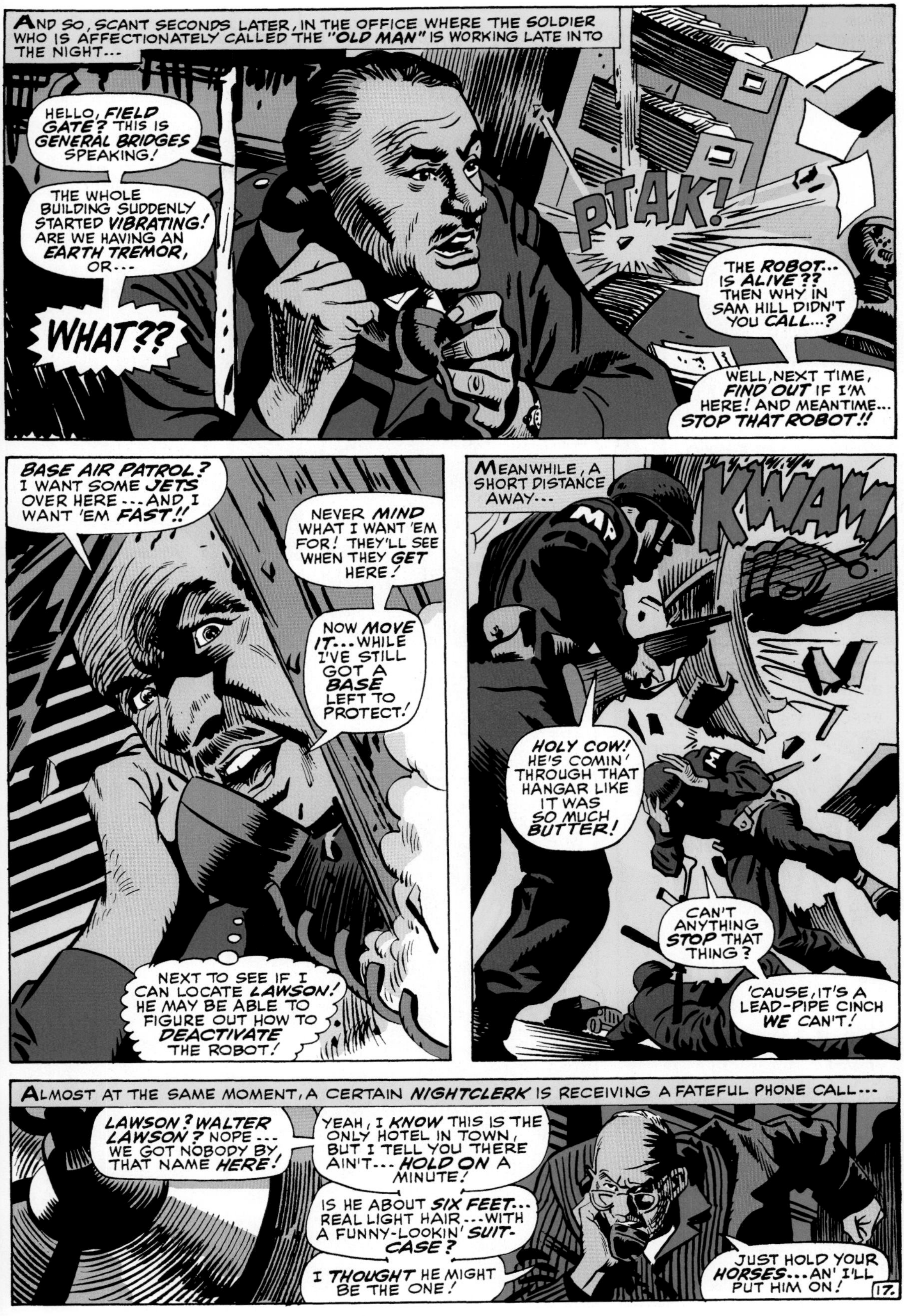
AND SO, SCANT SECONDS LATER, IN THE OFFICE WHERE THE SOLDIER WHO IS AFFECTIONATELY CALLED THE "OLD MAN" IS WORKING LATE INTO THE NIGHT...
HELLO, FIELD GATE? THIS IS GENERAL BRIDGES SPEAKING!
THE WHOLE BUILDING SUDDENLY STARTED VIBRATING! ARE WE HAVING AN EARTH TREMOR, OR---
WHAT??
PTAK!
THE ROBOT... IS ALIVE?? THEN WHY IN SAM HILL DIDN'T YOU CALL...?
WELL, NEXT TIME, FIND OUT IF I'M HERE! AND MEANTIME... STOP THAT ROBOT!!
BASE AIR PATROL? I WANT SOME JETS OVER HERE --- AND I WANT 'EM FAST!!
NEVER MIND WHAT I WANT 'EM FOR! THEY'LL SEE WHEN THEY GET HERE!
NOW MOVE IT... WHILE I'VE STILL GOT A BASE LEFT TO PROTECT!
NEXT TO SEE IF I CAN LOCATE LAWSON! HE MAY BE ABLE TO FIGURE OUT HOW TO DEACTIVATE THE ROBOT!
MEANWHILE, A SHORT DISTANCE AWAY...
KWAM
MP
HOLY COW! HE'S COMIN' THROUGH THAT HANGAR LIKE IT WAS SO MUCH BUTTER!
CAN'T ANYTHING STOP THAT THING?
'CAUSE, IT'S A LEAD-PIPE CINCH WE CAN'T!
ALMOST AT THE SAME MOMENT, A CERTAIN NIGHTCLERK IS RECEIVING A FATEFUL PHONE CALL...
LAWSON? WALTER LAWSON? NOPE... WE GOT NOBODY BY THAT NAME HERE!
YEAH, I KNOW THIS IS THE ONLY HOTEL IN TOWN, BUT I TELL YOU THERE AIN'T... HOLD ON A MINUTE!
IS HE ABOUT SIX FEET... REAL LIGHT HAIR... WITH A FUNNY-LOOKIN' SUIT-CASE?
I THOUGHT HE MIGHT BE THE ONE!
JUST HOLD YOUR HORSES... AN' I'LL PUT HIM ON!
17.

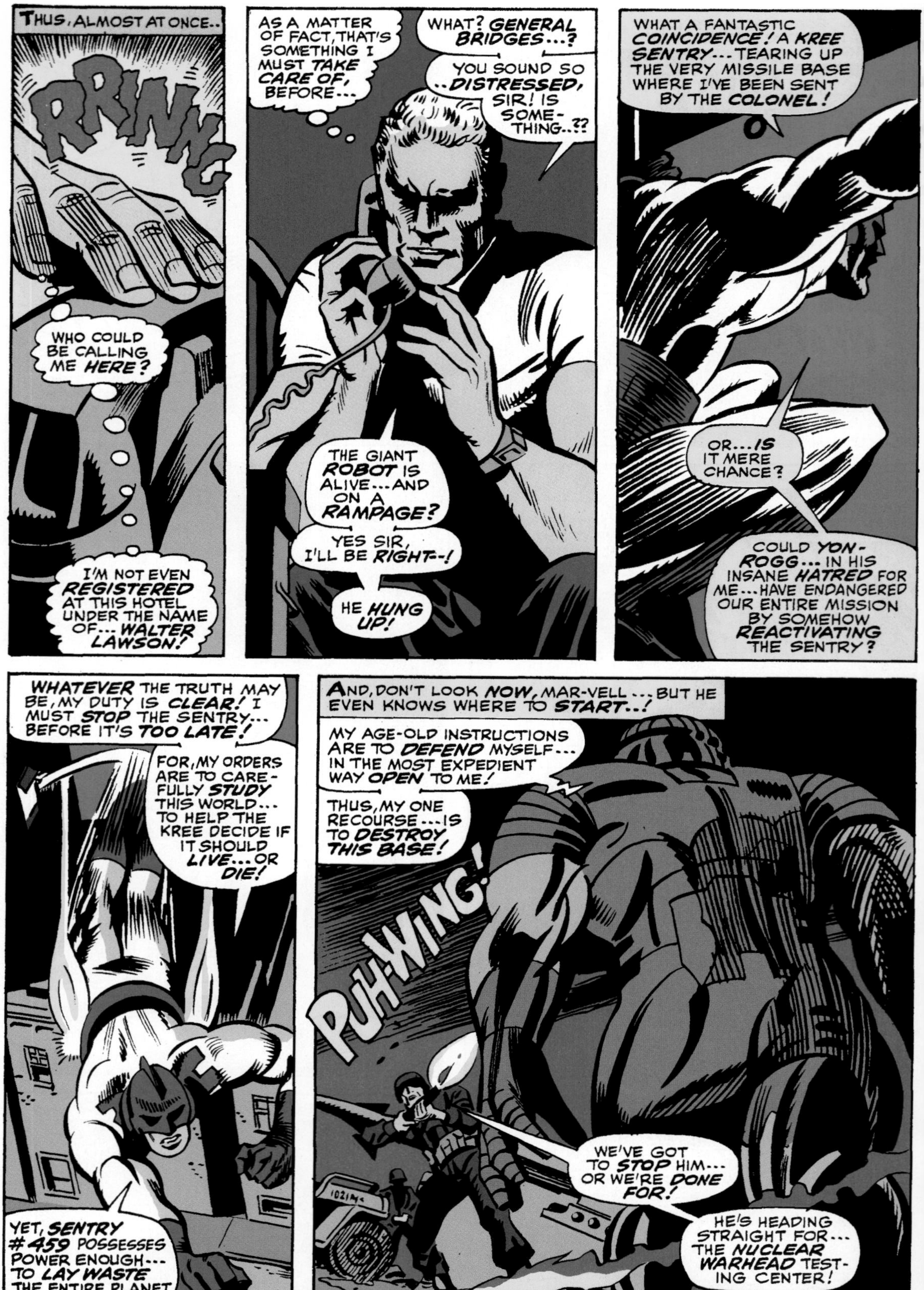
THUS, ALMOST AT ONCE..
RRINNG
WHO COULD BE CALLING ME HERE?
I'M NOT EVEN REGISTERED AT THIS HOTEL UNDER THE NAME OF... WALTER LAWSON!
AS A MATTER OF FACT, THAT'S SOMETHING I MUST TAKE CARE OF, BEFORE...
WHAT? GENERAL BRIDGES...?
YOU SOUND SO ..DISTRESSED, SIR! IS SOME-THING..??
THE GIANT ROBOT IS ALIVE... AND ON A RAMPAGE?
YES SIR, I'LL BE RIGHT--!
HE HUNG UP!
WHAT A FANTASTIC COINCIDENCE! A KREE SENTRY... TEARING UP THE VERY MISSILE BASE WHERE I'VE BEEN SENT BY THE COLONEL!
OR... IS IT MERE CHANCE?
COULD YON-ROGG... IN HIS INSANE HATRED FOR ME... HAVE ENDANGERED OUR ENTIRE MISSION BY SOMEHOW REACTIVATING THE SENTRY?
WHATEVER THE TRUTH MAY BE, MY DUTY IS CLEAR! I MUST STOP THE SENTRY... BEFORE IT'S TOO LATE!
FOR, MY ORDERS ARE TO CARE-FULLY STUDY THIS WORLD... TO HELP THE KREE DECIDE IF IT SHOULD LIVE... OR DIE!
YET, SENTRY #459 POSSESSES POWER ENOUGH... TO LAY WASTE THE ENTIRE PLANET BY HIMSELF!
AND, DON'T LOOK NOW, MAR-VELL... BUT HE EVEN KNOWS WHERE TO START..!
MY AGE-OLD INSTRUCTIONS ARE TO DEFEND MYSELF... IN THE MOST EXPEDIENT WAY OPEN TO ME!
THUS, MY ONE RECOURSE... IS TO DESTROY THIS BASE!
PUH-WING!
WE'VE GOT TO STOP HIM... OR WE'RE DONE FOR!
HE'S HEADING STRAIGHT FOR... THE NUCLEAR WARHEAD TEST-ING CENTER!
18

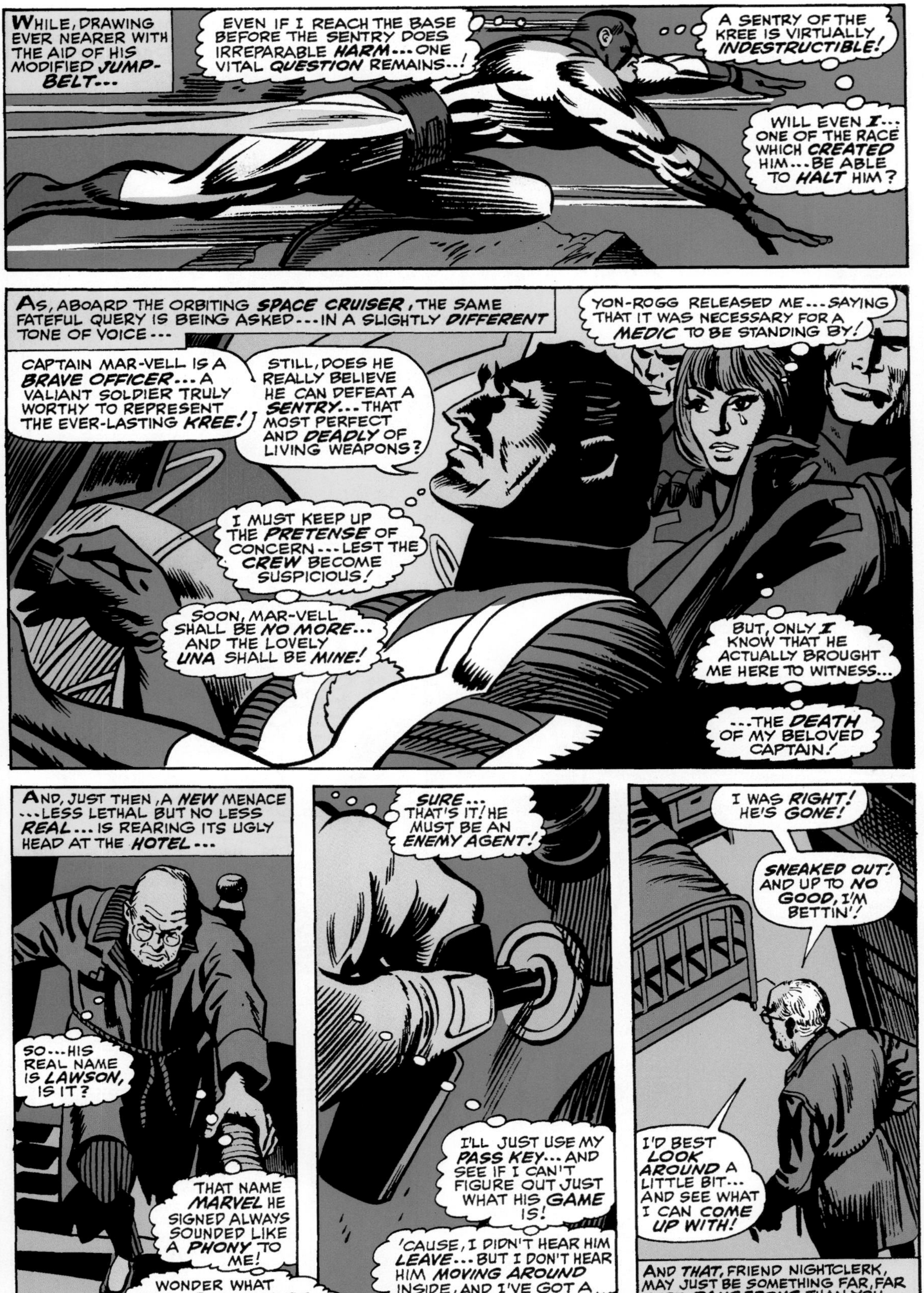

WHILE, DRAWING EVER NEARER WITH THE AID OF HIS MODIFIED JUMP-BELT...
EVEN IF I REACH THE BASE BEFORE THE SENTRY DOES IRREPARABLE HARM... ONE VITAL QUESTION REMAINS..!
A SENTRY OF THE KREE IS VIRTUALLY INDESTRUCTIBLE!
WILL EVEN I... ONE OF THE RACE WHICH CREATED HIM... BE ABLE TO HALT HIM?
AS, ABOARD THE ORBITING SPACE CRUISER, THE SAME FATEFUL QUERY IS BEING ASKED--- IN A SLIGHTLY DIFFERENT TONE OF VOICE---
CAPTAIN MAR-VELL IS A BRAVE OFFICER... A VALIANT SOLDIER TRULY WORTHY TO REPRESENT THE EVER-LASTING KREE!
STILL, DOES HE REALLY BELIEVE HE CAN DEFEAT A SENTRY... THAT MOST PERFECT AND DEADLY OF LIVING WEAPONS?
I MUST KEEP UP THE PRETENSE OF CONCERN--- LEST THE CREW BECOME SUSPICIOUS!
SOON, MAR-VELL SHALL BE NO MORE... AND THE LOVELY UNA SHALL BE MINE!
YON-ROGG RELEASED ME... SAYING THAT IT WAS NECESSARY FOR A MEDIC TO BE STANDING BY!
BUT, ONLY I KNOW THAT HE ACTUALLY BROUGHT ME HERE TO WITNESS...
...THE DEATH OF MY BELOVED CAPTAIN!
AND, JUST THEN, A NEW MENACE ...LESS LETHAL BUT NO LESS REAL... IS REARING ITS UGLY HEAD AT THE HOTEL...
SO... HIS REAL NAME IS LAWSON, IS IT?
THAT NAME MARVEL HE SIGNED ALWAYS SOUNDED LIKE A PHONY TO ME!
WONDER WHAT HE'S UP TO... MAYBE SPYING ON THE CAPE!?
SURE... THAT'S IT! HE MUST BE AN ENEMY AGENT!
I'LL JUST USE MY PASS KEY... AND SEE IF I CAN'T FIGURE OUT JUST WHAT HIS GAME IS!
'CAUSE, I DIDN'T HEAR HIM LEAVE... BUT I DON'T HEAR HIM MOVING AROUND INSIDE, AND I'VE GOT A HUNCH THAT...
I WAS RIGHT! HE'S GONE!
SNEAKED OUT! AND UP TO NO GOOD, I'M BETTIN'!
I'D BEST LOOK AROUND A LITTLE BIT... AND SEE WHAT I CAN COME UP WITH!
AND THAT, FRIEND NIGHTCLERK, MAY JUST BE SOMETHING FAR, FAR MORE DANGEROUS THAN YOU COULD POSSIBLY IMAGINE...
19.

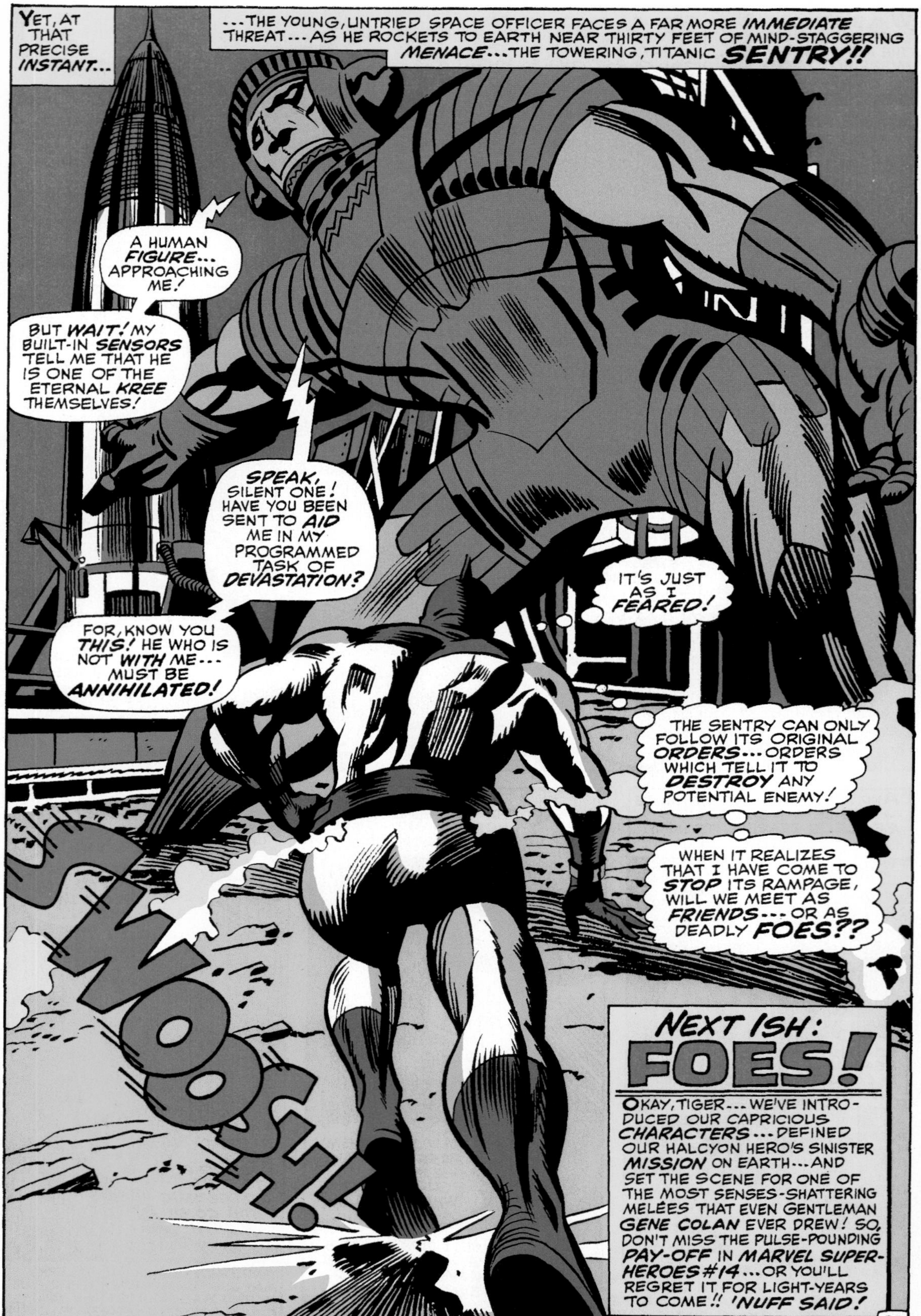

YET, AT THAT PRECISE INSTANT...
...THE YOUNG, UNTRIED SPACE OFFICER FACES A FAR MORE IMMEDIATE THREAT... AS HE ROCKETS TO EARTH NEAR THIRTY FEET OF MIND-STAGGERING MENACE... THE TOWERING, TITANIC SENTRY!!
A HUMAN FIGURE... APPROACHING ME!
BUT WAIT! MY BUILT-IN SENSORS TELL ME THAT HE IS ONE OF THE ETERNAL KREE THEMSELVES!
SPEAK, SILENT ONE! HAVE YOU BEEN SENT TO AID ME IN MY PROGRAMMED TASK OF DEVASTATION?
FOR, KNOW YOU THIS! HE WHO IS NOT WITH ME... MUST BE ANNIHILATED!
IT'S JUST AS I FEARED!
THE SENTRY CAN ONLY FOLLOW ITS ORIGINAL ORDERS... ORDERS WHICH TELL IT TO DESTROY ANY POTENTIAL ENEMY!
WHEN IT REALIZES THAT I HAVE COME TO STOP ITS RAMPAGE, WILL WE MEET AS FRIENDS... OR AS DEADLY FOES??
SWOOSH!
NEXT ISH: FOES!
OKAY, TIGER... WE'VE INTRODUCED OUR CAPRICIOUS CHARACTERS... DEFINED OUR HALCYON HERO'S SINISTER MISSION ON EARTH... AND SET THE SCENE FOR ONE OF THE MOST SENSES-SHATTERING MELÉES THAT EVEN GENTLEMAN GENE COLAN EVER DREW! SO, DON'T MISS THE PULSE-POUNDING PAY-OFF IN MARVEL SUPER-HEROES #14... OR YOU'LL REGRET IT FOR LIGHT-YEARS TO COME!! 'NUFF SAID!
20.

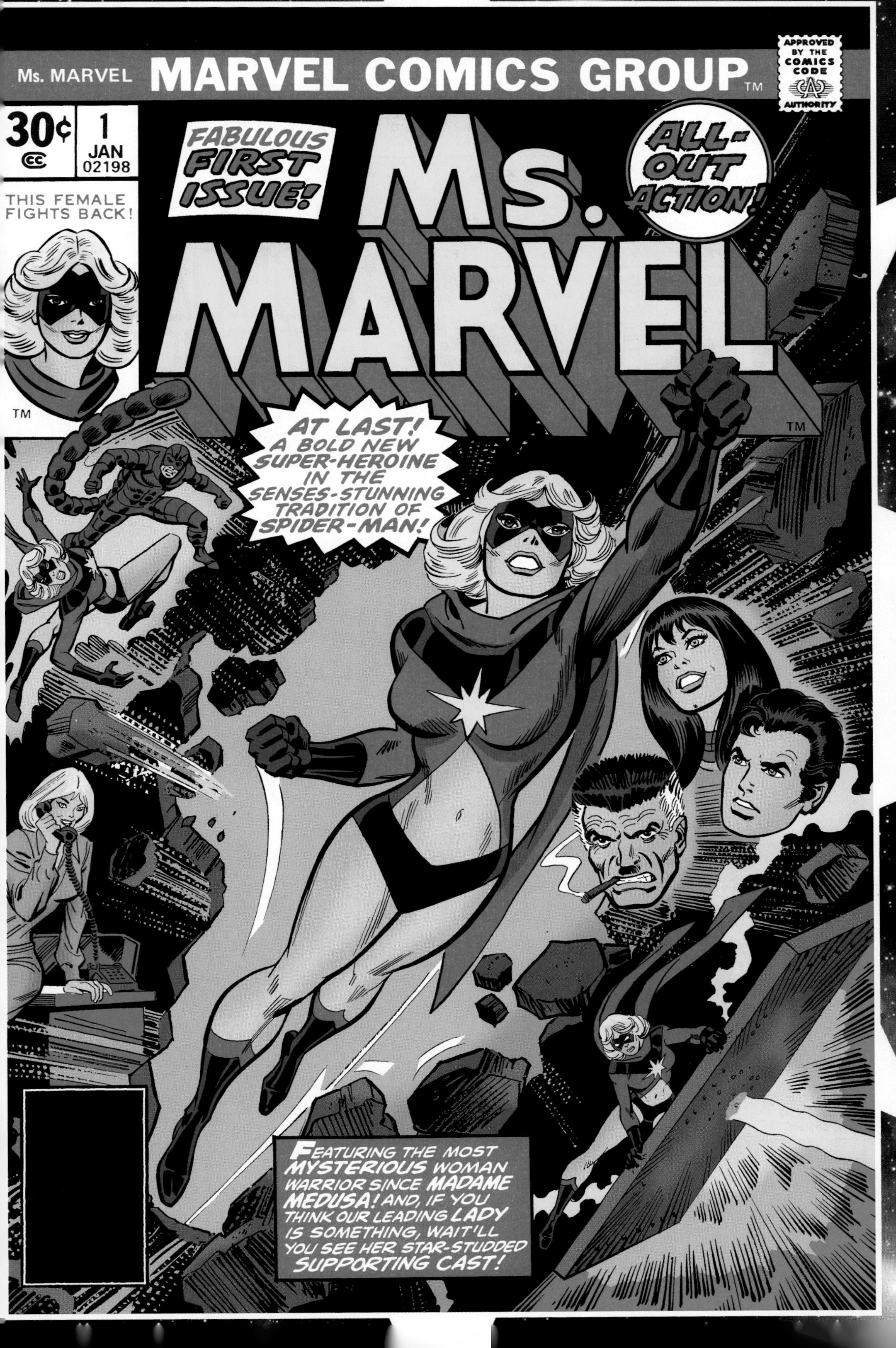
Ms. MARVEL
MARVEL COMICS GROUP TM
APPROVED BY THE COMICS CODE AUTHORITY
30¢ CC
1 JAN 02198
THIS FEMALE FIGHTS BACK!
TM
FABULOUS FIRST ISSUE!
Ms. MARVEL TM
ALL-OUT ACTION!
AT LAST! A BOLD NEW SUPER-HEROINE IN THE SENSES-STUNNING TRADITION OF SPIDER-MAN!
FEATURING THE MOST MYSTERIOUS WOMAN WARRIOR SINCE MADAME MEDUSA! AND, IF YOU THINK OUR LEADING LADY IS SOMETHING, WAIT'LL YOU SEE HER STAR-STUDDED SUPPORTING CAST!

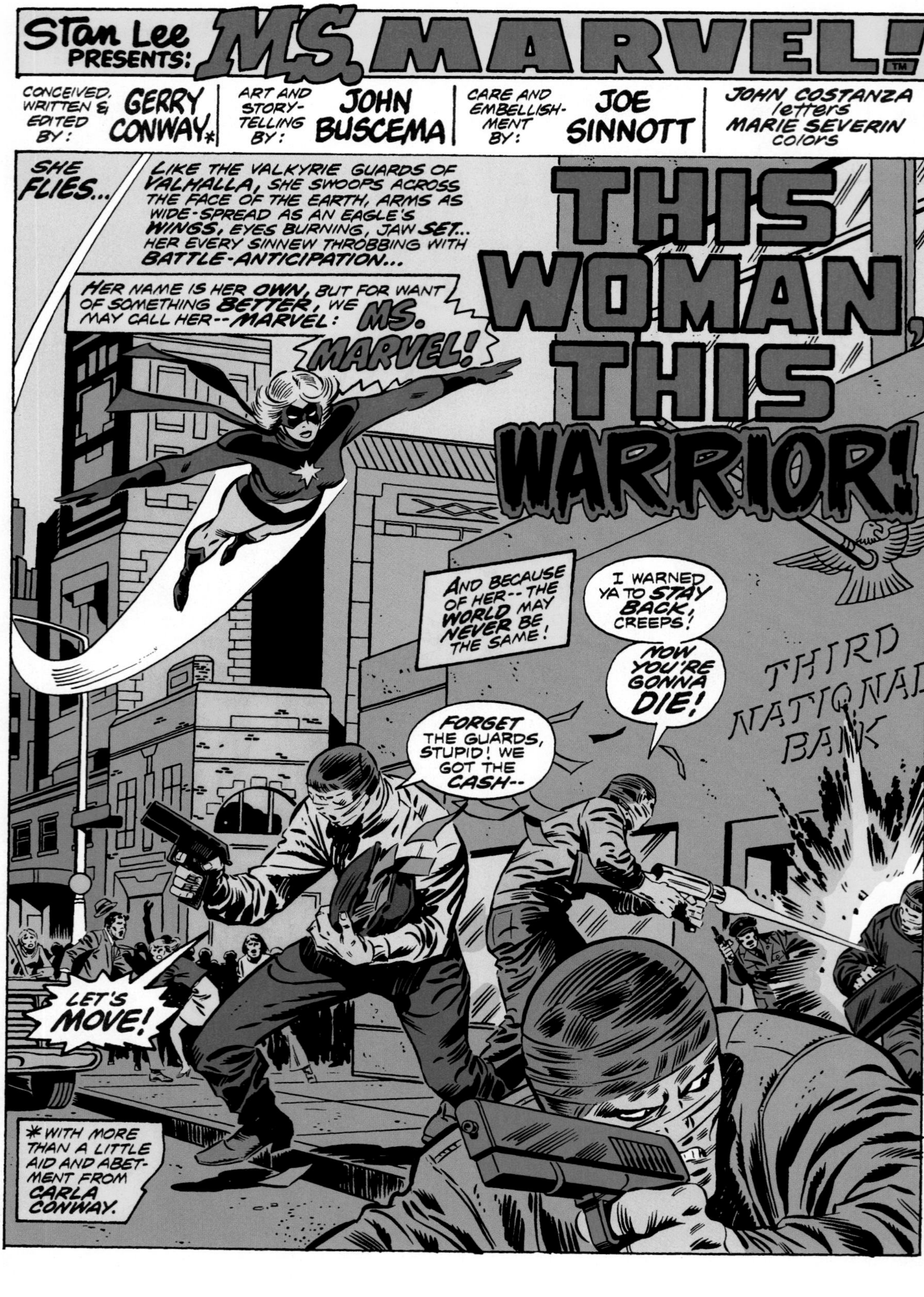
Stan Lee PRESENTS: MS. MARVEL! ™
CONCEIVED, WRITTEN & EDITED BY: GERRY CONWAY*
ART AND STORY-TELLING BY: JOHN BUSCEMA
CARE AND EMBELLISH-MENT BY: JOE SINNOTT
JOHN COSTANZA letters MARIE SEVERIN colors
SHE FLIES...
LIKE THE VALKYRIE GUARDS OF VALHALLA, SHE SWOOPS ACROSS THE FACE OF THE EARTH, ARMS AS WIDE-SPREAD AS AN EAGLE'S WINGS, EYES BURNING, JAW SET... HER EVERY SINNEW THROBBING WITH BATTLE-ANTICIPATION...
HER NAME IS HER OWN, BUT FOR WANT OF SOMETHING BETTER, WE MAY CALL HER--MARVEL: MS. MARVEL!
THIS WOMAN, THIS WARRIOR!
AND BECAUSE OF HER--THE WORLD MAY NEVER BE THE SAME!
I WARNED YA TO STAY BACK, CREEPS!
NOW YOU'RE GONNA DIE!
THIRD NATIONAL BANK
FORGET THE GUARDS, STUPID! WE GOT THE CASH--
LET'S MOVE!
*WITH MORE THAN A LITTLE AID AND ABET-MENT FROM CARLA CONWAY.

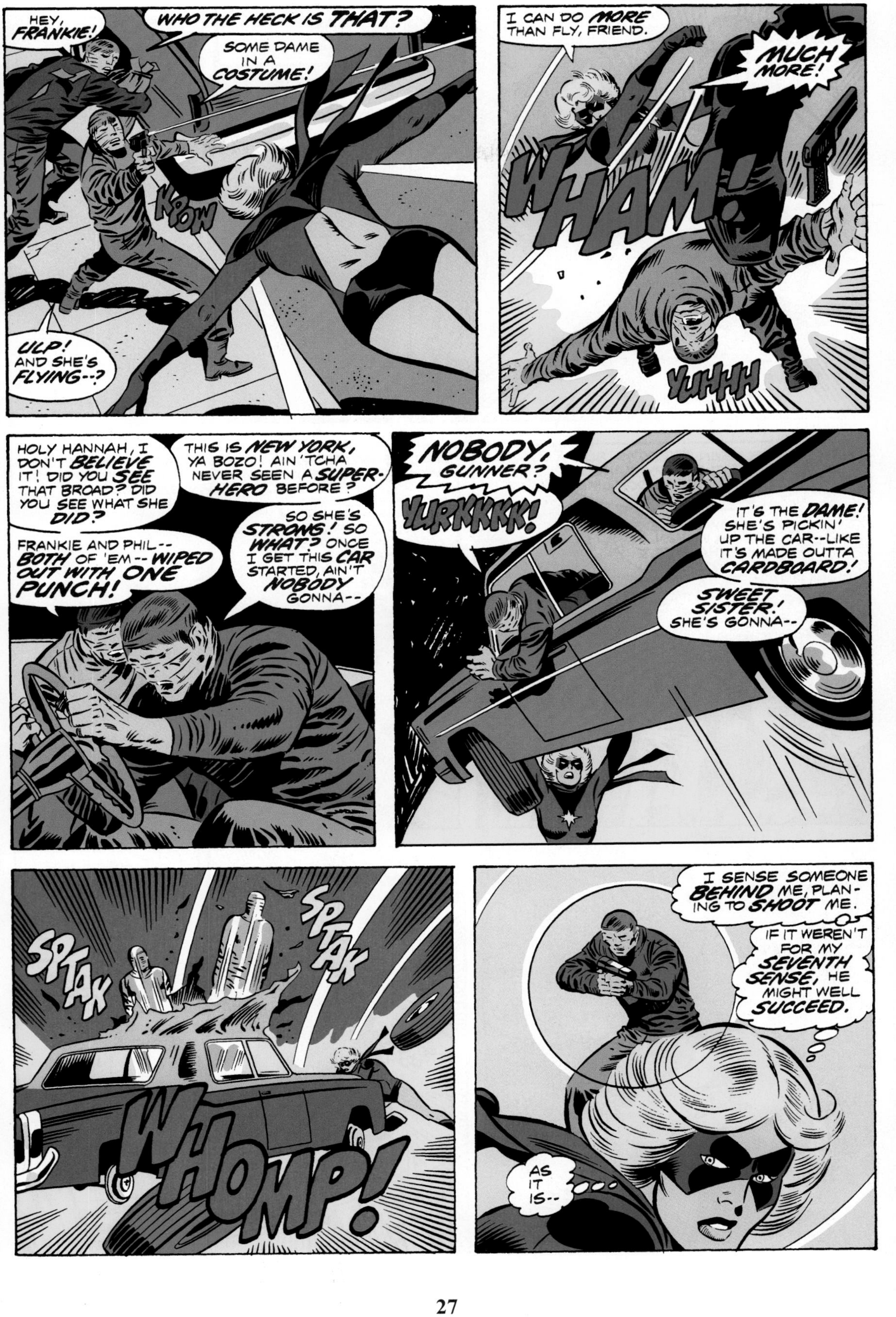
HEY, FRANKIE!
WHO THE HECK IS THAT?
SOME DAME IN A COSTUME!
KPOW
ULP! AND SHE'S FLYING--?
I CAN DO MORE THAN FLY, FRIEND.
MUCH MORE!
WHAM!
YUHHH
HOLY HANNAH, I DON'T BELIEVE IT! DID YOU SEE THAT BROAD? DID YOU SEE WHAT SHE DID?
THIS IS NEW YORK, YA BOZO! AIN'TCHA NEVER SEEN A SUPER-HERO BEFORE?
FRANKIE AND PHIL-- BOTH OF 'EM -- WIPED OUT WITH ONE PUNCH!
SO SHE'S STRONG! SO WHAT? ONCE I GET THIS CAR STARTED, AIN'T NOBODY GONNA--
NOBODY, GUNNER?
YURKKKK!
IT'S THE DAME! SHE'S PICKIN' UP THE CAR--LIKE IT'S MADE OUTTA CARDBOARD!
SWEET SISTER! SHE'S GONNA--
SPTAK
SPTAK
WHOMP!
I SENSE SOMEONE BEHIND ME, PLANING TO SHOOT ME.
IF IT WEREN'T FOR MY SEVENTH SENSE, HE MIGHT WELL SUCCEED.
AS IT IS--

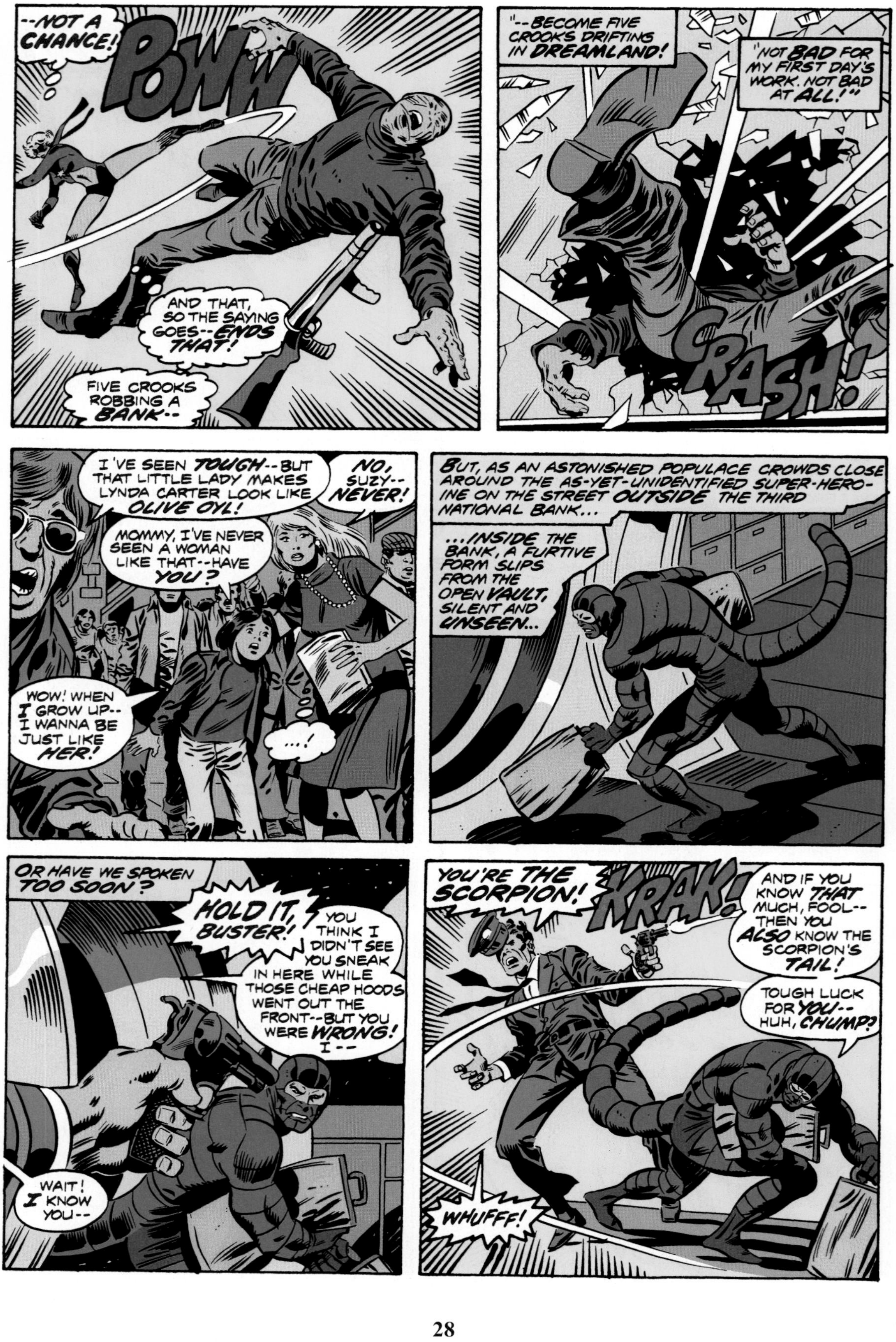
--NOT A CHANCE!
POWW
AND THAT, SO THE SAYING GOES--ENDS THAT!
FIVE CROOKS ROBBING A BANK--
"--BECOME FIVE CROOKS DRIFTING IN DREAMLAND!
"NOT BAD FOR MY FIRST DAY'S WORK. NOT BAD AT ALL!"
CRASH!
I'VE SEEN TOUGH--BUT THAT LITTLE LADY MAKES LYNDA CARTER LOOK LIKE OLIVE OYL!
NO, SUZY--NEVER!
MOMMY, I'VE NEVER SEEN A WOMAN LIKE THAT--HAVE YOU?
WOW! WHEN I GROW UP--I WANNA BE JUST LIKE HER!
...!
BUT, AS AN ASTONISHED POPULACE CROWDS CLOSE AROUND THE AS-YET-UNIDENTIFIED SUPER-HEROINE ON THE STREET OUTSIDE THE THIRD NATIONAL BANK...
...INSIDE THE BANK, A FURTIVE FORM SLIPS FROM THE OPEN VAULT, SILENT AND UNSEEN...
OR HAVE WE SPOKEN TOO SOON?
HOLD IT, BUSTER!
YOU THINK I DIDN'T SEE YOU SNEAK IN HERE WHILE THOSE CHEAP HOODS WENT OUT THE FRONT--BUT YOU WERE WRONG! I--
WAIT! I KNOW YOU--
YOU'RE THE SCORPION!
KRAK!
AND IF YOU KNOW THAT MUCH, FOOL--THEN YOU ALSO KNOW THE SCORPION'S TAIL!
TOUGH LUCK FOR YOU--HUH, CHUMP?
WHUFFF!

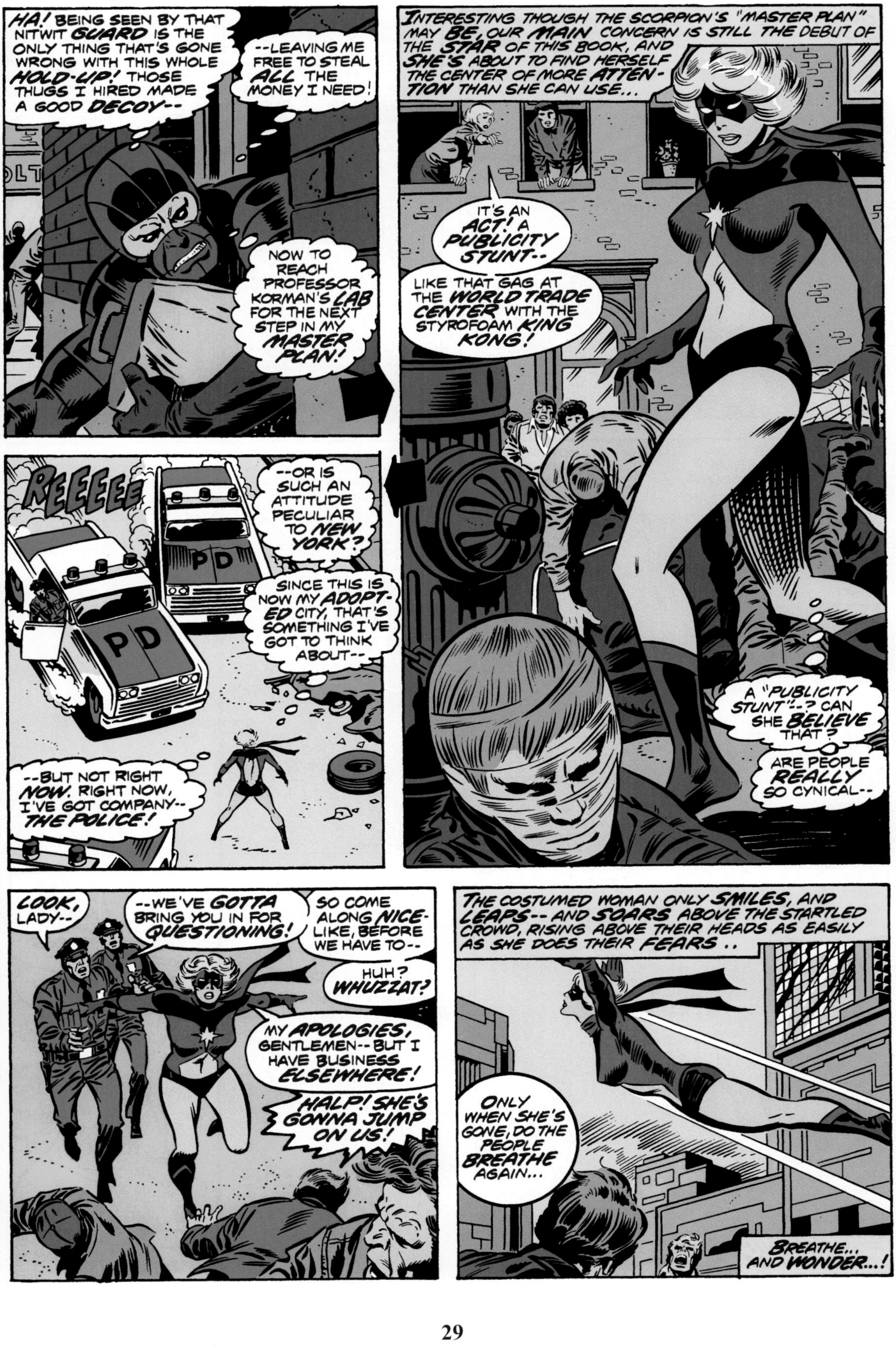
HA! BEING SEEN BY THAT NITWIT GUARD IS THE ONLY THING THAT'S GONE WRONG WITH THIS WHOLE HOLD-UP! THOSE THUGS I HIRED MADE A GOOD DECOY--
--LEAVING ME FREE TO STEAL ALL THE MONEY I NEED!
NOW TO REACH PROFESSOR KORMAN'S LAB FOR THE NEXT STEP IN MY MASTER PLAN!
INTERESTING THOUGH THE SCORPION'S "MASTER PLAN" MAY BE, OUR MAIN CONCERN IS STILL THE DEBUT OF THE STAR OF THIS BOOK, AND SHE'S ABOUT TO FIND HERSELF THE CENTER OF MORE ATTENTION THAN SHE CAN USE...
IT'S AN ACT! A PUBLICITY STUNT--
LIKE THAT GAG AT THE WORLD TRADE CENTER WITH THE STYROFOAM KING KONG!
A "PUBLICITY STUNT"--? CAN SHE BELIEVE THAT?
ARE PEOPLE REALLY SO CYNICAL--
REEEEE
--OR IS SUCH AN ATTITUDE PECULIAR TO NEW YORK?
SINCE THIS IS NOW MY ADOPTED CITY, THAT'S SOMETHING I'VE GOT TO THINK ABOUT--
PD
PD
--BUT NOT RIGHT NOW. RIGHT NOW, I'VE GOT COMPANY-- THE POLICE!
LOOK, LADY--
--WE'VE GOTTA BRING YOU IN FOR QUESTIONING!
SO COME ALONG NICE-LIKE, BEFORE WE HAVE TO--
HUH? WHUZZAT?
MY APOLOGIES, GENTLEMEN-- BUT I HAVE BUSINESS ELSEWHERE!
HALP! SHE'S GONNA JUMP ON US!
THE COSTUMED WOMAN ONLY SMILES, AND LEAPS-- AND SOARS ABOVE THE STARTLED CROWD, RISING ABOVE THEIR HEADS AS EASILY AS SHE DOES THEIR FEARS..
ONLY WHEN SHE'S GONE, DO THE PEOPLE BREATHE AGAIN...
BREATHE... AND WONDER...!

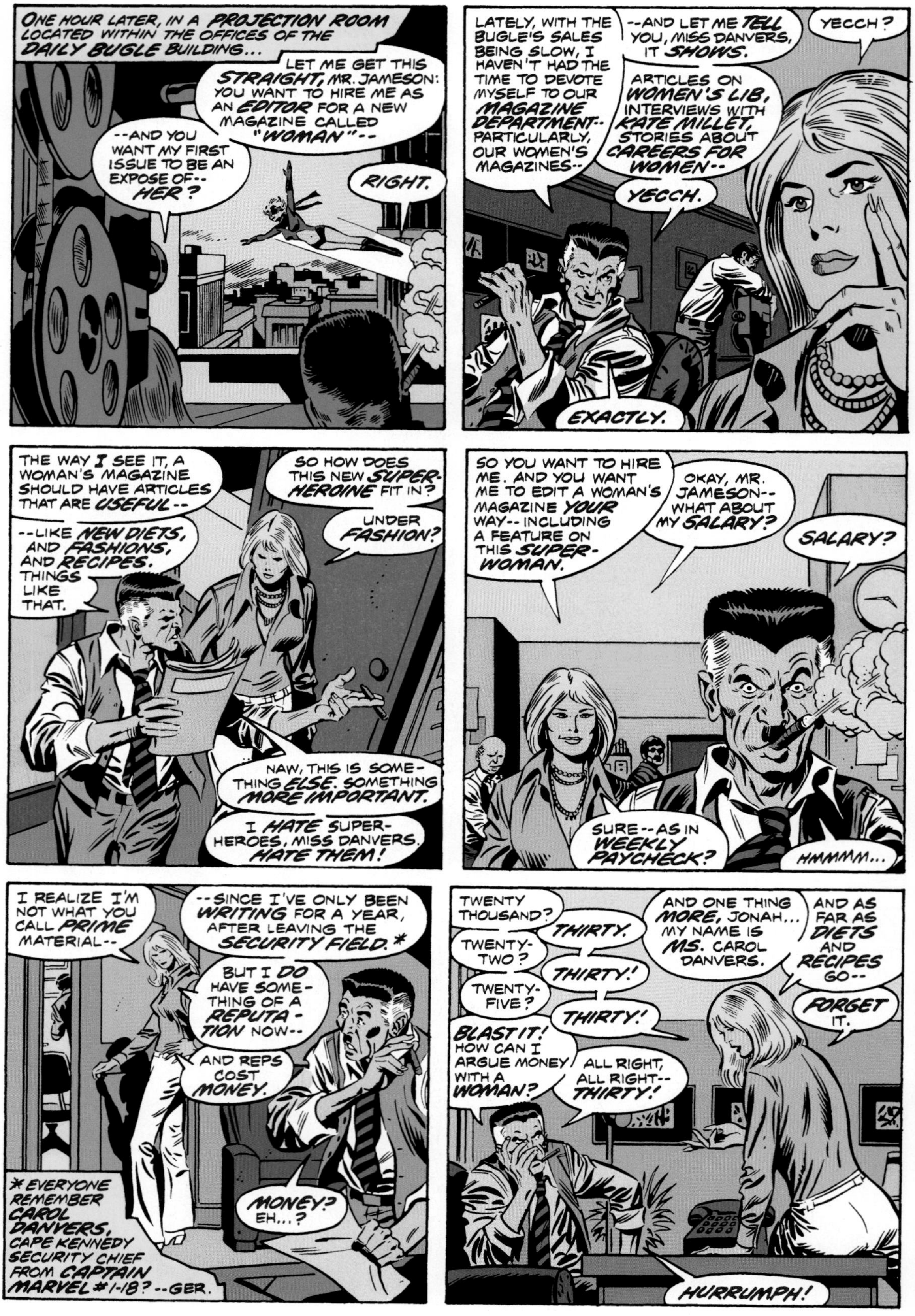
ONE HOUR LATER, IN A PROJECTION ROOM LOCATED WITHIN THE OFFICES OF THE DAILY BUGLE BUILDING...
LET ME GET THIS STRAIGHT, MR. JAMESON: YOU WANT TO HIRE ME AS AN EDITOR FOR A NEW MAGAZINE CALLED "WOMAN"--
--AND YOU WANT MY FIRST ISSUE TO BE AN EXPOSE OF-- HER?
RIGHT.
LATELY, WITH THE BUGLE'S SALES BEING SLOW, I HAVEN'T HAD THE TIME TO DEVOTE MYSELF TO OUR MAGAZINE DEPARTMENT-- PARTICULARLY, OUR WOMEN'S MAGAZINES--
--AND LET ME TELL YOU, MISS DANVERS, IT SHOWS.
ARTICLES ON WOMEN'S LIB, INTERVIEWS WITH KATE MILLET, STORIES ABOUT CAREERS FOR WOMEN--
YECCH.
YECCH?
EXACTLY.
THE WAY I SEE IT, A WOMAN'S MAGAZINE SHOULD HAVE ARTICLES THAT ARE USEFUL--
--LIKE NEW DIETS, AND FASHIONS, AND RECIPES. THINGS LIKE THAT.
SO HOW DOES THIS NEW SUPER-HEROINE FIT IN?
UNDER FASHION?
NAW, THIS IS SOME-THING ELSE. SOMETHING MORE IMPORTANT.
I HATE SUPER-HEROES, MISS DANVERS. HATE THEM!
SO YOU WANT TO HIRE ME. AND YOU WANT ME TO EDIT A WOMAN'S MAGAZINE YOUR WAY-- INCLUDING A FEATURE ON THIS SUPER-WOMAN.
OKAY, MR. JAMESON-- WHAT ABOUT MY SALARY?
SALARY?
SURE--AS IN WEEKLY PAYCHECK?
HMMMM...
I REALIZE I'M NOT WHAT YOU CALL PRIME MATERIAL--
--SINCE I'VE ONLY BEEN WRITING FOR A YEAR, AFTER LEAVING THE SECURITY FIELD.*
BUT I DO HAVE SOME-THING OF A REPUTA-TION NOW--
AND REPS COST MONEY.
MONEY? EH...?
*EVERYONE REMEMBER CAROL DANVERS, CAPE KENNEDY SECURITY CHIEF FROM CAPTAIN MARVEL #1-18? --GER.
TWENTY THOUSAND?
THIRTY.
TWENTY-TWO?
THIRTY!
TWENTY-FIVE?
THIRTY!
BLAST IT! HOW CAN I ARGUE MONEY WITH A WOMAN?
ALL RIGHT, ALL RIGHT-- THIRTY!
AND ONE THING MORE, JONAH... MY NAME IS MS. CAROL DANVERS.
AND AS FAR AS DIETS AND RECIPES GO--
FORGET IT.
HURRUMPH!

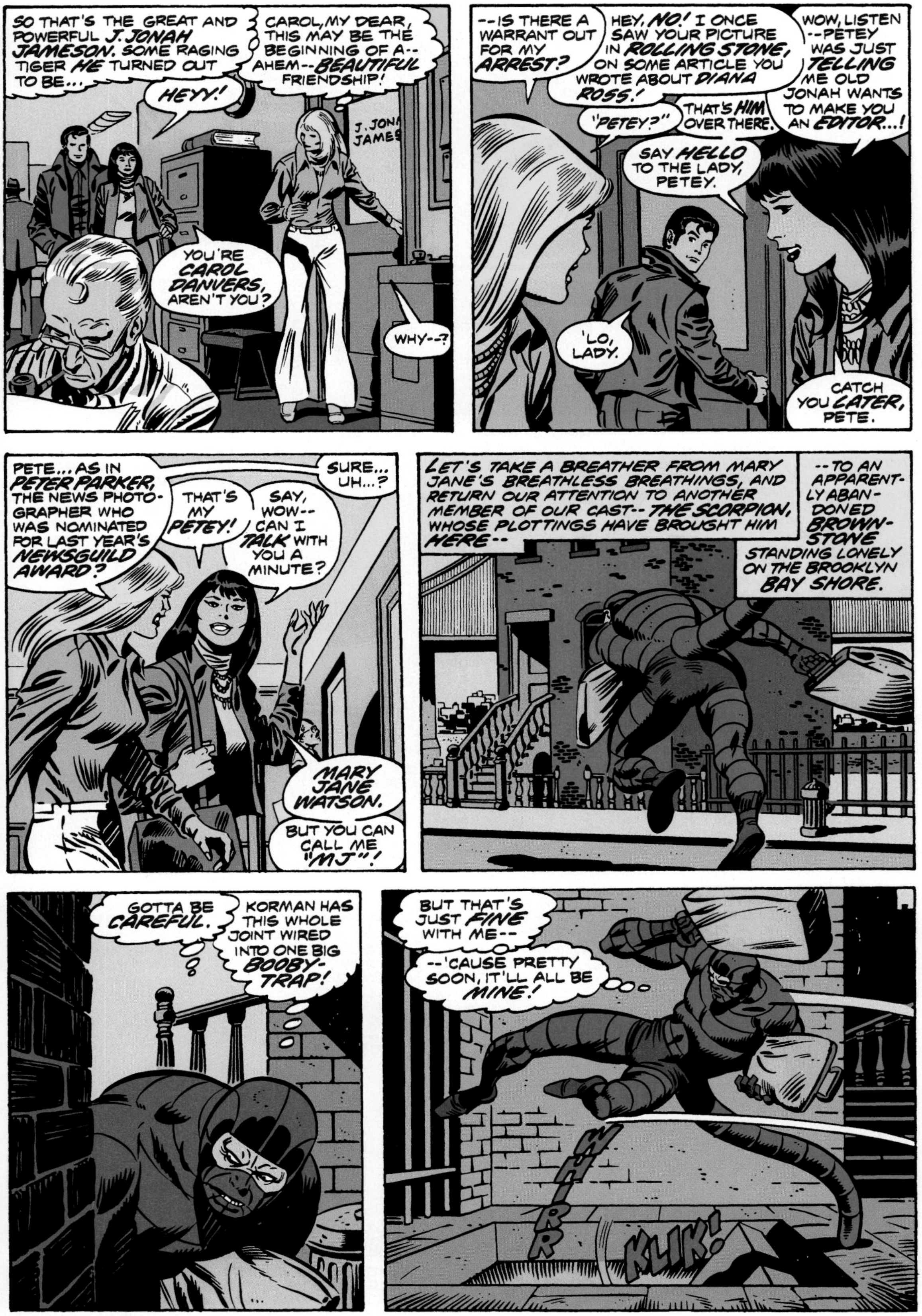

SO THAT'S THE GREAT AND POWERFUL J. JONAH JAMESON. SOME RAGING TIGER HE TURNED OUT TO BE...
CAROL, MY DEAR, THIS MAY BE THE BEGINNING OF A-- AHEM--BEAUTIFUL FRIENDSHIP!
HEYY!
J. JONA
JAMES
YOU'RE CAROL DANVERS, AREN'T YOU?
WHY--?
--IS THERE A WARRANT OUT FOR MY ARREST?
HEY, NO! I ONCE SAW YOUR PICTURE IN ROLLING STONE, ON SOME ARTICLE YOU WROTE ABOUT DIANA ROSS!
WOW, LISTEN--PETEY WAS JUST TELLING ME OLD JONAH WANTS TO MAKE YOU AN EDITOR...!
"PETEY?"
THAT'S HIM OVER THERE.
SAY HELLO TO THE LADY, PETEY.
'LO, LADY.
CATCH YOU LATER, PETE.
PETE... AS IN PETER PARKER, THE NEWS PHOTOGRAPHER WHO WAS NOMINATED FOR LAST YEAR'S NEWSGUILD AWARD?
THAT'S MY PETEY!
SURE... UH...?
SAY, WOW--CAN I TALK WITH YOU A MINUTE?
MARY JANE WATSON.
BUT YOU CAN CALL ME "MJ"!
LET'S TAKE A BREATHER FROM MARY JANE'S BREATHLESS BREATHINGS, AND RETURN OUR ATTENTION TO ANOTHER MEMBER OF OUR CAST--THE SCORPION, WHOSE PLOTTINGS HAVE BROUGHT HIM HERE--
--TO AN APPARENTLY ABANDONED BROWNSTONE STANDING LONELY ON THE BROOKLYN BAY SHORE.
GOTTA BE CAREFUL.
KORMAN HAS THIS WHOLE JOINT WIRED INTO ONE BIG BOOBY-TRAP!
BUT THAT'S JUST FINE WITH ME--
--'CAUSE PRETTY SOON, IT'LL ALL BE MINE!
WHIRR
KLIK!

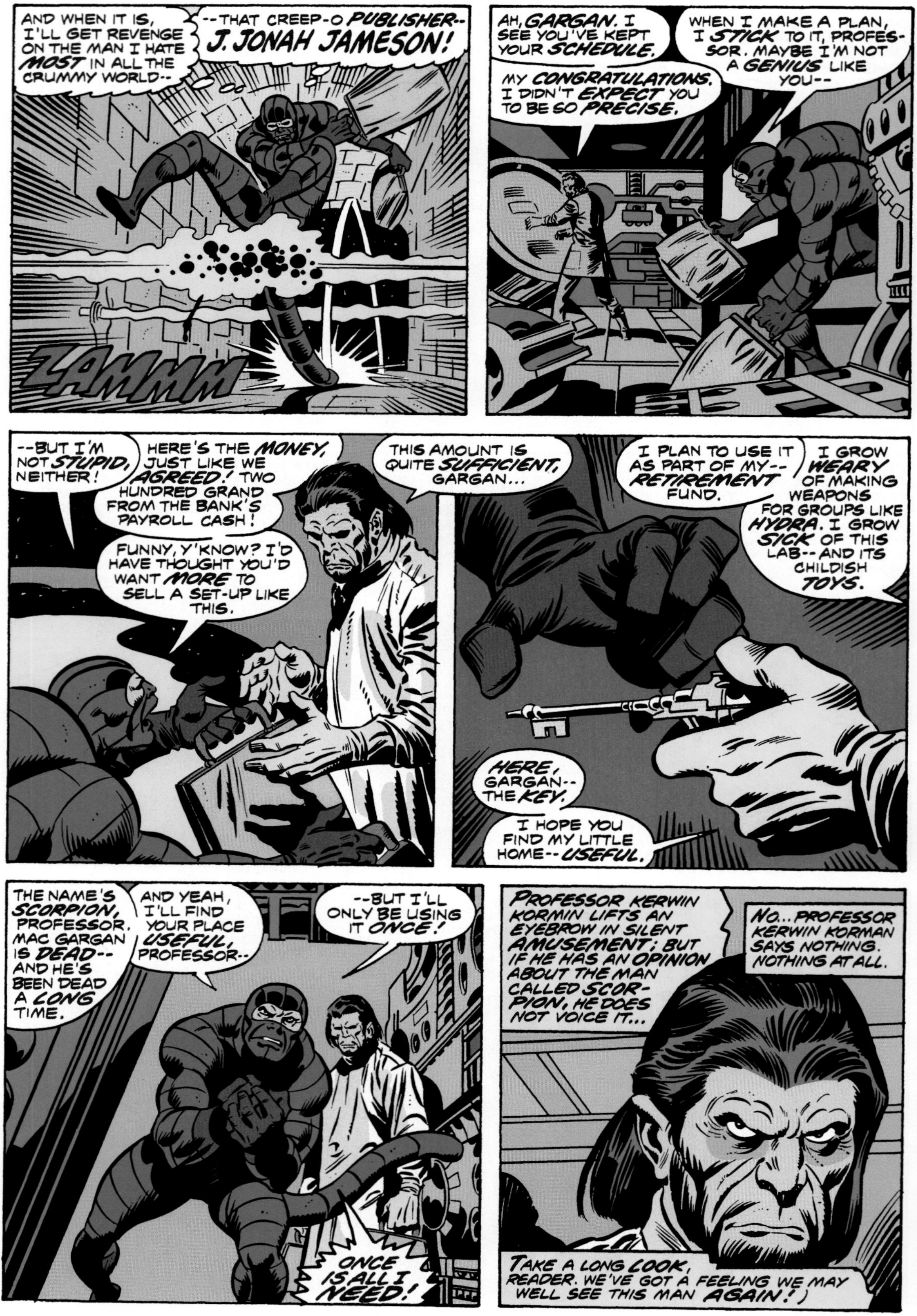
AND WHEN IT IS, I'LL GET REVENGE ON THE MAN I HATE MOST IN ALL THE CRUMMY WORLD--
--THAT CREEP-O PUBLISHER-- J. JONAH JAMESON!
ZAMMM
AH, GARGAN. I SEE YOU'VE KEPT YOUR SCHEDULE.
MY CONGRATULATIONS. I DIDN'T EXPECT YOU TO BE SO PRECISE.
WHEN I MAKE A PLAN, I STICK TO IT, PROFESSOR. MAYBE I'M NOT A GENIUS LIKE YOU--
--BUT I'M NOT STUPID, NEITHER!
HERE'S THE MONEY, JUST LIKE WE AGREED! TWO HUNDRED GRAND FROM THE BANK'S PAYROLL CASH!
FUNNY, Y'KNOW? I'D HAVE THOUGHT YOU'D WANT MORE TO SELL A SET-UP LIKE THIS.
THIS AMOUNT IS QUITE SUFFICIENT, GARGAN...
I PLAN TO USE IT AS PART OF MY-- RETIREMENT FUND.
I GROW WEARY OF MAKING WEAPONS FOR GROUPS LIKE HYDRA. I GROW SICK OF THIS LAB-- AND ITS CHILDISH TOYS.
HERE, GARGAN-- THE KEY.
I HOPE YOU FIND MY LITTLE HOME-- USEFUL.
THE NAME'S SCORPION, PROFESSOR. MAC GARGAN IS DEAD-- AND HE'S BEEN DEAD A LONG TIME.
AND YEAH, I'LL FIND YOUR PLACE USEFUL, PROFESSOR--
--BUT I'LL ONLY BE USING IT ONCE!
ONCE IS ALL I NEED!
PROFESSOR KERWIN KORMIN LIFTS AN EYEBROW IN SILENT AMUSEMENT; BUT IF HE HAS AN OPINION ABOUT THE MAN CALLED SCORPION, HE DOES NOT VOICE IT...
NO... PROFESSOR KERWIN KORMAN SAYS NOTHING. NOTHING AT ALL.
TAKE A LONG LOOK, READER. WE'VE GOT A FEELING WE MAY WELL SEE THIS MAN AGAIN!)

AND, SPEAKING OF SEEING PEOPLE AGAIN, ISN'T IT TIME WE *REJOINED* ONE OF THE STARS OF THIS *BOOK*--?

MS. DANVERS! THERE WAS A MAN TO SEE YOU-- SAID HIS NAME WAS *BARNETT.*

HE LEFT A *MESSAGE*-- SOMETHING ABOUT DINNER AT *SARDI'S*--?

SURE--

THANKS, HEWLIT. I'LL GIVE MIKE A CALL WHEN I GET *UPSTAIRS.*

CARE FOR SOME *COFFEE,* MARY JANE?

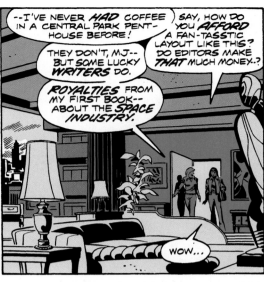

--I'VE NEVER *HAD* COFFEE IN A CENTRAL PARK PENT-HOUSE BEFORE!

THEY DON'T, MJ-- BUT SOME LUCKY *WRITERS* DO.

ROYALTIES FROM MY FIRST BOOK-- ABOUT THE *SPACE INDUSTRY.*

SAY, HOW DO YOU *AFFORD* A FAN-*TASSTIC* LAYOUT LIKE THIS? DO EDITORS MAKE *THAT* MUCH MONEY..?

WOW...

...THAT'S *RIGHT.* YOU WERE A *SECURITY CONSULTANT* AT CAPE KENNEDY, WEREN'T YOU?

I REMEMBER READING ABOUT YOU IN THE PAPERS, WHEN THAT WEIRD *CAPTAIN MARVEL* GUY FIRST SHOWED UP ON EARTH. *

WHY'D YOU *LEAVE* ALL THAT, CAROL-- AND HOWCUM YOU BECAME A *WRITER?*

NOT BECAUSE I *WANTED* TO, MJ--

* AGAIN, CM #1.--GER.

--BUT BECAUSE I *HAD* TO.

CAPTAIN MARVEL'S APPEARANCE AT THE CAPE--AND MY INABILITY TO *CAPTURE* HIM-- JUST ABOUT *DESTROYED* MY SECURITY FIELD CAREER.

I KEPT TRYING TO HOLD IT *TOGETHER,* UNTIL I FINALLY WENT BACK TO MY FIRST LOVE--

WRITING.

TURNS OUT I HAVE MORE TALENT FOR THE *PEN* THEN THE *SWORD*--AND I'LL TELL YOU, I'M A LOT HAPPIER THAN--

CAROL!

OHHHH

KRASH

I-I'M *ALL RIGHT,* MARY JANE. J-JUST A MIGRANE *HEADACHE*...

I'VE BEEN GETTING A LOT OF THEM... SINCE COMING TO *NEW YORK*...

YOU WANT ME TO CALL A *DOCTOR?*

NO!

NO... I'M SORRY ...BUT YOU BETTER JUST *GO*...

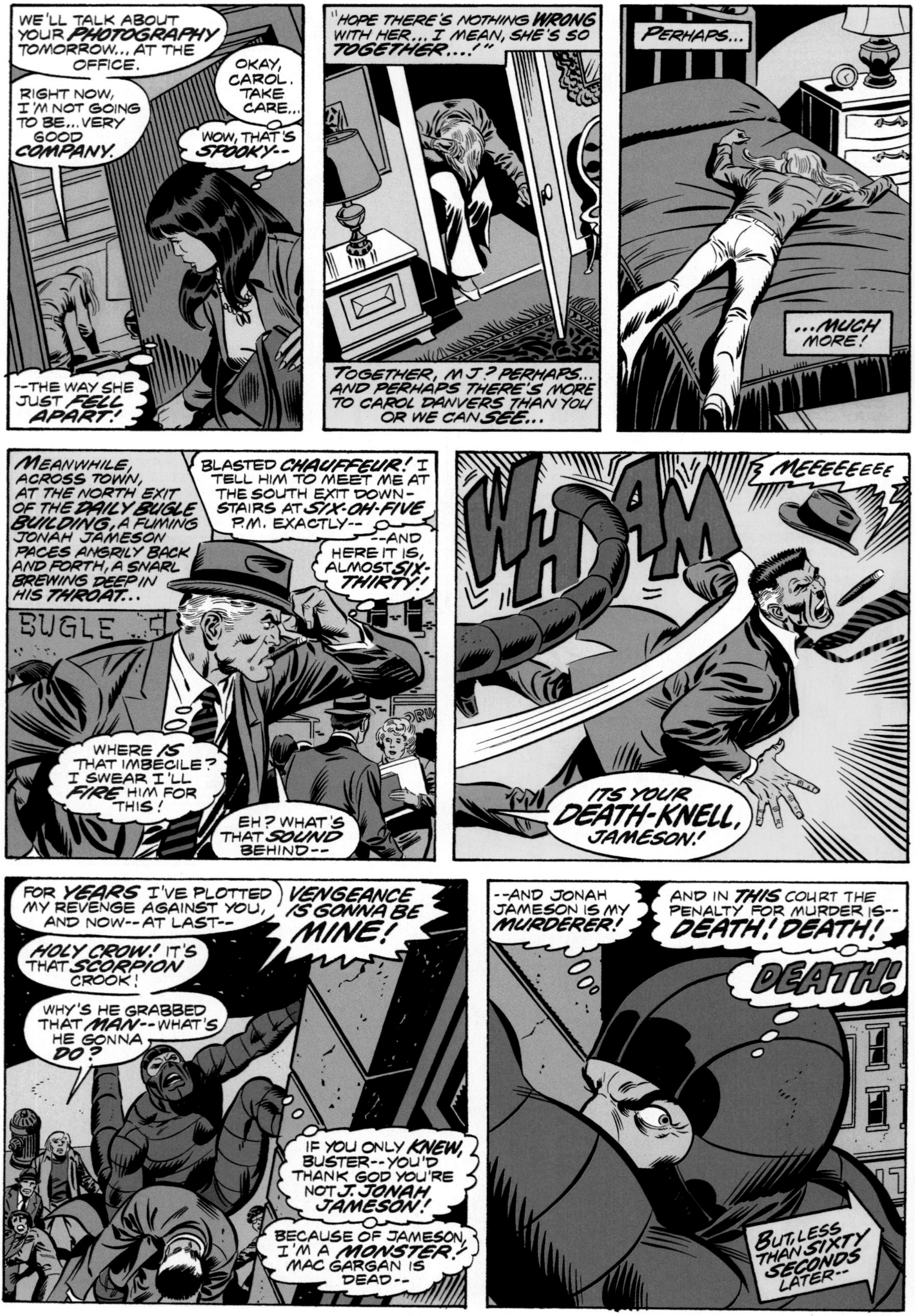
WE'LL TALK ABOUT YOUR PHOTOGRAPHY TOMORROW... AT THE OFFICE.
RIGHT NOW, I'M NOT GOING TO BE... VERY GOOD COMPANY.
OKAY, CAROL. TAKE CARE...
WOW, THAT'S SPOOKY--
--THE WAY SHE JUST FELL APART!
"HOPE THERE'S NOTHING WRONG WITH HER... I MEAN, SHE'S SO TOGETHER...!"
TOGETHER, M.J.? PERHAPS... AND PERHAPS THERE'S MORE TO CAROL DANVERS THAN YOU OR WE CAN SEE...
PERHAPS...
...MUCH MORE!
MEANWHILE, ACROSS TOWN, AT THE NORTH EXIT OF THE DAILY BUGLE BUILDING, A FUMING JONAH JAMESON PACES ANGRILY BACK AND FORTH, A SNARL BREWING DEEP IN HIS THROAT...
BLASTED CHAUFFEUR! I TELL HIM TO MEET ME AT THE SOUTH EXIT DOWN-STAIRS AT SIX-OH-FIVE P.M. EXACTLY--
--AND HERE IT IS, ALMOST SIX-THIRTY!
BUGLE
WHERE IS THAT IMBECILE? I SWEAR I'LL FIRE HIM FOR THIS!
EH? WHAT'S THAT SOUND BEHIND--
WHAM
MEEEEEEEEE
ITS YOUR DEATH-KNELL, JAMESON!
FOR YEARS I'VE PLOTTED MY REVENGE AGAINST YOU, AND NOW--AT LAST--
VENGEANCE IS GONNA BE MINE!
HOLY CROW! IT'S THAT SCORPION CROOK!
WHY'S HE GRABBED THAT MAN--WHAT'S HE GONNA DO?
IF YOU ONLY KNEW, BUSTER--YOU'D THANK GOD YOU'RE NOT J. JONAH JAMESON!
BECAUSE OF JAMESON, I'M A MONSTER! MAC GARGAN IS DEAD--
--AND JONAH JAMESON IS MY MURDERER!
AND IN THIS COURT THE PENALTY FOR MURDER IS--DEATH! DEATH!
DEATH!
BUT, LESS THAN SIXTY SECONDS LATER--

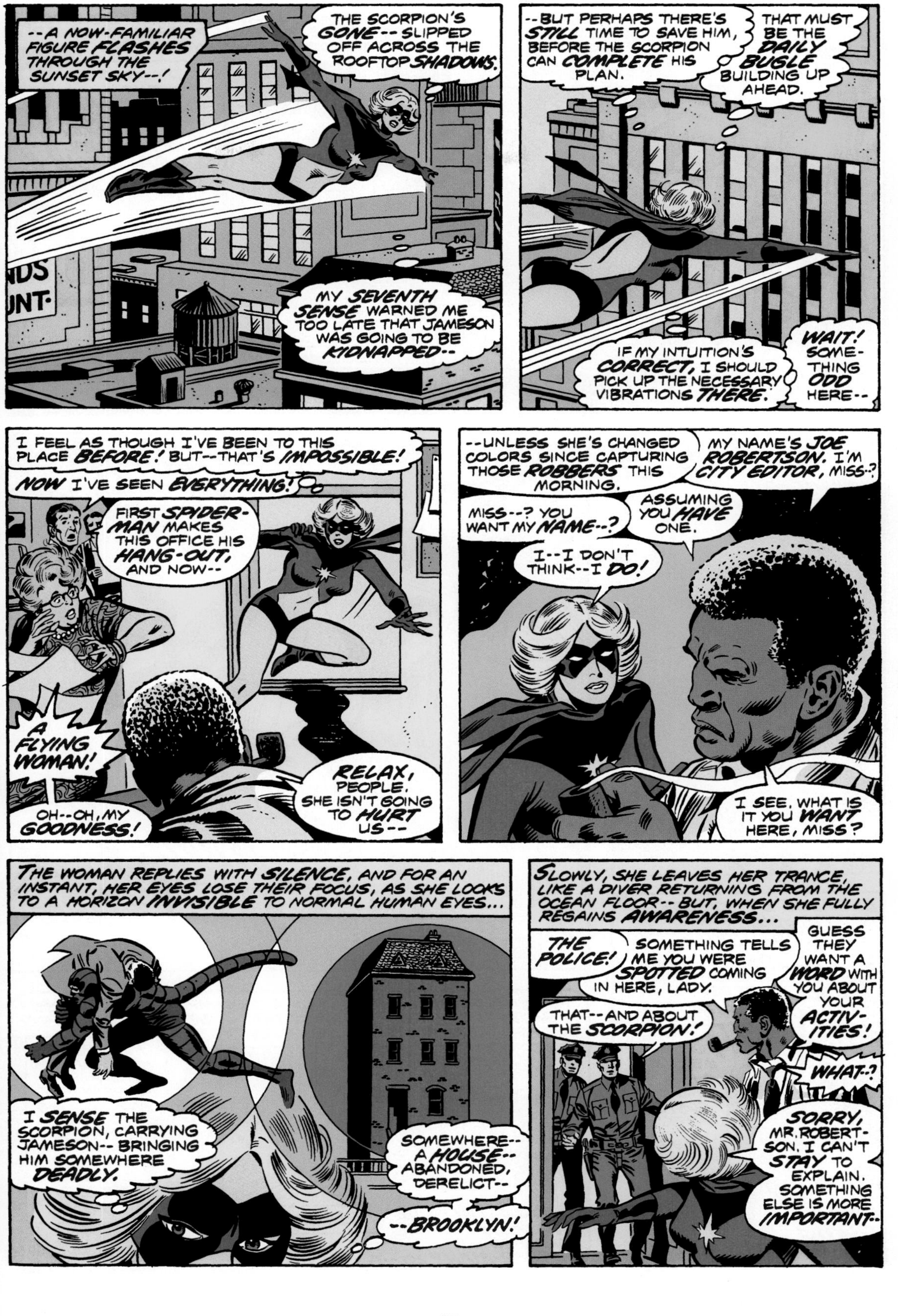
--A NOW-FAMILIAR FIGURE FLASHES THROUGH THE SUNSET SKY--!
THE SCORPION'S GONE--SLIPPED OFF ACROSS THE ROOFTOP SHADOWS.
MY SEVENTH SENSE WARNED ME TOO LATE THAT JAMESON WAS GOING TO BE KIDNAPPED--
--BUT PERHAPS THERE'S STILL TIME TO SAVE HIM, BEFORE THE SCORPION CAN COMPLETE HIS PLAN.
THAT MUST BE THE DAILY BUGLE BUILDING UP AHEAD.
IF MY INTUITION'S CORRECT, I SHOULD PICK UP THE NECESSARY VIBRATIONS THERE.
WAIT! SOMETHING ODD HERE--
I FEEL AS THOUGH I'VE BEEN TO THIS PLACE BEFORE! BUT--THAT'S IMPOSSIBLE!
NOW I'VE SEEN EVERYTHING!
FIRST SPIDER-MAN MAKES THIS OFFICE HIS HANG-OUT, AND NOW--
A FLYING WOMAN!
OH--OH, MY GOODNESS!
RELAX, PEOPLE. SHE ISN'T GOING TO HURT US--
--UNLESS SHE'S CHANGED COLORS SINCE CAPTURING THOSE ROBBERS THIS MORNING.
MY NAME'S JOE ROBERTSON. I'M CITY EDITOR, MISS--?
MISS--? YOU WANT MY NAME--?
ASSUMING YOU HAVE ONE.
I--I DON'T THINK--I DO!
I SEE. WHAT IS IT YOU WANT HERE, MISS?
THE WOMAN REPLIES WITH SILENCE, AND FOR AN INSTANT, HER EYES LOSE THEIR FOCUS, AS SHE LOOKS TO A HORIZON INVISIBLE TO NORMAL HUMAN EYES...
I SENSE THE SCORPION, CARRYING JAMESON--BRINGING HIM SOMEWHERE DEADLY.
SOMEWHERE--A HOUSE--ABANDONED, DERELICT--
--BROOKLYN!
SLOWLY, SHE LEAVES HER TRANCE, LIKE A DIVER RETURNING FROM THE OCEAN FLOOR--BUT, WHEN SHE FULLY REGAINS AWARENESS...
THE POLICE!
SOMETHING TELLS ME YOU WERE SPOTTED COMING IN HERE, LADY.
GUESS THEY WANT A WORD WITH YOU ABOUT YOUR ACTIVITIES!
THAT--AND ABOUT THE SCORPION!
WHAT--?
SORRY, MR. ROBERTSON. I CAN'T STAY TO EXPLAIN. SOMETHING ELSE IS MORE IMPORTANT--

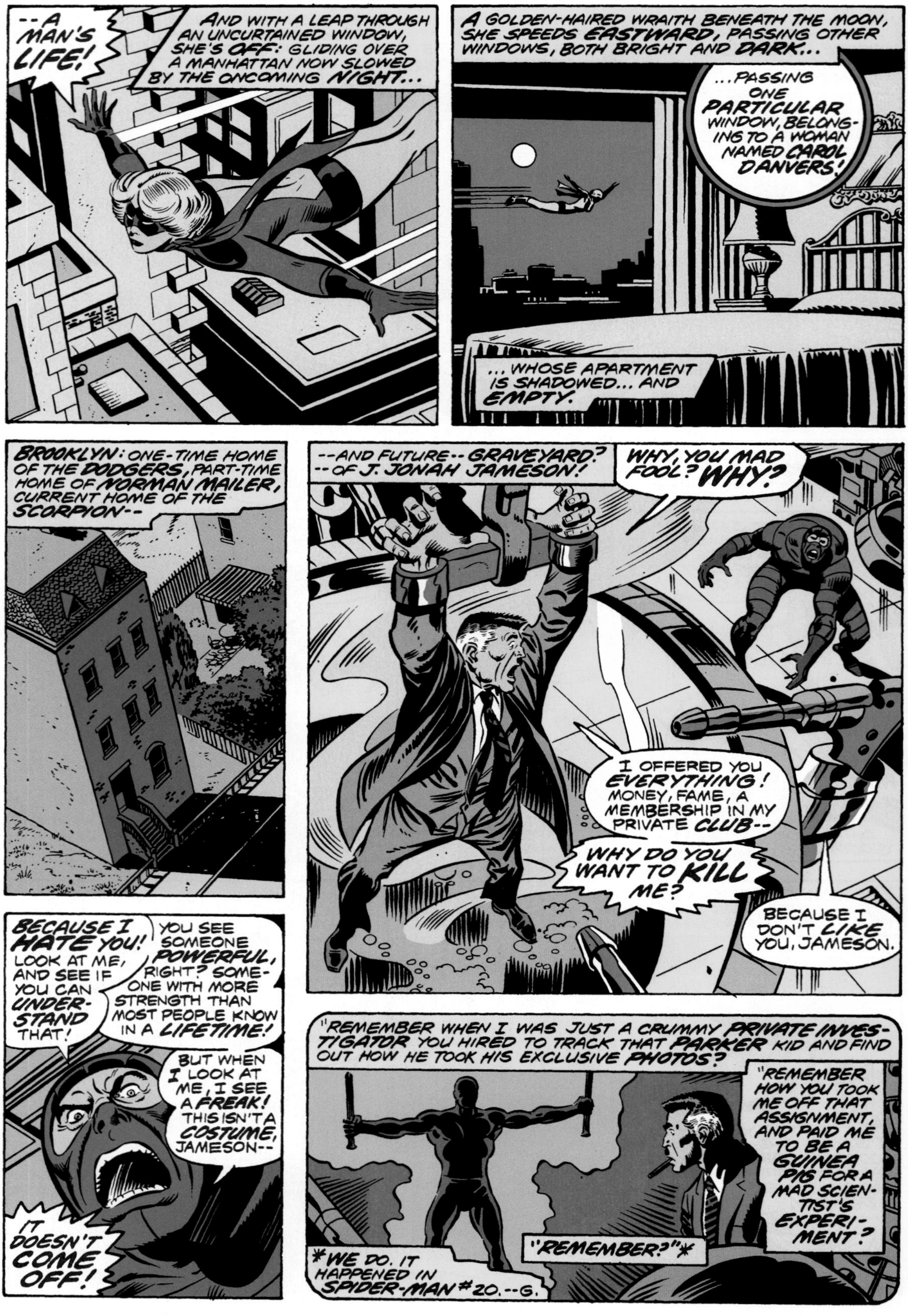

--A MAN'S LIFE!
AND WITH A LEAP THROUGH AN UNCURTAINED WINDOW, SHE'S OFF: GLIDING OVER A MANHATTAN NOW SLOWED BY THE ONCOMING NIGHT...
A GOLDEN-HAIRED WRAITH BENEATH THE MOON, SHE SPEEDS EASTWARD, PASSING OTHER WINDOWS, BOTH BRIGHT AND DARK...
...PASSING ONE PARTICULAR WINDOW, BELONGING TO A WOMAN NAMED CAROL DANVERS!
...WHOSE APARTMENT IS SHADOWED... AND EMPTY.
BROOKLYN: ONE-TIME HOME OF THE DODGERS, PART-TIME HOME OF NORMAN MAILER, CURRENT HOME OF THE SCORPION--
--AND FUTURE--GRAVEYARD? --OF J. JONAH JAMESON!
WHY, YOU MAD FOOL? WHY?
I OFFERED YOU EVERYTHING! MONEY, FAME, A MEMBERSHIP IN MY PRIVATE CLUB--
WHY DO YOU WANT TO KILL ME?
BECAUSE I DON'T LIKE YOU, JAMESON.
BECAUSE I HATE YOU! LOOK AT ME, AND SEE IF YOU CAN UNDERSTAND THAT!
YOU SEE SOMEONE POWERFUL, RIGHT? SOMEONE WITH MORE STRENGTH THAN MOST PEOPLE KNOW IN A LIFETIME!
BUT WHEN I LOOK AT ME, I SEE A FREAK! THIS ISN'T A COSTUME, JAMESON--
IT DOESN'T COME OFF!
"REMEMBER WHEN I WAS JUST A CRUMMY PRIVATE INVESTIGATOR YOU HIRED TO TRACK THAT PARKER KID AND FIND OUT HOW HE TOOK HIS EXCLUSIVE PHOTOS?
"REMEMBER HOW YOU TOOK ME OFF THAT ASSIGNMENT, AND PAID ME TO BE A GUINEA PIG FOR A MAD SCIENTIST'S EXPERIMENT?
"REMEMBER?"*
*WE DO. IT HAPPENED IN SPIDER-MAN #20.--G.

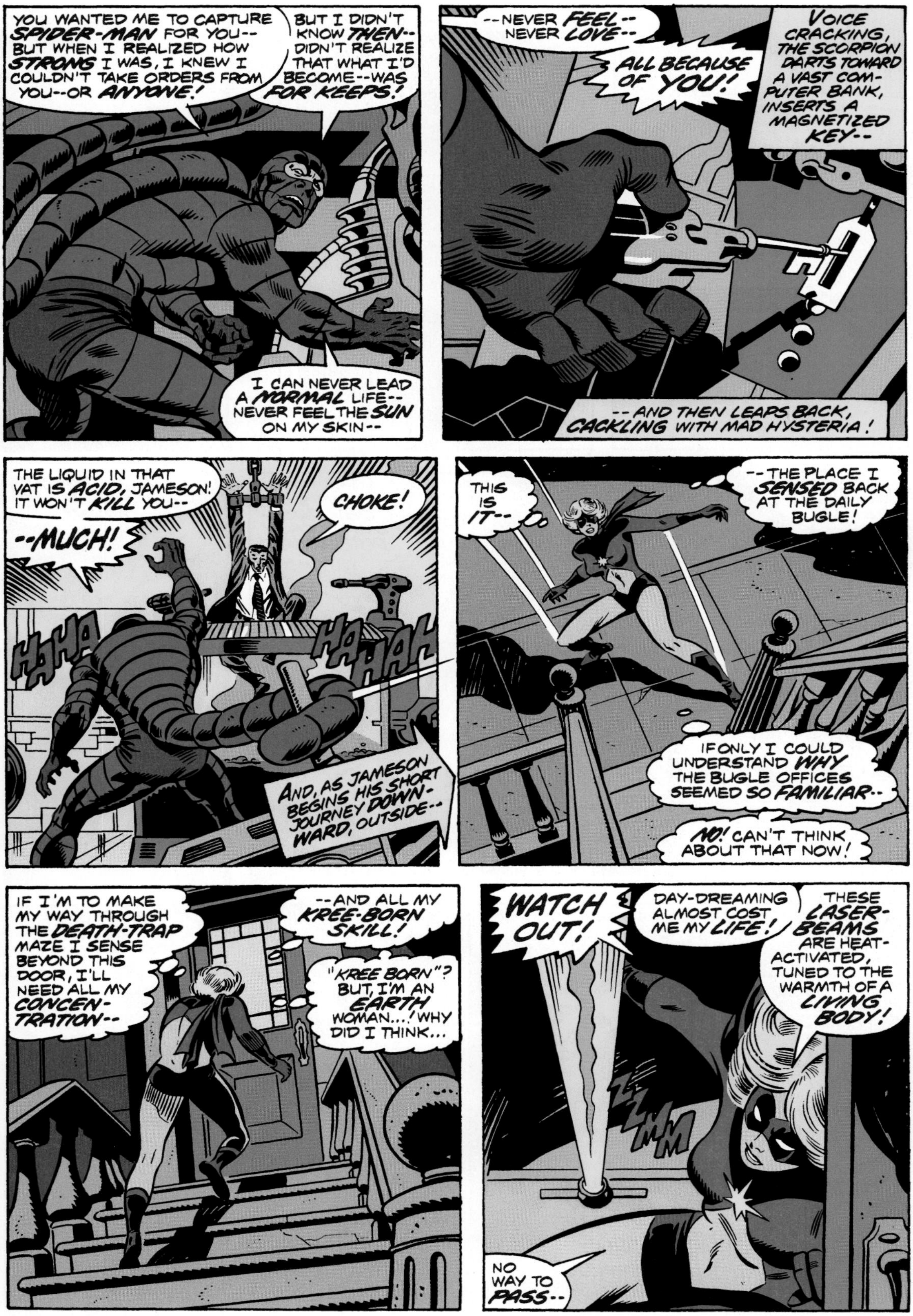

YOU WANTED ME TO CAPTURE SPIDER-MAN FOR YOU-- BUT WHEN I REALIZED HOW STRONG I WAS, I KNEW I COULDN'T TAKE ORDERS FROM YOU--OR ANYONE!
BUT I DIDN'T KNOW THEN-- DIDN'T REALIZE THAT WHAT I'D BECOME--WAS FOR KEEPS!
I CAN NEVER LEAD A NORMAL LIFE-- NEVER FEEL THE SUN ON MY SKIN--
--NEVER FEEL-- NEVER LOVE--
ALL BECAUSE OF YOU!
VOICE CRACKING, THE SCORPION DARTS TOWARD A VAST COMPUTER BANK, INSERTS A MAGNETIZED KEY--
--AND THEN LEAPS BACK, CACKLING WITH MAD HYSTERIA!
THE LIQUID IN THAT VAT IS ACID, JAMESON! IT WON'T KILL YOU--
--MUCH!
CHOKE!
HAHA
HAHAH
AND, AS JAMESON BEGINS HIS SHORT JOURNEY DOWNWARD, OUTSIDE--
THIS IS IT--
--THE PLACE I SENSED BACK AT THE DAILY BUGLE!
IF ONLY I COULD UNDERSTAND WHY THE BUGLE OFFICES SEEMED SO FAMILIAR--
NO! CAN'T THINK ABOUT THAT NOW!
IF I'M TO MAKE MY WAY THROUGH THE DEATH-TRAP MAZE I SENSE BEYOND THIS DOOR, I'LL NEED ALL MY CONCENTRATION--
--AND ALL MY KREE-BORN SKILL!
"KREE BORN"? BUT, I'M AN EARTH WOMAN...! WHY DID I THINK...
WATCH OUT!
DAY-DREAMING ALMOST COST ME MY LIFE!
THESE LASER-BEAMS ARE HEAT-ACTIVATED, TUNED TO THE WARMTH OF A LIVING BODY!
ZZMMM
NO WAY TO PASS--

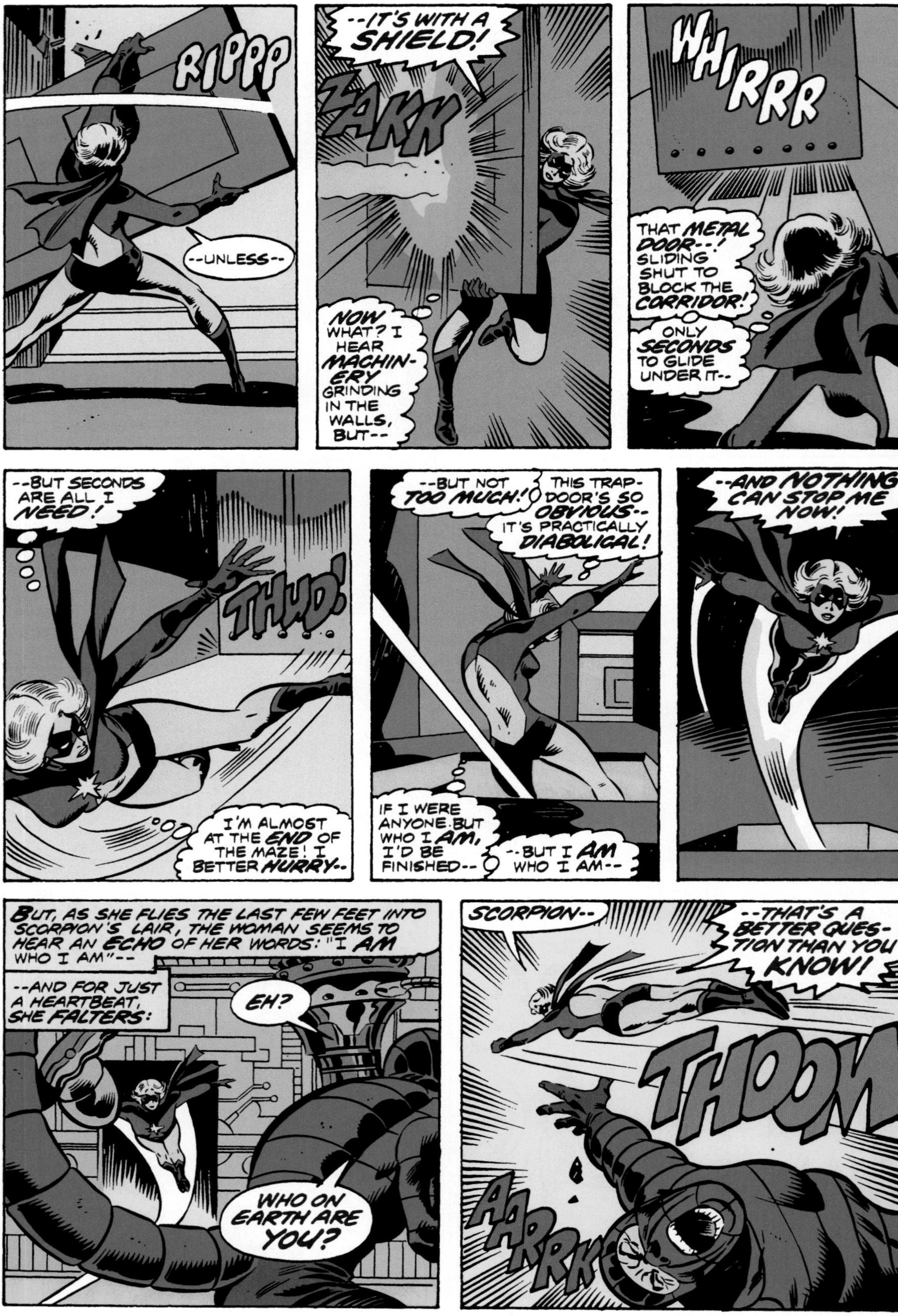
RIPPP
--UNLESS--
--IT'S WITH A SHIELD!
ZAKK
NOW WHAT? I HEAR MACHINERY GRINDING IN THE WALLS, BUT--
WHIRRR
THAT METAL DOOR--! SLIDING SHUT TO BLOCK THE CORRIDOR!
ONLY SECONDS TO GLIDE UNDER IT--
--BUT SECONDS ARE ALL I NEED!
THUD!
I'M ALMOST AT THE END OF THE MAZE! I BETTER HURRY--
--BUT NOT TOO MUCH!
THIS TRAP-DOOR'S SO OBVIOUS--IT'S PRACTICALLY DIABOLICAL!
IF I WERE ANYONE. BUT WHO I AM, I'D BE FINISHED--
--BUT I AM WHO I AM--
--AND NOTHING CAN STOP ME NOW!
BUT, AS SHE FLIES THE LAST FEW FEET INTO SCORPION'S LAIR, THE WOMAN SEEMS TO HEAR AN ECHO OF HER WORDS: "I AM WHO I AM"--
--AND FOR JUST A HEARTBEAT, SHE FALTERS:
EH?
WHO ON EARTH ARE YOU?
SCORPION--
--THAT'S A BETTER QUESTION THAN YOU KNOW!
THOOM
AARRK

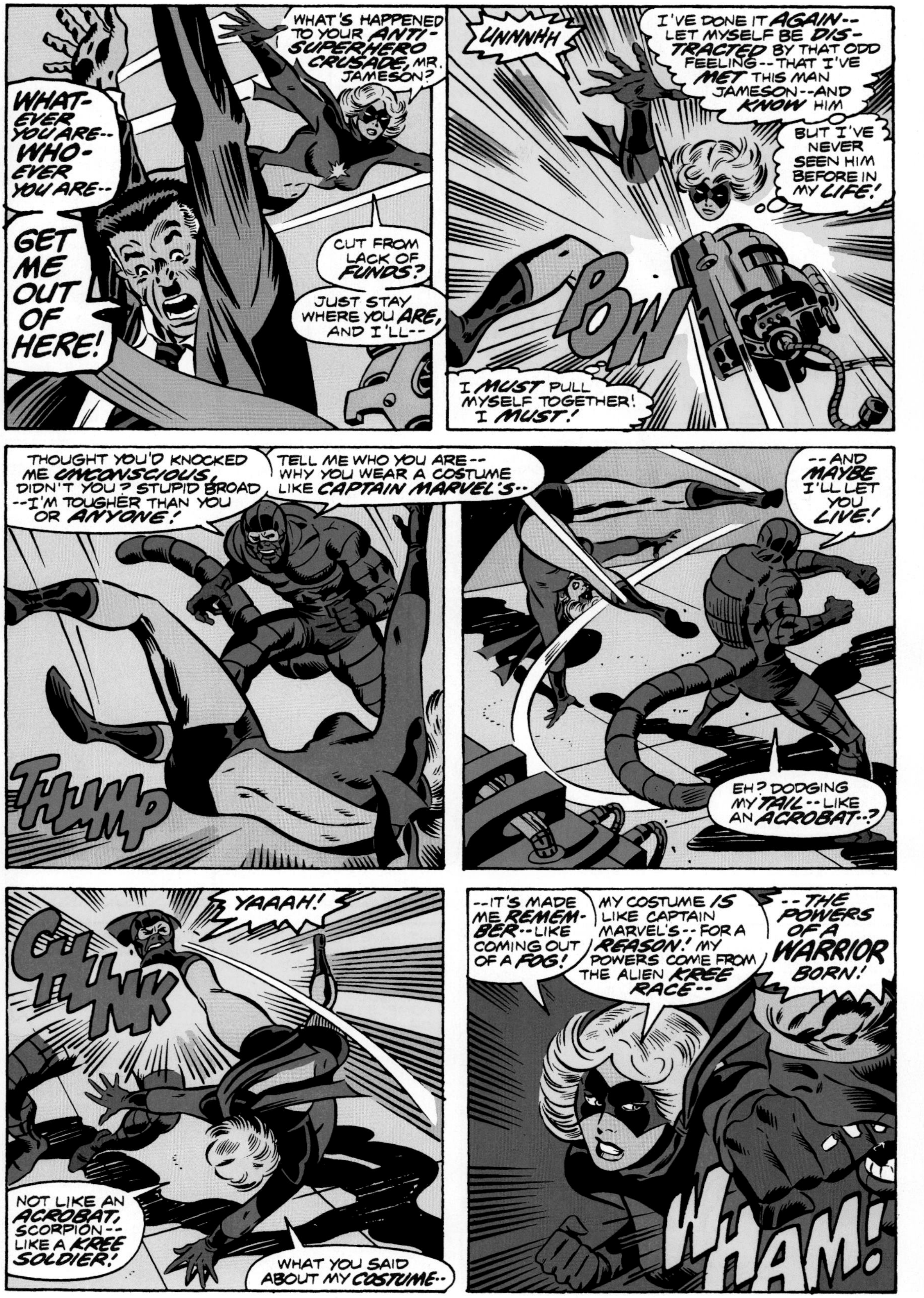
WHAT'S HAPPENED TO YOUR ANTI-SUPERHERO CRUSADE, MR. JAMESON?
WHAT-EVER YOU ARE-- WHO-EVER YOU ARE--
GET ME OUT OF HERE!
CUT FROM LACK OF FUNDS?
JUST STAY WHERE YOU ARE, AND I'LL--
UNNNHH
I'VE DONE IT AGAIN-- LET MYSELF BE DIS-TRACTED BY THAT ODD FEELING--THAT I'VE MET THIS MAN JAMESON--AND KNOW HIM
BUT I'VE NEVER SEEN HIM BEFORE IN MY LIFE!
POW
I MUST PULL MYSELF TOGETHER! I MUST!
THOUGHT YOU'D KNOCKED ME UNCONSCIOUS, DIDN'T YOU? STUPID BROAD --I'M TOUGHER THAN YOU OR ANYONE!
TELL ME WHO YOU ARE-- WHY YOU WEAR A COSTUME LIKE CAPTAIN MARVEL'S--
THUMP
--AND MAYBE I'LL LET YOU LIVE!
EH? DODGING MY TAIL--LIKE AN ACROBAT--?
YAAAH!
CHUNK
NOT LIKE AN ACROBAT, SCORPION-- LIKE A KREE SOLDIER!
WHAT YOU SAID ABOUT MY COSTUME--
--IT'S MADE ME REMEM-BER--LIKE COMING OUT OF A FOG!
MY COSTUME IS LIKE CAPTAIN MARVEL'S--FOR A REASON! MY POWERS COME FROM THE ALIEN KREE RACE--
--THE POWERS OF A WARRIOR BORN!
WHAM!

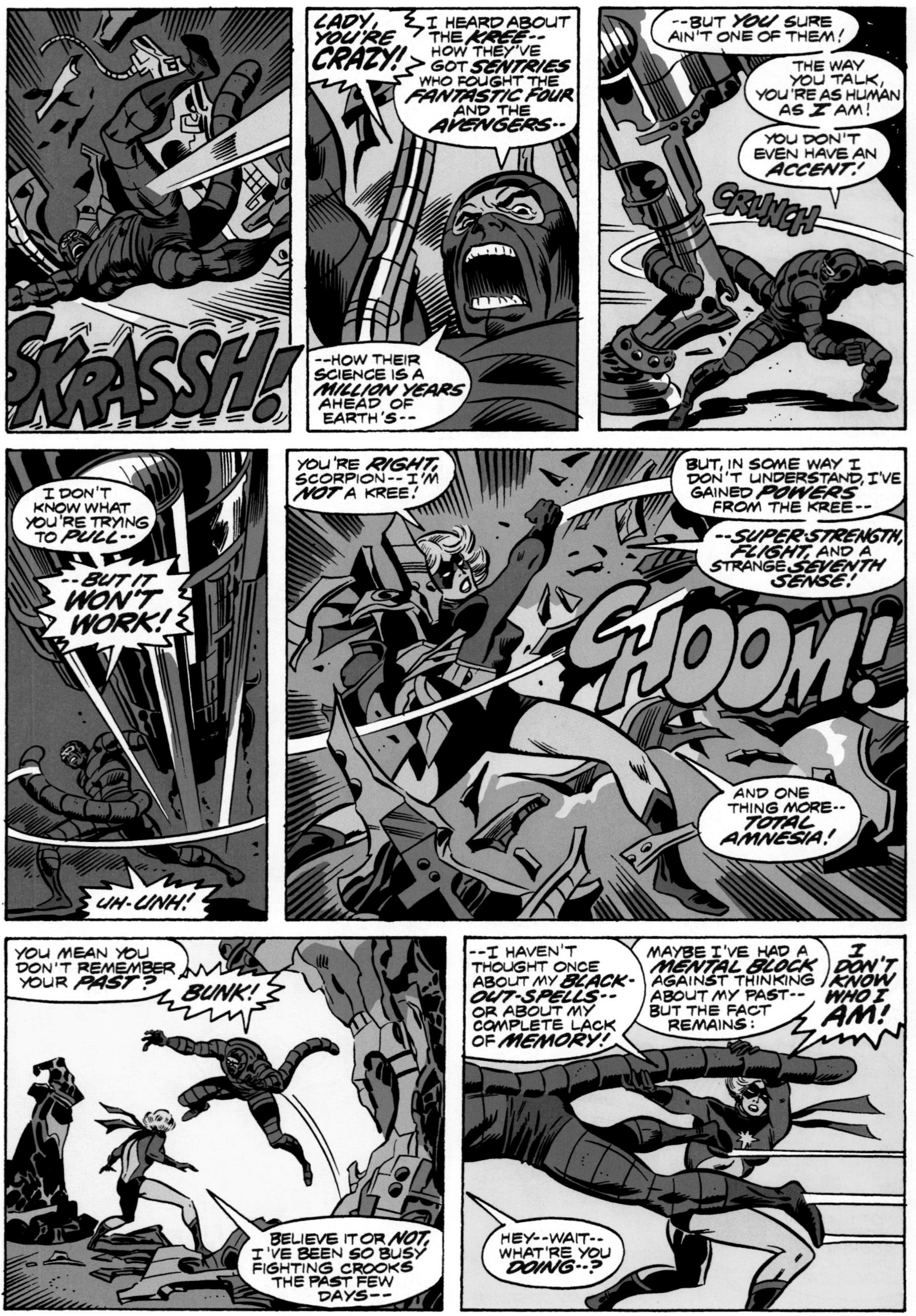
SKRASSH!
LADY, YOU'RE CRAZY!
I HEARD ABOUT THE KREE-- HOW THEY'VE GOT SENTRIES WHO FOUGHT THE FANTASTIC FOUR AND THE AVENGERS--
--HOW THEIR SCIENCE IS A MILLION YEARS AHEAD OF EARTH'S--
--BUT YOU SURE AIN'T ONE OF THEM!
THE WAY YOU TALK, YOU'RE AS HUMAN AS I AM!
YOU DON'T EVEN HAVE AN ACCENT!
CRUNCH
I DON'T KNOW WHAT YOU'RE TRYING TO PULL--
--BUT IT WON'T WORK!
UH-UNH!
YOU'RE RIGHT, SCORPION-- I'M NOT A KREE!
BUT, IN SOME WAY I DON'T UNDERSTAND, I'VE GAINED POWERS FROM THE KREE--
--SUPER-STRENGTH, FLIGHT, AND A STRANGE SEVENTH SENSE!
CHOOM!
AND ONE THING MORE-- TOTAL AMNESIA!
YOU MEAN YOU DON'T REMEMBER YOUR PAST?
BUNK!
BELIEVE IT OR NOT, I'VE BEEN SO BUSY FIGHTING CROOKS THE PAST FEW DAYS--
--I HAVEN'T THOUGHT ONCE ABOUT MY BLACK-OUT-SPELLS-- OR ABOUT MY COMPLETE LACK OF MEMORY!
MAYBE I'VE HAD A MENTAL BLOCK AGAINST THINKING ABOUT MY PAST-- BUT THE FACT REMAINS:
I DON'T KNOW WHO I AM!
HEY--WAIT-- WHAT'RE YOU DOING--?

DOING? WHAT DOES IT *LOOK* LIKE I'M DOING?

NOOOO

I'M *WINNING!*

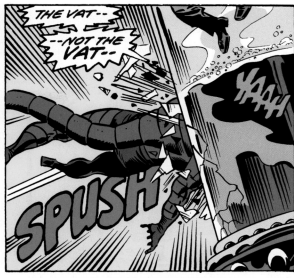

THE VAT-- --NOT THE VAT--

SPUSH

YAAH

LIQUID *EXPLODES* FROM THE VAT IN A CASCADE OF BUBBLING, BURNING *FURY*:

BEFORE THE SCOR-PION CAN FINISH HIS *SCREAM*, HE'S *INUNDATED* BY THE *SEETHING* ACID, AND THOUGH HIS GRAFTED-ON COSTUME PROTECTS HIM FROM THE FULL *FORCE* OF THE RAGING CHEMICAL--

--HE STILL *BURNS*-- --AND SHRIEKING, *FLEES!*

AAAAA

MY LORD...

...THE POOR *MAN*...

FOR HEAVEN'S *SAKE*, WOMAN, DON'T JUST STAND THERE--*LET ME DOWN!*

I'VE BEEN *CONSIDERING* IT, MR. JAMESON--

--AND I'VE DECIDED YOU CAN CALL ME-- *MS. MARVEL!*

WHAT?

MY COSTUME *TIES* ME TO CAPTAIN MARVEL, IN A WAY I DON'T YET *UNDERSTAND.*

TILL I *DO* UNDERSTAND, I'LL NEED A NAME--

--AND MS. MARVEL IS AS GOOD AS *ANY!*

YOU'RE *CRAZY!*

THAT'S SOMETHING I NEED TO FIND *OUT*, MR. JAMESON-- WHEN I LEARN *WHO* I AM, AND *WHERE* I COME FROM.

WAIT! MY HANDS ARE STILL *CHAINED!*

UNTIL THEN--TRY NOT TO MAKE *TOO* HASTY A JUDGE-MENT ABOUT ME, HMMM?

WHAT ABOUT MY HANDS?

BUT MS. MARVEL ONLY *SMILES*-- AND IS GONE!

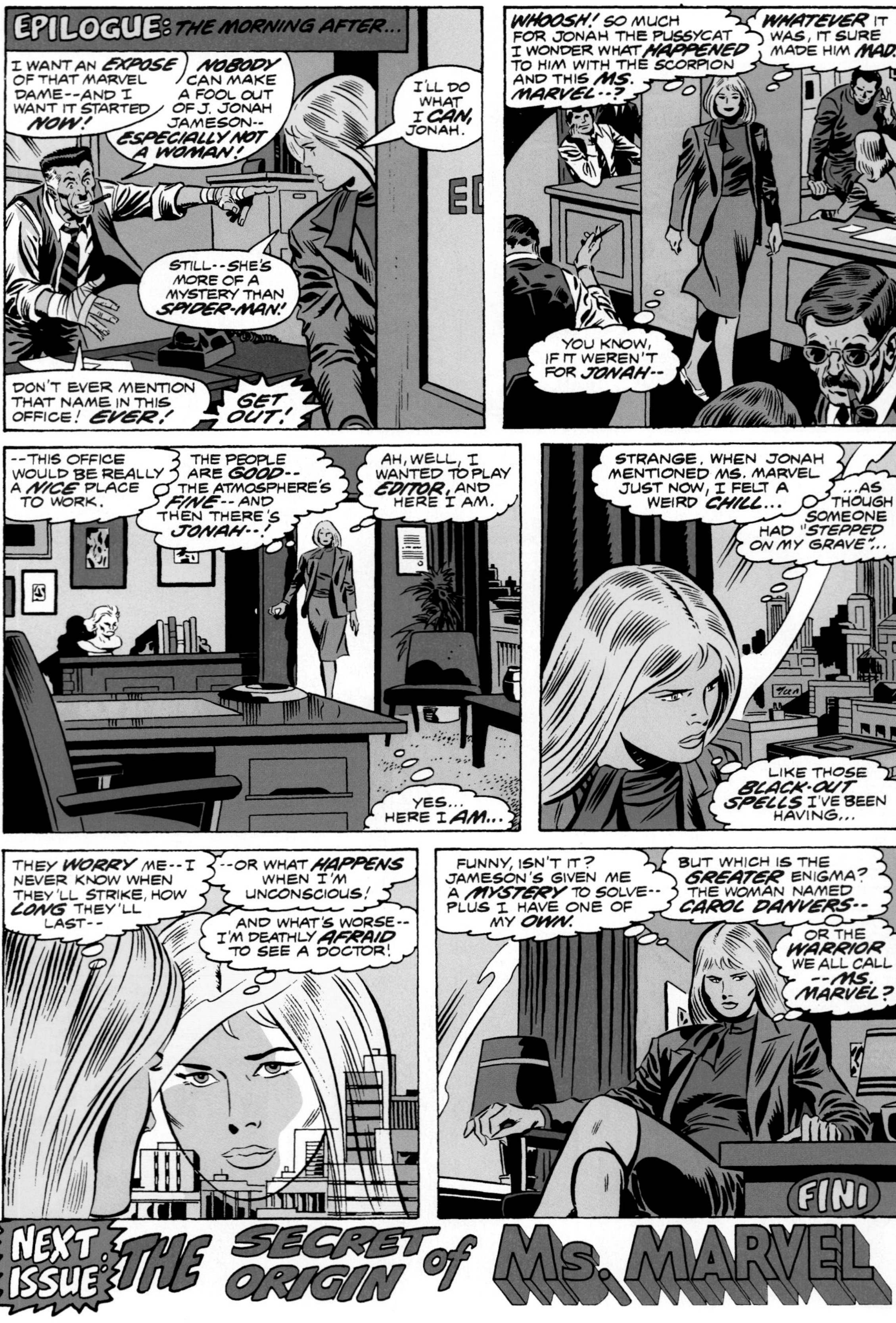
EPILOGUE: THE MORNING AFTER...
I WANT AN EXPOSE OF THAT MARVEL DAME--AND I WANT IT STARTED NOW!
NOBODY CAN MAKE A FOOL OUT OF J. JONAH JAMESON-- ESPECIALLY NOT A WOMAN!
I'LL DO WHAT I CAN, JONAH.
STILL--SHE'S MORE OF A MYSTERY THAN SPIDER-MAN!
DON'T EVER MENTION THAT NAME IN THIS OFFICE! EVER!
GET OUT!
WHOOSH! SO MUCH FOR JONAH THE PUSSYCAT I WONDER WHAT HAPPENED TO HIM WITH THE SCORPION AND THIS MS. MARVEL--?
WHATEVER IT WAS, IT SURE MADE HIM MAD.
YOU KNOW, IF IT WEREN'T FOR JONAH--
--THIS OFFICE WOULD BE REALLY A NICE PLACE TO WORK.
THE PEOPLE ARE GOOD-- THE ATMOSPHERE'S FINE--AND THEN THERE'S JONAH--!
AH, WELL, I WANTED TO PLAY EDITOR, AND HERE I AM.
YES... HERE I AM...
STRANGE, WHEN JONAH MENTIONED MS. MARVEL JUST NOW, I FELT A WEIRD CHILL...
...AS THOUGH SOMEONE HAD "STEPPED ON MY GRAVE"...
LIKE THOSE BLACK-OUT SPELLS I'VE BEEN HAVING...
THEY WORRY ME--I NEVER KNOW WHEN THEY'LL STRIKE, HOW LONG THEY'LL LAST--
--OR WHAT HAPPENS WHEN I'M UNCONSCIOUS!
AND WHAT'S WORSE--I'M DEATHLY AFRAID TO SEE A DOCTOR!
FUNNY, ISN'T IT? JAMESON'S GIVEN ME A MYSTERY TO SOLVE-- PLUS I HAVE ONE OF MY OWN.
BUT WHICH IS THE GREATER ENIGMA? THE WOMAN NAMED CAROL DANVERS--
--OR THE WARRIOR WE ALL CALL --MS. MARVEL?
FINI
NEXT ISSUE: THE SECRET ORIGIN of Ms. MARVEL

Ms. MARVEL TM
MARVEL® COMICS GROUP
APPROVED BY THE COMICS CODE AUTHORITY
35¢
19
AUG
02198
©1978 MARVEL COMICS GROUP
Ms. MARVEL TM
THIS ISSUE--AT LAST--
THE FEMALE FURY MEETS
CAPTAIN MARVEL!
AT THE MERCY OF RONAN!

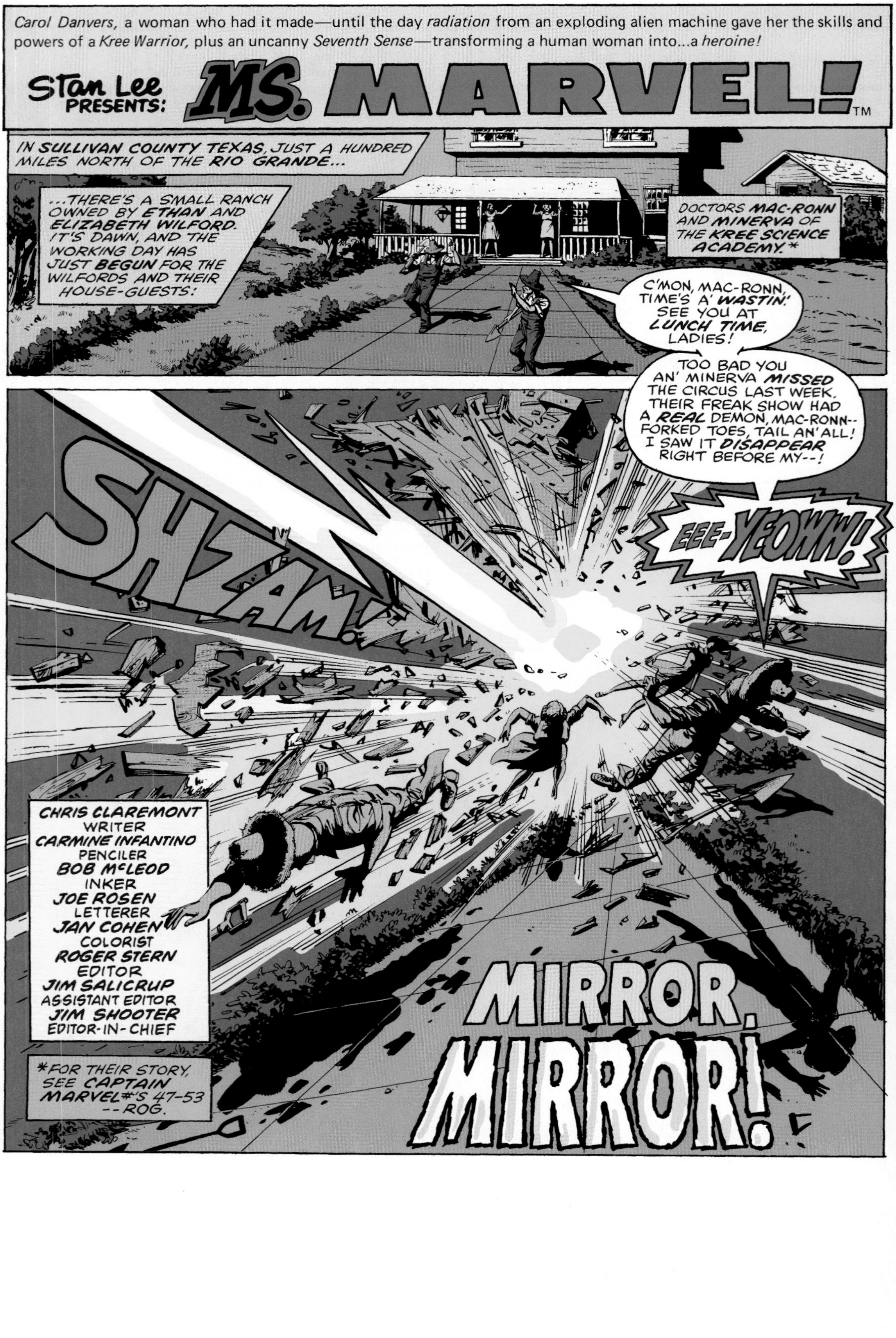

Carol Danvers, a woman who had it made—until the day radiation from an exploding alien machine gave her the skills and powers of a Kree Warrior, plus an uncanny Seventh Sense—transforming a human woman into...a heroine!
Stan Lee PRESENTS: MS. MARVEL! TM
IN SULLIVAN COUNTY TEXAS, JUST A HUNDRED MILES NORTH OF THE RIO GRANDE...
...THERE'S A SMALL RANCH OWNED BY ETHAN AND ELIZABETH WILFORD. IT'S DAWN, AND THE WORKING DAY HAS JUST BEGUN FOR THE WILFORDS AND THEIR HOUSE-GUESTS:
DOCTORS MAC-RONN AND MINERVA OF THE KREE SCIENCE ACADEMY.*
C'MON, MAC-RONN, TIME'S A' WASTIN'. SEE YOU AT LUNCH TIME, LADIES!
TOO BAD YOU AN' MINERVA MISSED THE CIRCUS LAST WEEK. THEIR FREAK SHOW HAD A REAL DEMON, MAC-RONN-- FORKED TOES, TAIL AN' ALL! I SAW IT DISAPPEAR RIGHT BEFORE MY--!
SHZAM!
EEE-YEOWW!
CHRIS CLAREMONT WRITER CARMINE INFANTINO PENCILER BOB McLEOD INKER JOE ROSEN LETTERER JAN COHEN COLORIST ROGER STERN EDITOR JIM SALICRUP ASSISTANT EDITOR JIM SHOOTER EDITOR-IN-CHIEF
*FOR THEIR STORY, SEE CAPTAIN MARVEL#'S 47-53 --ROG.
MIRROR, MIRROR!

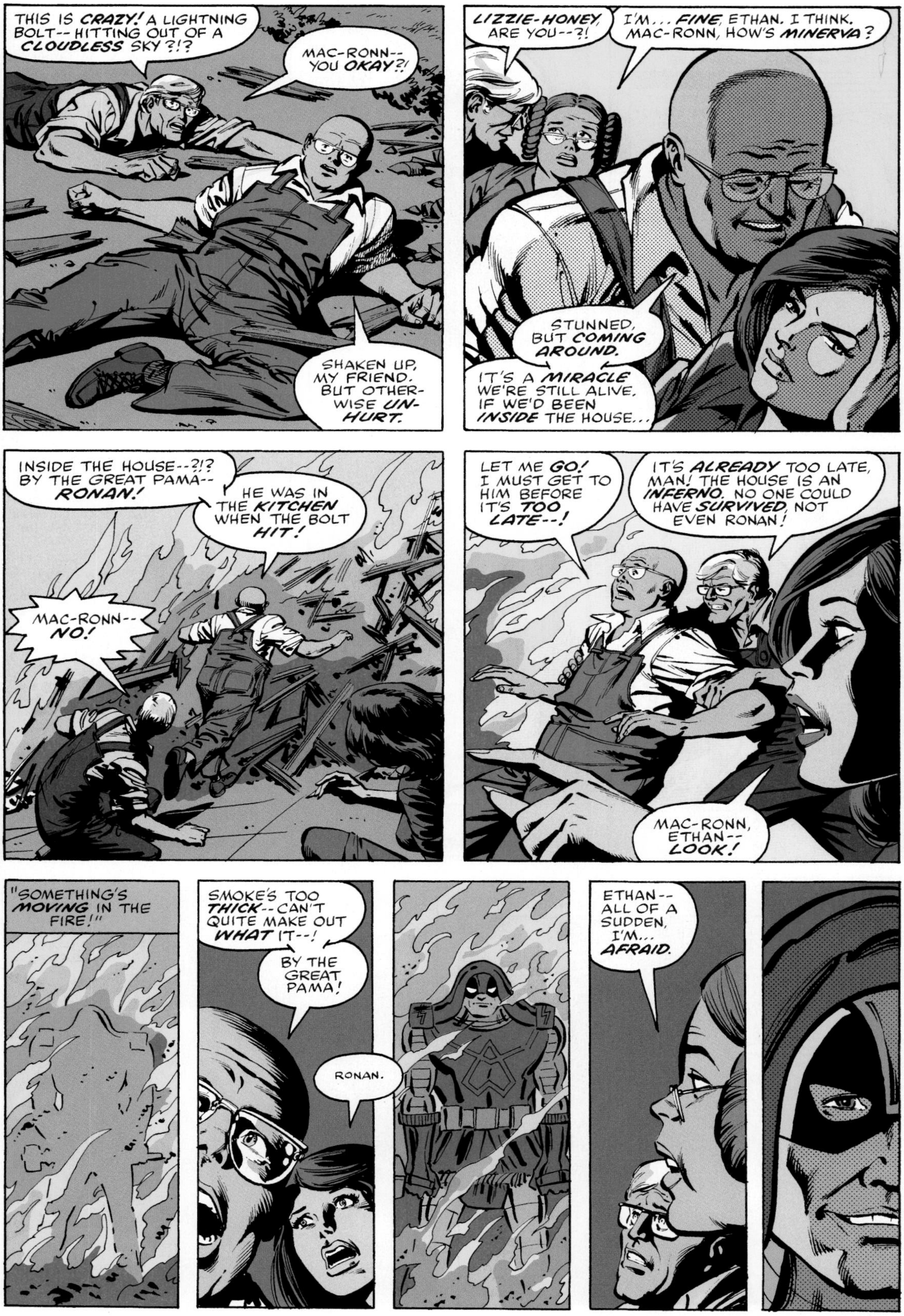

THIS IS CRAZY! A LIGHTNING BOLT-- HITTING OUT OF A CLOUDLESS SKY?!?
MAC-RONN-- YOU OKAY?!
SHAKEN UP, MY FRIEND. BUT OTHER-WISE UN-HURT.
LIZZIE-HONEY, ARE YOU--?!
I'M... FINE, ETHAN. I THINK. MAC-RONN, HOW'S MINERVA?
STUNNED, BUT COMING AROUND.
IT'S A MIRACLE WE'RE STILL ALIVE. IF WE'D BEEN INSIDE THE HOUSE...
INSIDE THE HOUSE--?!? BY THE GREAT PAMA-- RONAN!
HE WAS IN THE KITCHEN WHEN THE BOLT HIT!
MAC-RONN-- NO!
LET ME GO! I MUST GET TO HIM BEFORE IT'S TOO LATE--!
IT'S ALREADY TOO LATE, MAN! THE HOUSE IS AN INFERNO. NO ONE COULD HAVE SURVIVED, NOT EVEN RONAN!
MAC-RONN, ETHAN-- LOOK!
"SOMETHING'S MOVING IN THE FIRE!"
SMOKE'S TOO THICK--CAN'T QUITE MAKE OUT WHAT IT--!
BY THE GREAT PAMA!
RONAN.
ETHAN-- ALL OF A SUDDEN, I'M... AFRAID.

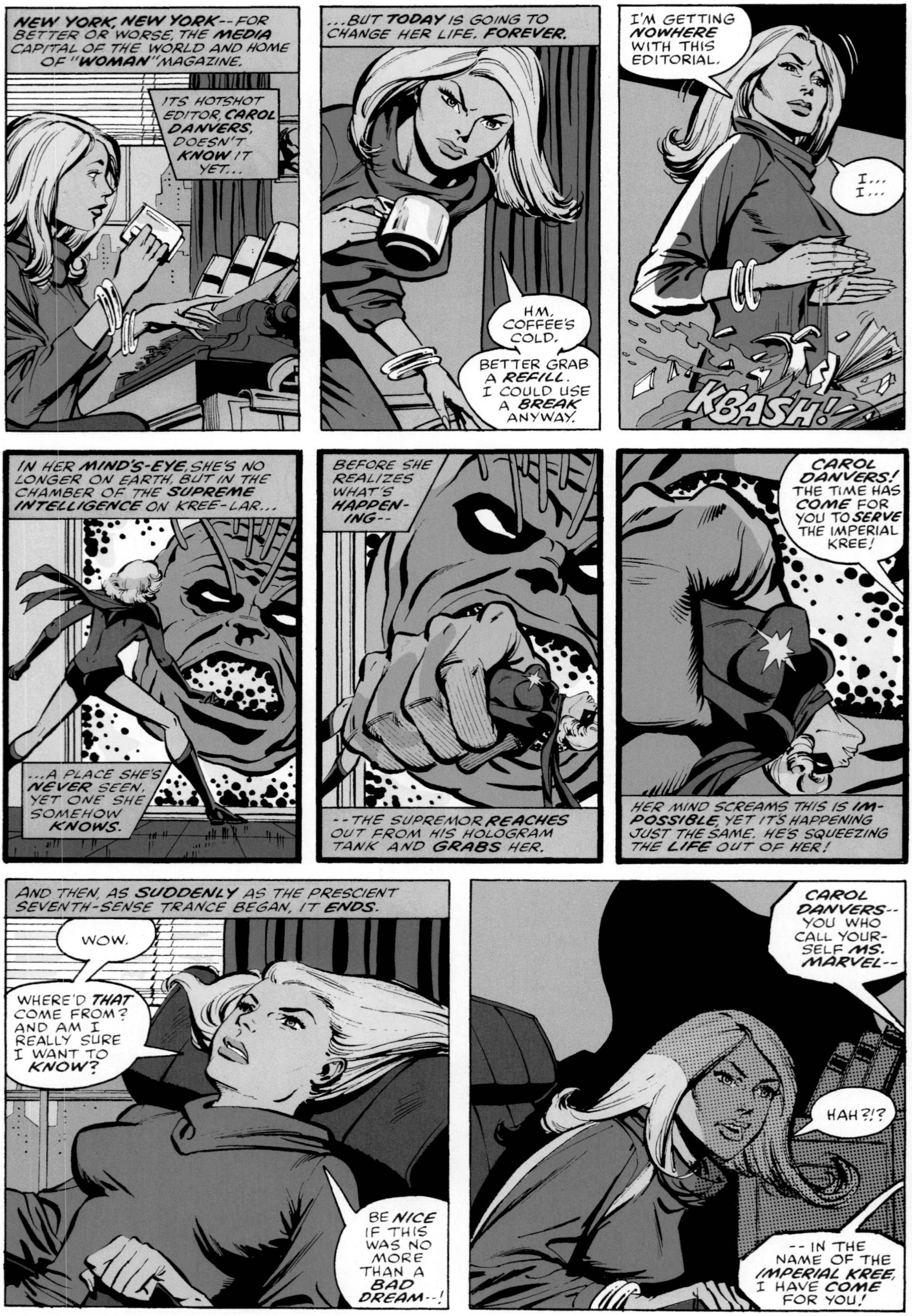

NEW YORK, NEW YORK--FOR BETTER OR WORSE, THE MEDIA CAPITAL OF THE WORLD AND HOME OF "WOMAN" MAGAZINE.
ITS HOTSHOT EDITOR, CAROL DANVERS, DOESN'T KNOW IT YET...
...BUT TODAY IS GOING TO CHANGE HER LIFE. FOREVER.
HM. COFFEE'S COLD.
BETTER GRAB A REFILL. I COULD USE A BREAK ANYWAY.
I'M GETTING NOWHERE WITH THIS EDITORIAL.
I... I...
KBASH!
IN HER MIND'S-EYE, SHE'S NO LONGER ON EARTH, BUT IN THE CHAMBER OF THE SUPREME INTELLIGENCE ON KREE-LAR...
...A PLACE SHE'S NEVER SEEN, YET ONE SHE SOMEHOW KNOWS.
BEFORE SHE REALIZES WHAT'S HAPPENING--
--THE SUPREMOR REACHES OUT FROM HIS HOLOGRAM TANK AND GRABS HER.
CAROL DANVERS! THE TIME HAS COME FOR YOU TO SERVE THE IMPERIAL KREE!
HER MIND SCREAMS THIS IS IMPOSSIBLE, YET IT'S HAPPENING JUST THE SAME. HE'S SQUEEZING THE LIFE OUT OF HER!
AND THEN, AS SUDDENLY AS THE PRESCIENT SEVENTH-SENSE TRANCE BEGAN, IT ENDS.
WOW.
WHERE'D THAT COME FROM? AND AM I REALLY SURE I WANT TO KNOW?
BE NICE IF THIS WAS NO MORE THAN A BAD DREAM--!
CAROL DANVERS--YOU WHO CALL YOURSELF MS. MARVEL--
HAH?!?
--IN THE NAME OF THE IMPERIAL KREE, I HAVE COME FOR YOU!

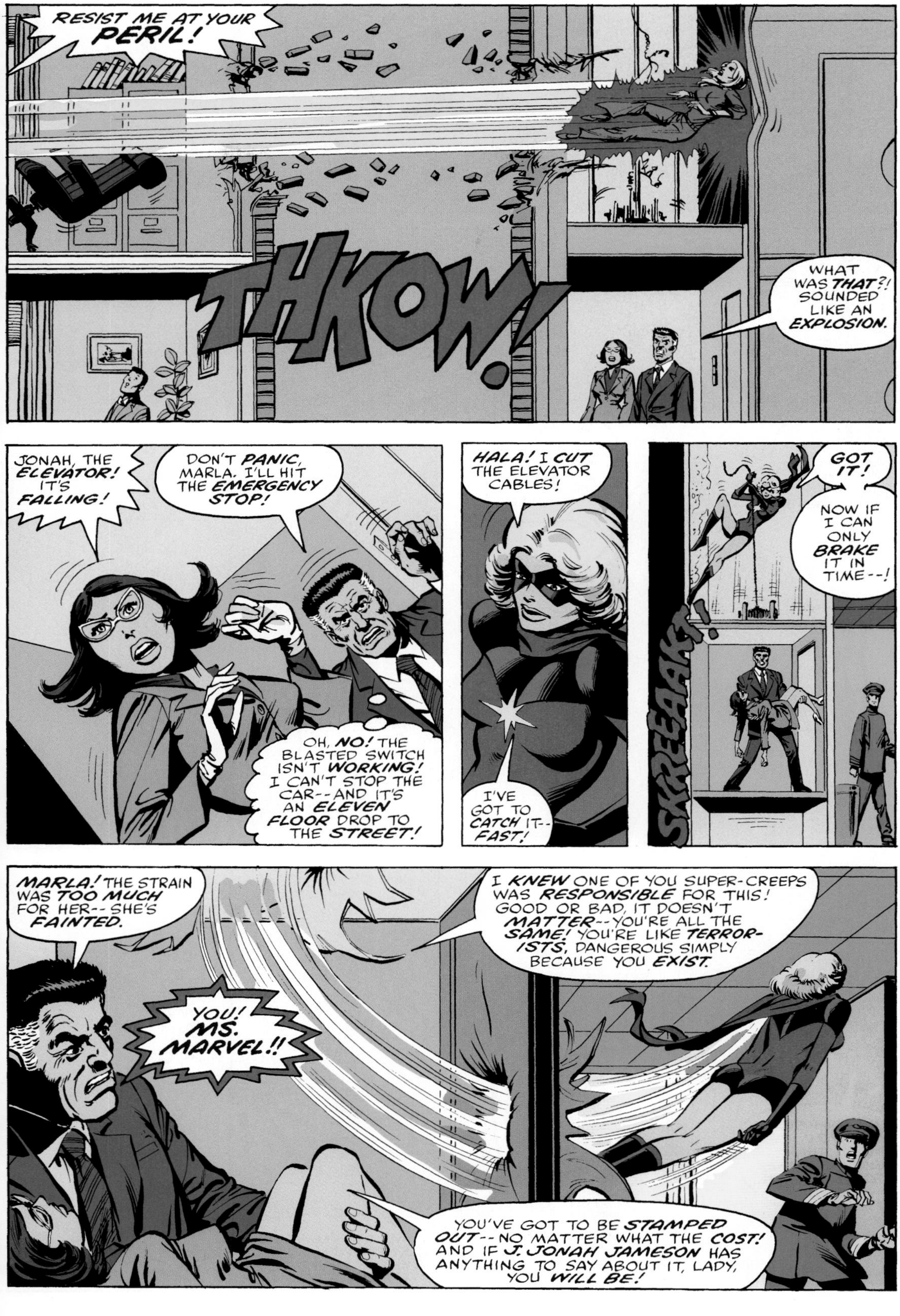
RESIST ME AT YOUR PERIL!
THKOW!
WHAT WAS THAT?! SOUNDED LIKE AN EXPLOSION.
JONAH, THE ELEVATOR! IT'S FALLING!
DON'T PANIC, MARLA. I'LL HIT THE EMERGENCY STOP!
OH, NO! THE BLASTED SWITCH ISN'T WORKING! I CAN'T STOP THE CAR--AND IT'S AN ELEVEN FLOOR DROP TO THE STREET!
HALA! I CUT THE ELEVATOR CABLES!
I'VE GOT TO CATCH IT--FAST!
GOT IT!
NOW IF I CAN ONLY BRAKE IT IN TIME--!
SKREEAAK!
MARLA! THE STRAIN WAS TOO MUCH FOR HER--SHE'S FAINTED.
YOU! MS. MARVEL!!
I KNEW ONE OF YOU SUPER-CREEPS WAS RESPONSIBLE FOR THIS! GOOD OR BAD, IT DOESN'T MATTER--YOU'RE ALL THE SAME! YOU'RE LIKE TERRORISTS, DANGEROUS SIMPLY BECAUSE YOU EXIST.
YOU'VE GOT TO BE STAMPED OUT--NO MATTER WHAT THE COST! AND IF J. JONAH JAMESON HAS ANYTHING TO SAY ABOUT IT, LADY, YOU WILL BE!

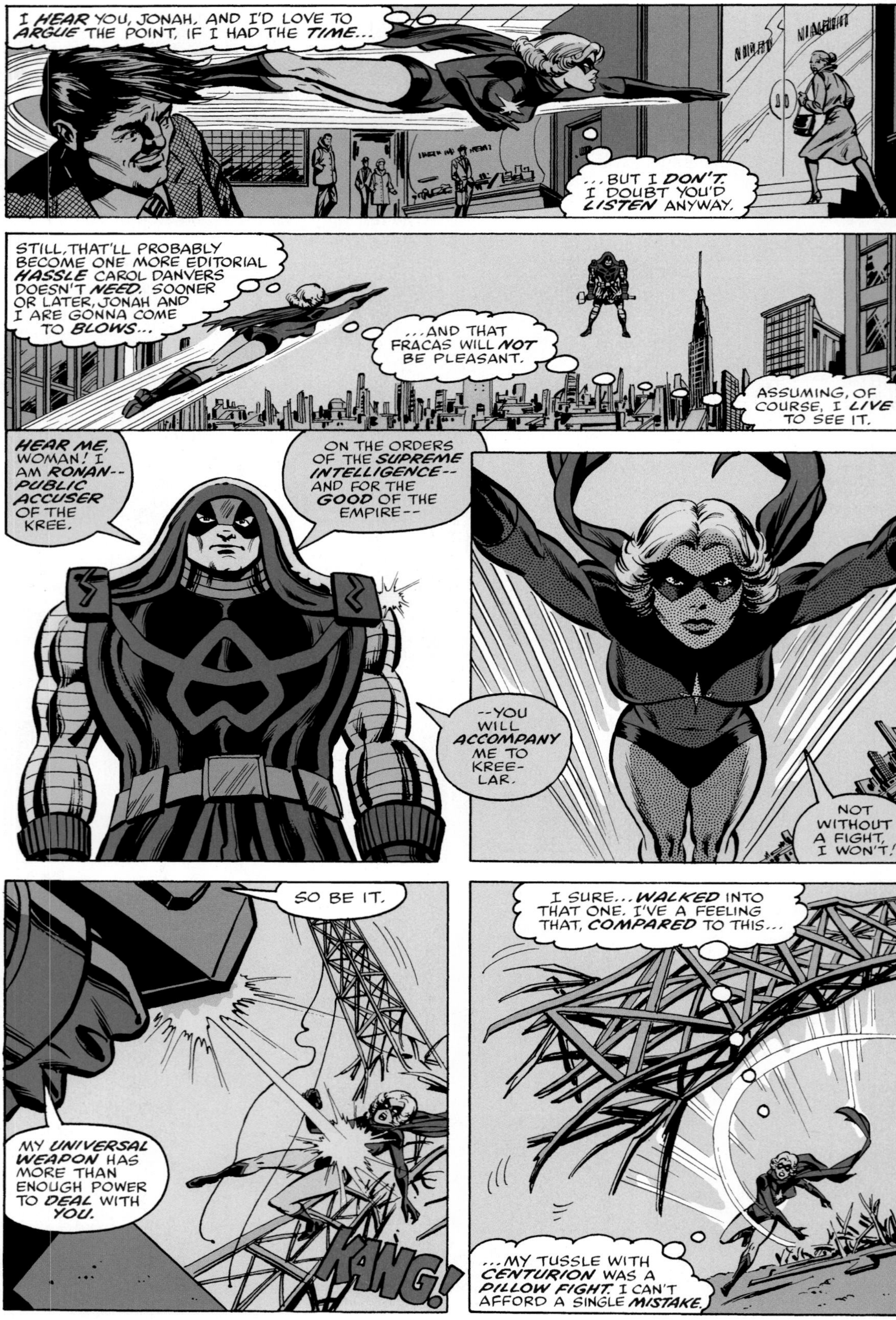

I HEAR YOU, JONAH, AND I'D LOVE TO ARGUE THE POINT, IF I HAD THE TIME...
...BUT I DON'T. I DOUBT YOU'D LISTEN ANYWAY.
STILL, THAT'LL PROBABLY BECOME ONE MORE EDITORIAL HASSLE CAROL DANVERS DOESN'T NEED. SOONER OR LATER, JONAH AND I ARE GONNA COME TO BLOWS...
...AND THAT FRACAS WILL NOT BE PLEASANT.
ASSUMING, OF COURSE, I LIVE TO SEE IT.
HEAR ME, WOMAN! I AM RONAN-- PUBLIC ACCUSER OF THE KREE.
ON THE ORDERS OF THE SUPREME INTELLIGENCE-- AND FOR THE GOOD OF THE EMPIRE--
--YOU WILL ACCOMPANY ME TO KREE-LAR.
NOT WITHOUT A FIGHT, I WON'T!
SO BE IT.
MY UNIVERSAL WEAPON HAS MORE THAN ENOUGH POWER TO DEAL WITH YOU.
KANG!
I SURE... WALKED INTO THAT ONE. I'VE A FEELING THAT, COMPARED TO THIS...
...MY TUSSLE WITH CENTURION WAS A PILLOW FIGHT. I CAN'T AFFORD A SINGLE MISTAKE.

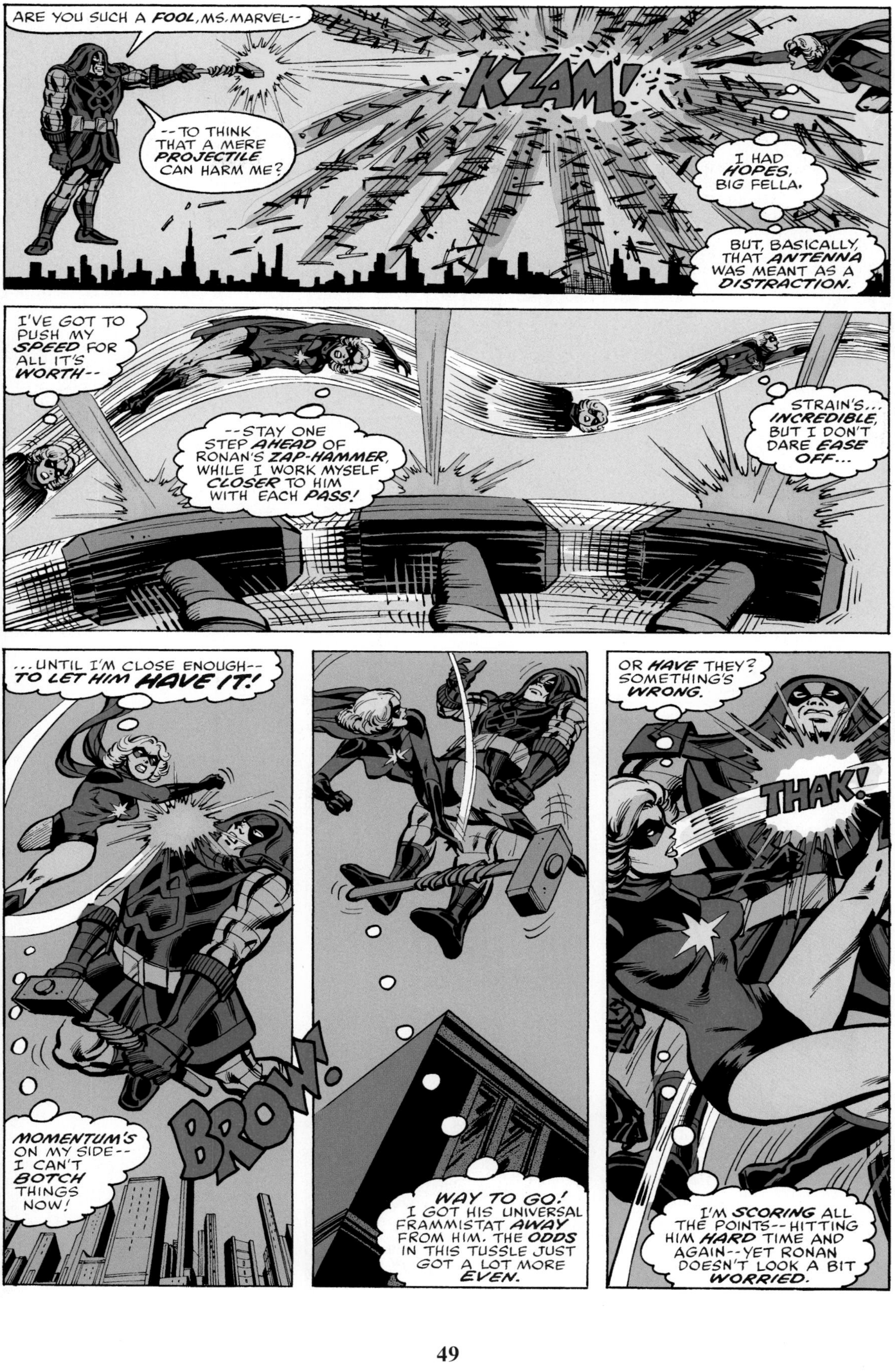
ARE YOU SUCH A FOOL, MS. MARVEL--
KZAM!
--TO THINK THAT A MERE PROJECTILE CAN HARM ME?
I HAD HOPES, BIG FELLA.
BUT, BASICALLY, THAT ANTENNA WAS MEANT AS A DISTRACTION.
I'VE GOT TO PUSH MY SPEED FOR ALL IT'S WORTH--
--STAY ONE STEP AHEAD OF RONAN'S ZAP-HAMMER, WHILE I WORK MYSELF CLOSER TO HIM WITH EACH PASS!
STRAIN'S... INCREDIBLE, BUT I DON'T DARE EASE OFF...
...UNTIL I'M CLOSE ENOUGH-- TO LET HIM HAVE IT!
BROW!
MOMENTUM'S ON MY SIDE-- I CAN'T BOTCH THINGS NOW!
WAY TO GO! I GOT HIS UNIVERSAL FRAMMISTAT AWAY FROM HIM. THE ODDS IN THIS TUSSLE JUST GOT A LOT MORE EVEN.
OR HAVE THEY? SOMETHING'S WRONG.
THAK!
I'M SCORING ALL THE POINTS--HITTING HIM HARD TIME AND AGAIN--YET RONAN DOESN'T LOOK A BIT WORRIED.

YOU FIGHT *WELL,* WARRIOR.

HALA! ELECTRICAL CHARGE SHOOTING THROUGH MY BODY! NERVES ON *FIRE*-- SO MUCH *PAIN!*

THOUGH YOU WERE *BORN* A TERRAN, YOUR *COURAGE* WOULD BRING HONOR TO A *KREE.*

BUT COURAGE COUNTS FOR *LITTLE* AGAINST RONAN.

MANAGED TO TWIST LOOSE-- *BLAST!* HE CAUGHT MY PUNCH, WITH SUCH *EASE!* HE'S BEEN *STRINGING* ME ALONG...

...*TEST-ING* ME TO FIND MY *LIMITS.*

MY-- *ARM!!*

RONAN IS *POWER PERSONIFIED,* WOMAN. DO NOT RESIST. MY *FRIGI-GRIP* WILL LOCK YOU IN *CRYOGENIC STASIS* IN SECONDS.

NO!!

SHATTERED ...ICE CASING...

...BUT MY ARM....IS *FROZEN* TO THE MARROW. THIS-- ON TOP OF THE *PUNISHMENT* IT TOOK FROM CENTURION*-- MAKES MY RIGHT SIDE... PRETTY MUCH *USE-LESS!*

*LAST ISH-- *ROG.*

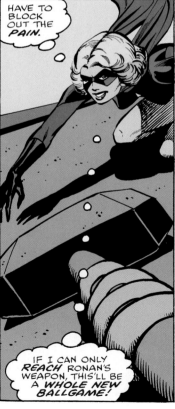

HAVE TO BLOCK OUT THE *PAIN.*

IF I CAN ONLY *REACH* RONAN'S WEAPON, THIS'LL BE A *WHOLE NEW BALLGAME!*

FOR *YOU,* MS. MARVEL, THE BATTLE IS *OVER.*

NO POWER ON EARTH CAN *SAVE* YOU NOW.

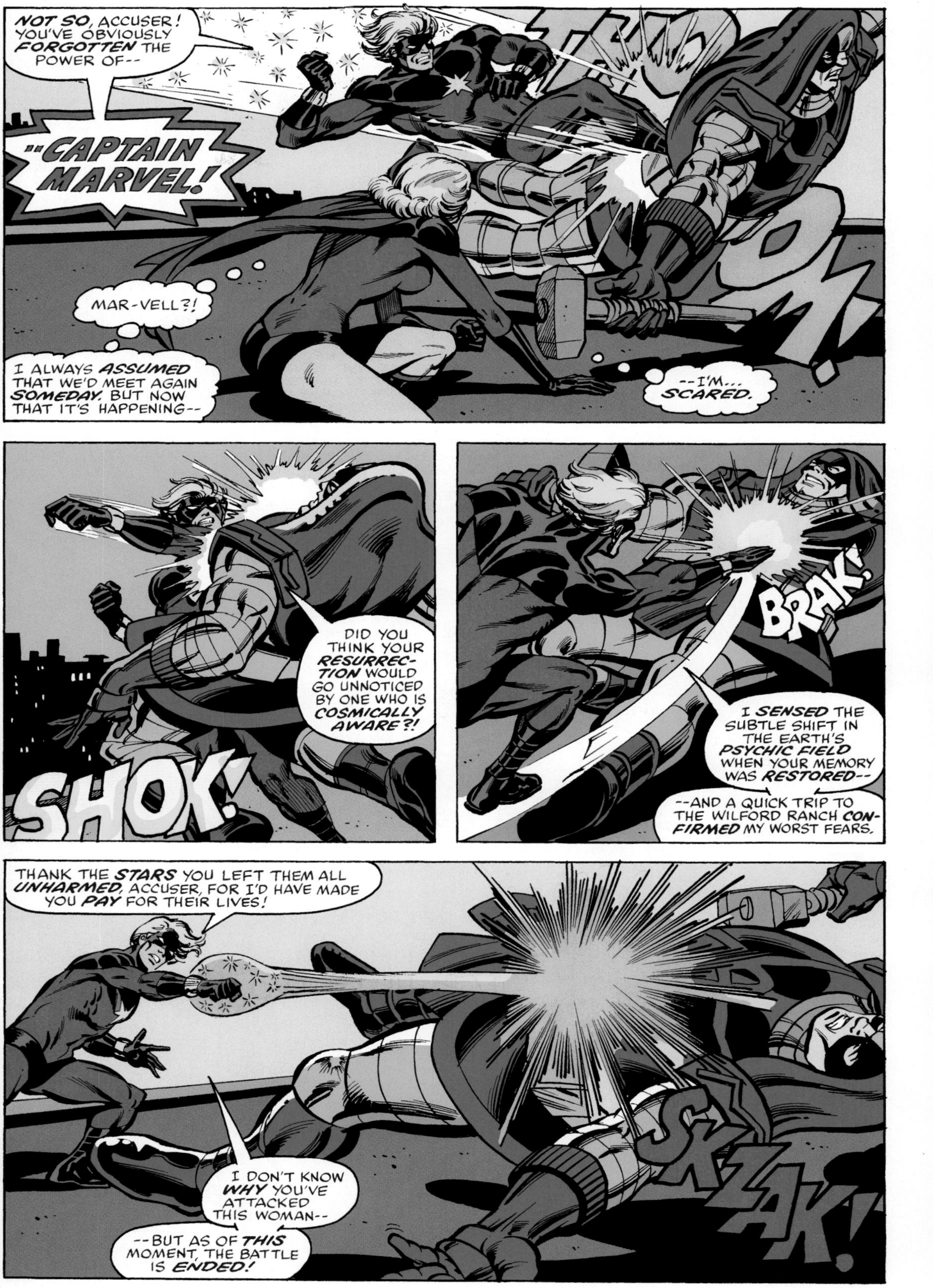
NOT SO, ACCUSER! YOU'VE OBVIOUSLY FORGOTTEN THE POWER OF--
--CAPTAIN MARVEL!
MAR-VELL?!
I ALWAYS ASSUMED THAT WE'D MEET AGAIN SOMEDAY. BUT NOW THAT IT'S HAPPENING--
--I'M... SCARED.
DID YOU THINK YOUR RESURREC-TION WOULD GO UNNOTICED BY ONE WHO IS COSMICALLY AWARE?!
SHOK!
BRAK!
I SENSED THE SUBTLE SHIFT IN THE EARTH'S PSYCHIC FIELD WHEN YOUR MEMORY WAS RESTORED--
--AND A QUICK TRIP TO THE WILFORD RANCH CON-FIRMED MY WORST FEARS.
THANK THE STARS YOU LEFT THEM ALL UNHARMED, ACCUSER, FOR I'D HAVE MADE YOU PAY FOR THEIR LIVES!
I DON'T KNOW WHY YOU'VE ATTACKED THIS WOMAN--
--BUT AS OF THIS MOMENT, THE BATTLE IS ENDED!
SKZAK!

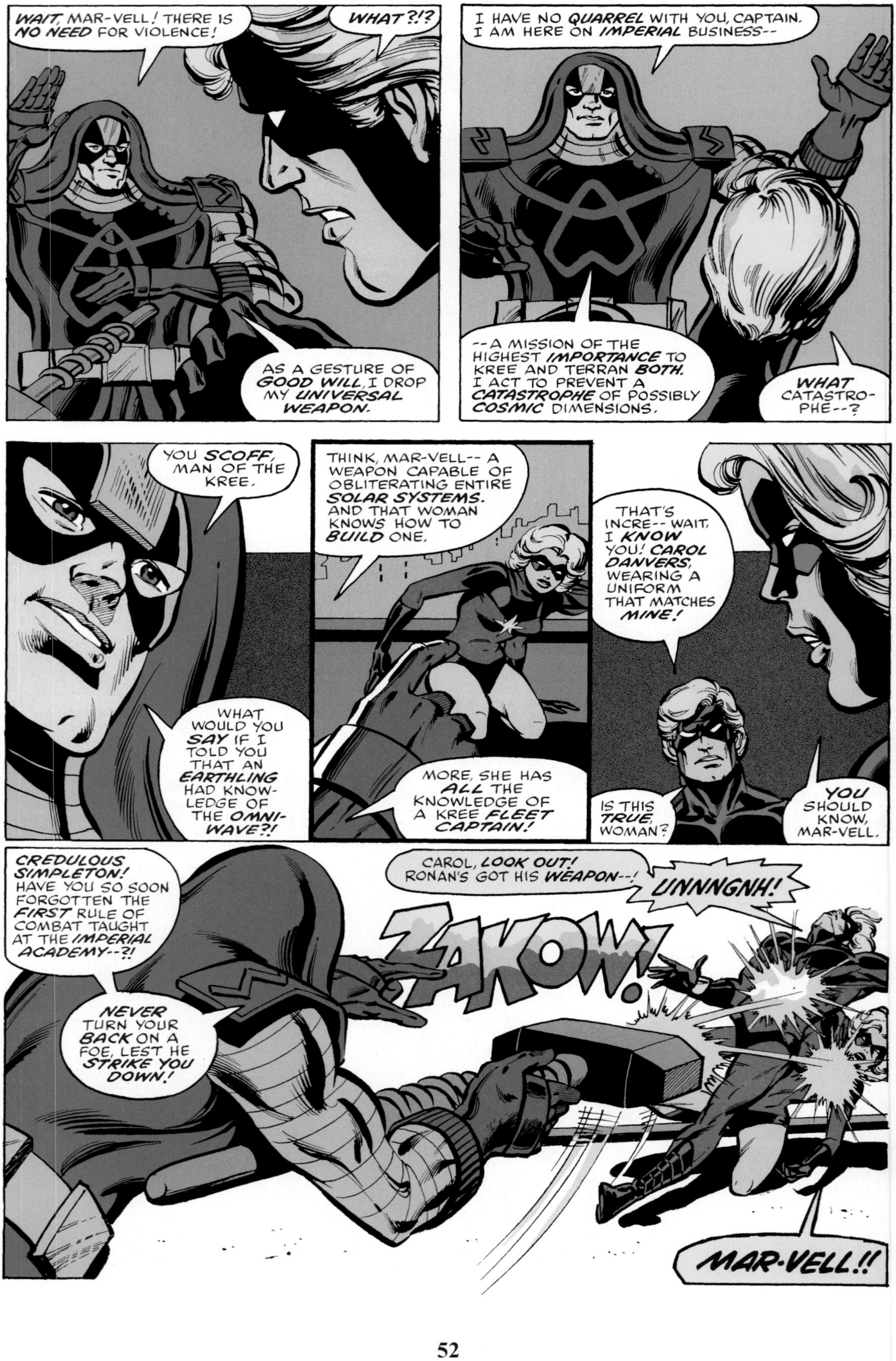

WAIT, MAR-VELL! THERE IS NO NEED FOR VIOLENCE!
WHAT?!?
AS A GESTURE OF GOOD WILL, I DROP MY UNIVERSAL WEAPON.
I HAVE NO QUARREL WITH YOU, CAPTAIN. I AM HERE ON IMPERIAL BUSINESS--
--A MISSION OF THE HIGHEST IMPORTANCE TO KREE AND TERRAN BOTH. I ACT TO PREVENT A CATASTROPHE OF POSSIBLY COSMIC DIMENSIONS.
WHAT CATASTRO-PHE--?
YOU SCOFF, MAN OF THE KREE.
WHAT WOULD YOU SAY IF I TOLD YOU THAT AN EARTHLING HAD KNOW-LEDGE OF THE OMNI-WAVE?!
THINK, MAR-VELL-- A WEAPON CAPABLE OF OBLITERATING ENTIRE SOLAR SYSTEMS. AND THAT WOMAN KNOWS HOW TO BUILD ONE.
MORE, SHE HAS ALL THE KNOWLEDGE OF A KREE FLEET CAPTAIN!
THAT'S INCRE-- WAIT, I KNOW YOU! CAROL DANVERS, WEARING A UNIFORM THAT MATCHES MINE!
IS THIS TRUE, WOMAN?
YOU SHOULD KNOW, MAR-VELL.
CREDULOUS SIMPLETON! HAVE YOU SO SOON FORGOTTEN THE FIRST RULE OF COMBAT TAUGHT AT THE IMPERIAL ACADEMY--?!
NEVER TURN YOUR BACK ON A FOE, LEST HE STRIKE YOU DOWN!
CAROL, LOOK OUT! RONAN'S GOT HIS WEAPON--!
UNNNGNH!
ZAKOW!
MAR-VELL!!

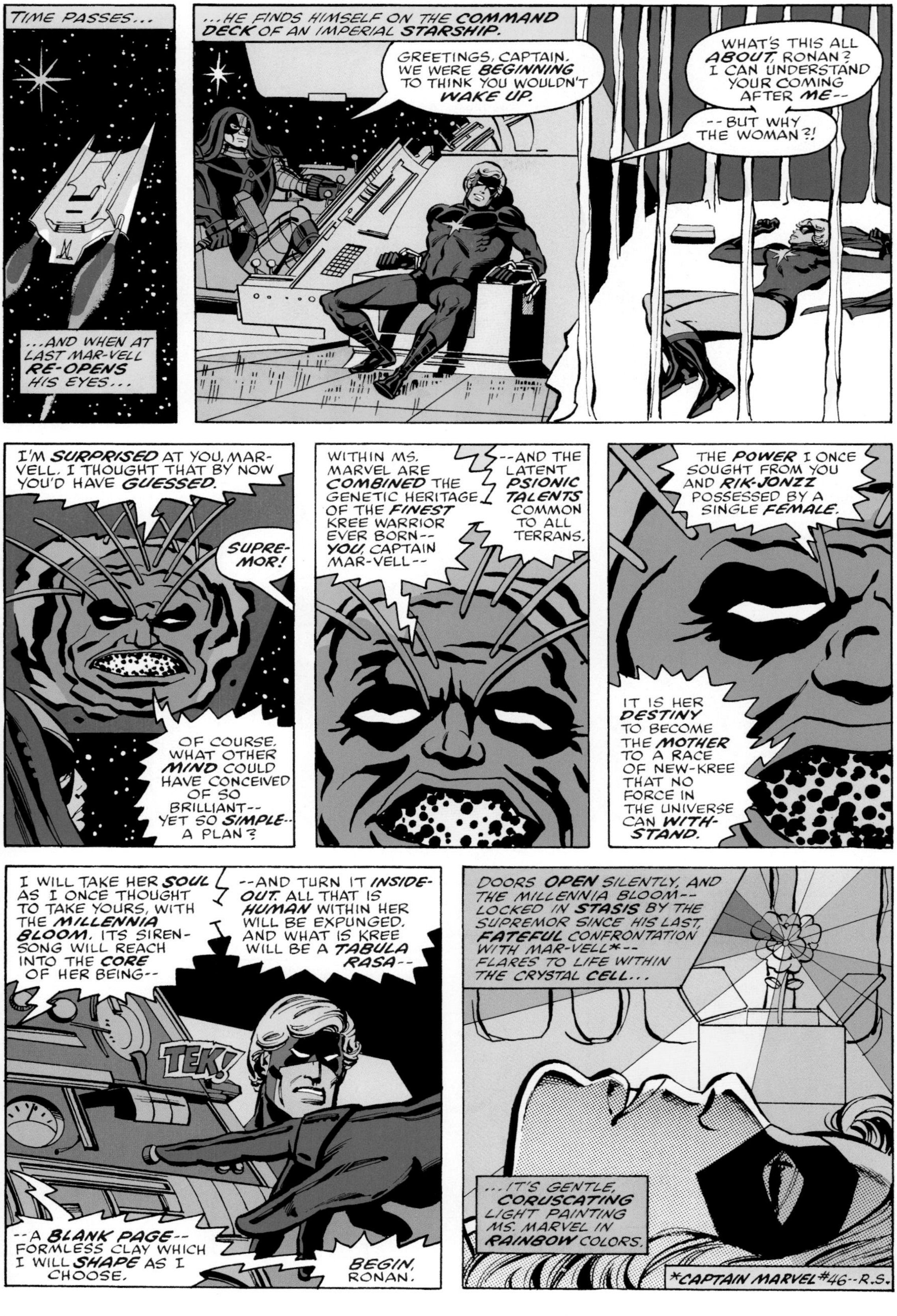

TIME PASSES...
...AND WHEN AT LAST MAR-VELL RE-OPENS HIS EYES...
...HE FINDS HIMSELF ON THE COMMAND DECK OF AN IMPERIAL STARSHIP.
GREETINGS, CAPTAIN. WE WERE BEGINNING TO THINK YOU WOULDN'T WAKE UP.
WHAT'S THIS ALL ABOUT, RONAN? I CAN UNDERSTAND YOUR COMING AFTER ME--
--BUT WHY THE WOMAN?!
I'M SURPRISED AT YOU, MAR-VELL. I THOUGHT THAT BY NOW YOU'D HAVE GUESSED.
SUPREMOR!
OF COURSE. WHAT OTHER MIND COULD HAVE CONCEIVED OF SO BRILLIANT--YET SO SIMPLE--A PLAN?
WITHIN MS. MARVEL ARE COMBINED THE GENETIC HERITAGE OF THE FINEST KREE WARRIOR EVER BORN--YOU, CAPTAIN MAR-VELL--
--AND THE LATENT PSIONIC TALENTS COMMON TO ALL TERRANS.
THE POWER I ONCE SOUGHT FROM YOU AND RIK-JONZZ POSSESSED BY A SINGLE FEMALE.
IT IS HER DESTINY TO BECOME THE MOTHER TO A RACE OF NEW-KREE THAT NO FORCE IN THE UNIVERSE CAN WITHSTAND.
I WILL TAKE HER SOUL AS I ONCE THOUGHT TO TAKE YOURS, WITH THE MILLENNIA BLOOM. ITS SIREN-SONG WILL REACH INTO THE CORE OF HER BEING--
--AND TURN IT INSIDE-OUT. ALL THAT IS HUMAN WITHIN HER WILL BE EXPUNGED, AND WHAT IS KREE WILL BE A TABULA RASA--
TEK!
--A BLANK PAGE--FORMLESS CLAY WHICH I WILL SHAPE AS I CHOOSE.
BEGIN, RONAN.
DOORS OPEN SILENTLY, AND THE MILLENNIA BLOOM--LOCKED IN STASIS BY THE SUPREMOR SINCE HIS LAST FATEFUL CONFRONTATION WITH MAR-VELL*--FLARES TO LIFE WITHIN THE CRYSTAL CELL...
...IT'S GENTLE, CORUSCATING LIGHT PAINTING MS. MARVEL IN RAINBOW COLORS.
*CAPTAIN MARVEL #46--R.S.

SLOWLY, STEADILY, THE LIGHTS GROW TO NEAR-**SOLAR** BRILLIANCE, MS. MARVEL CRYING OUT AS THE WORLD AROUND HER **DISSOLVES** UNDER THEIR ONSLAUGHT.

AND THEN, IT'S **HER** TURN, THE CHROMATIC SYMPHONY HITTING HER ON **EVERY** LEVEL OF PERCEPTION AT ONCE.

SHE'S **CAUGHT**, MIND AND BODY AND SOUL, UNABLE--**UNWILLING**--TO BREAK FREE AS THE LIGHT SHOW BUILDS TO A THUNDERING **CRESCENDO.**

TIME STOPS, REALITY LOSES ALL **MEANING** AND, SUDDENLY, SHE'S IN THE **SUPREMOR'S** CHAMBER--

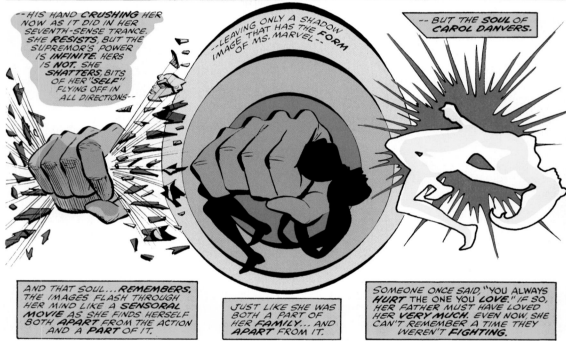

--HIS HAND **CRUSHING** HER NOW AS IT DID IN HER SEVENTH-SENSE TRANCE. SHE **RESISTS**, BUT THE SUPREMOR'S POWER IS **INFINITE.** HERS IS **NOT.** SHE **SHATTERS**, BITS OF HER "**SELF**" FLYING OFF IN ALL DIRECTIONS--

--LEAVING ONLY A SHADOW IMAGE THAT HAS THE **FORM** OF MS. MARVEL--

--BUT THE **SOUL** OF **CAROL DANVERS.**

AND THAT SOUL...**REMEMBERS.** THE IMAGES FLASH THROUGH HER MIND LIKE A **SENSORAL** MOVIE AS SHE FINDS HERSELF BOTH **APART** FROM THE ACTION AND A **PART** OF IT.

JUST LIKE SHE WAS BOTH A **PART** OF HER **FAMILY**... AND **APART** FROM IT.

SOMEONE ONCE SAID, "YOU ALWAYS **HURT** THE ONE YOU **LOVE.**" IF SO, HER FATHER MUST HAVE LOVED HER **VERY MUCH.** EVEN NOW, SHE CAN'T REMEMBER A TIME THEY WEREN'T **FIGHTING.**

...THIS DISCUSSION IS **OVER**, CAROL, MY DECISION IS **FINAL.**

NOT BEFORE YOU TELL ME **WHY**, DAD. YOU OWE ME **THAT** MUCH, AT LEAST.

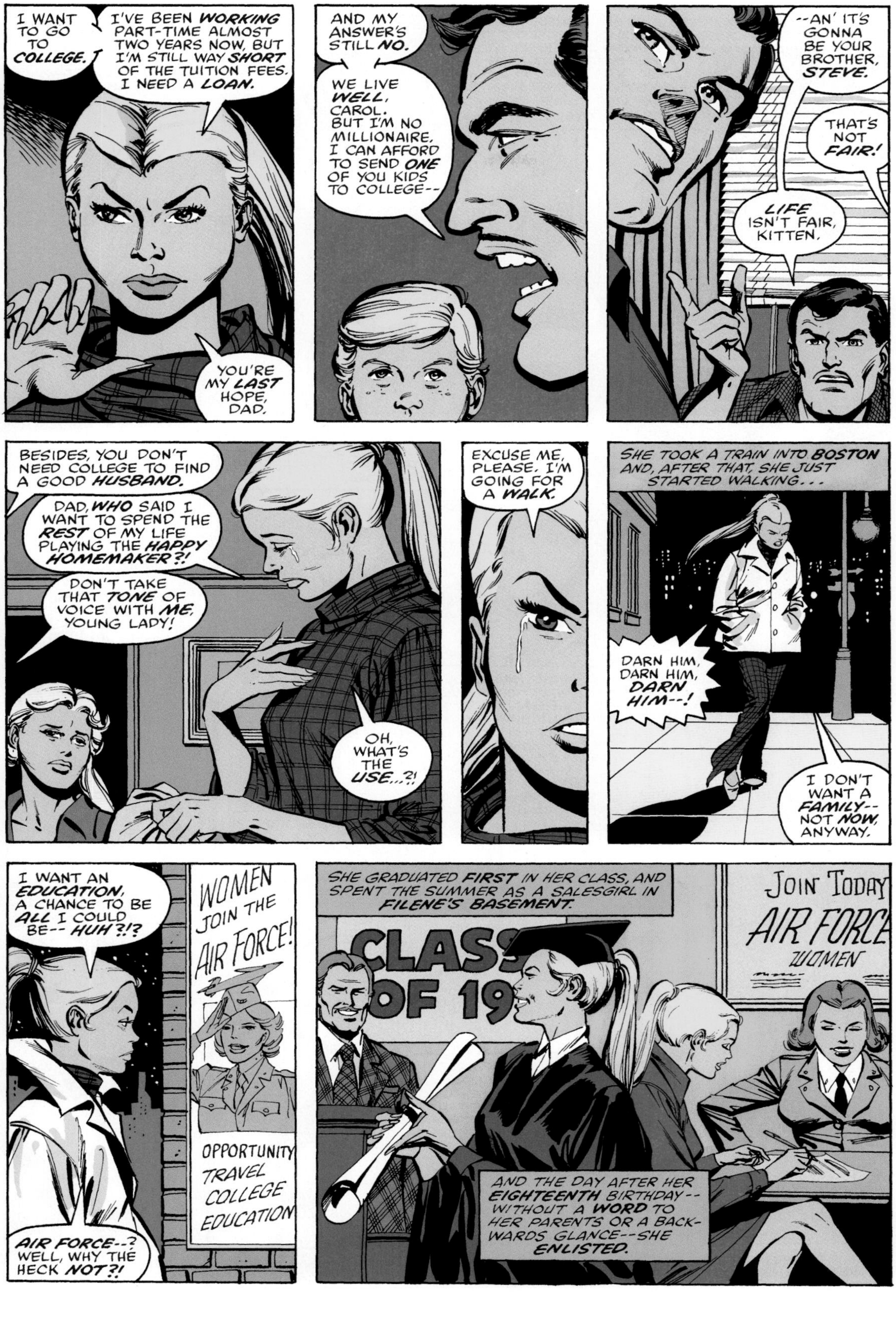
I WANT TO GO TO COLLEGE.
I'VE BEEN WORKING PART-TIME ALMOST TWO YEARS NOW, BUT I'M STILL WAY SHORT OF THE TUITION FEES. I NEED A LOAN.
YOU'RE MY LAST HOPE, DAD.
AND MY ANSWER'S STILL NO.
WE LIVE WELL, CAROL. BUT I'M NO MILLIONAIRE. I CAN AFFORD TO SEND ONE OF YOU KIDS TO COLLEGE--
--AN' IT'S GONNA BE YOUR BROTHER, STEVE.
THAT'S NOT FAIR!
LIFE ISN'T FAIR, KITTEN.
BESIDES, YOU DON'T NEED COLLEGE TO FIND A GOOD HUSBAND.
DAD, WHO SAID I WANT TO SPEND THE REST OF MY LIFE PLAYING THE HAPPY HOMEMAKER?!
DON'T TAKE THAT TONE OF VOICE WITH ME, YOUNG LADY!
OH, WHAT'S THE USE...?!
EXCUSE ME, PLEASE. I'M GOING FOR A WALK.
SHE TOOK A TRAIN INTO BOSTON AND, AFTER THAT, SHE JUST STARTED WALKING...
DARN HIM, DARN HIM, DARN HIM--!
I DON'T WANT A FAMILY-- NOT NOW, ANYWAY.
I WANT AN EDUCATION, A CHANCE TO BE ALL I COULD BE-- HUH?!?
WOMEN JOIN THE AIR FORCE!
OPPORTUNITY TRAVEL COLLEGE EDUCATION
AIR FORCE--? WELL, WHY THE HECK NOT?!
SHE GRADUATED FIRST IN HER CLASS, AND SPENT THE SUMMER AS A SALESGIRL IN FILENE'S BASEMENT.
CLASS OF 19
JOIN TODAY AIR FORCE WOMEN
AND THE DAY AFTER HER EIGHTEENTH BIRTHDAY-- WITHOUT A WORD TO HER PARENTS OR A BACKWARDS GLANCE--SHE ENLISTED.

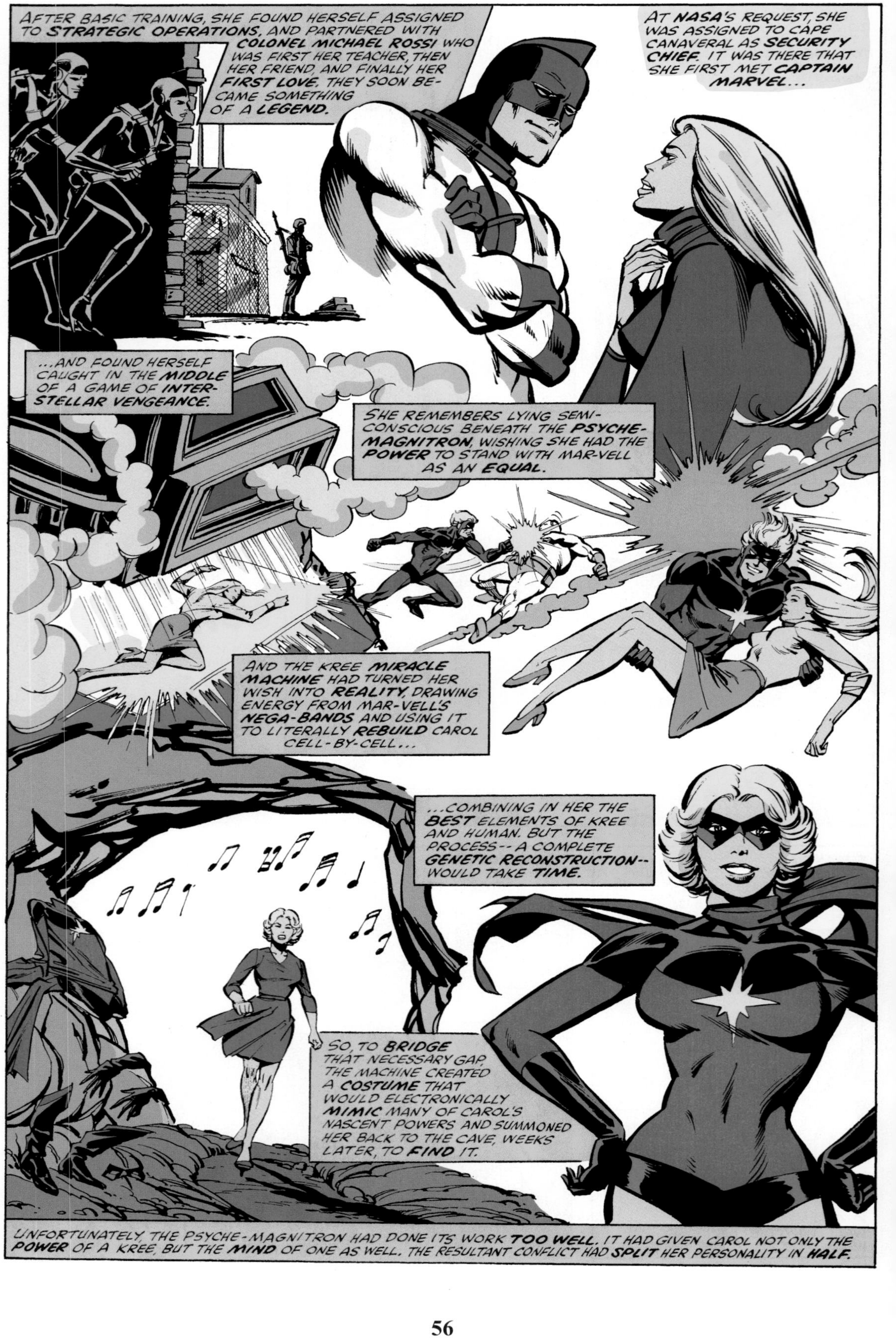
AFTER BASIC TRAINING, SHE FOUND HERSELF ASSIGNED TO STRATEGIC OPERATIONS, AND PARTNERED WITH COLONEL MICHAEL ROSSI WHO WAS FIRST HER TEACHER, THEN HER FRIEND, AND FINALLY HER FIRST LOVE. THEY SOON BECAME SOMETHING OF A LEGEND.
AT NASA'S REQUEST, SHE WAS ASSIGNED TO CAPE CANAVERAL AS SECURITY CHIEF. IT WAS THERE THAT SHE FIRST MET CAPTAIN MARVEL...
...AND FOUND HERSELF CAUGHT IN THE MIDDLE OF A GAME OF INTERSTELLAR VENGEANCE.
SHE REMEMBERS LYING SEMI-CONSCIOUS BENEATH THE PSYCHE-MAGNITRON, WISHING SHE HAD THE POWER TO STAND WITH MAR-VELL AS AN EQUAL.
AND THE KREE MIRACLE MACHINE HAD TURNED HER WISH INTO REALITY, DRAWING ENERGY FROM MAR-VELL'S NEGA-BANDS AND USING IT TO LITERALLY REBUILD CAROL CELL-BY-CELL...
...COMBINING IN HER THE BEST ELEMENTS OF KREE AND HUMAN. BUT THE PROCESS-- A COMPLETE GENETIC RECONSTRUCTION-- WOULD TAKE TIME.
SO, TO BRIDGE THAT NECESSARY GAP, THE MACHINE CREATED A COSTUME THAT WOULD ELECTRONICALLY MIMIC MANY OF CAROL'S NASCENT POWERS AND SUMMONED HER BACK TO THE CAVE, WEEKS LATER, TO FIND IT.
UNFORTUNATELY, THE PSYCHE-MAGNITRON HAD DONE ITS WORK TOO WELL. IT HAD GIVEN CAROL NOT ONLY THE POWER OF A KREE, BUT THE MIND OF ONE AS WELL. THE RESULTANT CONFLICT HAD SPLIT HER PERSONALITY IN HALF.

IN TIME, CAROL HAD MADE HER OWN *PEACE* WITH HERSELF, BUT NOW THE MILLENNIA BLOOM HAS *UNDONE* ALL THAT...

MY REFLECTION-- IT'S *CAROL DANVERS!*

HALA! SHE'S TURNING INTO A *DEMON*--! SHE WANTS ME *DEAD!*

NO, MONSTER! IF *ANYONE* DIES IN THIS NIGHTMARE--

--IT WILL *NOT* BE *MS. MARVEL!*

THERE'S NO *CRASH* AS THE MIRROR-MONSTER SHATTERS, ONLY THE WAIL OF A *LOST SOUL...*

...GIVING WAY TO THE *SOBS* OF A WOMAN PUSHED TO THE *LIMITS* OF HER SANITY, AND *FAR BEYOND.*

IT IS *DONE,* MAR-VELL. THE WOMAN IS *MINE.*

OH, CAROL.

WE ALL *EXPERIENCED* SOME OF WHAT YOU WENT THROUGH. I FEEL SOMEHOW... *RESPONSIBLE.*

AND NOW, THE SUPREMOR WILL *REMAKE* YOU IN HIS OWN IMAGE-- AS HE REMADE *RONAN*-- AND I AM *HELPLESS* TO STOP...EH?

BY THE *GREAT PAMA*--!

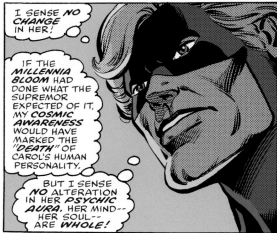

I SENSE *NO CHANGE* IN HER!

IF THE *MILLENNIA BLOOM* HAD DONE WHAT THE SUPREMOR EXPECTED OF IT, MY *COSMIC AWARENESS* WOULD HAVE MARKED THE *"DEATH"* OF CAROL'S HUMAN PERSONALITY.

BUT I SENSE *NO* ALTERATION IN HER *PSYCHIC AURA.* HER MIND-- HER SOUL-- ARE *WHOLE!*

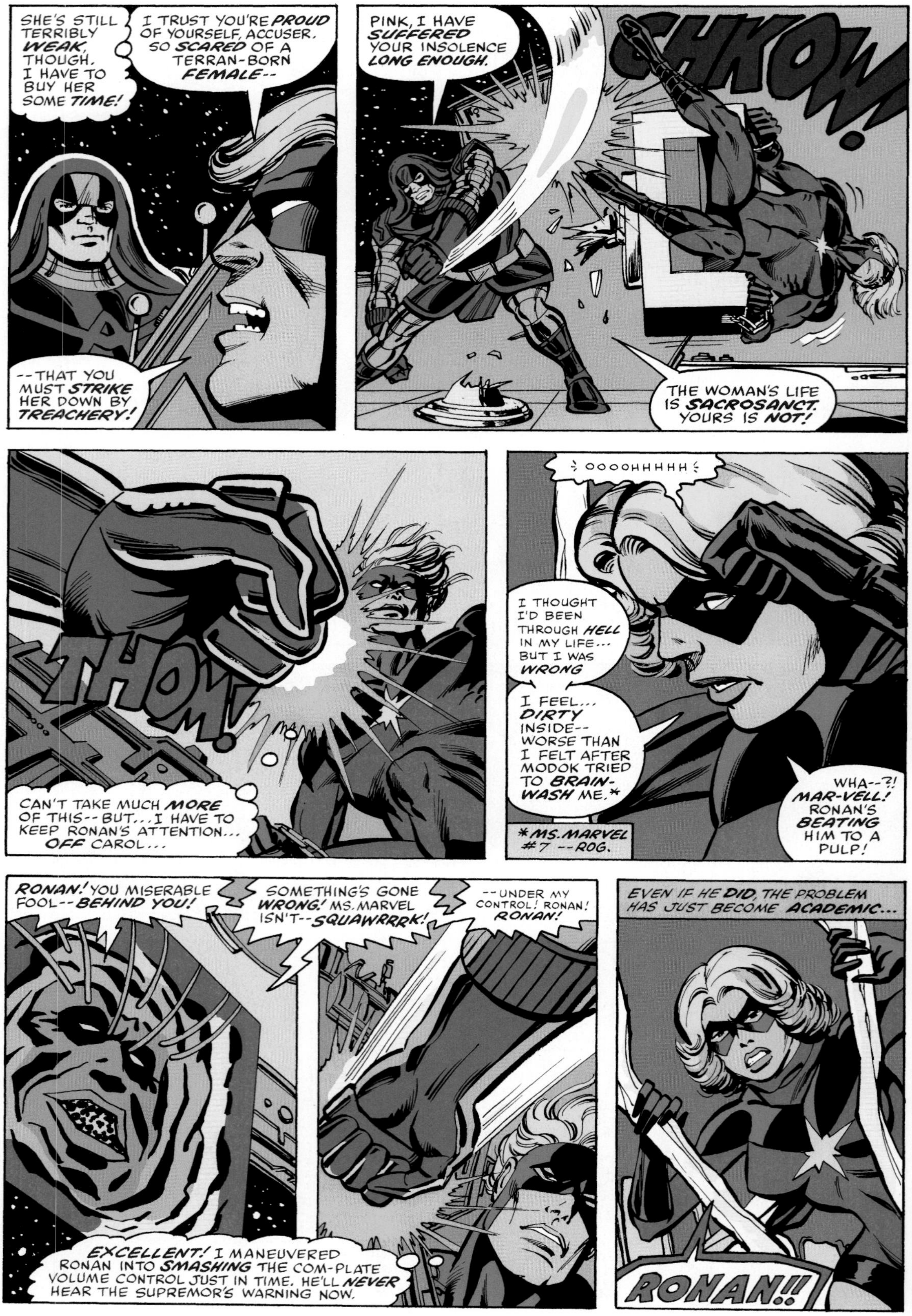

SHE'S STILL TERRIBLY WEAK, THOUGH. I HAVE TO BUY HER SOME TIME!
I TRUST YOU'RE PROUD OF YOURSELF, ACCUSER, SO SCARED OF A TERRAN-BORN FEMALE--
--THAT YOU MUST STRIKE HER DOWN BY TREACHERY!
PINK, I HAVE SUFFERED YOUR INSOLENCE LONG ENOUGH.
CHKOW!
THE WOMAN'S LIFE IS SACROSANCT. YOURS IS NOT!
THOM!
CAN'T TAKE MUCH MORE OF THIS-- BUT... I HAVE TO KEEP RONAN'S ATTENTION... OFF CAROL...
OOOOHHHHH
I THOUGHT I'D BEEN THROUGH HELL IN MY LIFE... BUT I WAS WRONG
I FEEL... DIRTY INSIDE-- WORSE THAN I FELT AFTER MODOK TRIED TO BRAIN-WASH ME.*
WHA--?! MAR-VELL! RONAN'S BEATING HIM TO A PULP!
*MS.MARVEL #7 --ROG.
RONAN! YOU MISERABLE FOOL--BEHIND YOU!
SOMETHING'S GONE WRONG! MS.MARVEL ISN'T--SQUAWRRRK!
--UNDER MY CONTROL! RONAN! RONAN!
EXCELLENT! I MANEUVERED RONAN INTO SMASHING THE COM-PLATE VOLUME CONTROL JUST IN TIME. HE'LL NEVER HEAR THE SUPREMOR'S WARNING NOW.
EVEN IF HE DID, THE PROBLEM HAS JUST BECOME ACADEMIC...
RONAN!!

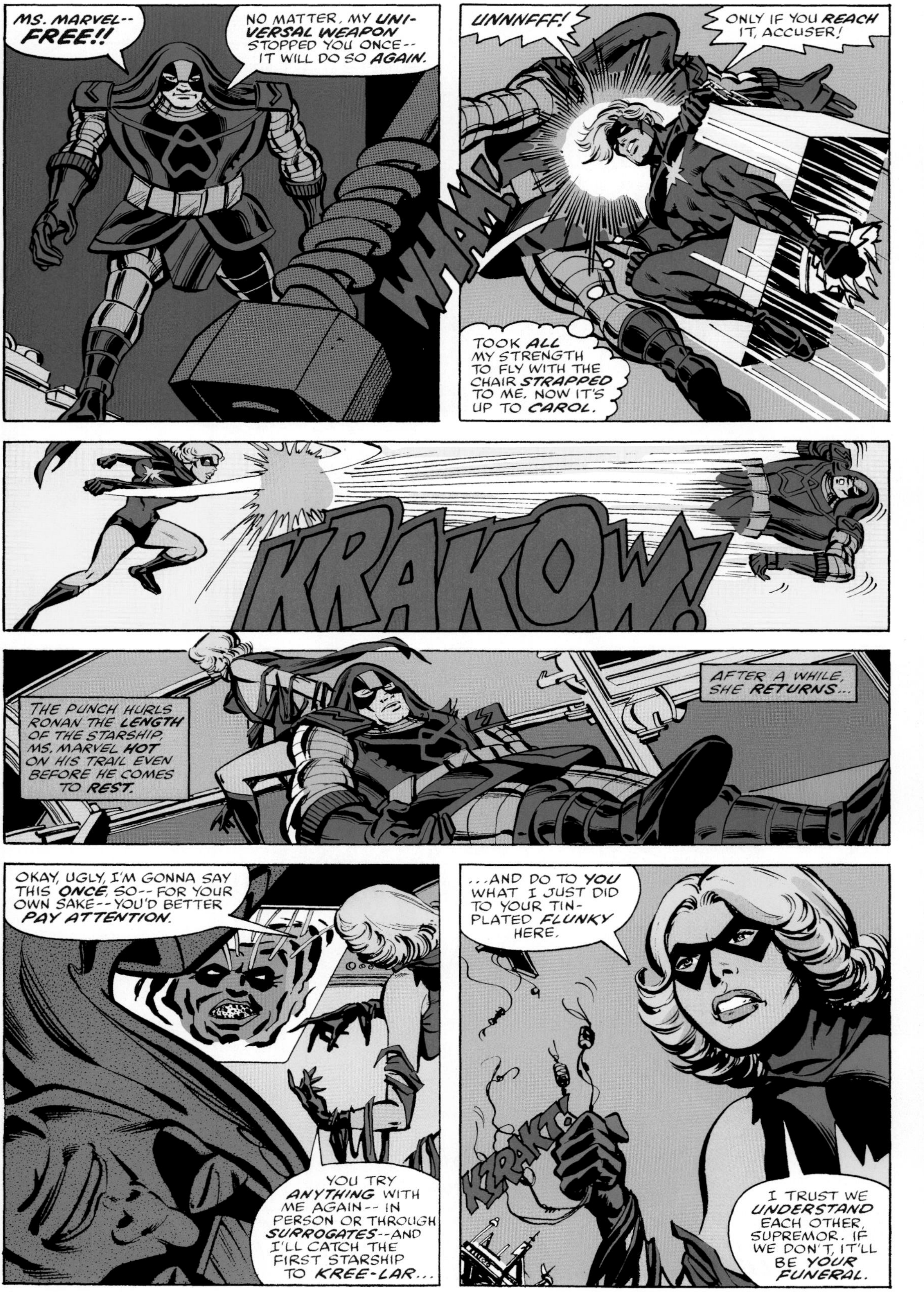

MS. MARVEL-- FREE!!
NO MATTER, MY UNIVERSAL WEAPON STOPPED YOU ONCE-- IT WILL DO SO AGAIN.
WHAM!
UNNNFFF!
ONLY IF YOU REACH IT, ACCUSER!
TOOK ALL MY STRENGTH TO FLY WITH THE CHAIR STRAPPED TO ME. NOW IT'S UP TO CAROL.
KRAKOW!
THE PUNCH HURLS RONAN THE LENGTH OF THE STARSHIP, MS. MARVEL HOT ON HIS TRAIL EVEN BEFORE HE COMES TO REST.
AFTER A WHILE, SHE RETURNS...
OKAY, UGLY, I'M GONNA SAY THIS ONCE, SO-- FOR YOUR OWN SAKE-- YOU'D BETTER PAY ATTENTION.
YOU TRY ANYTHING WITH ME AGAIN-- IN PERSON OR THROUGH SURROGATES--AND I'LL CATCH THE FIRST STARSHIP TO KREE-LAR...
...AND DO TO YOU WHAT I JUST DID TO YOUR TIN-PLATED FLUNKY HERE.
KRAKT!
I TRUST WE UNDERSTAND EACH OTHER, SUPREMOR. IF WE DON'T, IT'LL BE YOUR FUNERAL.

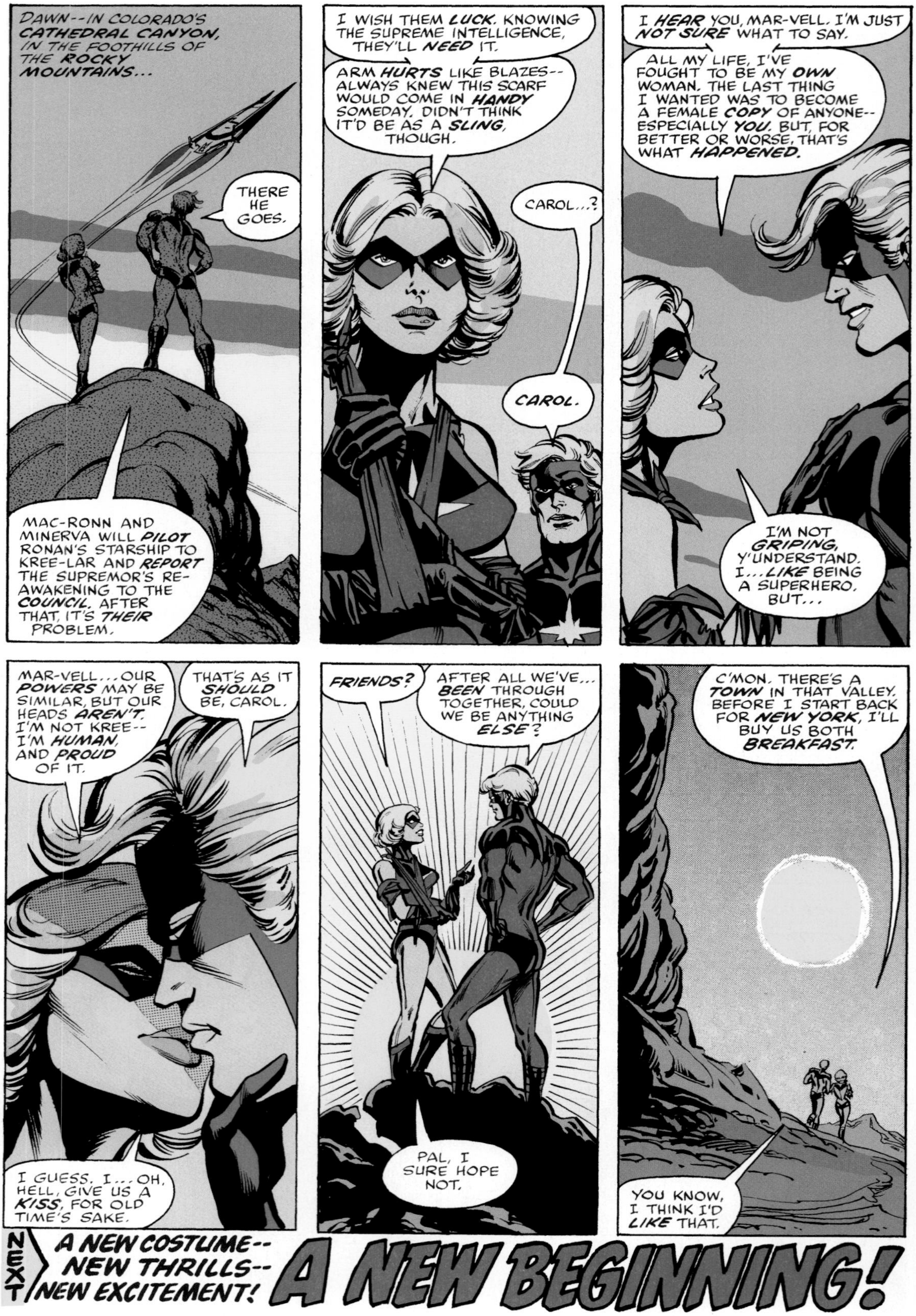
DAWN--IN COLORADO'S CATHEDRAL CANYON, IN THE FOOTHILLS OF THE ROCKY MOUNTAINS...
THERE HE GOES.
MAC-RONN AND MINERVA WILL PILOT RONAN'S STARSHIP TO KREE-LAR AND REPORT THE SUPREMOR'S RE-AWAKENING TO THE COUNCIL. AFTER THAT, IT'S THEIR PROBLEM.
I WISH THEM LUCK. KNOWING THE SUPREME INTELLIGENCE, THEY'LL NEED IT.
ARM HURTS LIKE BLAZES-- ALWAYS KNEW THIS SCARF WOULD COME IN HANDY SOMEDAY. DIDN'T THINK IT'D BE AS A SLING, THOUGH.
CAROL...?
CAROL.
I HEAR YOU, MAR-VELL. I'M JUST NOT SURE WHAT TO SAY.
ALL MY LIFE, I'VE FOUGHT TO BE MY OWN WOMAN. THE LAST THING I WANTED WAS TO BECOME A FEMALE COPY OF ANYONE-- ESPECIALLY YOU. BUT, FOR BETTER OR WORSE, THAT'S WHAT HAPPENED.
I'M NOT GRIPING, Y'UNDERSTAND. I...LIKE BEING A SUPERHERO, BUT...
MAR-VELL...OUR POWERS MAY BE SIMILAR, BUT OUR HEADS AREN'T. I'M NOT KREE-- I'M HUMAN, AND PROUD OF IT.
THAT'S AS IT SHOULD BE, CAROL.
I GUESS. I...OH, HELL, GIVE US A KISS, FOR OLD TIME'S SAKE.
FRIENDS?
AFTER ALL WE'VE... BEEN THROUGH TOGETHER, COULD WE BE ANYTHING ELSE?
PAL, I SURE HOPE NOT.
C'MON. THERE'S A TOWN IN THAT VALLEY. BEFORE I START BACK FOR NEW YORK, I'LL BUY US BOTH BREAKFAST.
YOU KNOW, I THINK I'D LIKE THAT.
NEXT
A NEW COSTUME-- NEW THRILLS-- NEW EXCITEMENT!
A NEW BEGINNING!

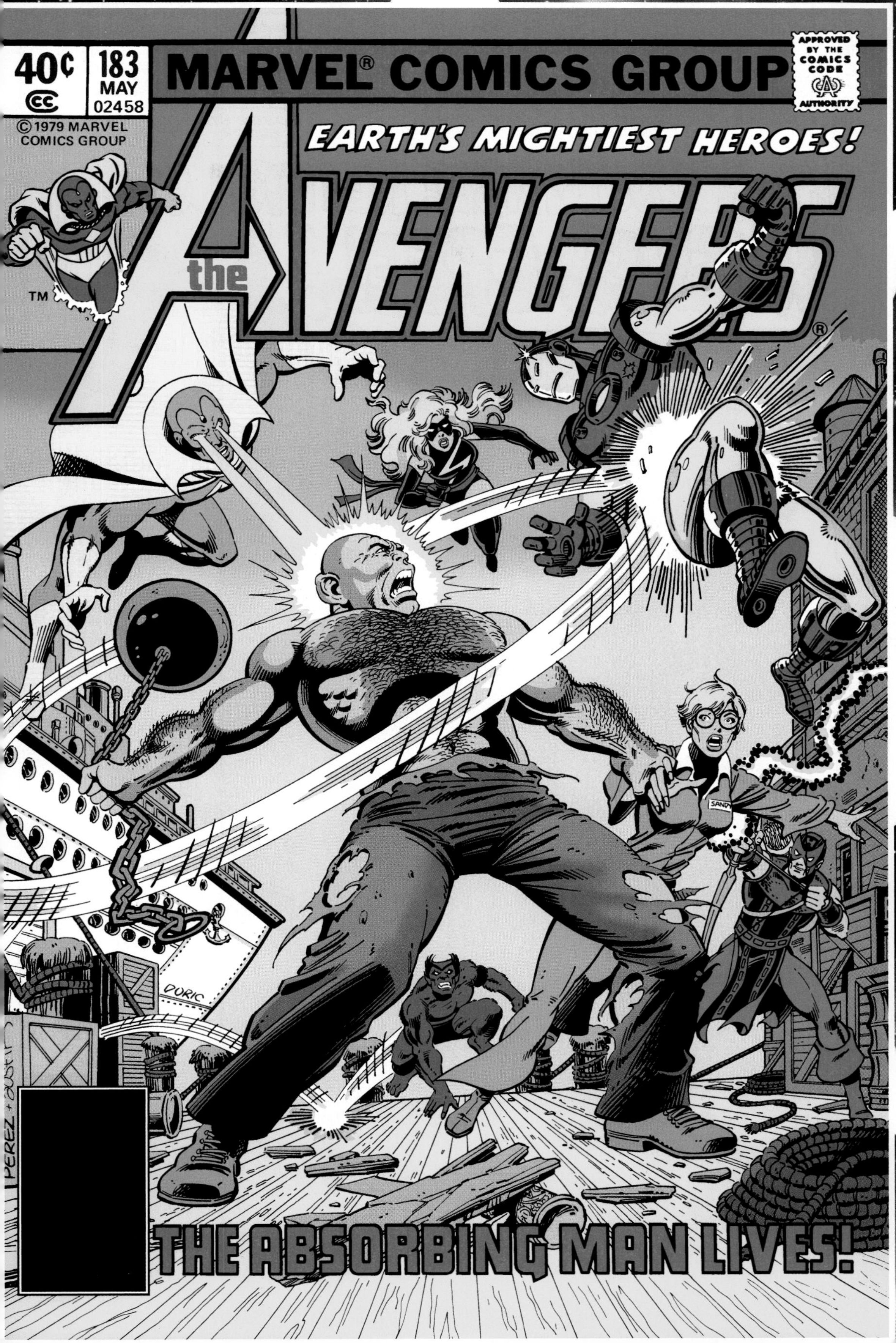

40¢
183
MAY
02458
© 1979 MARVEL COMICS GROUP
MARVEL® COMICS GROUP
APPROVED BY THE COMICS CODE AUTHORITY
EARTH'S MIGHTIEST HEROES!
THE AVENGERS®
TM
SANDY
DURIC
PEREZ + AUSTIN
THE ABSORBING MAN LIVES!

And there came a day when *Earth's mightiest heroes* found themselves *united* against a common threat. On that day, the *Avengers* were born—to fight the foes no *single* super-hero could withstand!

Stan Lee PRESENTS: THE MIGHTY AVENGERS!

| DAVID MICHELINIE WRITER | JOHN BYRNE PENCILS | KLAUS JANSON INKER | NOVAK-LETTERS SHAREN-COLORS | ROGER STERN EDITOR | JIM SHOOTER EDITOR-IN-CHIEF |

THE REDOUBTABLE RETURN OF CRUSHER CREEL!

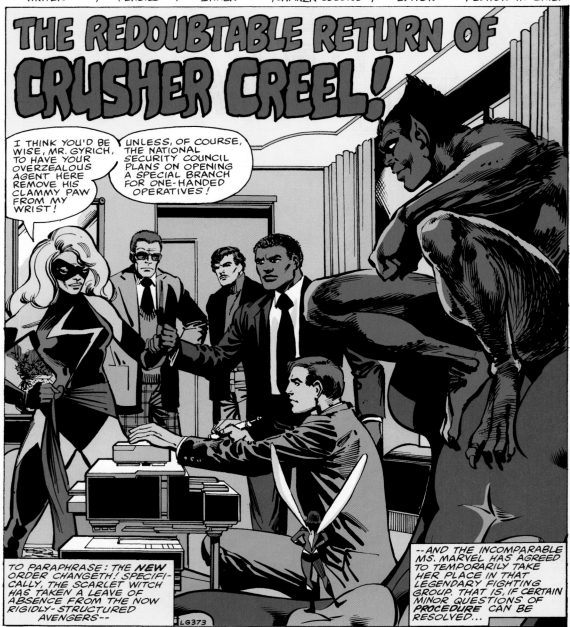

I THINK YOU'D BE WISE, MR. GYRICH, TO HAVE YOUR OVERZEALOUS AGENT HERE REMOVE HIS CLAMMY PAW FROM MY WRIST!

UNLESS, OF COURSE, THE NATIONAL SECURITY COUNCIL PLANS ON OPENING A SPECIAL BRANCH FOR ONE-HANDED OPERATIVES!

TO PARAPHRASE: THE **NEW** ORDER CHANGETH! SPECIFICALLY, THE SCARLET WITCH HAS TAKEN A LEAVE OF ABSENCE FROM THE NOW RIGIDLY-STRUCTURED AVENGERS--

--AND THE INCOMPARABLE MS. MARVEL HAS AGREED TO TEMPORARILY TAKE HER PLACE IN THAT LEGENDARY FIGHTING GROUP, THAT IS, IF CERTAIN MINOR QUESTIONS OF **PROCEDURE** CAN BE RESOLVED...

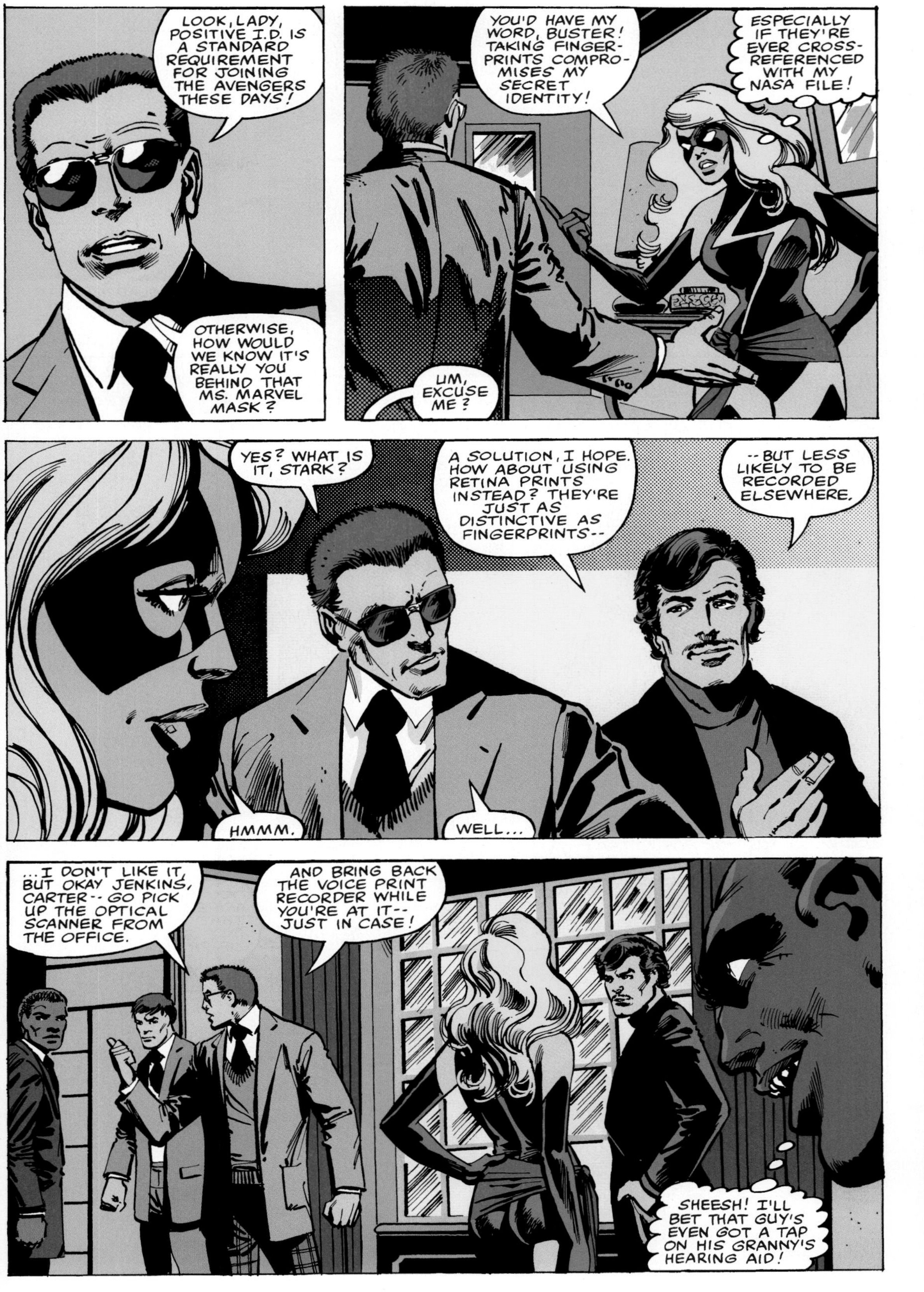
LOOK, LADY, POSITIVE I.D. IS A STANDARD REQUIREMENT FOR JOINING THE AVENGERS THESE DAYS!
OTHERWISE, HOW WOULD WE KNOW IT'S REALLY YOU BEHIND THAT MS. MARVEL MASK?
YOU'D HAVE MY WORD, BUSTER! TAKING FINGER-PRINTS COMPRO-MISES MY SECRET IDENTITY!
ESPECIALLY IF THEY'RE EVER CROSS-REFERENCED WITH MY NASA FILE!
UM, EXCUSE ME?
YES? WHAT IS IT, STARK?
A SOLUTION, I HOPE. HOW ABOUT USING RETINA PRINTS INSTEAD? THEY'RE JUST AS DISTINCTIVE AS FINGERPRINTS--
--BUT LESS LIKELY TO BE RECORDED ELSEWHERE.
HMMM.
WELL...
...I DON'T LIKE IT, BUT OKAY JENKINS, CARTER-- GO PICK UP THE OPTICAL SCANNER FROM THE OFFICE.
AND BRING BACK THE VOICE PRINT RECORDER WHILE YOU'RE AT IT-- JUST IN CASE!
SHEESH! I'LL BET THAT GUY'S EVEN GOT A TAP ON HIS GRANNY'S HEARING AID!

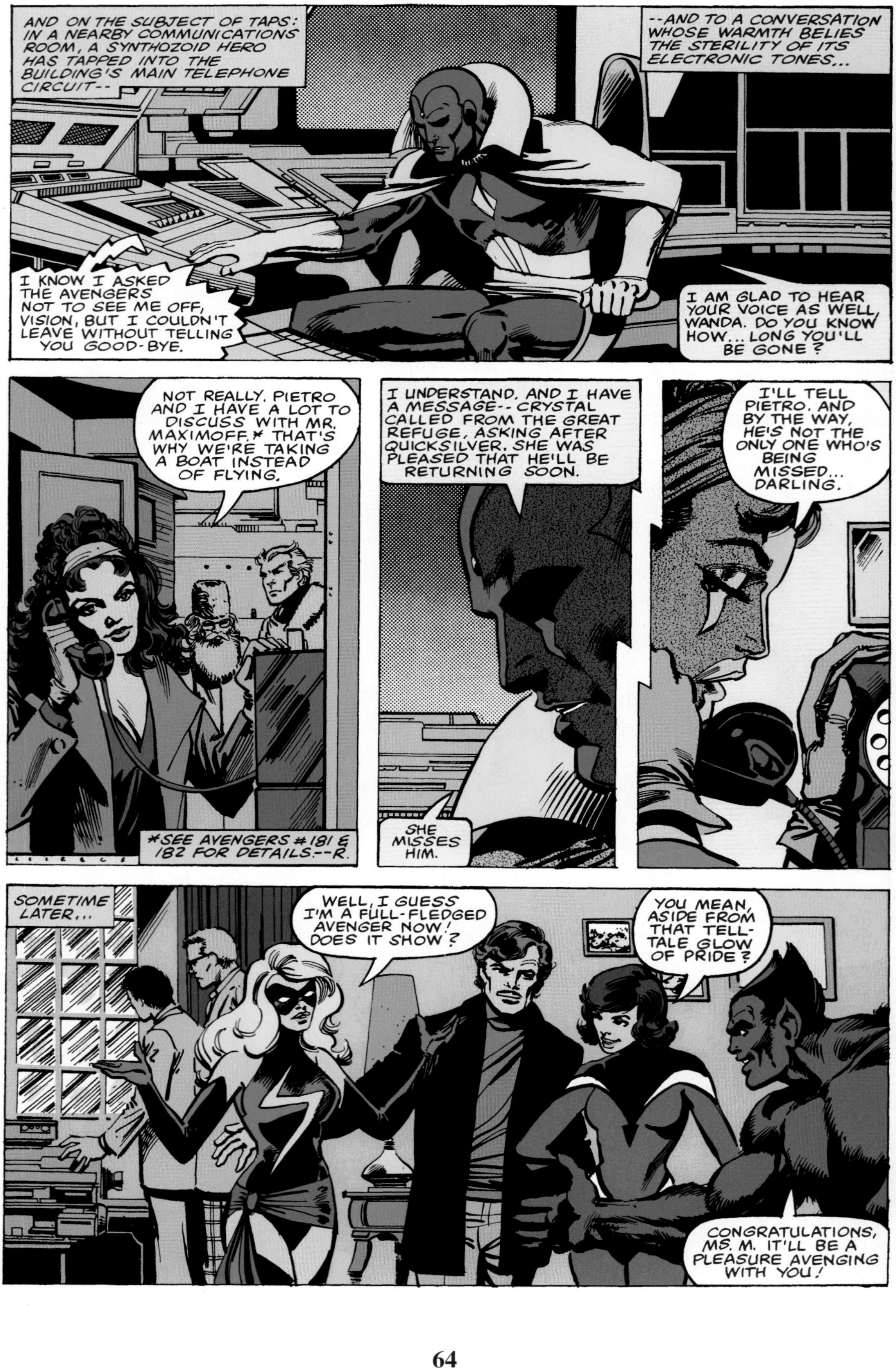
AND ON THE SUBJECT OF TAPS: IN A NEARBY COMMUNICATIONS ROOM, A SYNTHOZOID HERO HAS TAPPED INTO THE BUILDING'S MAIN TELEPHONE CIRCUIT--
--AND TO A CONVERSATION WHOSE WARMTH BELIES THE STERILITY OF ITS ELECTRONIC TONES...
I KNOW I ASKED THE AVENGERS NOT TO SEE ME OFF, VISION, BUT I COULDN'T LEAVE WITHOUT TELLING YOU GOOD-BYE.
I AM GLAD TO HEAR YOUR VOICE AS WELL, WANDA. DO YOU KNOW HOW... LONG YOU'LL BE GONE?
NOT REALLY. PIETRO AND I HAVE A LOT TO DISCUSS WITH MR. MAXIMOFF.* THAT'S WHY WE'RE TAKING A BOAT INSTEAD OF FLYING.
*SEE AVENGERS #181 & 182 FOR DETAILS.--R.
I UNDERSTAND. AND I HAVE A MESSAGE-- CRYSTAL CALLED FROM THE GREAT REFUGE, ASKING AFTER QUICKSILVER. SHE WAS PLEASED THAT HE'LL BE RETURNING SOON.
SHE MISSES HIM.
I'LL TELL PIETRO. AND BY THE WAY, HE'S NOT THE ONLY ONE WHO'S BEING MISSED... DARLING.
SOMETIME LATER...
WELL, I GUESS I'M A FULL-FLEDGED AVENGER NOW! DOES IT SHOW?
YOU MEAN, ASIDE FROM THAT TELL-TALE GLOW OF PRIDE?
CONGRATULATIONS, MS. M. IT'LL BE A PLEASURE AVENGING WITH YOU!

MOMENTS PASS, SMALL TALK IS MADE, AND THE NEWEST MEMBER OF THE WORLD'S GREATEST SUPERTEAM IS SHOWN TO HER QUARTERS--

--AS THE SPONSOR OF THAT SELFSAME GROUP RETIRES TO HIS...

I HOPE MS. MARVEL WILL BE A VALUABLE ASSET. GOD KNOWS--

-- WITH ALL THE RESTRICTIONS THE GOVERNMENT'S HEAPED ON US LATELY, WE CAN USE ALL THE HELP WE CAN GET!

TONY, M'MAN, SOMETIMES I THINK YOU BITE OFF MORE THAN YOU CAN CHEW!

AND SOMETIMES I THINK YOU JUST NEED A GOOD, STIFF MARTINI TO WASH IT DOWN WITH!

BUT THEN...

AW, DAGNAB IT!

WHHRRRRR

EH, LOOKS LIKE I'M NOT THE ONLY ONE WITH PROBLEMS TODAY!

EES NO GOOD, BERNIE. THE HYDRAULIC LIFT, SHE NO WORK NO MORE.

WHRRRRRRRRRRR

BLAST! AN' THIS WAS OUR LAST PICK-UP, TOO!

CAN I BE OF HELP, GENTLEMEN?

HUH? WHAZZAT?

I'M AFRAID THIS IS ALL MY FAULT, ANYWAY. I HELPED MR. STARK CLEAN OUT HIS LAB LAST WEEK--

-- AND I GUESS YOUR TRUCK JUST WASN'T BUILT TO HANDLE A HALF-TON OF ELECTRONIC SCRAPS!

KRRUNK

FORTU- NATELY, THOUGH, MY ARMOR WAS!

THERE. THAT SHOULD DO IT.

SHKRUBALANKALANG

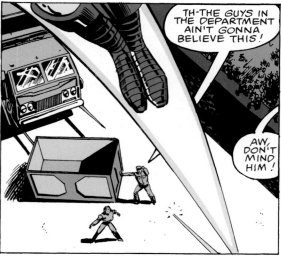

TH-THE GUYS IN THE DEPARTMENT AIN'T GONNA BELIEVE THIS!

AW, DON'T MIND HIM!

THERE ARE A LOT OF WEIRD CHARACTERS HANGING AROUND THIS PLACE!

QUÉ--?

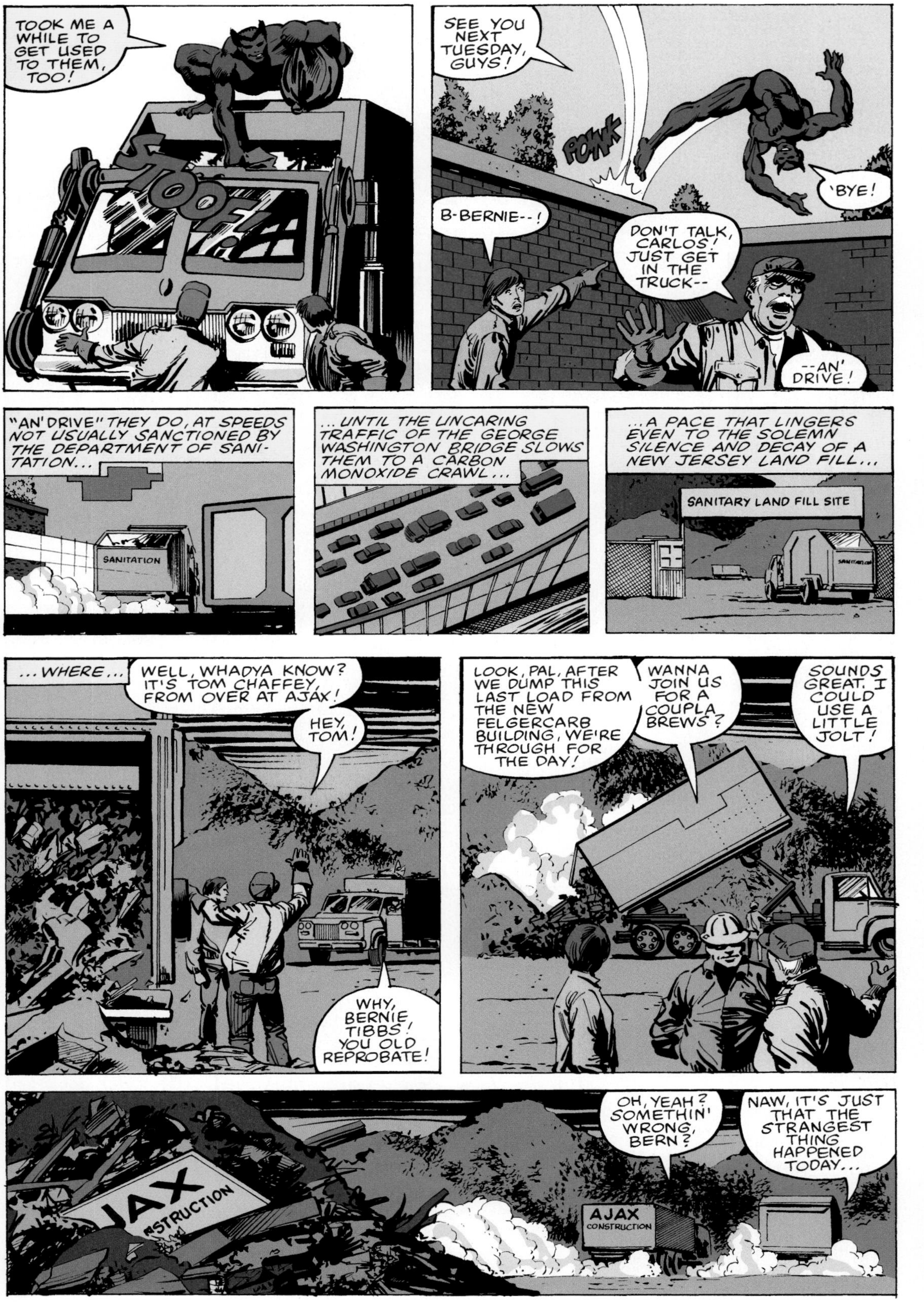
TOOK ME A WHILE TO GET USED TO THEM, TOO!
STOOF!
SEE YOU NEXT TUESDAY, GUYS!
POINK
'BYE!
B-BERNIE--!
DON'T TALK, CARLOS! JUST GET IN THE TRUCK--
--AN' DRIVE!
"AN' DRIVE" THEY DO, AT SPEEDS NOT USUALLY SANCTIONED BY THE DEPARTMENT OF SANITATION...
SANITATION
...UNTIL THE UNCARING TRAFFIC OF THE GEORGE WASHINGTON BRIDGE SLOWS THEM TO A CARBON MONOXIDE CRAWL...
...A PACE THAT LINGERS EVEN TO THE SOLEMN SILENCE AND DECAY OF A NEW JERSEY LAND FILL...
SANITARY LAND FILL SITE
...WHERE...
WELL, WHADYA KNOW? IT'S TOM CHAFFEY, FROM OVER AT AJAX!
HEY, TOM!
WHY, BERNIE TIBBS! YOU OLD REPROBATE!
LOOK, PAL, AFTER WE DUMP THIS LAST LOAD FROM THE NEW FELGERCARB BUILDING, WE'RE THROUGH FOR THE DAY!
WANNA JOIN US FOR A COUPLA BREWS?
SOUNDS GREAT. I COULD USE A LITTLE JOLT!
JAX
STRUCTION
AJAX
CONSTRUCTION
OH, YEAH? SOMETHIN' WRONG, BERN?
NAW, IT'S JUST THAT THE STRANGEST THING HAPPENED TODAY...

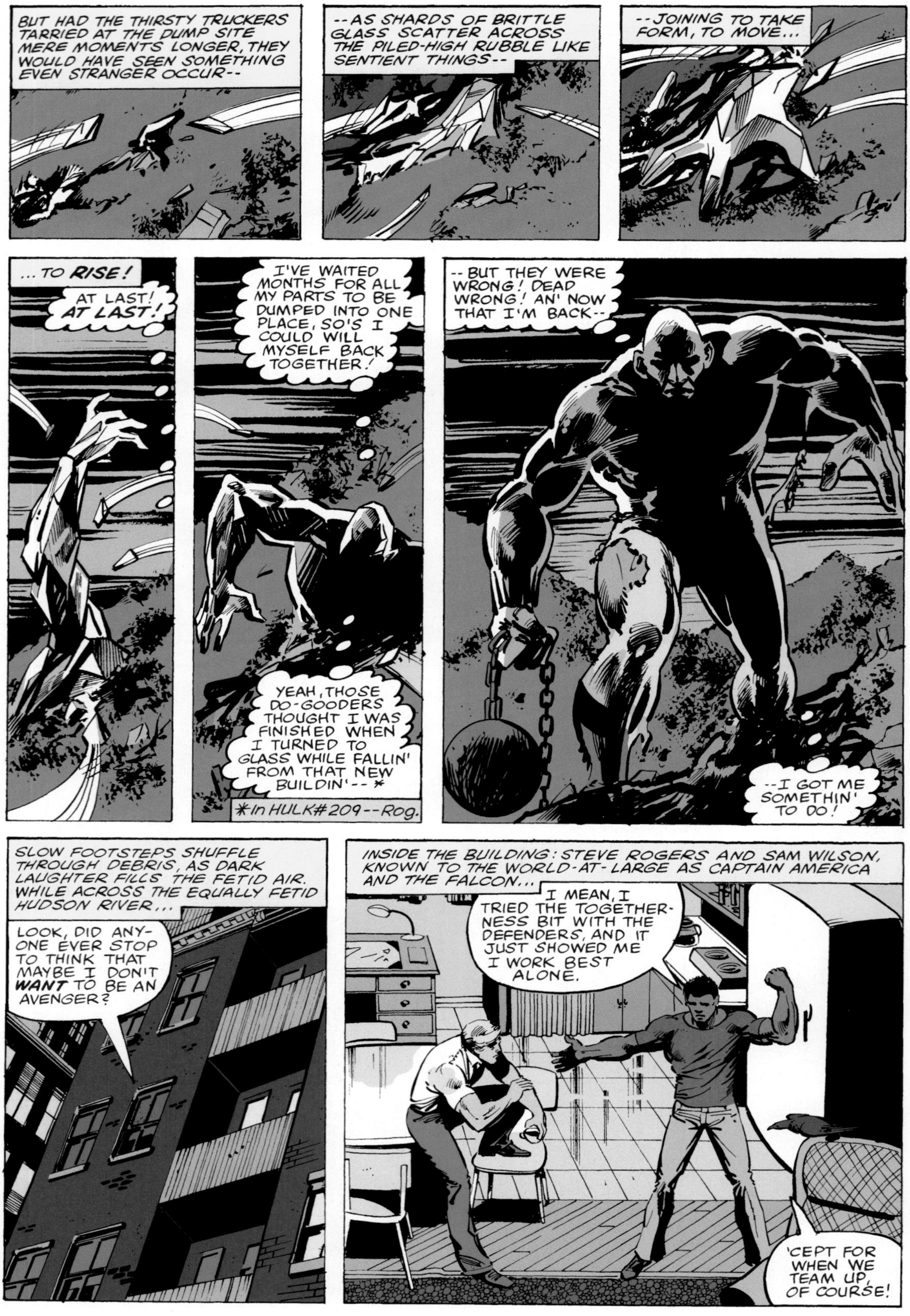
BUT HAD THE THIRSTY TRUCKERS TARRIED AT THE DUMP SITE MERE MOMENTS LONGER, THEY WOULD HAVE SEEN SOMETHING EVEN STRANGER OCCUR--
--AS SHARDS OF BRITTLE GLASS SCATTER ACROSS THE PILED-HIGH RUBBLE LIKE SENTIENT THINGS--
--JOINING TO TAKE FORM, TO MOVE...
...TO RISE!
AT LAST! AT LAST!
I'VE WAITED MONTHS FOR ALL MY PARTS TO BE DUMPED INTO ONE PLACE, SO'S I COULD WILL MYSELF BACK TOGETHER!
YEAH, THOSE DO-GOODERS THOUGHT I WAS FINISHED WHEN I TURNED TO GLASS WHILE FALLIN' FROM THAT NEW BUILDIN'--*
*In HULK #209--Rog.
--BUT THEY WERE WRONG! DEAD WRONG! AN' NOW THAT I'M BACK--
--I GOT ME SOMETHIN' TO DO!
SLOW FOOTSTEPS SHUFFLE THROUGH DEBRIS, AS DARK LAUGHTER FILLS THE FETID AIR. WHILE ACROSS THE EQUALLY FETID HUDSON RIVER...
LOOK, DID ANYONE EVER STOP TO THINK THAT MAYBE I DON'T WANT TO BE AN AVENGER?
INSIDE THE BUILDING: STEVE ROGERS AND SAM WILSON, KNOWN TO THE WORLD-AT-LARGE AS CAPTAIN AMERICA AND THE FALCON...
I MEAN, I TRIED THE TOGETHERNESS BIT WITH THE DEFENDERS, AND IT JUST SHOWED ME I WORK BEST ALONE.
'CEPT FOR WHEN WE TEAM UP, OF COURSE!

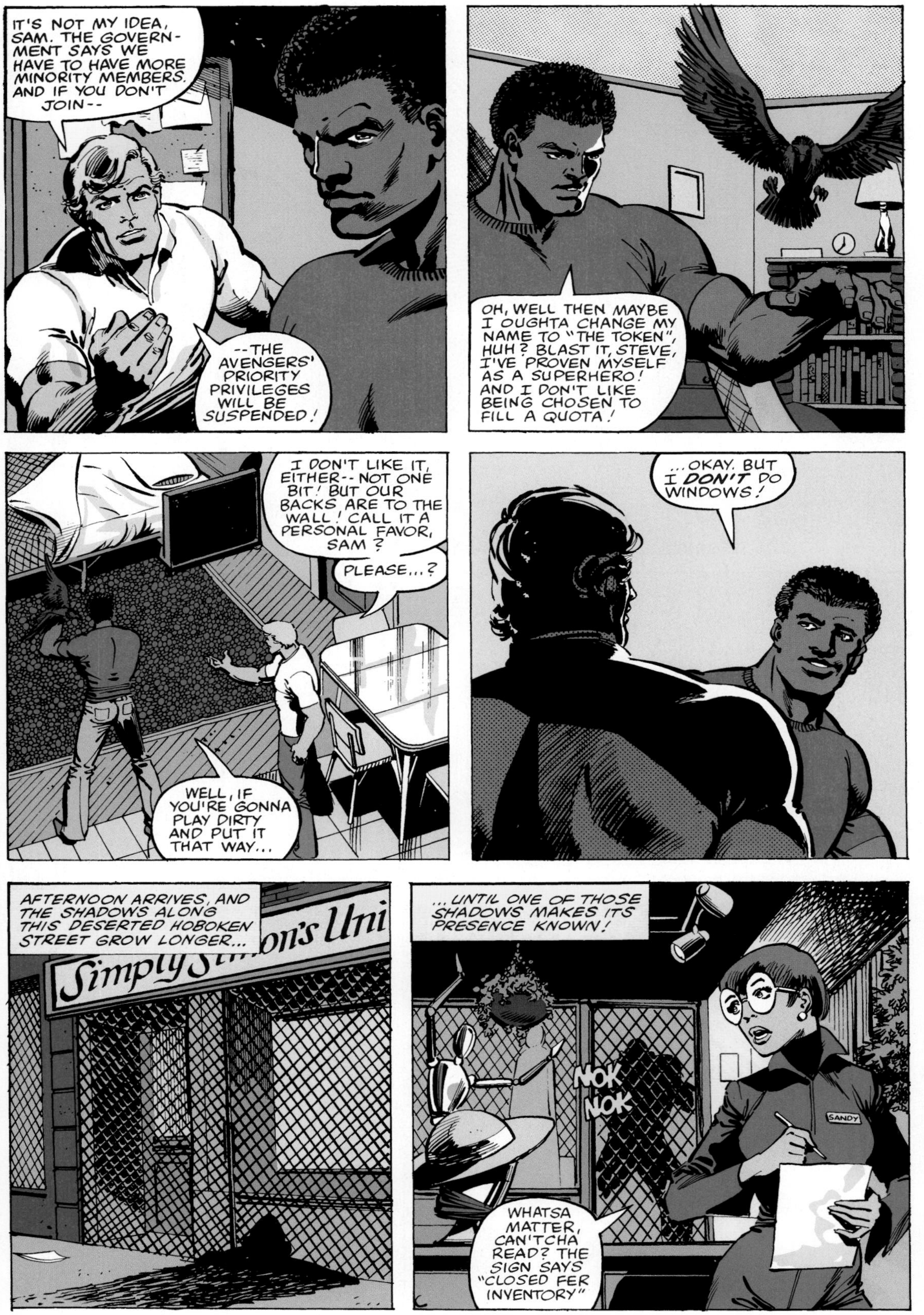
IT'S NOT MY IDEA, SAM. THE GOVERNMENT SAYS WE HAVE TO HAVE MORE MINORITY MEMBERS. AND IF YOU DON'T JOIN--
--THE AVENGERS' PRIORITY PRIVILEGES WILL BE SUSPENDED!
OH, WELL THEN MAYBE I OUGHTA CHANGE MY NAME TO "THE TOKEN", HUH? BLAST IT, STEVE, I'VE PROVEN MYSELF AS A SUPERHERO! AND I DON'T LIKE BEING CHOSEN TO FILL A QUOTA!
I DON'T LIKE IT, EITHER-- NOT ONE BIT! BUT OUR BACKS ARE TO THE WALL! CALL IT A PERSONAL FAVOR, SAM?
PLEASE...?
WELL, IF YOU'RE GONNA PLAY DIRTY AND PUT IT THAT WAY...
...OKAY. BUT I DON'T DO WINDOWS!
AFTERNOON ARRIVES, AND THE SHADOWS ALONG THIS DESERTED HOBOKEN STREET GROW LONGER...
...UNTIL ONE OF THOSE SHADOWS MAKES ITS PRESENCE KNOWN!
NOK NOK
SANDY
WHATSA MATTER, CAN'TCHA READ? THE SIGN SAYS "CLOSED FER INVENTORY"

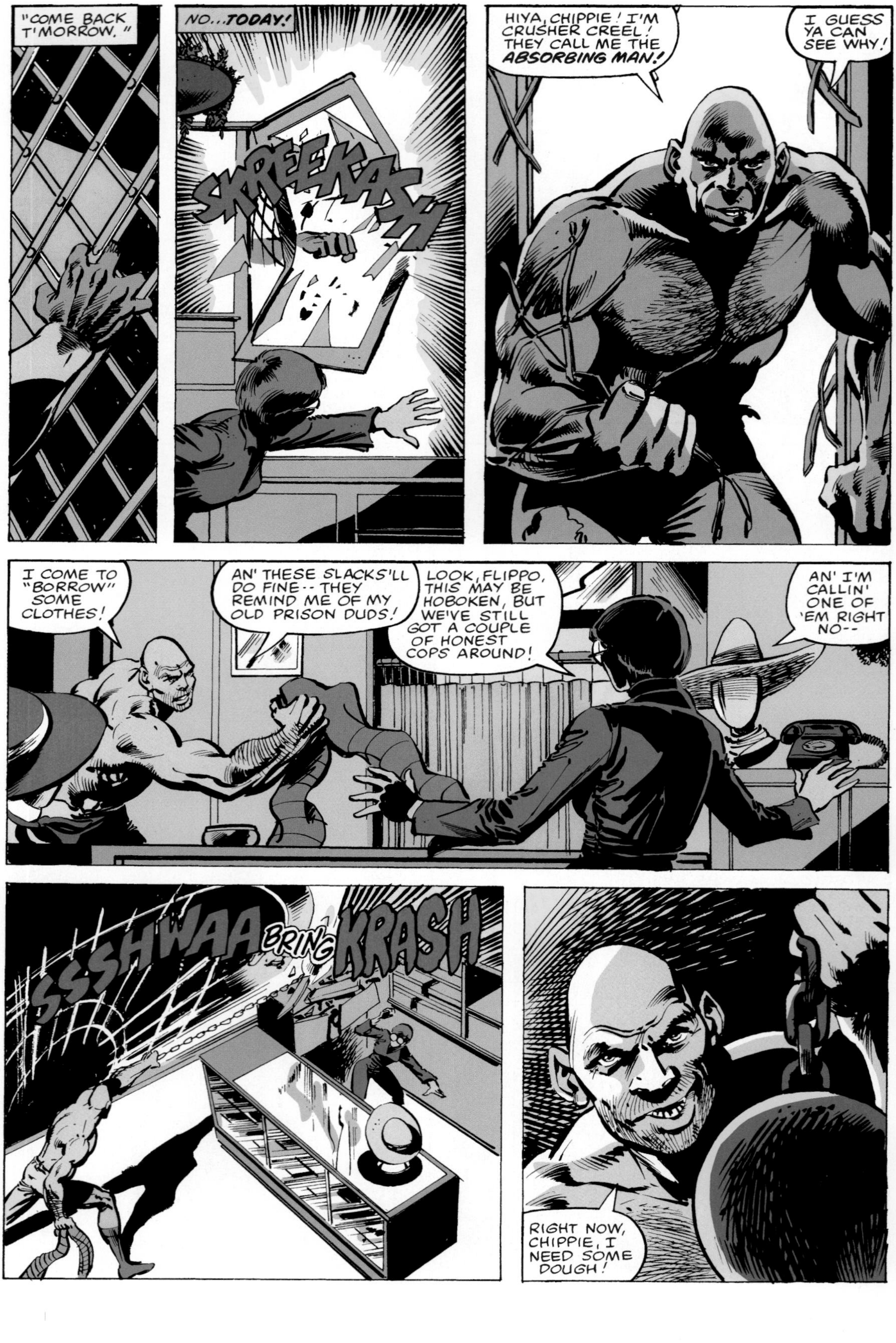
"COME BACK T'MORROW."
NO... TODAY!
SKREEKASH
HIYA, CHIPPIE! I'M CRUSHER CREEL! THEY CALL ME THE ABSORBING MAN!
I GUESS YA CAN SEE WHY!
I COME TO "BORROW" SOME CLOTHES!
AN' THESE SLACKS'LL DO FINE-- THEY REMIND ME OF MY OLD PRISON DUDS!
LOOK, FLIPPO, THIS MAY BE HOBOKEN, BUT WE'VE STILL GOT A COUPLE OF HONEST COPS AROUND!
AN' I'M CALLIN' ONE OF 'EM RIGHT NO--
SSSHWAA BRING KRASH
RIGHT NOW, CHIPPIE, I NEED SOME DOUGH!

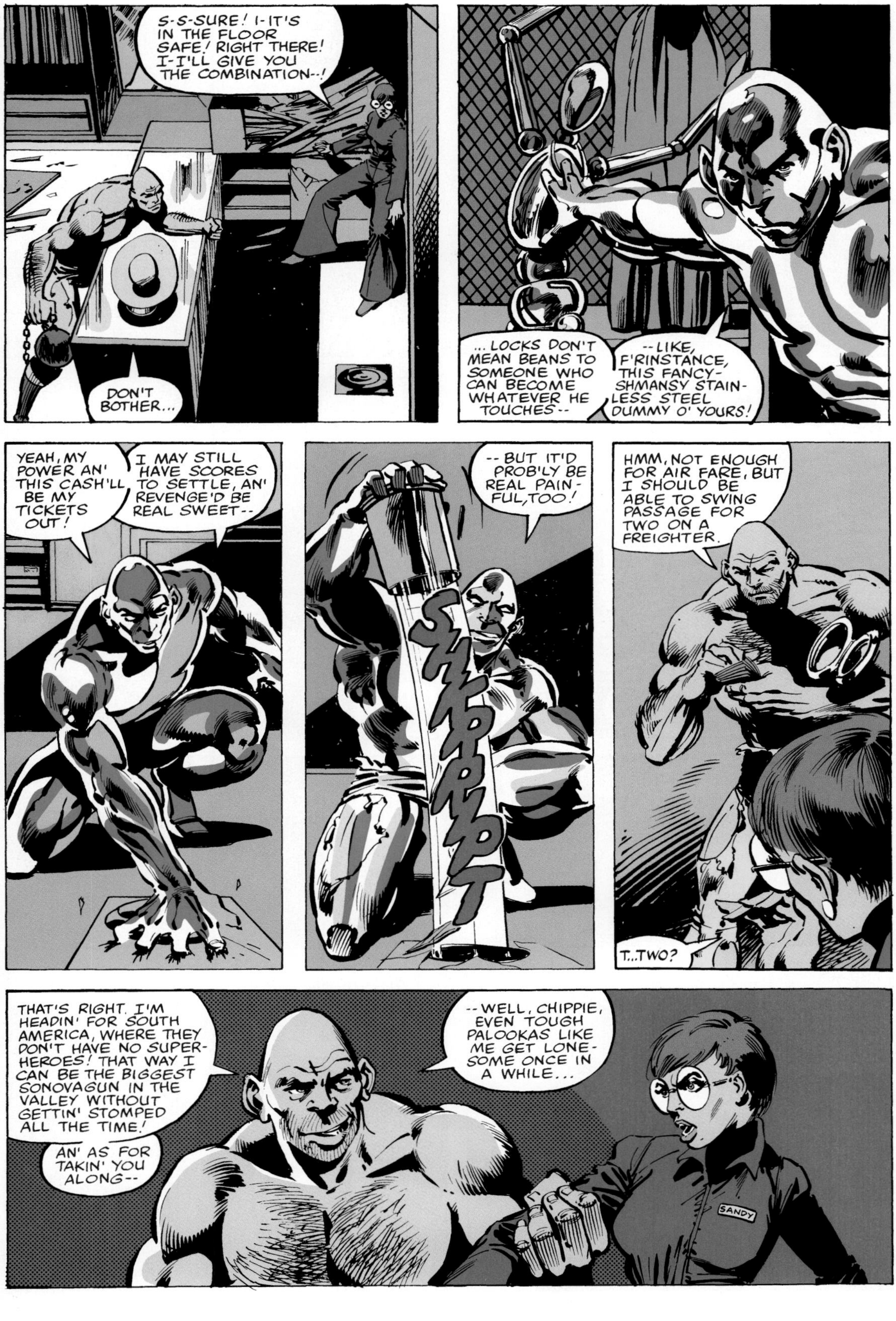
S-S-SURE! I-IT'S IN THE FLOOR SAFE! RIGHT THERE! I-I'LL GIVE YOU THE COMBINATION--!
DON'T BOTHER...
...LOCKS DON'T MEAN BEANS TO SOMEONE WHO CAN BECOME WHATEVER HE TOUCHES--
--LIKE, F'RINSTANCE, THIS FANCY-SHMANSY STAINLESS STEEL DUMMY O' YOURS!
YEAH, MY POWER AN' THIS CASH'LL BE MY TICKETS OUT!
I MAY STILL HAVE SCORES TO SETTLE, AN' REVENGE'D BE REAL SWEET--
--BUT IT'D PROB'LY BE REAL PAINFUL, TOO!
SKRRRPT
HMM, NOT ENOUGH FOR AIR FARE, BUT I SHOULD BE ABLE TO SWING PASSAGE FOR TWO ON A FREIGHTER.
T...TWO?
THAT'S RIGHT. I'M HEADIN' FOR SOUTH AMERICA, WHERE THEY DON'T HAVE NO SUPER-HEROES! THAT WAY I CAN BE THE BIGGEST SONOVAGUN IN THE VALLEY WITHOUT GETTIN' STOMPED ALL THE TIME!
AN' AS FOR TAKIN' YOU ALONG--
--WELL, CHIPPIE, EVEN TOUGH PALOOKAS LIKE ME GET LONESOME ONCE IN A WHILE...
SANDY

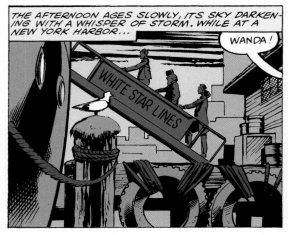

THE AFTERNOON AGES SLOWLY, ITS SKY DARKENING WITH A WHISPER OF STORM. WHILE AT A NEW YORK HARBOR...

WHITE STAR LINES

WANDA!

HEY, WANDA!

WHA--CLINT?! BUT I TOLD THE AVENGERS NOT TO SEE ME OFF!

SO WHO'S A FULL-TIME AVENGER? ANYWAY--

--I JUST WANTED TO WISH YOU BON VOYAGE AND BRING YOU THIS YAHTZEE GAME.

IN CASE YOU GET BORED COUNTIN' WHITECAPS!

CLINT BARTON, YOU'RE IMPOSSIBLE!

AND A DOLL, THANKS.

THEN, AS THE GLEAMING OCEAN LINER IS TOWED OUT TO SEA...

THE VISION IS ONE LUCKY MACHINE--

--THAT'S A HECKUVA LADY HE'S GOT THERE!

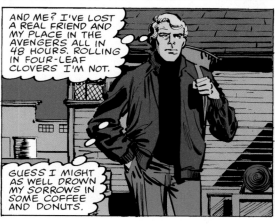

AND ME? I'VE LOST A REAL FRIEND AND MY PLACE IN THE AVENGERS ALL IN 48 HOURS. ROLLING IN FOUR-LEAF CLOVERS I'M NOT.

GUESS I MIGHT AS WELL DROWN MY SORROWS IN SOME COFFEE AND DONUTS.

AH, ON SECOND THOUGHT, UNTIL I FIND GAINFUL EMPLOYMENT, I'D BETTER MAKE THAT JUST COFFEE!

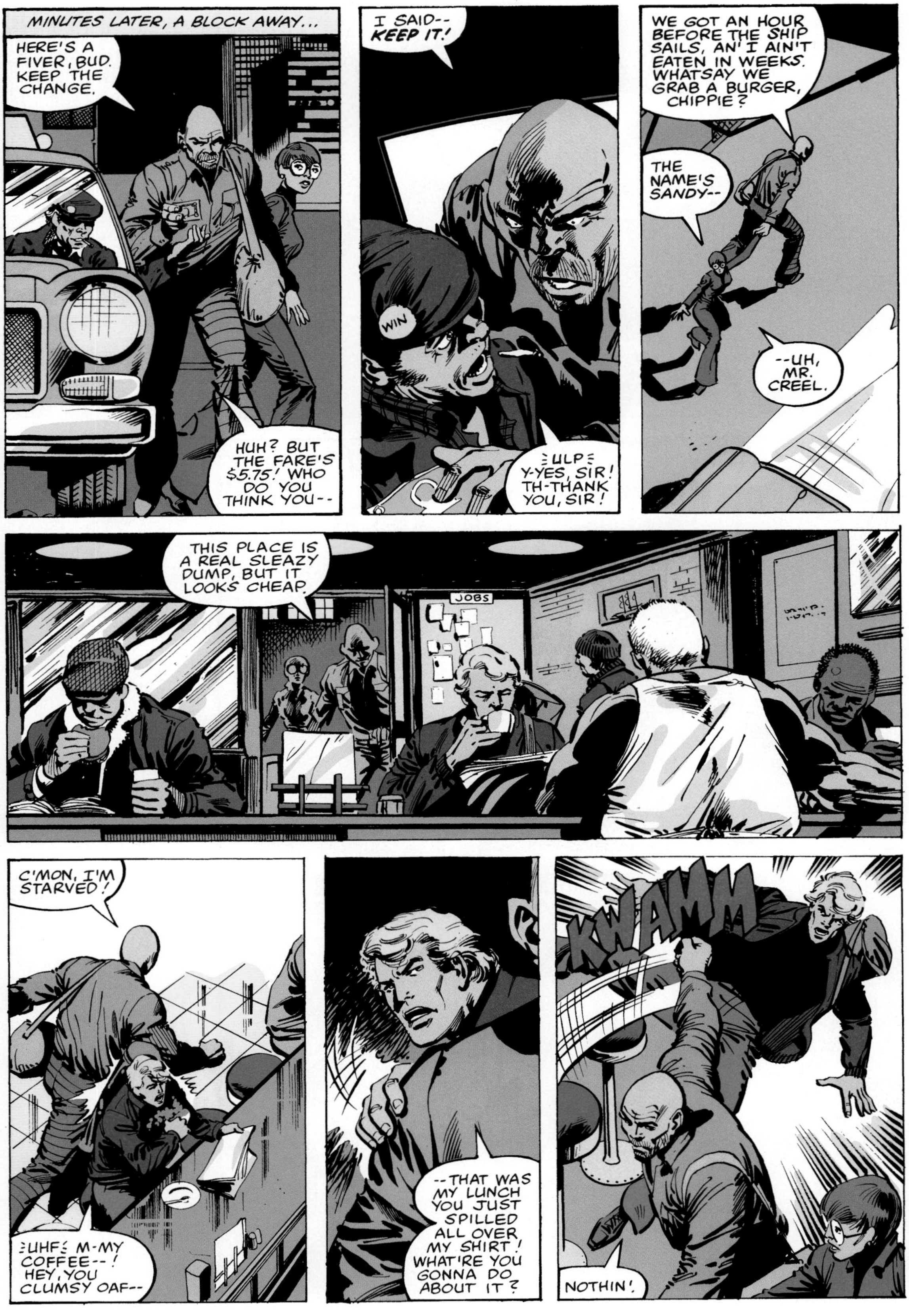
MINUTES LATER, A BLOCK AWAY...
HERE'S A FIVER, BUD. KEEP THE CHANGE.
HUH? BUT THE FARE'S $5.75! WHO DO YOU THINK YOU--
I SAID-- KEEP IT!
ULP Y-YES, SIR! TH-THANK YOU, SIR!
WE GOT AN HOUR BEFORE THE SHIP SAILS, AN' I AIN'T EATEN IN WEEKS. WHATSAY WE GRAB A BURGER, CHIPPIE?
THE NAME'S SANDY--
--UH, MR. CREEL.
THIS PLACE IS A REAL SLEAZY DUMP, BUT IT LOOKS CHEAP.
JOBS
C'MON, I'M STARVED!
UHF M-MY COFFEE--! HEY, YOU CLUMSY OAF--
--THAT WAS MY LUNCH YOU JUST SPILLED ALL OVER MY SHIRT! WHAT'RE YOU GONNA DO ABOUT IT?
KWAMM
NOTHIN'.

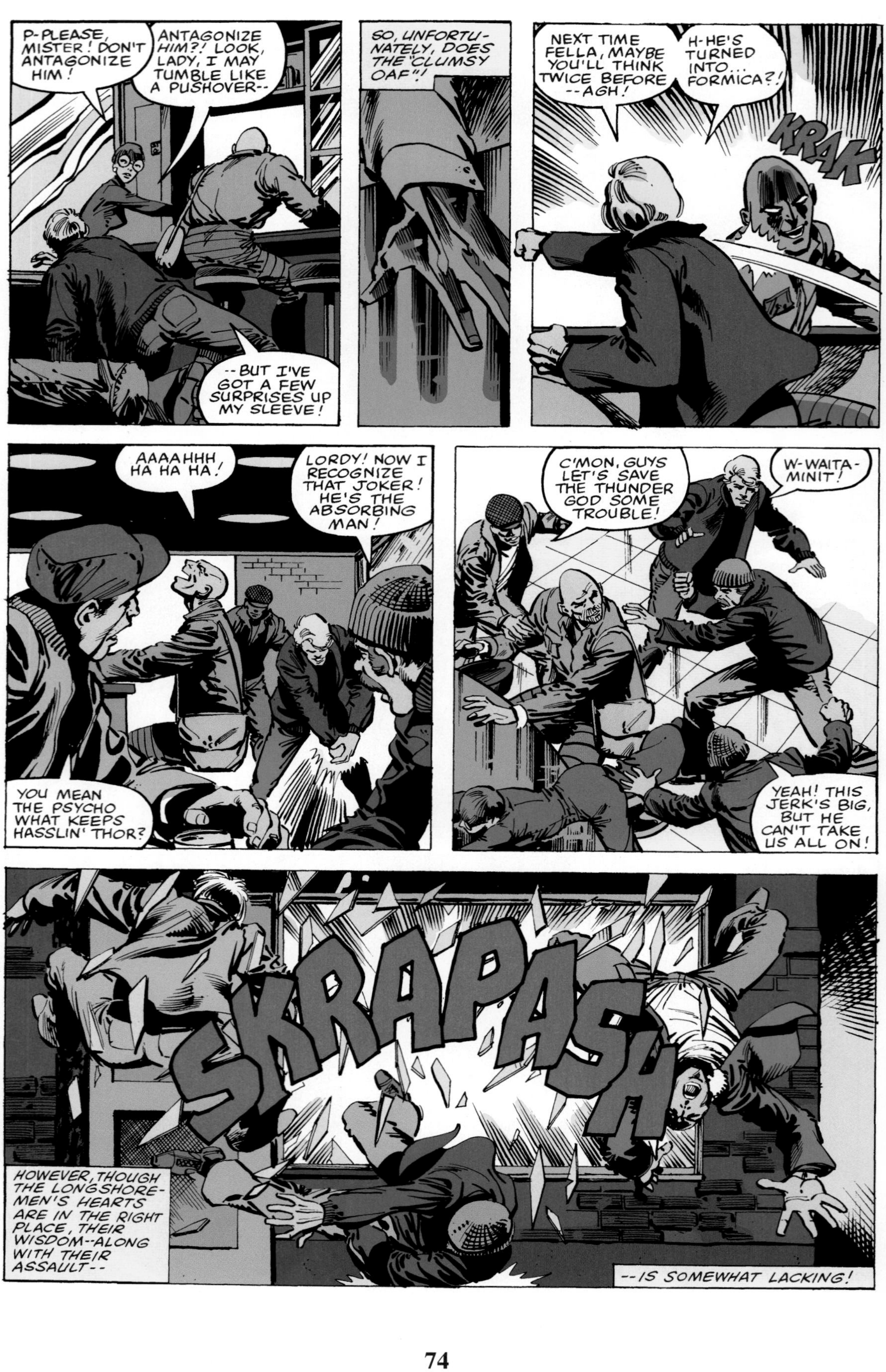
P-PLEASE, MISTER! DON'T ANTAGONIZE HIM!
ANTAGONIZE HIM?! LOOK, LADY, I MAY TUMBLE LIKE A PUSHOVER--
--BUT I'VE GOT A FEW SURPRISES UP MY SLEEVE!
SO, UNFORTUNATELY, DOES THE "CLUMSY OAF"!
NEXT TIME FELLA, MAYBE YOU'LL THINK TWICE BEFORE --AGH!
H-HE'S TURNED INTO... FORMICA?!
KRAK
AAAAHHH HA HA HA!
LORDY! NOW I RECOGNIZE THAT JOKER! HE'S THE ABSORBING MAN!
YOU MEAN THE PSYCHO WHAT KEEPS HASSLIN' THOR?
C'MON, GUYS LET'S SAVE THE THUNDER GOD SOME TROUBLE!
W-WAITA-MINIT!
YEAH! THIS JERK'S BIG, BUT HE CAN'T TAKE US ALL ON!
SKRAPASH
HOWEVER, THOUGH THE LONGSHOREMEN'S HEARTS ARE IN THE RIGHT PLACE, THEIR WISDOM--ALONG WITH THEIR ASSAULT--
--IS SOMEWHAT LACKING!

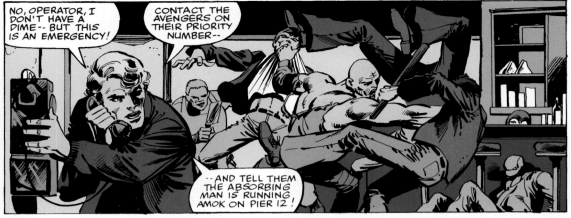

NO, OPERATOR, I DON'T HAVE A DIME-- BUT THIS IS AN EMERGENCY!

CONTACT THE AVENGERS ON THEIR PRIORITY NUMBER--

--AND TELL THEM THE ABSORBING MAN IS RUNNING AMOK ON PIER 12!

MEANWHILE, I'LL SEE WHAT I CAN DO TO KEEP HIM HERE!

THLUBB

BACK OFF, CREEPS! THIS AIN'T NONE O' YOUR AFFAIR!

I GOT 'IM! I GOT 'IM!

YOU KEEP 'IM! YOU KEEP 'IM!

SUDDENLY...

HUH? A NET?!

SHHWIP

SHHWIP

THAT'S RIGHT, SPONGY! COURTESY OF HAWKEYE, EVERYONE'S FAVORITE MODERN-DAY ROBIN HOOD!

CRIPES! THERE MUST BE A SUPER-CLOWN ON EVERY CORNER IN THIS BURG!

BUT I AIN'T *FALLIN'* THIS TIME! SO TURNIN' TO *GLASS* WON'T HURT ME--

--IT'LL *SAVE* ME! ALL I GOTTA DO IS *FLEX* AN' YOUR NET GETS SHREDDED LIKE SPAGHETTI!

MAYBE SO, CREEL--

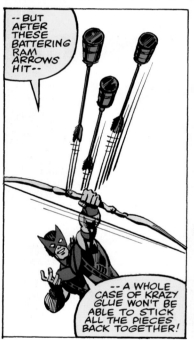

--BUT AFTER THESE BATTERING RAM ARROWS HIT--

--A WHOLE CASE OF *KRAZY GLUE* WON'T BE ABLE TO STICK ALL THE PIECES BACK TOGETHER!

WRONG, STUPE! ONCE I TOUCH THIS TIRE BUFFER, I'LL *ABSORB* EVERYTHING I NEED TO--

THAMP

THAMP

--BOUNCE RIGHT *BACK!* HA HA HA!

BUT THEN...

GIVE IT UP, CREEL! *REPULSORS* PACK A LOT MORE PUNCH THAN ARROWS--

--AND I HATE THE SMELL OF BURNING *RUBBER!*

WHO--?!

SSHHRRAK

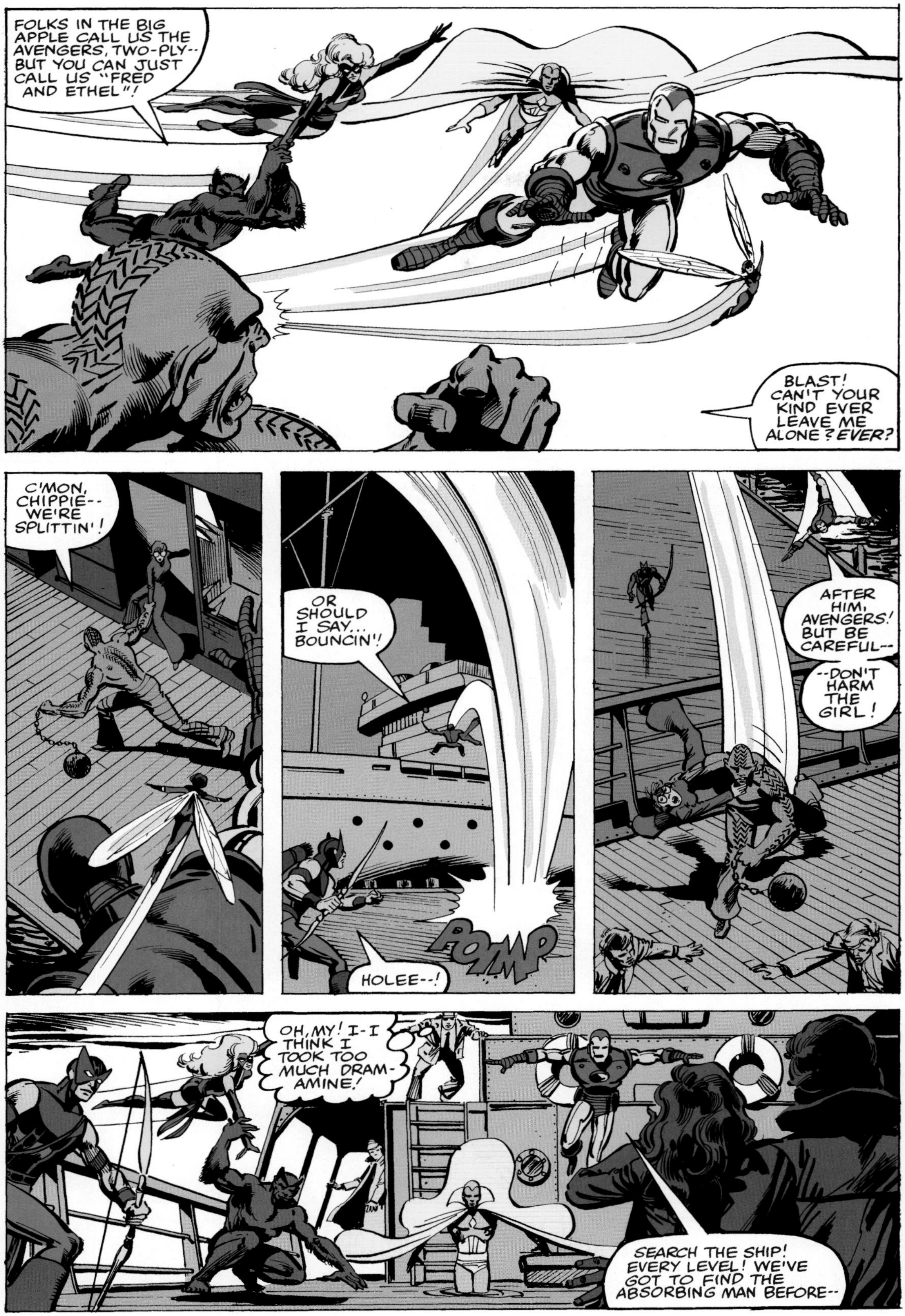
FOLKS IN THE BIG APPLE CALL US THE AVENGERS, TWO-PLY-- BUT YOU CAN JUST CALL US "FRED AND ETHEL"!
BLAST! CAN'T YOUR KIND EVER LEAVE ME ALONE? EVER?
C'MON, CHIPPIE-- WE'RE SPLITTIN'!
OR SHOULD I SAY... BOUNCIN'!
POMP
HOLEE--!
AFTER HIM, AVENGERS! BUT BE CAREFUL--
--DON'T HARM THE GIRL!
OH, MY! I-I THINK I TOOK TOO MUCH DRAM-AMINE!
SEARCH THE SHIP! EVERY LEVEL! WE'VE GOT TO FIND THE ABSORBING MAN BEFORE--

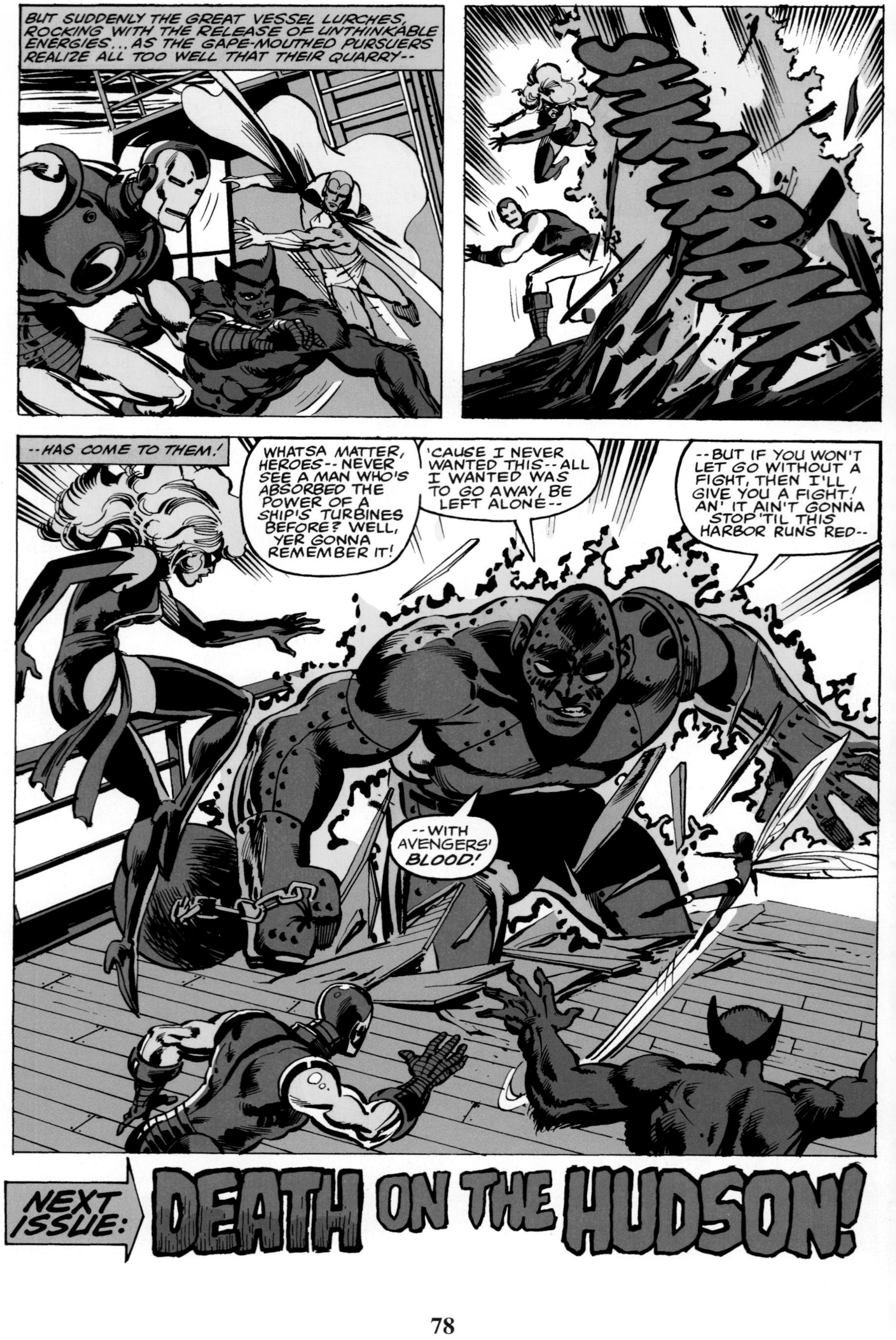
BUT SUDDENLY THE GREAT VESSEL LURCHES, ROCKING WITH THE RELEASE OF UNTHINKABLE ENERGIES... AS THE GAPE-MOUTHED PURSUERS REALIZE ALL TOO WELL THAT THEIR QUARRY--
SHHRRAAM
--HAS COME TO THEM!
WHATSA MATTER, HEROES--NEVER SEE A MAN WHO'S ABSORBED THE POWER OF A SHIP'S TURBINES BEFORE? WELL, YER GONNA REMEMBER IT!
'CAUSE I NEVER WANTED THIS--ALL I WANTED WAS TO GO AWAY, BE LEFT ALONE--
--BUT IF YOU WON'T LET GO WITHOUT A FIGHT, THEN I'LL GIVE YOU A FIGHT! AN' IT AIN'T GONNA STOP 'TIL THIS HARBOR RUNS RED--
--WITH AVENGERS' BLOOD!

NEXT ISSUE: DEATH ON THE HUDSON!

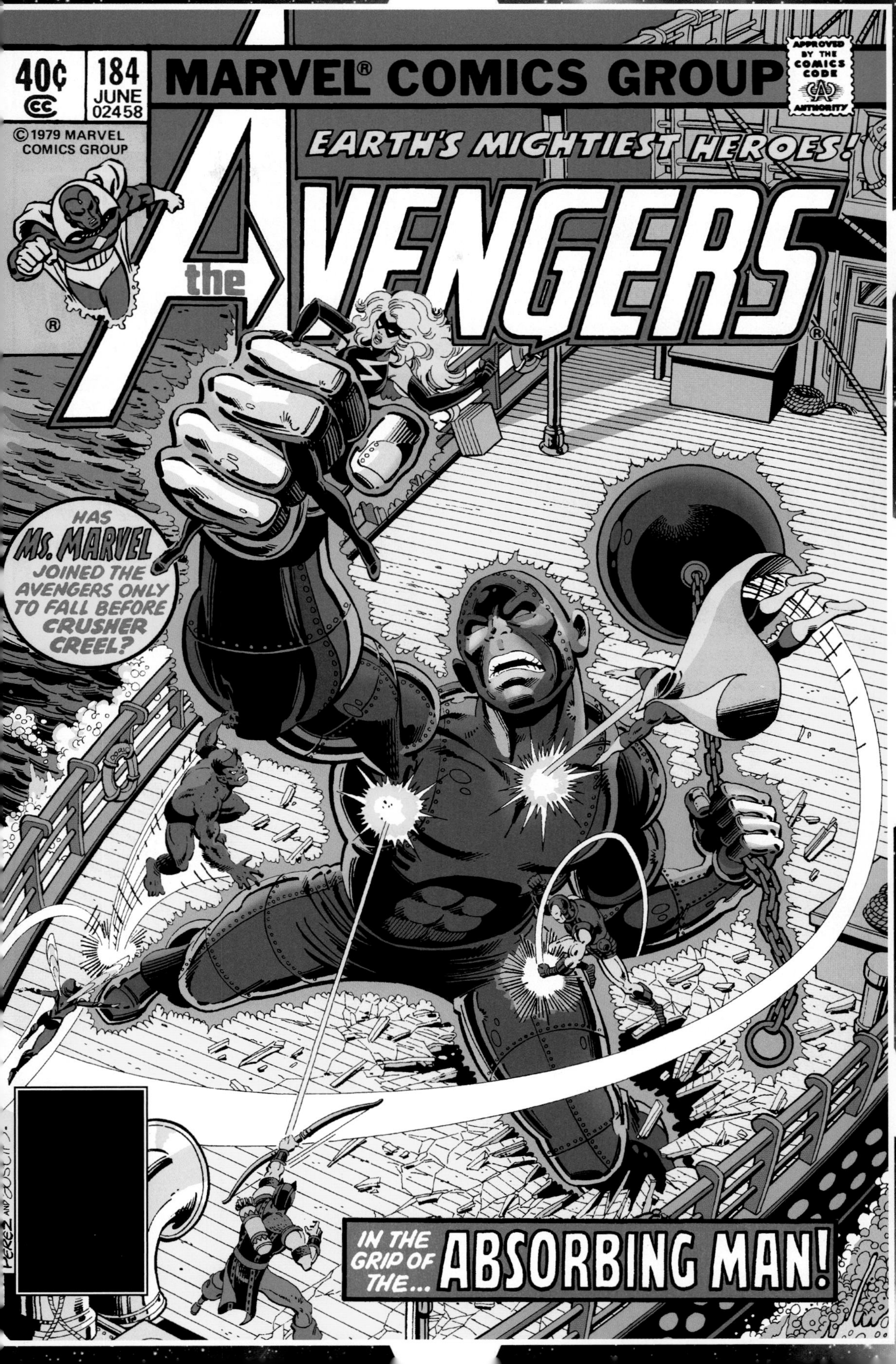

40¢
184
JUNE
02458
MARVEL® COMICS GROUP
APPROVED BY THE COMICS CODE AUTHORITY
©1979 MARVEL COMICS GROUP
EARTH'S MIGHTIEST HEROES!
the AVENGERS®
HAS MS. MARVEL JOINED THE AVENGERS ONLY TO FALL BEFORE CRUSHER CREEL?
IN THE GRIP OF THE... ABSORBING MAN!

And there came a day when *Earth's mightiest heroes* found themselves *united* against a common threat. On that day, the *Avengers* were born—to fight the foes no *single* superhero could withstand!

Stan Lee PRESENTS: THE MIGHTY AVENGERS!®

DAVID MICHELINIE WRITER / JOHN BYRNE CHOREOGRAPHY/PENCILS / D. HANDS INKS / B. SHAREN COLORS / D. ALBERS LETTERS / ROGER STERN EDITOR / J. SHOOTER EDITOR in CHIEF

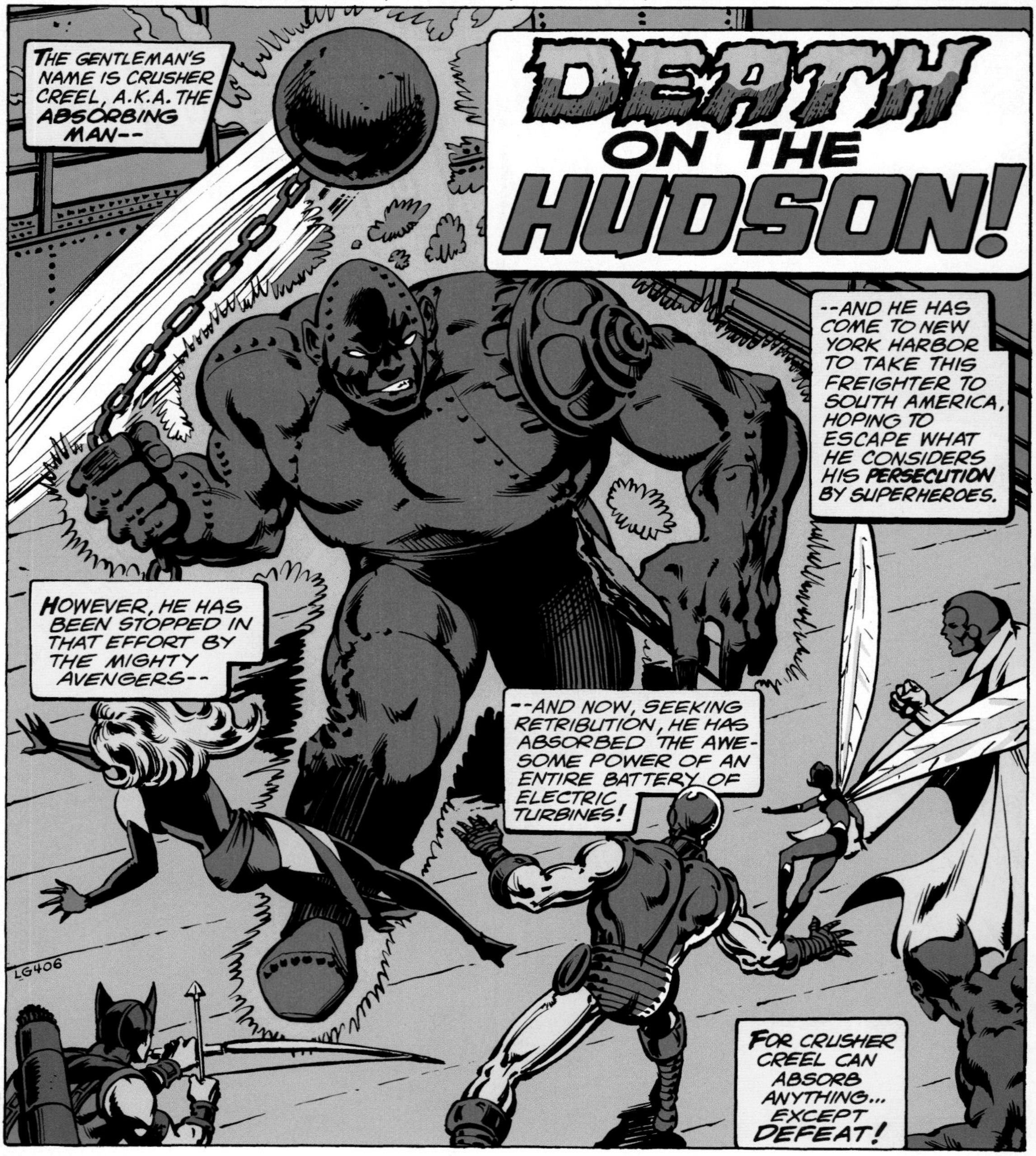

THE GENTLEMAN'S NAME IS CRUSHER CREEL, A.K.A. THE ABSORBING MAN--
DEATH ON THE HUDSON!
--AND HE HAS COME TO NEW YORK HARBOR TO TAKE THIS FREIGHTER TO SOUTH AMERICA, HOPING TO ESCAPE WHAT HE CONSIDERS HIS PERSECUTION BY SUPERHEROES.
HOWEVER, HE HAS BEEN STOPPED IN THAT EFFORT BY THE MIGHTY AVENGERS--
--AND NOW, SEEKING RETRIBUTION, HE HAS ABSORBED THE AWESOME POWER OF AN ENTIRE BATTERY OF ELECTRIC TURBINES!
FOR CRUSHER CREEL CAN ABSORB ANYTHING... EXCEPT DEFEAT!
LG406

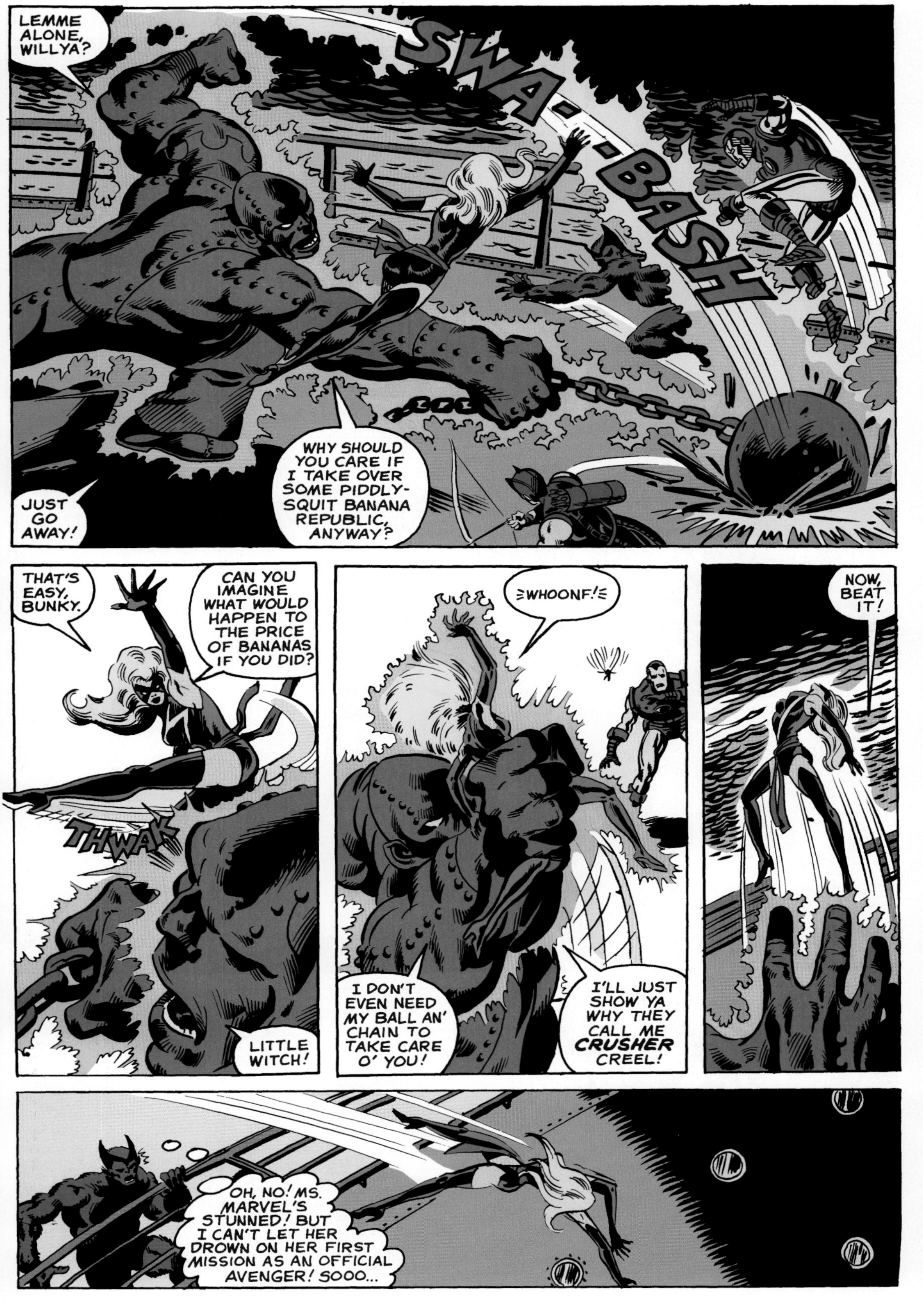
LEMME ALONE, WILLYA?
SWA-BASH
JUST GO AWAY!
WHY SHOULD YOU CARE IF I TAKE OVER SOME PIDDLY-SQUIT BANANA REPUBLIC, ANYWAY?
THAT'S EASY, BUNKY.
CAN YOU IMAGINE WHAT WOULD HAPPEN TO THE PRICE OF BANANAS IF YOU DID?
THWAK
LITTLE WITCH!
WHOONF!
I DON'T EVEN NEED MY BALL AN' CHAIN TO TAKE CARE O' YOU!
I'LL JUST SHOW YA WHY THEY CALL ME CRUSHER CREEL!
NOW, BEAT IT!
OH, NO! MS. MARVEL'S STUNNED! BUT I CAN'T LET HER DROWN ON HER FIRST MISSION AS AN OFFICIAL AVENGER! SOOO...

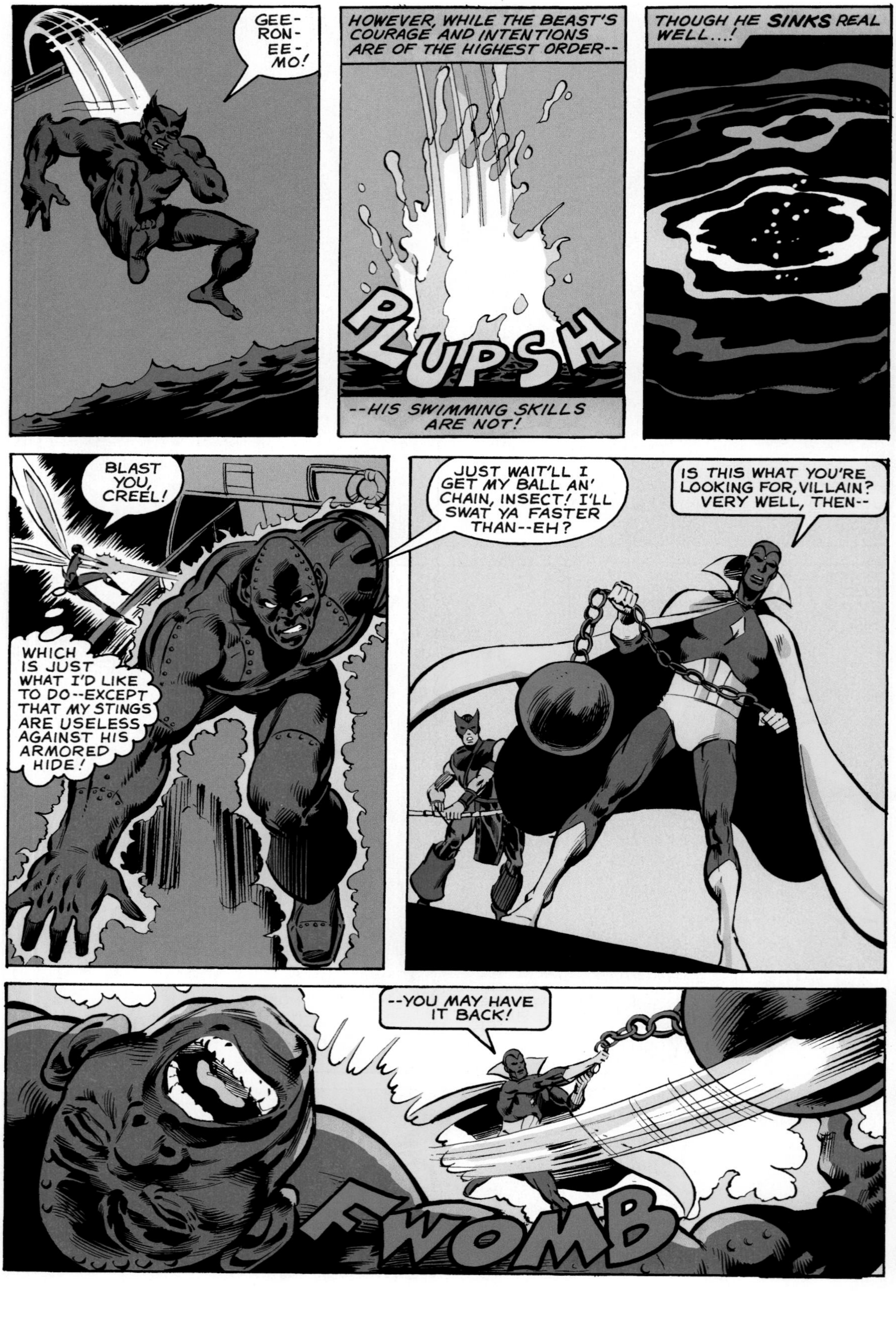
GEE-RON-EE-MO!
HOWEVER, WHILE THE BEAST'S COURAGE AND INTENTIONS ARE OF THE HIGHEST ORDER--
PLUPSH
--HIS SWIMMING SKILLS ARE NOT!
THOUGH HE SINKS REAL WELL...!
BLAST YOU, CREEL!
WHICH IS JUST WHAT I'D LIKE TO DO--EXCEPT THAT MY STINGS ARE USELESS AGAINST HIS ARMORED HIDE!
JUST WAIT'LL I GET MY BALL AN' CHAIN, INSECT! I'LL SWAT YA FASTER THAN--EH?
IS THIS WHAT YOU'RE LOOKING FOR, VILLAIN? VERY WELL, THEN--
--YOU MAY HAVE IT BACK!
FWOMB

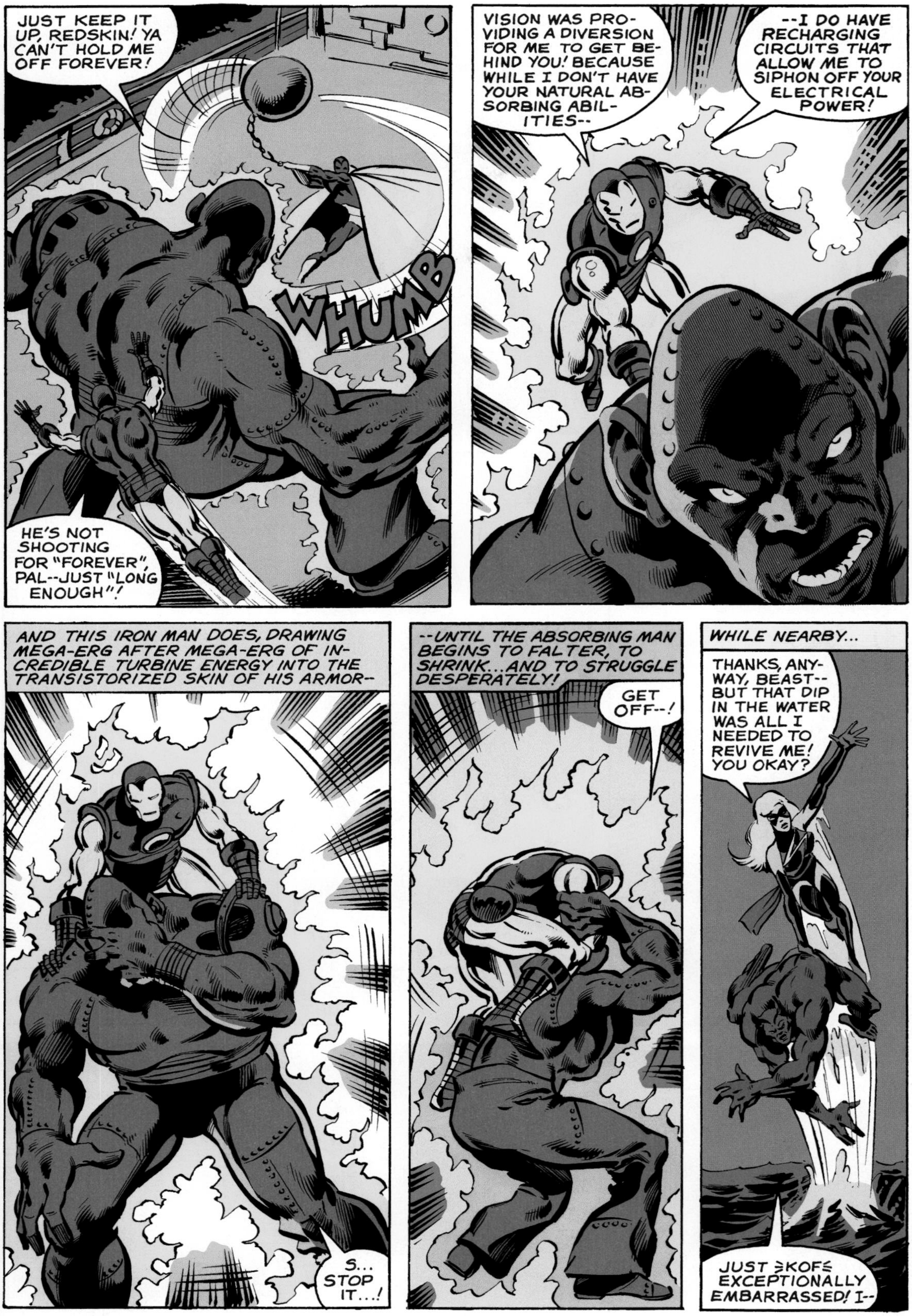

JUST KEEP IT UP, REDSKIN! YA CAN'T HOLD ME OFF FOREVER!
WHUMB
HE'S NOT SHOOTING FOR "FOREVER", PAL--JUST "LONG ENOUGH"!
VISION WAS PROVIDING A DIVERSION FOR ME TO GET BEHIND YOU! BECAUSE WHILE I DON'T HAVE YOUR NATURAL ABSORBING ABILITIES--
--I DO HAVE RECHARGING CIRCUITS THAT ALLOW ME TO SIPHON OFF YOUR ELECTRICAL POWER!
AND THIS IRON MAN DOES, DRAWING MEGA-ERG AFTER MEGA-ERG OF INCREDIBLE TURBINE ENERGY INTO THE TRANSISTORIZED SKIN OF HIS ARMOR--
S... STOP IT...!
--UNTIL THE ABSORBING MAN BEGINS TO FALTER, TO SHRINK...AND TO STRUGGLE DESPERATELY!
GET OFF--!
WHILE NEARBY...
THANKS, ANYWAY, BEAST--BUT THAT DIP IN THE WATER WAS ALL I NEEDED TO REVIVE ME! YOU OKAY?
JUST ≷KOF≶ EXCEPTIONALLY EMBARRASSED! I--

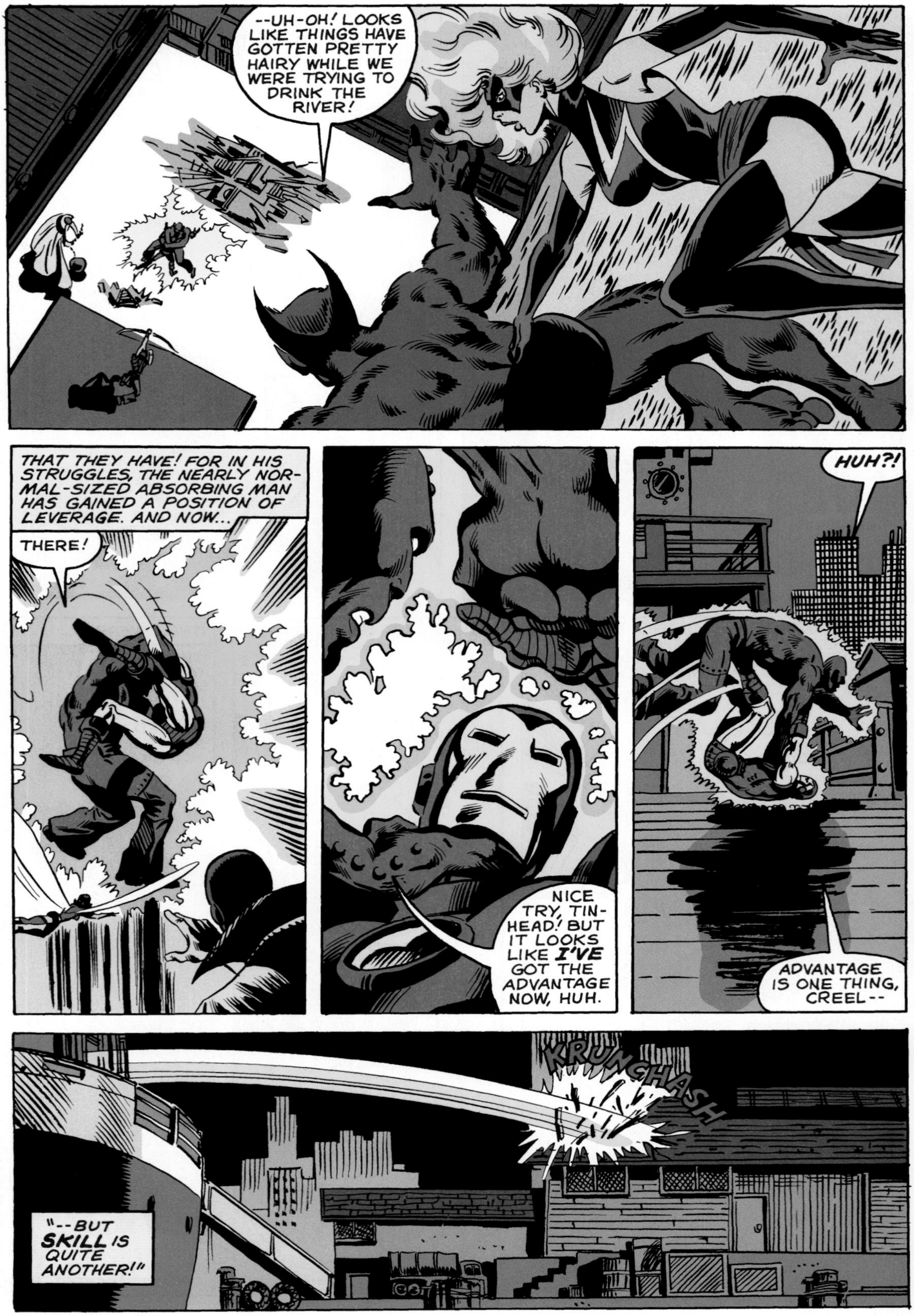
--UH-OH! LOOKS LIKE THINGS HAVE GOTTEN PRETTY HAIRY WHILE WE WERE TRYING TO DRINK THE RIVER!
THAT THEY HAVE! FOR IN HIS STRUGGLES, THE NEARLY NORMAL-SIZED ABSORBING MAN HAS GAINED A POSITION OF LEVERAGE. AND NOW...
THERE!
NICE TRY, TIN-HEAD! BUT IT LOOKS LIKE I'VE GOT THE ADVANTAGE NOW, HUH.
HUH?!
ADVANTAGE IS ONE THING, CREEL--
KRUNCHASH
"--BUT SKILL IS QUITE ANOTHER!"

THERE HE IS, MS. M! DROP ME!

UH, ARE YOU SURE THIS IS GOING TO WORK, BEAST?

AM I SURE? HEY, IS GEORGIE JESSEL JEWISH?

IRON MAN! WHAT--?

STAY BACK! MY STORAGE COMPONENTS HAVE NEVER HAD TO COPE WITH THIS MUCH POWER BEFORE!

I'VE GOT TO GET OUT OF THE ATMOSPHERE, DISCHARGE THE EXCESS!

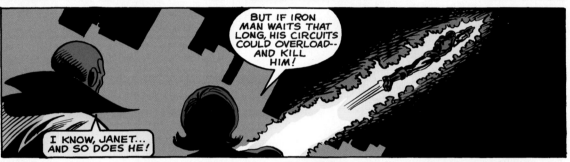

BUT IF IRON MAN WAITS THAT LONG, HIS CIRCUITS COULD OVERLOAD-- AND KILL HIM!

I KNOW, JANET... AND SO DOES HE!

I REALIZE IT'S RISKY HOLDING THE CHARGE THIS LONG--

ESPECIALLY SINCE MY ARMOR'S BEEN MALFUNCTIONING LATELY ANYWAY!*

*SEE RECENT ISSUES OF IRON MAN FOR DETAILS--R.

BUT IF I UNLOADED THIS BUILT-UP POWER IN A POPULATED AREA, THE RESULTS COULD BE DISASTROUS! I JUST HOPE I'M HIGH ENOUGH NOW-- BECAUSE IF I HOLD OUT ONE SECOND LONGER, I'M DEAD! GOT... TO...

--RELEASE!

AND FOR THE BRIEFEST OF MOMENTS, FOR THOSE NEW YORKERS SENTIENT ENOUGH TO RAISE THEIR EYES FROM THE GRITTY PAVEMENTS, A NEW STAR BLAZES OVER THE MANHATTAN SKYLINE...

WHILE TEN MINUTES *EARLIER*, IN THE PORTION OF THAT SKYLINE OCCUPIED BY AVENGERS' MANSION...

CAPTAIN AMERICA'S BEEN GONE TWO HOURS ALREADY!

JUST HOW LONG DOES IT TAKE TO RECRUIT A NEW AVENGER, ANYWAY?

AS LONG AS IT TAKES, SIR.

HMM, VERY SAGACIOUS, JARVIS.

I ONLY MEANT THAT THE AVENGERS DO THINGS IN THEIR OWN WAY, MR. GYRICH. AND IN THEIR OWN TIME.

AT LEAST... THEY USED TO.

WE STILL DO, JARVIS.

WHO-- MASTER CAP!

WELL, IT'S ABOUT TIME. I HAVE SOME FORMS FOR THE FALCON TO FILL OUT.

YASSUH, I SHO'BE GLAD T'DO THAT LI'L THING.

CAREFUL, FALC-- MR. GYRICH MIGHT THINK YOU DON'T LIKE HIM!

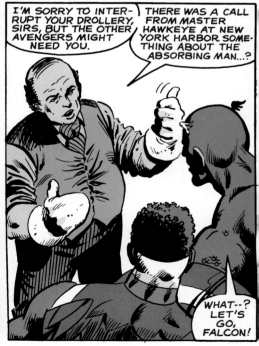

I'M SORRY TO INTERRUPT YOUR DROLLERY, SIRS, BUT THE OTHER AVENGERS MIGHT NEED YOU.

THERE WAS A CALL FROM MASTER HAWKEYE AT NEW YORK HARBOR SOMETHING ABOUT THE ABSORBING MAN...?

WHAT--? LET'S GO, FALCON!

W-WAITAMIN-IT! WHAT ABOUT PROCEDURES? THE FORMS--?

SORRY, "MASSUH," BUT WHEN CAP GETS A BEE IN HIS BONNET--

--THERE "JUS' AIN'T NO STOPPIN' THAT CHIL'. NOSSUH!"

GEEZ, CAP, THIS BEING A *TOKEN'S* STARTING TO WEAR PRETTY THIN PRETTY FAST.

I KNOW, SAM--SO FORGET IT!

IF WE'RE GOING TO MAKE THIS PARTNERSHIP WORK, YOU'RE GOING TO HAVE TO ACCEPT A LOT OF THINGS-- STARTING NOW.

THERE ARE LIVES AT STAKE.

I, UH, GET THE POINT, CAP. AND I'M SORRY.

COME ON, REDWING. LOOKS LIKE WE'RE AVENGERS NOW!

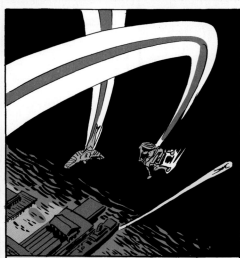

THE JOURNEY VIA SKY-CYCLE AND AIR-FOIL HAD TAKEN EIGHT MINUTES, BRINGING THE TWO HEROES TO THE WEST SIDE DOCKS IN TIME TO SEE AN OMINOUSLY GLOWING IRON MAN STREAKING SKYWARD...

...AND THEN...

YOUR ARRIVAL IS MOST TIMELY, CAPTAIN--AS WILL BE YOUR AID.

HI, FALCON. I LIKE YOUR BIRD!

THAT'S THE GUY WHO'S TAKING MY PLACE IN THE AVENGERS, EH? HE DOESN'T LOOK SO TOUGH TO ME!

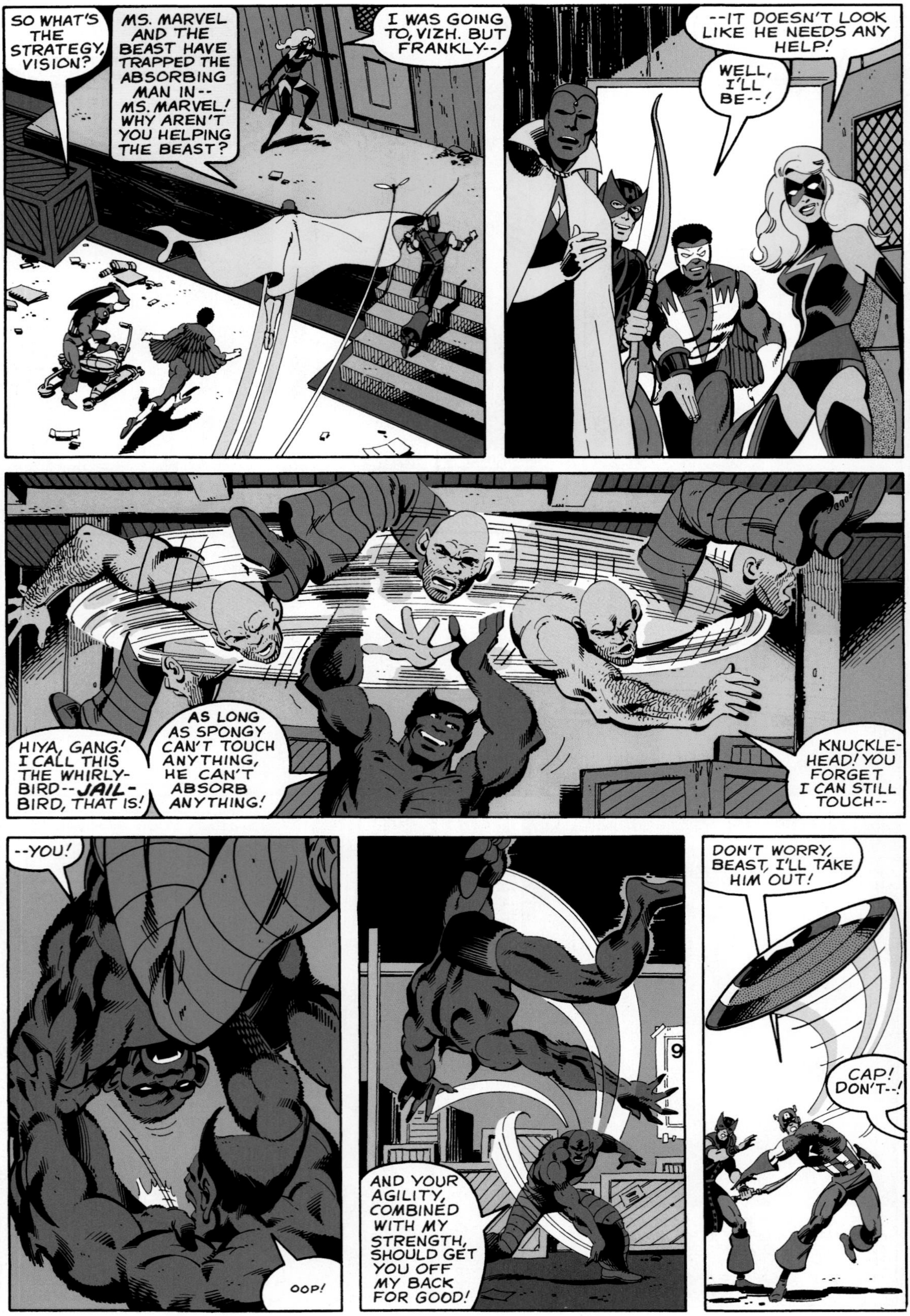
SO WHAT'S THE STRATEGY, VISION?
MS. MARVEL AND THE BEAST HAVE TRAPPED THE ABSORBING MAN IN-- MS. MARVEL! WHY AREN'T YOU HELPING THE BEAST?
I WAS GOING TO, VIZH. BUT FRANKLY--
--IT DOESN'T LOOK LIKE HE NEEDS ANY HELP!
WELL, I'LL BE--!
HIYA, GANG! I CALL THIS THE WHIRLY-BIRD--JAIL-BIRD, THAT IS!
AS LONG AS SPONGY CAN'T TOUCH ANYTHING, HE CAN'T ABSORB ANYTHING!
KNUCKLE-HEAD! YOU FORGET I CAN STILL TOUCH--
--YOU!
OOP!
AND YOUR AGILITY, COMBINED WITH MY STRENGTH, SHOULD GET YOU OFF MY BACK FOR GOOD!
DON'T WORRY, BEAST, I'LL TAKE HIM OUT!
CAP! DON'T--!

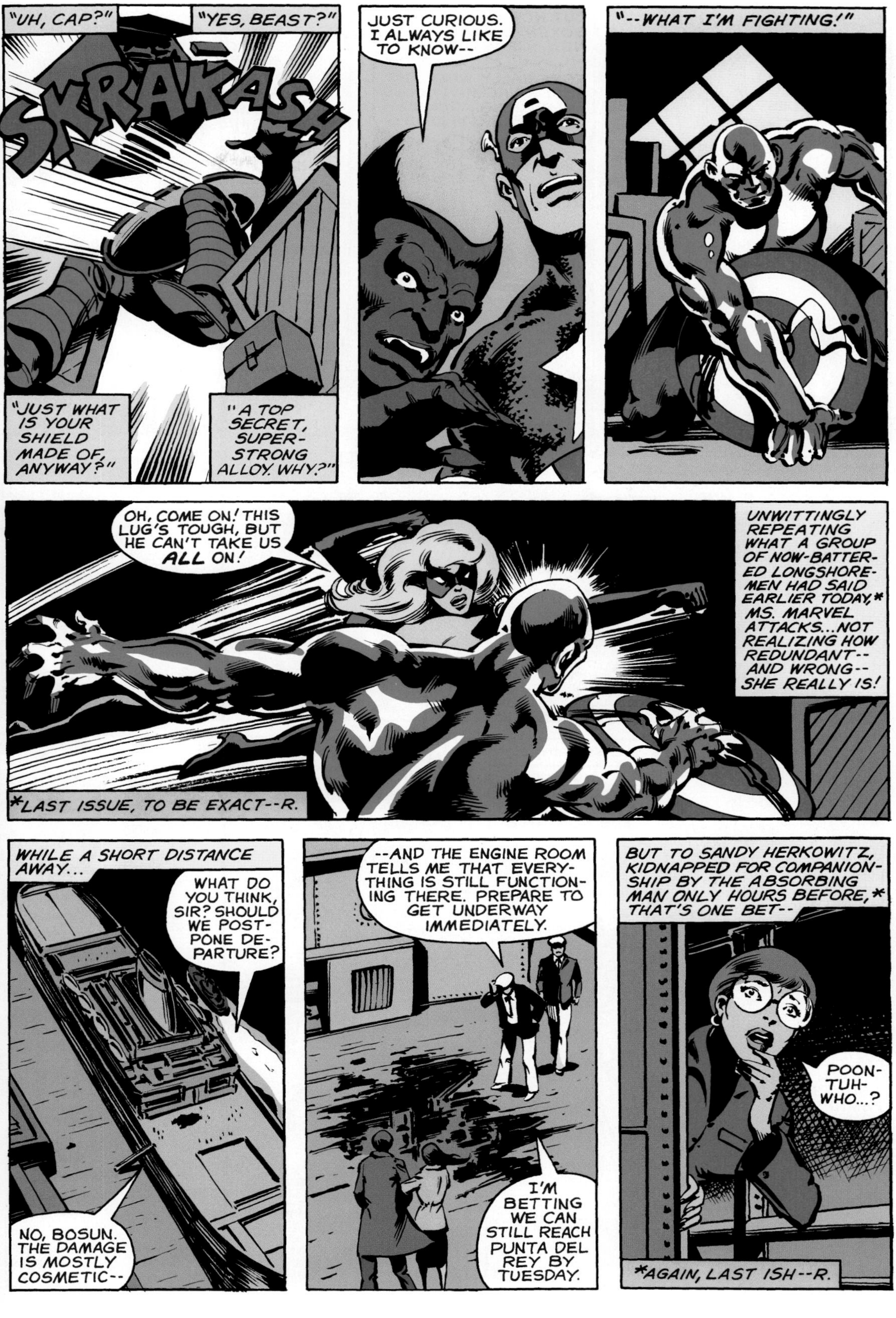
"UH, CAP?"
"YES, BEAST?"
SKRAKASH
"JUST WHAT IS YOUR SHIELD MADE OF, ANYWAY?"
"A TOP SECRET, SUPER-STRONG ALLOY. WHY?"
JUST CURIOUS. I ALWAYS LIKE TO KNOW--
"--WHAT I'M FIGHTING!"
OH, COME ON! THIS LUG'S TOUGH, BUT HE CAN'T TAKE US ALL ON!
UNWITTINGLY REPEATING WHAT A GROUP OF NOW-BATTERED LONGSHOREMEN HAD SAID EARLIER TODAY,* MS. MARVEL ATTACKS...NOT REALIZING HOW REDUNDANT--AND WRONG--SHE REALLY IS!
*LAST ISSUE, TO BE EXACT--R.
WHILE A SHORT DISTANCE AWAY...
WHAT DO YOU THINK, SIR? SHOULD WE POSTPONE DEPARTURE?
NO, BOSUN. THE DAMAGE IS MOSTLY COSMETIC--
--AND THE ENGINE ROOM TELLS ME THAT EVERYTHING IS STILL FUNCTIONING THERE. PREPARE TO GET UNDERWAY IMMEDIATELY.
I'M BETTING WE CAN STILL REACH PUNTA DEL REY BY TUESDAY.
BUT TO SANDY HERKOWITZ, KIDNAPPED FOR COMPANIONSHIP BY THE ABSORBING MAN ONLY HOURS BEFORE,* THAT'S ONE BET--
POON-TUH-WHO...?
*AGAIN, LAST ISH--R.

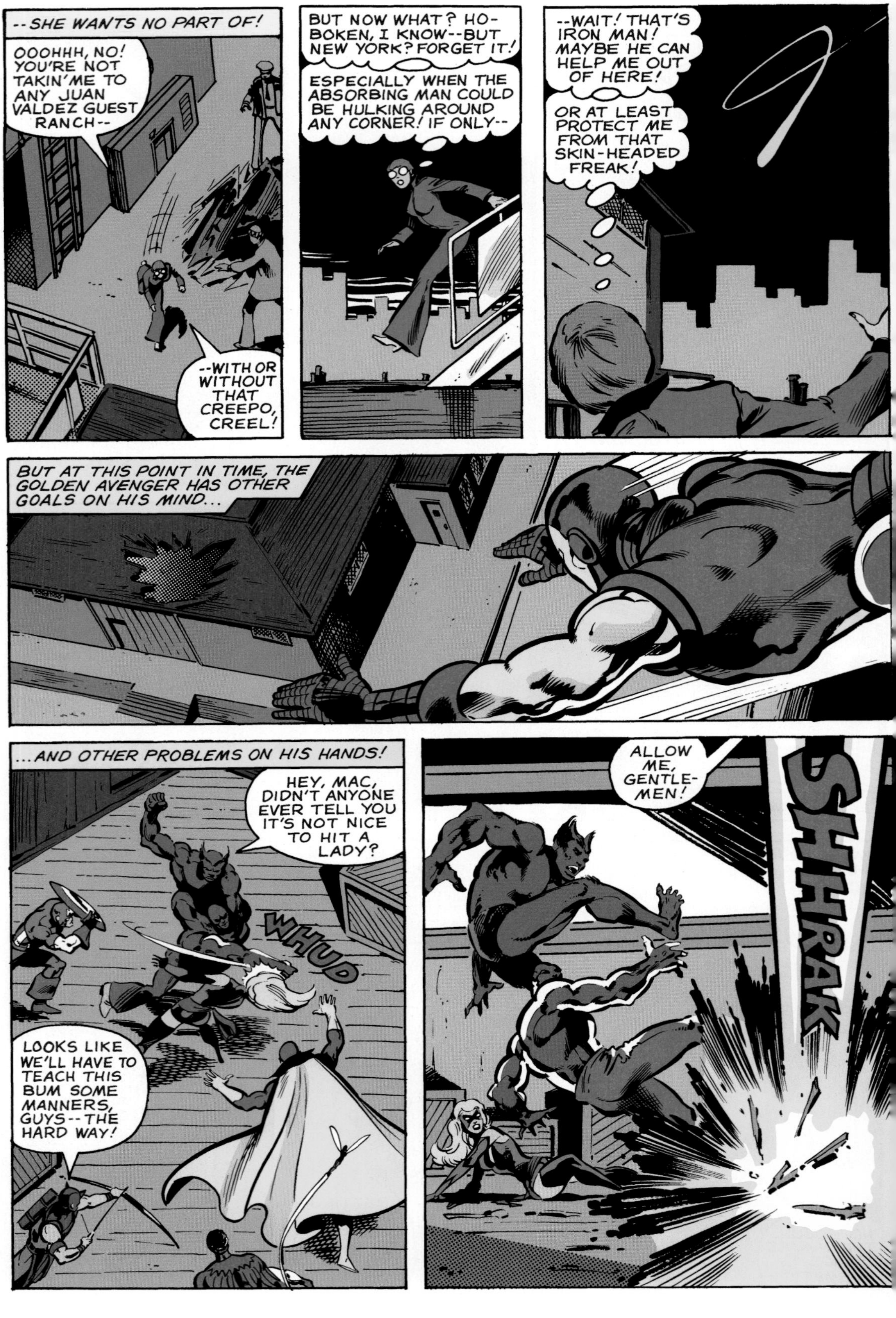
--SHE WANTS NO PART OF!
OOOHHH, NO! YOU'RE NOT TAKIN' ME TO ANY JUAN VALDEZ GUEST RANCH--
--WITH OR WITHOUT THAT CREEPO, CREEL!
BUT NOW WHAT? HO-BOKEN, I KNOW--BUT NEW YORK? FORGET IT!
ESPECIALLY WHEN THE ABSORBING MAN COULD BE HULKING AROUND ANY CORNER! IF ONLY--
--WAIT! THAT'S IRON MAN! MAYBE HE CAN HELP ME OUT OF HERE!
OR AT LEAST PROTECT ME FROM THAT SKIN-HEADED FREAK!
BUT AT THIS POINT IN TIME, THE GOLDEN AVENGER HAS OTHER GOALS ON HIS MIND...
...AND OTHER PROBLEMS ON HIS HANDS!
HEY, MAC, DIDN'T ANYONE EVER TELL YOU IT'S NOT NICE TO HIT A LADY?
WHUD
LOOKS LIKE WE'LL HAVE TO TEACH THIS BUM SOME MANNERS, GUYS--THE HARD WAY!
ALLOW ME, GENTLE-MEN!
SHHRAK

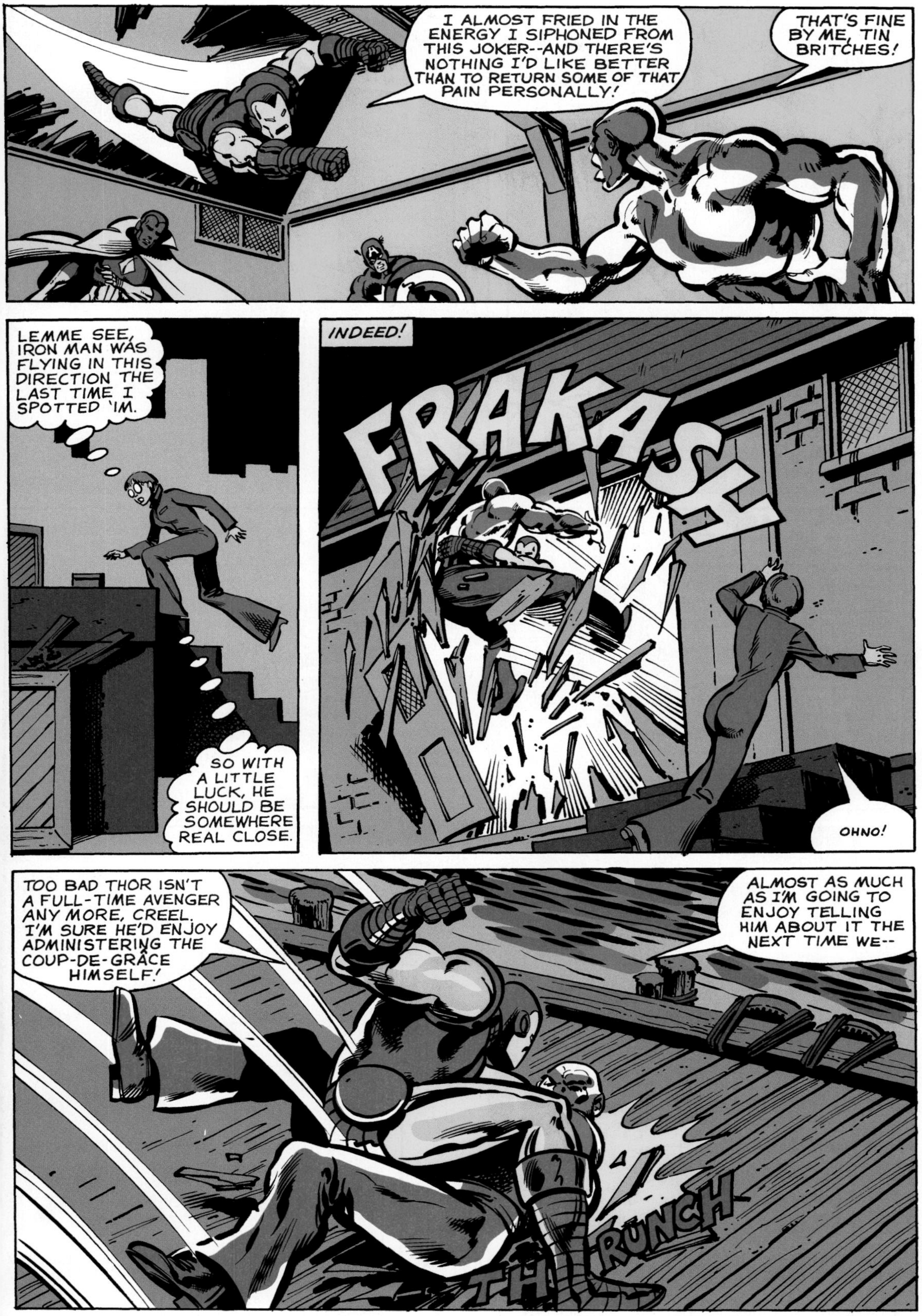
I ALMOST FRIED IN THE ENERGY I SIPHONED FROM THIS JOKER--AND THERE'S NOTHING I'D LIKE BETTER THAN TO RETURN SOME OF THAT PAIN PERSONALLY!
THAT'S FINE BY ME, TIN BRITCHES!
LEMME SEE, IRON MAN WAS FLYING IN THIS DIRECTION THE LAST TIME I SPOTTED 'IM.
SO WITH A LITTLE LUCK, HE SHOULD BE SOMEWHERE REAL CLOSE.
INDEED!
FRAKASH
OHNO!
TOO BAD THOR ISN'T A FULL-TIME AVENGER ANY MORE, CREEL. I'M SURE HE'D ENJOY ADMINISTERING THE COUP-DE-GRÂCE HIMSELF!
ALMOST AS MUCH AS I'M GOING TO ENJOY TELLING HIM ABOUT IT THE NEXT TIME WE--
THRUNCH

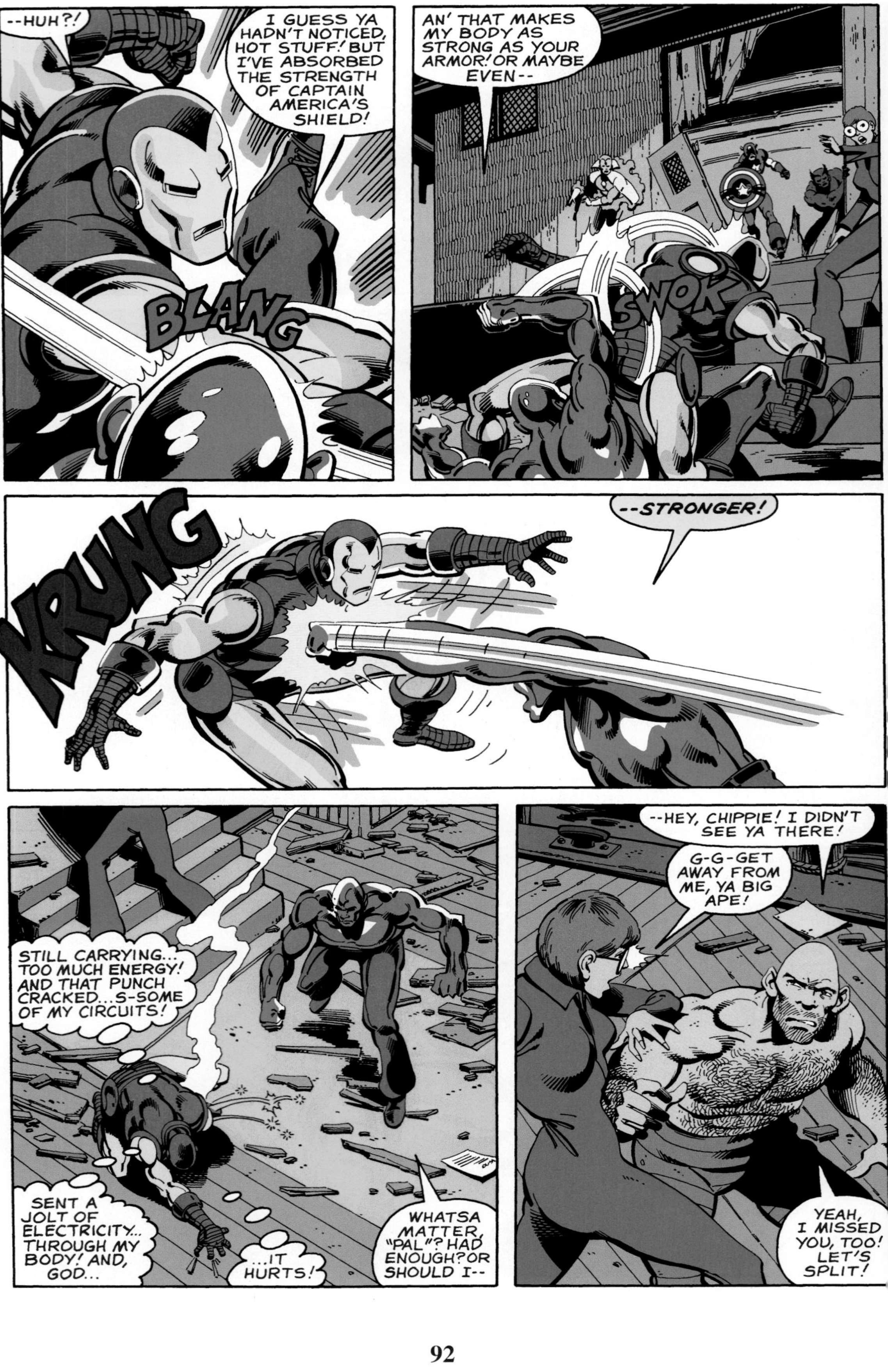
--HUH?!
I GUESS YA HADN'T NOTICED, HOT STUFF! BUT I'VE ABSORBED THE STRENGTH OF CAPTAIN AMERICA'S SHIELD!
BLANG
AN' THAT MAKES MY BODY AS STRONG AS YOUR ARMOR! OR MAYBE EVEN--
SWOK
KRUNG
--STRONGER!
STILL CARRYING... TOO MUCH ENERGY! AND THAT PUNCH CRACKED... S-SOME OF MY CIRCUITS!
SENT A JOLT OF ELECTRICITY... THROUGH MY BODY! AND, GOD...
...IT HURTS!
WHATSA MATTER, "PAL"? HAD ENOUGH? OR SHOULD I--
--HEY, CHIPPIE! I DIDN'T SEE YA THERE!
G-G-GET AWAY FROM ME, YA BIG APE!
YEAH, I MISSED YOU, TOO! LET'S SPLIT!

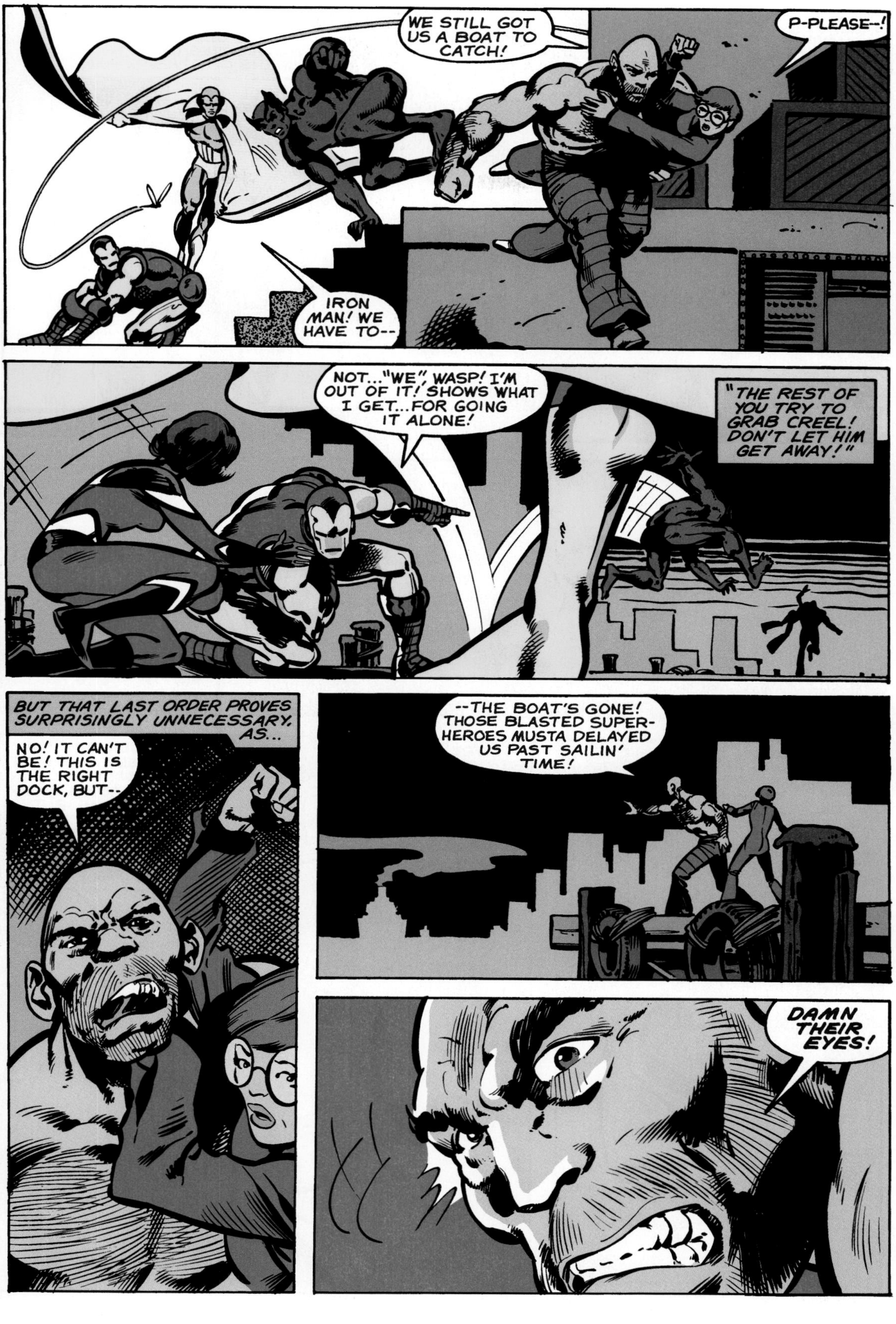
WE STILL GOT US A BOAT TO CATCH!
P-PLEASE--!
IRON MAN! WE HAVE TO--
NOT..."WE", WASP! I'M OUT OF IT! SHOWS WHAT I GET...FOR GOING IT ALONE!
"THE REST OF YOU TRY TO GRAB CREEL! DON'T LET HIM GET AWAY!"
BUT THAT LAST ORDER PROVES SURPRISINGLY UNNECESSARY, AS...
NO! IT CAN'T BE! THIS IS THE RIGHT DOCK, BUT--
--THE BOAT'S GONE! THOSE BLASTED SUPER-HEROES MUSTA DELAYED US PAST SAILIN' TIME!
DAMN THEIR EYES!

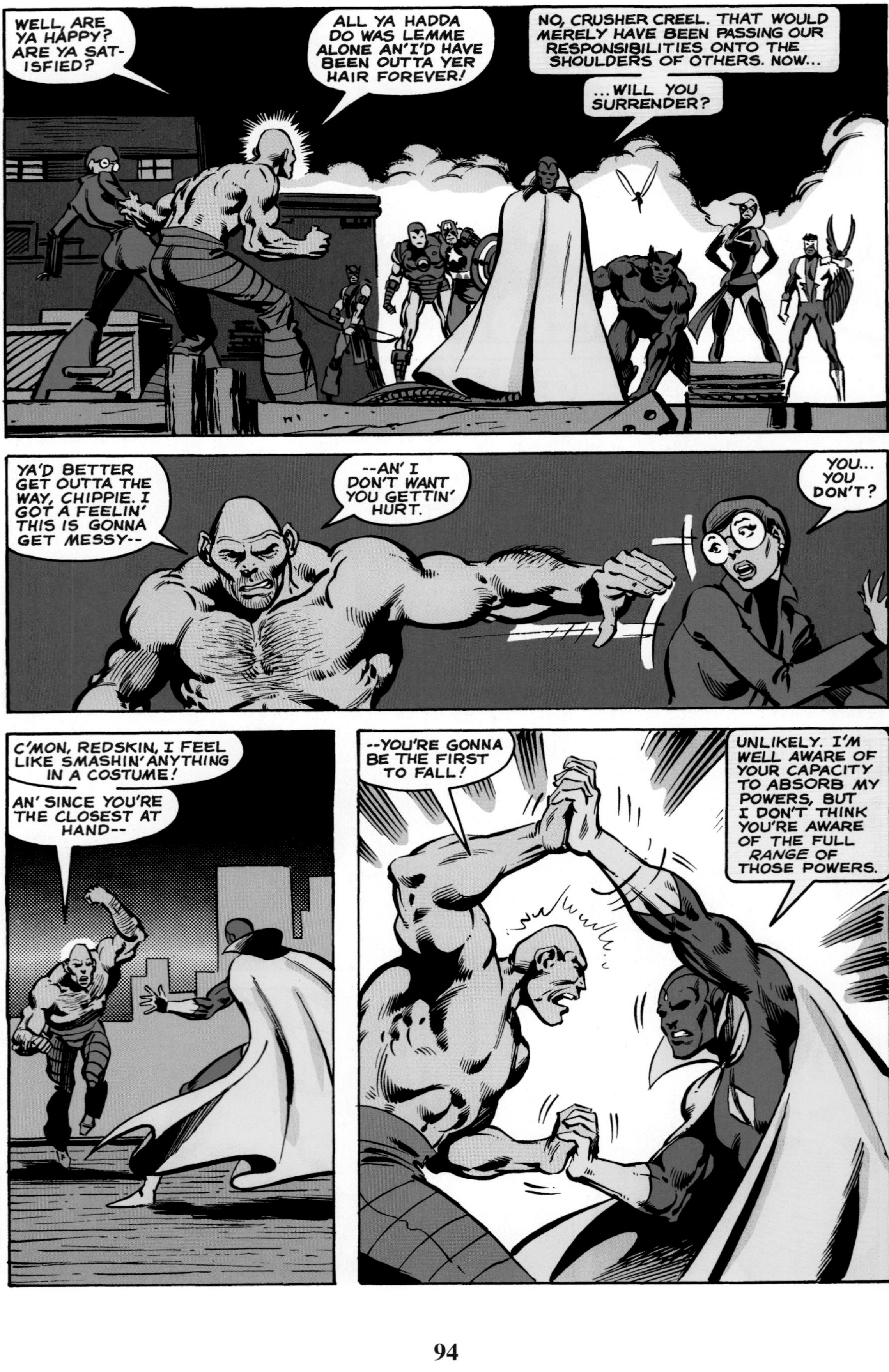
WELL, ARE YA HAPPY? ARE YA SATISFIED?
ALL YA HADDA DO WAS LEMME ALONE AN'I'D HAVE BEEN OUTTA YER HAIR FOREVER!
NO, CRUSHER CREEL. THAT WOULD MERELY HAVE BEEN PASSING OUR RESPONSIBILITIES ONTO THE SHOULDERS OF OTHERS. NOW...
...WILL YOU SURRENDER?
YA'D BETTER GET OUTTA THE WAY, CHIPPIE. I GOT A FEELIN' THIS IS GONNA GET MESSY--
--AN' I DON'T WANT YOU GETTIN' HURT.
YOU... YOU DON'T?
C'MON, REDSKIN, I FEEL LIKE SMASHIN' ANYTHING IN A COSTUME!
AN' SINCE YOU'RE THE CLOSEST AT HAND--
--YOU'RE GONNA BE THE FIRST TO FALL!
UNLIKELY. I'M WELL AWARE OF YOUR CAPACITY TO ABSORB MY POWERS, BUT I DON'T THINK YOU'RE AWARE OF THE FULL RANGE OF THOSE POWERS.

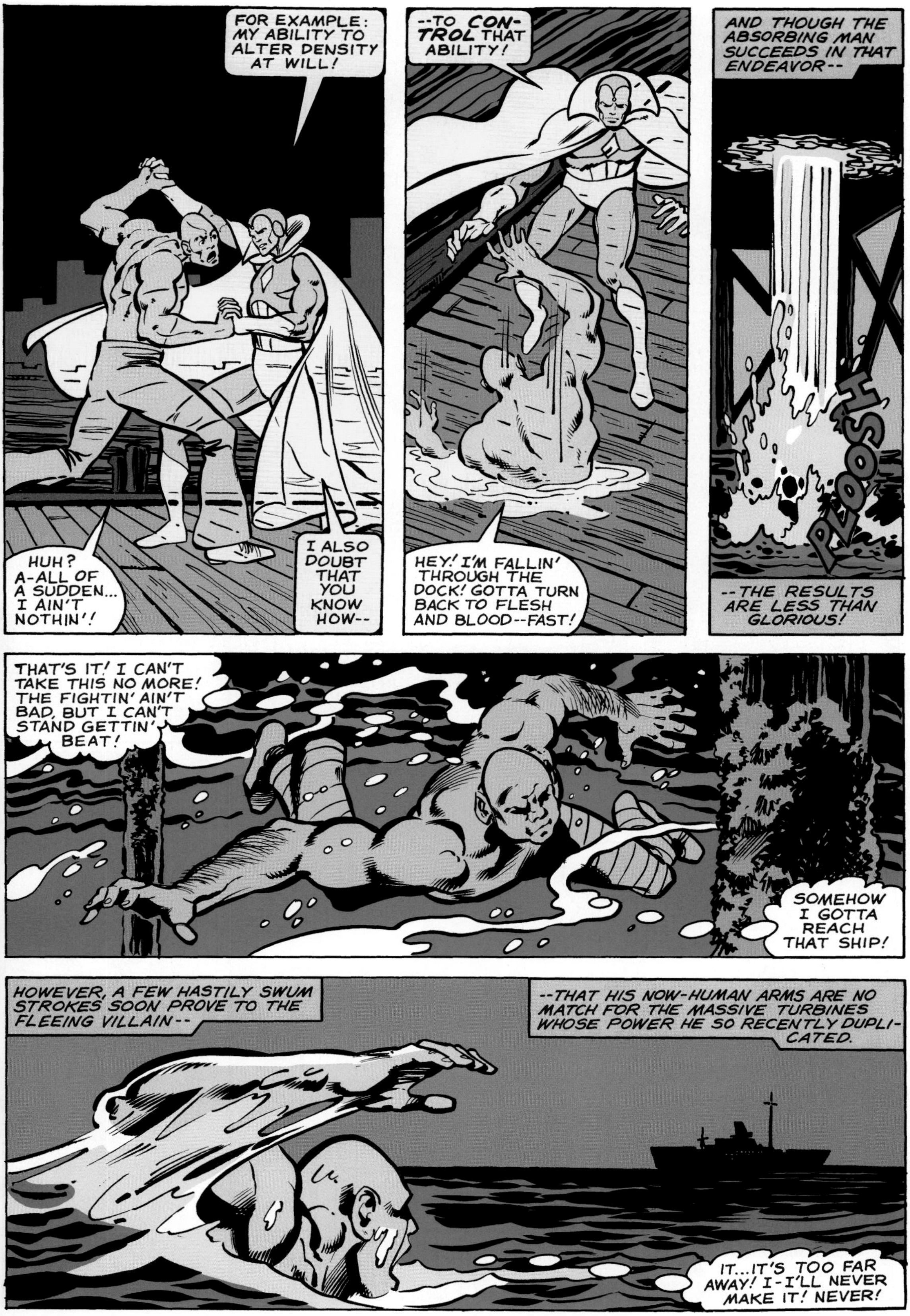

FOR EXAMPLE: MY ABILITY TO ALTER DENSITY AT WILL!
HUH? A-ALL OF A SUDDEN... I AIN'T NOTHIN'!
I ALSO DOUBT THAT YOU KNOW HOW--
--TO CONTROL THAT ABILITY!
HEY! I'M FALLIN' THROUGH THE DOCK! GOTTA TURN BACK TO FLESH AND BLOOD--FAST!
AND THOUGH THE ABSORBING MAN SUCCEEDS IN THAT ENDEAVOR--
PLOOSH
--THE RESULTS ARE LESS THAN GLORIOUS!
THAT'S IT! I CAN'T TAKE THIS NO MORE! THE FIGHTIN' AIN'T BAD, BUT I CAN'T STAND GETTIN' BEAT!
SOMEHOW I GOTTA REACH THAT SHIP!
HOWEVER, A FEW HASTILY SWUM STROKES SOON PROVE TO THE FLEEING VILLAIN--
--THAT HIS NOW-HUMAN ARMS ARE NO MATCH FOR THE MASSIVE TURBINES WHOSE POWER HE SO RECENTLY DUPLICATED.
IT...IT'S TOO FAR AWAY! I-I'LL NEVER MAKE IT! NEVER!

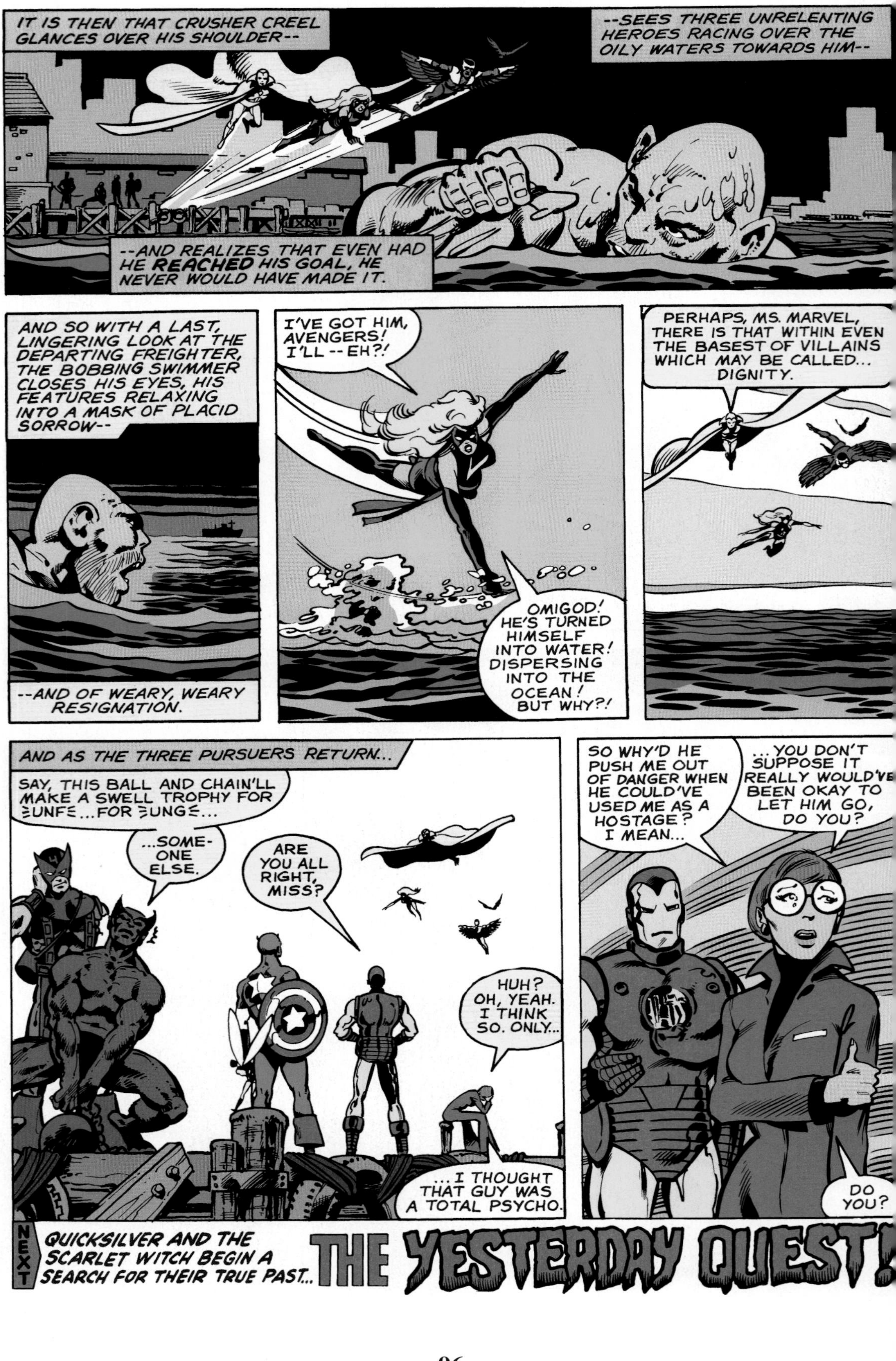
IT IS THEN THAT CRUSHER CREEL GLANCES OVER HIS SHOULDER--
--SEES THREE UNRELENTING HEROES RACING OVER THE OILY WATERS TOWARDS HIM--
--AND REALIZES THAT EVEN HAD HE REACHED HIS GOAL, HE NEVER WOULD HAVE MADE IT.
AND SO WITH A LAST, LINGERING LOOK AT THE DEPARTING FREIGHTER, THE BOBBING SWIMMER CLOSES HIS EYES, HIS FEATURES RELAXING INTO A MASK OF PLACID SORROW--
--AND OF WEARY, WEARY RESIGNATION.
I'VE GOT HIM, AVENGERS! I'LL -- EH?!
OMIGOD! HE'S TURNED HIMSELF INTO WATER! DISPERSING INTO THE OCEAN! BUT WHY?!
PERHAPS, MS. MARVEL, THERE IS THAT WITHIN EVEN THE BASEST OF VILLAINS WHICH MAY BE CALLED... DIGNITY.
AND AS THE THREE PURSUERS RETURN...
SAY, THIS BALL AND CHAIN'LL MAKE A SWELL TROPHY FOR ... FOR ...
...SOME-ONE ELSE.
ARE YOU ALL RIGHT, MISS?
HUH? OH, YEAH. I THINK SO. ONLY...
...I THOUGHT THAT GUY WAS A TOTAL PSYCHO.
SO WHY'D HE PUSH ME OUT OF DANGER WHEN HE COULD'VE USED ME AS A HOSTAGE? I MEAN...
...YOU DON'T SUPPOSE IT REALLY WOULD'VE BEEN OKAY TO LET HIM GO, DO YOU?
DO YOU?
NEXT
QUICKSILVER AND THE SCARLET WITCH BEGIN A SEARCH FOR THEIR TRUE PAST...
THE YESTERDAY QUEST!

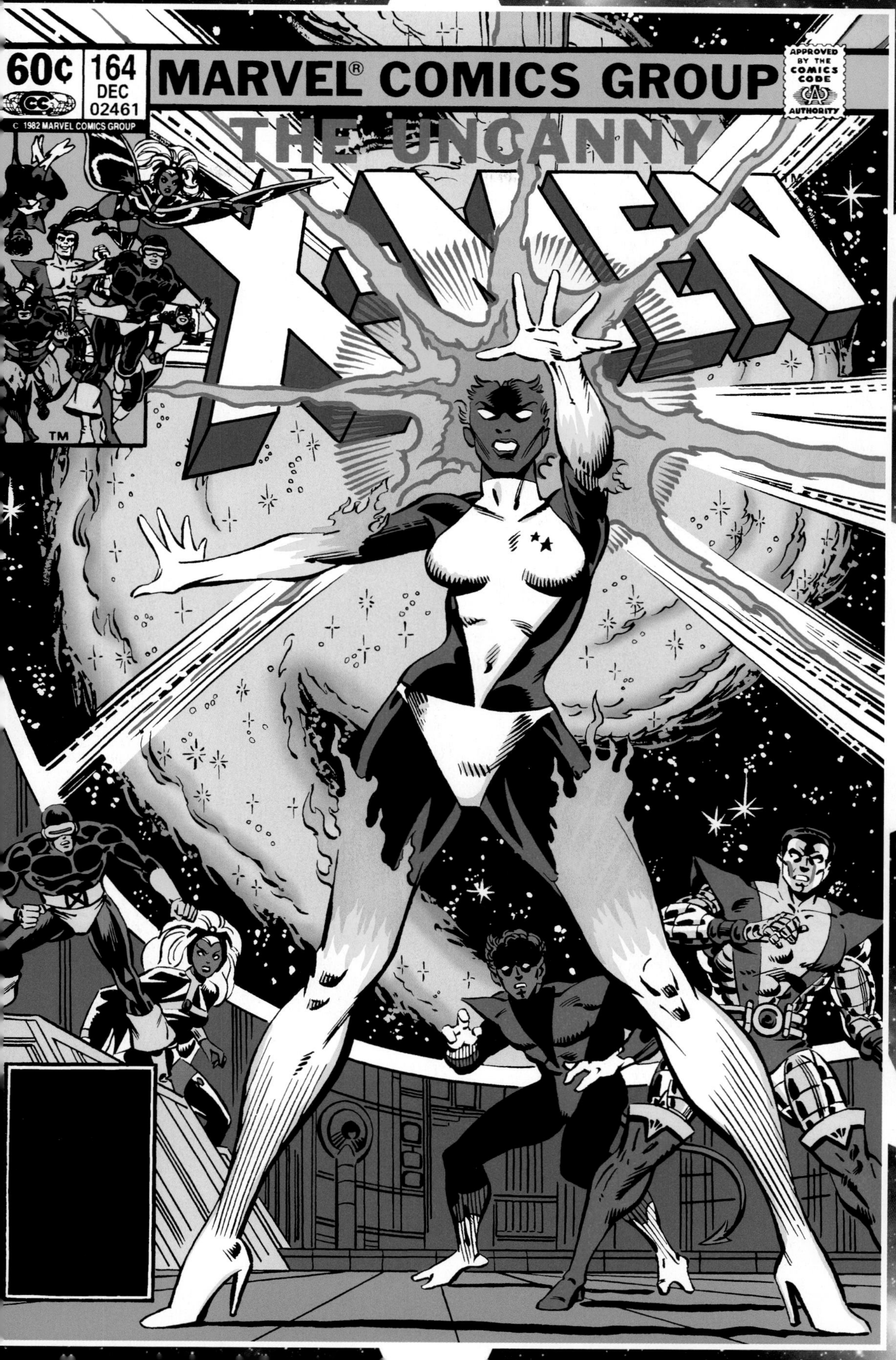
60¢
164
DEC
02461
© 1982 MARVEL COMICS GROUP
MARVEL® COMICS GROUP
APPROVED BY THE COMICS CODE AUTHORITY
THE UNCANNY
X-MEN
TM

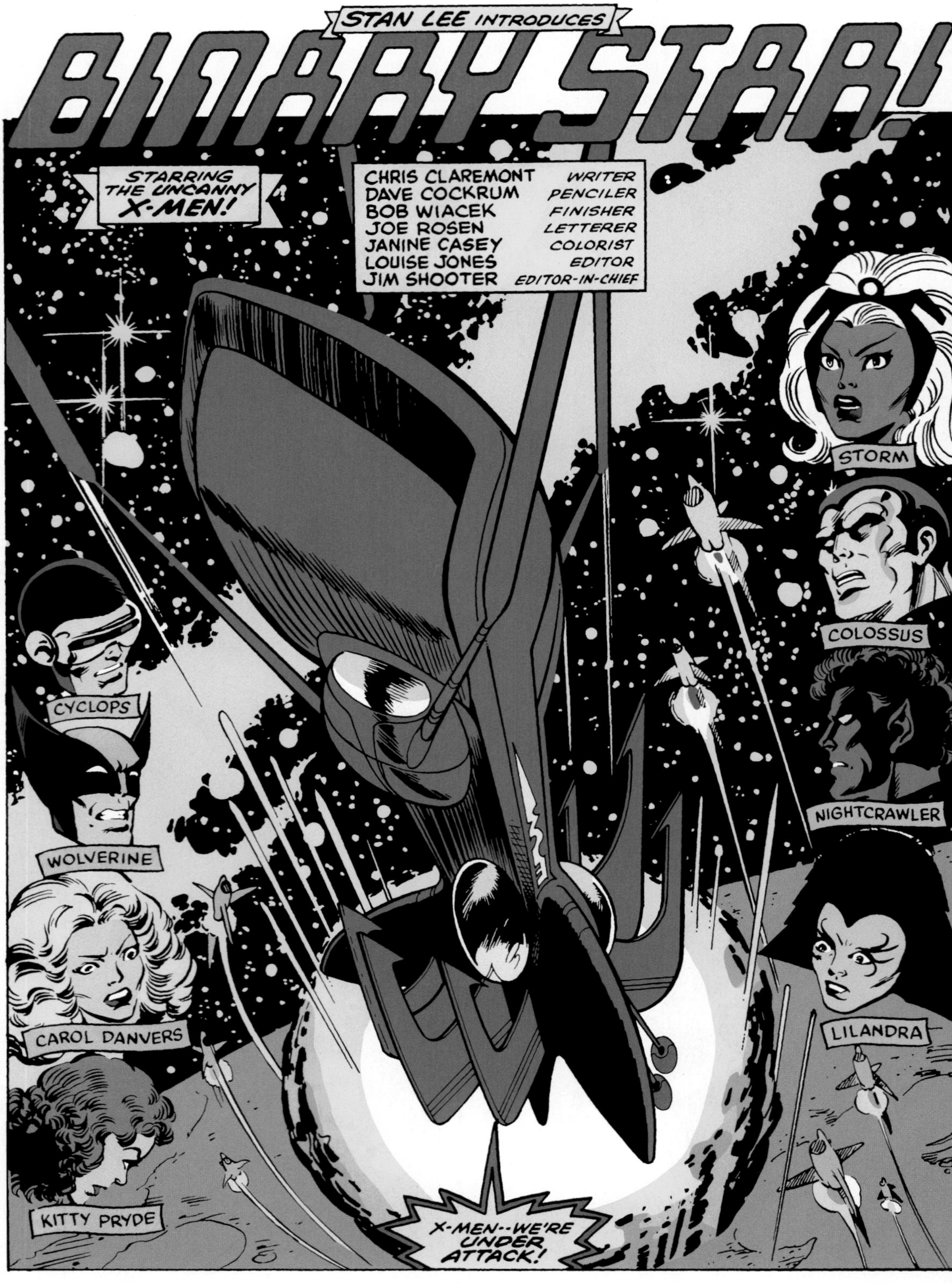
STAN LEE INTRODUCES
BINARY STAR!
STARRING THE UNCANNY X-MEN!
CHRIS CLAREMONT WRITER
DAVE COCKRUM PENCILER
BOB WIACEK FINISHER
JOE ROSEN LETTERER
JANINE CASEY COLORIST
LOUISE JONES EDITOR
JIM SHOOTER EDITOR-IN-CHIEF
STORM
COLOSSUS
NIGHTCRAWLER
LILANDRA
CYCLOPS
WOLVERINE
CAROL DANVERS
KITTY PRYDE
X-MEN--WE'RE UNDER ATTACK!

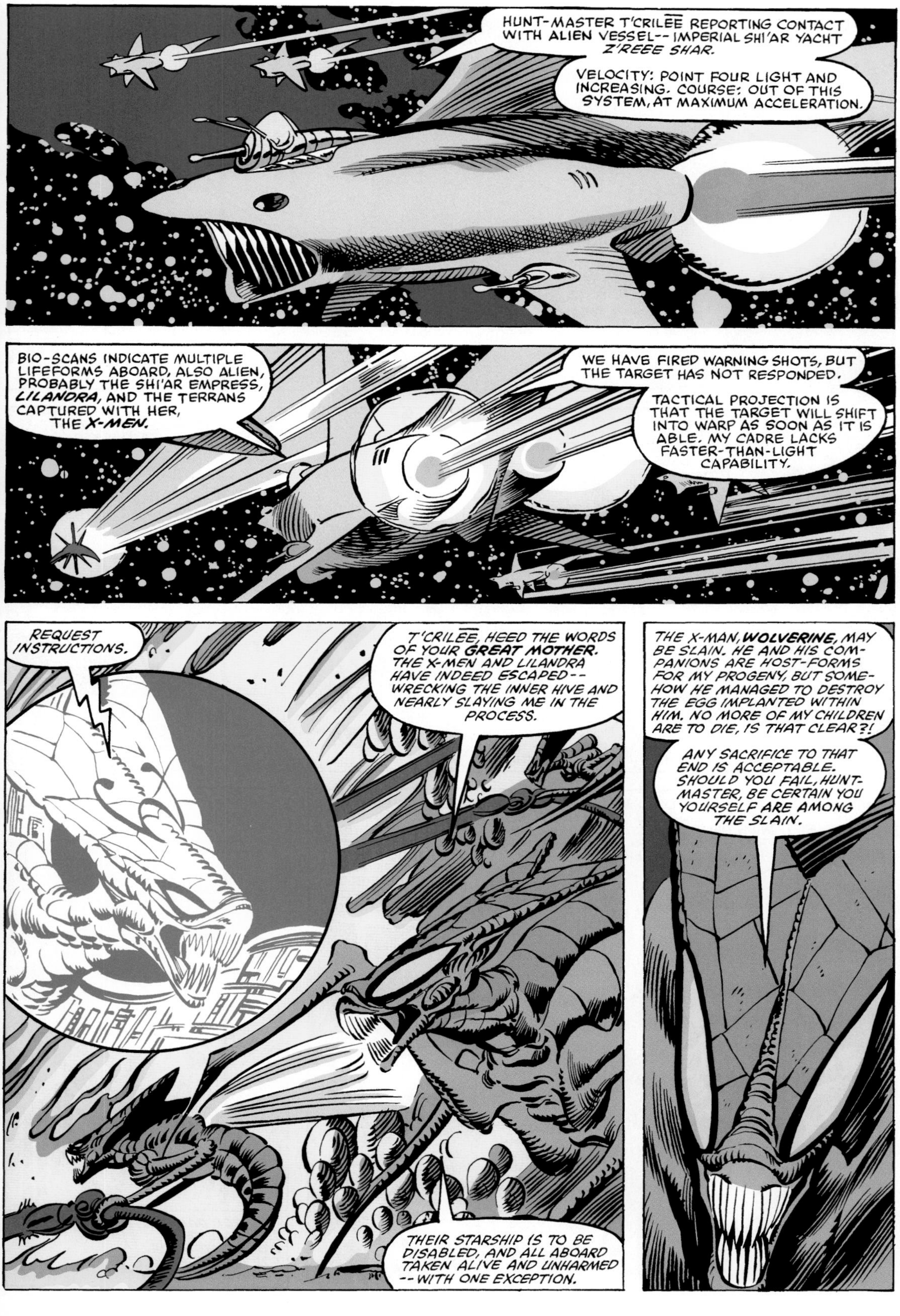
HUNT-MASTER T'CRILEE REPORTING CONTACT WITH ALIEN VESSEL--IMPERIAL SHI'AR YACHT Z'REEE SHAR.
VELOCITY: POINT FOUR LIGHT AND INCREASING. COURSE: OUT OF THIS SYSTEM, AT MAXIMUM ACCELERATION.
BIO-SCANS INDICATE MULTIPLE LIFEFORMS ABOARD, ALSO ALIEN, PROBABLY THE SHI'AR EMPRESS, LILANDRA, AND THE TERRANS CAPTURED WITH HER, THE X-MEN.
WE HAVE FIRED WARNING SHOTS, BUT THE TARGET HAS NOT RESPONDED.
TACTICAL PROJECTION IS THAT THE TARGET WILL SHIFT INTO WARP AS SOON AS IT IS ABLE. MY CADRE LACKS FASTER-THAN-LIGHT CAPABILITY.
REQUEST INSTRUCTIONS.
T'CRILEE, HEED THE WORDS OF YOUR GREAT MOTHER. THE X-MEN AND LILANDRA HAVE INDEED ESCAPED--WRECKING THE INNER HIVE AND NEARLY SLAYING ME IN THE PROCESS.
THEIR STARSHIP IS TO BE DISABLED, AND ALL ABOARD TAKEN ALIVE AND UNHARMED--WITH ONE EXCEPTION.
THE X-MAN, WOLVERINE, MAY BE SLAIN. HE AND HIS COMPANIONS ARE HOST-FORMS FOR MY PROGENY, BUT SOMEHOW HE MANAGED TO DESTROY THE EGG IMPLANTED WITHIN HIM. NO MORE OF MY CHILDREN ARE TO DIE, IS THAT CLEAR?!
ANY SACRIFICE TO THAT END IS ACCEPTABLE. SHOULD YOU FAIL, HUNT-MASTER, BE CERTAIN YOU YOURSELF ARE AMONG THE SLAIN.

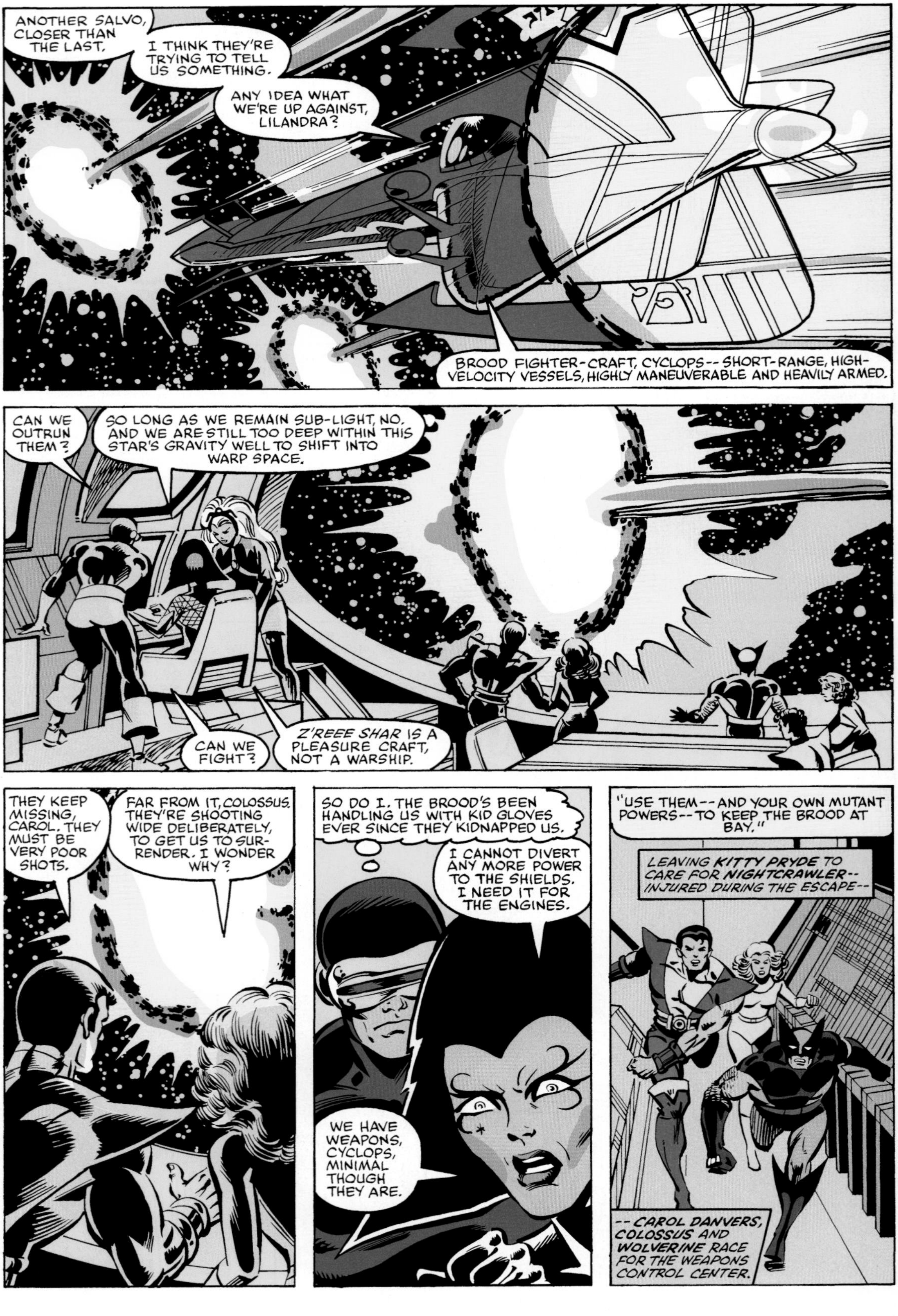
ANOTHER SALVO, CLOSER THAN THE LAST.
I THINK THEY'RE TRYING TO TELL US SOMETHING.
ANY IDEA WHAT WE'RE UP AGAINST, LILANDRA?
BROOD FIGHTER-CRAFT, CYCLOPS-- SHORT-RANGE, HIGH-VELOCITY VESSELS, HIGHLY MANEUVERABLE AND HEAVILY ARMED.
CAN WE OUTRUN THEM?
SO LONG AS WE REMAIN SUB-LIGHT, NO. AND WE ARE STILL TOO DEEP WITHIN THIS STAR'S GRAVITY WELL TO SHIFT INTO WARP SPACE.
CAN WE FIGHT?
Z'REEE SHAR IS A PLEASURE CRAFT, NOT A WARSHIP.
THEY KEEP MISSING, CAROL. THEY MUST BE VERY POOR SHOTS.
FAR FROM IT, COLOSSUS. THEY'RE SHOOTING WIDE DELIBERATELY, TO GET US TO SURRENDER. I WONDER WHY?
SO DO I. THE BROOD'S BEEN HANDLING US WITH KID GLOVES EVER SINCE THEY KIDNAPPED US.
I CANNOT DIVERT ANY MORE POWER TO THE SHIELDS. I NEED IT FOR THE ENGINES.
WE HAVE WEAPONS, CYCLOPS, MINIMAL THOUGH THEY ARE.
"USE THEM--AND YOUR OWN MUTANT POWERS--TO KEEP THE BROOD AT BAY."
LEAVING KITTY PRYDE TO CARE FOR NIGHTCRAWLER-- INJURED DURING THE ESCAPE--
--CAROL DANVERS, COLOSSUS AND WOLVERINE RACE FOR THE WEAPONS CONTROL CENTER.

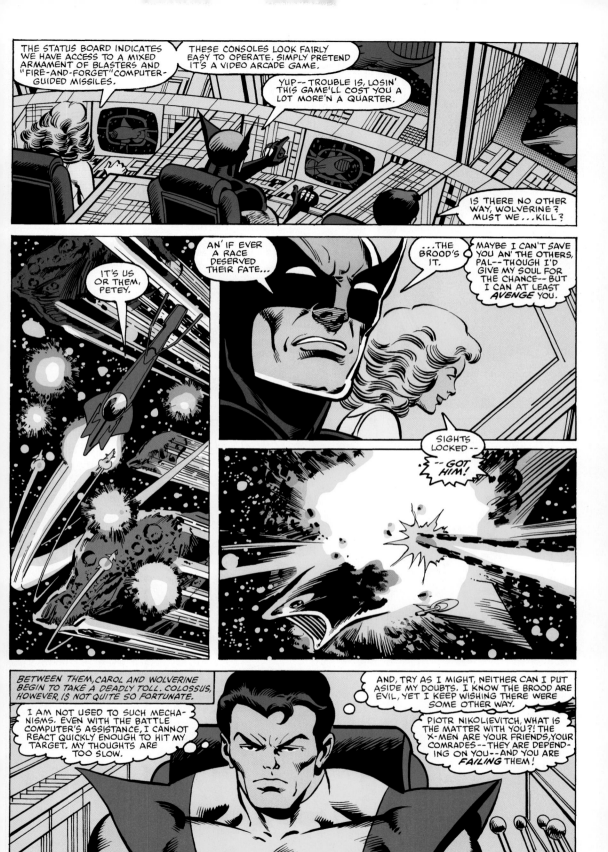

THE STATUS BOARD INDICATES WE HAVE ACCESS TO A MIXED ARMAMENT OF BLASTERS AND "FIRE-AND-FORGET" COMPUTER-GUIDED MISSILES.

THESE CONSOLES LOOK FAIRLY EASY TO OPERATE. SIMPLY PRETEND IT'S A VIDEO ARCADE GAME.

YUP-- TROUBLE IS, LOSIN' THIS GAME'LL COST YOU A LOT MORE'N A QUARTER.

IS THERE NO OTHER WAY, WOLVERINE? MUST WE...KILL?

IT'S US OR THEM, PETEY.

AN' IF EVER A RACE DESERVED THEIR FATE...

...THE BROOD'S IT.

MAYBE I CAN'T SAVE YOU AN' THE OTHERS, PAL-- THOUGH I'D GIVE MY SOUL FOR THE CHANCE-- BUT I CAN AT LEAST AVENGE YOU.

SIGHTS LOCKED--

--GOT HIM!

BETWEEN THEM, CAROL AND WOLVERINE BEGIN TO TAKE A DEADLY TOLL. COLOSSUS, HOWEVER, IS NOT QUITE SO FORTUNATE.

I AM NOT USED TO SUCH MECHANISMS. EVEN WITH THE BATTLE COMPUTER'S ASSISTANCE, I CANNOT REACT QUICKLY ENOUGH TO HIT MY TARGET. MY THOUGHTS ARE TOO SLOW.

AND, TRY AS I MIGHT, NEITHER CAN I PUT ASIDE MY DOUBTS. I KNOW THE BROOD ARE EVIL, YET I KEEP WISHING THERE WERE SOME OTHER WAY.

PIOTR NIKOLIEVITCH, WHAT IS THE MATTER WITH YOU?! THE X-MEN ARE YOUR FRIENDS, YOUR COMRADES-- THEY ARE DEPENDING ON YOU-- AND YOU ARE FAILING THEM!

101

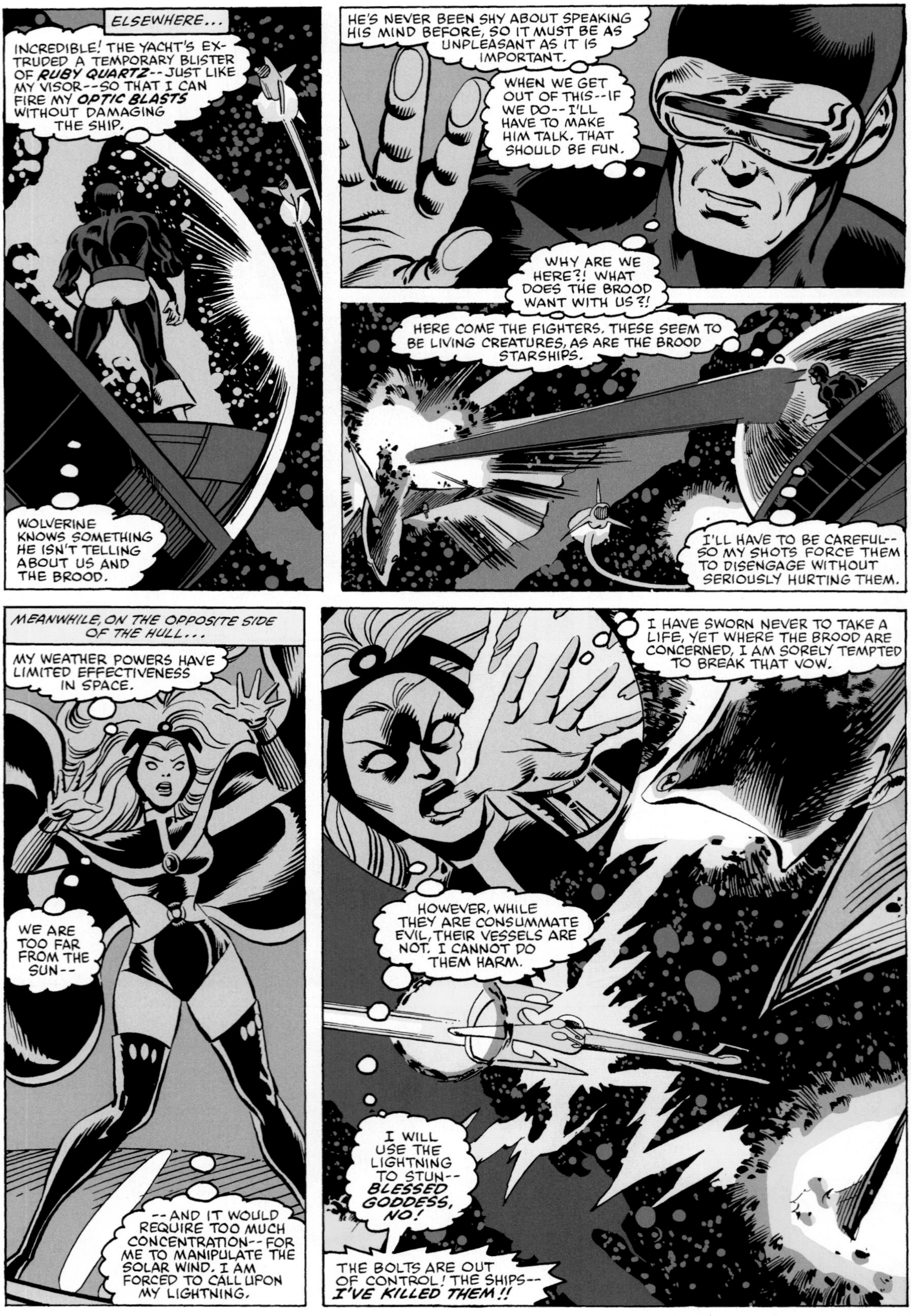
ELSEWHERE...
INCREDIBLE! THE YACHT'S EXTRUDED A TEMPORARY BLISTER OF RUBY QUARTZ--JUST LIKE MY VISOR--SO THAT I CAN FIRE MY OPTIC BLASTS WITHOUT DAMAGING THE SHIP.
WOLVERINE KNOWS SOMETHING HE ISN'T TELLING ABOUT US AND THE BROOD.
HE'S NEVER BEEN SHY ABOUT SPEAKING HIS MIND BEFORE, SO IT MUST BE AS UNPLEASANT AS IT IS IMPORTANT.
WHEN WE GET OUT OF THIS--IF WE DO--I'LL HAVE TO MAKE HIM TALK. THAT SHOULD BE FUN.
WHY ARE WE HERE?! WHAT DOES THE BROOD WANT WITH US?!
HERE COME THE FIGHTERS. THESE SEEM TO BE LIVING CREATURES, AS ARE THE BROOD STARSHIPS.
I'LL HAVE TO BE CAREFUL--SO MY SHOTS FORCE THEM TO DISENGAGE WITHOUT SERIOUSLY HURTING THEM.
MEANWHILE, ON THE OPPOSITE SIDE OF THE HULL...
MY WEATHER POWERS HAVE LIMITED EFFECTIVENESS IN SPACE.
WE ARE TOO FAR FROM THE SUN--
--AND IT WOULD REQUIRE TOO MUCH CONCENTRATION--FOR ME TO MANIPULATE THE SOLAR WIND. I AM FORCED TO CALL UPON MY LIGHTNING.
I HAVE SWORN NEVER TO TAKE A LIFE, YET WHERE THE BROOD ARE CONCERNED, I AM SORELY TEMPTED TO BREAK THAT VOW.
HOWEVER, WHILE THEY ARE CONSUMMATE EVIL, THEIR VESSELS ARE NOT. I CANNOT DO THEM HARM.
I WILL USE THE LIGHTNING TO STUN--BLESSED GODDESS, NO!
THE BOLTS ARE OUT OF CONTROL! THE SHIPS--I'VE KILLED THEM!!

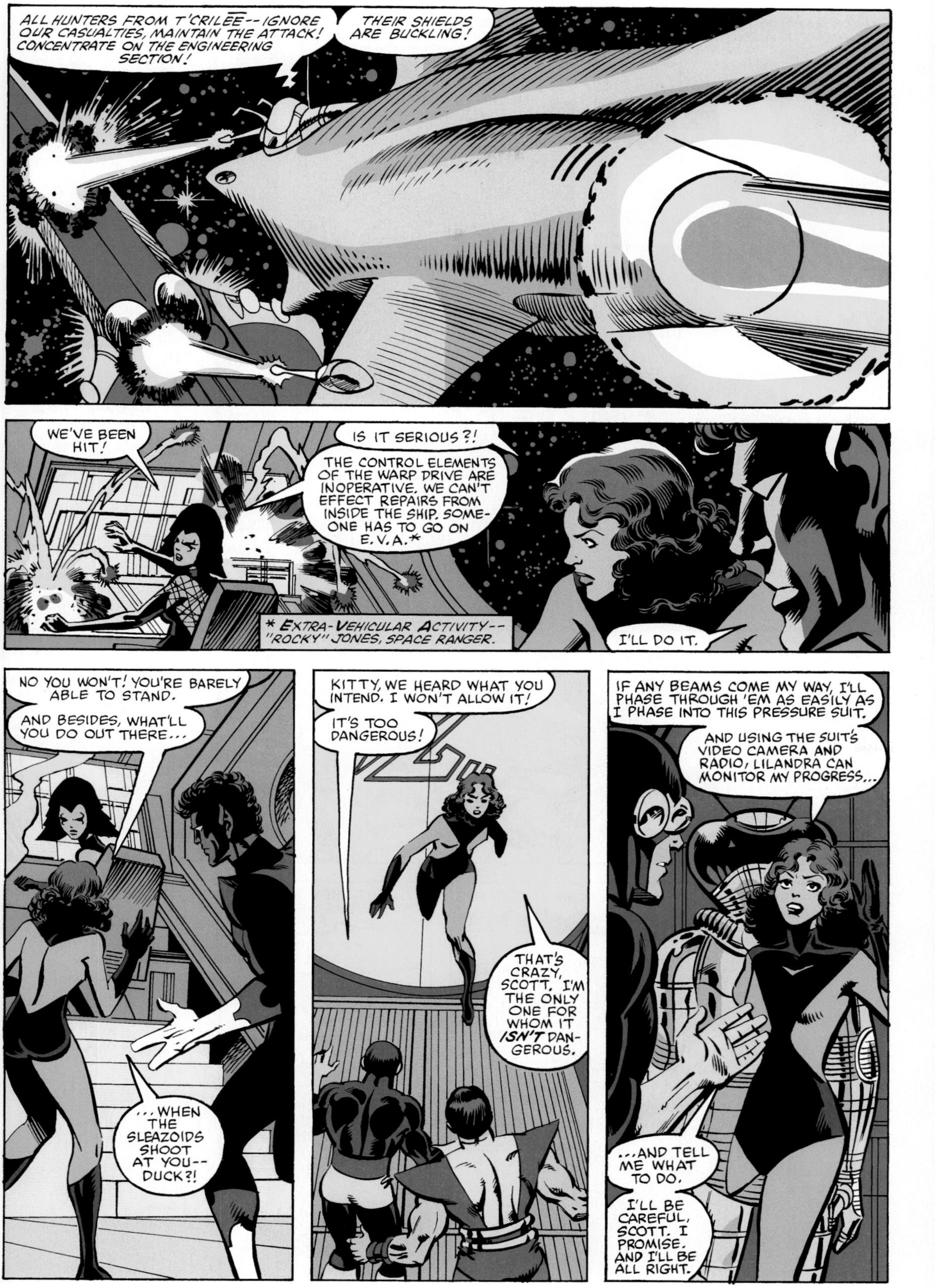
ALL HUNTERS FROM T'CRILEE--IGNORE OUR CASUALTIES, MAINTAIN THE ATTACK! CONCENTRATE ON THE ENGINEERING SECTION!
THEIR SHIELDS ARE BUCKLING!
WE'VE BEEN HIT!
IS IT SERIOUS?!
THE CONTROL ELEMENTS OF THE WARP DRIVE ARE INOPERATIVE. WE CAN'T EFFECT REPAIRS FROM INSIDE THE SHIP. SOMEONE HAS TO GO ON E.V.A.*
* EXTRA-VEHICULAR ACTIVITY-- "ROCKY" JONES, SPACE RANGER.
I'LL DO IT.
NO YOU WON'T! YOU'RE BARELY ABLE TO STAND.
AND BESIDES, WHAT'LL YOU DO OUT THERE...
...WHEN THE SLEAZOIDS SHOOT AT YOU--DUCK?!
KITTY, WE HEARD WHAT YOU INTEND. I WON'T ALLOW IT!
IT'S TOO DANGEROUS!
THAT'S CRAZY, SCOTT. I'M THE ONLY ONE FOR WHOM IT ISN'T DANGEROUS.
IF ANY BEAMS COME MY WAY, I'LL PHASE THROUGH 'EM AS EASILY AS I PHASE INTO THIS PRESSURE SUIT.
AND USING THE SUIT'S VIDEO CAMERA AND RADIO, LILANDRA CAN MONITOR MY PROGRESS...
...AND TELL ME WHAT TO DO.
I'LL BE CAREFUL, SCOTT. I PROMISE. AND I'LL BE ALL RIGHT.

AFTER MAKING CERTAIN SHE HAS THE NECESSARY EQUIPMENT AND THAT IT'S FUNCTIONING PROPERLY...

...KITTY PHASES THROUGH THE PRIMARY HULL.

WOW!

"STAR WARS" WAS NEVER LIKE THIS!

THE BUSTED MODULE IS AFT, BENEATH THE SOLAR FINS.

I WANT TO RUN, BUT I CAN'T. I'M NOT USING A SAFETY LINE. ONE MISSTEP'LL THROW ME OFF INTO SPACE...

...AND THE OTHERS WON'T BE ABLE TO STOP AND COME BACK FOR ME.

AT THAT MOMENT, IN WEAPONS CONTROL...

WHAT THE--?!?

MY VISION SUDDENLY WENT BLURRY-- I SAW COLORS, IMAGES I NEVER DREAMED POSSIBLE.

BUT EVERYTHING'S NORMAL NOW. PROBABLY STRESS-- A DELAYED REACTION TO THE TREATMENT I RECEIVED FROM THE BROOD.

ON THE YACHT'S HULL-- AN X-MAN-- THE YOUNGLING!

USE STUN AND 'PRESSOR BEAMS ON HER! TRY TO KNOCK HER LOOSE. ONCE SHE'S IN FREE SPACE, WE CAN EASILY TAKE HER PRISONER.

SPAWN OF THE BLOODMOON-- MY BOLTS HAVE NO EFFECT!

÷WHEW!÷

I KNOW I'VE BEEN THROUGH MOMENTS LIKE THIS BEFORE...

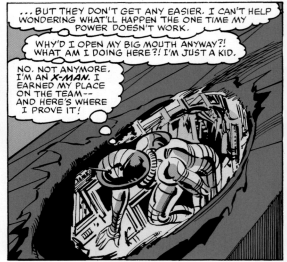

...BUT THEY DON'T GET ANY EASIER. I CAN'T HELP WONDERING WHAT'LL HAPPEN THE ONE TIME MY POWER DOESN'T WORK.

WHY'D I OPEN MY BIG MOUTH ANYWAY?! WHAT AM I DOING HERE?! I'M JUST A KID.

NO. NOT ANYMORE. I'M AN X-MAN. I EARNED MY PLACE ON THE TEAM-- AND HERE'S WHERE I PROVE IT!

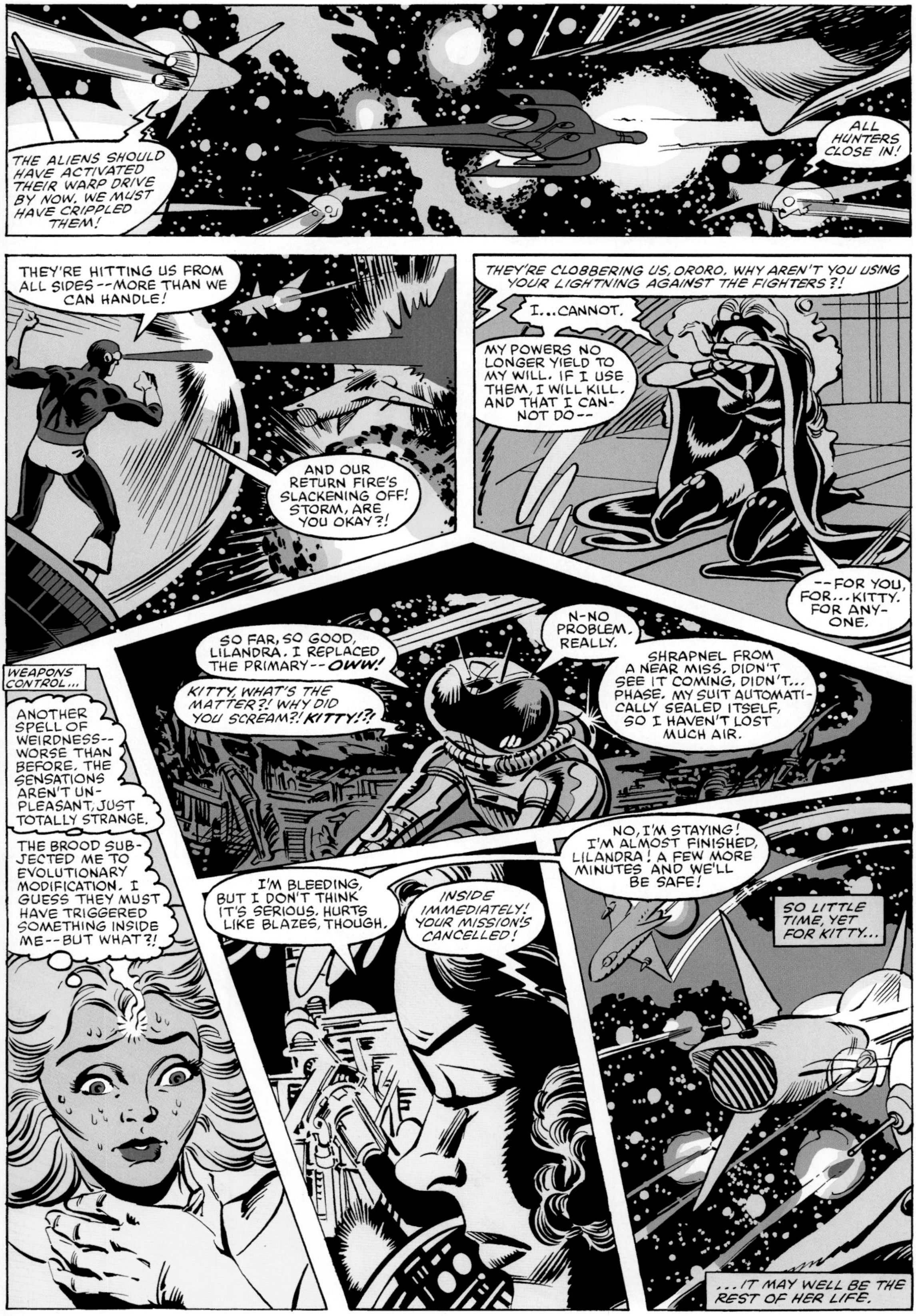

THE ALIENS SHOULD HAVE ACTIVATED THEIR WARP DRIVE BY NOW. WE MUST HAVE CRIPPLED THEM!
ALL HUNTERS CLOSE IN!
THEY'RE HITTING US FROM ALL SIDES--MORE THAN WE CAN HANDLE!
AND OUR RETURN FIRE'S SLACKENING OFF! STORM, ARE YOU OKAY?!
THEY'RE CLOBBERING US, ORORO. WHY AREN'T YOU USING YOUR LIGHTNING AGAINST THE FIGHTERS?!
I...CANNOT.
MY POWERS NO LONGER YIELD TO MY WILL. IF I USE THEM, I WILL KILL. AND THAT I CANNOT DO--
--FOR YOU, FOR...KITTY. FOR ANYONE.
WEAPONS CONTROL...
ANOTHER SPELL OF WEIRDNESS--WORSE THAN BEFORE. THE SENSATIONS AREN'T UNPLEASANT, JUST TOTALLY STRANGE.
THE BROOD SUBJECTED ME TO EVOLUTIONARY MODIFICATION. I GUESS THEY MUST HAVE TRIGGERED SOMETHING INSIDE ME--BUT WHAT?!
SO FAR, SO GOOD, LILANDRA. I REPLACED THE PRIMARY--OWW!
KITTY, WHAT'S THE MATTER?! WHY DID YOU SCREAM?! KITTY!?!
N-NO PROBLEM, REALLY.
SHRAPNEL FROM A NEAR MISS. DIDN'T SEE IT COMING, DIDN'T... PHASE. MY SUIT AUTOMATICALLY SEALED ITSELF, SO I HAVEN'T LOST MUCH AIR.
I'M BLEEDING, BUT I DON'T THINK IT'S SERIOUS. HURTS LIKE BLAZES, THOUGH.
INSIDE IMMEDIATELY! YOUR MISSION'S CANCELLED!
NO, I'M STAYING! I'M ALMOST FINISHED, LILANDRA! A FEW MORE MINUTES AND WE'LL BE SAFE!
SO LITTLE TIME, YET FOR KITTY...
...IT MAY WELL BE THE REST OF HER LIFE.

THE SAME, IN A WAY, HOLDS TRUE FOR CAROL.

YEARS AGO, A FREAK ACCIDENT COMBINED THE BEST GENETIC ELEMENTS OF HUMAN AND THE ANCIENT, STAR-FARING **KREE** TO TRANSFORM HER INTO MS. MARVEL.

AND WHILE SHE LATER LOST HER SUPER-POWERS TO THE MUTANT ROGUE, THOSE HYBRID GENES REMAINED. NOW, THANKS TO THE BROOD'S MEDDLING, THEIR UNTAPPED POTENTIAL IS BEING REALIZED, WITH A VENGEANCE.

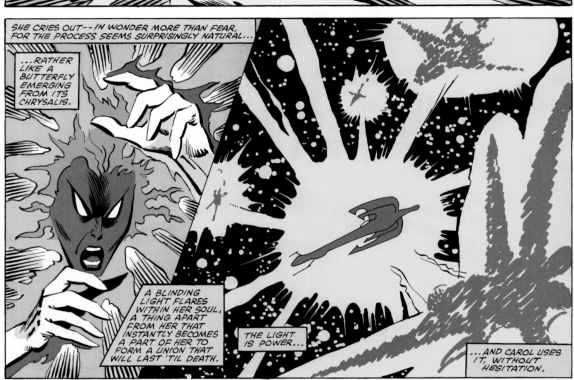

SHE CRIES OUT-- IN WONDER MORE THAN FEAR, FOR THE PROCESS SEEMS SURPRISINGLY NATURAL...

...RATHER LIKE A BUTTERFLY EMERGING FROM ITS CHRYSALIS.

A BLINDING LIGHT FLARES WITHIN HER SOUL, A THING APART FROM HER THAT INSTANTLY BECOMES A PART OF HER TO FORM A UNION THAT WILL LAST 'TIL DEATH.

THE LIGHT IS POWER...

...AND CAROL USES IT, WITHOUT HESITATION.

EVERYTHING'S FIXED! THROW THE SWITCH, LILANDRA!

THROW US INTO WARP!

BLESS YOU, CHILD! WE'RE ON OUR WAY!

KITTY, ARE YOU THERE?!

KITTY!!!

PROFESSOR XAVIER'S SCHOOL FOR GIFTED YOUNGSTERS -- SALEM CENTER, NEW YORK.

THE TITLE IS SOMETHING OF A MISNOMER THESE DAYS. THOUGH THE MANSION HAS BEEN REBUILT-- BETTER THAN BEFORE, COURTESY OF CONSTRUCTION ROBOTS PROVIDED BY LILANDRA--

-- THE SCHOOL IS, IN TRUTH, NO MORE.

AS A YOUNG MAN, CHARLES XAVIER HAD A DREAM, OF AN EARTH WHERE HUMANITY AND MUTANTKIND LIVED TOGETHER IN PEACE. TO FULFILL THAT DREAM--

-- AND TO PROTECT THE WORLD FROM THE DEPREDATIONS OF EVIL MUTANTS-- HE FORMED THIS SCHOOL, WHOSE STUDENTS BECAME THE UNCANNY X-MEN. UNSUNG HEROES, FEARED, OFTEN HATED, BY THE VERY PEOPLE THEY WERE SWORN TO SAVE.

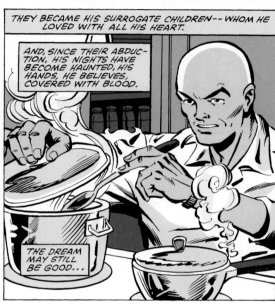

THEY BECAME HIS SURROGATE CHILDREN-- WHOM HE LOVED WITH ALL HIS HEART.

AND, SINCE THEIR ABDUCTION, HIS NIGHTS HAVE BECOME HAUNTED, HIS HANDS, HE BELIEVES, COVERED WITH BLOOD.

THE DREAM MAY STILL BE GOOD...

...BUT THIS DREAMER IS DONE.

YOU CALL ME, PROFESSOR?

DINNER'S READY, ILLYANA.

GREAT! I'M STARVED!

THE GIRL IS ILLYANA RASPUTIN, COLOSSUS' SISTER.

I'VE BEEN EXPLORING THE HOUSE. IT'S ALMOST EXACTLY AS I REMEMBER IT...

...THOUGH IT'S A BIT SPOOKY WITH JUST THE TWO OF US HERE.

MOIRA WILL BE BACK ON MONDAY.

THAT'S WONDERFUL! I LIKE DR. MACTAGGERT A LOT.

I'M SURE SHE'LL BE PLEASED TO HEAR THAT.

I LIKE YOU, TOO, PROFESSOR. HONEST.

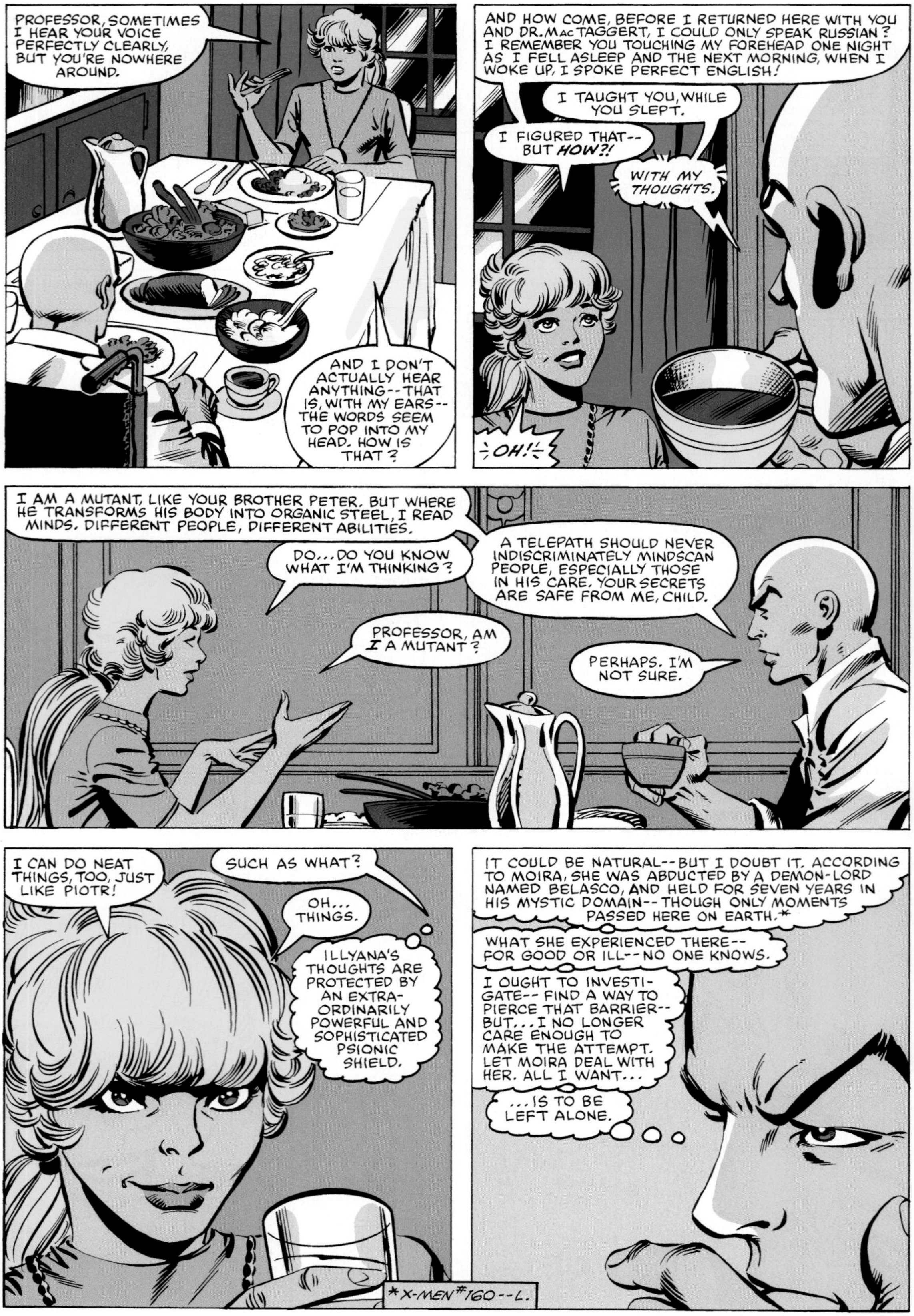
PROFESSOR, SOMETIMES I HEAR YOUR VOICE PERFECTLY CLEARLY, BUT YOU'RE NOWHERE AROUND.
AND I DON'T ACTUALLY HEAR ANYTHING--THAT IS, WITH MY EARS--THE WORDS SEEM TO POP INTO MY HEAD. HOW IS THAT?
AND HOW COME, BEFORE I RETURNED HERE WITH YOU AND DR. MacTAGGERT, I COULD ONLY SPEAK RUSSIAN? I REMEMBER YOU TOUCHING MY FOREHEAD ONE NIGHT AS I FELL ASLEEP AND THE NEXT MORNING, WHEN I WOKE UP, I SPOKE PERFECT ENGLISH!
I TAUGHT YOU, WHILE YOU SLEPT.
I FIGURED THAT--BUT HOW?!
WITH MY THOUGHTS.
OH!
I AM A MUTANT, LIKE YOUR BROTHER PETER. BUT WHERE HE TRANSFORMS HIS BODY INTO ORGANIC STEEL, I READ MINDS. DIFFERENT PEOPLE, DIFFERENT ABILITIES.
DO...DO YOU KNOW WHAT I'M THINKING?
A TELEPATH SHOULD NEVER INDISCRIMINATELY MINDSCAN PEOPLE, ESPECIALLY THOSE IN HIS CARE. YOUR SECRETS ARE SAFE FROM ME, CHILD.
PROFESSOR, AM I A MUTANT?
PERHAPS. I'M NOT SURE.
I CAN DO NEAT THINGS, TOO, JUST LIKE PIOTR!
SUCH AS WHAT?
OH... THINGS.
ILLYANA'S THOUGHTS ARE PROTECTED BY AN EXTRAORDINARILY POWERFUL AND SOPHISTICATED PSIONIC SHIELD.
IT COULD BE NATURAL--BUT I DOUBT IT. ACCORDING TO MOIRA, SHE WAS ABDUCTED BY A DEMON-LORD NAMED BELASCO, AND HELD FOR SEVEN YEARS IN HIS MYSTIC DOMAIN--THOUGH ONLY MOMENTS PASSED HERE ON EARTH.*
WHAT SHE EXPERIENCED THERE--FOR GOOD OR ILL--NO ONE KNOWS.
I OUGHT TO INVESTIGATE--FIND A WAY TO PIERCE THAT BARRIER--BUT...I NO LONGER CARE ENOUGH TO MAKE THE ATTEMPT. LET MOIRA DEAL WITH HER. ALL I WANT...
...IS TO BE LEFT ALONE.
*X-MEN #160--L.

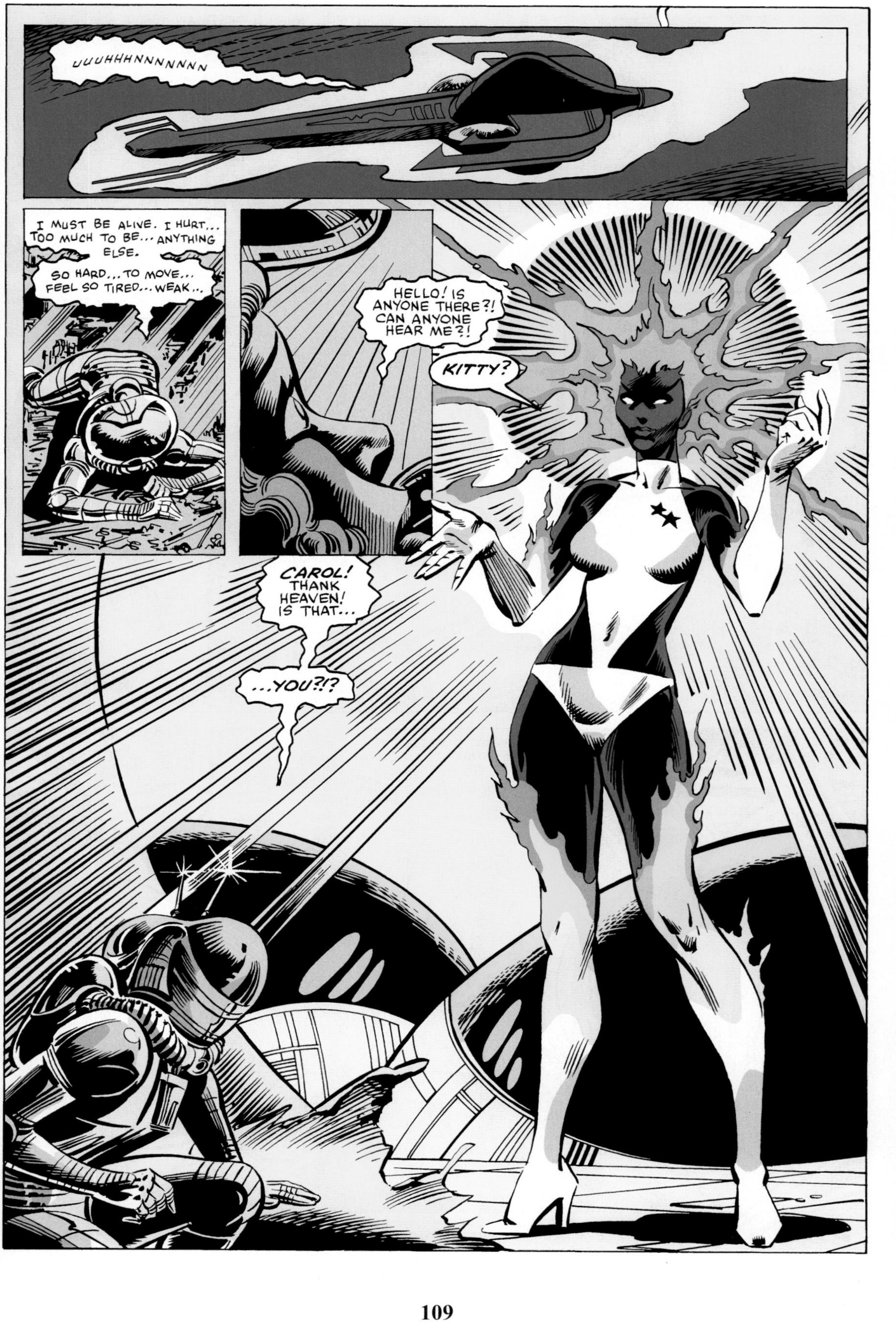
UUUHHHNNNNNNN
I MUST BE ALIVE. I HURT... TOO MUCH TO BE... ANYTHING ELSE.
SO HARD... TO MOVE... FEEL SO TIRED... WEAK...
HELLO! IS ANYONE THERE?! CAN ANYONE HEAR ME?!
KITTY?
CAROL! THANK HEAVEN! IS THAT...
...YOU?!?

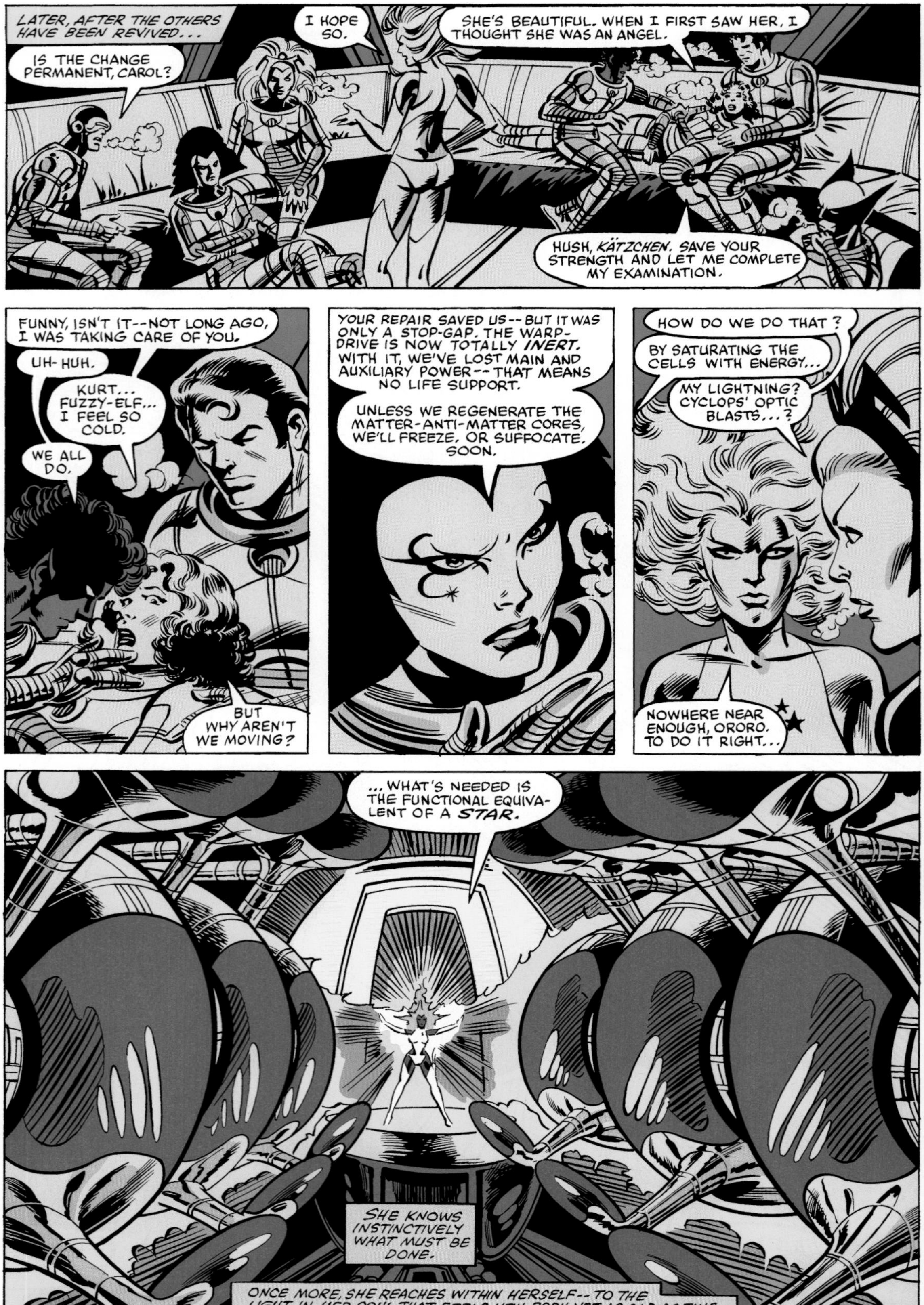
LATER, AFTER THE OTHERS HAVE BEEN REVIVED...
IS THE CHANGE PERMANENT, CAROL?
I HOPE SO.
SHE'S BEAUTIFUL. WHEN I FIRST SAW HER, I THOUGHT SHE WAS AN ANGEL.
HUSH, KÄTZCHEN. SAVE YOUR STRENGTH AND LET ME COMPLETE MY EXAMINATION.
FUNNY, ISN'T IT--NOT LONG AGO, I WAS TAKING CARE OF YOU.
UH-HUH.
KURT... FUZZY-ELF... I FEEL SO COLD.
WE ALL DO.
BUT WHY AREN'T WE MOVING?
YOUR REPAIR SAVED US--BUT IT WAS ONLY A STOP-GAP. THE WARP-DRIVE IS NOW TOTALLY INERT. WITH IT, WE'VE LOST MAIN AND AUXILIARY POWER--THAT MEANS NO LIFE SUPPORT.
UNLESS WE REGENERATE THE MATTER-ANTI-MATTER CORES, WE'LL FREEZE, OR SUFFOCATE. SOON.
HOW DO WE DO THAT?
BY SATURATING THE CELLS WITH ENERGY...
MY LIGHTNING? CYCLOPS' OPTIC BLASTS...?
NOWHERE NEAR ENOUGH, ORORO. TO DO IT RIGHT...
...WHAT'S NEEDED IS THE FUNCTIONAL EQUIVALENT OF A STAR.
SHE KNOWS INSTINCTIVELY WHAT MUST BE DONE.
ONCE MORE, SHE REACHES WITHIN HERSELF--TO THE LIGHT IN HER SOUL THAT FEELS NEW-BORN, YET AS OLD AS TIME...

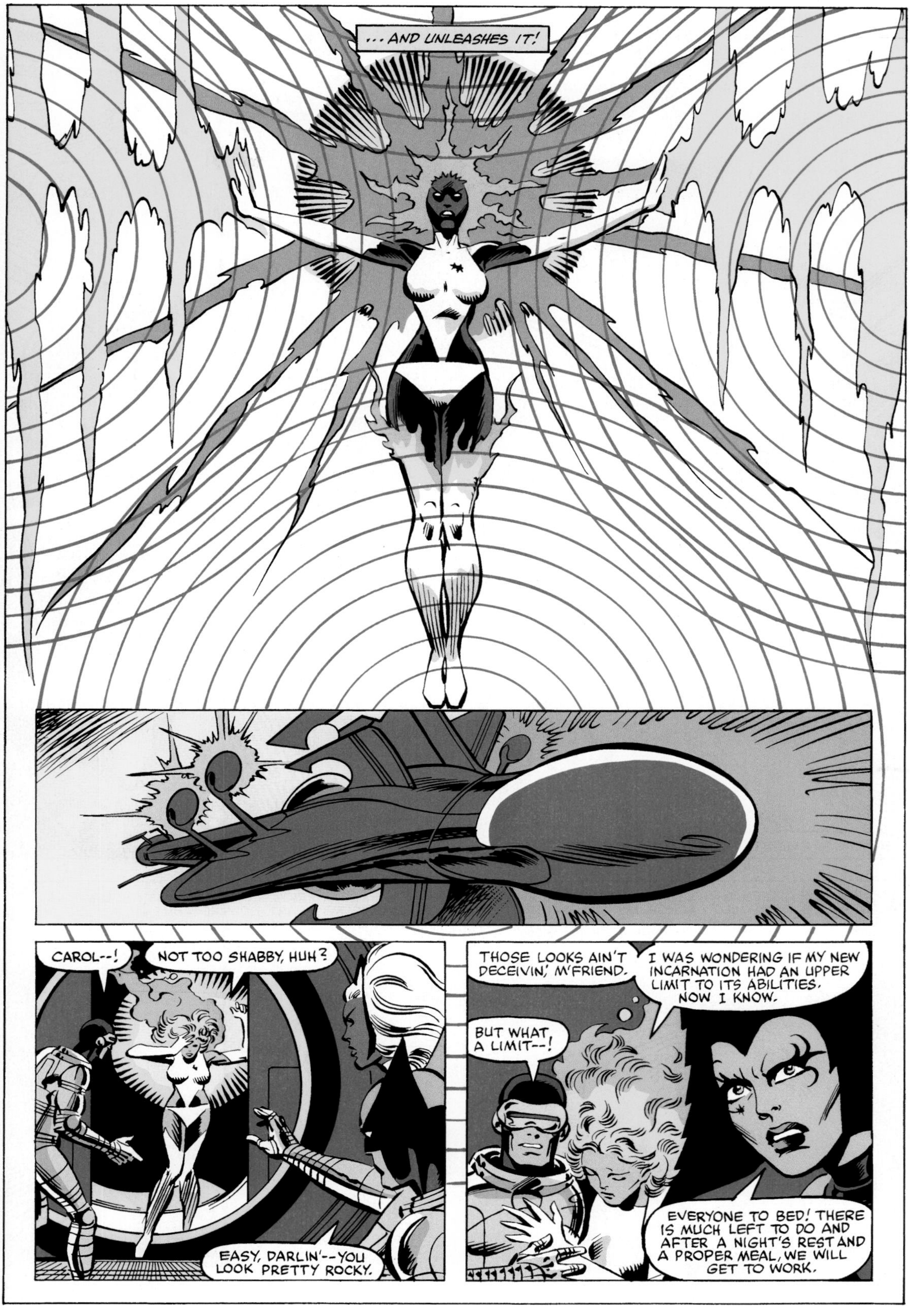
...AND UNLEASHES IT!
CAROL--!
NOT TOO SHABBY, HUH?
EASY, DARLIN'--YOU LOOK PRETTY ROCKY.
THOSE LOOKS AIN'T DECEIVIN,' M'FRIEND.
I WAS WONDERING IF MY NEW INCARNATION HAD AN UPPER LIMIT TO ITS ABILITIES. NOW I KNOW.
BUT WHAT A LIMIT--!
EVERYONE TO BED! THERE IS MUCH LEFT TO DO AND AFTER A NIGHT'S REST AND A PROPER MEAL, WE WILL GET TO WORK.

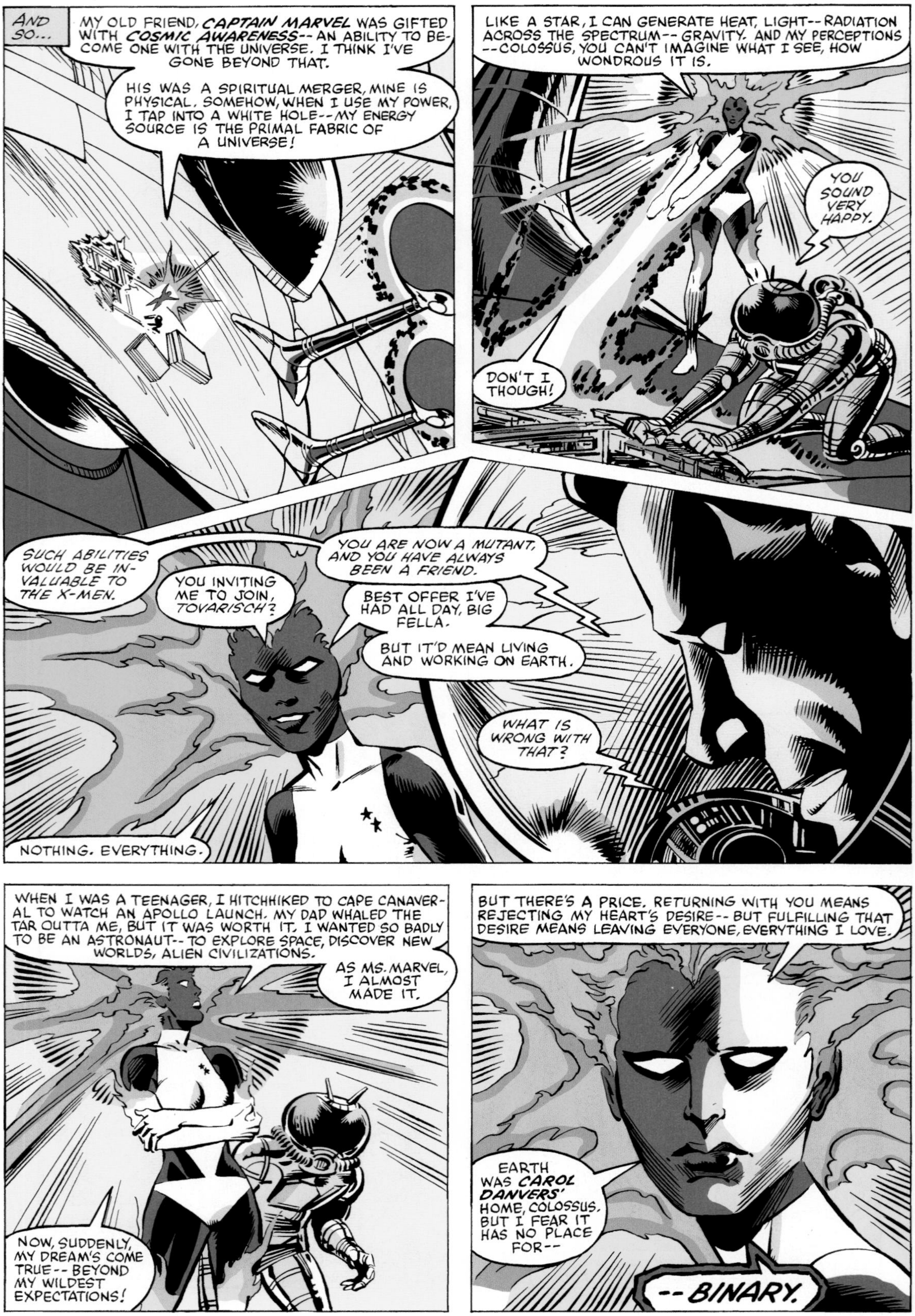
AND SO...
MY OLD FRIEND, CAPTAIN MARVEL WAS GIFTED WITH COSMIC AWARENESS-- AN ABILITY TO BECOME ONE WITH THE UNIVERSE. I THINK I'VE GONE BEYOND THAT.
HIS WAS A SPIRITUAL MERGER, MINE IS PHYSICAL. SOMEHOW, WHEN I USE MY POWER, I TAP INTO A WHITE HOLE--MY ENERGY SOURCE IS THE PRIMAL FABRIC OF A UNIVERSE!
LIKE A STAR, I CAN GENERATE HEAT, LIGHT--RADIATION ACROSS THE SPECTRUM-- GRAVITY. AND MY PERCEPTIONS --COLOSSUS, YOU CAN'T IMAGINE WHAT I SEE, HOW WONDROUS IT IS.
YOU SOUND VERY HAPPY.
DON'T I THOUGH!
SUCH ABILITIES WOULD BE INVALUABLE TO THE X-MEN.
YOU INVITING ME TO JOIN, TOVARISCH?
YOU ARE NOW A MUTANT, AND YOU HAVE ALWAYS BEEN A FRIEND.
BEST OFFER I'VE HAD ALL DAY, BIG FELLA.
BUT IT'D MEAN LIVING AND WORKING ON EARTH.
WHAT IS WRONG WITH THAT?
NOTHING. EVERYTHING.
WHEN I WAS A TEENAGER, I HITCHHIKED TO CAPE CANAVERAL TO WATCH AN APOLLO LAUNCH. MY DAD WHALED THE TAR OUTTA ME, BUT IT WAS WORTH IT. I WANTED SO BADLY TO BE AN ASTRONAUT-- TO EXPLORE SPACE, DISCOVER NEW WORLDS, ALIEN CIVILIZATIONS.
AS MS. MARVEL, I ALMOST MADE IT.
NOW, SUDDENLY, MY DREAM'S COME TRUE-- BEYOND MY WILDEST EXPECTATIONS!
BUT THERE'S A PRICE. RETURNING WITH YOU MEANS REJECTING MY HEART'S DESIRE-- BUT FULFILLING THAT DESIRE MEANS LEAVING EVERYONE, EVERYTHING I LOVE.
EARTH WAS CAROL DANVERS' HOME, COLOSSUS. BUT I FEAR IT HAS NO PLACE FOR--
--BINARY.

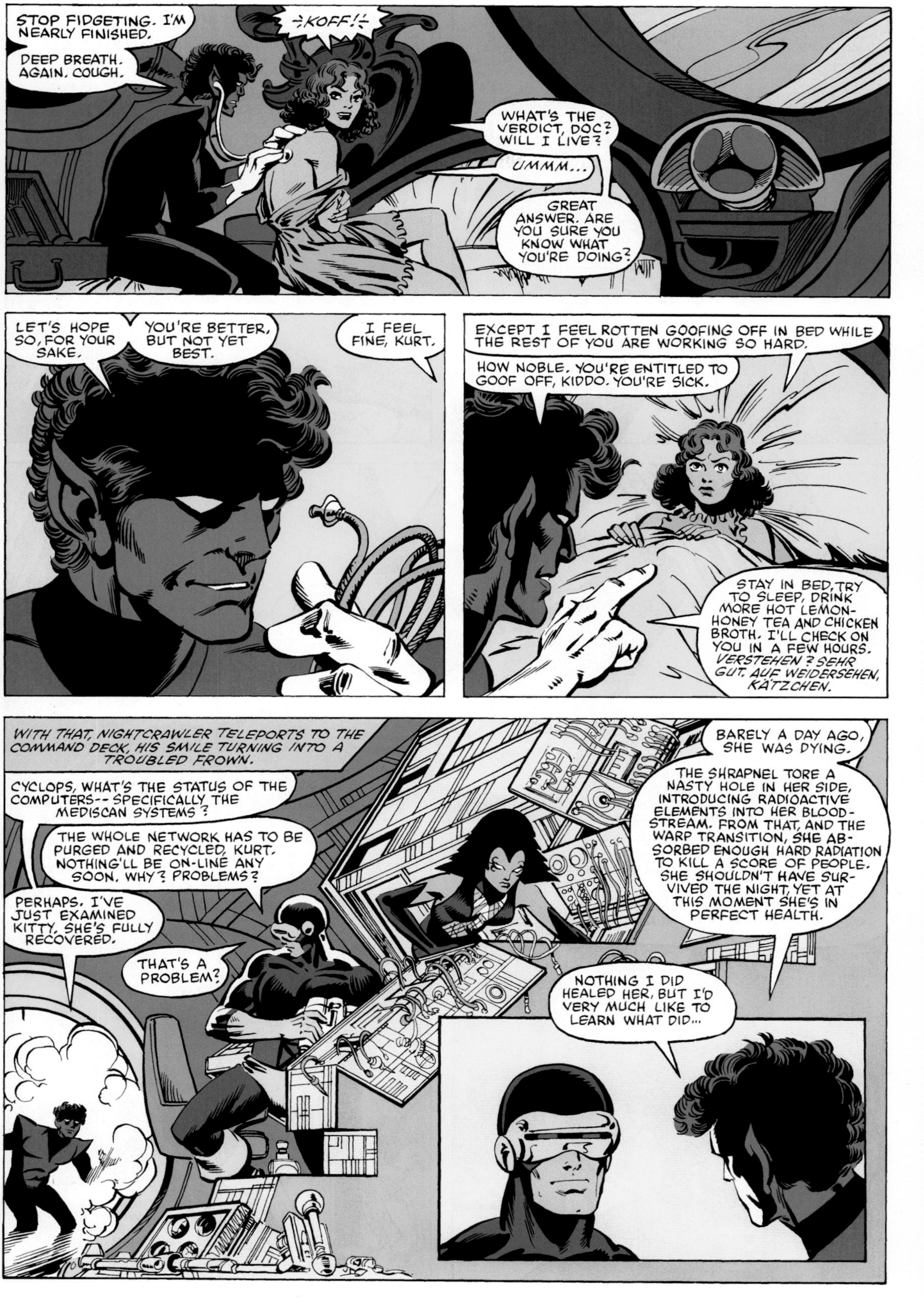
STOP FIDGETING. I'M NEARLY FINISHED.
DEEP BREATH. AGAIN. COUGH.
KOFF!
WHAT'S THE VERDICT, DOC? WILL I LIVE?
UMMM...
GREAT ANSWER. ARE YOU SURE YOU KNOW WHAT YOU'RE DOING?
LET'S HOPE SO, FOR YOUR SAKE.
YOU'RE BETTER, BUT NOT YET BEST.
I FEEL FINE, KURT.
EXCEPT I FEEL ROTTEN GOOFING OFF IN BED WHILE THE REST OF YOU ARE WORKING SO HARD.
HOW NOBLE. YOU'RE ENTITLED TO GOOF OFF, KIDDO. YOU'RE SICK.
STAY IN BED, TRY TO SLEEP, DRINK MORE HOT LEMON-HONEY TEA AND CHICKEN BROTH. I'LL CHECK ON YOU IN A FEW HOURS. VERSTEHEN? SEHR GUT. AUF WEIDERSEHEN, KÄTZCHEN.
WITH THAT, NIGHTCRAWLER TELEPORTS TO THE COMMAND DECK, HIS SMILE TURNING INTO A TROUBLED FROWN.
CYCLOPS, WHAT'S THE STATUS OF THE COMPUTERS-- SPECIFICALLY, THE MEDISCAN SYSTEMS?
THE WHOLE NETWORK HAS TO BE PURGED AND RECYCLED, KURT. NOTHING'LL BE ON-LINE ANY SOON. WHY? PROBLEMS?
PERHAPS. I'VE JUST EXAMINED KITTY. SHE'S FULLY RECOVERED.
THAT'S A PROBLEM?
BARELY A DAY AGO, SHE WAS DYING.
THE SHRAPNEL TORE A NASTY HOLE IN HER SIDE, INTRODUCING RADIOACTIVE ELEMENTS INTO HER BLOOD-STREAM. FROM THAT, AND THE WARP TRANSITION, SHE AB-SORBED ENOUGH HARD RADIATION TO KILL A SCORE OF PEOPLE. SHE SHOULDN'T HAVE SUR-VIVED THE NIGHT, YET AT THIS MOMENT SHE'S IN PERFECT HEALTH.
NOTHING I DID HEALED HER, BUT I'D VERY MUCH LIKE TO LEARN WHAT DID...

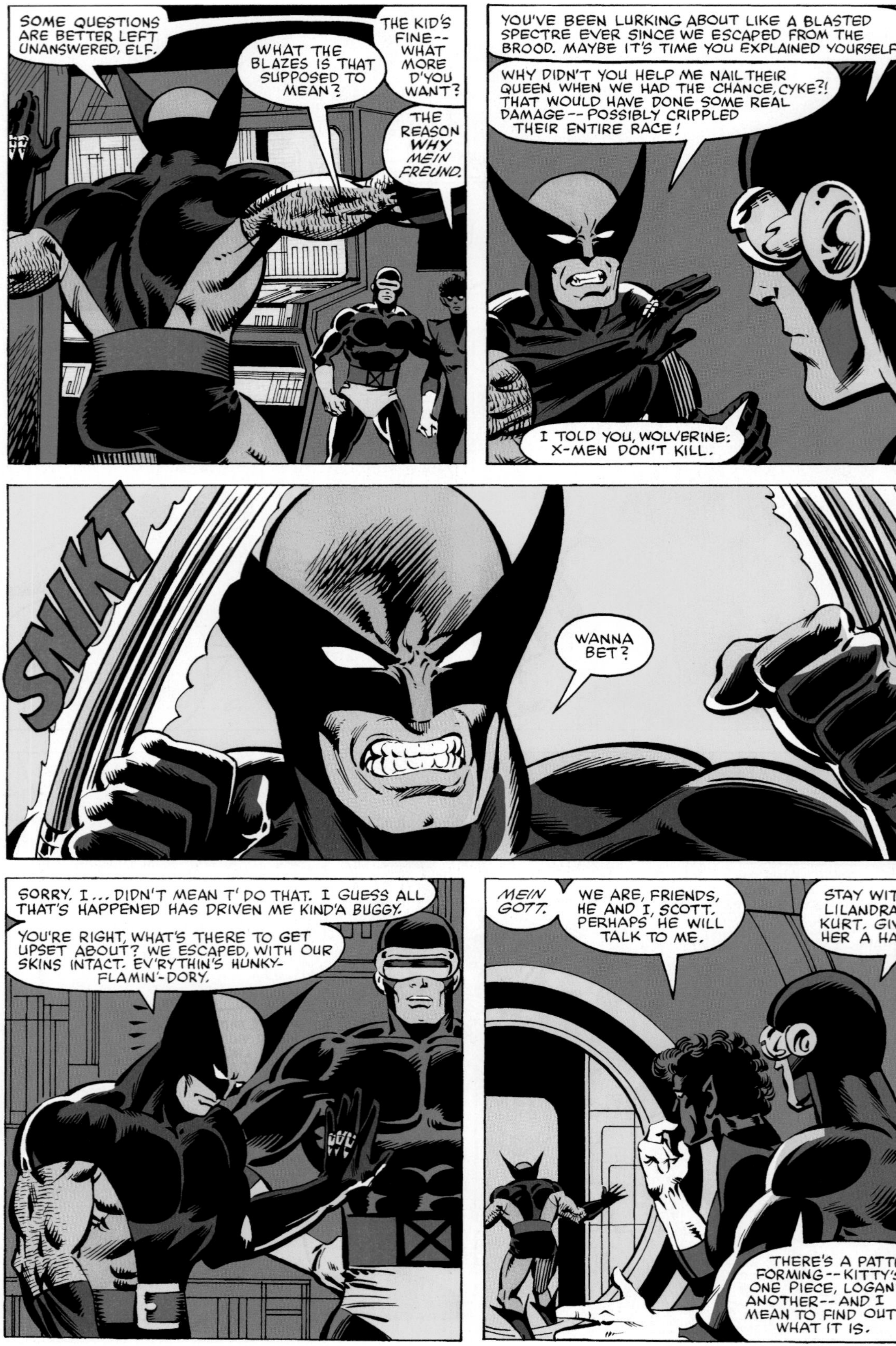
SOME QUESTIONS ARE BETTER LEFT UNANSWERED, ELF.
WHAT THE BLAZES IS THAT SUPPOSED TO MEAN?
THE KID'S FINE-- WHAT MORE D'YOU WANT?
THE REASON WHY MEIN FREUND.
YOU'VE BEEN LURKING ABOUT LIKE A BLASTED SPECTRE EVER SINCE WE ESCAPED FROM THE BROOD. MAYBE IT'S TIME YOU EXPLAINED YOURSELF.
WHY DIDN'T YOU HELP ME NAIL THEIR QUEEN WHEN WE HAD THE CHANCE, CYKE?! THAT WOULD HAVE DONE SOME REAL DAMAGE--POSSIBLY CRIPPLED THEIR ENTIRE RACE!
I TOLD YOU, WOLVERINE: X-MEN DON'T KILL.
SNIKT
WANNA BET?
SORRY. I... DIDN'T MEAN T' DO THAT. I GUESS ALL THAT'S HAPPENED HAS DRIVEN ME KIND'A BUGGY.
YOU'RE RIGHT, WHAT'S THERE TO GET UPSET ABOUT? WE ESCAPED, WITH OUR SKINS INTACT. EV'RYTHIN'S HUNKY-FLAMIN'-DORY.
MEIN GOTT.
WE ARE, FRIENDS, HE AND I, SCOTT. PERHAPS HE WILL TALK TO ME.
STAY WITH LILANDRA, KURT. GIVE HER A HAND.
THERE'S A PATTERN FORMING--KITTY'S ONE PIECE, LOGAN'S ANOTHER--AND I MEAN TO FIND OUT WHAT IT IS.

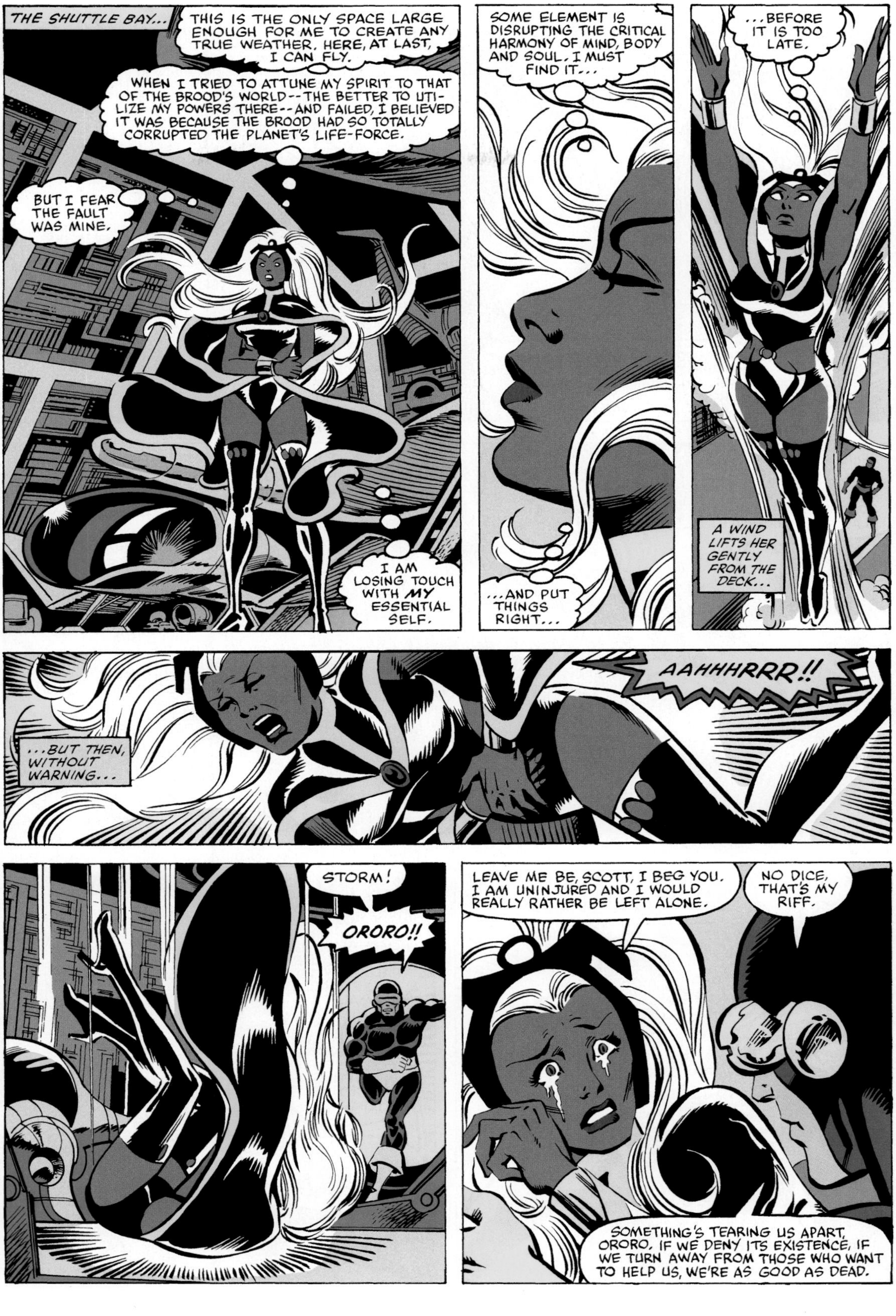
THE SHUTTLE BAY...
THIS IS THE ONLY SPACE LARGE ENOUGH FOR ME TO CREATE ANY TRUE WEATHER. HERE, AT LAST, I CAN FLY.
WHEN I TRIED TO ATTUNE MY SPIRIT TO THAT OF THE BROOD'S WORLD--THE BETTER TO UTILIZE MY POWERS THERE--AND FAILED, I BELIEVED IT WAS BECAUSE THE BROOD HAD SO TOTALLY CORRUPTED THE PLANET'S LIFE-FORCE.
BUT I FEAR THE FAULT WAS MINE.
I AM LOSING TOUCH WITH MY ESSENTIAL SELF.
SOME ELEMENT IS DISRUPTING THE CRITICAL HARMONY OF MIND, BODY AND SOUL. I MUST FIND IT...
...AND PUT THINGS RIGHT...
...BEFORE IT IS TOO LATE.
A WIND LIFTS HER GENTLY FROM THE DECK...
...BUT THEN, WITHOUT WARNING...
AAHHHRRR!!
STORM!
ORORO!!
LEAVE ME BE, SCOTT, I BEG YOU. I AM UNINJURED AND I WOULD REALLY RATHER BE LEFT ALONE.
NO DICE, THAT'S MY RIFF.
SOMETHING'S TEARING US APART, ORORO. IF WE DENY ITS EXISTENCE, IF WE TURN AWAY FROM THOSE WHO WANT TO HELP US, WE'RE AS GOOD AS DEAD.

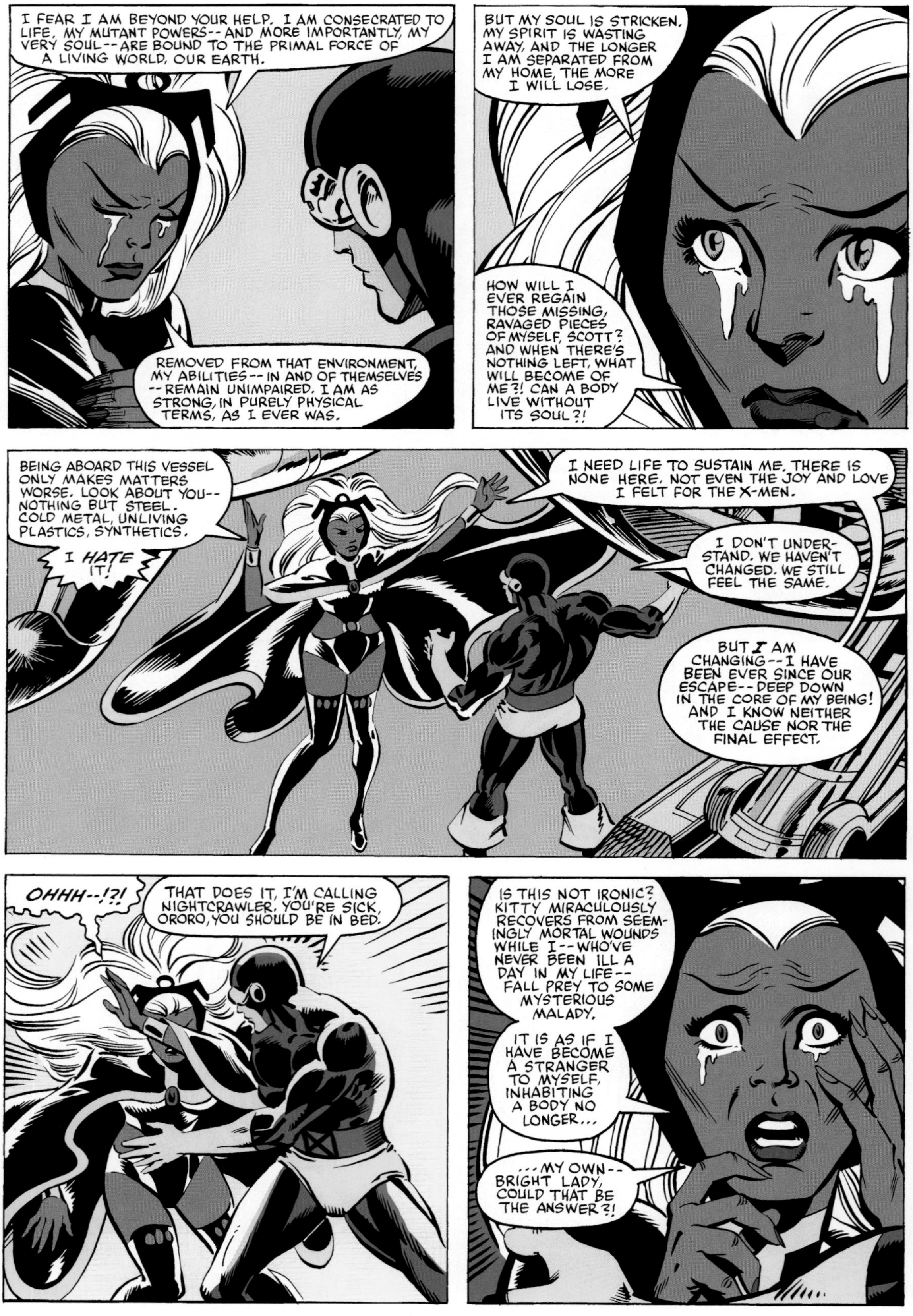
I FEAR I AM BEYOND YOUR HELP. I AM CONSECRATED TO LIFE. MY MUTANT POWERS-- AND MORE IMPORTANTLY, MY VERY SOUL--ARE BOUND TO THE PRIMAL FORCE OF A LIVING WORLD, OUR EARTH.
REMOVED FROM THAT ENVIRONMENT, MY ABILITIES-- IN AND OF THEMSELVES --REMAIN UNIMPAIRED. I AM AS STRONG, IN PURELY PHYSICAL TERMS, AS I EVER WAS.
BUT MY SOUL IS STRICKEN, MY SPIRIT IS WASTING AWAY, AND THE LONGER I AM SEPARATED FROM MY HOME, THE MORE I WILL LOSE.
HOW WILL I EVER REGAIN THOSE MISSING, RAVAGED PIECES OF MYSELF, SCOTT? AND WHEN THERE'S NOTHING LEFT, WHAT WILL BECOME OF ME?! CAN A BODY LIVE WITHOUT ITS SOUL?!
BEING ABOARD THIS VESSEL ONLY MAKES MATTERS WORSE. LOOK ABOUT YOU-- NOTHING BUT STEEL. COLD METAL, UNLIVING PLASTICS, SYNTHETICS.
I HATE IT!
I NEED LIFE TO SUSTAIN ME. THERE IS NONE HERE. NOT EVEN THE JOY AND LOVE I FELT FOR THE X-MEN.
I DON'T UNDERSTAND. WE HAVEN'T CHANGED. WE STILL FEEL THE SAME.
BUT I AM CHANGING-- I HAVE BEEN EVER SINCE OUR ESCAPE-- DEEP DOWN IN THE CORE OF MY BEING! AND I KNOW NEITHER THE CAUSE NOR THE FINAL EFFECT.
OHHH--!?!
THAT DOES IT, I'M CALLING NIGHTCRAWLER. YOU'RE SICK, ORORO, YOU SHOULD BE IN BED.
IS THIS NOT IRONIC? KITTY MIRACULOUSLY RECOVERS FROM SEEMINGLY MORTAL WOUNDS WHILE I--WHO'VE NEVER BEEN ILL A DAY IN MY LIFE-- FALL PREY TO SOME MYSTERIOUS MALADY.
IT IS AS IF I HAVE BECOME A STRANGER TO MYSELF, INHABITING A BODY NO LONGER...
...MY OWN-- BRIGHT LADY, COULD THAT BE THE ANSWER?!

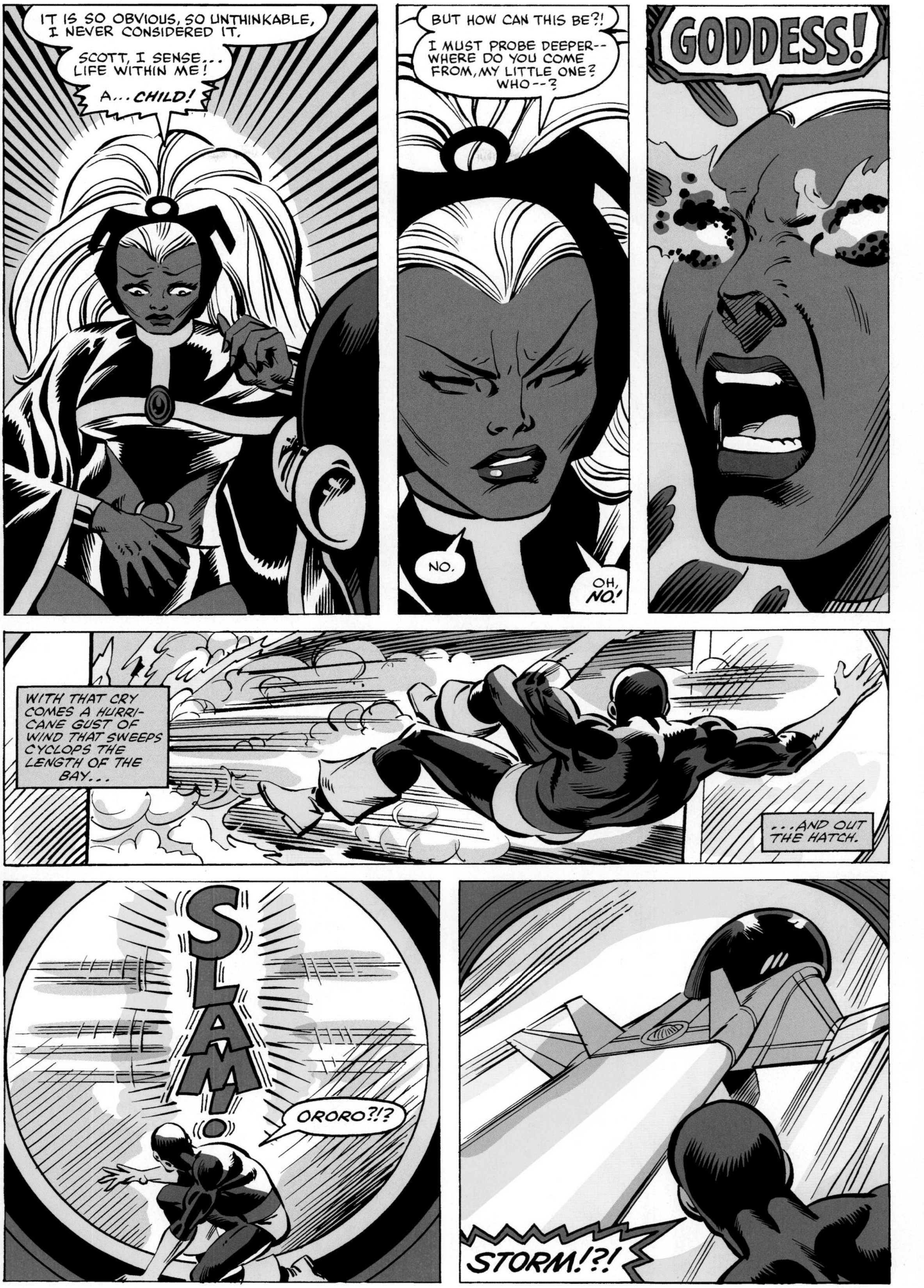
IT IS SO OBVIOUS, SO UNTHINKABLE, I NEVER CONSIDERED IT.
SCOTT, I SENSE... LIFE WITHIN ME!
A... CHILD!
BUT HOW CAN THIS BE?!
I MUST PROBE DEEPER-- WHERE DO YOU COME FROM, MY LITTLE ONE? WHO--?
NO.
OH, NO!
GODDESS!
WITH THAT CRY COMES A HURRICANE GUST OF WIND THAT SWEEPS CYCLOPS THE LENGTH OF THE BAY...
...AND OUT THE HATCH.
SLAM!
ORORO?!?
STORM!?!

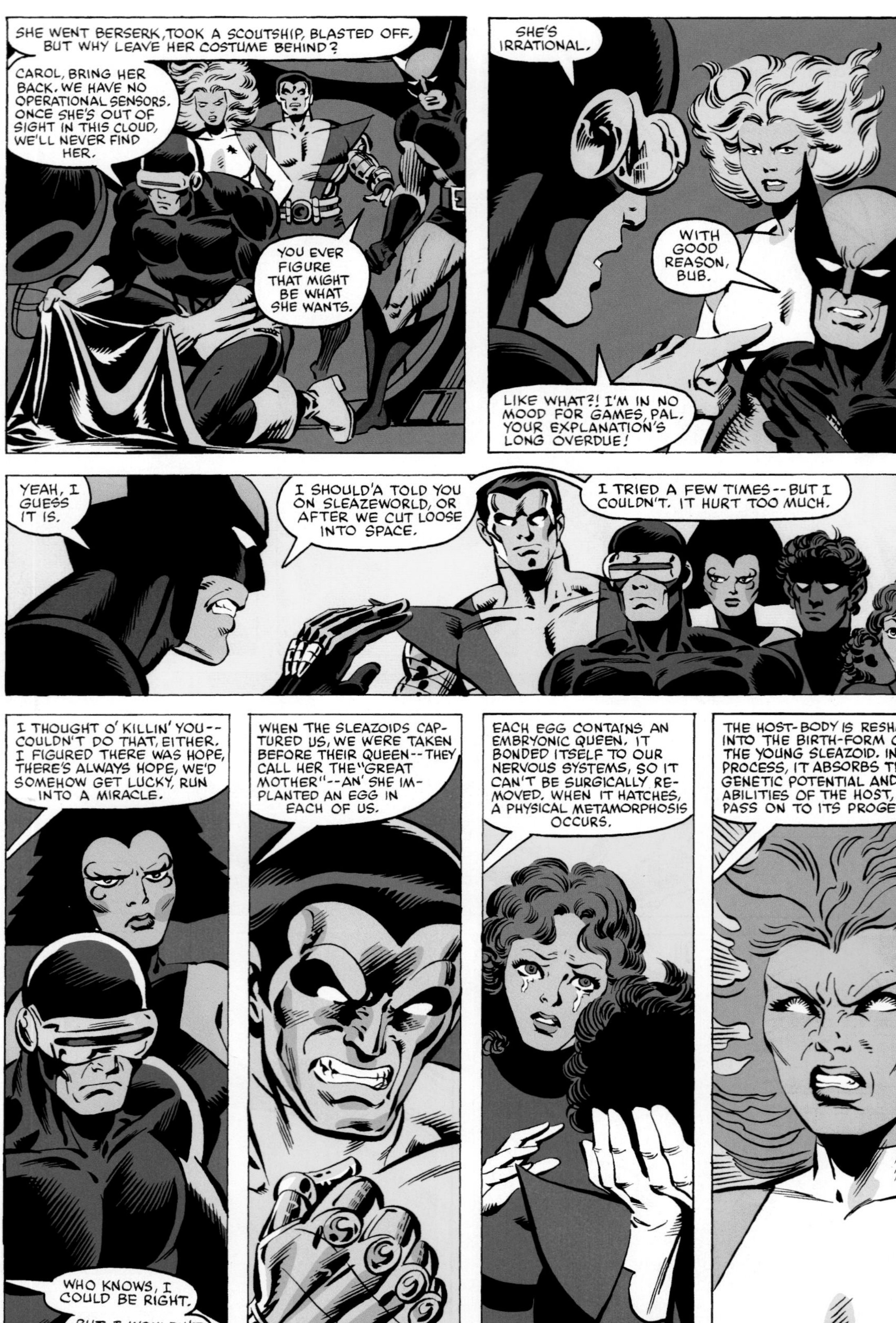
SHE WENT BERSERK, TOOK A SCOUTSHIP, BLASTED OFF. BUT WHY LEAVE HER COSTUME BEHIND?
CAROL, BRING HER BACK. WE HAVE NO OPERATIONAL SENSORS. ONCE SHE'S OUT OF SIGHT IN THIS CLOUD, WE'LL NEVER FIND HER.
YOU EVER FIGURE THAT MIGHT BE WHAT SHE WANTS.
SHE'S IRRATIONAL.
WITH GOOD REASON, BUB.
LIKE WHAT?! I'M IN NO MOOD FOR GAMES, PAL. YOUR EXPLANATION'S LONG OVERDUE!
YEAH, I GUESS IT IS.
I SHOULD'A TOLD YOU ON SLEAZEWORLD, OR AFTER WE CUT LOOSE INTO SPACE.
I TRIED A FEW TIMES--BUT I COULDN'T. IT HURT TOO MUCH.
I THOUGHT O' KILLIN' YOU--COULDN'T DO THAT, EITHER. I FIGURED THERE WAS HOPE, THERE'S ALWAYS HOPE, WE'D SOMEHOW GET LUCKY, RUN INTO A MIRACLE.
WHO KNOWS, I COULD BE RIGHT.
BUT I WOULDN'T COUNT ON IT.
WHEN THE SLEAZOIDS CAPTURED US, WE WERE TAKEN BEFORE THEIR QUEEN--THEY CALL HER THE "GREAT MOTHER"--AN' SHE IMPLANTED AN EGG IN EACH OF US.
EACH EGG CONTAINS AN EMBRYONIC QUEEN. IT BONDED ITSELF TO OUR NERVOUS SYSTEMS, SO IT CAN'T BE SURGICALLY REMOVED. WHEN IT HATCHES, A PHYSICAL METAMORPHOSIS OCCURS.
THE HOST-BODY IS RESHAPED INTO THE BIRTH-FORM OF THE YOUNG SLEAZOID. IN THE PROCESS, IT ABSORBS THE GENETIC POTENTIAL AND ABILITIES OF THE HOST, TO PASS ON TO ITS PROGENY.

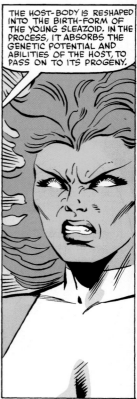

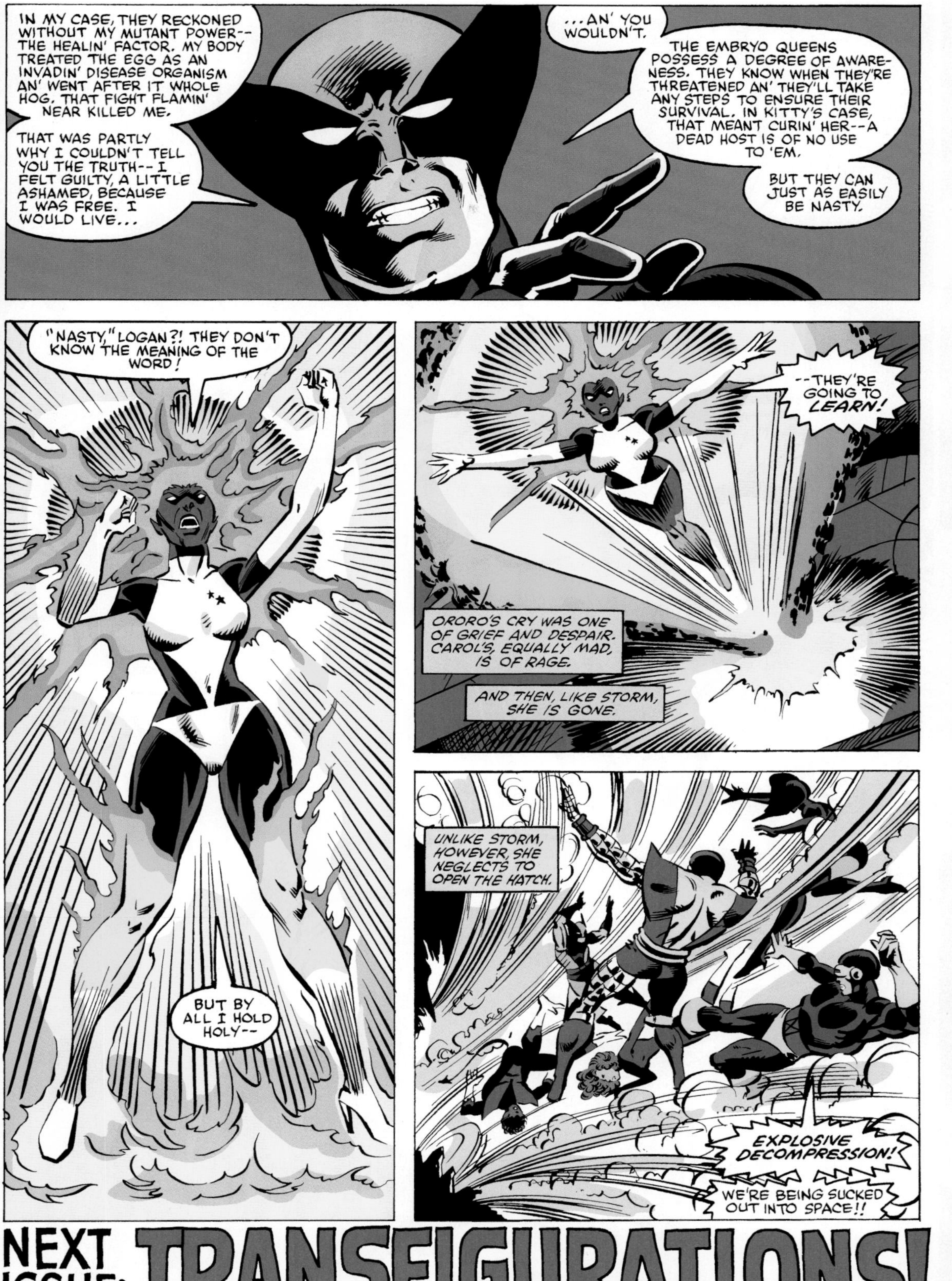

IN MY CASE, THEY RECKONED WITHOUT MY MUTANT POWER-- THE HEALIN' FACTOR. MY BODY TREATED THE EGG AS AN INVADIN' DISEASE ORGANISM AN' WENT AFTER IT WHOLE HOG. THAT FIGHT FLAMIN' NEAR KILLED ME.
THAT WAS PARTLY WHY I COULDN'T TELL YOU THE TRUTH-- I FELT GUILTY, A LITTLE ASHAMED, BECAUSE I WAS FREE. I WOULD LIVE...
...AN' YOU WOULDN'T.
THE EMBRYO QUEENS POSSESS A DEGREE OF AWARENESS. THEY KNOW WHEN THEY'RE THREATENED AN' THEY'LL TAKE ANY STEPS TO ENSURE THEIR SURVIVAL. IN KITTY'S CASE, THAT MEANT CURIN' HER--A DEAD HOST IS OF NO USE TO 'EM.
BUT THEY CAN JUST AS EASILY BE NASTY.
"NASTY," LOGAN?! THEY DON'T KNOW THE MEANING OF THE WORD!
BUT BY ALL I HOLD HOLY--
--THEY'RE GOING TO LEARN!
ORORO'S CRY WAS ONE OF GRIEF AND DESPAIR. CAROL'S, EQUALLY MAD, IS OF RAGE.
AND THEN, LIKE STORM, SHE IS GONE.
UNLIKE STORM, HOWEVER, SHE NEGLECTS TO OPEN THE HATCH.
EXPLOSIVE DECOMPRESSION!
WE'RE BEING SUCKED OUT INTO SPACE!!

NEXT ISSUE: TRANSFIGURATIONS!

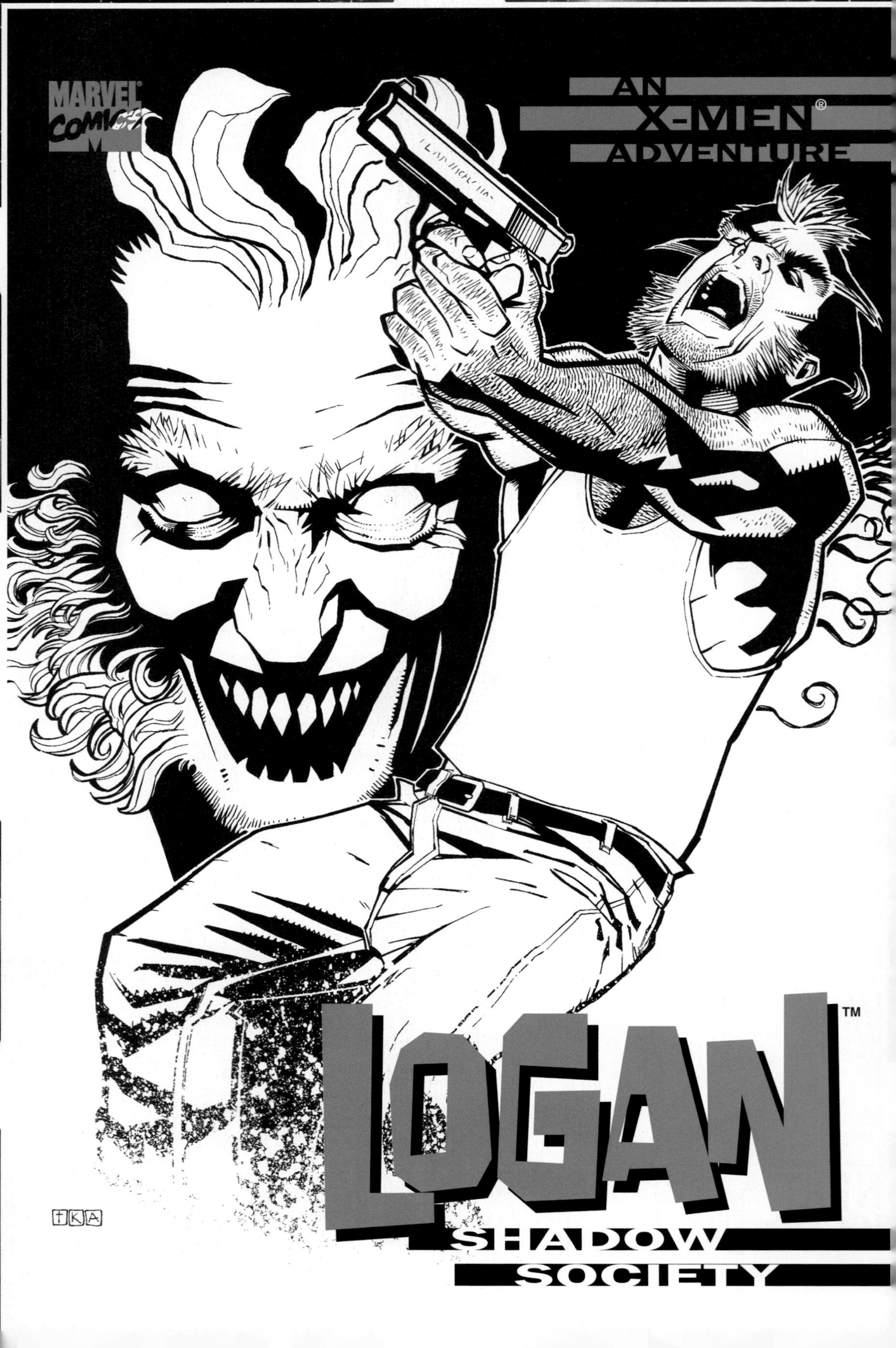
MARVEL COMICS
AN X-MEN® ADVENTURE
LOGAN™
SHADOW SOCIETY
TKA

STAN LEE presents

LOGAN

SHADOW SOCIETY

HOWARD MACKIE
plot

MARK JASON
script

TOMM COKER
& KEITH AIKEN
with OCTAVIO CARIELLO
artists

RICHARD STARKINGS
and COMICRAFT/EM
lettering

COMICRAFT'S
JOHN G. ROSHELL
book design

CHRISTIE SCHEELE
color art

MALIBU'S HUES
color separations

MARK BERNARDO
& MARK POWERS
editors

DAN HOSEK
assistant editor

BOB HARRAS
editor in chief

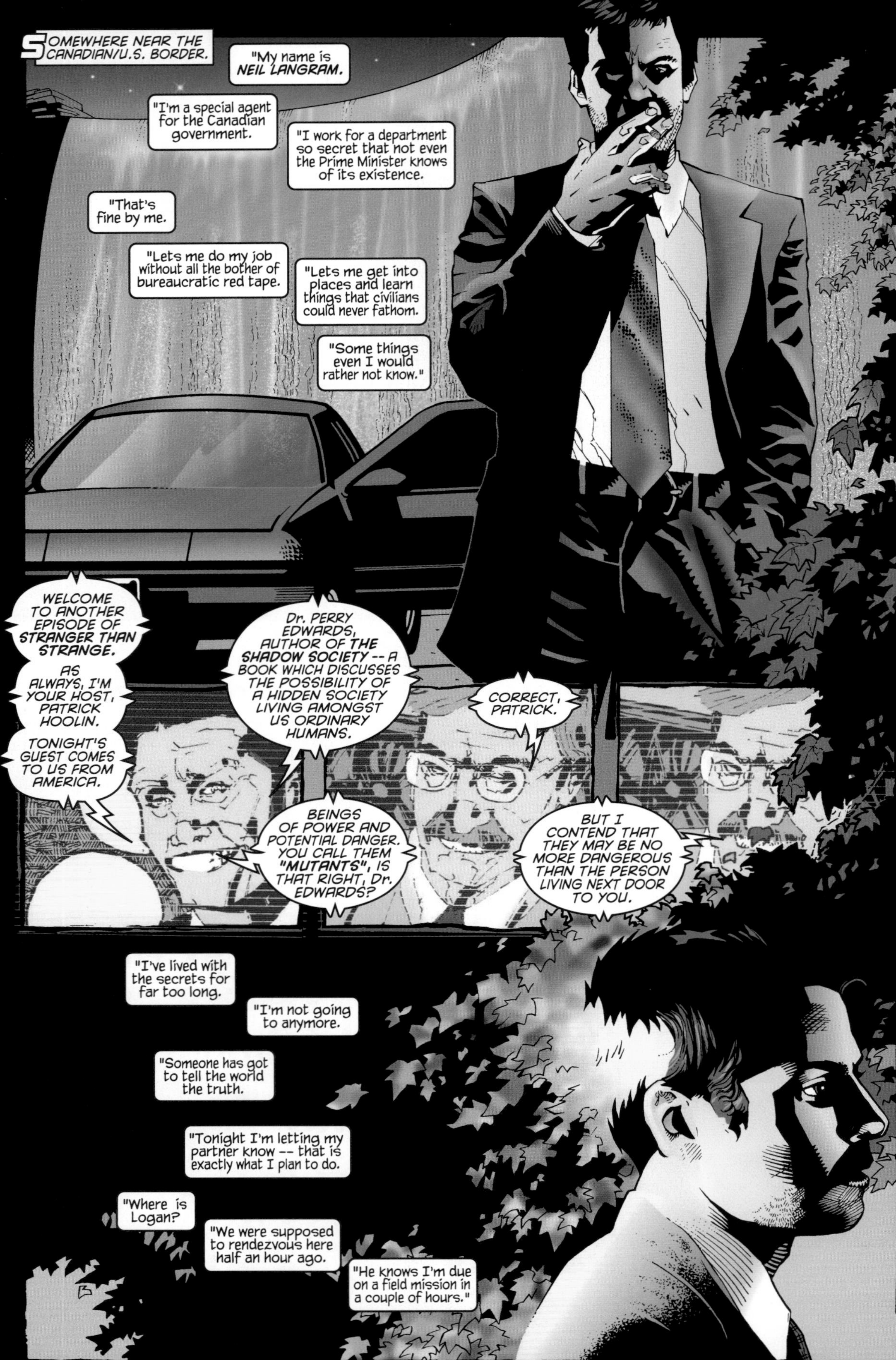
SOMEWHERE NEAR THE CANADIAN/U.S. BORDER.
"My name is NEIL LANGRAM.
"I'm a special agent for the Canadian government.
"I work for a department so secret that not even the Prime Minister knows of its existence.
"That's fine by me.
"Lets me do my job without all the bother of bureaucratic red tape.
"Lets me get into places and learn things that civilians could never fathom.
"Some things even I would rather not know."
WELCOME TO ANOTHER EPISODE OF STRANGER THAN STRANGE.
AS ALWAYS, I'M YOUR HOST, PATRICK HOOLIN.
TONIGHT'S GUEST COMES TO US FROM AMERICA.
Dr. PERRY EDWARDS, AUTHOR OF THE SHADOW SOCIETY -- A BOOK WHICH DISCUSSES THE POSSIBILITY OF A HIDDEN SOCIETY LIVING AMONGST US ORDINARY HUMANS.
BEINGS OF POWER AND POTENTIAL DANGER. YOU CALL THEM "MUTANTS", IS THAT RIGHT, Dr. EDWARDS?
CORRECT, PATRICK.
BUT I CONTEND THAT THEY MAY BE NO MORE DANGEROUS THAN THE PERSON LIVING NEXT DOOR TO YOU.
"I've lived with the secrets for far too long.
"I'm not going to anymore.
"Someone has got to tell the world the truth.
"Tonight I'm letting my partner know -- that is exactly what I plan to do.
"Where is Logan?
"We were supposed to rendezvous here half an hour ago.
"He knows I'm due on a field mission in a couple of hours."

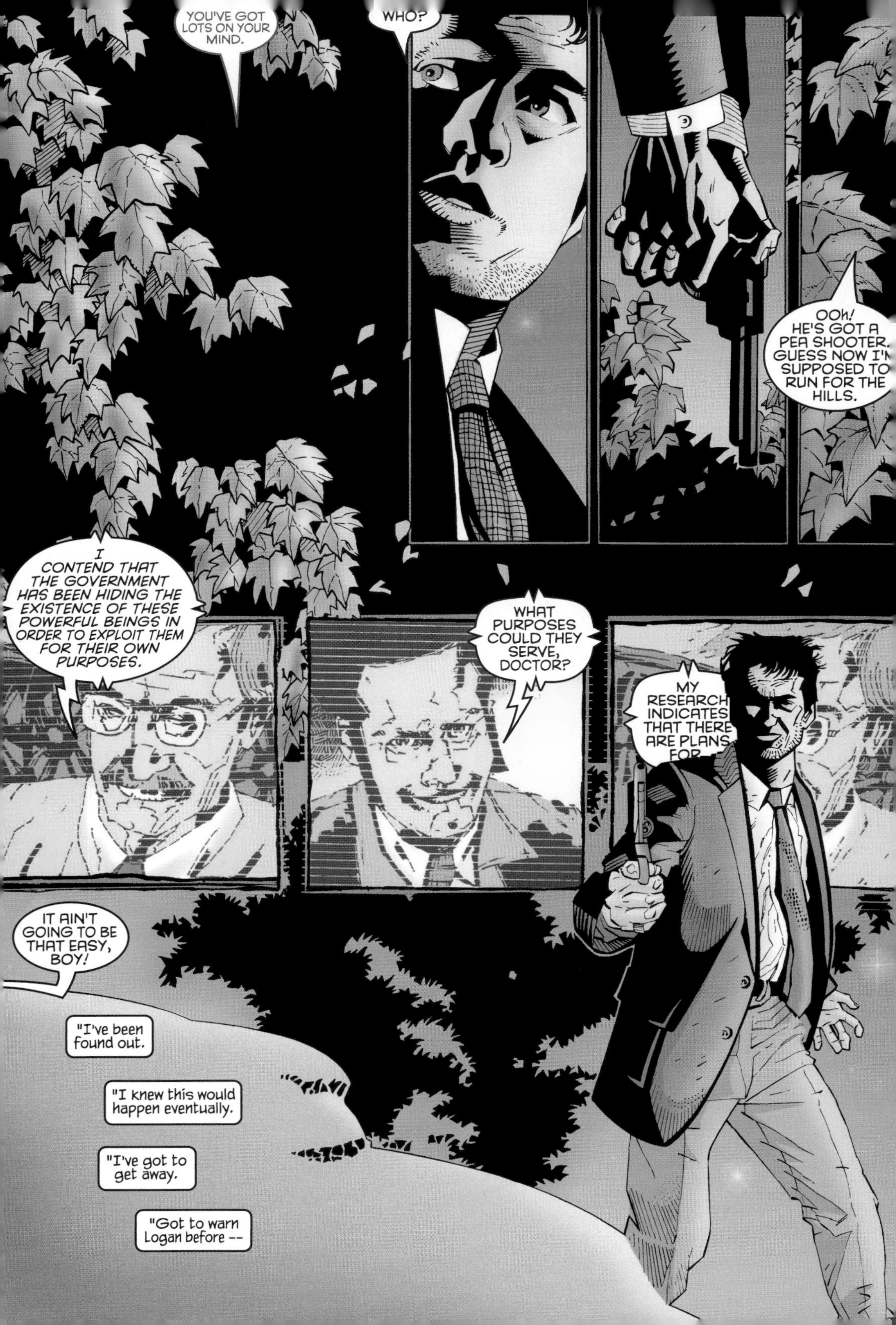
YOU'VE GOT LOTS ON YOUR MIND.
WHO?
OOh! HE'S GOT A PEA SHOOTER. GUESS NOW I'M SUPPOSED TO RUN FOR THE HILLS.
I CONTEND THAT THE GOVERNMENT HAS BEEN HIDING THE EXISTENCE OF THESE POWERFUL BEINGS IN ORDER TO EXPLOIT THEM FOR THEIR OWN PURPOSES.
WHAT PURPOSES COULD THEY SERVE, DOCTOR?
MY RESEARCH INDICATES THAT THERE ARE PLANS FOR--
IT AIN'T GOING TO BE THAT EASY, BOY!
"I've been found out.
"I knew this would happen eventually.
"I've got to get away.
"Got to warn Logan before --

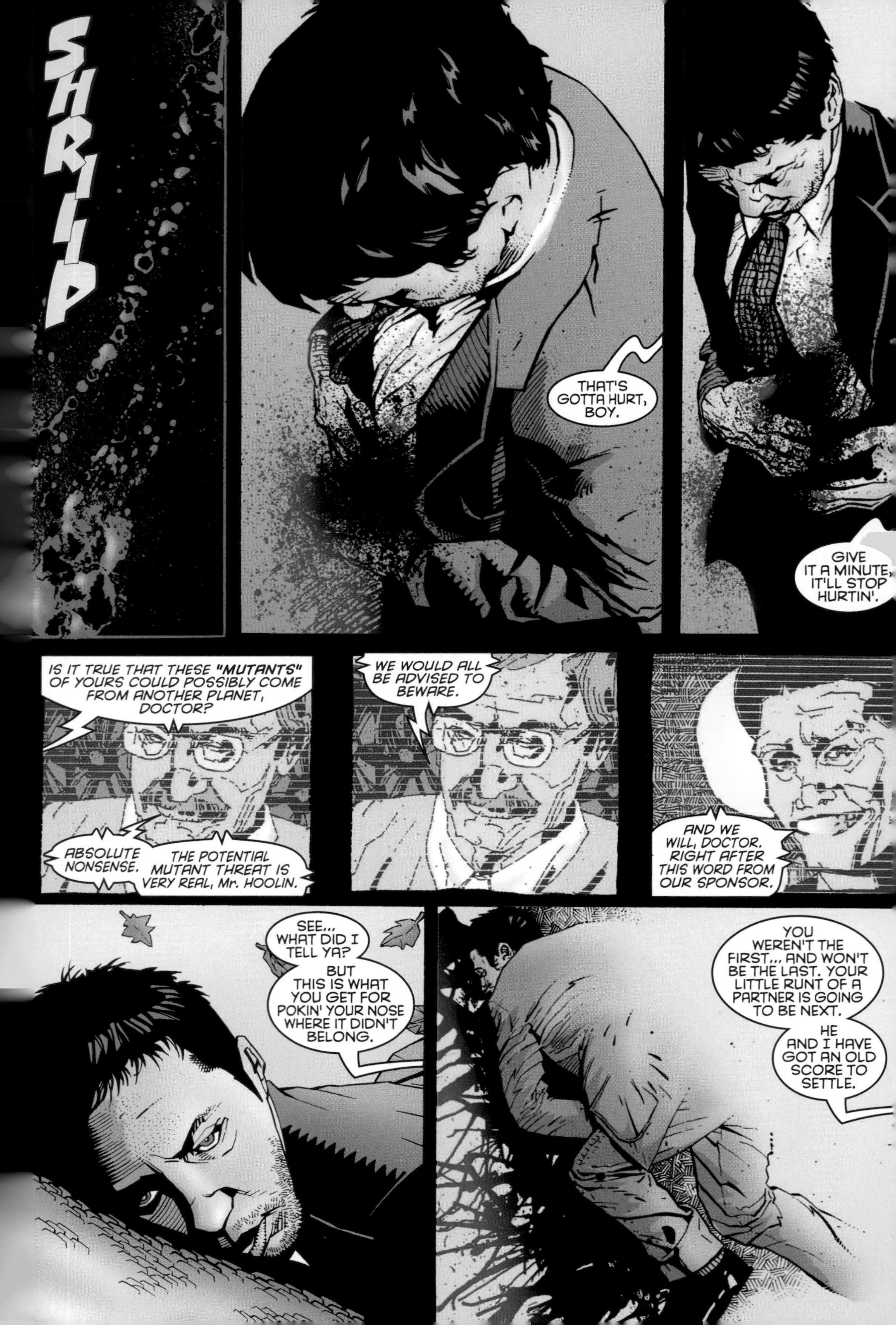
SHRIIIP
THAT'S GOTTA HURT, BOY.
GIVE IT A MINUTE, IT'LL STOP HURTIN'.
IS IT TRUE THAT THESE "MUTANTS" OF YOURS COULD POSSIBLY COME FROM ANOTHER PLANET, DOCTOR?
ABSOLUTE NONSENSE.
THE POTENTIAL MUTANT THREAT IS VERY REAL, Mr. HOOLIN.
WE WOULD ALL BE ADVISED TO BEWARE.
AND WE WILL, DOCTOR. RIGHT AFTER THIS WORD FROM OUR SPONSOR.
SEE... WHAT DID I TELL YA?
BUT THIS IS WHAT YOU GET FOR POKIN' YOUR NOSE WHERE IT DIDN'T BELONG.
YOU WEREN'T THE FIRST... AND WON'T BE THE LAST. YOUR LITTLE RUNT OF A PARTNER IS GOING TO BE NEXT.
HE AND I HAVE GOT AN OLD SCORE TO SETTLE.

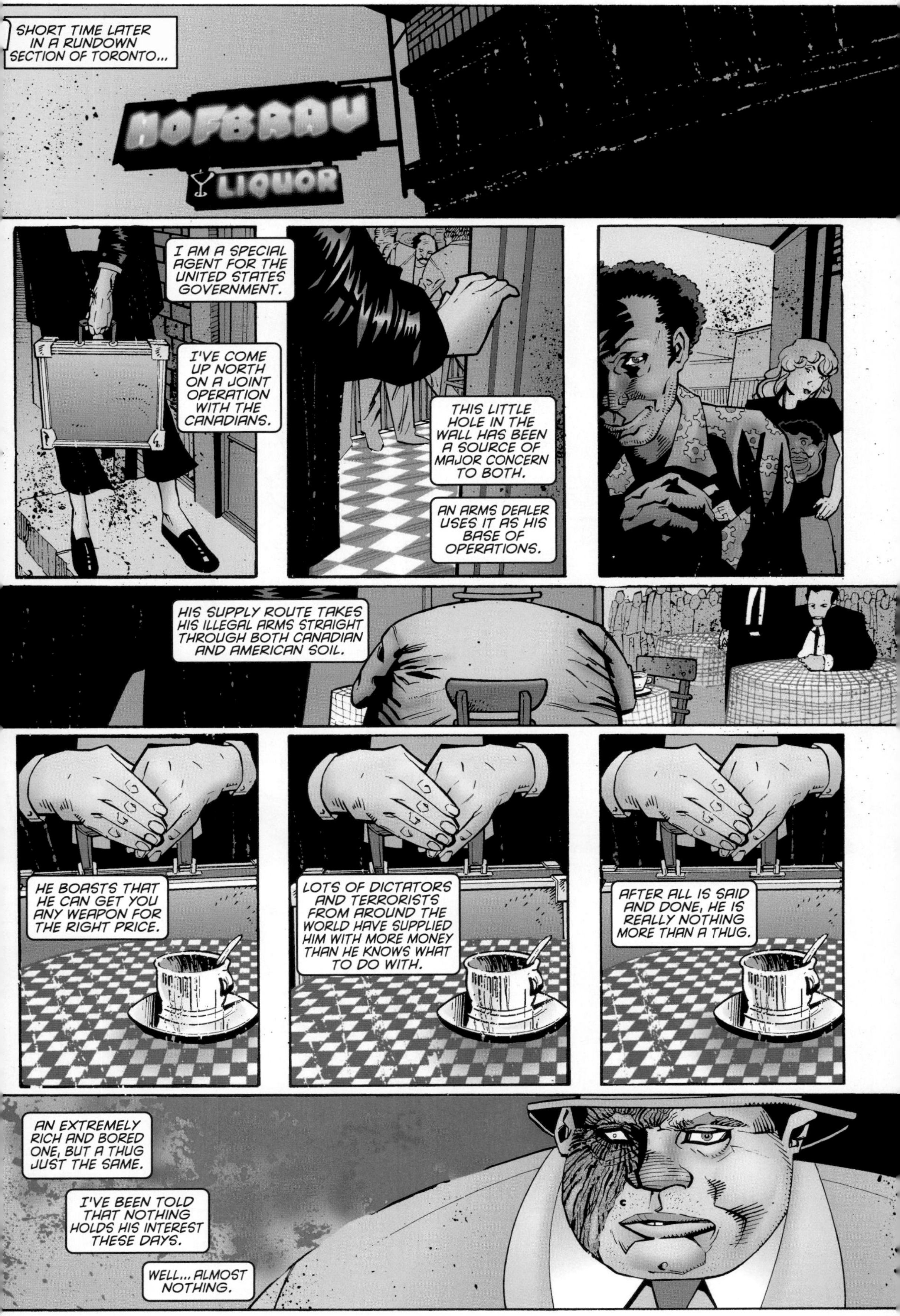
SHORT TIME LATER IN A RUNDOWN SECTION OF TORONTO...
HOFBRAU
LIQUOR
I AM A SPECIAL AGENT FOR THE UNITED STATES GOVERNMENT.
I'VE COME UP NORTH ON A JOINT OPERATION WITH THE CANADIANS.
THIS LITTLE HOLE IN THE WALL HAS BEEN A SOURCE OF MAJOR CONCERN TO BOTH.
AN ARMS DEALER USES IT AS HIS BASE OF OPERATIONS.
HIS SUPPLY ROUTE TAKES HIS ILLEGAL ARMS STRAIGHT THROUGH BOTH CANADIAN AND AMERICAN SOIL.
HE BOASTS THAT HE CAN GET YOU ANY WEAPON FOR THE RIGHT PRICE.
LOTS OF DICTATORS AND TERRORISTS FROM AROUND THE WORLD HAVE SUPPLIED HIM WITH MORE MONEY THAN HE KNOWS WHAT TO DO WITH.
AFTER ALL IS SAID AND DONE, HE IS REALLY NOTHING MORE THAN A THUG.
AN EXTREMELY RICH AND BORED ONE, BUT A THUG JUST THE SAME.
I'VE BEEN TOLD THAT NOTHING HOLDS HIS INTEREST THESE DAYS.
WELL... ALMOST NOTHING.

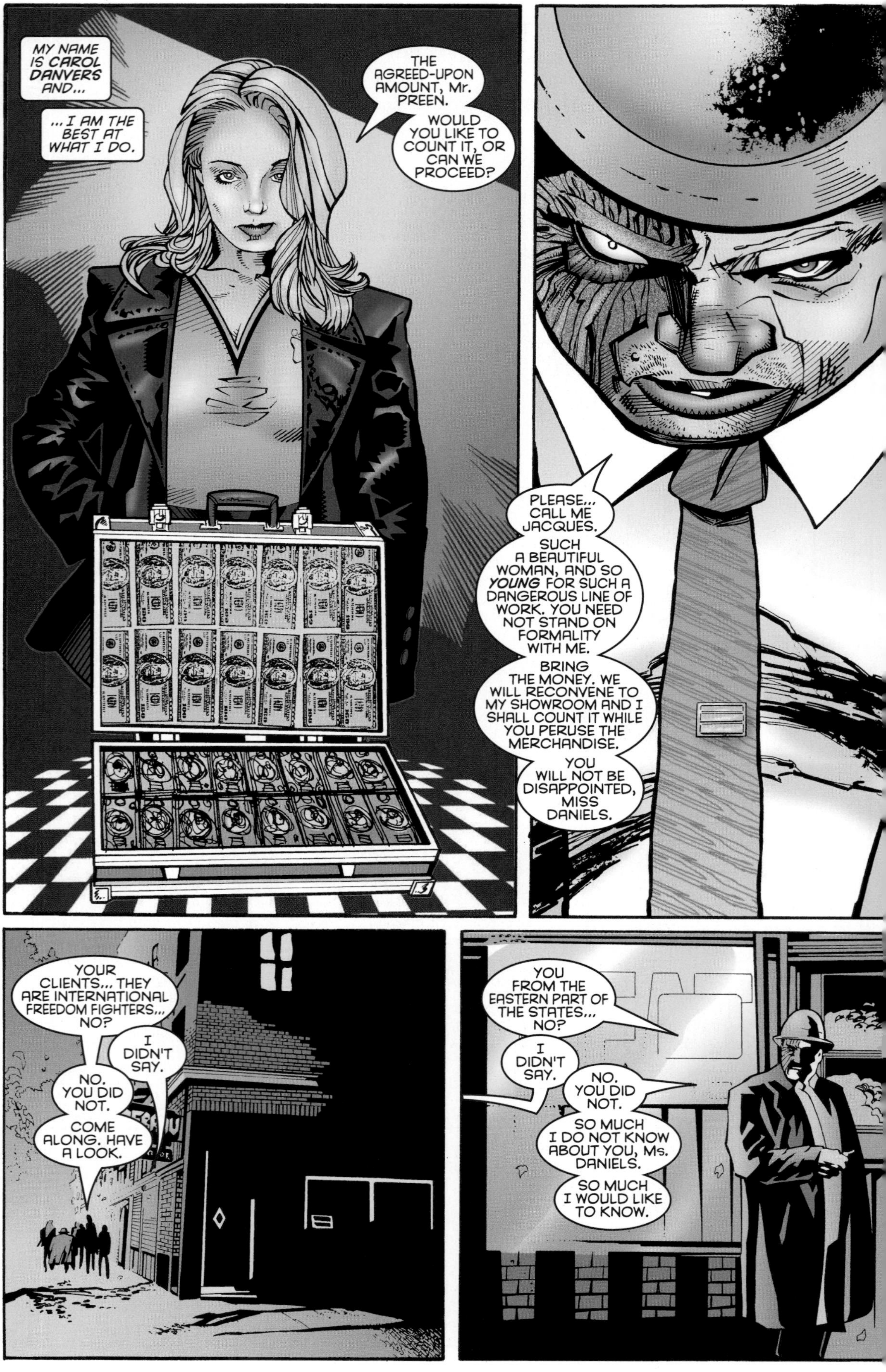

MY NAME IS CAROL DANVERS AND...
...I AM THE BEST AT WHAT I DO.
THE AGREED-UPON AMOUNT, Mr. PREEN.
WOULD YOU LIKE TO COUNT IT, OR CAN WE PROCEED?
PLEASE... CALL ME JACQUES.
SUCH A BEAUTIFUL WOMAN, AND SO YOUNG FOR SUCH A DANGEROUS LINE OF WORK. YOU NEED NOT STAND ON FORMALITY WITH ME.
BRING THE MONEY. WE WILL RECONVENE TO MY SHOWROOM AND I SHALL COUNT IT WHILE YOU PERUSE THE MERCHANDISE.
YOU WILL NOT BE DISAPPOINTED, MISS DANIELS.
YOUR CLIENTS... THEY ARE INTERNATIONAL FREEDOM FIGHTERS... NO?
I DIDN'T SAY.
NO. YOU DID NOT.
COME ALONG. HAVE A LOOK.
YOU FROM THE EASTERN PART OF THE STATES... NO?
I DIDN'T SAY.
NO. YOU DID NOT.
SO MUCH I DO NOT KNOW ABOUT YOU, Ms. DANIELS.
SO MUCH I WOULD LIKE TO KNOW.

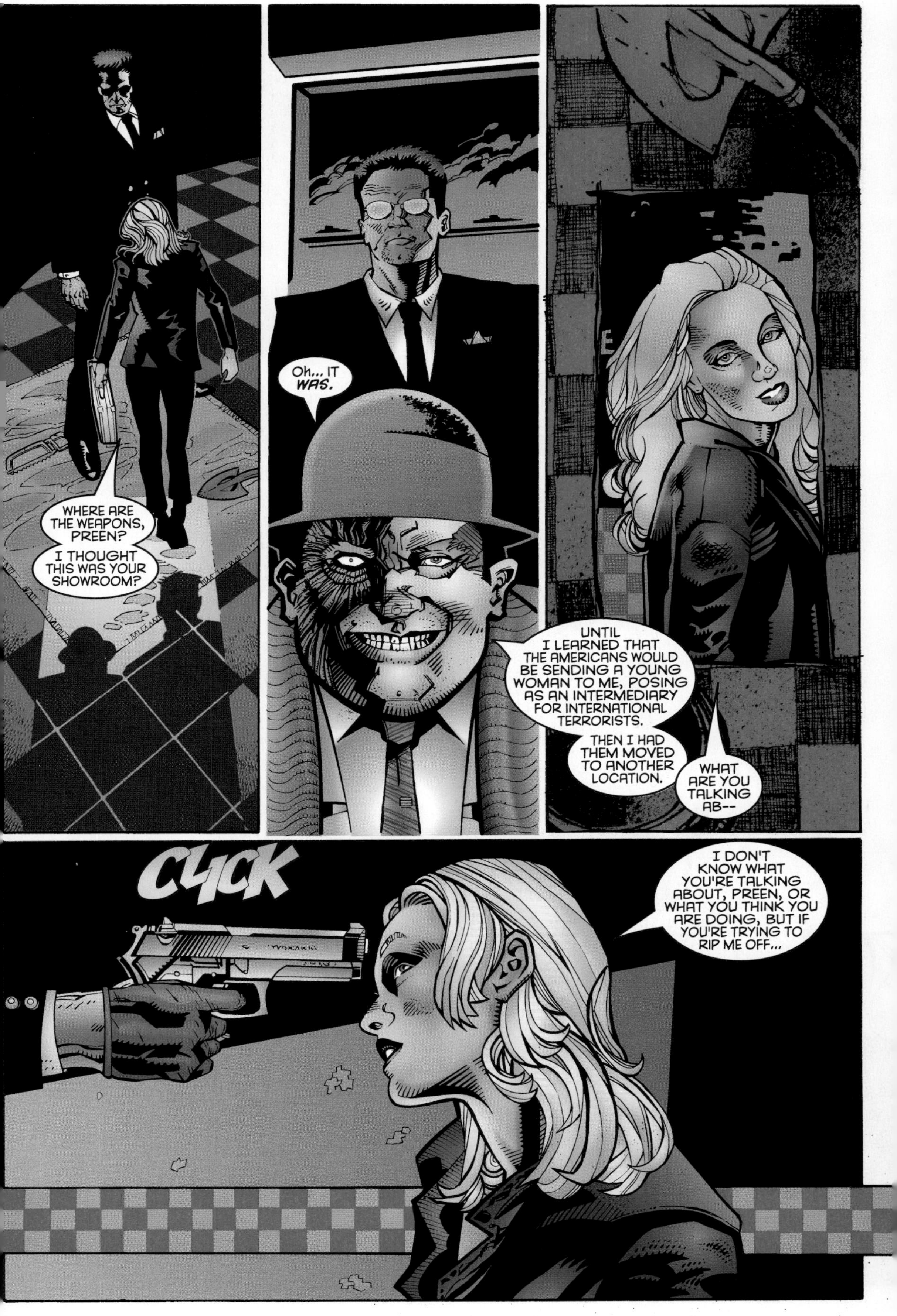
WHERE ARE THE WEAPONS, PREEN?
I THOUGHT THIS WAS YOUR SHOWROOM?
Oh... IT *WAS.*
UNTIL I LEARNED THAT THE AMERICANS WOULD BE SENDING A YOUNG WOMAN TO ME, POSING AS AN INTERMEDIARY FOR INTERNATIONAL TERRORISTS.
THEN I HAD THEM MOVED TO ANOTHER LOCATION.
WHAT ARE YOU TALKING AB--
CLICK
I DON'T KNOW WHAT YOU'RE TALKING ABOUT, PREEN, OR WHAT YOU THINK YOU ARE DOING, BUT IF YOU'RE TRYING TO RIP ME OFF...

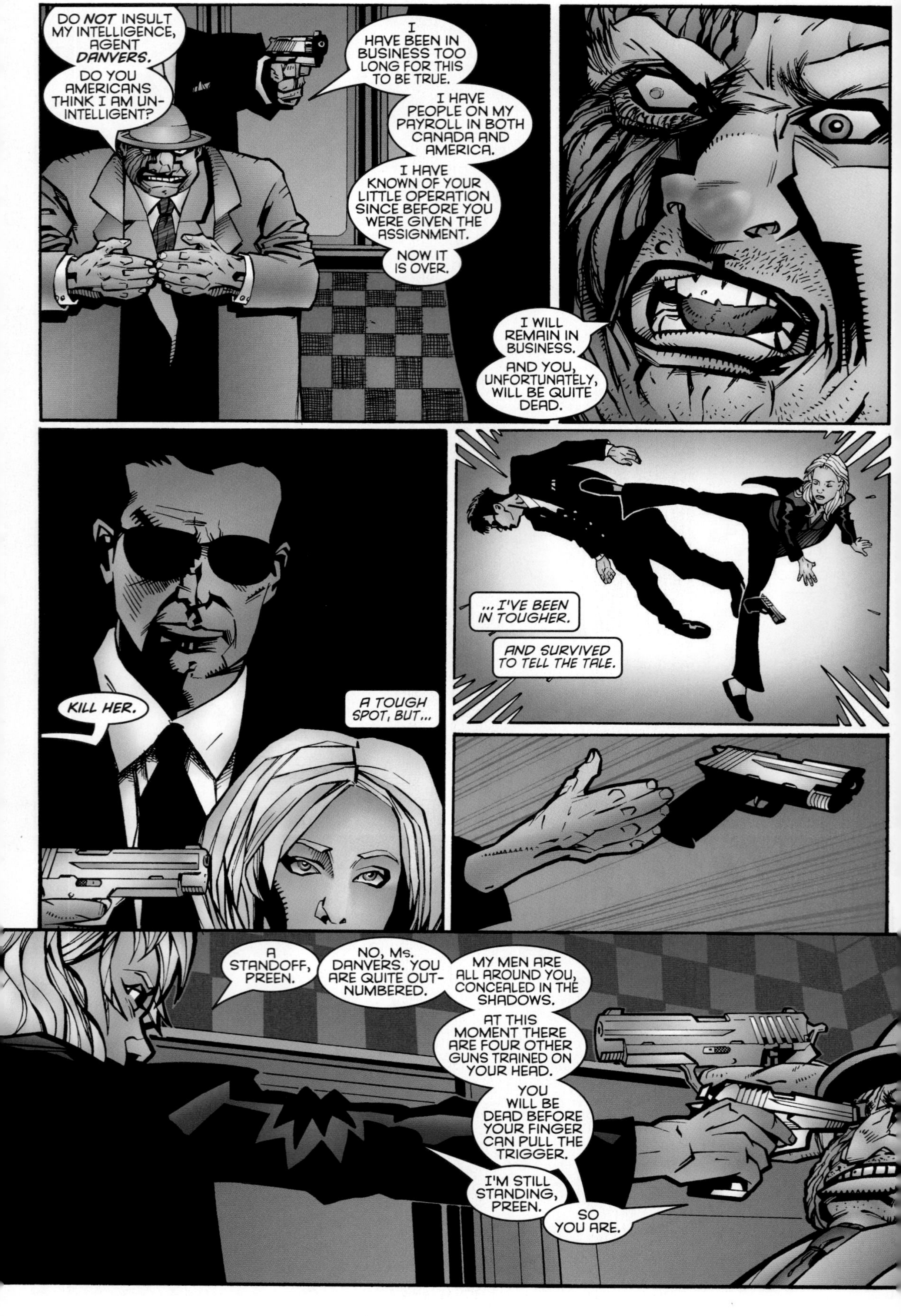
DO *NOT* INSULT MY INTELLIGENCE, AGENT *DANVERS.*
DO YOU AMERICANS THINK I AM UN-INTELLIGENT?
I HAVE BEEN IN BUSINESS TOO LONG FOR THIS TO BE TRUE.
I HAVE PEOPLE ON MY PAYROLL IN BOTH CANADA AND AMERICA.
I HAVE KNOWN OF YOUR LITTLE OPERATION SINCE BEFORE YOU WERE GIVEN THE ASSIGNMENT.
NOW IT IS OVER.
I WILL REMAIN IN BUSINESS.
AND YOU, UNFORTUNATELY, WILL BE QUITE DEAD.
KILL HER.
A TOUGH SPOT, BUT...
...I'VE BEEN IN TOUGHER.
AND SURVIVED TO TELL THE TALE.
A STANDOFF, PREEN.
NO, Ms. DANVERS. YOU ARE QUITE OUT-NUMBERED.
MY MEN ARE ALL AROUND YOU, CONCEALED IN THE SHADOWS.
AT THIS MOMENT THERE ARE FOUR OTHER GUNS TRAINED ON YOUR HEAD.
YOU WILL BE DEAD BEFORE YOUR FINGER CAN PULL THE TRIGGER.
I'M STILL STANDING, PREEN.
SO YOU ARE.

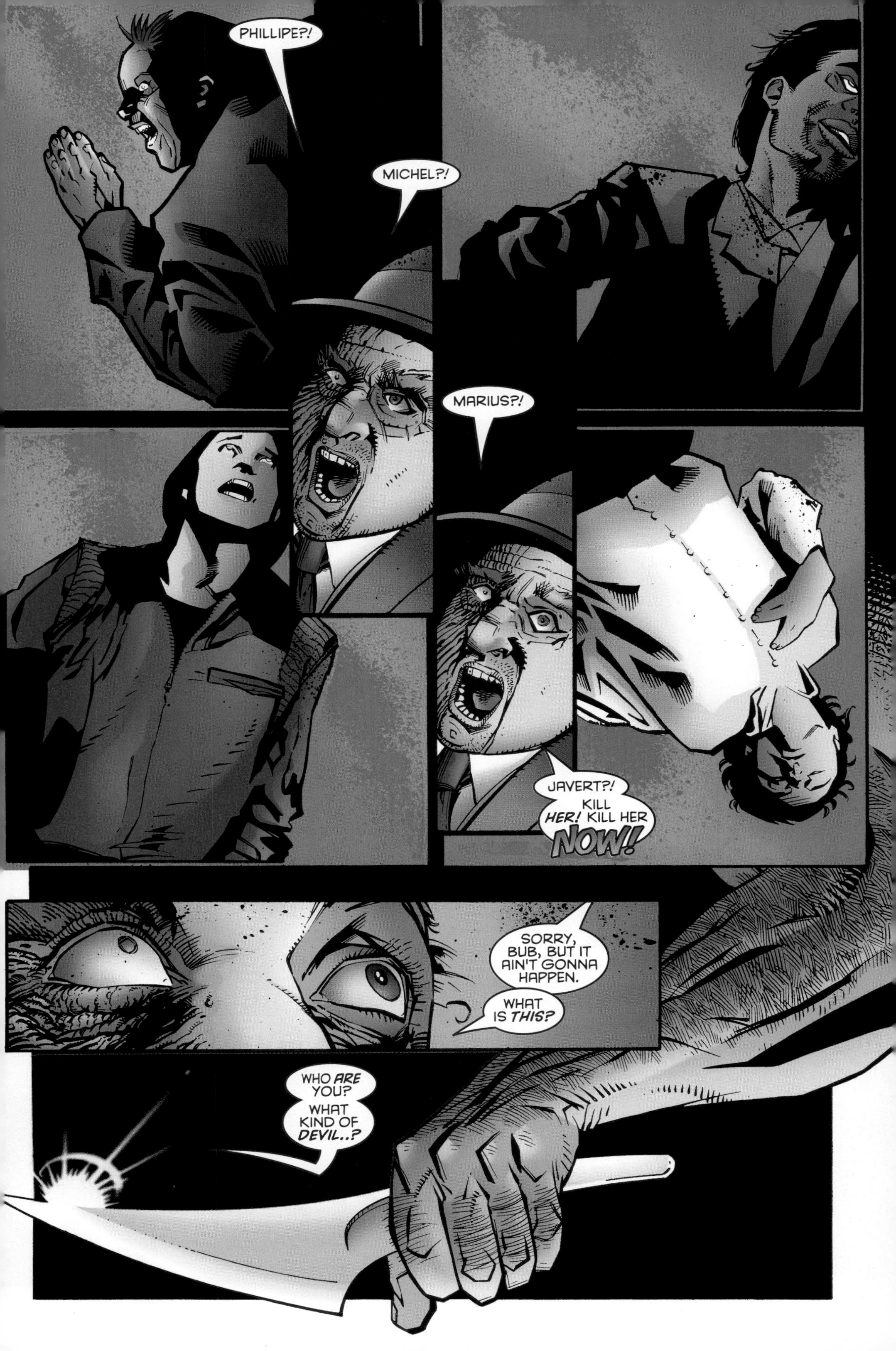
PHILLIPE?!
MICHEL?!
MARIUS?!
JAVERT?! KILL HER! KILL HER NOW!!
SORRY, BUB, BUT IT AIN'T GONNA HAPPEN.
WHAT IS THIS?
WHO ARE YOU? WHAT KIND OF DEVIL..?

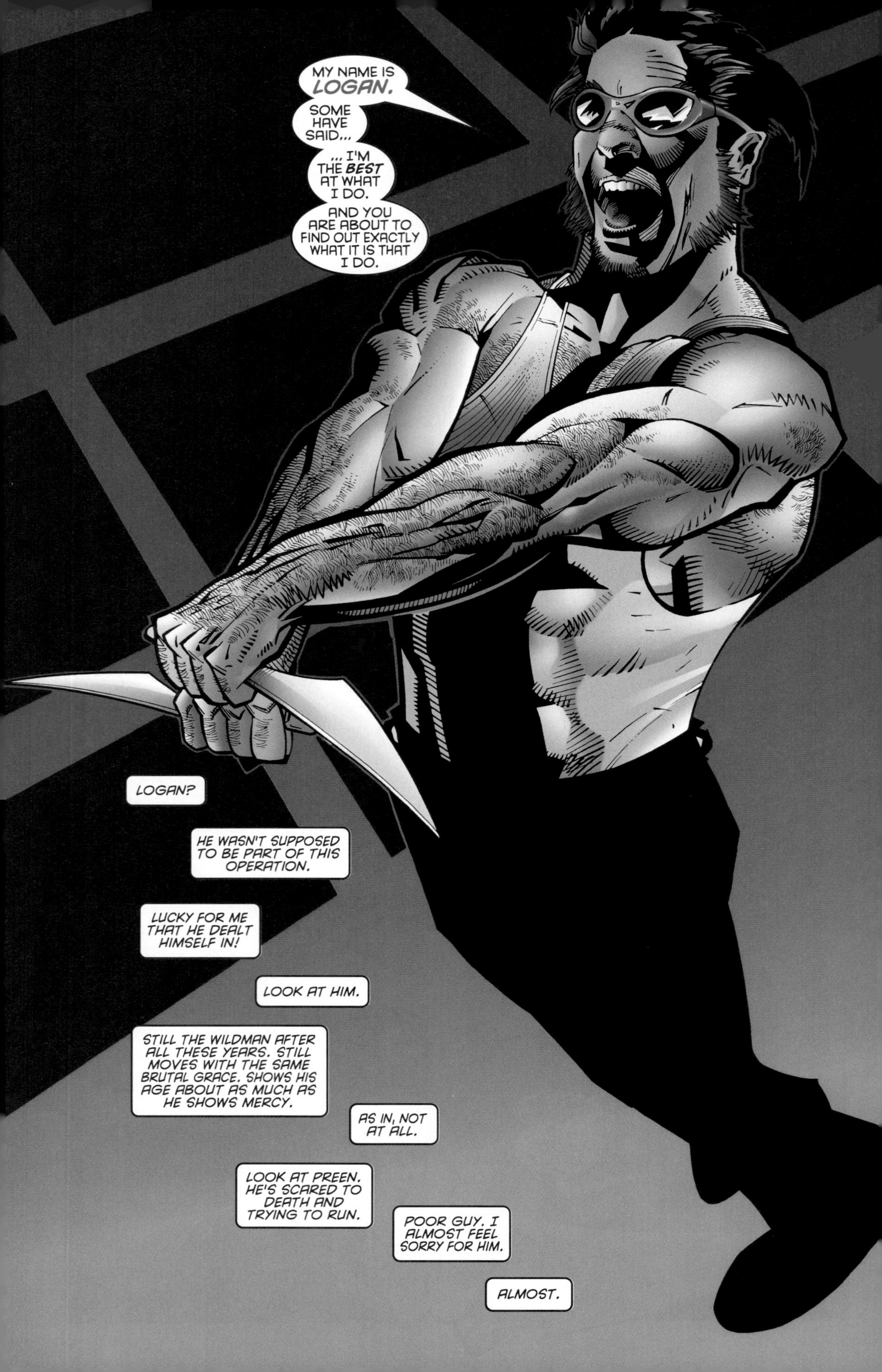
MY NAME IS LOGAN.
SOME HAVE SAID...
...I'M THE BEST AT WHAT I DO.
AND YOU ARE ABOUT TO FIND OUT EXACTLY WHAT IT IS THAT I DO.
LOGAN?
HE WASN'T SUPPOSED TO BE PART OF THIS OPERATION.
LUCKY FOR ME THAT HE DEALT HIMSELF IN!
LOOK AT HIM.
STILL THE WILDMAN AFTER ALL THESE YEARS. STILL MOVES WITH THE SAME BRUTAL GRACE. SHOWS HIS AGE ABOUT AS MUCH AS HE SHOWS MERCY.
AS IN, NOT AT ALL.
LOOK AT PREEN. HE'S SCARED TO DEATH AND TRYING TO RUN.
POOR GUY. I ALMOST FEEL SORRY FOR HIM.
ALMOST.

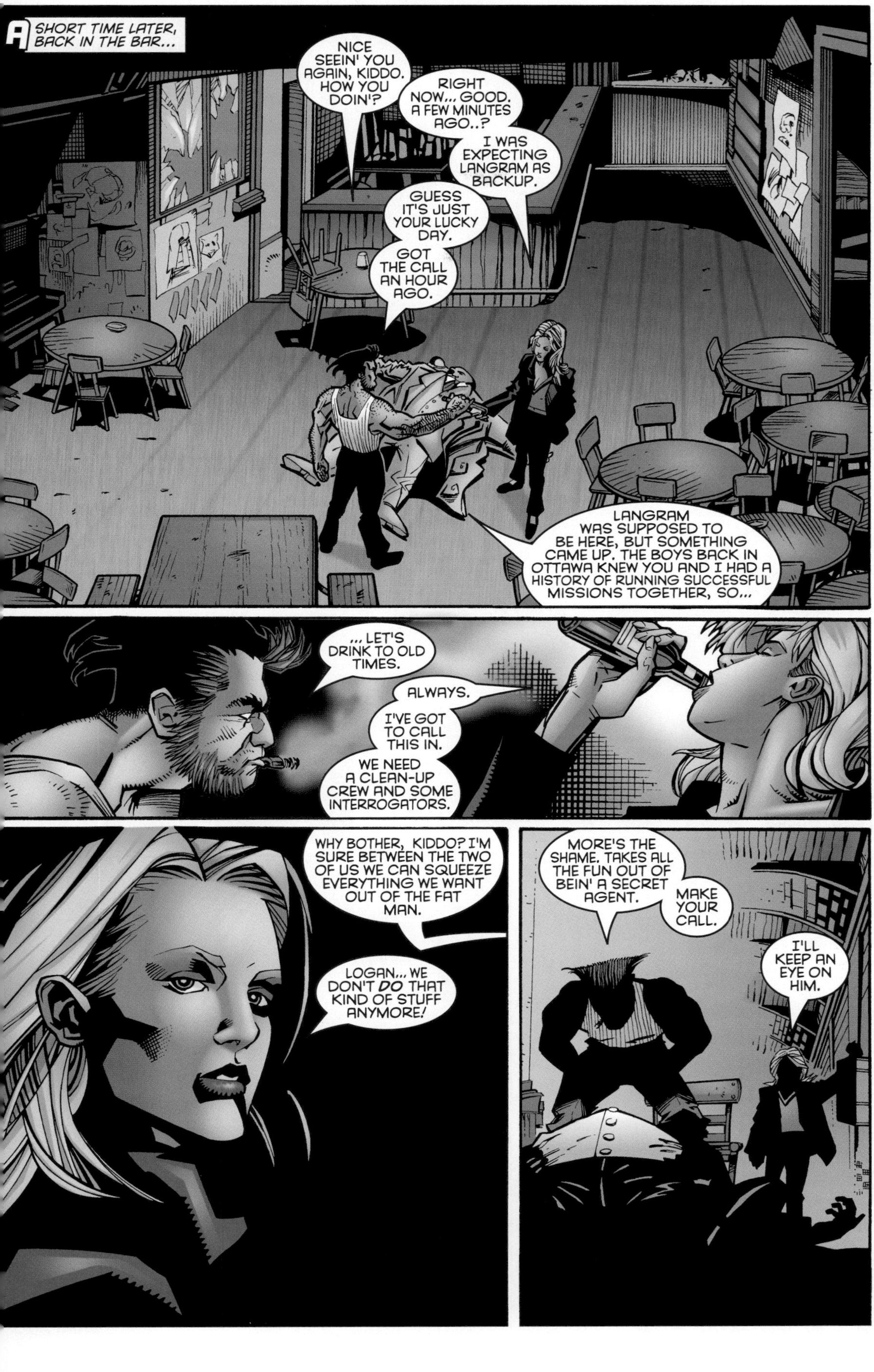
A SHORT TIME LATER, BACK IN THE BAR...
NICE SEEIN' YOU AGAIN, KIDDO. HOW YOU DOIN'?
RIGHT NOW... GOOD. A FEW MINUTES AGO..?
I WAS EXPECTING LANGRAM AS BACKUP.
GUESS IT'S JUST YOUR LUCKY DAY.
GOT THE CALL AN HOUR AGO.
LANGRAM WAS SUPPOSED TO BE HERE, BUT SOMETHING CAME UP. THE BOYS BACK IN OTTAWA KNEW YOU AND I HAD A HISTORY OF RUNNING SUCCESSFUL MISSIONS TOGETHER, SO...
...LET'S DRINK TO OLD TIMES.
ALWAYS.
I'VE GOT TO CALL THIS IN.
WE NEED A CLEAN-UP CREW AND SOME INTERROGATORS.
WHY BOTHER, KIDDO? I'M SURE BETWEEN THE TWO OF US WE CAN SQUEEZE EVERYTHING WE WANT OUT OF THE FAT MAN.
LOGAN... WE DON'T DO THAT KIND OF STUFF ANYMORE!
MORE'S THE SHAME. TAKES ALL THE FUN OUT OF BEIN' A SECRET AGENT.
MAKE YOUR CALL.
I'LL KEEP AN EYE ON HIM.

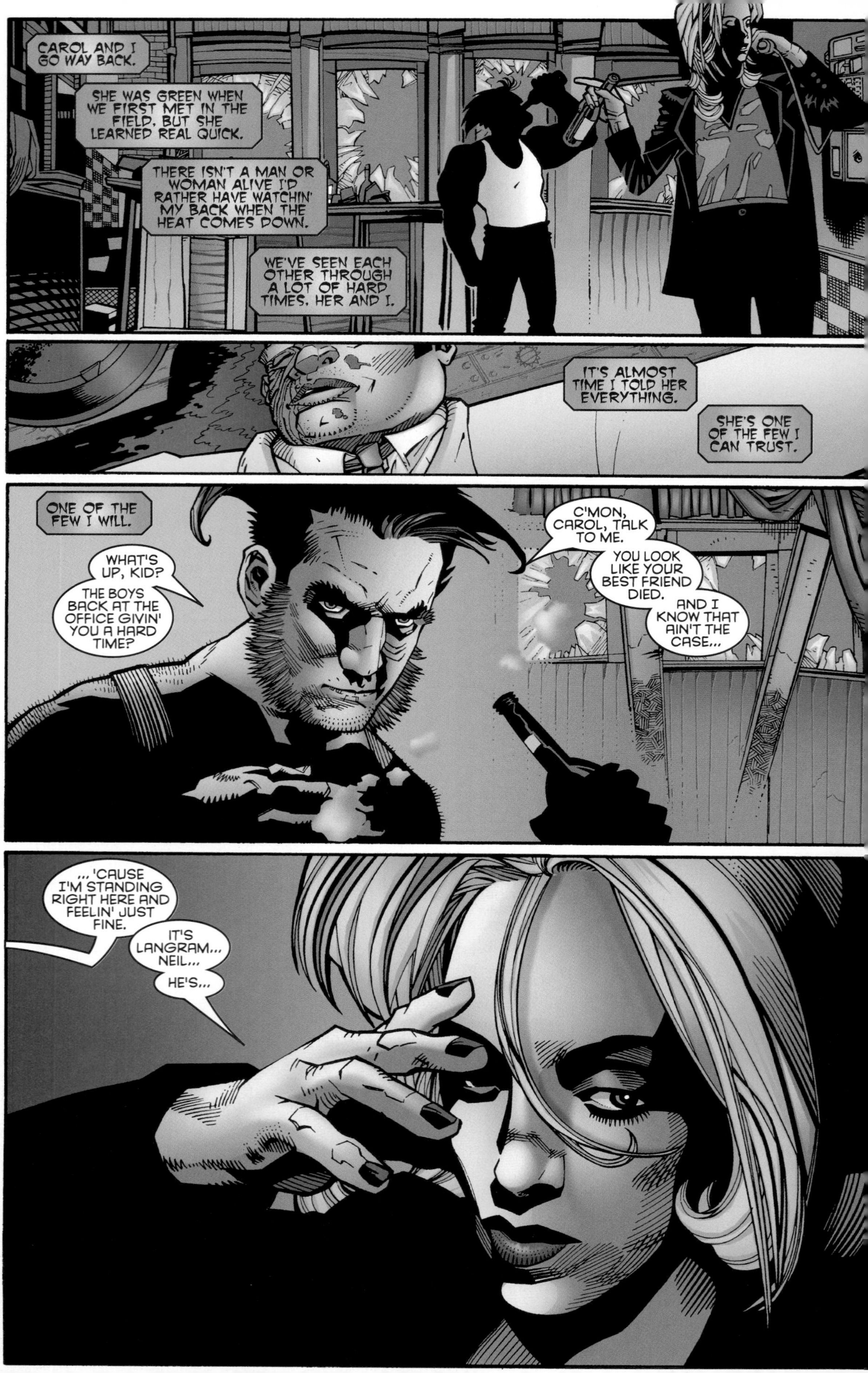
CAROL AND I GO WAY BACK.
SHE WAS GREEN WHEN WE FIRST MET IN THE FIELD, BUT SHE LEARNED REAL QUICK.
THERE ISN'T A MAN OR WOMAN ALIVE I'D RATHER HAVE WATCHIN' MY BACK WHEN THE HEAT COMES DOWN.
WE'VE SEEN EACH OTHER THROUGH A LOT OF HARD TIMES. HER AND I.
IT'S ALMOST TIME I TOLD HER EVERYTHING.
SHE'S ONE OF THE FEW I CAN TRUST.
ONE OF THE FEW I WILL.
WHAT'S UP, KID?
THE BOYS BACK AT THE OFFICE GIVIN' YOU A HARD TIME?
C'MON, CAROL, TALK TO ME.
YOU LOOK LIKE YOUR BEST FRIEND DIED.
AND I KNOW THAT AIN'T THE CASE...
...'CAUSE I'M STANDING RIGHT HERE AND FEELIN' JUST FINE.
IT'S LANGRAM... NEIL...
HE'S...

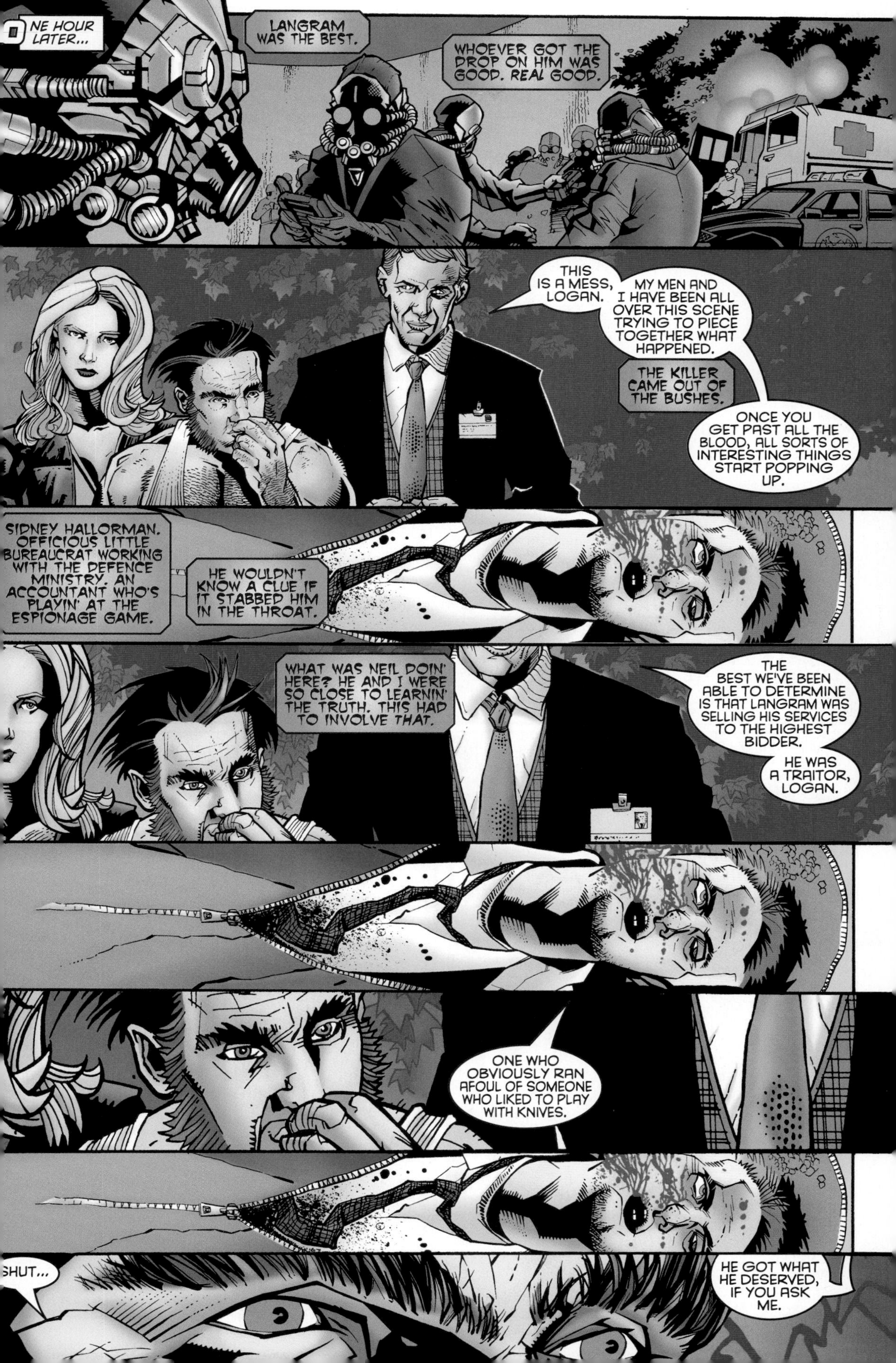
ONE HOUR LATER...
LANGRAM WAS THE BEST.
WHOEVER GOT THE DROP ON HIM WAS GOOD. REAL GOOD.
THIS IS A MESS, LOGAN.
MY MEN AND I HAVE BEEN ALL OVER THIS SCENE TRYING TO PIECE TOGETHER WHAT HAPPENED.
THE KILLER CAME OUT OF THE BUSHES.
ONCE YOU GET PAST ALL THE BLOOD, ALL SORTS OF INTERESTING THINGS START POPPING UP.
SIDNEY HALLORMAN. OFFICIOUS LITTLE BUREAUCRAT WORKING WITH THE DEFENCE MINISTRY. AN ACCOUNTANT WHO'S PLAYIN' AT THE ESPIONAGE GAME.
HE WOULDN'T KNOW A CLUE IF IT STABBED HIM IN THE THROAT.
WHAT WAS NEIL DOIN' HERE? HE AND I WERE SO CLOSE TO LEARNIN' THE TRUTH. THIS HAD TO INVOLVE THAT.
THE BEST WE'VE BEEN ABLE TO DETERMINE IS THAT LANGRAM WAS SELLING HIS SERVICES TO THE HIGHEST BIDDER.
HE WAS A TRAITOR, LOGAN.
ONE WHO OBVIOUSLY RAN AFOUL OF SOMEONE WHO LIKED TO PLAY WITH KNIVES.
SHUT...
HE GOT WHAT HE DESERVED, IF YOU ASK ME.

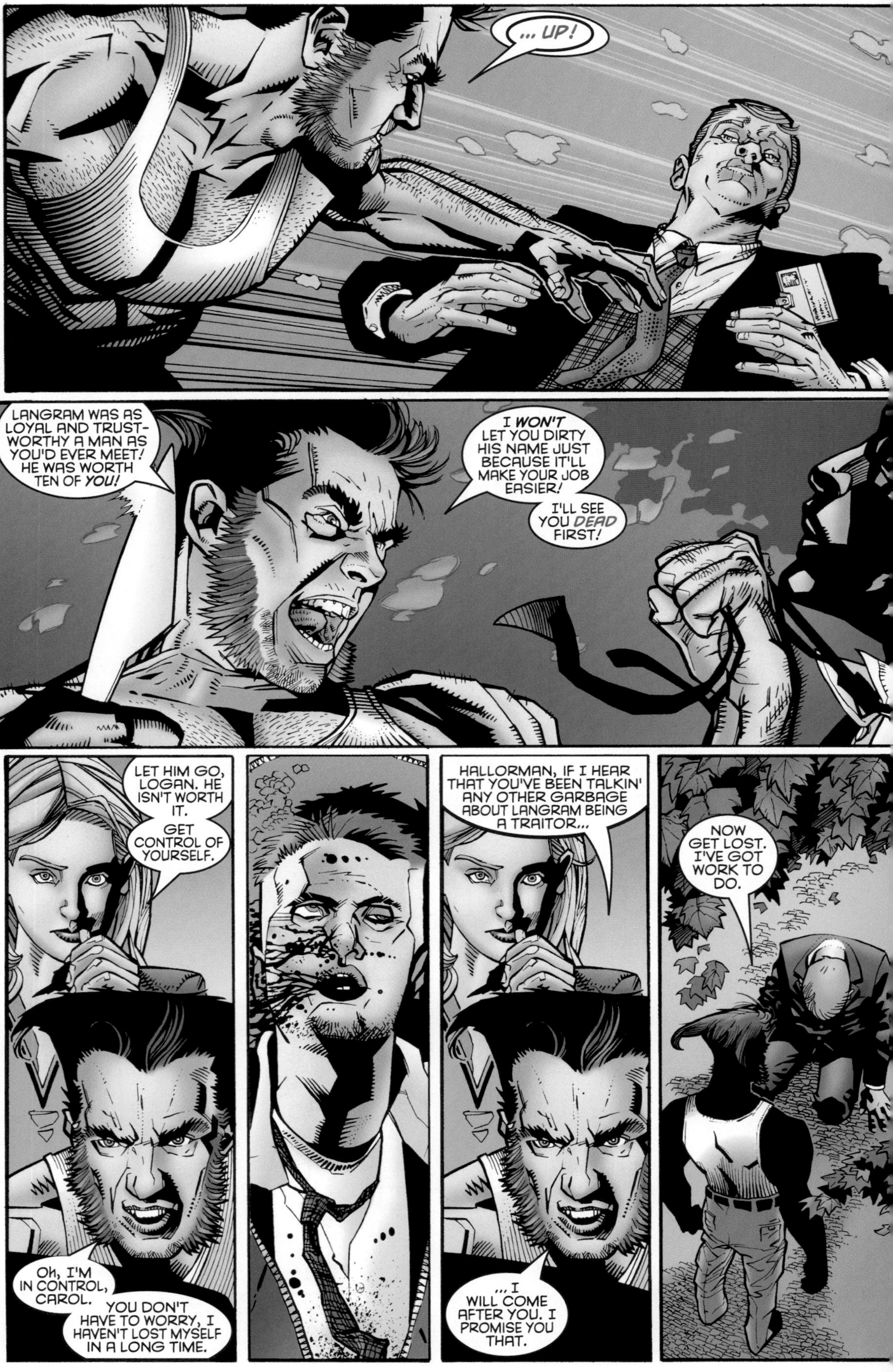
... UP!
LANGRAM WAS AS LOYAL AND TRUST-WORTHY A MAN AS YOU'D EVER MEET! HE WAS WORTH TEN OF YOU!
I WON'T LET YOU DIRTY HIS NAME JUST BECAUSE IT'LL MAKE YOUR JOB EASIER!
I'LL SEE YOU DEAD FIRST!
LET HIM GO, LOGAN. HE ISN'T WORTH IT.
GET CONTROL OF YOURSELF.
Oh, I'M IN CONTROL, CAROL.
YOU DON'T HAVE TO WORRY, I HAVEN'T LOST MYSELF IN A LONG TIME.
HALLORMAN, IF I HEAR THAT YOU'VE BEEN TALKIN' ANY OTHER GARBAGE ABOUT LANGRAM BEING A TRAITOR...
... I WILL COME AFTER YOU. I PROMISE YOU THAT.
NOW GET LOST. I'VE GOT WORK TO DO.

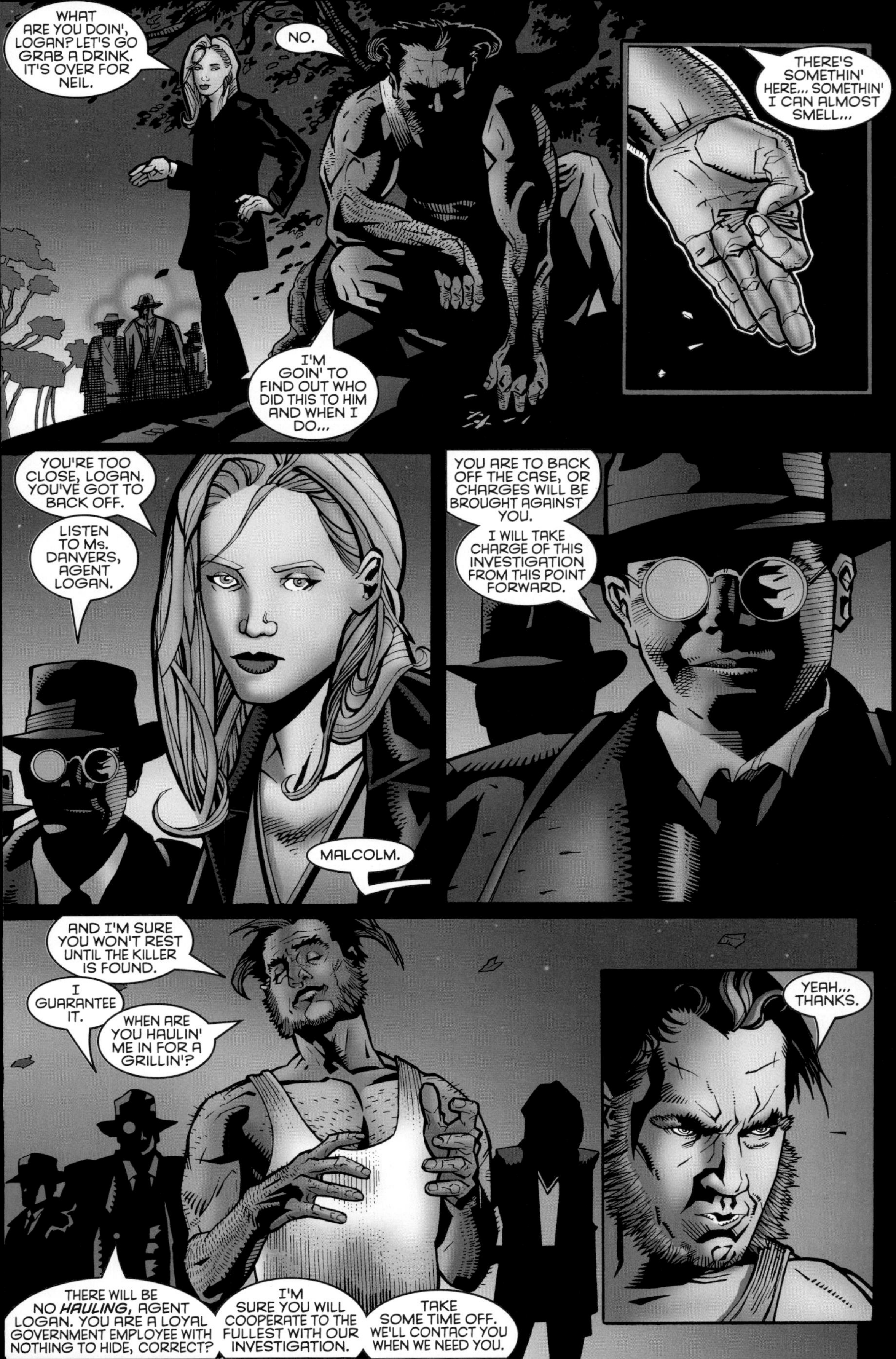

WHAT ARE YOU DOIN', LOGAN? LET'S GO GRAB A DRINK. IT'S OVER FOR NEIL.
NO.
I'M GOIN' TO FIND OUT WHO DID THIS TO HIM AND WHEN I DO...
THERE'S SOMETHIN' HERE... SOMETHIN' I CAN ALMOST SMELL...
YOU'RE TOO CLOSE, LOGAN. YOU'VE GOT TO BACK OFF.
LISTEN TO Ms. DANVERS, AGENT LOGAN.
MALCOLM.
YOU ARE TO BACK OFF THE CASE, OR CHARGES WILL BE BROUGHT AGAINST YOU.
I WILL TAKE CHARGE OF THIS INVESTIGATION FROM THIS POINT FORWARD.
AND I'M SURE YOU WON'T REST UNTIL THE KILLER IS FOUND.
I GUARANTEE IT.
WHEN ARE YOU HAULIN' ME IN FOR A GRILLIN'?
THERE WILL BE NO *HAULING,* AGENT LOGAN. YOU ARE A LOYAL GOVERNMENT EMPLOYEE WITH NOTHING TO HIDE, CORRECT?
I'M SURE YOU WILL COOPERATE TO THE FULLEST WITH OUR INVESTIGATION.
TAKE SOME TIME OFF. WE'LL CONTACT YOU WHEN WE NEED YOU.
YEAH... THANKS.

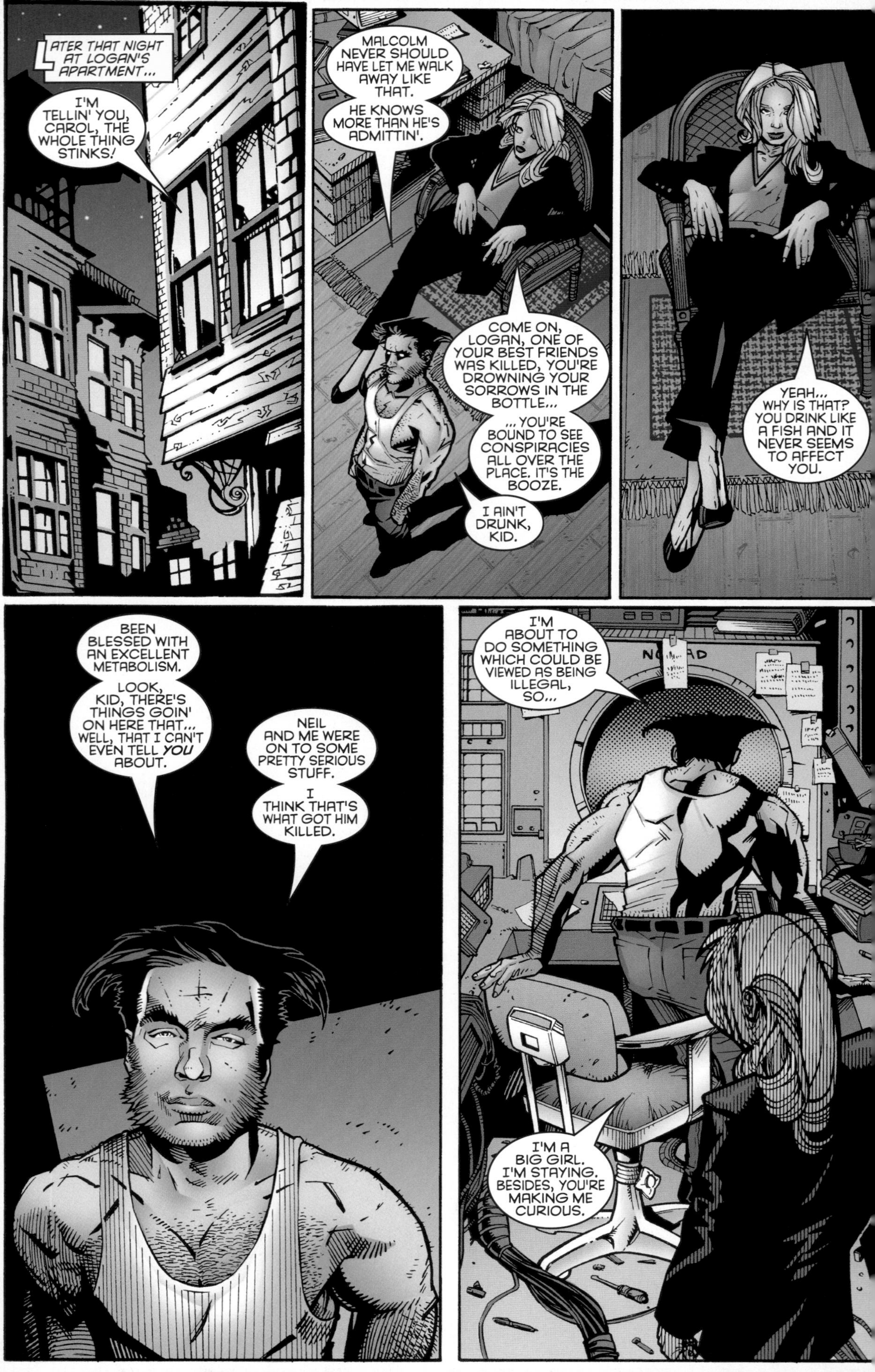
LATER THAT NIGHT AT LOGAN'S APARTMENT...
I'M TELLIN' YOU, CAROL, THE WHOLE THING STINKS!
MALCOLM NEVER SHOULD HAVE LET ME WALK AWAY LIKE THAT.
HE KNOWS MORE THAN HE'S ADMITTIN'.
COME ON, LOGAN, ONE OF YOUR BEST FRIENDS WAS KILLED, YOU'RE DROWNING YOUR SORROWS IN THE BOTTLE...
...YOU'RE BOUND TO SEE CONSPIRACIES ALL OVER THE PLACE. IT'S THE BOOZE.
I AIN'T DRUNK, KID.
YEAH... WHY IS THAT? YOU DRINK LIKE A FISH AND IT NEVER SEEMS TO AFFECT YOU.
BEEN BLESSED WITH AN EXCELLENT METABOLISM.
LOOK, KID, THERE'S THINGS GOIN' ON HERE THAT... WELL, THAT I CAN'T EVEN TELL YOU ABOUT.
NEIL AND ME WERE ON TO SOME PRETTY SERIOUS STUFF.
I THINK THAT'S WHAT GOT HIM KILLED.
I'M ABOUT TO DO SOMETHING WHICH COULD BE VIEWED AS BEING ILLEGAL, SO...
I'M A BIG GIRL. I'M STAYING. BESIDES, YOU'RE MAKING ME CURIOUS.

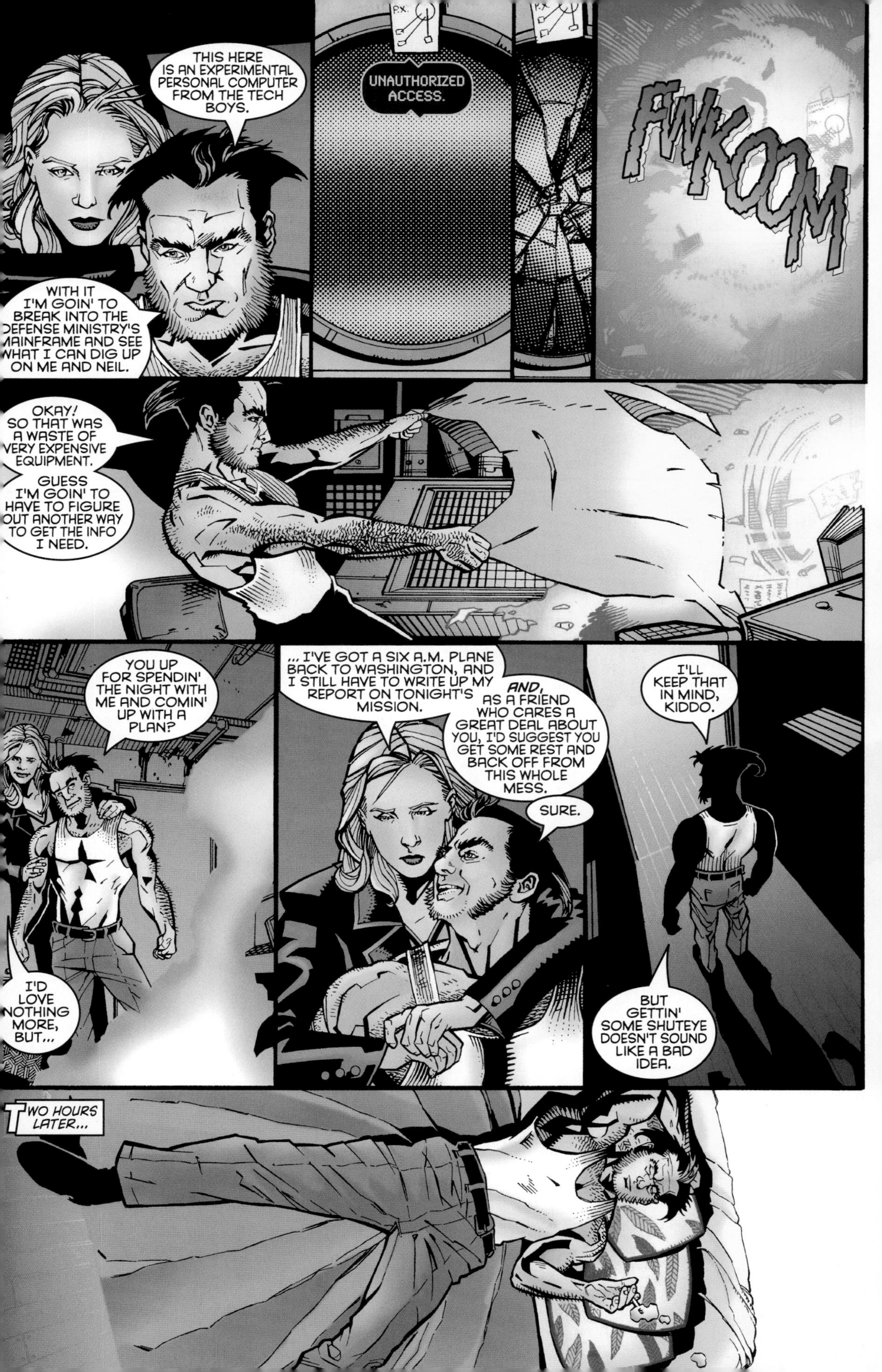

THIS HERE IS AN EXPERIMENTAL PERSONAL COMPUTER FROM THE TECH BOYS.
WITH IT I'M GOIN' TO BREAK INTO THE DEFENSE MINISTRY'S MAINFRAME AND SEE WHAT I CAN DIG UP ON ME AND NEIL.
UNAUTHORIZED ACCESS.
FWKOOM
OKAY! SO THAT WAS A WASTE OF VERY EXPENSIVE EQUIPMENT.
GUESS I'M GOIN' TO HAVE TO FIGURE OUT ANOTHER WAY TO GET THE INFO I NEED.
YOU UP FOR SPENDIN' THE NIGHT WITH ME AND COMIN' UP WITH A PLAN?
I'D LOVE NOTHING MORE, BUT...
... I'VE GOT A SIX A.M. PLANE BACK TO WASHINGTON, AND I STILL HAVE TO WRITE UP MY REPORT ON TONIGHT'S MISSION.
AND, AS A FRIEND WHO CARES A GREAT DEAL ABOUT YOU, I'D SUGGEST YOU GET SOME REST AND BACK OFF FROM THIS WHOLE MESS.
SURE.
I'LL KEEP THAT IN MIND, KIDDO.
BUT GETTIN' SOME SHUTEYE DOESN'T SOUND LIKE A BAD IDEA.
TWO HOURS LATER...

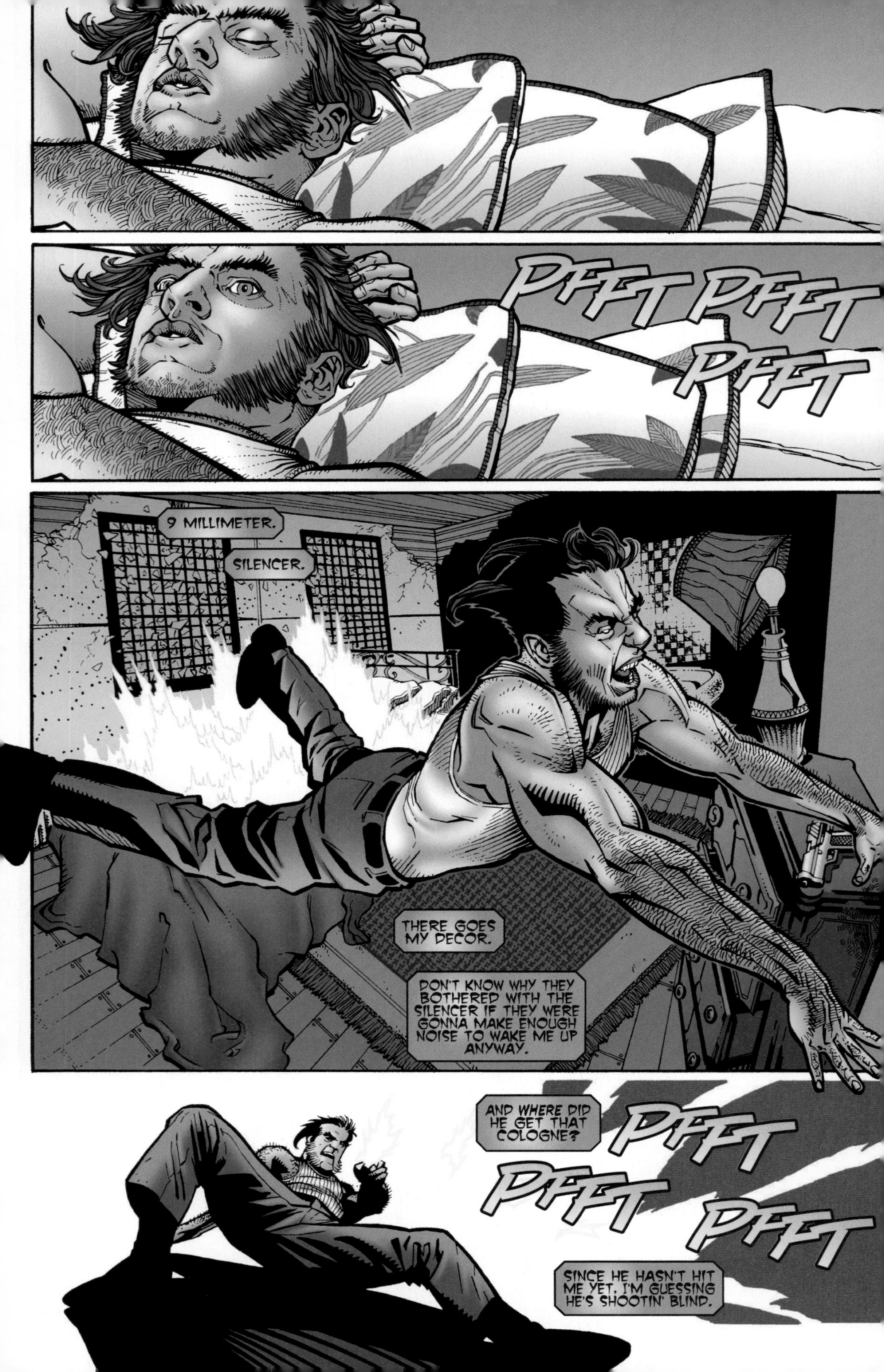
PFFT PFFT
PFFT
9 MILLIMETER.
SILENCER.
THERE GOES MY DECOR.
DON'T KNOW WHY THEY BOTHERED WITH THE SILENCER IF THEY WERE GONNA MAKE ENOUGH NOISE TO WAKE ME UP ANYWAY.
AND WHERE DID HE GET THAT COLOGNE?
PFFT
PFFT
PFFT
SINCE HE HASN'T HIT ME YET, I'M GUESSING HE'S SHOOTIN' BLIND.

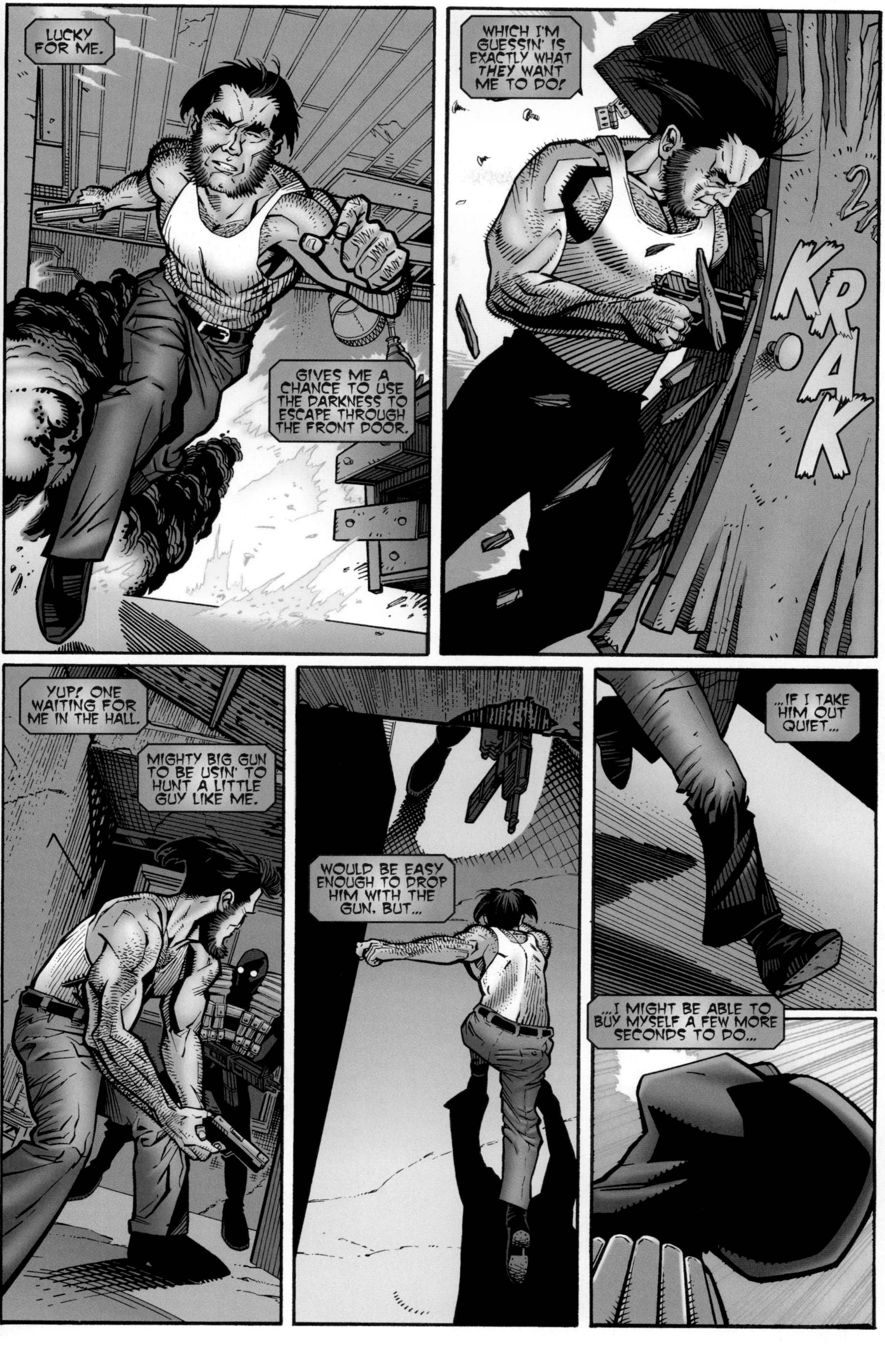
LUCKY FOR ME.
GIVES ME A CHANCE TO USE THE DARKNESS TO ESCAPE THROUGH THE FRONT DOOR.
WHICH I'M GUESSIN' IS EXACTLY WHAT THEY WANT ME TO DO!
KRAK
YUP! ONE WAITING FOR ME IN THE HALL.
MIGHTY BIG GUN TO BE USIN' TO HUNT A LITTLE GUY LIKE ME.
WOULD BE EASY ENOUGH TO DROP HIM WITH THE GUN. BUT...
...IF I TAKE HIM OUT QUIET...
...I MIGHT BE ABLE TO BUY MYSELF A FEW MORE SECONDS TO DO...

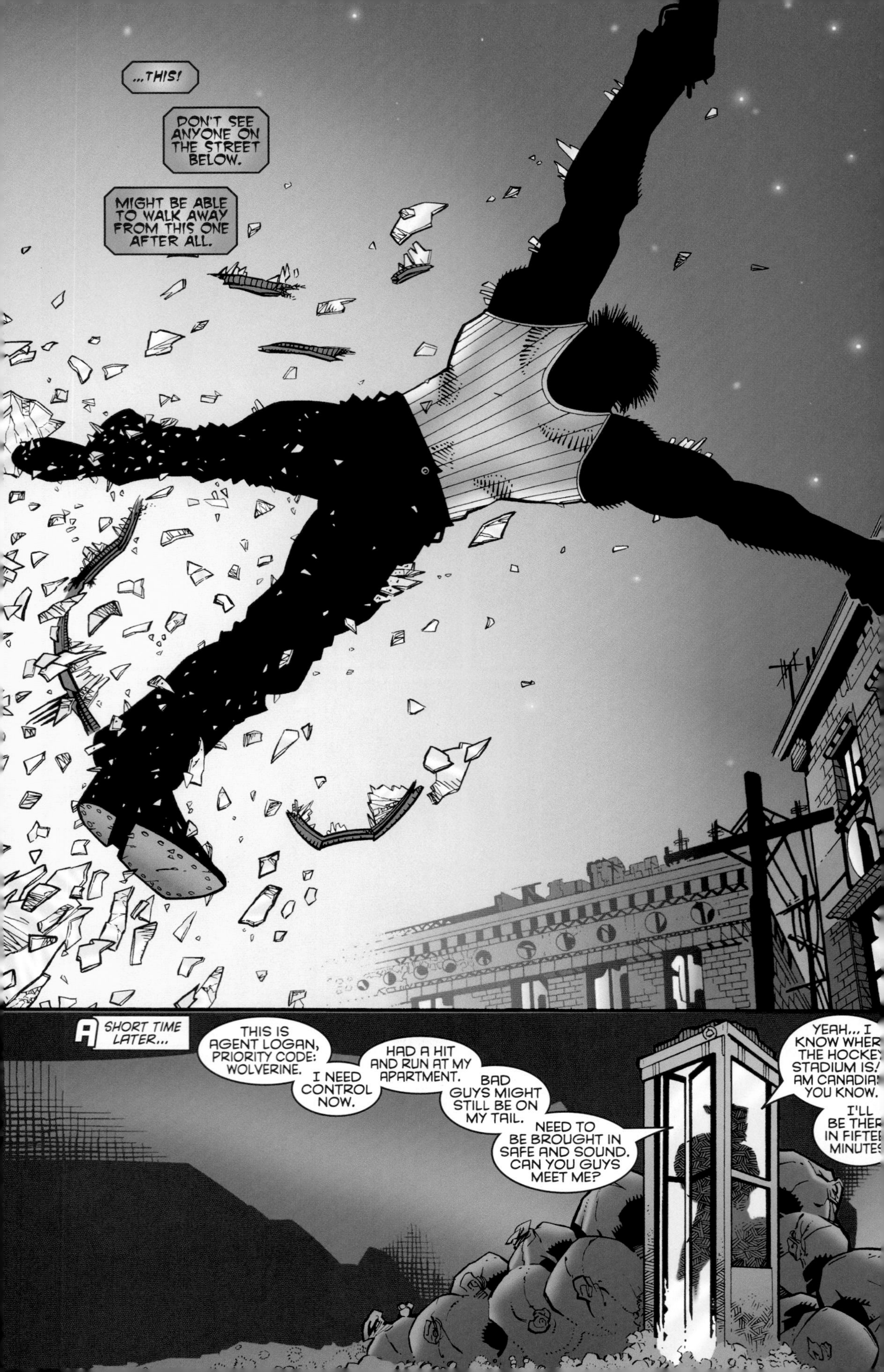
...THIS!
DON'T SEE ANYONE ON THE STREET BELOW.
MIGHT BE ABLE TO WALK AWAY FROM THIS ONE AFTER ALL.
A SHORT TIME LATER...
THIS IS AGENT LOGAN, PRIORITY CODE: WOLVERINE.
I NEED CONTROL NOW.
HAD A HIT AND RUN AT MY APARTMENT.
BAD GUYS MIGHT STILL BE ON MY TAIL.
NEED TO BE BROUGHT IN SAFE AND SOUND. CAN YOU GUYS MEET ME?
YEAH... I KNOW WHER THE HOCKE STADIUM IS! AM CANADIA YOU KNOW.
I'LL BE THER IN FIFTE MINUTE

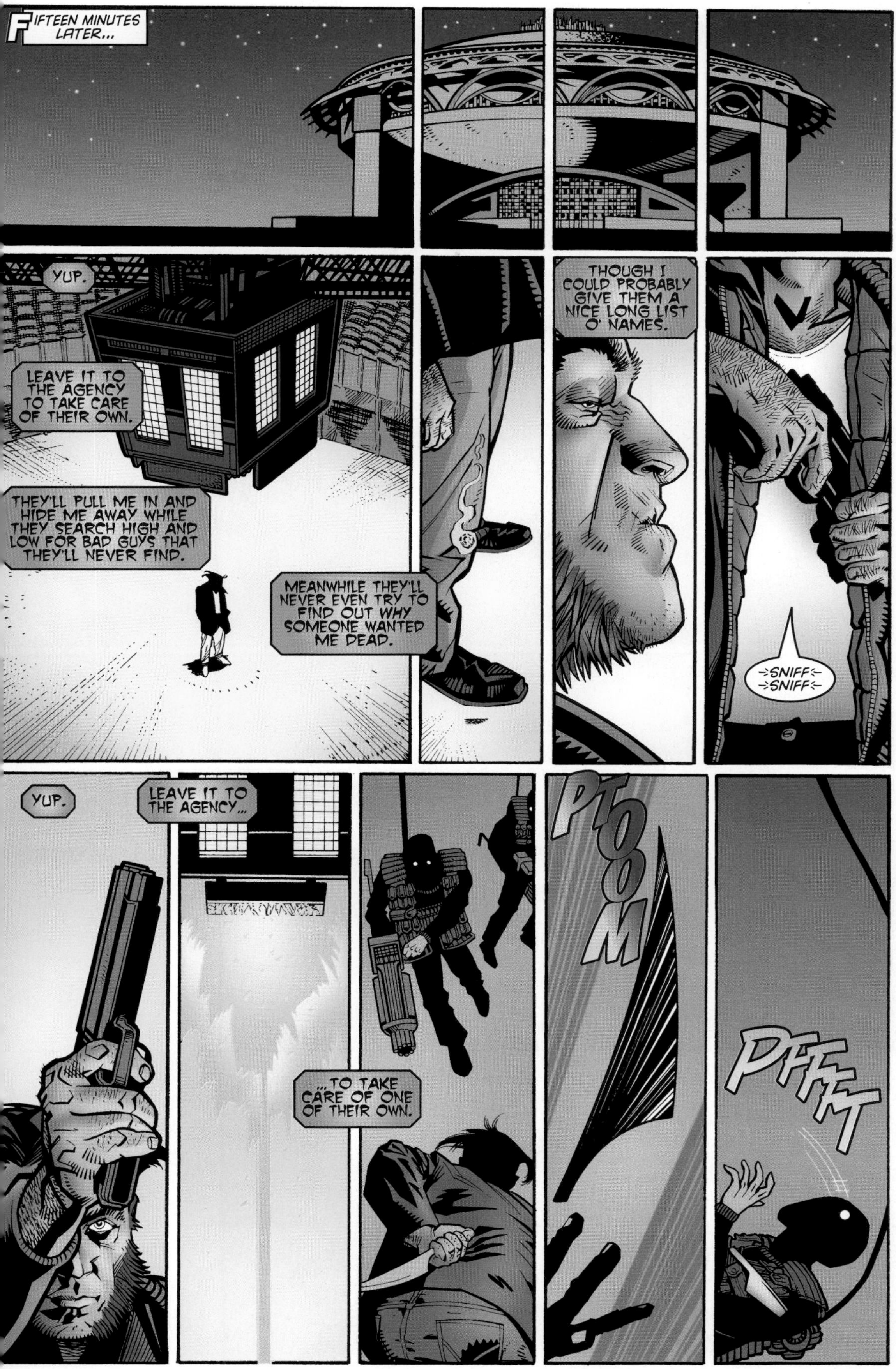

FIFTEEN MINUTES LATER...
YUP.
LEAVE IT TO THE AGENCY TO TAKE CARE OF THEIR OWN.
THEY'LL PULL ME IN AND HIDE ME AWAY WHILE THEY SEARCH HIGH AND LOW FOR BAD GUYS THAT THEY'LL NEVER FIND.
MEANWHILE THEY'LL NEVER EVEN TRY TO FIND OUT WHY SOMEONE WANTED ME DEAD.
THOUGH I COULD PROBABLY GIVE THEM A NICE LONG LIST O' NAMES.
SNIFF SNIFF
YUP.
LEAVE IT TO THE AGENCY...
...TO TAKE CARE OF ONE OF THEIR OWN.
PTOOOM
PFFFT

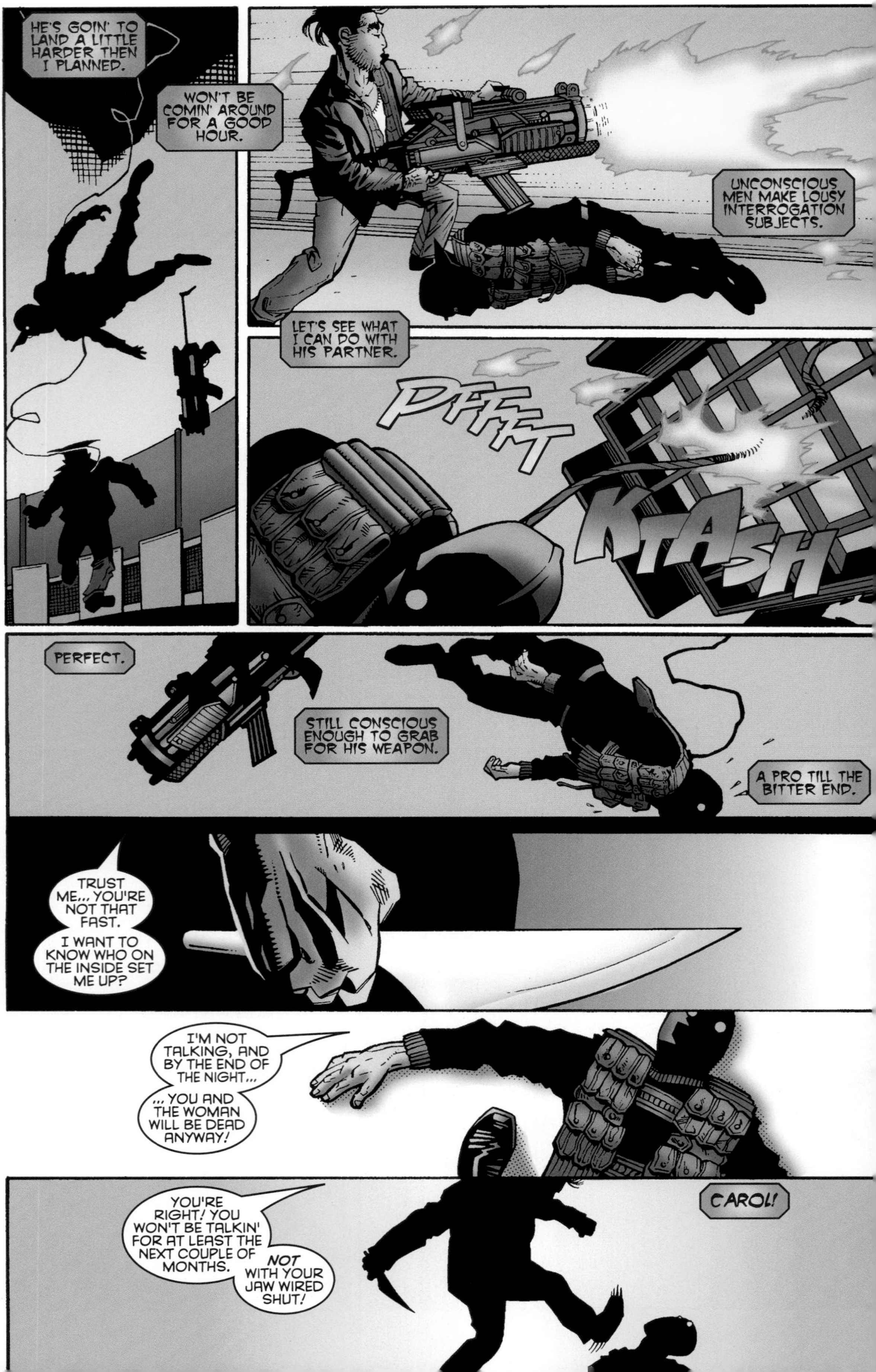
HE'S GOIN' TO LAND A LITTLE HARDER THEN I PLANNED.
WON'T BE COMIN' AROUND FOR A GOOD HOUR.
UNCONSCIOUS MEN MAKE LOUSY INTERROGATION SUBJECTS.
LET'S SEE WHAT I CAN DO WITH HIS PARTNER.
PFFFT
KTASH
PERFECT.
STILL CONSCIOUS ENOUGH TO GRAB FOR HIS WEAPON.
A PRO TILL THE BITTER END.
TRUST ME... YOU'RE NOT THAT FAST.
I WANT TO KNOW WHO ON THE INSIDE SET ME UP?
I'M NOT TALKING, AND BY THE END OF THE NIGHT...
...YOU AND THE WOMAN WILL BE DEAD ANYWAY!
YOU'RE RIGHT! YOU WON'T BE TALKIN' FOR AT LEAST THE NEXT COUPLE OF MONTHS.
NOT WITH YOUR JAW WIRED SHUT!
CAROL!

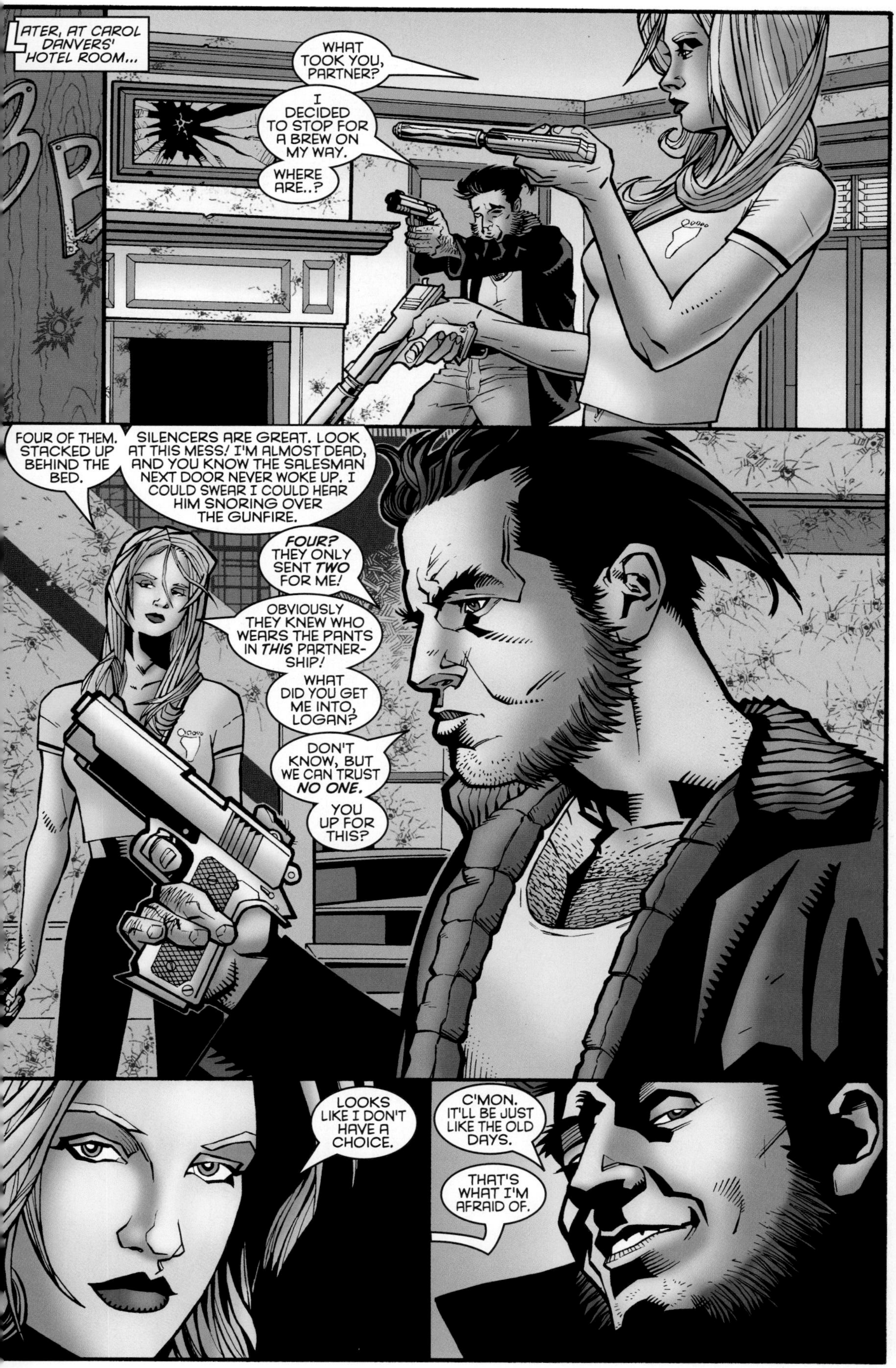
LATER, AT CAROL DANVERS' HOTEL ROOM...
WHAT TOOK YOU, PARTNER?
I DECIDED TO STOP FOR A BREW ON MY WAY.
WHERE ARE..?
FOUR OF THEM. STACKED UP BEHIND THE BED.
SILENCERS ARE GREAT. LOOK AT THIS MESS! I'M ALMOST DEAD, AND YOU KNOW THE SALESMAN NEXT DOOR NEVER WOKE UP. I COULD SWEAR I COULD HEAR HIM SNORING OVER THE GUNFIRE.
FOUR? THEY ONLY SENT TWO FOR ME!
OBVIOUSLY THEY KNEW WHO WEARS THE PANTS IN THIS PARTNER-SHIP!
WHAT DID YOU GET ME INTO, LOGAN?
DON'T KNOW, BUT WE CAN TRUST NO ONE.
YOU UP FOR THIS?
LOOKS LIKE I DON'T HAVE A CHOICE.
C'MON. IT'LL BE JUST LIKE THE OLD DAYS.
THAT'S WHAT I'M AFRAID OF.

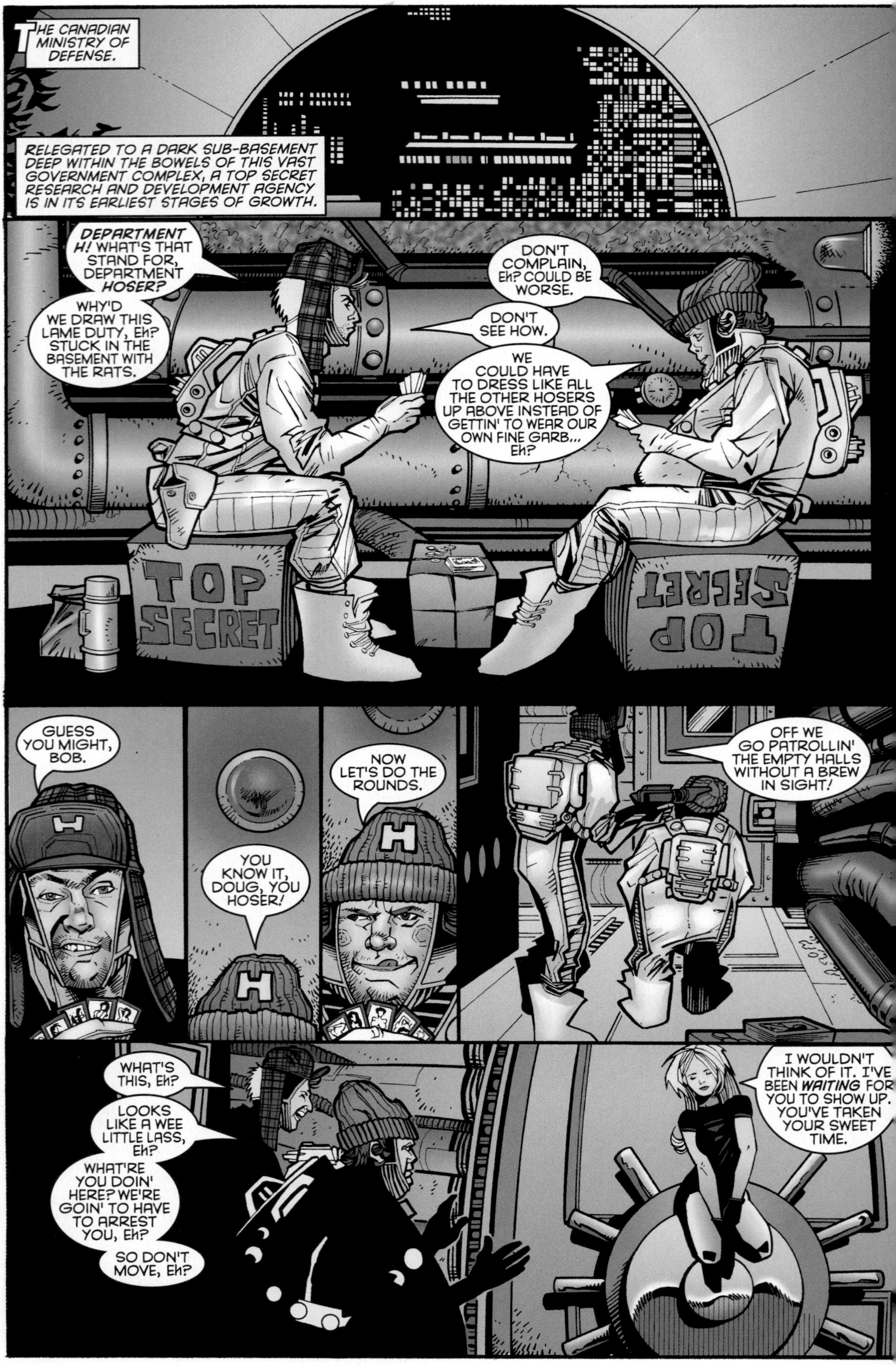
THE CANADIAN MINISTRY OF DEFENSE.
RELEGATED TO A DARK SUB-BASEMENT DEEP WITHIN THE BOWELS OF THIS VAST GOVERNMENT COMPLEX, A TOP SECRET RESEARCH AND DEVELOPMENT AGENCY IS IN ITS EARLIEST STAGES OF GROWTH.
DEPARTMENT H! WHAT'S THAT STAND FOR, DEPARTMENT HOSER?
WHY'D WE DRAW THIS LAME DUTY, Eh? STUCK IN THE BASEMENT WITH THE RATS.
DON'T COMPLAIN, Eh? COULD BE WORSE.
DON'T SEE HOW.
WE COULD HAVE TO DRESS LIKE ALL THE OTHER HOSERS UP ABOVE INSTEAD OF GETTIN' TO WEAR OUR OWN FINE GARB... Eh?
TOP SECRET
TOP SECRET
GUESS YOU MIGHT, BOB.
YOU KNOW IT, DOUG, YOU HOSER!
NOW LET'S DO THE ROUNDS.
OFF WE GO PATROLLIN' THE EMPTY HALLS WITHOUT A BREW IN SIGHT!
WHAT'S THIS, Eh?
LOOKS LIKE A WEE LITTLE LASS, Eh?
WHAT'RE YOU DOIN' HERE? WE'RE GOIN' TO HAVE TO ARREST YOU, Eh?
SO DON'T MOVE, Eh?
I WOULDN'T THINK OF IT. I'VE BEEN WAITING FOR YOU TO SHOW UP. YOU'VE TAKEN YOUR SWEET TIME.

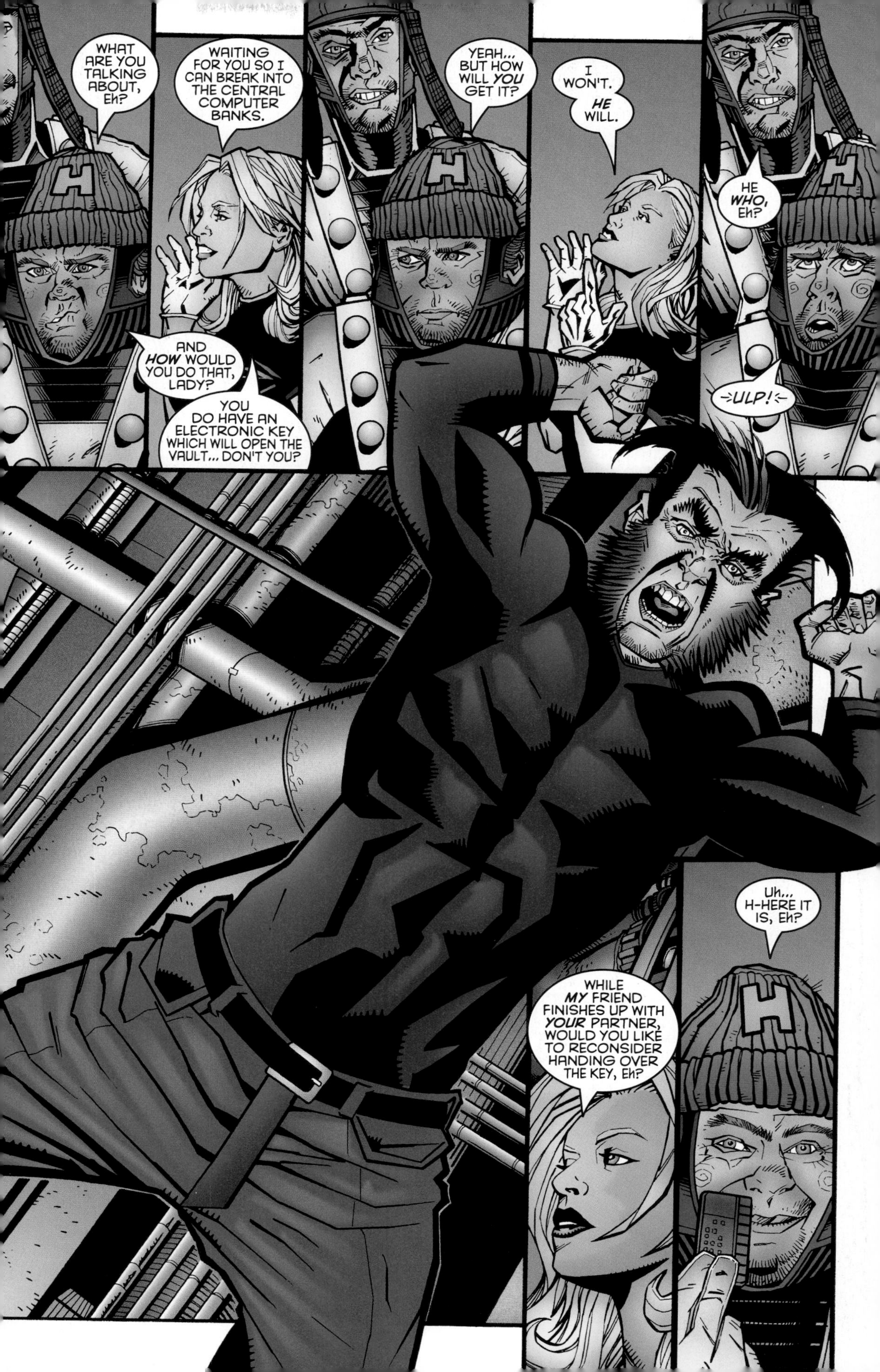
WHAT ARE YOU TALKING ABOUT, Eh?
WAITING FOR YOU SO I CAN BREAK INTO THE CENTRAL COMPUTER BANKS.
YEAH... BUT HOW WILL YOU GET IT?
I WON'T. HE WILL.
HE WHO, Eh?
AND HOW WOULD YOU DO THAT, LADY?
YOU DO HAVE AN ELECTRONIC KEY WHICH WILL OPEN THE VAULT... DON'T YOU?
ULP!
Uh... H-HERE IT IS, Eh?
WHILE MY FRIEND FINISHES UP WITH YOUR PARTNER, WOULD YOU LIKE TO RECONSIDER HANDING OVER THE KEY, Eh?

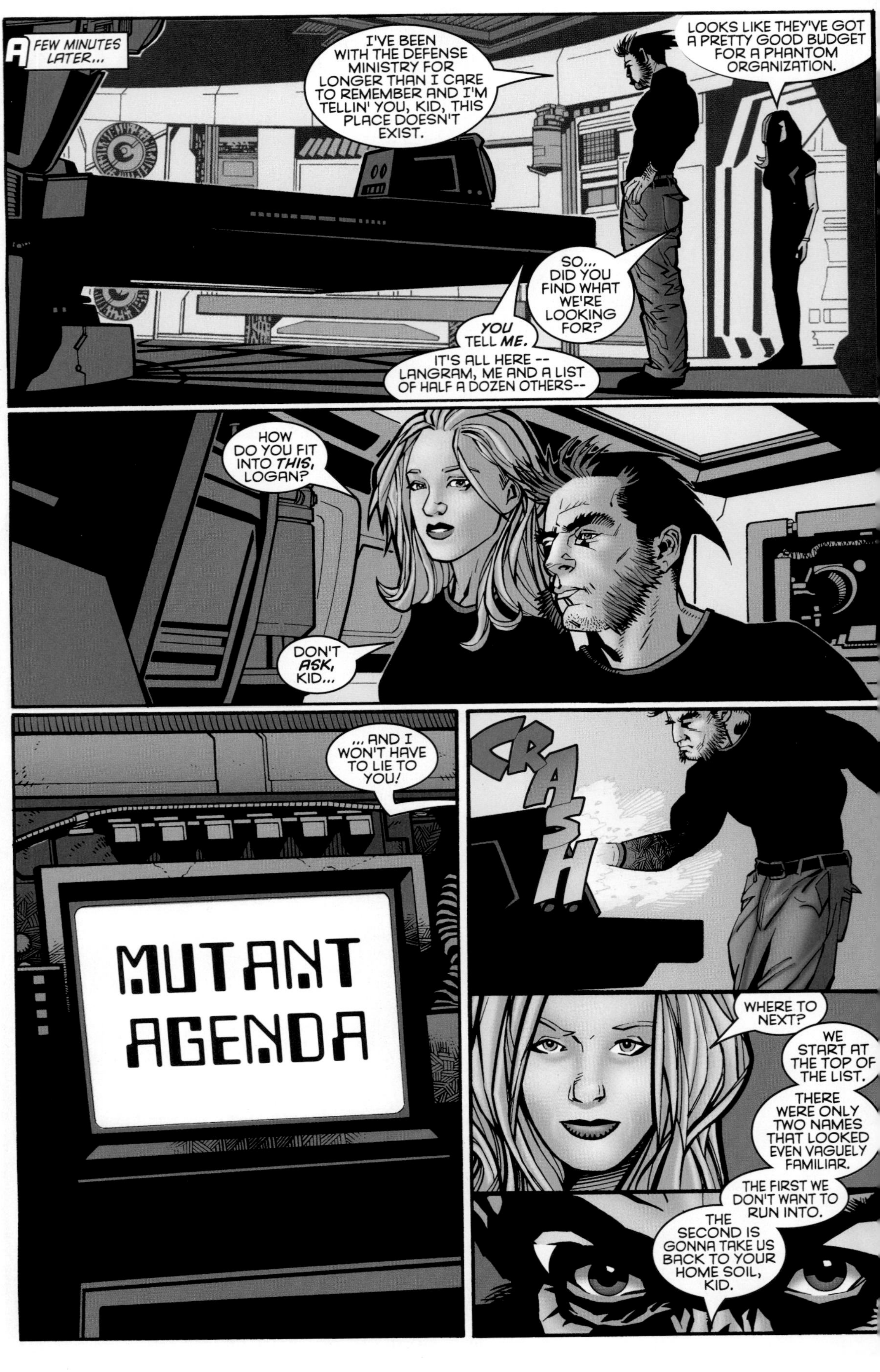
A FEW MINUTES LATER...
I'VE BEEN WITH THE DEFENSE MINISTRY FOR LONGER THAN I CARE TO REMEMBER AND I'M TELLIN' YOU, KID, THIS PLACE DOESN'T EXIST.
LOOKS LIKE THEY'VE GOT A PRETTY GOOD BUDGET FOR A PHANTOM ORGANIZATION.
SO... DID YOU FIND WHAT WE'RE LOOKING FOR?
YOU TELL ME.
IT'S ALL HERE -- LANGRAM, ME AND A LIST OF HALF A DOZEN OTHERS--
HOW DO YOU FIT INTO THIS, LOGAN?
DON'T ASK, KID...
...AND I WON'T HAVE TO LIE TO YOU!
MUTANT AGENDA
CRASH
WHERE TO NEXT?
WE START AT THE TOP OF THE LIST.
THERE WERE ONLY TWO NAMES THAT LOOKED EVEN VAGUELY FAMILIAR.
THE FIRST WE DON'T WANT TO RUN INTO.
THE SECOND IS GONNA TAKE US BACK TO YOUR HOME SOIL, KID.

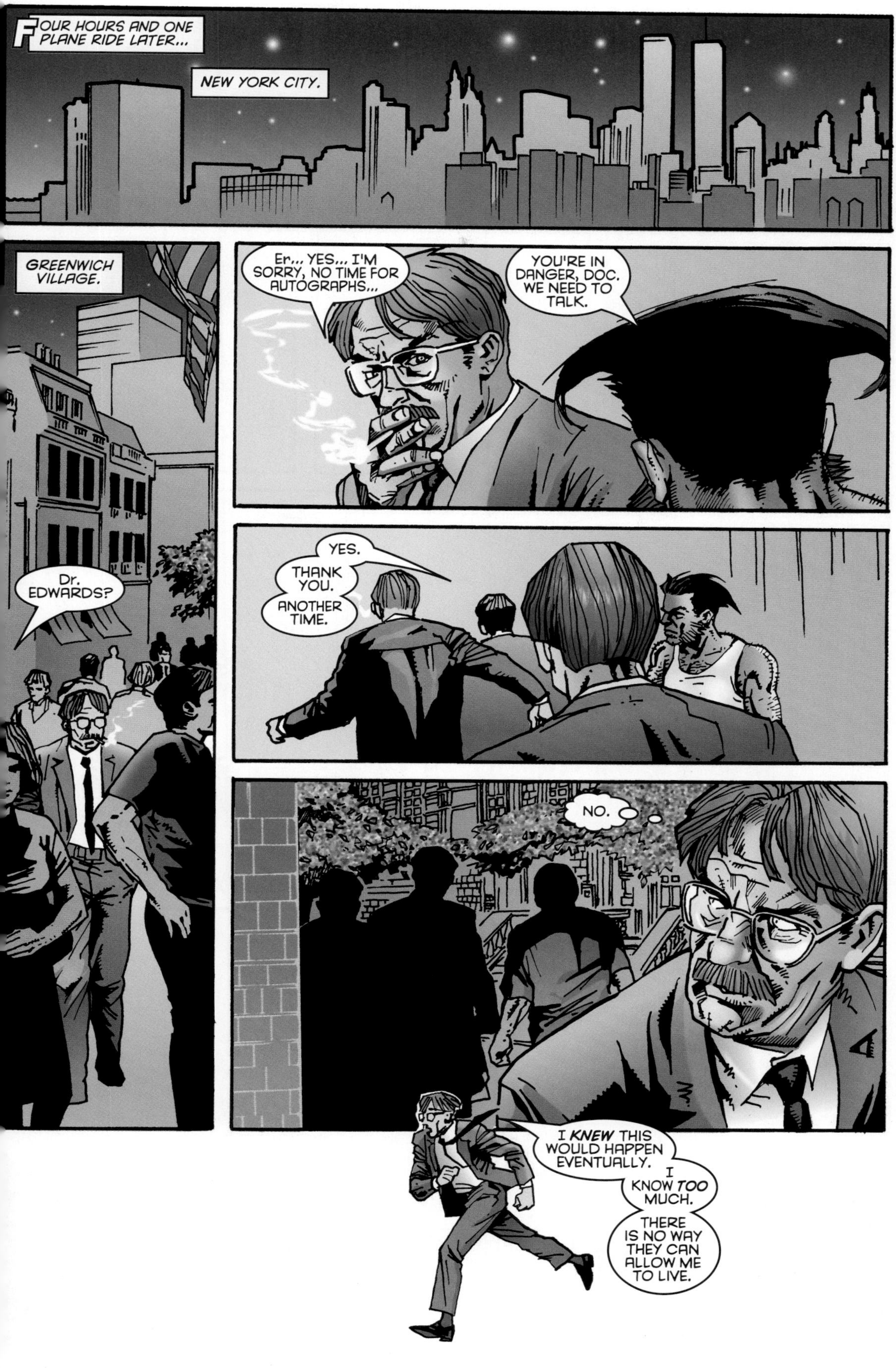
FOUR HOURS AND ONE PLANE RIDE LATER...
NEW YORK CITY.
GREENWICH VILLAGE.
Dr. EDWARDS?
Er... YES... I'M SORRY, NO TIME FOR AUTOGRAPHS...
YOU'RE IN DANGER, DOC. WE NEED TO TALK.
YES.
THANK YOU.
ANOTHER TIME.
NO.
I KNEW THIS WOULD HAPPEN EVENTUALLY.
I KNOW TOO MUCH.
THERE IS NO WAY THEY CAN ALLOW ME TO LIVE.

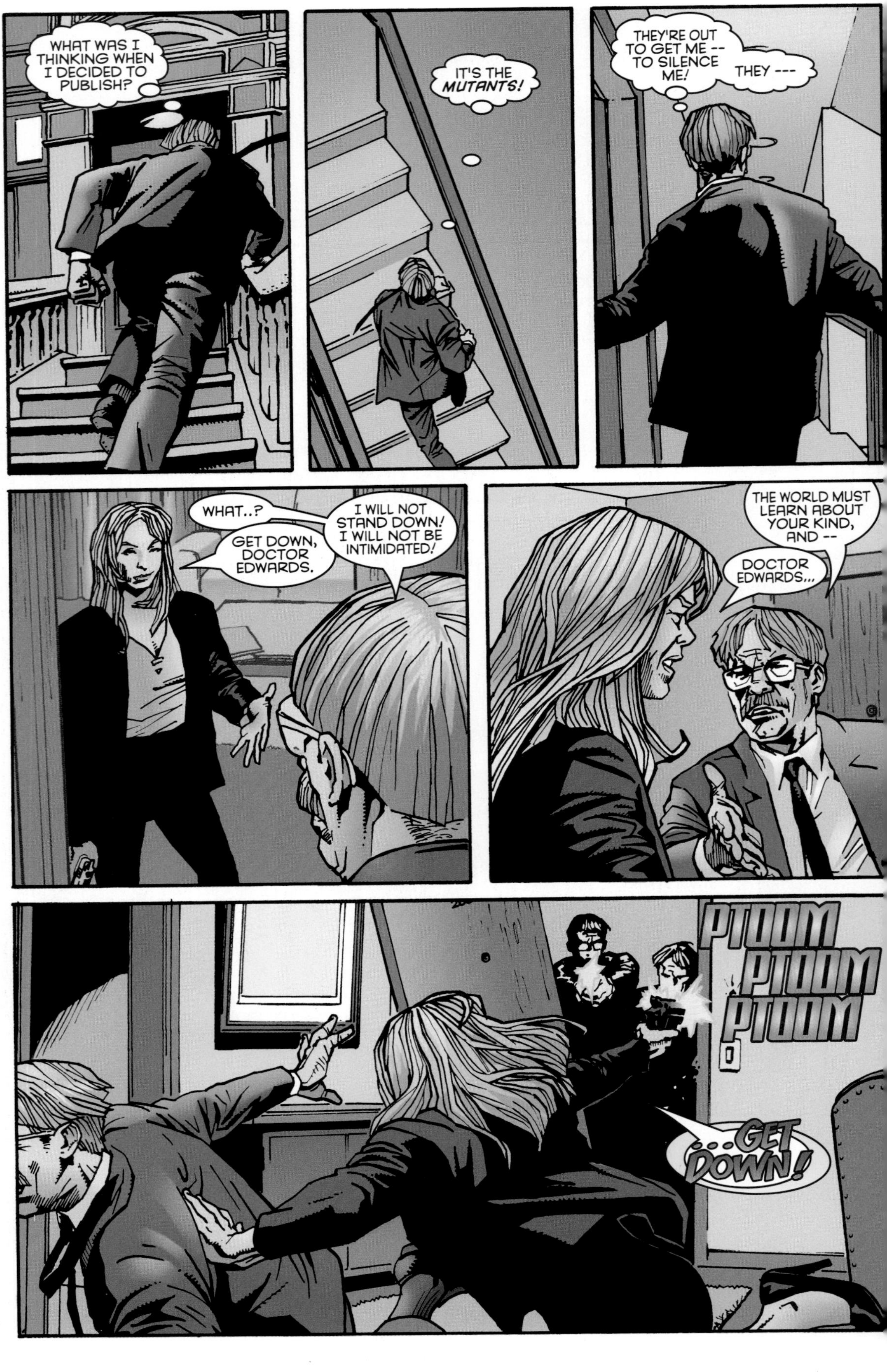
WHAT WAS I THINKING WHEN I DECIDED TO PUBLISH?
IT'S THE MUTANTS!
THEY'RE OUT TO GET ME -- TO SILENCE ME!
THEY ---
WHAT..?
GET DOWN, DOCTOR EDWARDS.
I WILL NOT STAND DOWN! I WILL NOT BE INTIMIDATED!
THE WORLD MUST LEARN ABOUT YOUR KIND, AND --
DOCTOR EDWARDS...
PTOOM PTOOM PTOOM
...GET DOWN!

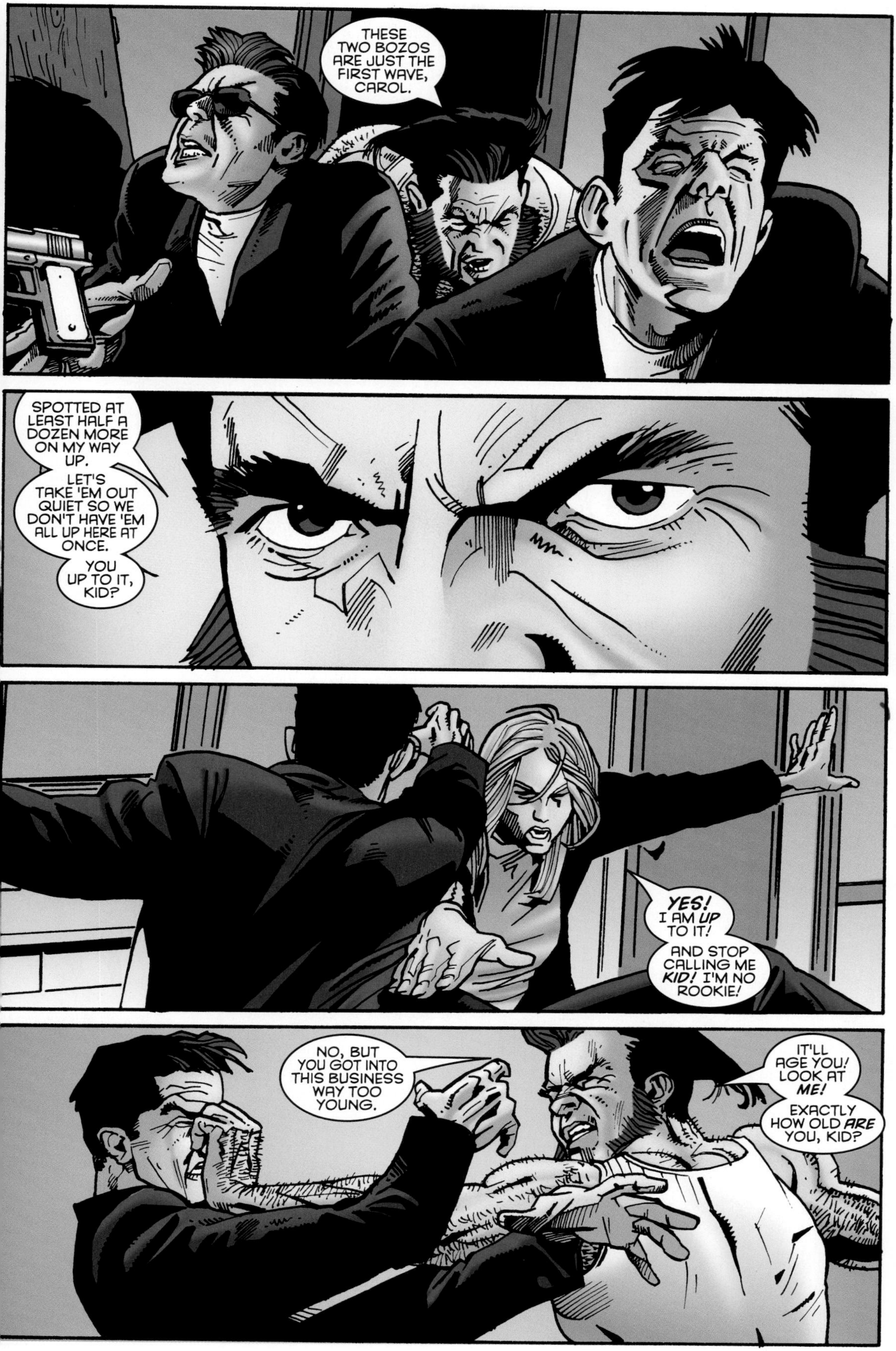
THESE TWO BOZOS ARE JUST THE FIRST WAVE, CAROL.
SPOTTED AT LEAST HALF A DOZEN MORE ON MY WAY UP.
LET'S TAKE 'EM OUT QUIET SO WE DON'T HAVE 'EM ALL UP HERE AT ONCE.
YOU UP TO IT, KID?
YES! I AM UP TO IT!
AND STOP CALLING ME KID! I'M NO ROOKIE!
NO, BUT YOU GOT INTO THIS BUSINESS WAY TOO YOUNG.
IT'LL AGE YOU! LOOK AT ME!
EXACTLY HOW OLD ARE YOU, KID?

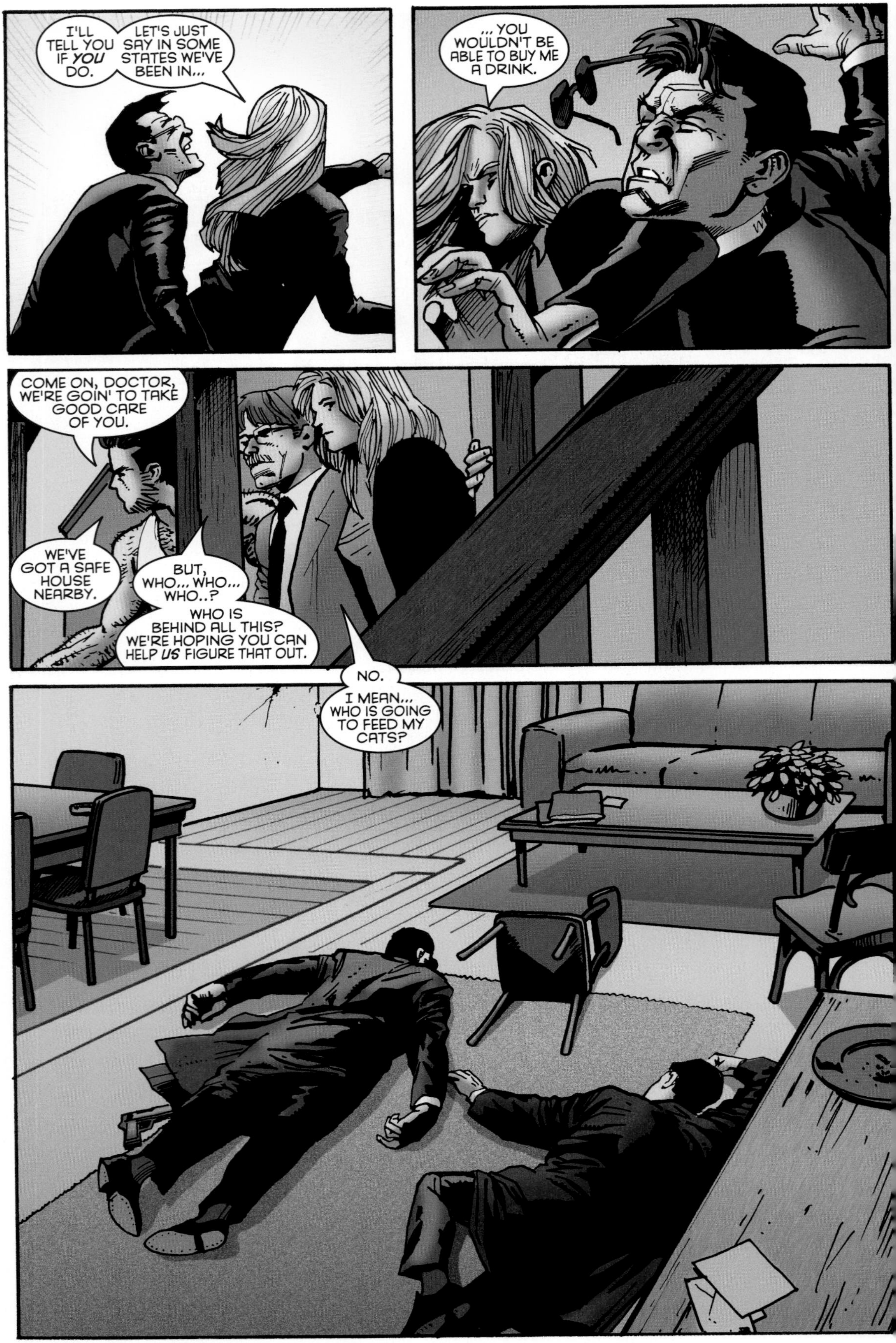
I'LL TELL YOU IF YOU DO.
LET'S JUST SAY IN SOME STATES WE'VE BEEN IN...
... YOU WOULDN'T BE ABLE TO BUY ME A DRINK.
COME ON, DOCTOR, WE'RE GOIN' TO TAKE GOOD CARE OF YOU.
WE'VE GOT A SAFE HOUSE NEARBY.
BUT, WHO... WHO... WHO..?
WHO IS BEHIND ALL THIS? WE'RE HOPING YOU CAN HELP US FIGURE THAT OUT.
NO.
I MEAN... WHO IS GOING TO FEED MY CATS?

A SHORT TIME LATER...

GET AWAY FROM ME! I AM *GOING* TO THE POLICE!

I WOULDN'T ADVISE DOING THAT.

I AM NOT INTERESTED IN *YOUR* ADVICE, YOUNG LADY.

WE'RE ONLY TRYIN' TO KEEP YOU ALIVE, DOC.

KEEP ME *ALIVE?*

I WANT TO KNOW -- *WHO* DO YOU THINK IS TRYING TO KILL *ME?* AND *WHY?*

YOU AND US BOTH, DOC.

'CAUSE WHOEVER WANTS YOU DEAD WANTS TO OFF *ME,* TOO.

YOUR NAME, ALONG WITH MINE AND A FEW OTHERS, TURNED UP IN A GOVERNMENT DATA BANK. THE FILE WAS CALLED *"THE MUTANT AGENDA"* AND IT LOOKED LIKE IT HAS WORLDWIDE RAMIFICATIONS.

WORLDWIDE?

EVEN I NEVER DREAMED...

BUT OF COURSE IT WOULD BE WORLDWIDE. HOW SMALL-MINDED I WAS TO ASSUME IT WAS CONFINED TO THE UNITED STATES.

THIS IS BIGGER THAN I HAD EVER IMAGINED.

AND I'M ON THE BRINK OF EXPOSING THEM ALL.

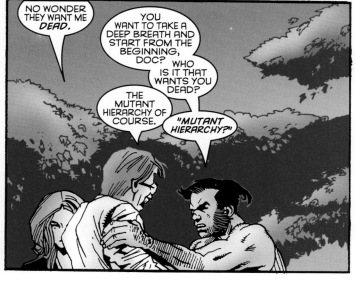

NO WONDER THEY WANT ME *DEAD.*

YOU WANT TO TAKE A DEEP BREATH AND START FROM THE BEGINNING, DOC? WHO IS IT THAT WANTS YOU DEAD?

THE MUTANT HIERARCHY OF COURSE.

"MUTANT HIERARCHY?"

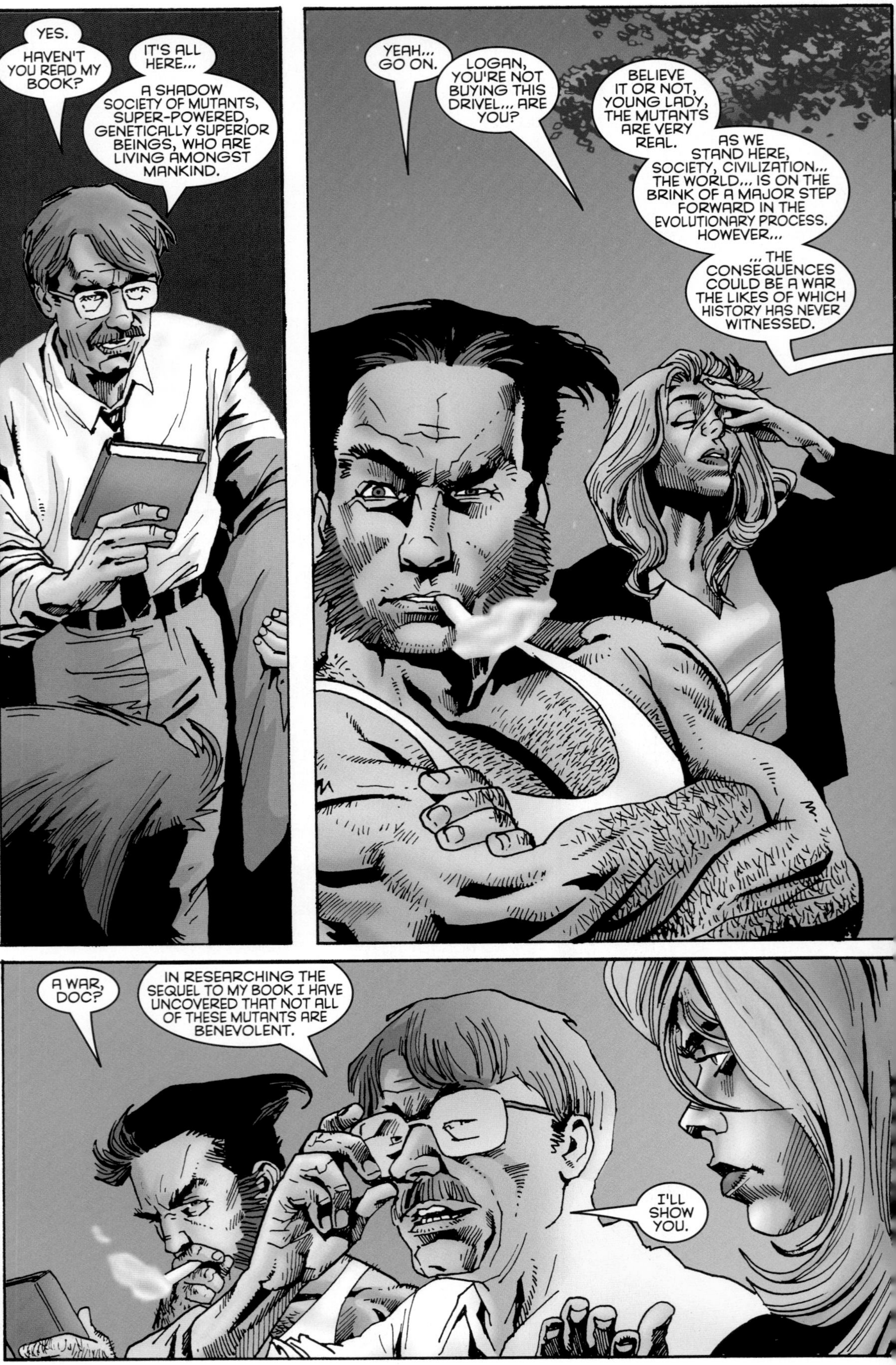
YES.
HAVEN'T YOU READ MY BOOK?
IT'S ALL HERE...
A SHADOW SOCIETY OF MUTANTS, SUPER-POWERED, GENETICALLY SUPERIOR BEINGS, WHO ARE LIVING AMONGST MANKIND.
YEAH... GO ON.
LOGAN, YOU'RE NOT BUYING THIS DRIVEL... ARE YOU?
BELIEVE IT OR NOT, YOUNG LADY, THE MUTANTS ARE VERY REAL.
AS WE STAND HERE, SOCIETY, CIVILIZATION... THE WORLD... IS ON THE BRINK OF A MAJOR STEP FORWARD IN THE EVOLUTIONARY PROCESS. HOWEVER...
... THE CONSEQUENCES COULD BE A WAR THE LIKES OF WHICH HISTORY HAS NEVER WITNESSED.
A WAR, DOC?
IN RESEARCHING THE SEQUEL TO MY BOOK I HAVE UNCOVERED THAT NOT ALL OF THESE MUTANTS ARE BENEVOLENT.
I'LL SHOW YOU.

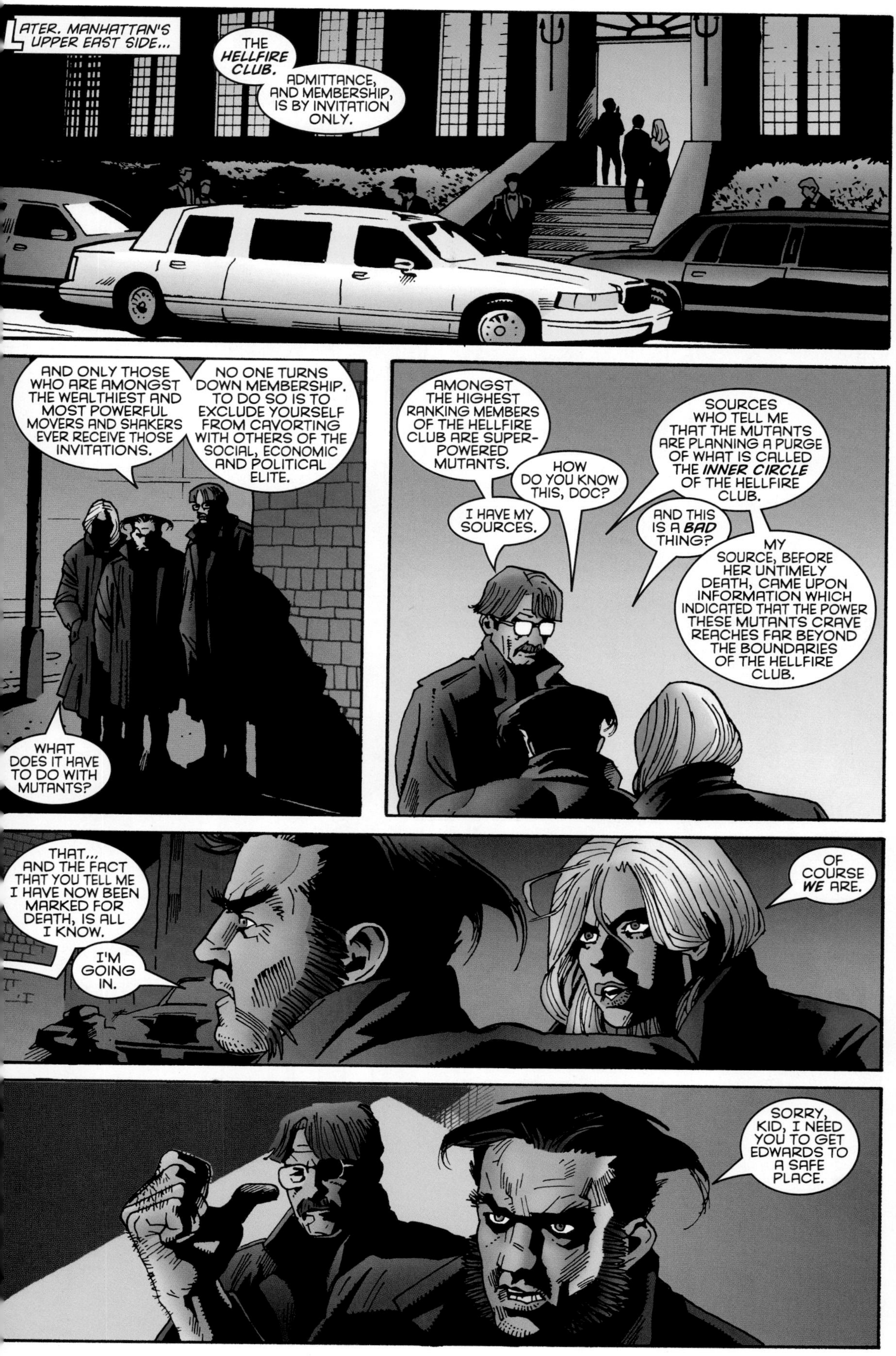
LATER. MANHATTAN'S UPPER EAST SIDE...
THE HELLFIRE CLUB.
ADMITTANCE, AND MEMBERSHIP, IS BY INVITATION ONLY.
AND ONLY THOSE WHO ARE AMONGST THE WEALTHIEST AND MOST POWERFUL MOVERS AND SHAKERS EVER RECEIVE THOSE INVITATIONS.
NO ONE TURNS DOWN MEMBERSHIP. TO DO SO IS TO EXCLUDE YOURSELF FROM CAVORTING WITH OTHERS OF THE SOCIAL, ECONOMIC AND POLITICAL ELITE.
WHAT DOES IT HAVE TO DO WITH MUTANTS?
AMONGST THE HIGHEST RANKING MEMBERS OF THE HELLFIRE CLUB ARE SUPER-POWERED MUTANTS.
HOW DO YOU KNOW THIS, DOC?
I HAVE MY SOURCES.
SOURCES WHO TELL ME THAT THE MUTANTS ARE PLANNING A PURGE OF WHAT IS CALLED THE INNER CIRCLE OF THE HELLFIRE CLUB.
AND THIS IS A BAD THING?
MY SOURCE, BEFORE HER UNTIMELY DEATH, CAME UPON INFORMATION WHICH INDICATED THAT THE POWER THESE MUTANTS CRAVE REACHES FAR BEYOND THE BOUNDARIES OF THE HELLFIRE CLUB.
THAT... AND THE FACT THAT YOU TELL ME I HAVE NOW BEEN MARKED FOR DEATH, IS ALL I KNOW.
I'M GOING IN.
OF COURSE WE ARE.
SORRY, KID, I NEED YOU TO GET EDWARDS TO A SAFE PLACE.

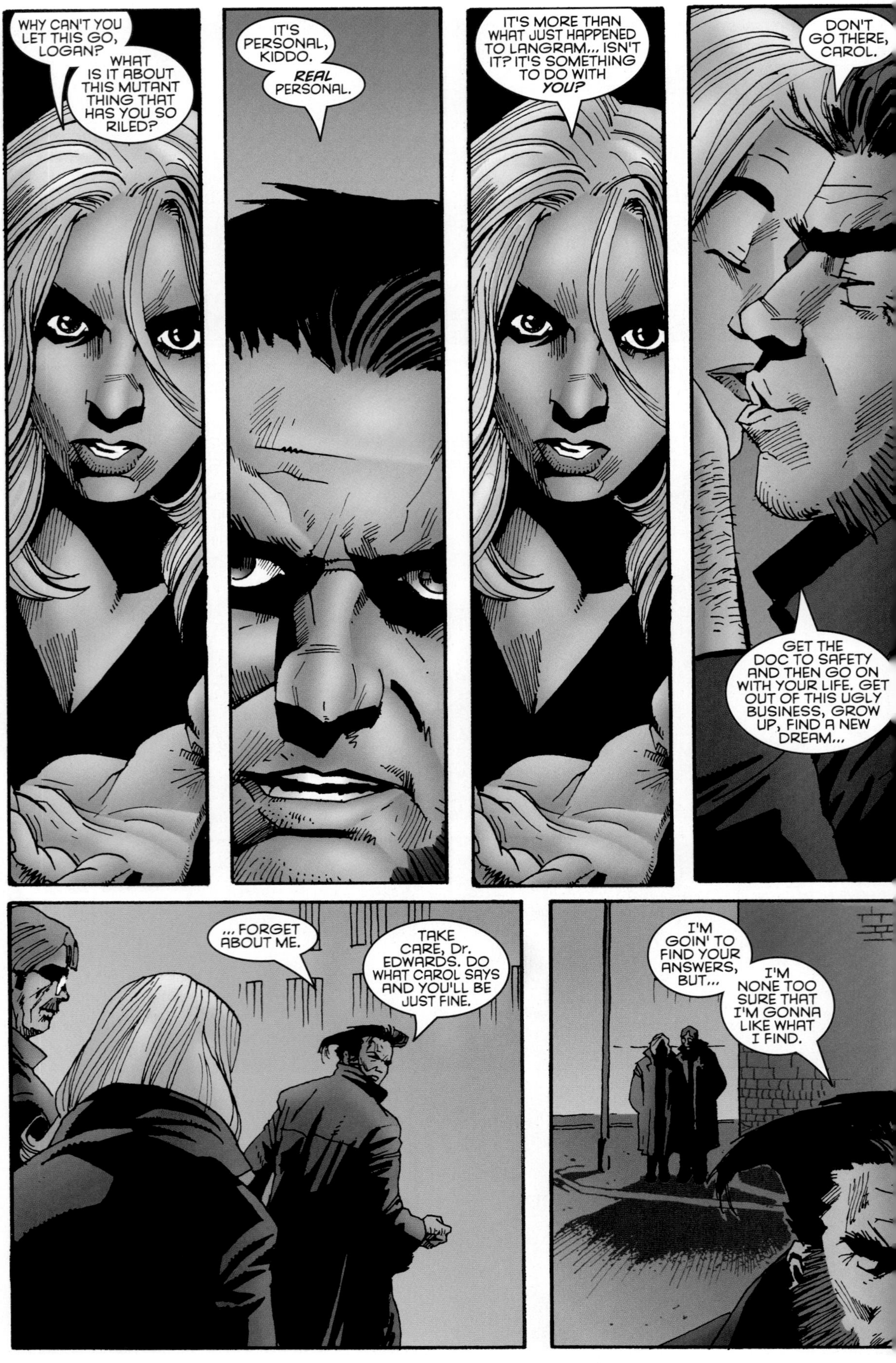
WHY CAN'T YOU LET THIS GO, LOGAN?
WHAT IS IT ABOUT THIS MUTANT THING THAT HAS YOU SO RILED?
IT'S PERSONAL, KIDDO.
REAL PERSONAL.
IT'S MORE THAN WHAT JUST HAPPENED TO LANGRAM... ISN'T IT? IT'S SOMETHING TO DO WITH YOU?
DON'T GO THERE, CAROL.
GET THE DOC TO SAFETY AND THEN GO ON WITH YOUR LIFE. GET OUT OF THIS UGLY BUSINESS, GROW UP, FIND A NEW DREAM...
...FORGET ABOUT ME.
TAKE CARE, Dr. EDWARDS. DO WHAT CAROL SAYS AND YOU'LL BE JUST FINE.
I'M GOIN' TO FIND YOUR ANSWERS, BUT...
I'M NONE TOO SURE THAT I'M GONNA LIKE WHAT I FIND.

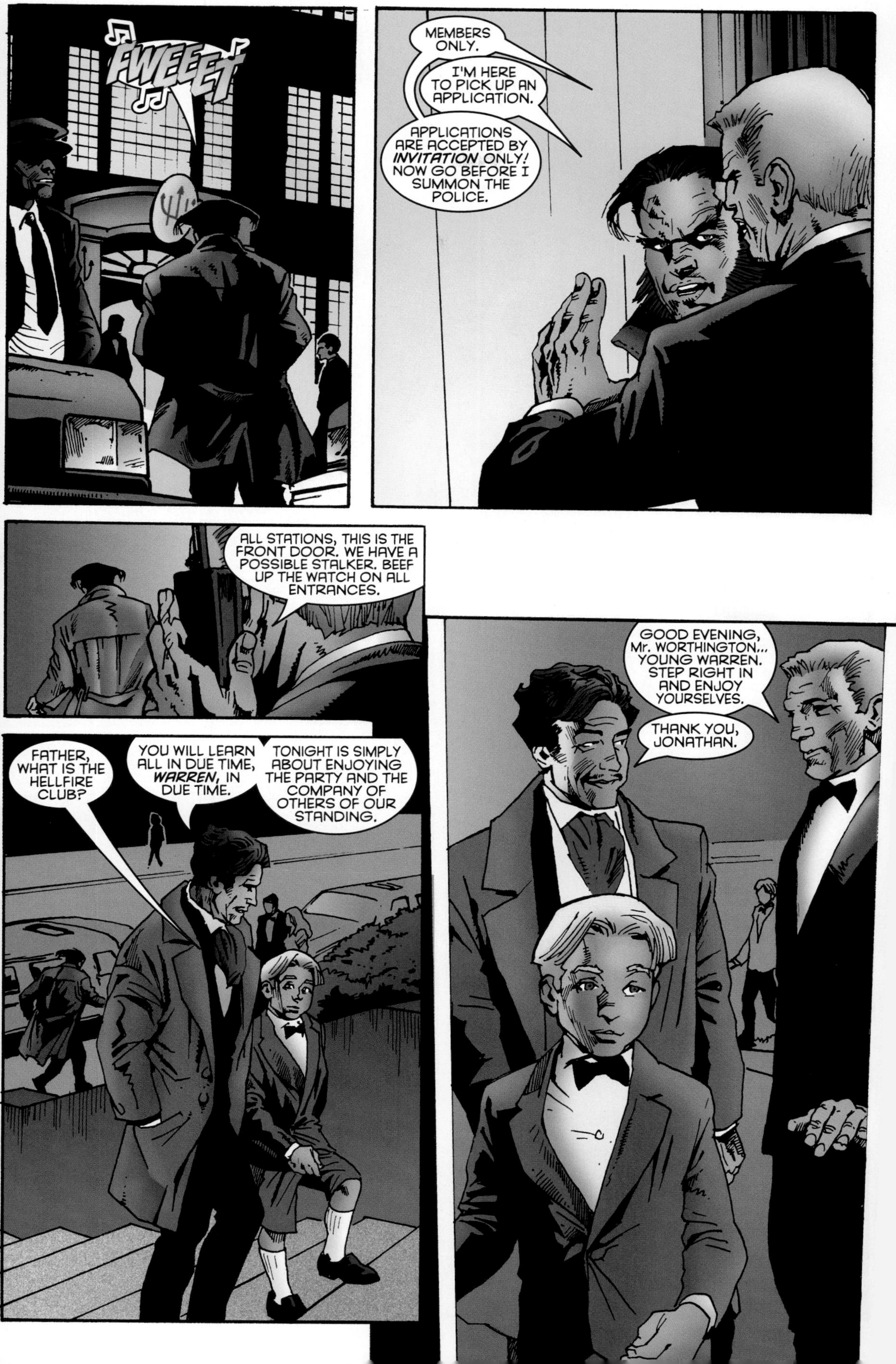
FWEEET
MEMBERS ONLY.
I'M HERE TO PICK UP AN APPLICATION.
APPLICATIONS ARE ACCEPTED BY INVITATION ONLY! NOW GO BEFORE I SUMMON THE POLICE.
ALL STATIONS, THIS IS THE FRONT DOOR. WE HAVE A POSSIBLE STALKER. BEEF UP THE WATCH ON ALL ENTRANCES.
FATHER, WHAT IS THE HELLFIRE CLUB?
YOU WILL LEARN ALL IN DUE TIME, WARREN, IN DUE TIME.
TONIGHT IS SIMPLY ABOUT ENJOYING THE PARTY AND THE COMPANY OF OTHERS OF OUR STANDING.
GOOD EVENING, Mr. WORTHINGTON... YOUNG WARREN. STEP RIGHT IN AND ENJOY YOURSELVES.
THANK YOU, JONATHAN.

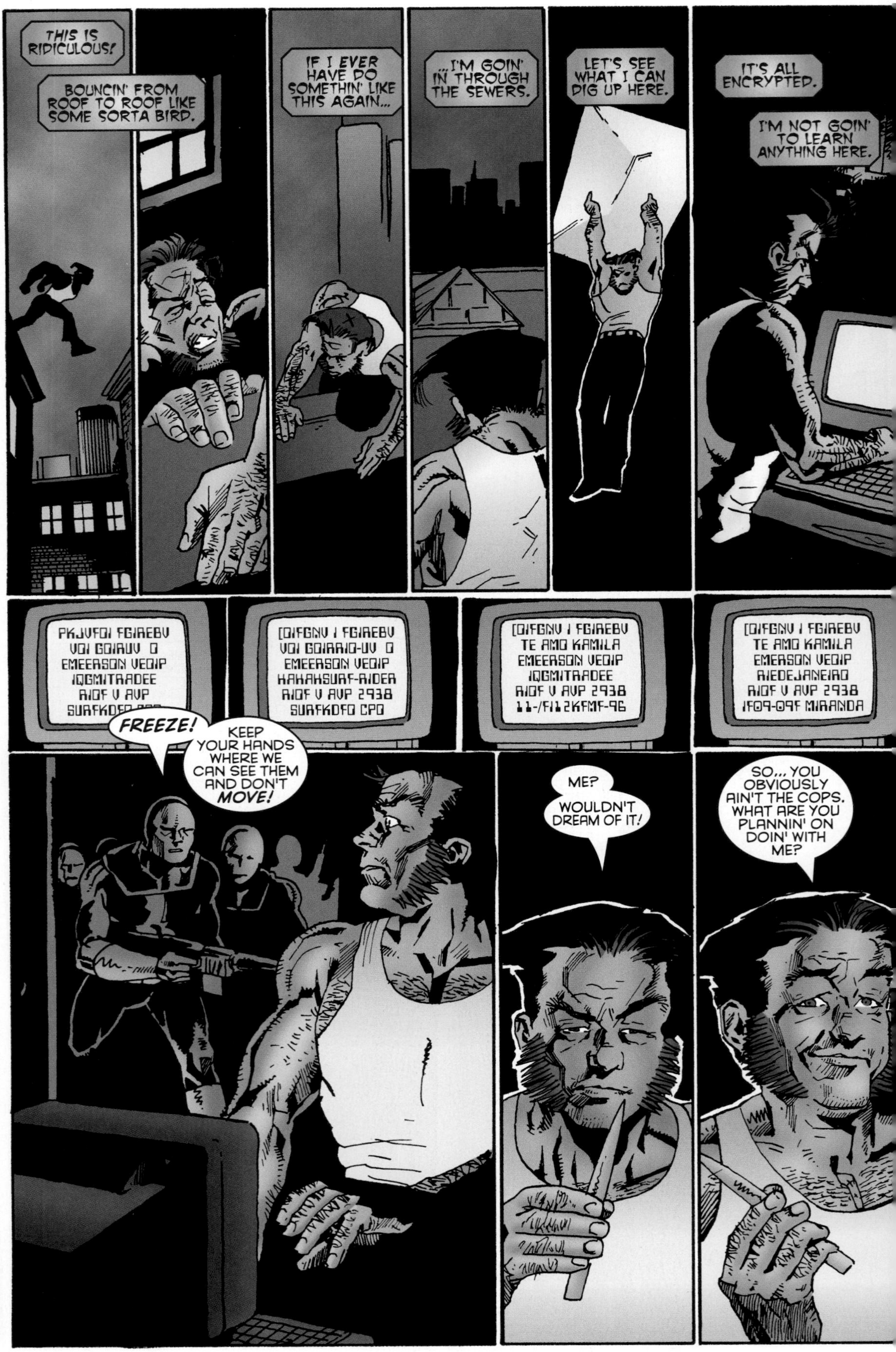
THIS IS RIDICULOUS!
BOUNCIN' FROM ROOF TO ROOF LIKE SOME SORTA BIRD.
IF I EVER HAVE DO SOMETHIN' LIKE THIS AGAIN...
...I'M GOIN' IN THROUGH THE SEWERS.
LET'S SEE WHAT I CAN DIG UP HERE.
IT'S ALL ENCRYPTED.
I'M NOT GOIN' TO LEARN ANYTHING HERE.
PKJVFOI FGIREBV
VOI GOIRUV O
EMEERSON VEOIP
IQGMITRADEE
RIOF V AVP
[OIFGNV I FGIREBV
VOI GOIRRIO-UV O
EMEERSON VEOIP
HAHAHSURF-RIDER
RIOF V AVP 2938
SURFKOFO CPO
[OIFGNV I FGIREBV
TE AMO KAMILA
EMEERSON VEOIP
IQGMITRADEE
RIOF V AVP 2938
[OIFGNV I FGIREBV
TE AMO KAMILA
EMEERSON VEOIP
RIEDEJANEIRO
RIOF V AVP 2938
IFO9-O9F MIRANDA
FREEZE!
KEEP YOUR HANDS WHERE WE CAN SEE THEM AND DON'T MOVE!
ME?
WOULDN'T DREAM OF IT!
SO... YOU OBVIOUSLY AIN'T THE COPS. WHAT ARE YOU PLANNIN' ON DOIN' WITH ME?

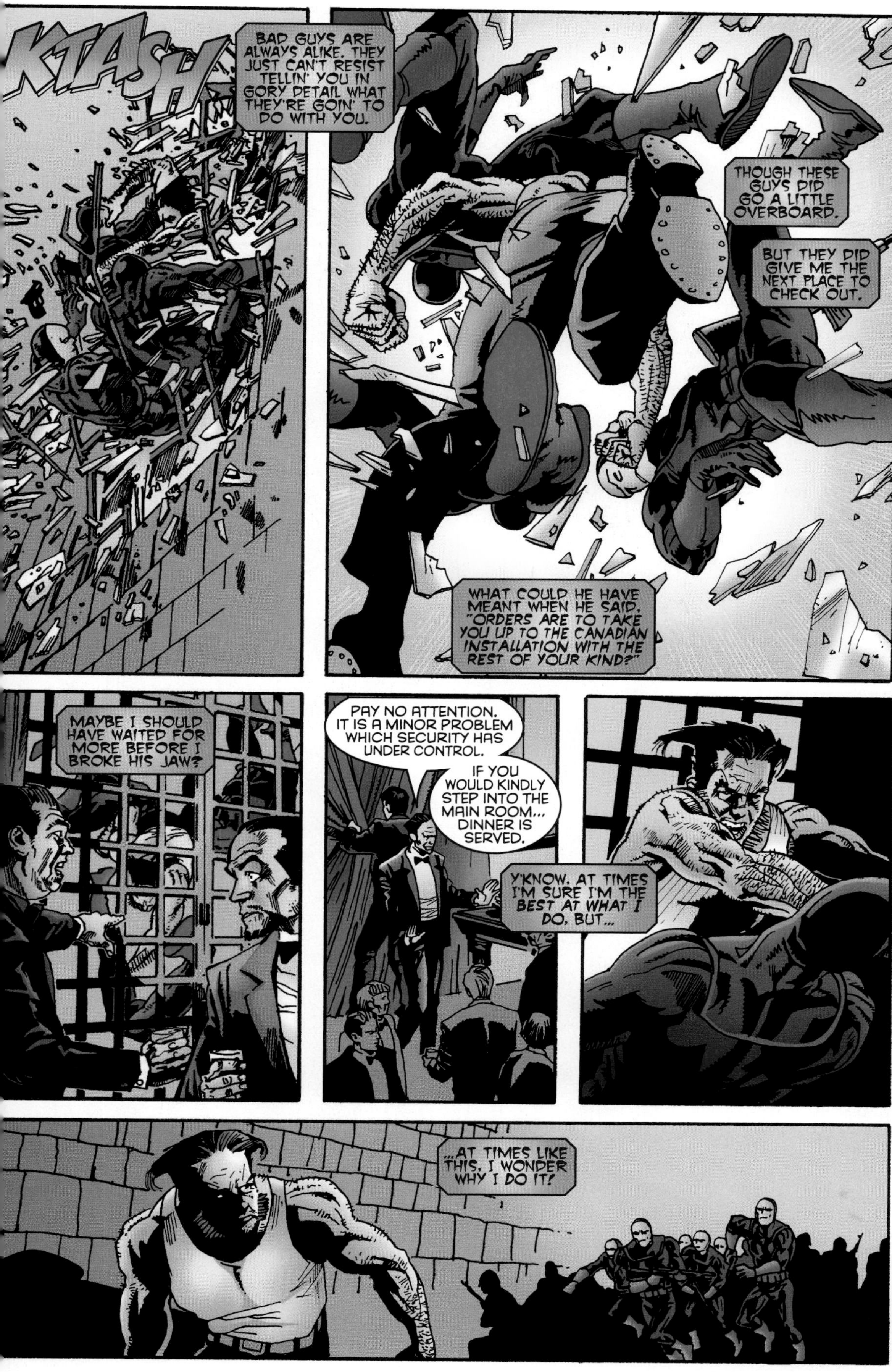
KTASH
BAD GUYS ARE ALWAYS ALIKE. THEY JUST CAN'T RESIST TELLIN' YOU IN GORY DETAIL WHAT THEY'RE GOIN' TO DO WITH YOU.
THOUGH THESE GUYS DID GO A LITTLE OVERBOARD.
BUT THEY DID GIVE ME THE NEXT PLACE TO CHECK OUT.
WHAT COULD HE HAVE MEANT WHEN HE SAID, "ORDERS ARE TO TAKE YOU UP TO THE CANADIAN INSTALLATION WITH THE REST OF YOUR KIND?"
MAYBE I SHOULD HAVE WAITED FOR MORE BEFORE I BROKE HIS JAW?
PAY NO ATTENTION. IT IS A MINOR PROBLEM WHICH SECURITY HAS UNDER CONTROL.
IF YOU WOULD KINDLY STEP INTO THE MAIN ROOM... DINNER IS SERVED.
Y'KNOW, AT TIMES I'M SURE I'M THE BEST AT WHAT I DO, BUT...
...AT TIMES LIKE THIS, I WONDER WHY I DO IT!

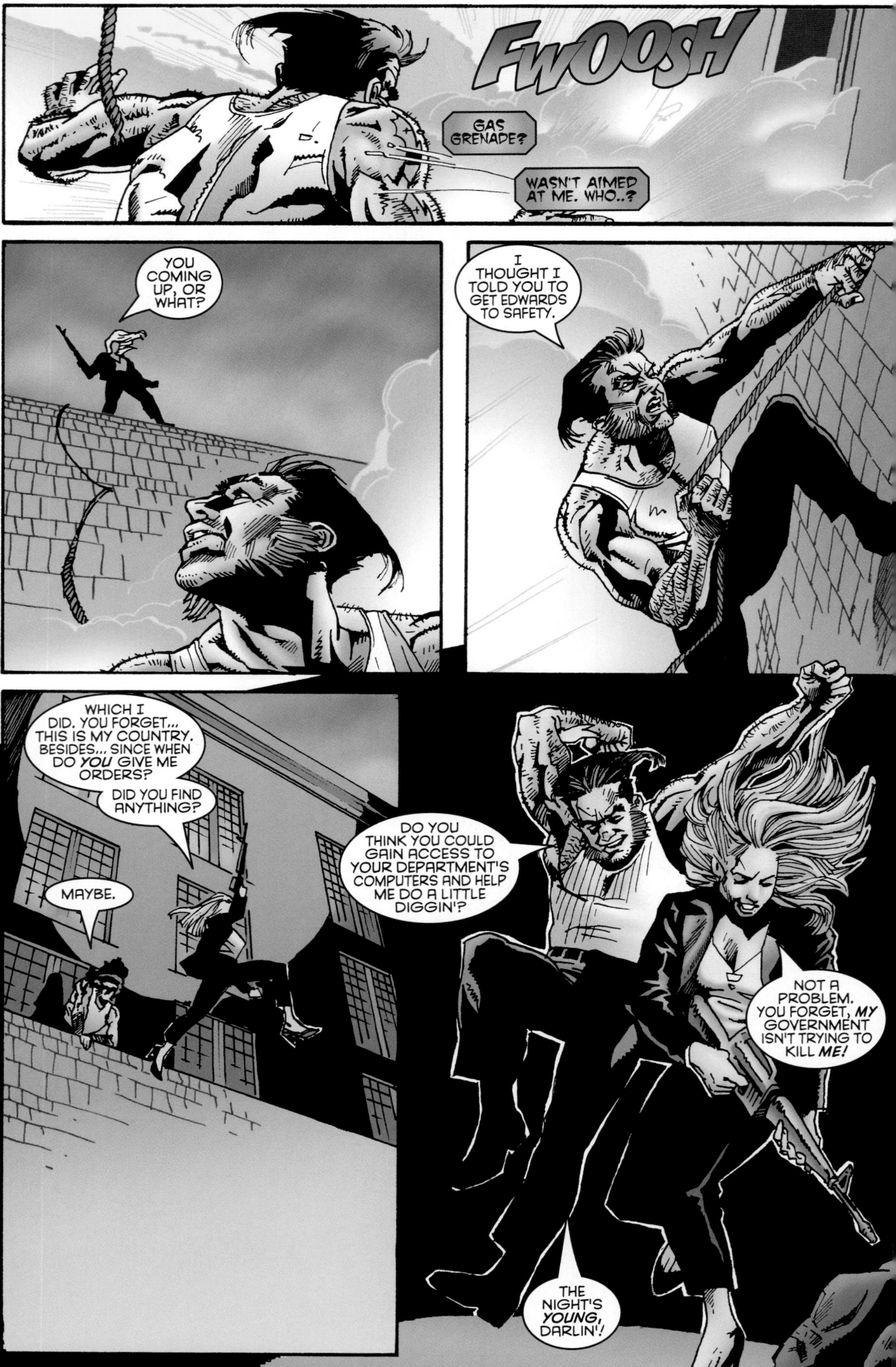
FWOOSH
GAS GRENADE?
WASN'T AIMED AT ME. WHO..?
YOU COMING UP, OR WHAT?
I THOUGHT I TOLD YOU TO GET EDWARDS TO SAFETY.
WHICH I DID. YOU FORGET... THIS IS MY COUNTRY. BESIDES... SINCE WHEN DO YOU GIVE ME ORDERS?
DID YOU FIND ANYTHING?
MAYBE.
DO YOU THINK YOU COULD GAIN ACCESS TO YOUR DEPARTMENT'S COMPUTERS AND HELP ME DO A LITTLE DIGGIN'?
NOT A PROBLEM. YOU FORGET, MY GOVERNMENT ISN'T TRYING TO KILL ME!
THE NIGHT'S YOUNG, DARLIN'!

A WINDOW HIGH ABOVE THE HELLFIRE CLUB COURTYARD...

WILL HE TAKE THE BAIT?

COUNT ON IT.

THE RUNT IS GOOD ENOUGH TO FOLLOW THE TRAIL I'VE GIVEN HIM. HE'LL BE THERE.

HE DOES SHOW INITIATIVE.

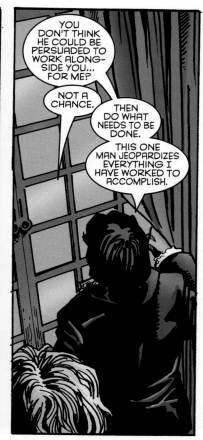

YOU DON'T THINK HE COULD BE PERSUADED TO WORK ALONGSIDE YOU... FOR ME?

NOT A CHANCE.

THEN DO WHAT NEEDS TO BE DONE.

THIS ONE MAN JEOPARDIZES EVERYTHING I HAVE WORKED TO ACCOMPLISH.

THE ENTIRE INNER CIRCLE IS WITHIN MY GRASP.

AND AFTER ALL..?

IT IS IMPERATIVE THAT THE EXISTENCE OF MUTANTKIND NOT BE MADE PUBLIC UNTIL I AND MY COMPATRIOTS ARE READY TO ACT DECISIVELY.

THIS ENTIRE OPERATION HAS TURNED INTO A DEBACLE. SALVAGE THAT WHICH YOU CAN AND CLEAN UP THE REST.

CAN'T THINK OF ANYONE I'D RATHER CLEAN UP, MR. SHAW.

THE LITTLE GUY AND ME HAVE GOT A MAJOR SCORE TO SETTLE.

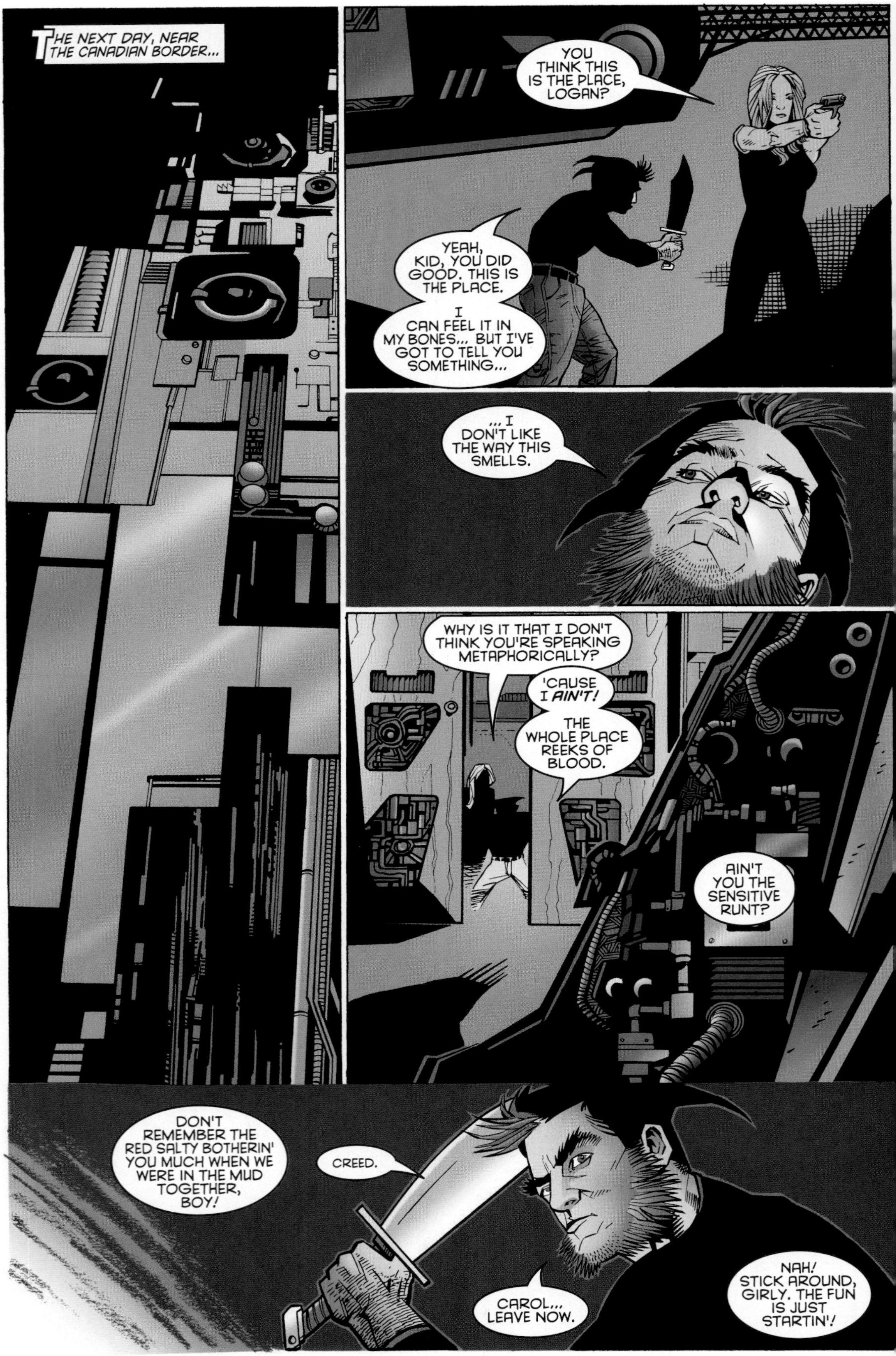
THE NEXT DAY, NEAR THE CANADIAN BORDER...
YOU THINK THIS IS THE PLACE, LOGAN?
YEAH, KID, YOU DID GOOD. THIS IS THE PLACE.
I CAN FEEL IT IN MY BONES... BUT I'VE GOT TO TELL YOU SOMETHING...
...I DON'T LIKE THE WAY THIS SMELLS.
WHY IS IT THAT I DON'T THINK YOU'RE SPEAKING METAPHORICALLY?
'CAUSE I AIN'T!
THE WHOLE PLACE REEKS OF BLOOD.
AIN'T YOU THE SENSITIVE RUNT?
DON'T REMEMBER THE RED SALTY BOTHERIN' YOU MUCH WHEN WE WERE IN THE MUD TOGETHER, BOY!
CREED.
CAROL... LEAVE NOW.
NAH! STICK AROUND, GIRLY. THE FUN IS JUST STARTIN'!

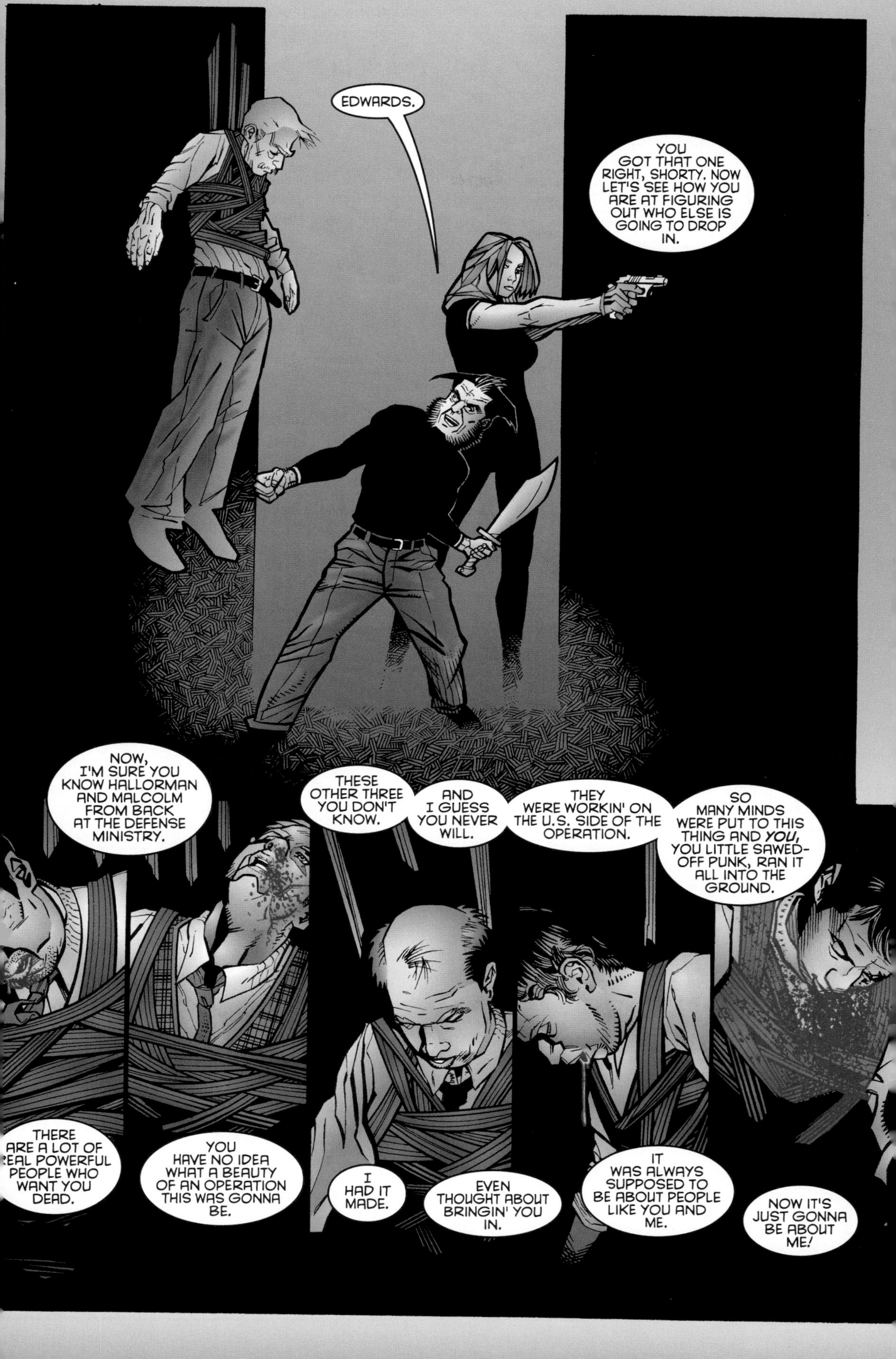
EDWARDS.
YOU GOT THAT ONE RIGHT, SHORTY. NOW LET'S SEE HOW YOU ARE AT FIGURING OUT WHO ELSE IS GOING TO DROP IN.
NOW, I'M SURE YOU KNOW HALLORMAN AND MALCOLM FROM BACK AT THE DEFENSE MINISTRY.
THESE OTHER THREE YOU DON'T KNOW.
AND I GUESS YOU NEVER WILL.
THEY WERE WORKIN' ON THE U.S. SIDE OF THE OPERATION.
SO MANY MINDS WERE PUT TO THIS THING AND *YOU*, YOU LITTLE SAWED-OFF PUNK, RAN IT ALL INTO THE GROUND.
THERE ARE A LOT OF REAL POWERFUL PEOPLE WHO WANT YOU DEAD.
YOU HAVE NO IDEA WHAT A BEAUTY OF AN OPERATION THIS WAS GONNA BE.
I HAD IT MADE.
EVEN THOUGHT ABOUT BRINGIN' YOU IN.
IT WAS ALWAYS SUPPOSED TO BE ABOUT PEOPLE LIKE YOU AND ME.
NOW IT'S JUST GONNA BE ABOUT ME!

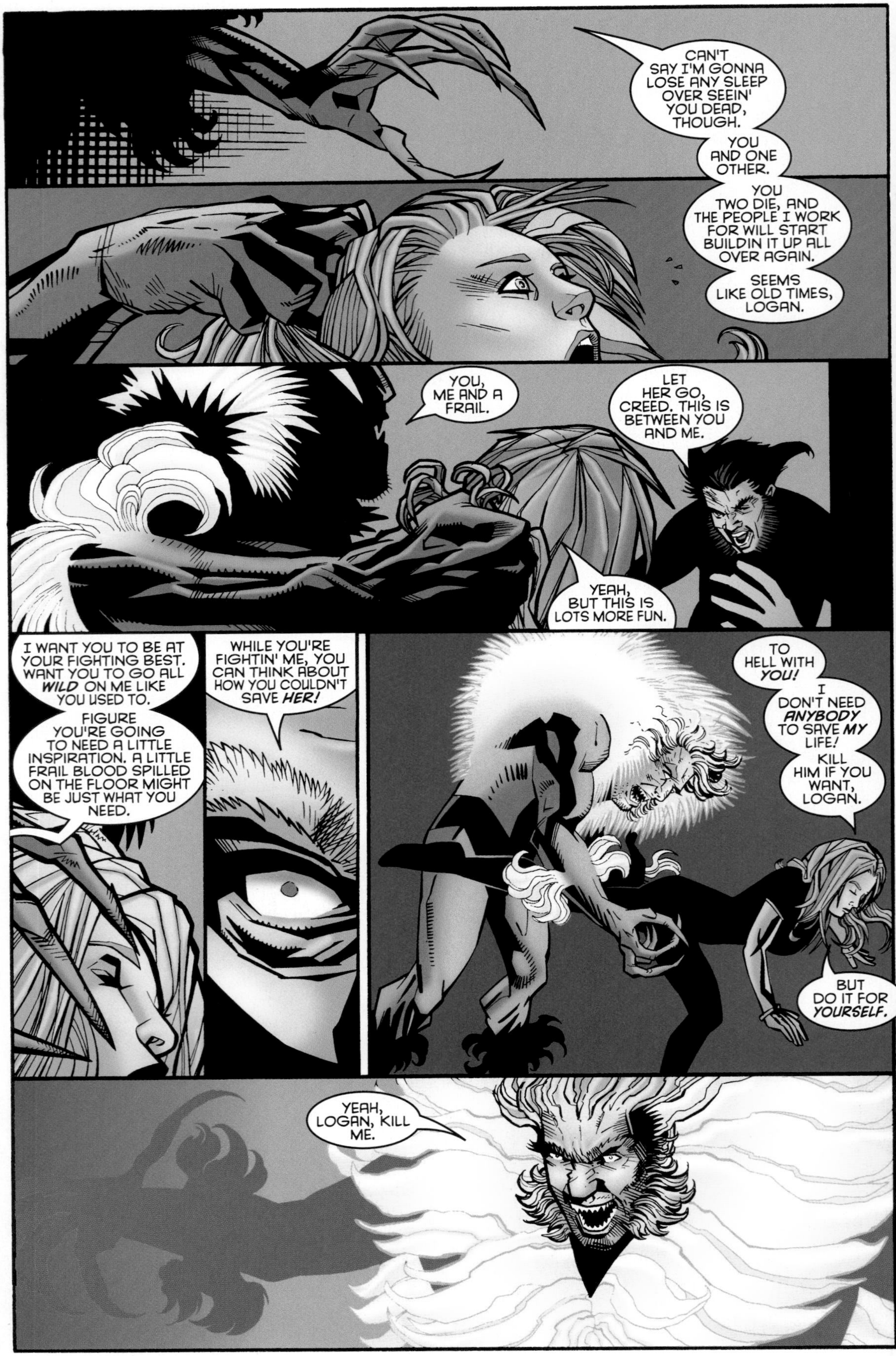
CAN'T SAY I'M GONNA LOSE ANY SLEEP OVER SEEIN' YOU DEAD, THOUGH.
YOU AND ONE OTHER.
YOU TWO DIE, AND THE PEOPLE I WORK FOR WILL START BUILDIN IT UP ALL OVER AGAIN.
SEEMS LIKE OLD TIMES, LOGAN.
YOU, ME AND A FRAIL.
LET HER GO, CREED. THIS IS BETWEEN YOU AND ME.
YEAH, BUT THIS IS LOTS MORE FUN.
I WANT YOU TO BE AT YOUR FIGHTING BEST. WANT YOU TO GO ALL WILD ON ME LIKE YOU USED TO.
FIGURE YOU'RE GOING TO NEED A LITTLE INSPIRATION. A LITTLE FRAIL BLOOD SPILLED ON THE FLOOR MIGHT BE JUST WHAT YOU NEED.
WHILE YOU'RE FIGHTIN' ME, YOU CAN THINK ABOUT HOW YOU COULDN'T SAVE HER!
TO HELL WITH YOU!
I DON'T NEED ANYBODY TO SAVE MY LIFE!
KILL HIM IF YOU WANT, LOGAN.
BUT DO IT FOR YOURSELF.
YEAH, LOGAN, KILL ME.

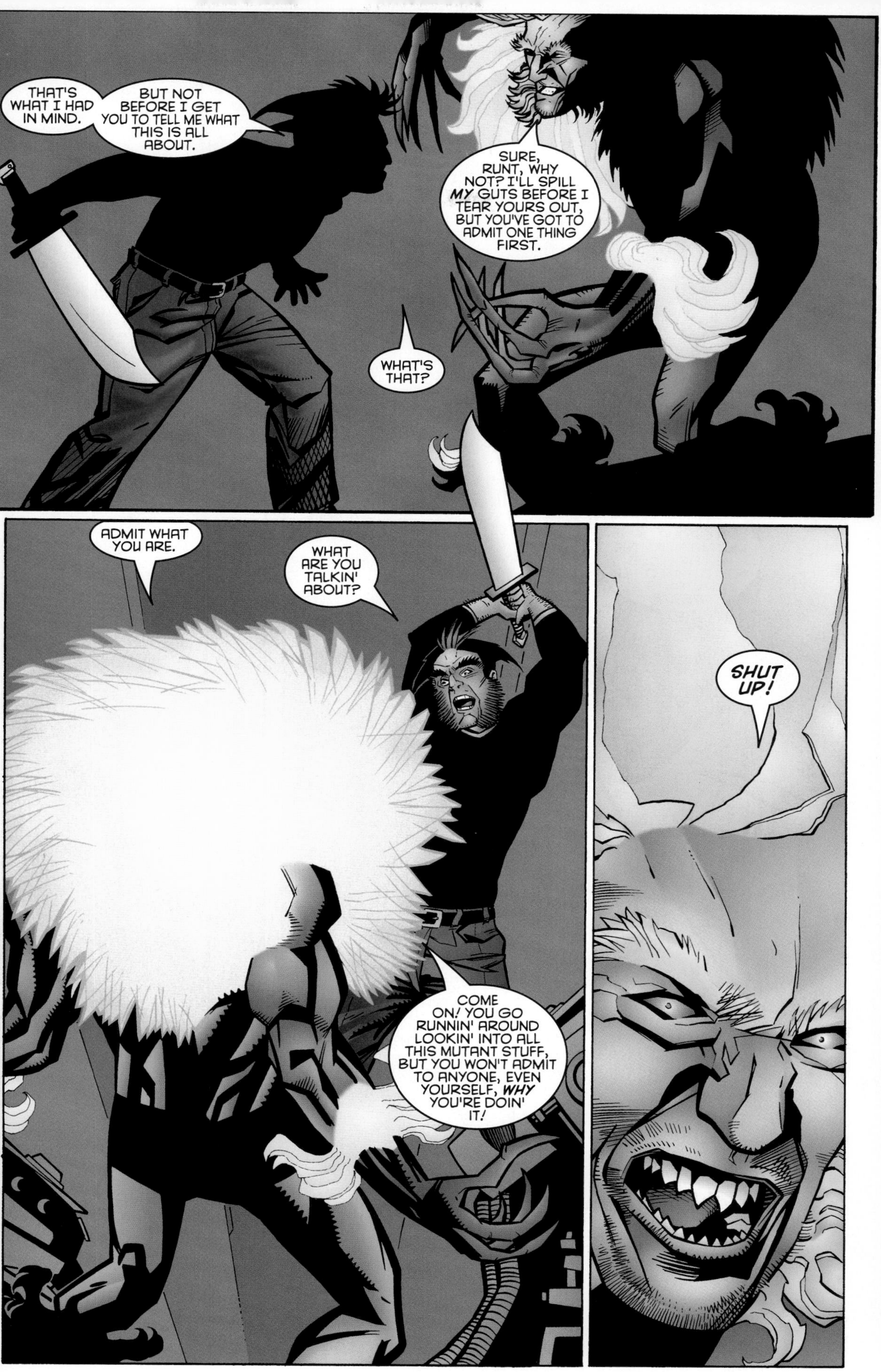
THAT'S WHAT I HAD IN MIND.
BUT NOT BEFORE I GET YOU TO TELL ME WHAT THIS IS ALL ABOUT.
SURE, RUNT, WHY NOT? I'LL SPILL MY GUTS BEFORE I TEAR YOURS OUT, BUT YOU'VE GOT TO ADMIT ONE THING FIRST.
WHAT'S THAT?
ADMIT WHAT YOU ARE.
WHAT ARE YOU TALKIN' ABOUT?
COME ON! YOU GO RUNNIN' AROUND LOOKIN' INTO ALL THIS MUTANT STUFF, BUT YOU WON'T ADMIT TO ANYONE, EVEN YOURSELF, WHY YOU'RE DOIN' IT!
SHUT UP!

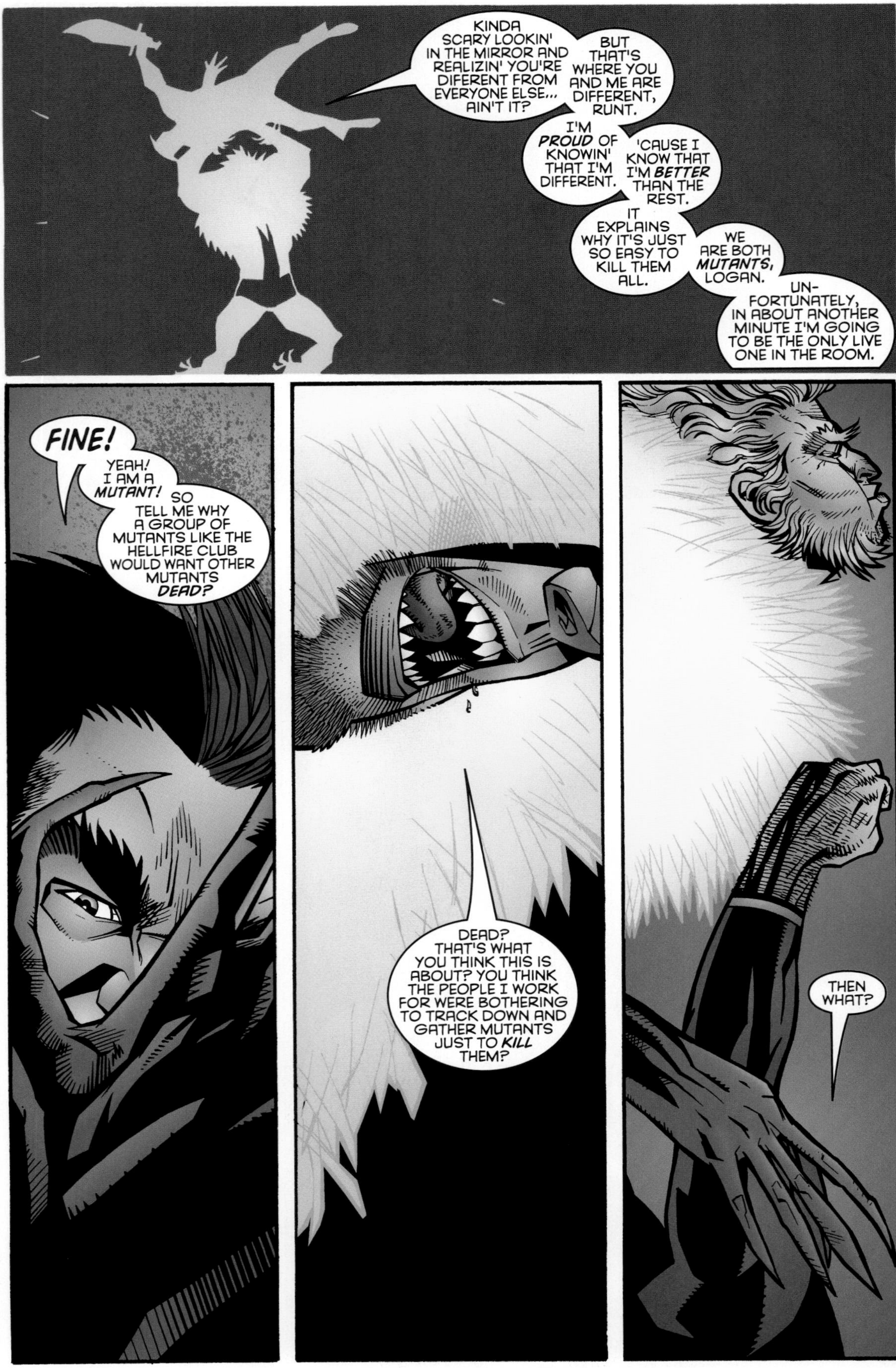
KINDA SCARY LOOKIN' IN THE MIRROR AND REALIZIN' YOU'RE DIFERENT FROM EVERYONE ELSE... AIN'T IT?
BUT THAT'S WHERE YOU AND ME ARE DIFFERENT, RUNT.
I'M PROUD OF KNOWIN' THAT I'M DIFFERENT.
'CAUSE I KNOW THAT I'M BETTER THAN THE REST.
IT EXPLAINS WHY IT'S JUST SO EASY TO KILL THEM ALL.
WE ARE BOTH MUTANTS, LOGAN.
UN-FORTUNATELY, IN ABOUT ANOTHER MINUTE I'M GOING TO BE THE ONLY LIVE ONE IN THE ROOM.
FINE!
YEAH! I AM A MUTANT!
SO TELL ME WHY A GROUP OF MUTANTS LIKE THE HELLFIRE CLUB WOULD WANT OTHER MUTANTS DEAD?
DEAD? THAT'S WHAT YOU THINK THIS IS ABOUT? YOU THINK THE PEOPLE I WORK FOR WERE BOTHERING TO TRACK DOWN AND GATHER MUTANTS JUST TO KILL THEM?
THEN WHAT?

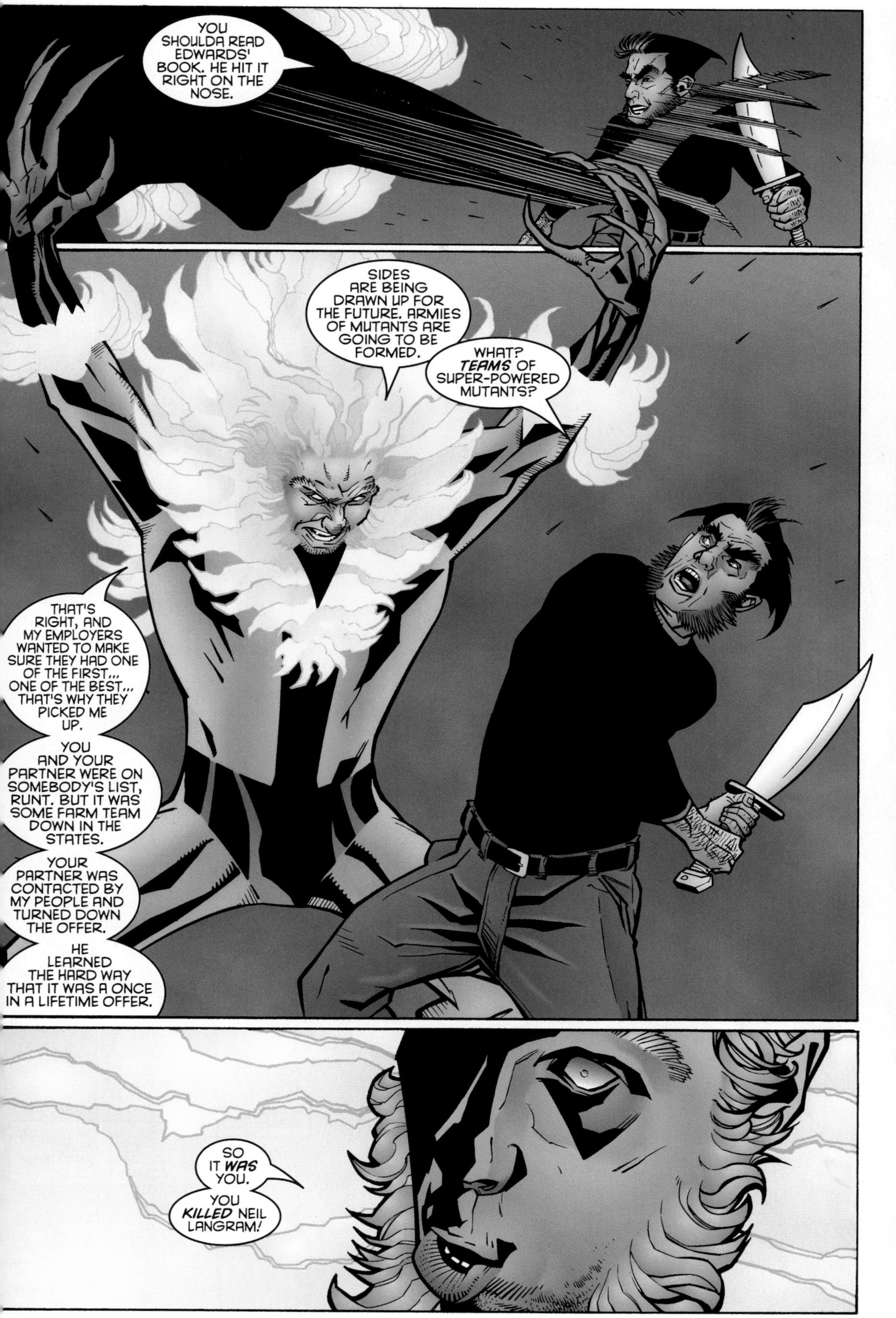
YOU SHOULDA READ EDWARDS' BOOK. HE HIT IT RIGHT ON THE NOSE.
SIDES ARE BEING DRAWN UP FOR THE FUTURE. ARMIES OF MUTANTS ARE GOING TO BE FORMED.
WHAT? *TEAMS* OF SUPER-POWERED MUTANTS?
THAT'S RIGHT, AND MY EMPLOYERS WANTED TO MAKE SURE THEY HAD ONE OF THE FIRST... ONE OF THE BEST... THAT'S WHY THEY PICKED ME UP.
YOU AND YOUR PARTNER WERE ON SOMEBODY'S LIST, RUNT. BUT IT WAS SOME FARM TEAM DOWN IN THE STATES.
YOUR PARTNER WAS CONTACTED BY MY PEOPLE AND TURNED DOWN THE OFFER.
HE LEARNED THE HARD WAY THAT IT WAS A ONCE IN A LIFETIME OFFER.
SO IT *WAS* YOU.
YOU *KILLED* NEIL LANGRAM!

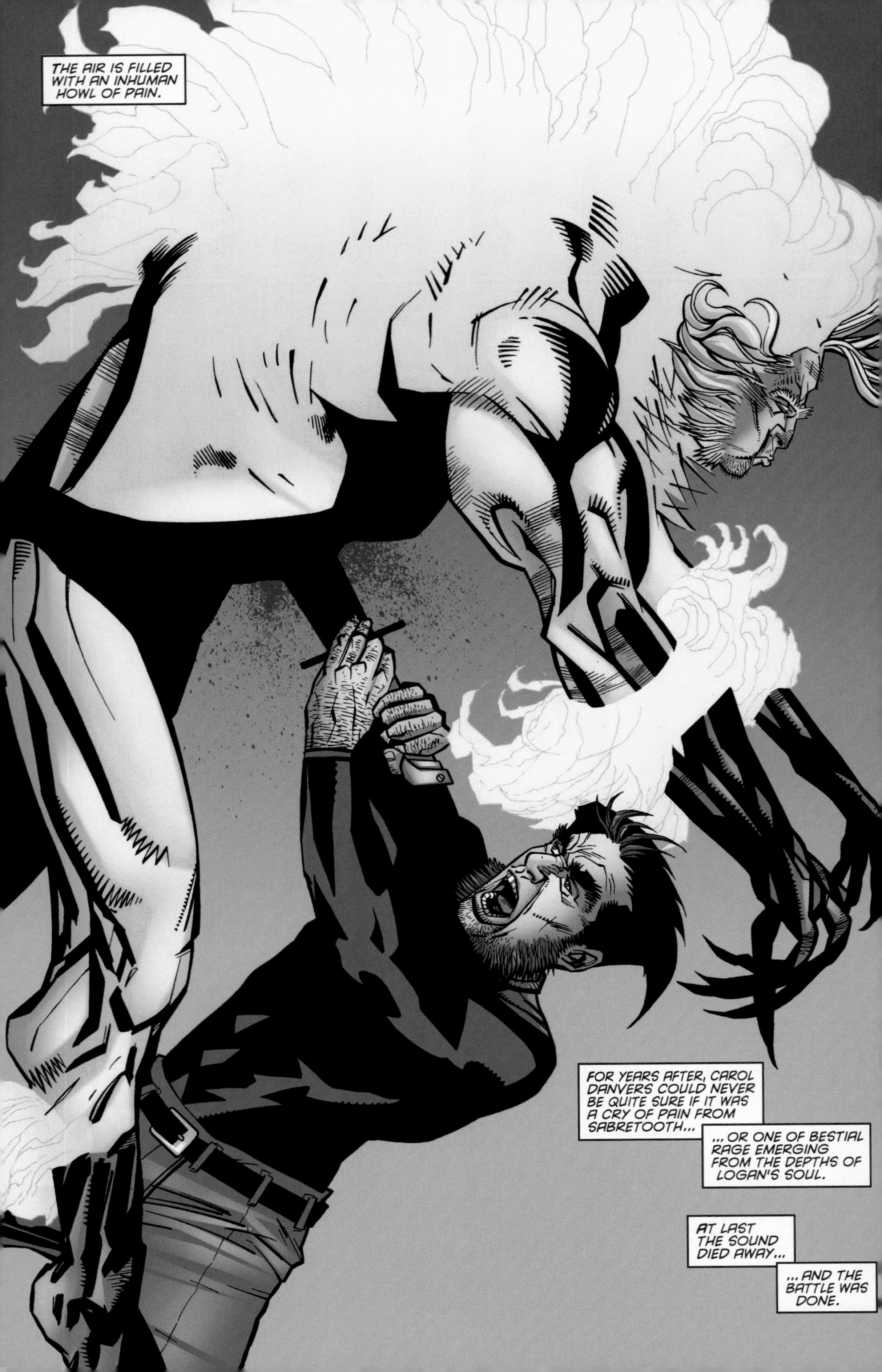
THE AIR IS FILLED WITH AN INHUMAN HOWL OF PAIN.
FOR YEARS AFTER, CAROL DANVERS COULD NEVER BE QUITE SURE IF IT WAS A CRY OF PAIN FROM SABRETOOTH...
...OR ONE OF BESTIAL RAGE EMERGING FROM THE DEPTHS OF LOGAN'S SOUL.
AT LAST THE SOUND DIED AWAY...
...AND THE BATTLE WAS DONE.

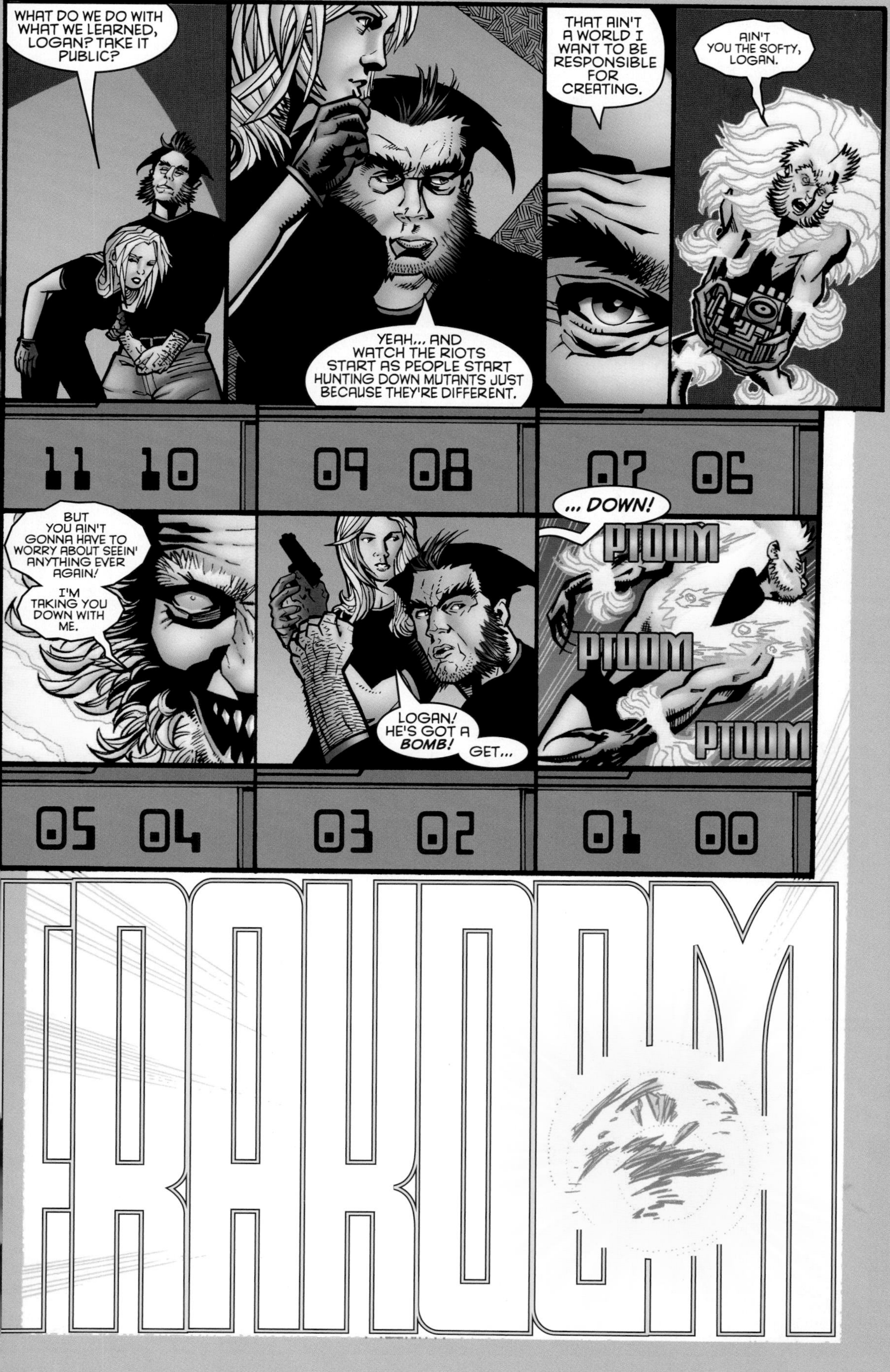
WHAT DO WE DO WITH WHAT WE LEARNED, LOGAN? TAKE IT PUBLIC?
YEAH... AND WATCH THE RIOTS START AS PEOPLE START HUNTING DOWN MUTANTS JUST BECAUSE THEY'RE DIFFERENT.
THAT AIN'T A WORLD I WANT TO BE RESPONSIBLE FOR CREATING.
AIN'T YOU THE SOFTY, LOGAN.
11 10
09 08
07 06
BUT YOU AIN'T GONNA HAVE TO WORRY ABOUT SEEIN' ANYTHING EVER AGAIN!
I'M TAKING YOU DOWN WITH ME.
LOGAN! HE'S GOT A BOMB!
GET...
... DOWN!
PTOOM
PTOOM
PTOOM
05 04
03 02
01 00
KRAKOOM

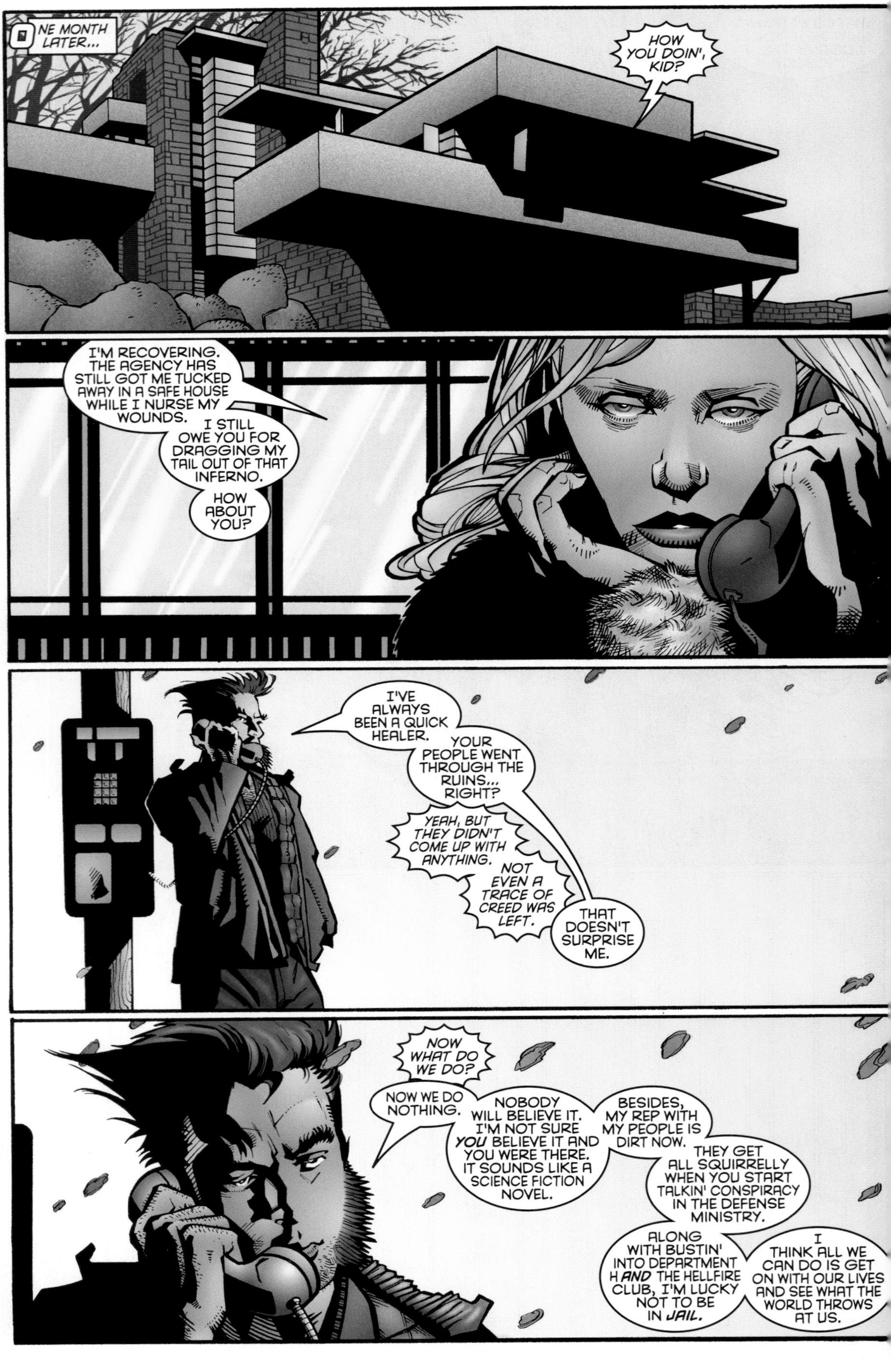
ONE MONTH LATER...
HOW YOU DOIN', KID?
I'M RECOVERING. THE AGENCY HAS STILL GOT ME TUCKED AWAY IN A SAFE HOUSE WHILE I NURSE MY WOUNDS.
I STILL OWE YOU FOR DRAGGING MY TAIL OUT OF THAT INFERNO.
HOW ABOUT YOU?
I'VE ALWAYS BEEN A QUICK HEALER.
YOUR PEOPLE WENT THROUGH THE RUINS... RIGHT?
YEAH, BUT THEY DIDN'T COME UP WITH ANYTHING.
NOT EVEN A TRACE OF CREED WAS LEFT.
THAT DOESN'T SURPRISE ME.
NOW WHAT DO WE DO?
NOW WE DO NOTHING.
NOBODY WILL BELIEVE IT. I'M NOT SURE YOU BELIEVE IT AND YOU WERE THERE. IT SOUNDS LIKE A SCIENCE FICTION NOVEL.
BESIDES, MY REP WITH MY PEOPLE IS DIRT NOW.
THEY GET ALL SQUIRRELLY WHEN YOU START TALKIN' CONSPIRACY IN THE DEFENSE MINISTRY.
ALONG WITH BUSTIN' INTO DEPARTMENT H AND THE HELLFIRE CLUB, I'M LUCKY NOT TO BE IN JAIL.
I THINK ALL WE CAN DO IS GET ON WITH OUR LIVES AND SEE WHAT THE WORLD THROWS AT US.

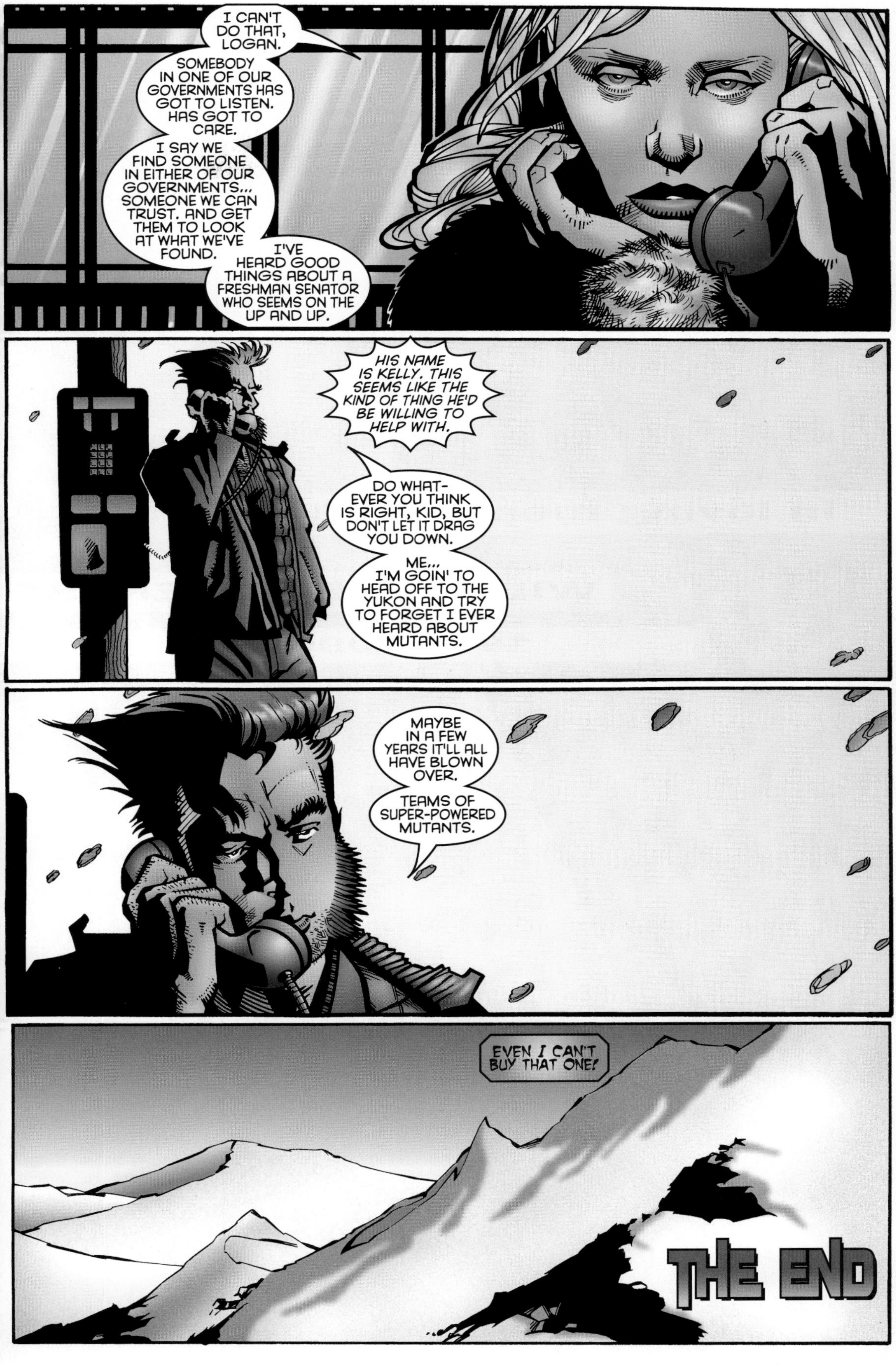
I CAN'T DO THAT, LOGAN.
SOMEBODY IN ONE OF OUR GOVERNMENTS HAS GOT TO LISTEN. HAS GOT TO CARE.
I SAY WE FIND SOMEONE IN EITHER OF OUR GOVERNMENTS... SOMEONE WE CAN TRUST. AND GET THEM TO LOOK AT WHAT WE'VE FOUND.
I'VE HEARD GOOD THINGS ABOUT A FRESHMAN SENATOR WHO SEEMS ON THE UP AND UP.
HIS NAME IS KELLY. THIS SEEMS LIKE THE KIND OF THING HE'D BE WILLING TO HELP WITH.
DO WHATEVER YOU THINK IS RIGHT, KID, BUT DON'T LET IT DRAG YOU DOWN.
ME... I'M GOIN' TO HEAD OFF TO THE YUKON AND TRY TO FORGET I EVER HEARD ABOUT MUTANTS.
MAYBE IN A FEW YEARS IT'LL ALL HAVE BLOWN OVER.
TEAMS OF SUPER-POWERED MUTANTS.
EVEN I CAN'T BUY THAT ONE!
THE END

in loving memory of

WILLIAM E. AIKEN, SR

1941-1996

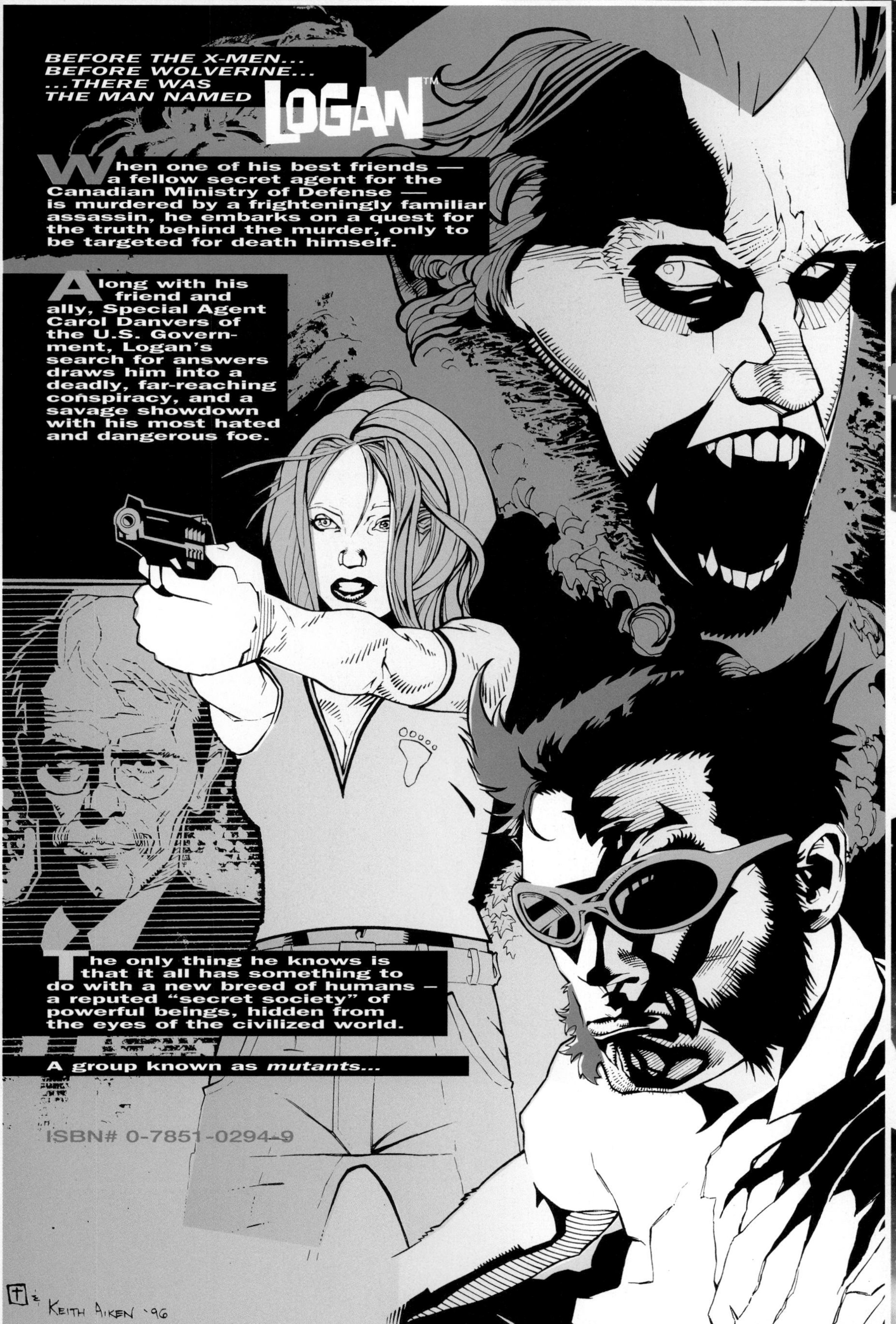
BEFORE THE X-MEN...
BEFORE WOLVERINE...
...THERE WAS
THE MAN NAMED LOGAN™
When one of his best friends — a fellow secret agent for the Canadian Ministry of Defense — is murdered by a frighteningly familiar assassin, he embarks on a quest for the truth behind the murder, only to be targeted for death himself.
Along with his friend and ally, Special Agent Carol Danvers of the U.S. Government, Logan's search for answers draws him into a deadly, far-reaching conspiracy, and a savage showdown with his most hated and dangerous foe.
The only thing he knows is that it all has something to do with a new breed of humans — a reputed "secret society" of powerful beings, hidden from the eyes of the civilized world.
A group known as *mutants*...
ISBN# 0-7851-0294-9
Keith Aiken '96

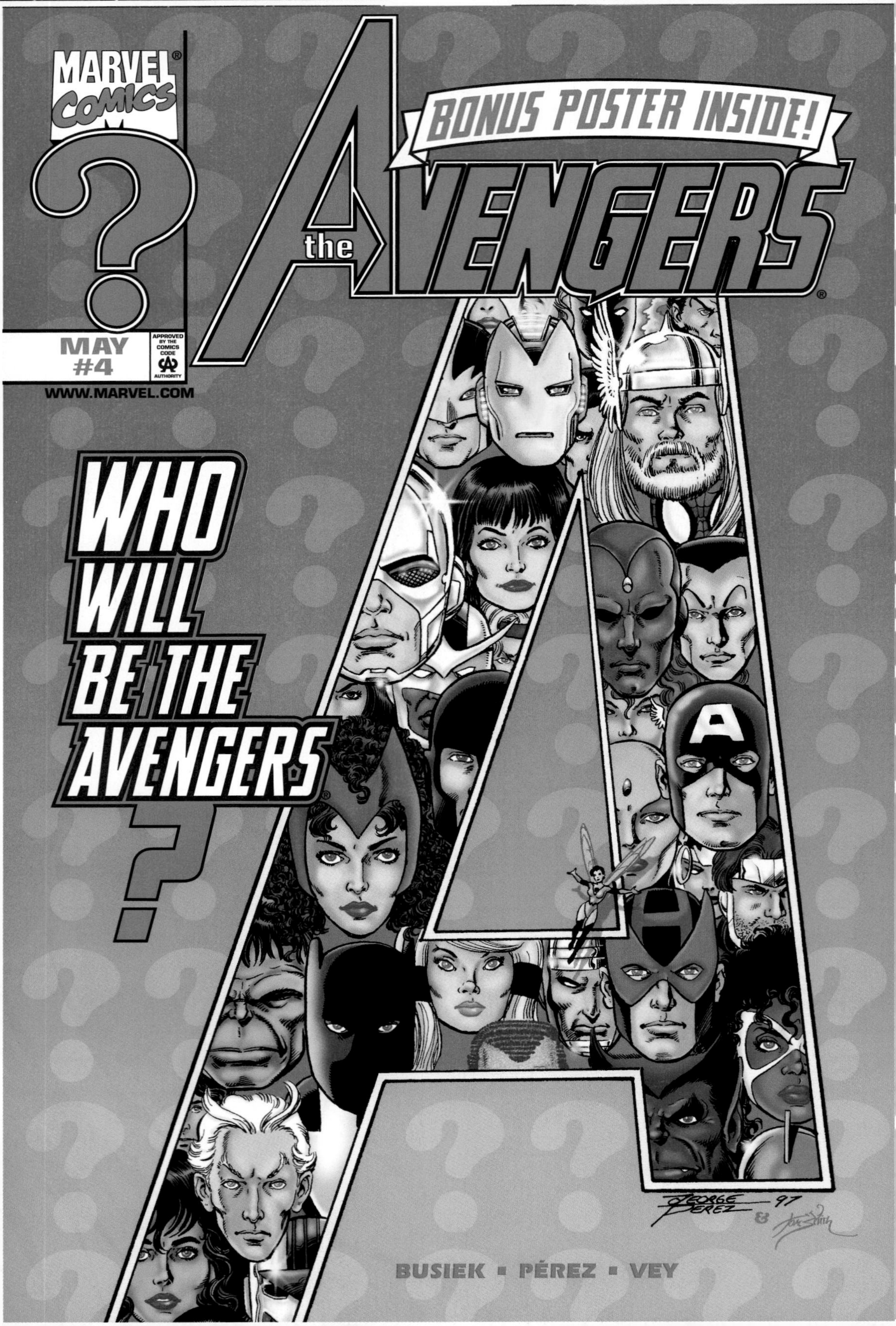
MARVEL COMICS
MAY #4
APPROVED BY THE COMICS CODE AUTHORITY
WWW.MARVEL.COM
BONUS POSTER INSIDE!
the AVENGERS
WHO WILL BE THE AVENGERS?
GEORGE PEREZ 97
BUSIEK • PÉREZ • VEY

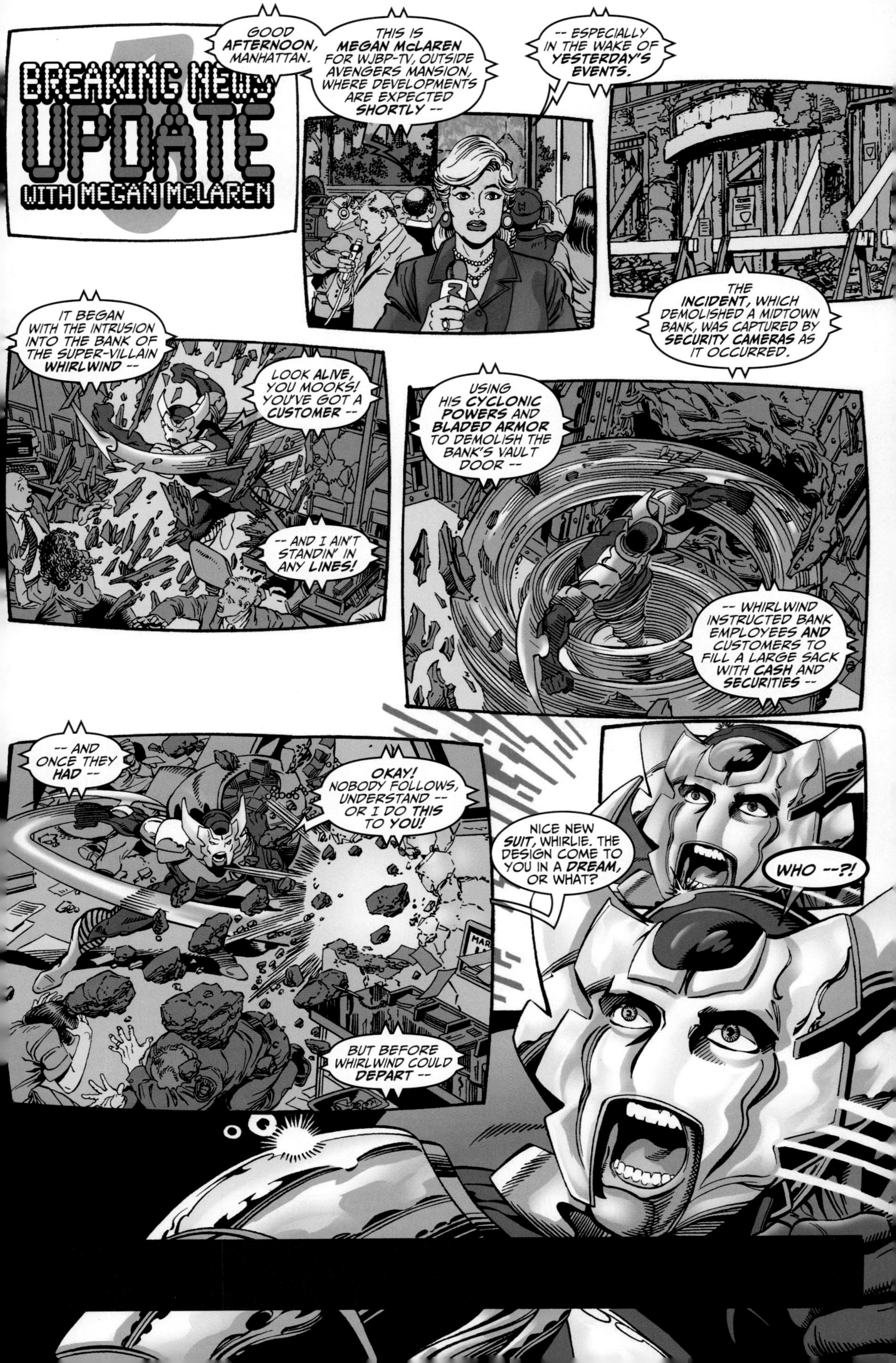
BREAKING NEWS UPDATE
WITH MEGAN McLAREN
GOOD AFTERNOON, MANHATTAN.
THIS IS MEGAN McLAREN FOR WJBP-TV, OUTSIDE AVENGERS MANSION, WHERE DEVELOPMENTS ARE EXPECTED SHORTLY --
-- ESPECIALLY IN THE WAKE OF YESTERDAY'S EVENTS.
THE INCIDENT, WHICH DEMOLISHED A MIDTOWN BANK, WAS CAPTURED BY SECURITY CAMERAS AS IT OCCURRED.
IT BEGAN WITH THE INTRUSION INTO THE BANK OF THE SUPER-VILLAIN WHIRLWIND --
LOOK ALIVE, YOU MOOKS! YOU'VE GOT A CUSTOMER --
-- AND I AIN'T STANDIN' IN ANY LINES!
USING HIS CYCLONIC POWERS AND BLADED ARMOR TO DEMOLISH THE BANK'S VAULT DOOR --
-- WHIRLWIND INSTRUCTED BANK EMPLOYEES AND CUSTOMERS TO FILL A LARGE SACK WITH CASH AND SECURITIES --
-- AND ONCE THEY HAD --
OKAY! NOBODY FOLLOWS, UNDERSTAND -- OR I DO THIS TO YOU!
BUT BEFORE WHIRLWIND COULD DEPART --
NICE NEW SUIT, WHIRLIE. THE DESIGN COME TO YOU IN A DREAM, OR WHAT?
WHO --?!

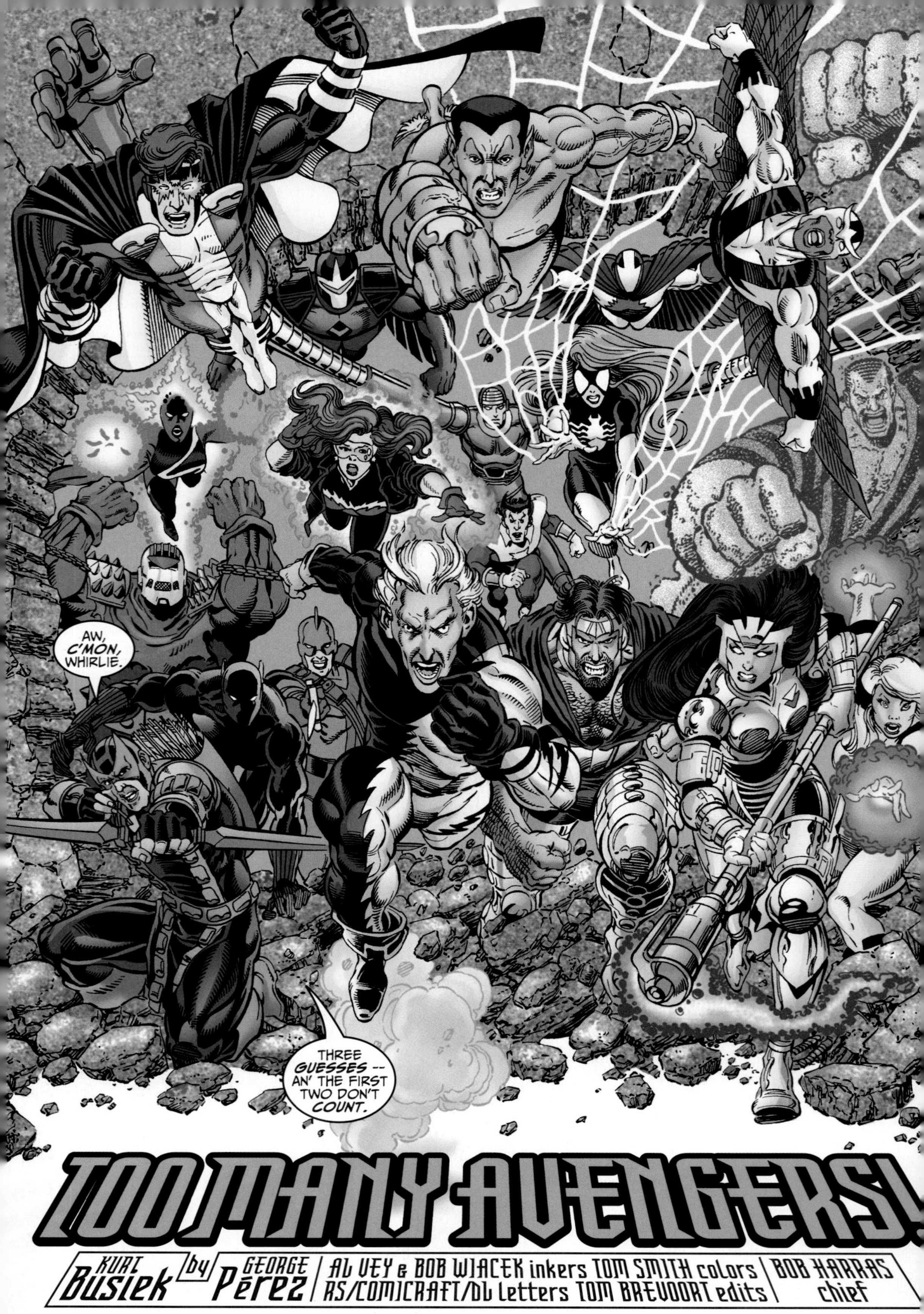
AW, C'MON, WHIRLIE.
THREE GUESSES -- AN' THE FIRST TWO DON'T COUNT.
TOO MANY AVENGERS!
KURT BUSIEK by GEORGE PÉREZ
AL VEY & BOB WIACEK inkers TOM SMITH colors
RS/COMICRAFT/DL letters TOM BREVOORT edits
BOB HARRAS chief

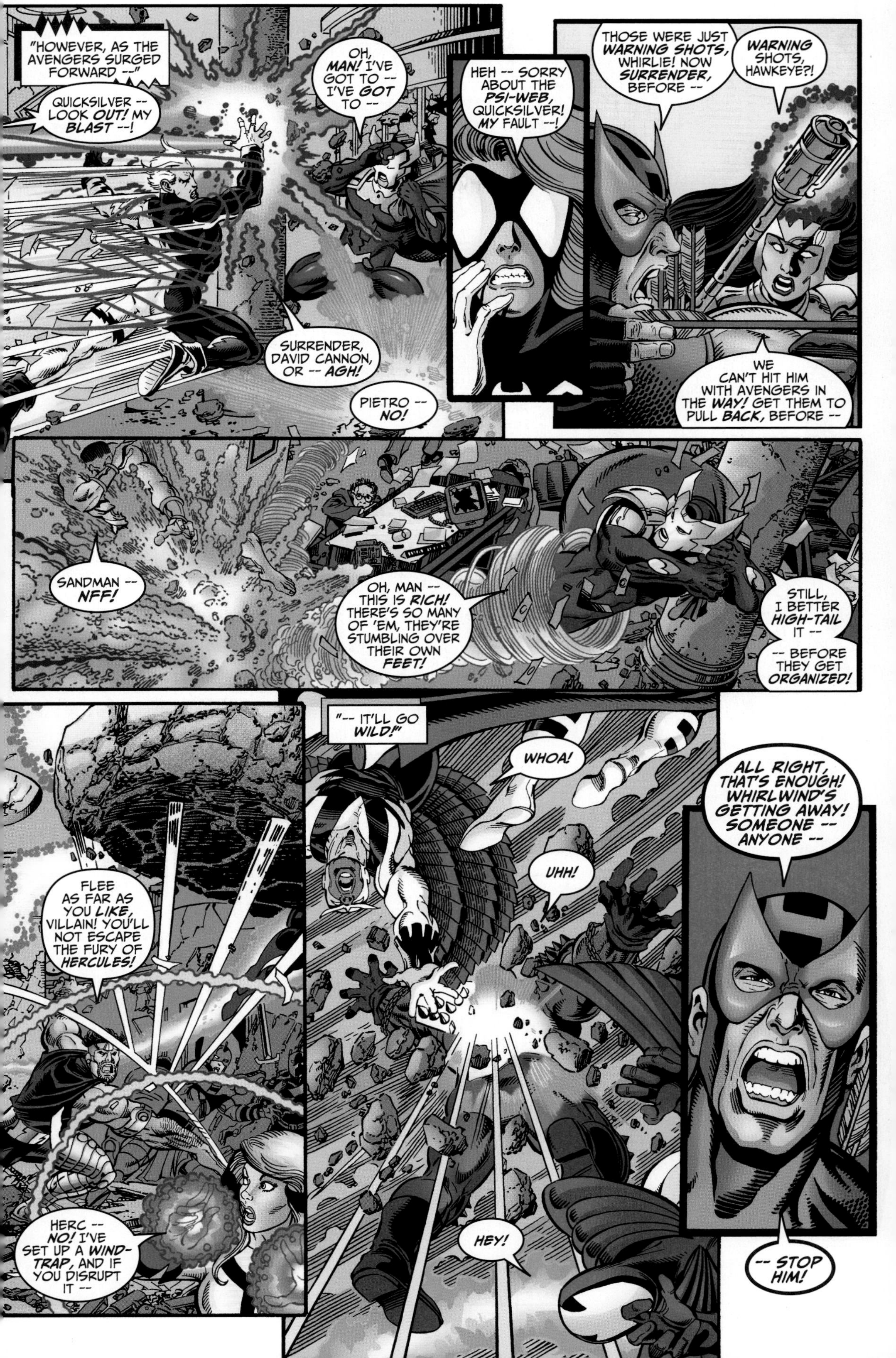
"HOWEVER, AS THE AVENGERS SURGED FORWARD --"
QUICKSILVER -- LOOK OUT! MY BLAST --!
OH, MAN! I'VE GOT TO -- I'VE GOT TO --
SURRENDER, DAVID CANNON, OR -- AGH!
PIETRO -- NO!
HEH -- SORRY ABOUT THE PSI-WEB, QUICKSILVER! MY FAULT --!
THOSE WERE JUST WARNING SHOTS, WHIRLIE! NOW SURRENDER, BEFORE --
WARNING SHOTS, HAWKEYE?!
WE CAN'T HIT HIM WITH AVENGERS IN THE WAY! GET THEM TO PULL BACK, BEFORE --
SANDMAN -- NFF!
OH, MAN -- THIS IS RICH! THERE'S SO MANY OF 'EM, THEY'RE STUMBLING OVER THEIR OWN FEET!
STILL, I BETTER HIGH-TAIL IT --
-- BEFORE THEY GET ORGANIZED!
FLEE AS FAR AS YOU LIKE, VILLAIN! YOU'LL NOT ESCAPE THE FURY OF HERCULES!
HERC -- NO! I'VE SET UP A WIND-TRAP, AND IF YOU DISRUPT IT --
"-- IT'LL GO WILD!"
WHOA!
UHH!
HEY!
ALL RIGHT, THAT'S ENOUGH! WHIRLWIND'S GETTING AWAY! SOMEONE -- ANYONE --
-- STOP HIM!

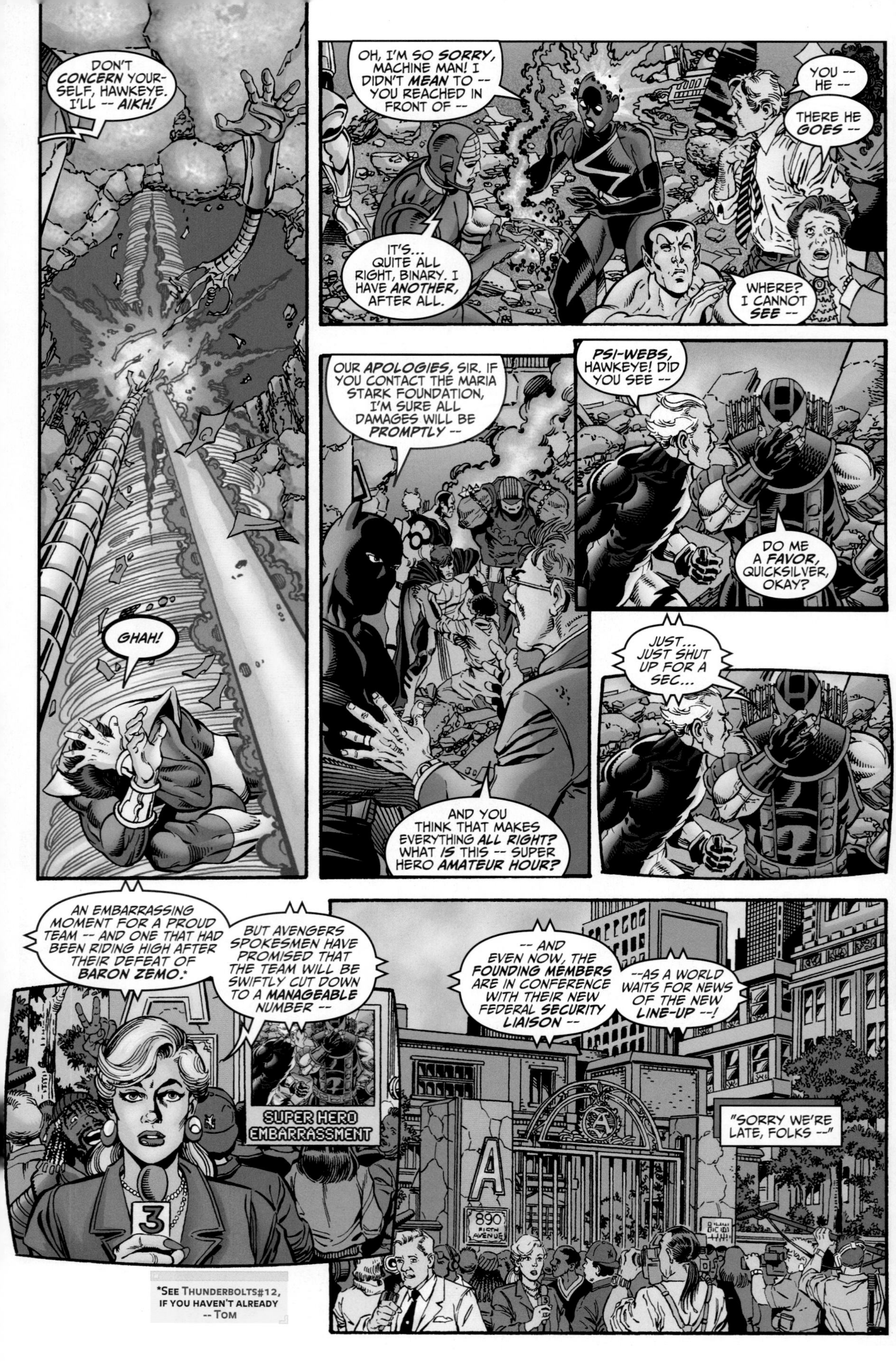

DON'T CONCERN YOURSELF, HAWKEYE. I'LL -- AIKH!
GHAH!
OH, I'M SO SORRY, MACHINE MAN! I DIDN'T MEAN TO -- YOU REACHED IN FRONT OF --
IT'S... QUITE ALL RIGHT, BINARY. I HAVE ANOTHER, AFTER ALL.
YOU -- HE --
THERE HE GOES --
WHERE? I CANNOT SEE --
OUR APOLOGIES, SIR. IF YOU CONTACT THE MARIA STARK FOUNDATION, I'M SURE ALL DAMAGES WILL BE PROMPTLY --
AND YOU THINK THAT MAKES EVERYTHING ALL RIGHT? WHAT IS THIS -- SUPER HERO AMATEUR HOUR?
PSI-WEBS, HAWKEYE! DID YOU SEE --
DO ME A FAVOR, QUICKSILVER, OKAY?
JUST... JUST SHUT UP FOR A SEC...
AN EMBARRASSING MOMENT FOR A PROUD TEAM -- AND ONE THAT HAD BEEN RIDING HIGH AFTER THEIR DEFEAT OF BARON ZEMO.*
BUT AVENGERS SPOKESMEN HAVE PROMISED THAT THE TEAM WILL BE SWIFTLY CUT DOWN TO A MANAGEABLE NUMBER --
SUPER HERO EMBARRASSMENT
3
*SEE THUNDERBOLTS #12, IF YOU HAVEN'T ALREADY -- TOM
-- AND EVEN NOW, THE FOUNDING MEMBERS ARE IN CONFERENCE WITH THEIR NEW FEDERAL SECURITY LIAISON --
--AS A WORLD WAITS FOR NEWS OF THE NEW LINE-UP --!
"SORRY WE'RE LATE, FOLKS --"
A
890 FIFTH AVENUE

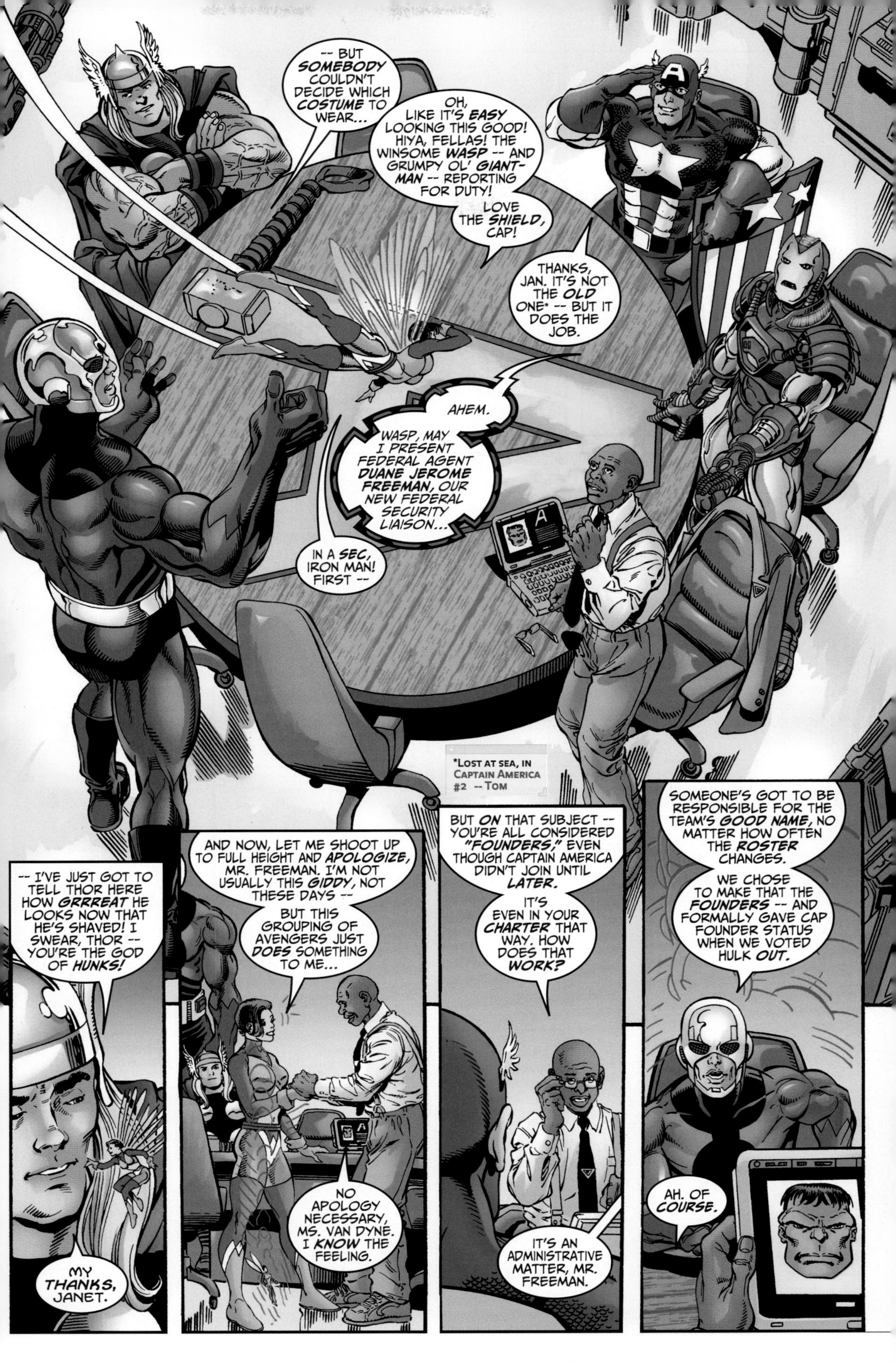

-- BUT SOMEBODY COULDN'T DECIDE WHICH COSTUME TO WEAR...
OH, LIKE IT'S EASY LOOKING THIS GOOD! HIYA, FELLAS! THE WINSOME WASP -- AND GRUMPY OL' GIANT-MAN -- REPORTING FOR DUTY!
LOVE THE SHIELD, CAP!
THANKS, JAN. IT'S NOT THE OLD ONE* -- BUT IT DOES THE JOB.
AHEM.
WASP, MAY I PRESENT FEDERAL AGENT DUANE JEROME FREEMAN, OUR NEW FEDERAL SECURITY LIAISON...
IN A SEC, IRON MAN! FIRST --
*LOST AT SEA, IN CAPTAIN AMERICA #2 -- TOM
-- I'VE JUST GOT TO TELL THOR HERE HOW GRRREAT HE LOOKS NOW THAT HE'S SHAVED! I SWEAR, THOR -- YOU'RE THE GOD OF HUNKS!
MY THANKS, JANET.
AND NOW, LET ME SHOOT UP TO FULL HEIGHT AND APOLOGIZE, MR. FREEMAN. I'M NOT USUALLY THIS GIDDY, NOT THESE DAYS --
BUT THIS GROUPING OF AVENGERS JUST DOES SOMETHING TO ME...
NO APOLOGY NECESSARY, MS. VAN DYNE. I KNOW THE FEELING.
BUT ON THAT SUBJECT -- YOU'RE ALL CONSIDERED "FOUNDERS," EVEN THOUGH CAPTAIN AMERICA DIDN'T JOIN UNTIL LATER.
IT'S EVEN IN YOUR CHARTER THAT WAY. HOW DOES THAT WORK?
IT'S AN ADMINISTRATIVE MATTER, MR. FREEMAN.
SOMEONE'S GOT TO BE RESPONSIBLE FOR THE TEAM'S GOOD NAME, NO MATTER HOW OFTEN THE ROSTER CHANGES.
WE CHOSE TO MAKE THAT THE FOUNDERS -- AND FORMALLY GAVE CAP FOUNDER STATUS WHEN WE VOTED HULK OUT.
AH. OF COURSE.

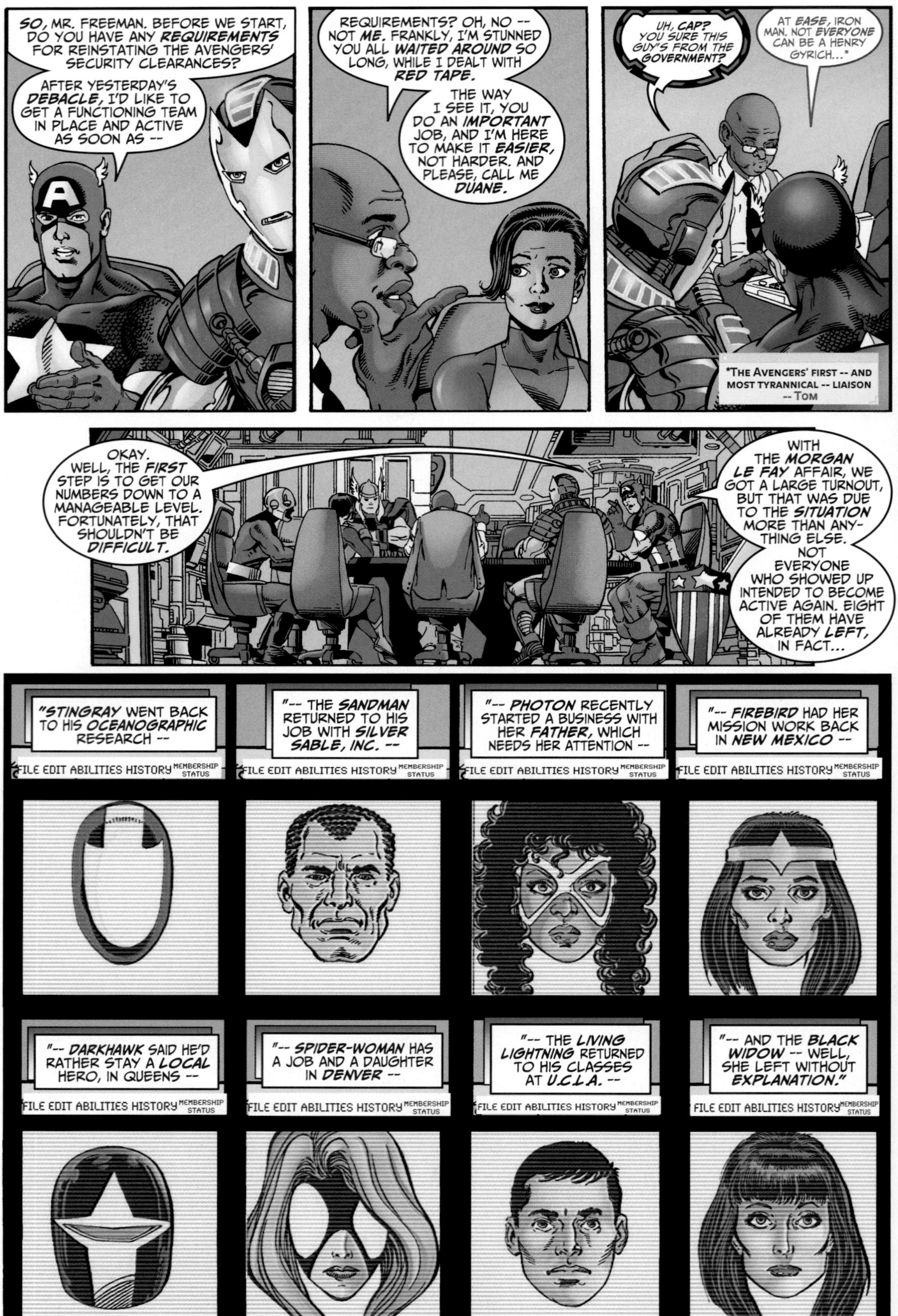

SO, MR. FREEMAN. BEFORE WE START, DO YOU HAVE ANY REQUIREMENTS FOR REINSTATING THE AVENGERS' SECURITY CLEARANCES?
AFTER YESTERDAY'S DEBACLE, I'D LIKE TO GET A FUNCTIONING TEAM IN PLACE AND ACTIVE AS SOON AS --
REQUIREMENTS? OH, NO -- NOT ME. FRANKLY, I'M STUNNED YOU ALL WAITED AROUND SO LONG, WHILE I DEALT WITH RED TAPE.
THE WAY I SEE IT, YOU DO AN IMPORTANT JOB, AND I'M HERE TO MAKE IT EASIER, NOT HARDER. AND PLEASE, CALL ME DUANE.
UH, CAP? YOU SURE THIS GUY'S FROM THE GOVERNMENT?
AT EASE, IRON MAN. NOT EVERYONE CAN BE A HENRY GYRICH...*
*THE AVENGERS' FIRST -- AND MOST TYRANNICAL -- LIAISON -- TOM
OKAY. WELL, THE FIRST STEP IS TO GET OUR NUMBERS DOWN TO A MANAGEABLE LEVEL. FORTUNATELY, THAT SHOULDN'T BE DIFFICULT.
WITH THE MORGAN LE FAY AFFAIR, WE GOT A LARGE TURNOUT, BUT THAT WAS DUE TO THE SITUATION MORE THAN ANYTHING ELSE.
NOT EVERYONE WHO SHOWED UP INTENDED TO BECOME ACTIVE AGAIN. EIGHT OF THEM HAVE ALREADY LEFT, IN FACT...
"STINGRAY WENT BACK TO HIS OCEANOGRAPHIC RESEARCH --
FILE EDIT ABILITIES HISTORY MEMBERSHIP STATUS
"-- THE SANDMAN RETURNED TO HIS JOB WITH SILVER SABLE, INC. --
FILE EDIT ABILITIES HISTORY MEMBERSHIP STATUS
"-- PHOTON RECENTLY STARTED A BUSINESS WITH HER FATHER, WHICH NEEDS HER ATTENTION --
FILE EDIT ABILITIES HISTORY MEMBERSHIP STATUS
"-- FIREBIRD HAD HER MISSION WORK BACK IN NEW MEXICO --
FILE EDIT ABILITIES HISTORY MEMBERSHIP STATUS
"-- DARKHAWK SAID HE'D RATHER STAY A LOCAL HERO, IN QUEENS --
FILE EDIT ABILITIES HISTORY MEMBERSHIP STATUS
"-- SPIDER-WOMAN HAS A JOB AND A DAUGHTER IN DENVER --
FILE EDIT ABILITIES HISTORY MEMBERSHIP STATUS
"-- THE LIVING LIGHTNING RETURNED TO HIS CLASSES AT U.C.L.A. --
FILE EDIT ABILITIES HISTORY MEMBERSHIP STATUS
"-- AND THE BLACK WIDOW -- WELL, SHE LEFT WITHOUT EXPLANATION."
FILE EDIT ABILITIES HISTORY MEMBERSHIP STATUS

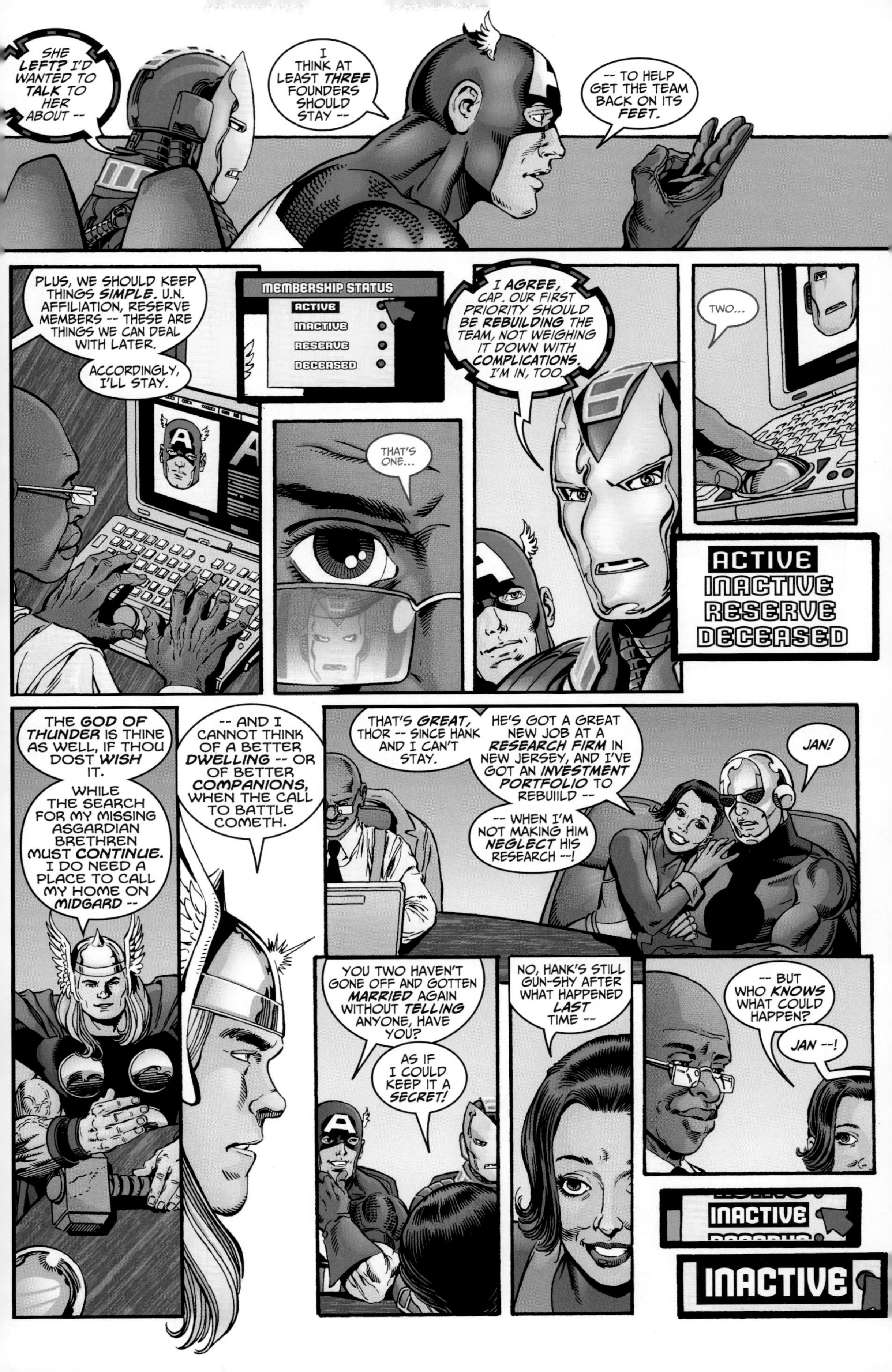
SHE LEFT? I'D WANTED TO TALK TO HER ABOUT --
I THINK AT LEAST THREE FOUNDERS SHOULD STAY --
-- TO HELP GET THE TEAM BACK ON ITS FEET.
PLUS, WE SHOULD KEEP THINGS SIMPLE. U.N. AFFILIATION, RESERVE MEMBERS -- THESE ARE THINGS WE CAN DEAL WITH LATER.
ACCORDINGLY, I'LL STAY.
MEMBERSHIP STATUS
ACTIVE
INACTIVE
RESERVE
DECEASED
THAT'S ONE...
I AGREE, CAP. OUR FIRST PRIORITY SHOULD BE REBUILDING THE TEAM, NOT WEIGHING IT DOWN WITH COMPLICATIONS. I'M IN, TOO.
TWO...
ACTIVE
INACTIVE
RESERVE
DECEASED
THE GOD OF THUNDER IS THINE AS WELL, IF THOU DOST WISH IT.
WHILE THE SEARCH FOR MY MISSING ASGARDIAN BRETHREN MUST CONTINUE. I DO NEED A PLACE TO CALL MY HOME ON MIDGARD --
-- AND I CANNOT THINK OF A BETTER DWELLING -- OR OF BETTER COMPANIONS, WHEN THE CALL TO BATTLE COMETH.
THAT'S GREAT, THOR -- SINCE HANK AND I CAN'T STAY.
HE'S GOT A GREAT NEW JOB AT A RESEARCH FIRM IN NEW JERSEY, AND I'VE GOT AN INVESTMENT PORTFOLIO TO REBUIILD --
-- WHEN I'M NOT MAKING HIM NEGLECT HIS RESEARCH --!
JAN!
YOU TWO HAVEN'T GONE OFF AND GOTTEN MARRIED AGAIN WITHOUT TELLING ANYONE, HAVE YOU?
AS IF I COULD KEEP IT A SECRET!
NO, HANK'S STILL GUN-SHY AFTER WHAT HAPPENED LAST TIME --
-- BUT WHO KNOWS WHAT COULD HAPPEN?
JAN --!
INACTIVE
INACTIVE

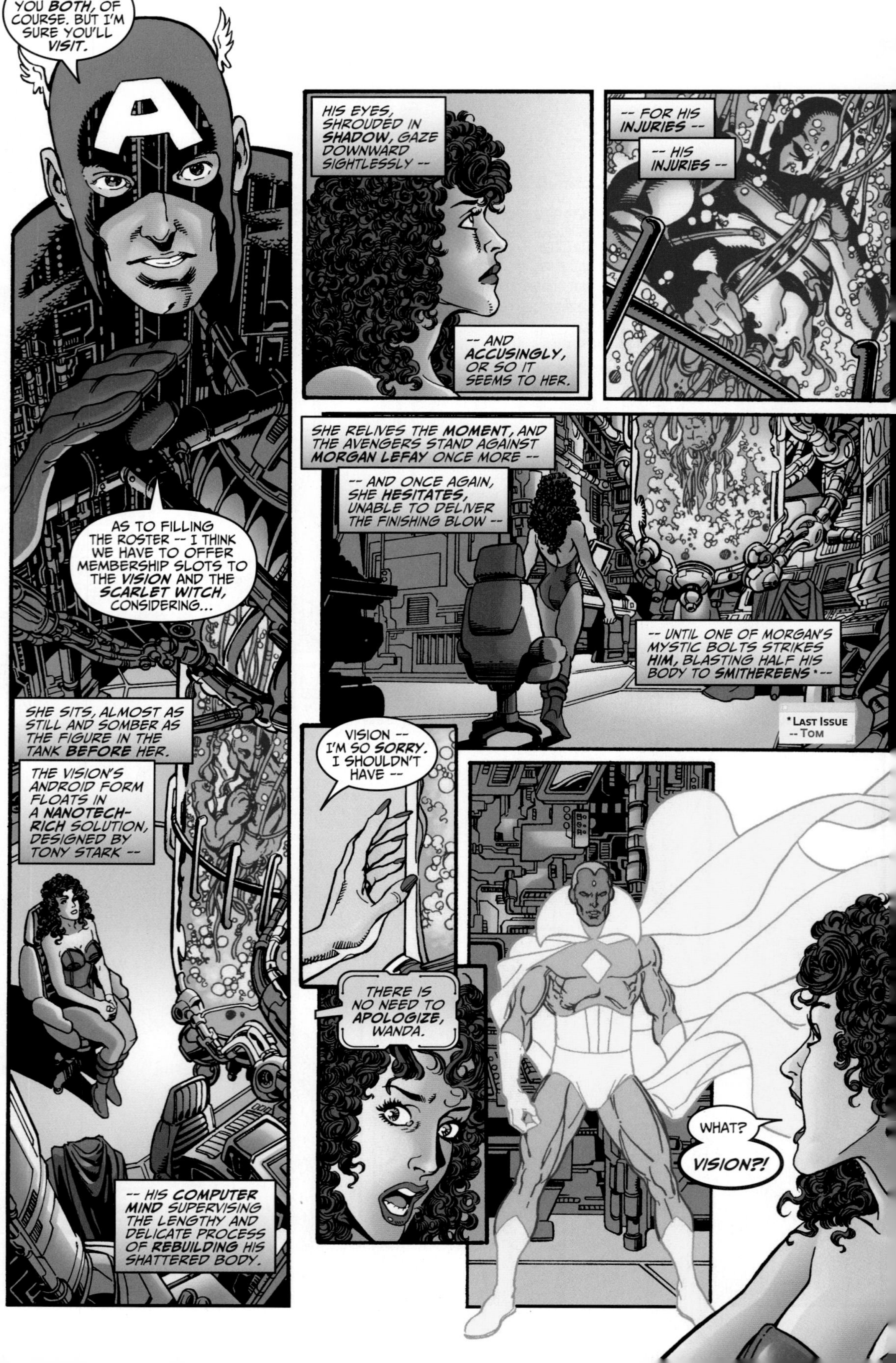
WELL, WE'LL MISS YOU BOTH, OF COURSE. BUT I'M SURE YOU'LL VISIT.
AS TO FILLING THE ROSTER -- I THINK WE HAVE TO OFFER MEMBERSHIP SLOTS TO THE VISION AND THE SCARLET WITCH, CONSIDERING...
HIS EYES, SHROUDED IN SHADOW, GAZE DOWNWARD SIGHTLESSLY --
-- AND ACCUSINGLY, OR SO IT SEEMS TO HER.
-- FOR HIS INJURIES --
-- HIS INJURIES --
SHE RELIVES THE MOMENT, AND THE AVENGERS STAND AGAINST MORGAN LEFAY ONCE MORE --
-- AND ONCE AGAIN, SHE HESITATES, UNABLE TO DELIVER THE FINISHING BLOW --
-- UNTIL ONE OF MORGAN'S MYSTIC BOLTS STRIKES HIM, BLASTING HALF HIS BODY TO SMITHEREENS* --
*LAST ISSUE -- TOM
SHE SITS, ALMOST AS STILL AND SOMBER AS THE FIGURE IN THE TANK BEFORE HER.
THE VISION'S ANDROID FORM FLOATS IN A NANOTECH-RICH SOLUTION, DESIGNED BY TONY STARK --
-- HIS COMPUTER MIND SUPERVISING THE LENGTHY AND DELICATE PROCESS OF REBUILDING HIS SHATTERED BODY.
VISION -- I'M SO SORRY. I SHOULDN'T HAVE --
THERE IS NO NEED TO APOLOGIZE, WANDA.
WHAT?
VISION?!

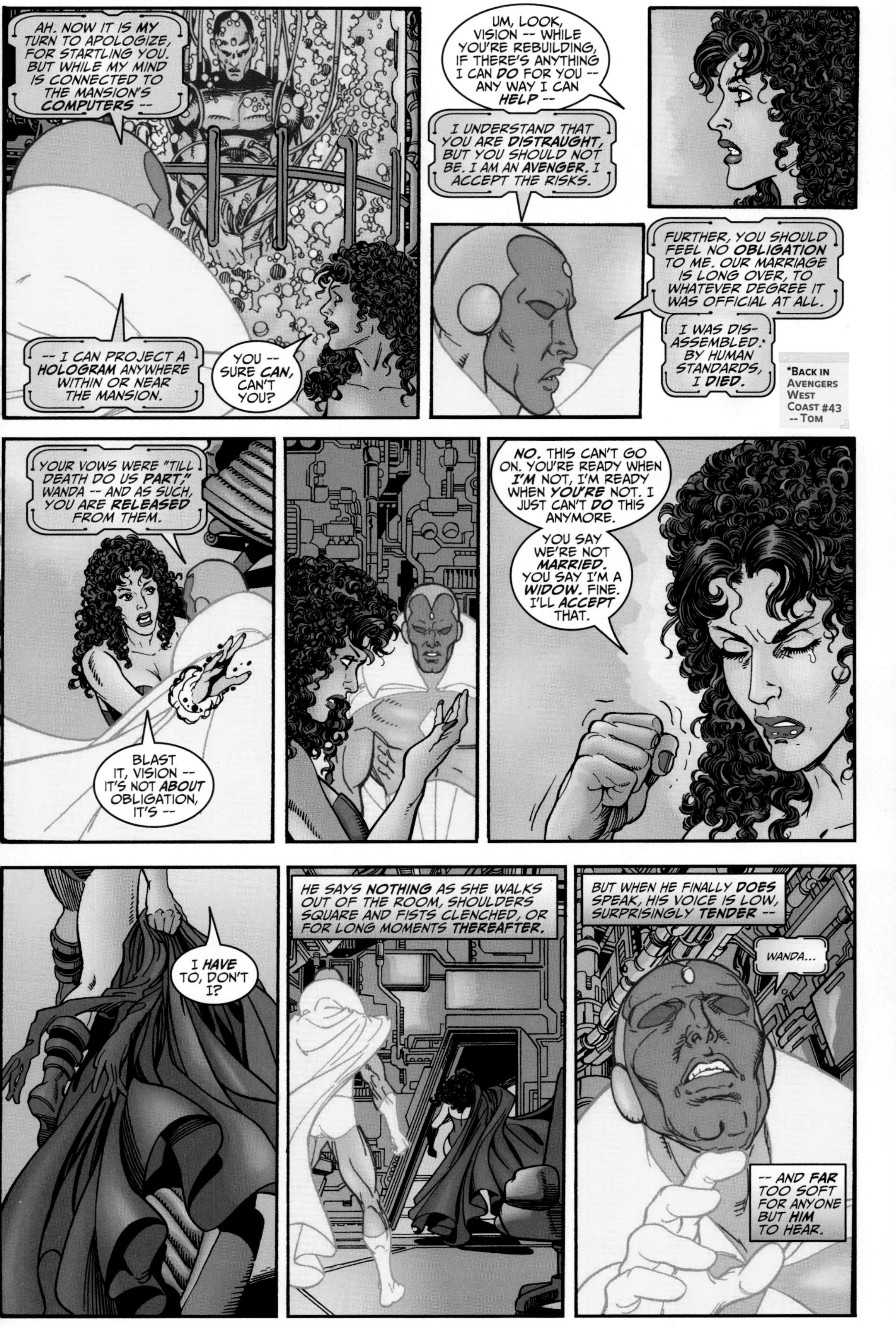
AH. NOW IT IS MY TURN TO APOLOGIZE, FOR STARTLING YOU. BUT WHILE MY MIND IS CONNECTED TO THE MANSION'S COMPUTERS --
-- I CAN PROJECT A HOLOGRAM ANYWHERE WITHIN OR NEAR THE MANSION.
YOU -- SURE CAN, CAN'T YOU?
UM, LOOK, VISION -- WHILE YOU'RE REBUILDING, IF THERE'S ANYTHING I CAN DO FOR YOU -- ANY WAY I CAN HELP --
I UNDERSTAND THAT YOU ARE DISTRAUGHT, BUT YOU SHOULD NOT BE. I AM AN AVENGER. I ACCEPT THE RISKS.
FURTHER, YOU SHOULD FEEL NO OBLIGATION TO ME. OUR MARRIAGE IS LONG OVER, TO WHATEVER DEGREE IT WAS OFFICIAL AT ALL.
I WAS DIS-ASSEMBLED.* BY HUMAN STANDARDS, I DIED.
*Back in Avengers West Coast #43 -- Tom
YOUR VOWS WERE "TILL DEATH DO US PART," WANDA -- AND AS SUCH, YOU ARE RELEASED FROM THEM.
BLAST IT, VISION -- IT'S NOT ABOUT OBLIGATION, IT'S --
NO. THIS CAN'T GO ON. YOU'RE READY WHEN I'M NOT, I'M READY WHEN YOU'RE NOT. I JUST CAN'T DO THIS ANYMORE.
YOU SAY WE'RE NOT MARRIED. YOU SAY I'M A WIDOW. FINE. I'LL ACCEPT THAT.
I HAVE TO, DON'T I?
HE SAYS NOTHING AS SHE WALKS OUT OF THE ROOM, SHOULDERS SQUARE AND FISTS CLENCHED, OR FOR LONG MOMENTS THEREAFTER.
BUT WHEN HE FINALLY DOES SPEAK, HIS VOICE IS LOW, SURPRISINGLY TENDER --
WANDA...
-- AND FAR TOO SOFT FOR ANYONE BUT HIM TO HEAR.

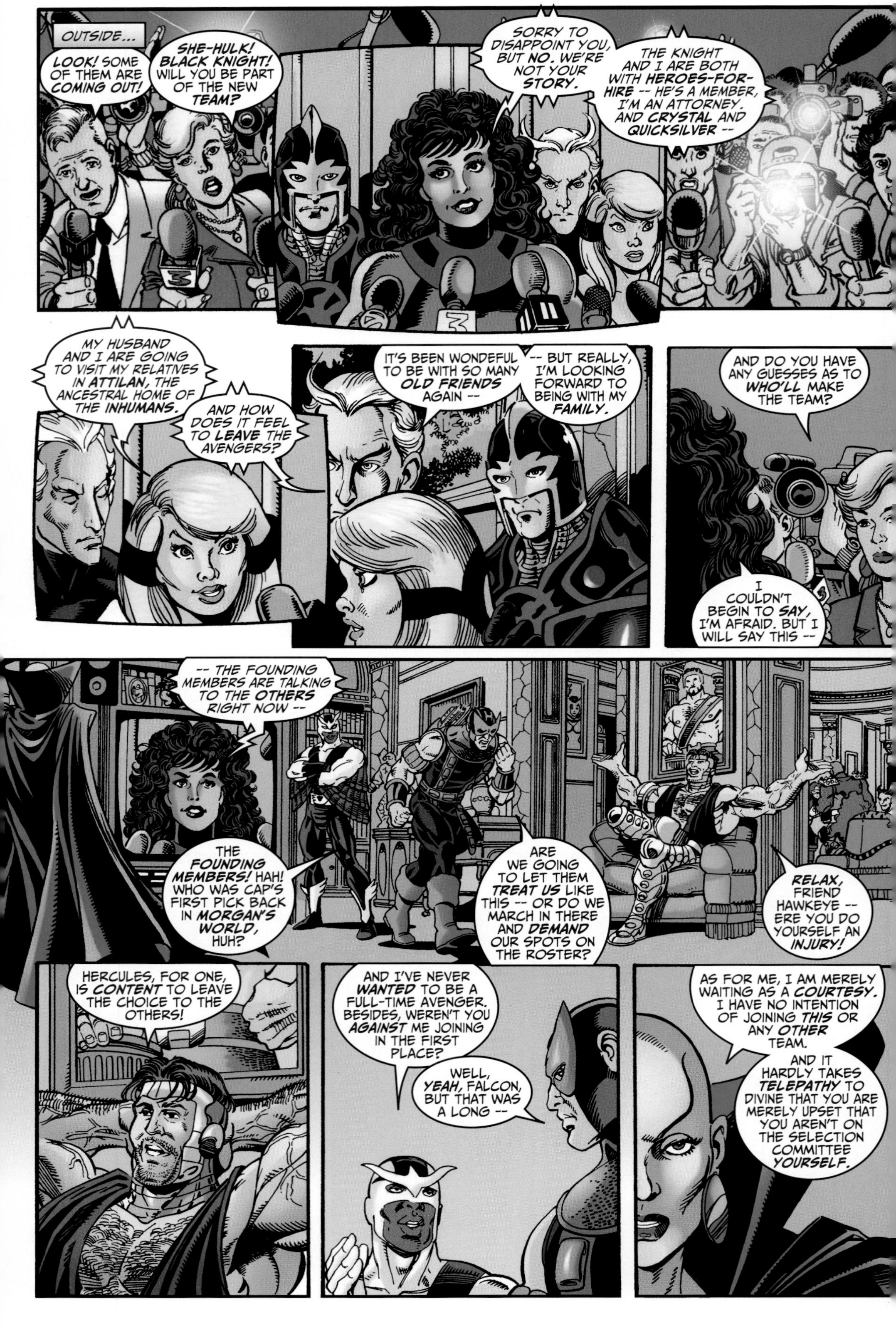
OUTSIDE...
LOOK! SOME OF THEM ARE COMING OUT!
SHE-HULK! BLACK KNIGHT! WILL YOU BE PART OF THE NEW TEAM?
SORRY TO DISAPPOINT YOU, BUT NO. WE'RE NOT YOUR STORY.
THE KNIGHT AND I ARE BOTH WITH HEROES-FOR-HIRE -- HE'S A MEMBER, I'M AN ATTORNEY. AND CRYSTAL AND QUICKSILVER --
MY HUSBAND AND I ARE GOING TO VISIT MY RELATIVES IN ATTILAN, THE ANCESTRAL HOME OF THE INHUMANS.
AND HOW DOES IT FEEL TO LEAVE THE AVENGERS?
IT'S BEEN WONDEFUL TO BE WITH SO MANY OLD FRIENDS AGAIN --
-- BUT REALLY, I'M LOOKING FORWARD TO BEING WITH MY FAMILY.
AND DO YOU HAVE ANY GUESSES AS TO WHO'LL MAKE THE TEAM?
I COULDN'T BEGIN TO SAY, I'M AFRAID. BUT I WILL SAY THIS --
-- THE FOUNDING MEMBERS ARE TALKING TO THE OTHERS RIGHT NOW --
THE FOUNDING MEMBERS! HAH! WHO WAS CAP'S FIRST PICK BACK IN MORGAN'S WORLD, HUH?
ARE WE GOING TO LET THEM TREAT US LIKE THIS -- OR DO WE MARCH IN THERE AND DEMAND OUR SPOTS ON THE ROSTER?
RELAX, FRIEND HAWKEYE -- ERE YOU DO YOURSELF AN INJURY!
HERCULES, FOR ONE, IS CONTENT TO LEAVE THE CHOICE TO THE OTHERS!
AND I'VE NEVER WANTED TO BE A FULL-TIME AVENGER. BESIDES, WEREN'T YOU AGAINST ME JOINING IN THE FIRST PLACE?
WELL, YEAH, FALCON, BUT THAT WAS A LONG --
AS FOR ME, I AM MERELY WAITING AS A COURTESY. I HAVE NO INTENTION OF JOINING THIS OR ANY OTHER TEAM.
AND IT HARDLY TAKES TELEPATHY TO DIVINE THAT YOU ARE MERELY UPSET THAT YOU AREN'T ON THE SELECTION COMMITTEE YOURSELF.

WELL, *NEWS FLASH*, MOONDRAGON -- I WASN'T TALKING TO *YOU!*

LOOK AT' EM. NO ROOM ON *THIS* TEAM, I GUESS. NONE AT ALL.

NO SKIN OFF *MY* NOSE, OF COURSE -- I'M STILL *UNDERAGE*. BUT YOU JUST TURNED EIGHTEEN, FIRESTAR. DO YOU --

TO BE *HONEST*, ELVIN, I'D BE HAPPY GOING BACK TO THE NEW WARRIORS, TOO --

-- BUT VANCE HAS DREAMED OF BEING AN AVENGER HIS ENTIRE *LIFE*. HE DOESN'T WANT TO *GIVE UP* -- EVEN IF THERE'S NO REAL --

HEY! HEY, *ANGEL!*

C'MON, C'MON -- WE GOTTA *GO!* I JUST HEARD SOMETHING ON THE POLICE BAND, AND THIS COULD BE OUR *SHOT!*

HUH?

YOU WANT ME TO *COME ALONG*, JUSTICE?

NO OFFENSE MEANT, RAGE, BUT THIS ISN'T A *WARRIORS* GIG -- IT'S *AVENGERS* BUSINESS!

AND WHAT HAVE WE *HERE?*

LOOKS LIKE THE *JUNIOR LEAGUE'S* GOT SOMETHIN' COOKIN'. THEY'RE GOOD KIDS -- IT'S TOO BAD THEY CAN'T --

-- HEY NOW. HEY, THERE'S AN IDEA...

"ATHENA? PALLAS? NIKE?"

"OH, COME ON. DO I LOOK GREEK TO YOU?"

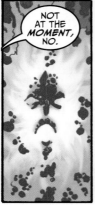

NOT AT THE *MOMENT*, NO.

CORONA? *FLARE?* BLAZE?

TAKEN, I DON'T THINK SO --

-- AND I DON'T *THINK* SO.

SO WHAT'S THE SCORE? GIVE IT TO ME *STRAIGHT*.

STRAIGHT YOU *WANT*, MY DEAR MS. DANVERS -- STRAIGHT YOU *GET*. IT APPEARS THAT YOUR POWERS HAVE *DEFINITELY* DECREASED.

FROM THESE READINGS, I DOUBT YOU'LL EVEN BE ABLE TO SHIFT INTO YOUR *BINARY* FORM AGAIN. I'M *SORRY*.

DON'T BE. IT'S NOT YOUR FAULT. BESIDES, YOU'RE ONLY CONFIRMING WHAT I ALREADY *KNEW*. I'VE BEEN FEELING IT FOR WEEKS.

JUST DO ME A FAVOR, BEAST, AND DON'T *TELL* ANYONE. HEY, WOULD A FIGHTER-PLANE WORK? ONE OF THE OLD *WARBIRDS*, MAYBE?

FOR AN EX-U.S.A.F. CUTIE WHO *FLIES*? HOW OUTRÉ CAN YOU GET? BUT HEY, SO YOU GO FROM *PHENOMENALLY* POWERFUL TO MERELY *INCREDIBLY* POWERFUL. WHERE'S THE HARM IN TELLING --

NO, BEAST. *YOU'VE* GOT THE X-MEN, I WANT ON *THIS* TEAM -- AND I'M *NOT* GOING TO RISK JEOPARDIZING IT. NOW WHAT'VE YOU *GOT*?

UH, BEFORE YOU *LOOK* --

WARRIOR WOMAN? REGALIA? STUKA? BLITZKRIEG?

HEY, I'M CALLED THE *BEAST!* WHAT DO I KNOW FROM NAMES?

REGALIA NIMBUS DYNAMO MARVELLE BLITZKRIEG WARRIOR WOMAN GALACTICA SHRIKE PITFIRE HURRICANE STUKA ZERO

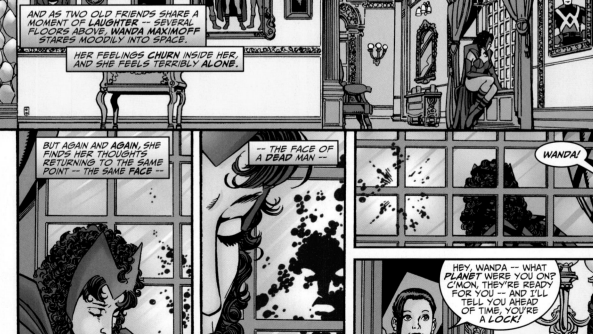

AND AS TWO OLD FRIENDS SHARE A MOMENT OF *LAUGHTER* -- SEVERAL FLOORS ABOVE, *WANDA MAXIMOFF* STARES MOODILY INTO SPACE.

HER FEELINGS *CHURN* INSIDE HER, AND SHE FEELS TERRIBLY *ALONE*.

BUT AGAIN AND *AGAIN*, SHE FINDS HER THOUGHTS RETURNING TO THE SAME POINT -- THE SAME *FACE* --

-- THE FACE OF A *DEAD MAN* --

WANDA!

HEY, WANDA -- WHAT *PLANET* WERE YOU ON? C'MON, THEY'RE READY FOR YOU -- AND I'LL TELL YOU AHEAD OF TIME, YOU'RE A *LOCK!*

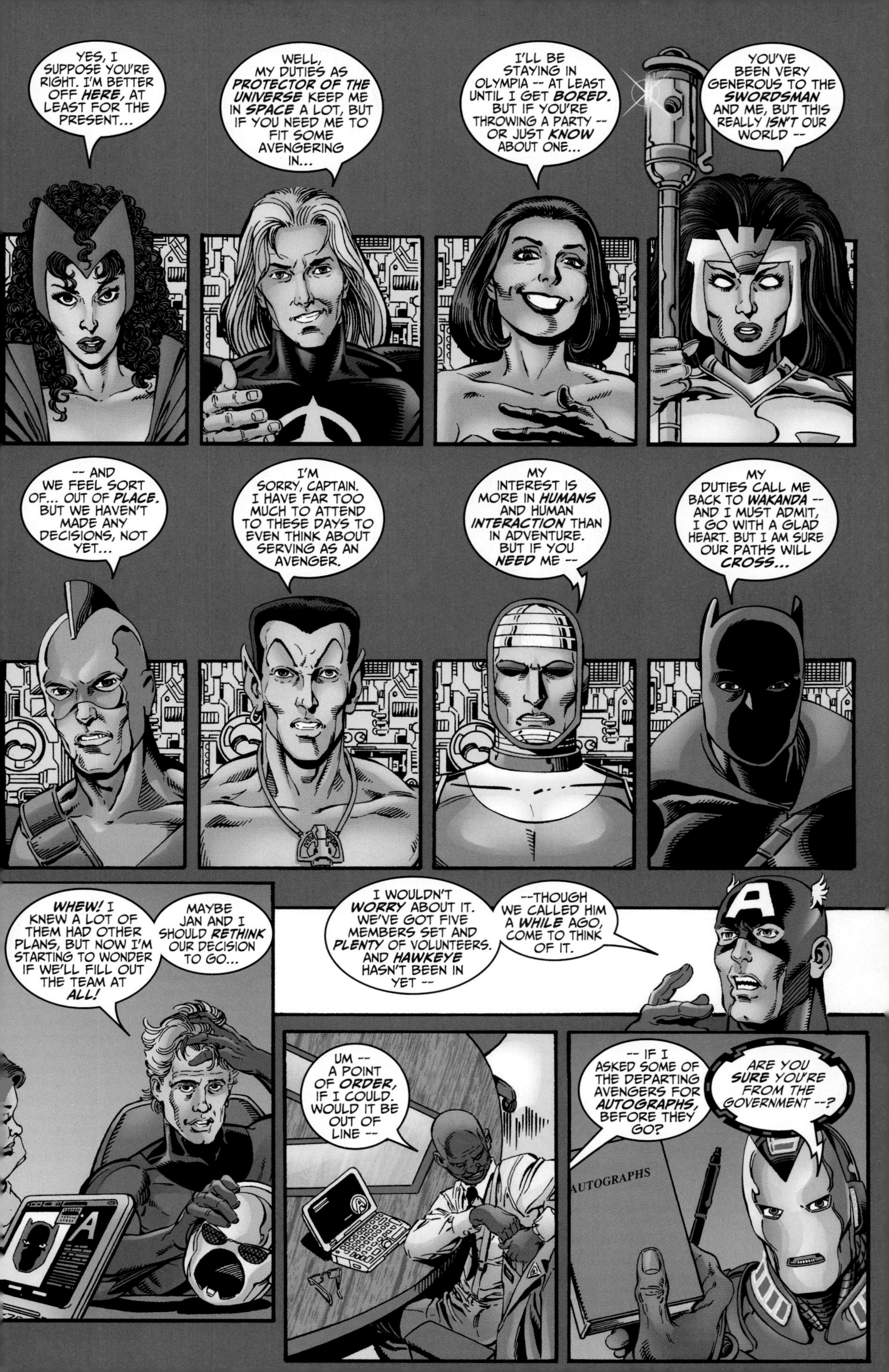
YES, I SUPPOSE YOU'RE RIGHT. I'M BETTER OFF HERE, AT LEAST FOR THE PRESENT...
WELL, MY DUTIES AS PROTECTOR OF THE UNIVERSE KEEP ME IN SPACE A LOT, BUT IF YOU NEED ME TO FIT SOME AVENGERING IN...
I'LL BE STAYING IN OLYMPIA -- AT LEAST UNTIL I GET BORED. BUT IF YOU'RE THROWING A PARTY -- OR JUST KNOW ABOUT ONE...
YOU'VE BEEN VERY GENEROUS TO THE SWORDSMAN AND ME, BUT THIS REALLY ISN'T OUR WORLD --
-- AND WE FEEL SORT OF... OUT OF PLACE. BUT WE HAVEN'T MADE ANY DECISIONS, NOT YET...
I'M SORRY, CAPTAIN. I HAVE FAR TOO MUCH TO ATTEND TO THESE DAYS TO EVEN THINK ABOUT SERVING AS AN AVENGER.
MY INTEREST IS MORE IN HUMANS AND HUMAN INTERACTION THAN IN ADVENTURE. BUT IF YOU NEED ME --
MY DUTIES CALL ME BACK TO WAKANDA -- AND I MUST ADMIT, I GO WITH A GLAD HEART. BUT I AM SURE OUR PATHS WILL CROSS...
WHEW! I KNEW A LOT OF THEM HAD OTHER PLANS, BUT NOW I'M STARTING TO WONDER IF WE'LL FILL OUT THE TEAM AT ALL!
MAYBE JAN AND I SHOULD RETHINK OUR DECISION TO GO...
I WOULDN'T WORRY ABOUT IT. WE'VE GOT FIVE MEMBERS SET AND PLENTY OF VOLUNTEERS. AND HAWKEYE HASN'T BEEN IN YET --
--THOUGH WE CALLED HIM A WHILE AGO, COME TO THINK OF IT.
UM -- A POINT OF ORDER, IF I COULD. WOULD IT BE OUT OF LINE --
-- IF I ASKED SOME OF THE DEPARTING AVENGERS FOR AUTOGRAPHS, BEFORE THEY GO?
ARE YOU SURE YOU'RE FROM THE GOVERNMENT --?
AUTOGRAPHS

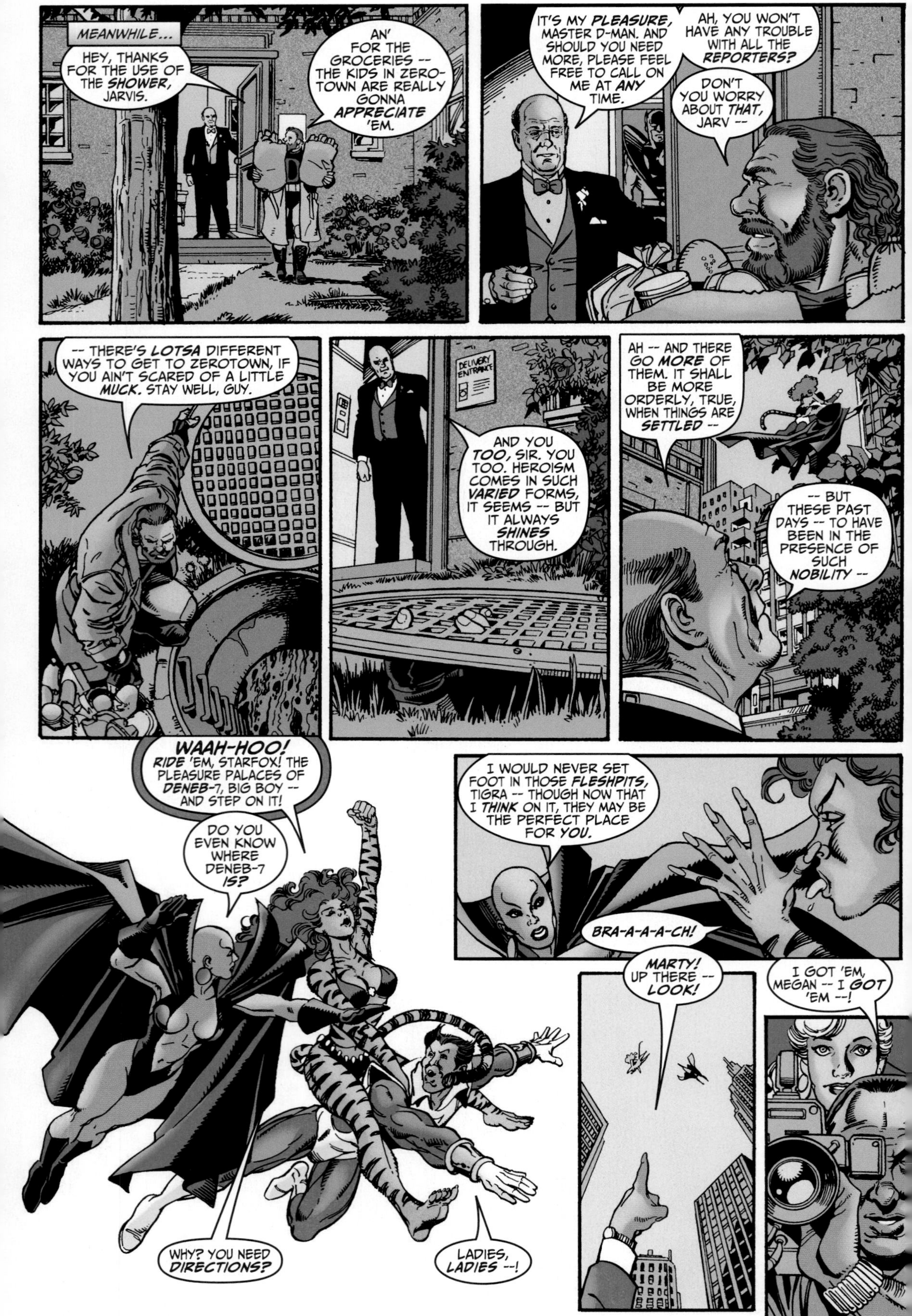
MEANWHILE...
HEY, THANKS FOR THE USE OF THE SHOWER, JARVIS.
AN' FOR THE GROCERIES -- THE KIDS IN ZERO-TOWN ARE REALLY GONNA APPRECIATE 'EM.
IT'S MY PLEASURE, MASTER D-MAN. AND SHOULD YOU NEED MORE, PLEASE FEEL FREE TO CALL ON ME AT ANY TIME.
AH, YOU WON'T HAVE ANY TROUBLE WITH ALL THE REPORTERS?
DON'T YOU WORRY ABOUT THAT, JARV --
-- THERE'S LOTSA DIFFERENT WAYS TO GET TO ZEROTOWN, IF YOU AIN'T SCARED OF A LITTLE MUCK. STAY WELL, GUY.
DELIVERY ENTRANCE
AND YOU TOO, SIR. YOU TOO. HEROISM COMES IN SUCH VARIED FORMS, IT SEEMS -- BUT IT ALWAYS SHINES THROUGH.
AH -- AND THERE GO MORE OF THEM. IT SHALL BE MORE ORDERLY, TRUE, WHEN THINGS ARE SETTLED --
-- BUT THESE PAST DAYS -- TO HAVE BEEN IN THE PRESENCE OF SUCH NOBILITY --
WAAH-HOO! RIDE 'EM, STARFOX! THE PLEASURE PALACES OF DENEB-7, BIG BOY -- AND STEP ON IT!
DO YOU EVEN KNOW WHERE DENEB-7 IS?
WHY? YOU NEED DIRECTIONS?
LADIES, LADIES --!
I WOULD NEVER SET FOOT IN THOSE FLESHPITS, TIGRA -- THOUGH NOW THAT I THINK ON IT, THEY MAY BE THE PERFECT PLACE FOR YOU.
BRA-A-A-CH!
MARTY! UP THERE -- LOOK!
I GOT 'EM, MEGAN -- I GOT 'EM --!

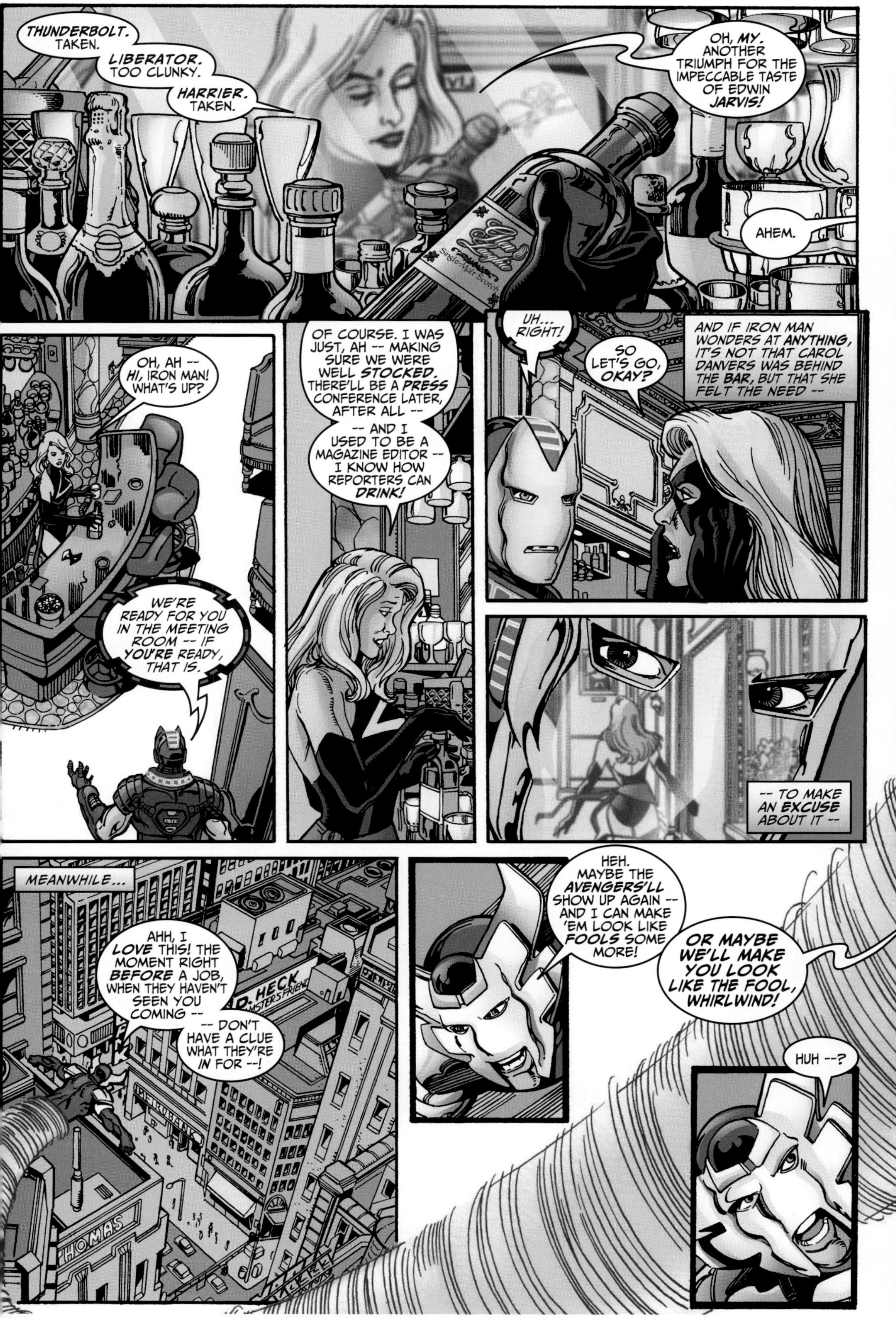
THUNDERBOLT. TAKEN.
LIBERATOR. TOO CLUNKY.
HARRIER. TAKEN.
OH, MY. ANOTHER TRIUMPH FOR THE IMPECCABLE TASTE OF EDWIN JARVIS!
Glen Laughie Single-Malt Scotch
AHEM.
OH, AH -- HI, IRON MAN! WHAT'S UP?
WE'RE READY FOR YOU IN THE MEETING ROOM -- IF YOU'RE READY, THAT IS.
OF COURSE. I WAS JUST, AH -- MAKING SURE WE WERE WELL STOCKED. THERE'LL BE A PRESS CONFERENCE LATER, AFTER ALL --
-- AND I USED TO BE A MAGAZINE EDITOR -- I KNOW HOW REPORTERS CAN DRINK!
UH... RIGHT!
SO LET'S GO, OKAY?
AND IF IRON MAN WONDERS AT ANYTHING, IT'S NOT THAT CAROL DANVERS WAS BEHIND THE BAR, BUT THAT SHE FELT THE NEED --
-- TO MAKE AN EXCUSE ABOUT IT --
MEANWHILE...
AHH, I LOVE THIS! THE MOMENT RIGHT BEFORE A JOB, WHEN THEY HAVEN'T SEEN YOU COMING --
-- DON'T HAVE A CLUE WHAT THEY'RE IN FOR --!
D. HECK
METROBANK
HOMAS
HEH. MAYBE THE AVENGERS'LL SHOW UP AGAIN -- AND I CAN MAKE 'EM LOOK LIKE FOOLS SOME MORE!
OR MAYBE WE'LL MAKE YOU LOOK LIKE THE FOOL, WHIRLWIND!
HUH --?

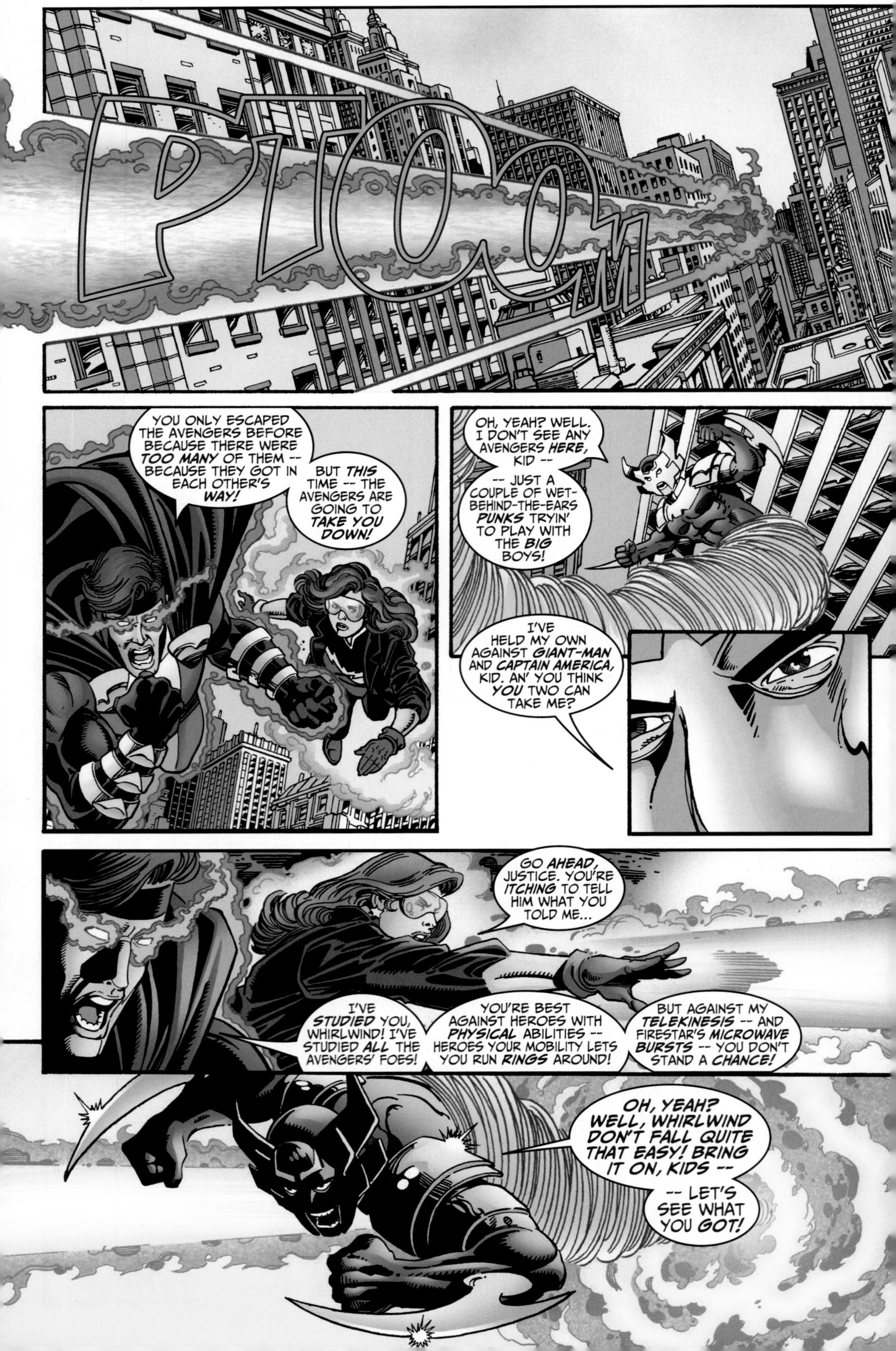
PTOOOM
YOU ONLY ESCAPED THE AVENGERS BEFORE BECAUSE THERE WERE TOO MANY OF THEM -- BECAUSE THEY GOT IN EACH OTHER'S WAY!
BUT THIS TIME -- THE AVENGERS ARE GOING TO TAKE YOU DOWN!
OH, YEAH? WELL. I DON'T SEE ANY AVENGERS HERE, KID --
-- JUST A COUPLE OF WET-BEHIND-THE-EARS PUNKS TRYIN' TO PLAY WITH THE BIG BOYS!
I'VE HELD MY OWN AGAINST GIANT-MAN AND CAPTAIN AMERICA, KID. AN' YOU THINK YOU TWO CAN TAKE ME?
GO AHEAD, JUSTICE. YOU'RE ITCHING TO TELL HIM WHAT YOU TOLD ME...
I'VE STUDIED YOU, WHIRLWIND! I'VE STUDIED ALL THE AVENGERS' FOES!
YOU'RE BEST AGAINST HEROES WITH PHYSICAL ABILITIES -- HEROES YOUR MOBILITY LETS YOU RUN RINGS AROUND!
BUT AGAINST MY TELEKINESIS -- AND FIRESTAR'S MICROWAVE BURSTS -- YOU DON'T STAND A CHANCE!
OH, YEAH? WELL, WHIRLWIND DON'T FALL QUITE THAT EASY! BRING IT ON, KIDS --
-- LET'S SEE WHAT YOU GOT!

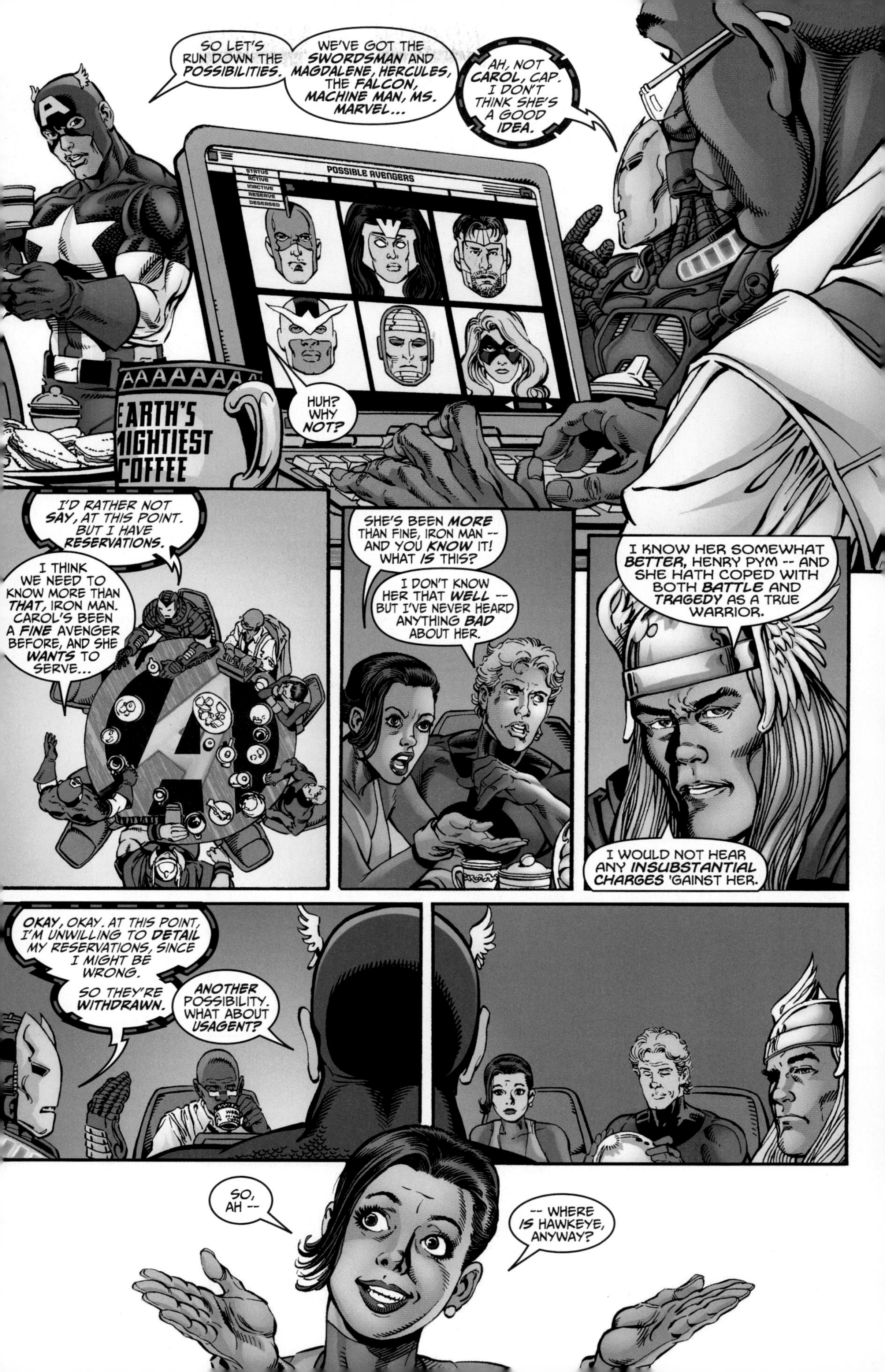
SO LET'S RUN DOWN THE POSSIBILITIES.
WE'VE GOT THE SWORDSMAN AND MAGDALENE, HERCULES, THE FALCON, MACHINE MAN, MS. MARVEL...
AH, NOT CAROL, CAP. I DON'T THINK SHE'S A GOOD IDEA.
POSSIBLE AVENGERS
STATUS
ACTIVE
INACTIVE
RESERVE
DESERSED
HUH? WHY NOT?
EARTH'S MIGHTIEST COFFEE
I'D RATHER NOT SAY, AT THIS POINT. BUT I HAVE RESERVATIONS.
I THINK WE NEED TO KNOW MORE THAN THAT, IRON MAN. CAROL'S BEEN A FINE AVENGER BEFORE, AND SHE WANTS TO SERVE...
SHE'S BEEN MORE THAN FINE, IRON MAN -- AND YOU KNOW IT! WHAT IS THIS?
I DON'T KNOW HER THAT WELL -- BUT I'VE NEVER HEARD ANYTHING BAD ABOUT HER.
I KNOW HER SOMEWHAT BETTER, HENRY PYM -- AND SHE HATH COPED WITH BOTH BATTLE AND TRAGEDY AS A TRUE WARRIOR.
I WOULD NOT HEAR ANY INSUBSTANTIAL CHARGES 'GAINST HER.
OKAY, OKAY. AT THIS POINT, I'M UNWILLING TO DETAIL MY RESERVATIONS, SINCE I MIGHT BE WRONG.
SO THEY'RE WITHDRAWN.
ANOTHER POSSIBILITY. WHAT ABOUT USAGENT?
SO, AH --
-- WHERE IS HAWKEYE, ANYWAY?

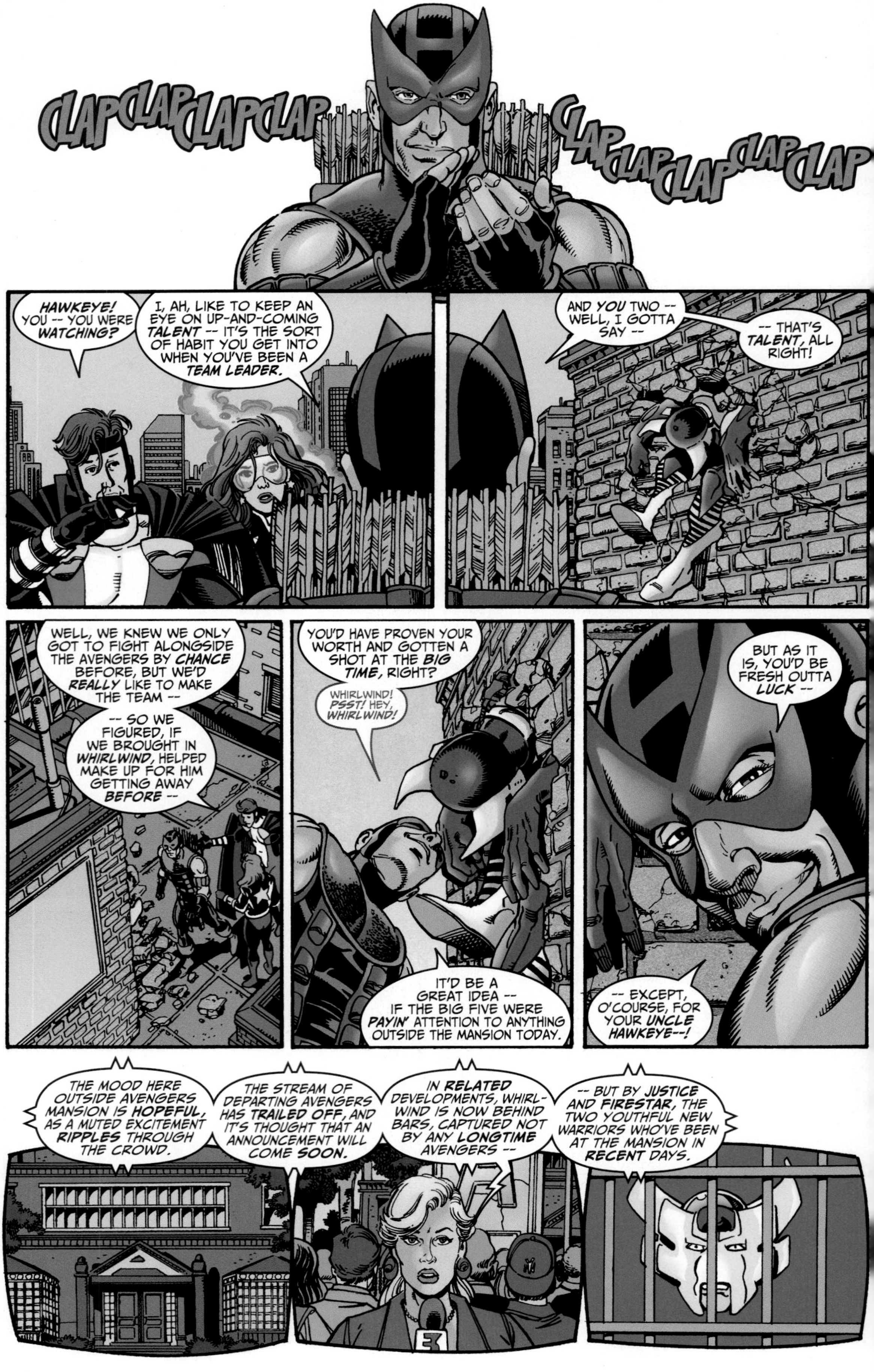
CLAPCLAPCLAPCLAP
CLAPCLAPCLAPCLAPCLAP
HAWKEYE! YOU -- YOU WERE WATCHING?
I, AH, LIKE TO KEEP AN EYE ON UP-AND-COMING TALENT -- IT'S THE SORT OF HABIT YOU GET INTO WHEN YOU'VE BEEN A TEAM LEADER.
AND YOU TWO -- WELL, I GOTTA SAY --
-- THAT'S TALENT, ALL RIGHT!
WELL, WE KNEW WE ONLY GOT TO FIGHT ALONGSIDE THE AVENGERS BY CHANCE BEFORE, BUT WE'D REALLY LIKE TO MAKE THE TEAM --
-- SO WE FIGURED, IF WE BROUGHT IN WHIRLWIND, HELPED MAKE UP FOR HIM GETTING AWAY BEFORE --
YOU'D HAVE PROVEN YOUR WORTH AND GOTTEN A SHOT AT THE BIG TIME, RIGHT?
WHIRLWIND! PSST! HEY, WHIRLWIND!
IT'D BE A GREAT IDEA -- IF THE BIG FIVE WERE PAYIN' ATTENTION TO ANYTHING OUTSIDE THE MANSION TODAY.
BUT AS IT IS, YOU'D BE FRESH OUTTA LUCK --
-- EXCEPT, O'COURSE, FOR YOUR UNCLE HAWKEYE--!
THE MOOD HERE OUTSIDE AVENGERS MANSION IS HOPEFUL, AS A MUTED EXCITEMENT RIPPLES THROUGH THE CROWD.
THE STREAM OF DEPARTING AVENGERS HAS TRAILED OFF, AND IT'S THOUGHT THAT AN ANNOUNCEMENT WILL COME SOON.
IN RELATED DEVELOPMENTS, WHIRLWIND IS NOW BEHIND BARS, CAPTURED NOT BY ANY LONGTIME AVENGERS --
-- BUT BY JUSTICE AND FIRESTAR, THE TWO YOUTHFUL NEW WARRIORS WHO'VE BEEN AT THE MANSION IN RECENT DAYS.

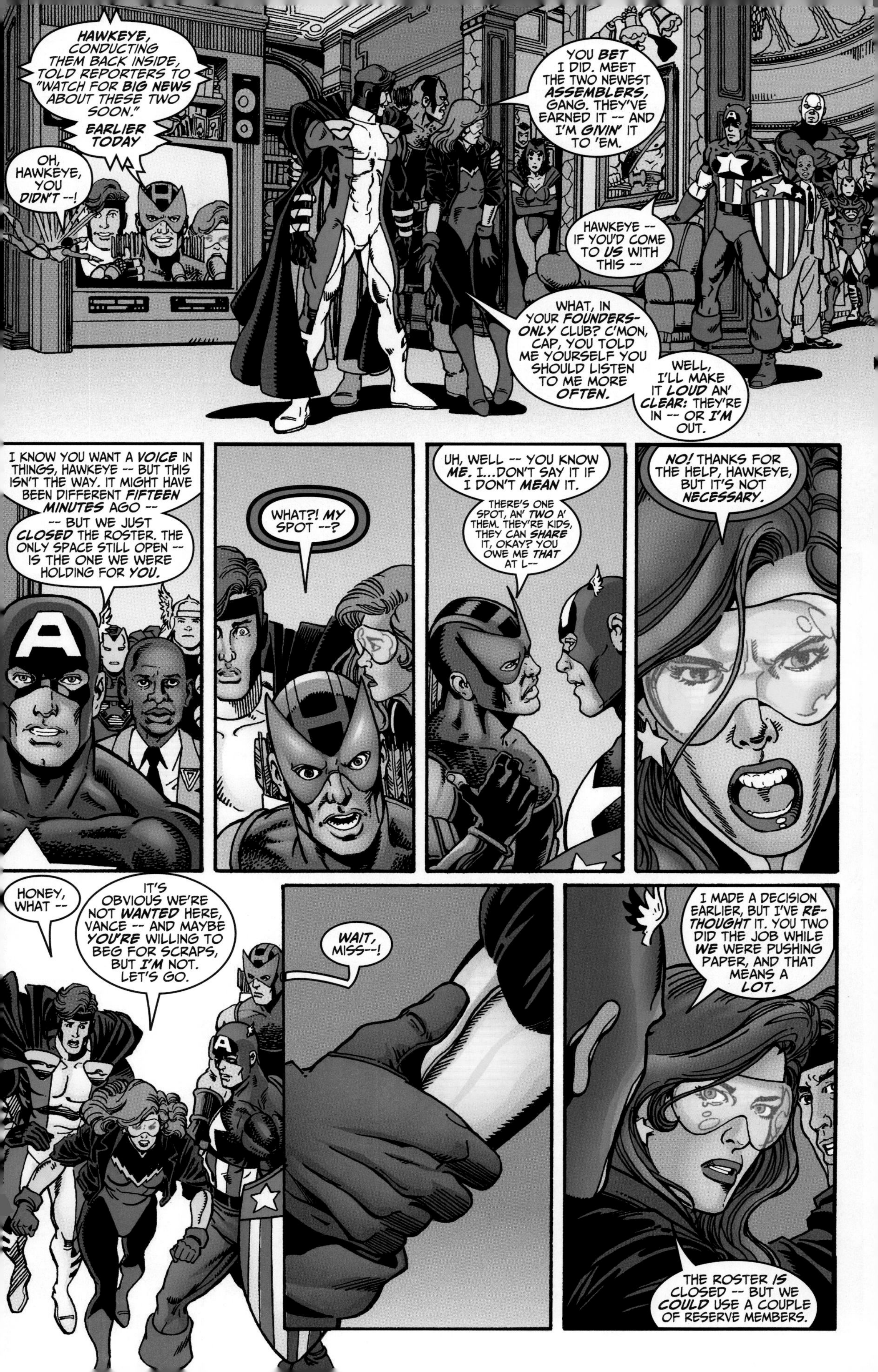
HAWKEYE, CONDUCTING THEM BACK INSIDE, TOLD REPORTERS TO "WATCH FOR BIG NEWS ABOUT THESE TWO SOON."
EARLIER TODAY
OH, HAWKEYE, YOU DIDN'T --!
YOU BET I DID. MEET THE TWO NEWEST ASSEMBLERS, GANG. THEY'VE EARNED IT -- AND I'M GIVIN' IT TO 'EM.
HAWKEYE -- IF YOU'D COME TO US WITH THIS --
WHAT, IN YOUR FOUNDERS-ONLY CLUB? C'MON, CAP, YOU TOLD ME YOURSELF YOU SHOULD LISTEN TO ME MORE OFTEN.
WELL, I'LL MAKE IT LOUD AN' CLEAR: THEY'RE IN -- OR I'M OUT.
I KNOW YOU WANT A VOICE IN THINGS, HAWKEYE -- BUT THIS ISN'T THE WAY. IT MIGHT HAVE BEEN DIFFERENT FIFTEEN MINUTES AGO --
-- BUT WE JUST CLOSED THE ROSTER. THE ONLY SPACE STILL OPEN -- IS THE ONE WE WERE HOLDING FOR YOU.
WHAT?! MY SPOT --?
UH, WELL -- YOU KNOW ME. I...DON'T SAY IT IF I DON'T MEAN IT.
THERE'S ONE SPOT, AN' TWO A' THEM. THEY'RE KIDS, THEY CAN SHARE IT, OKAY? YOU OWE ME THAT AT L--
NO! THANKS FOR THE HELP, HAWKEYE, BUT IT'S NOT NECESSARY.
HONEY, WHAT --
IT'S OBVIOUS WE'RE NOT WANTED HERE, VANCE -- AND MAYBE YOU'RE WILLING TO BEG FOR SCRAPS, BUT I'M NOT. LET'S GO.
WAIT, MISS--!
I MADE A DECISION EARLIER, BUT I'VE RE-THOUGHT IT. YOU TWO DID THE JOB WHILE WE WERE PUSHING PAPER, AND THAT MEANS A LOT.
THE ROSTER IS CLOSED -- BUT WE COULD USE A COUPLE OF RESERVE MEMBERS.

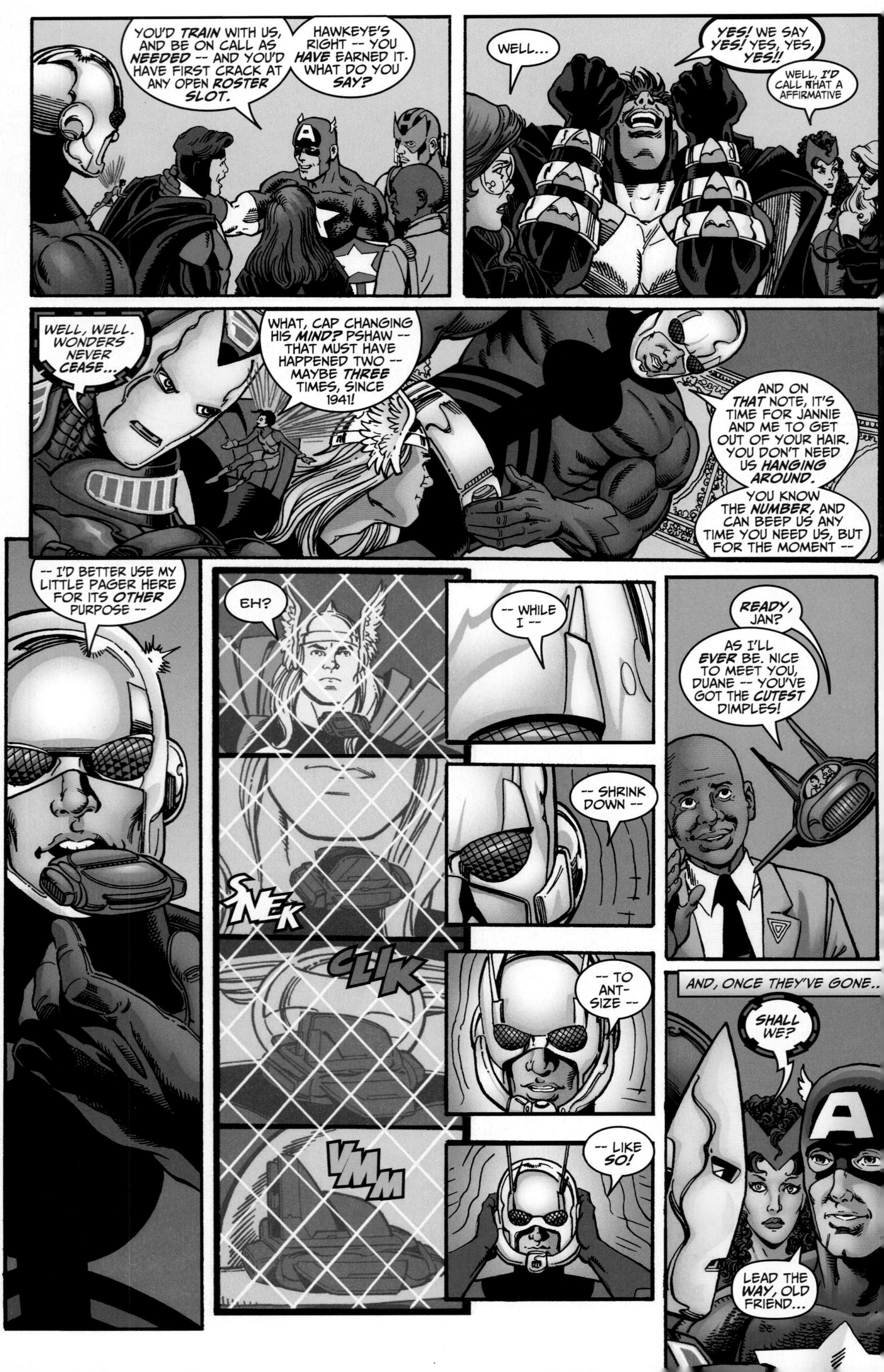
YOU'D TRAIN WITH US, AND BE ON CALL AS NEEDED -- AND YOU'D HAVE FIRST CRACK AT ANY OPEN ROSTER SLOT.
HAWKEYE'S RIGHT -- YOU HAVE EARNED IT. WHAT DO YOU SAY?
WELL...
YES! WE SAY YES! YES, YES, YES!!
WELL, I'D CALL THAT A AFFIRMATIVE
WELL, WELL. WONDERS NEVER CEASE...
WHAT, CAP CHANGING HIS MIND? PSHAW -- THAT MUST HAVE HAPPENED TWO -- MAYBE THREE TIMES, SINCE 1941!
AND ON THAT NOTE, IT'S TIME FOR JANNIE AND ME TO GET OUT OF YOUR HAIR. YOU DON'T NEED US HANGING AROUND.
YOU KNOW THE NUMBER, AND CAN BEEP US ANY TIME YOU NEED US, BUT FOR THE MOMENT --
-- I'D BETTER USE MY LITTLE PAGER HERE FOR ITS OTHER PURPOSE --
EH?
SNEK
CLIK
VMM
-- WHILE I --
-- SHRINK DOWN --
-- TO ANT-SIZE --
-- LIKE SO!
READY, JAN?
AS I'LL EVER BE. NICE TO MEET YOU, DUANE -- YOU'VE GOT THE CUTEST DIMPLES!
AND, ONCE THEY'VE GONE...
SHALL WE?
LEAD THE WAY, OLD FRIEND...

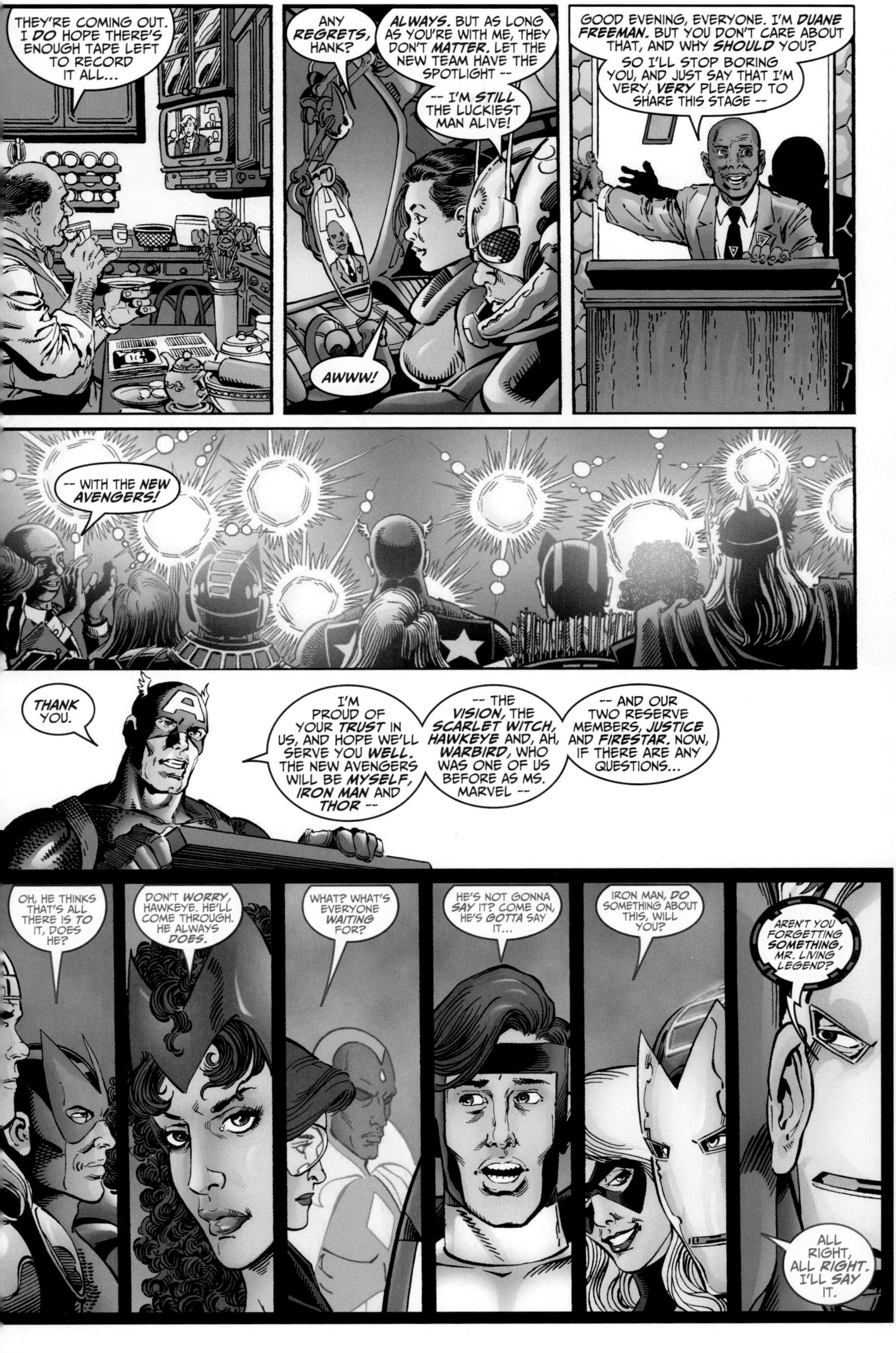
THEY'RE COMING OUT. I DO HOPE THERE'S ENOUGH TAPE LEFT TO RECORD IT ALL...
ANY REGRETS, HANK?
ALWAYS. BUT AS LONG AS YOU'RE WITH ME, THEY DON'T MATTER. LET THE NEW TEAM HAVE THE SPOTLIGHT --
-- I'M STILL THE LUCKIEST MAN ALIVE!
AWWW!
GOOD EVENING, EVERYONE. I'M DUANE FREEMAN. BUT YOU DON'T CARE ABOUT THAT, AND WHY SHOULD YOU?
SO I'LL STOP BORING YOU, AND JUST SAY THAT I'M VERY, VERY PLEASED TO SHARE THIS STAGE --
-- WITH THE NEW AVENGERS!
THANK YOU.
I'M PROUD OF YOUR TRUST IN US, AND HOPE WE'LL SERVE YOU WELL. THE NEW AVENGERS WILL BE MYSELF, IRON MAN AND THOR --
-- THE VISION, THE SCARLET WITCH, HAWKEYE AND, AH, WARBIRD, WHO WAS ONE OF US BEFORE AS MS. MARVEL --
-- AND OUR TWO RESERVE MEMBERS, JUSTICE AND FIRESTAR. NOW, IF THERE ARE ANY QUESTIONS...
OH, HE THINKS THAT'S ALL THERE IS TO IT, DOES HE?
DON'T WORRY, HAWKEYE. HE'LL COME THROUGH. HE ALWAYS DOES.
WHAT? WHAT'S EVERYONE WAITING FOR?
HE'S NOT GONNA SAY IT? COME ON, HE'S GOTTA SAY IT...
IRON MAN, DO SOMETHING ABOUT THIS, WILL YOU?
AREN'T YOU FORGETTING SOMETHING, MR. LIVING LEGEND?
ALL RIGHT, ALL RIGHT. I'LL SAY IT.

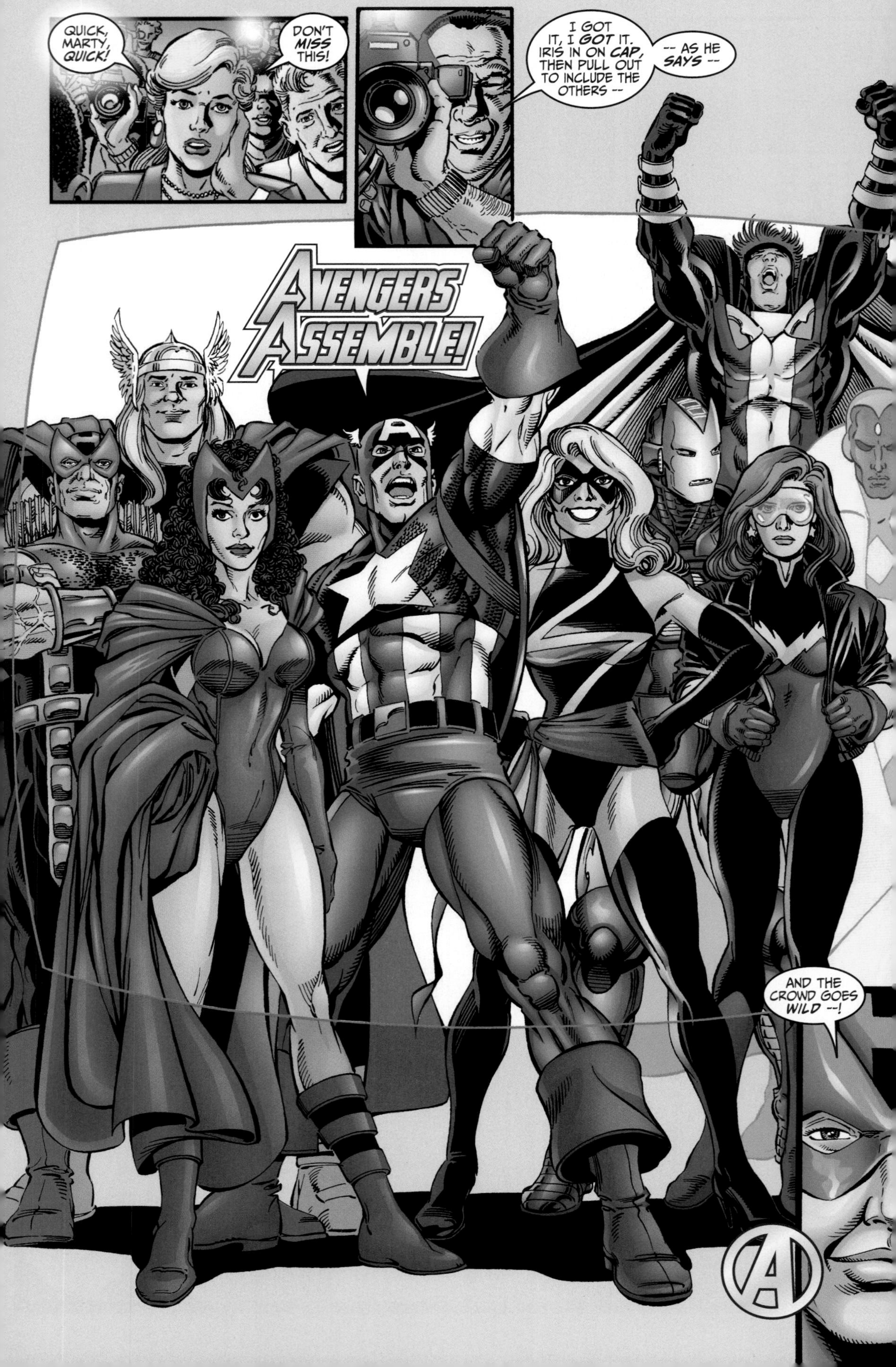
QUICK, MARTY, QUICK!
DON'T MISS THIS!
I GOT IT, I GOT IT. IRIS IN ON CAP, THEN PULL OUT TO INCLUDE THE OTHERS --
-- AS HE SAYS --
AVENGERS ASSEMBLE!
AND THE CROWD GOES WILD --!

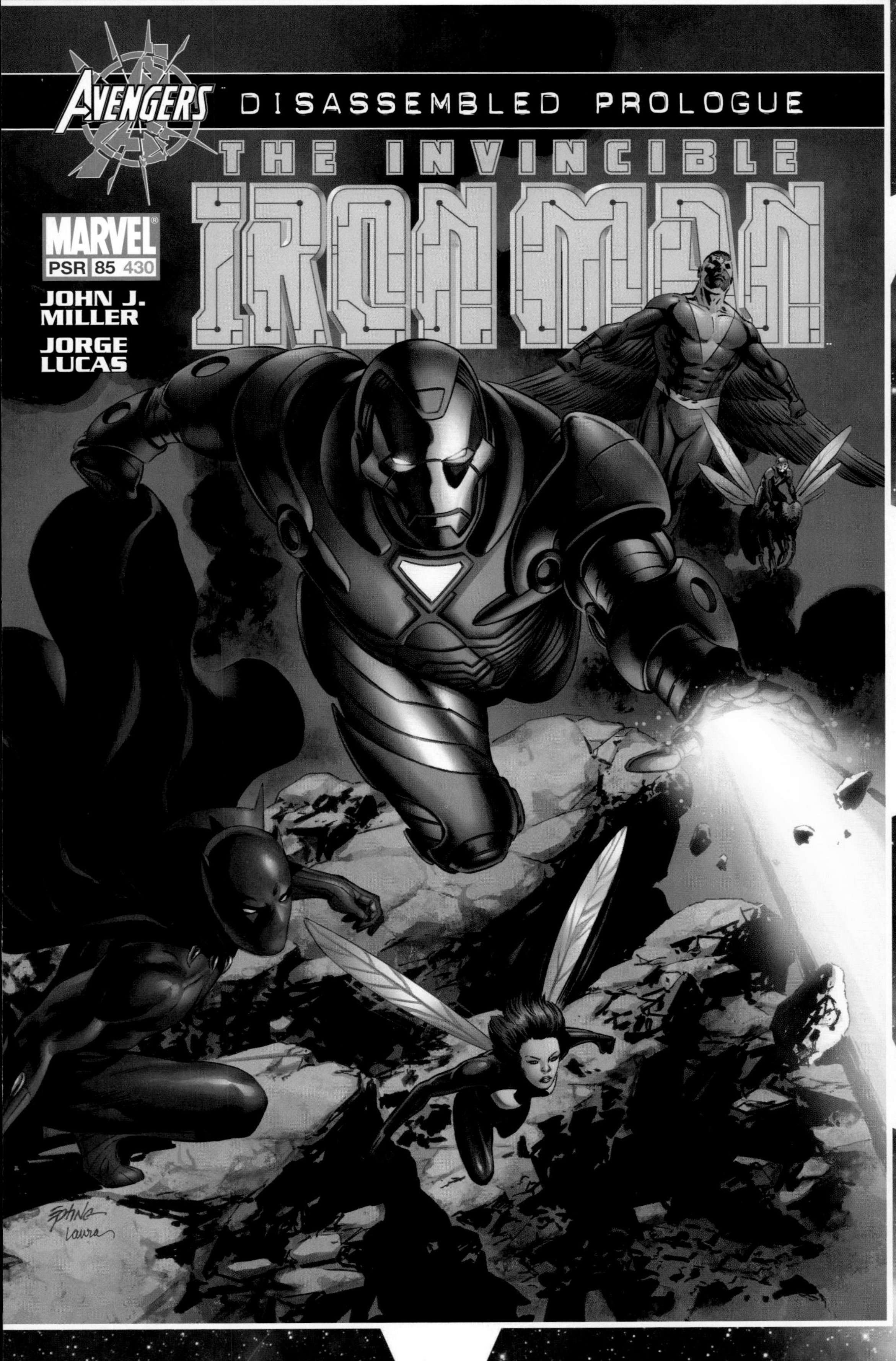
AVENGERS
DISASSEMBLED PROLOGUE
THE INVINCIBLE
IRON MAN
MARVEL
PSR 85 430
JOHN J. MILLER
JORGE LUCAS

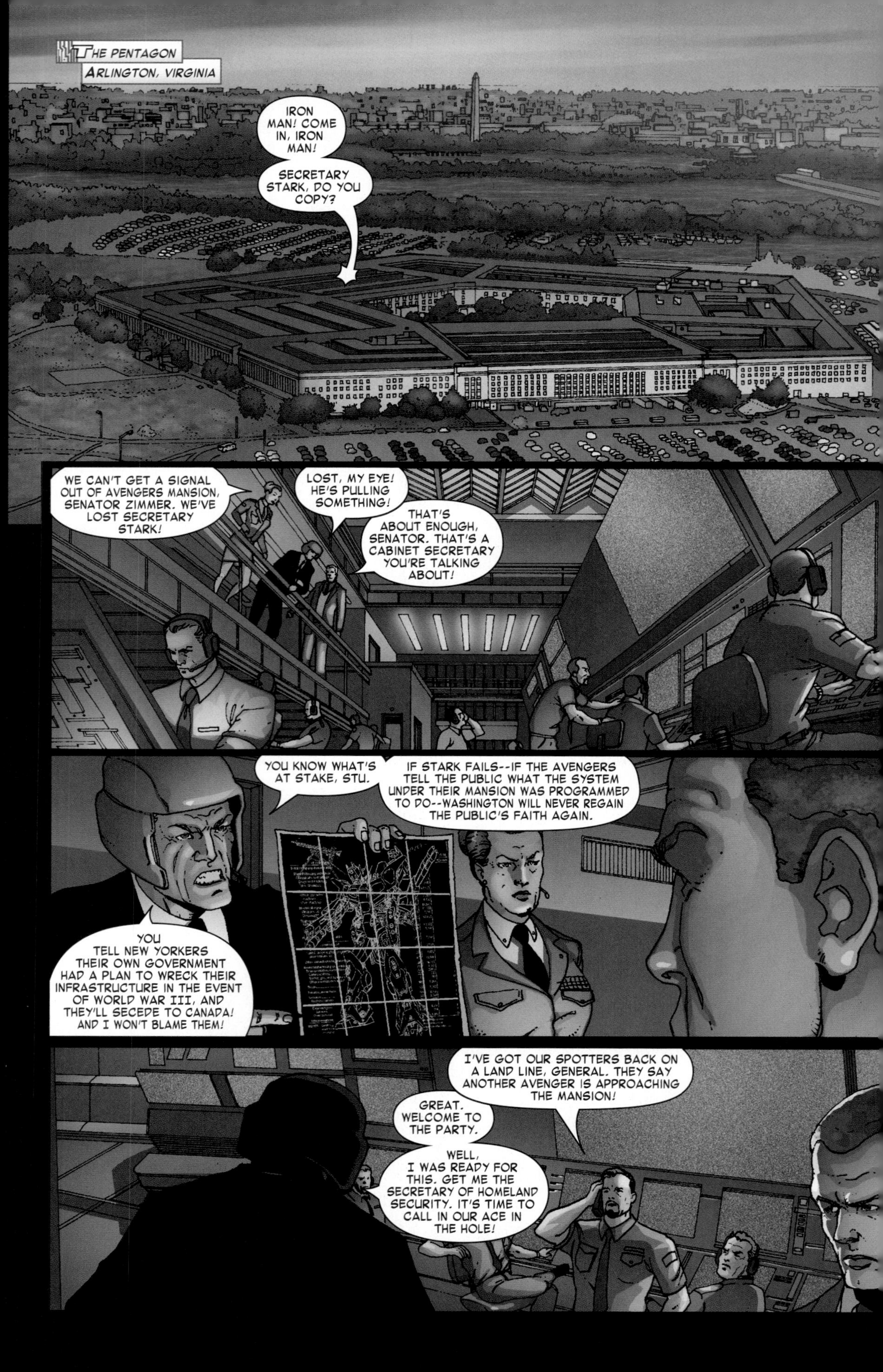
THE PENTAGON
ARLINGTON, VIRGINIA
IRON MAN! COME IN, IRON MAN!
SECRETARY STARK, DO YOU COPY?
WE CAN'T GET A SIGNAL OUT OF AVENGERS MANSION, SENATOR ZIMMER. WE'VE LOST SECRETARY STARK!
LOST, MY EYE! HE'S PULLING SOMETHING!
THAT'S ABOUT ENOUGH, SENATOR. THAT'S A CABINET SECRETARY YOU'RE TALKING ABOUT!
YOU KNOW WHAT'S AT STAKE, STU.
IF STARK FAILS--IF THE AVENGERS TELL THE PUBLIC WHAT THE SYSTEM UNDER THEIR MANSION WAS PROGRAMMED TO DO--WASHINGTON WILL NEVER REGAIN THE PUBLIC'S FAITH AGAIN.
YOU TELL NEW YORKERS THEIR OWN GOVERNMENT HAD A PLAN TO WRECK THEIR INFRASTRUCTURE IN THE EVENT OF WORLD WAR III, AND THEY'LL SECEDE TO CANADA! AND I WON'T BLAME THEM!
I'VE GOT OUR SPOTTERS BACK ON A LAND LINE, GENERAL. THEY SAY ANOTHER AVENGER IS APPROACHING THE MANSION!
GREAT. WELCOME TO THE PARTY.
WELL, I WAS READY FOR THIS. GET ME THE SECRETARY OF HOMELAND SECURITY. IT'S TIME TO CALL IN OUR ACE IN THE HOLE!

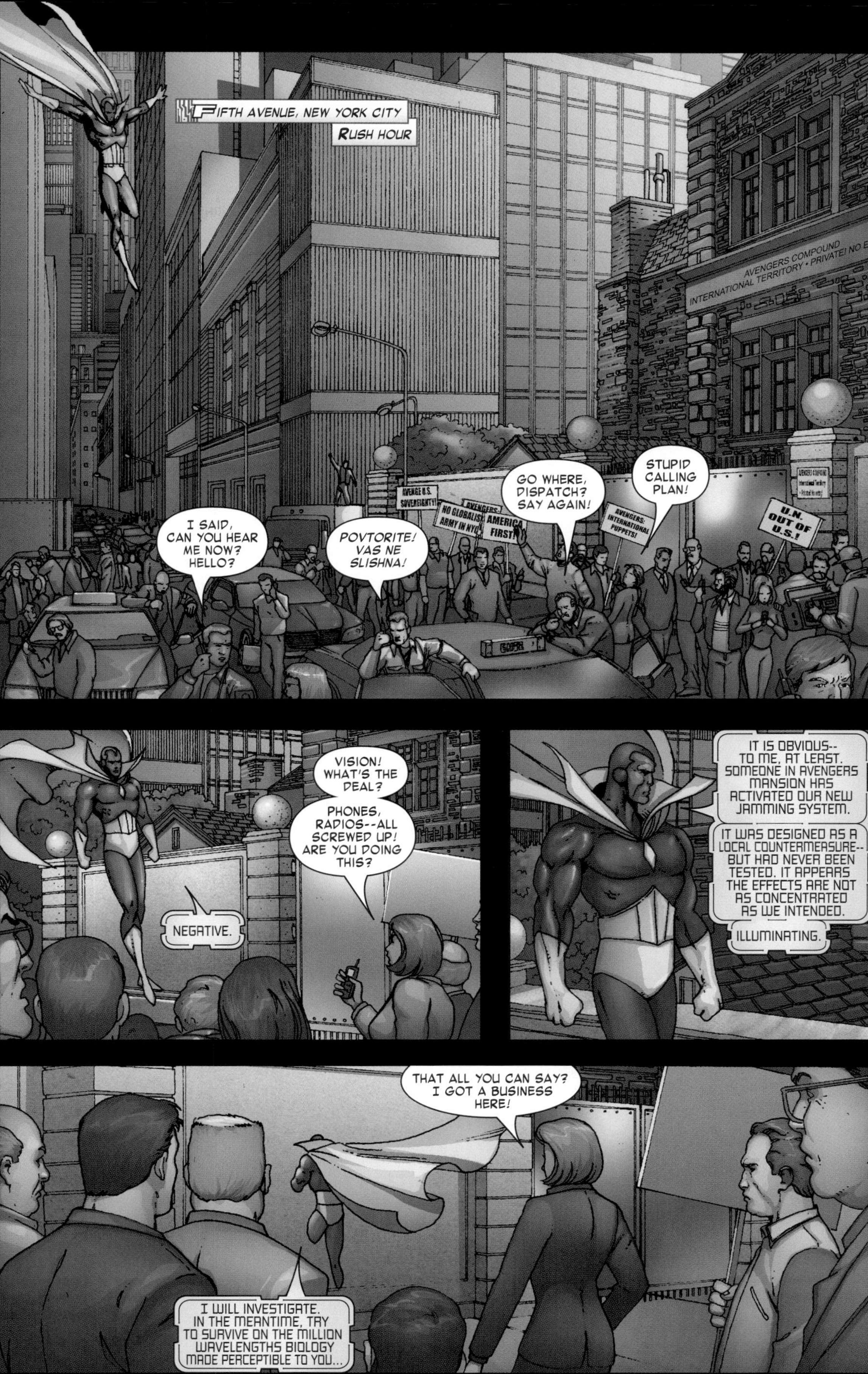
FIFTH AVENUE, NEW YORK CITY
RUSH HOUR
AVENGERS COMPOUND INTERNATIONAL TERRITORY • PRIVATE! NO E
AVENGE U.S. SOVEREIGNTY!
NO GLOBALIST ARMY IN NYC!
AMERICA FIRST!
AVENGERS: INTERNATIONAL PUPPETS!
U.N. OUT OF U.S.!
I SAID, CAN YOU HEAR ME NOW? HELLO?
POVTORITE! VAS NE SLISHNA!
GO WHERE, DISPATCH? SAY AGAIN!
STUPID CALLING PLAN!
VISION! WHAT'S THE DEAL?
PHONES, RADIOS--ALL SCREWED UP! ARE YOU DOING THIS?
NEGATIVE.
IT IS OBVIOUS-- TO ME, AT LEAST. SOMEONE IN AVENGERS MANSION HAS ACTIVATED OUR NEW JAMMING SYSTEM.
IT WAS DESIGNED AS A LOCAL COUNTERMEASURE-- BUT HAD NEVER BEEN TESTED. IT APPEARS THE EFFECTS ARE NOT AS CONCENTRATED AS WE INTENDED.
ILLUMINATING.
THAT ALL YOU CAN SAY? I GOT A BUSINESS HERE!
I WILL INVESTIGATE. IN THE MEANTIME, TRY TO SURVIVE ON THE MILLION WAVELENGTHS BIOLOGY MADE PERCEPTIBLE TO YOU...

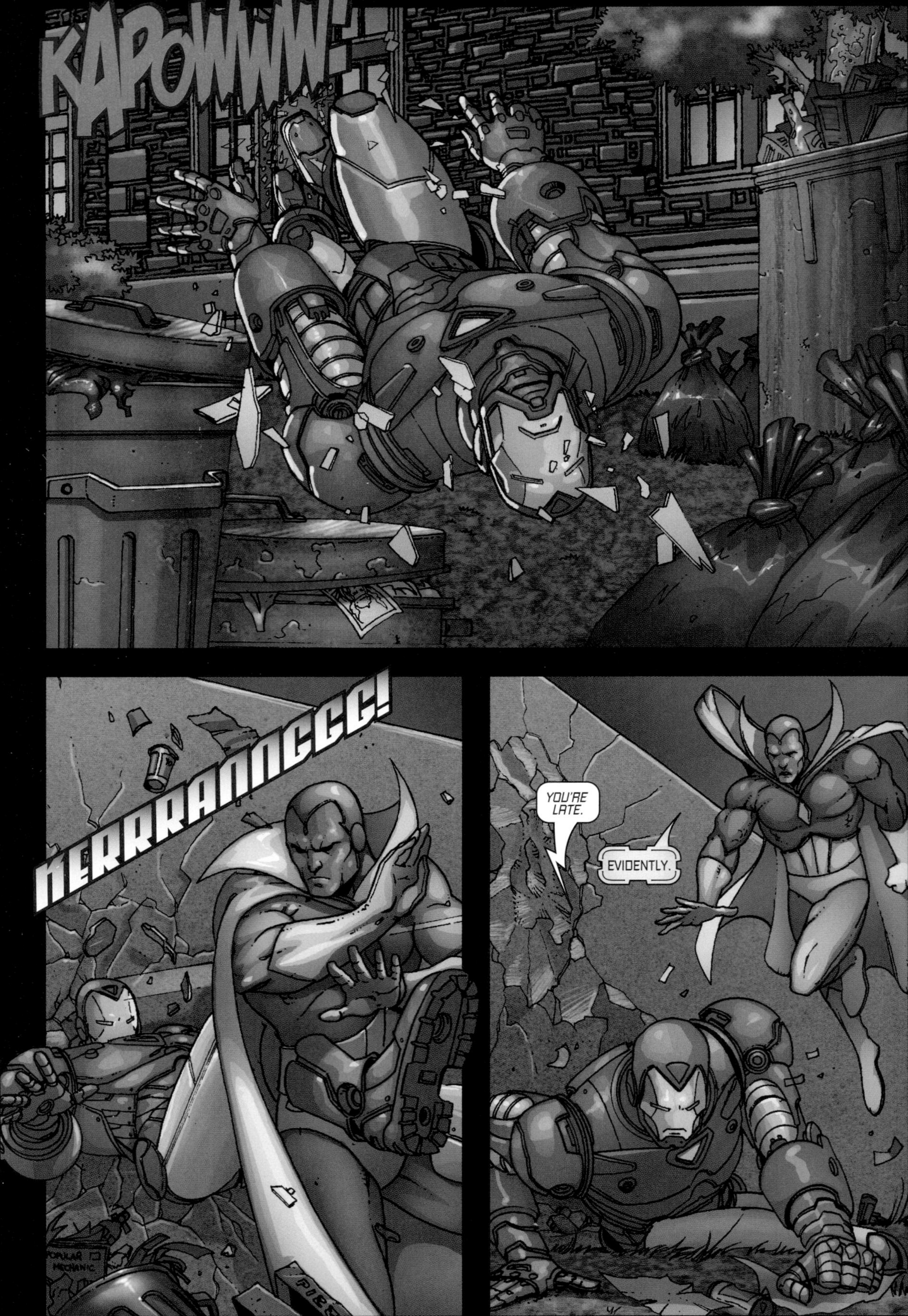
KAPOWWW!
KERRRANNCCC!
YOU'RE LATE.
EVIDENTLY.

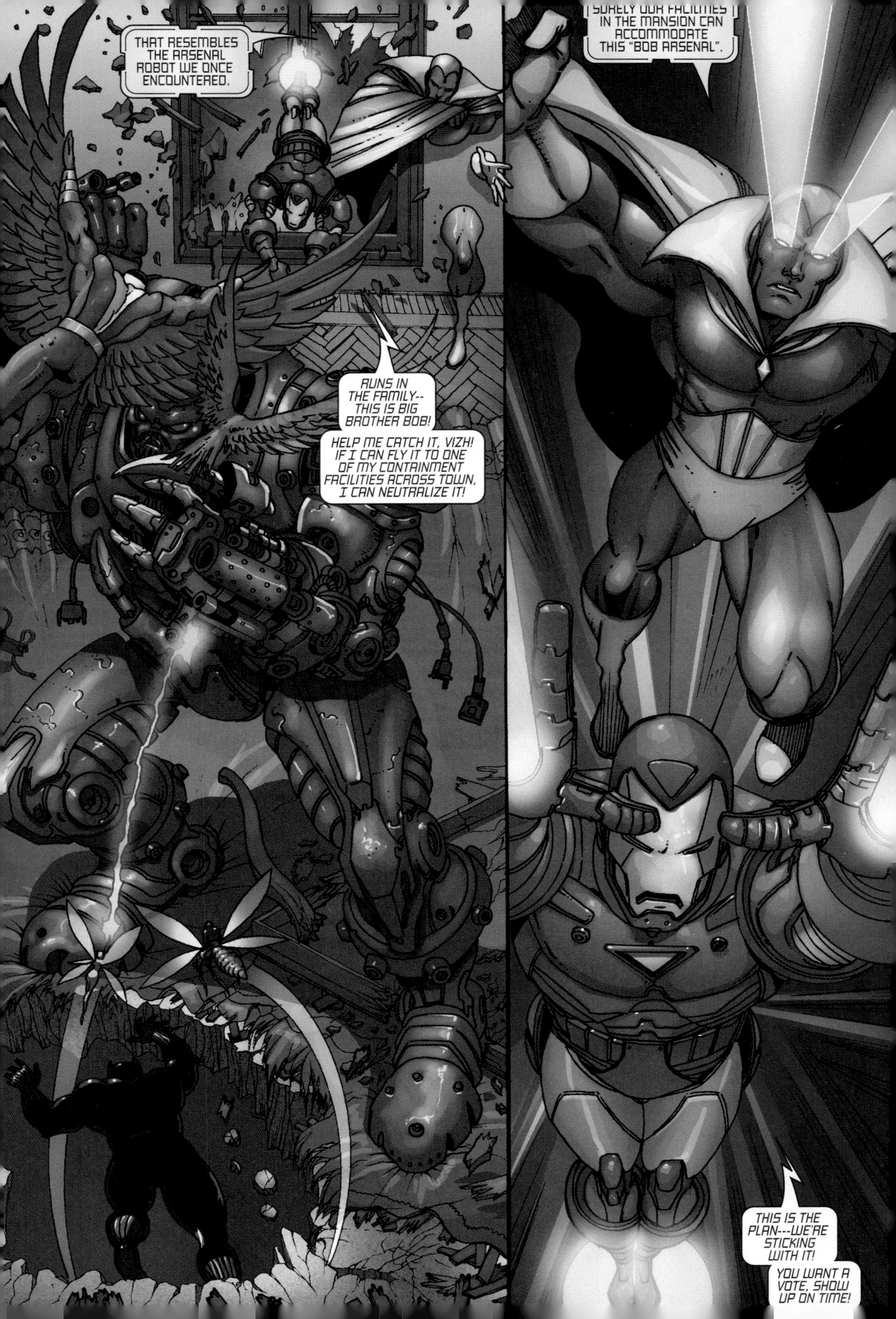
THAT RESEMBLES THE ARSENAL ROBOT WE ONCE ENCOUNTERED.
RUNS IN THE FAMILY-- THIS IS BIG BROTHER BOB!
HELP ME CATCH IT, VIZH! IF I CAN FLY IT TO ONE OF MY CONTAINMENT FACILITIES ACROSS TOWN, I CAN NEUTRALIZE IT!
SURELY OUR FACILITIES IN THE MANSION CAN ACCOMMODATE THIS "BOB ARSENAL".
THIS IS THE PLAN---WE'RE STICKING WITH IT!
YOU WANT A VOTE, SHOW UP ON TIME!

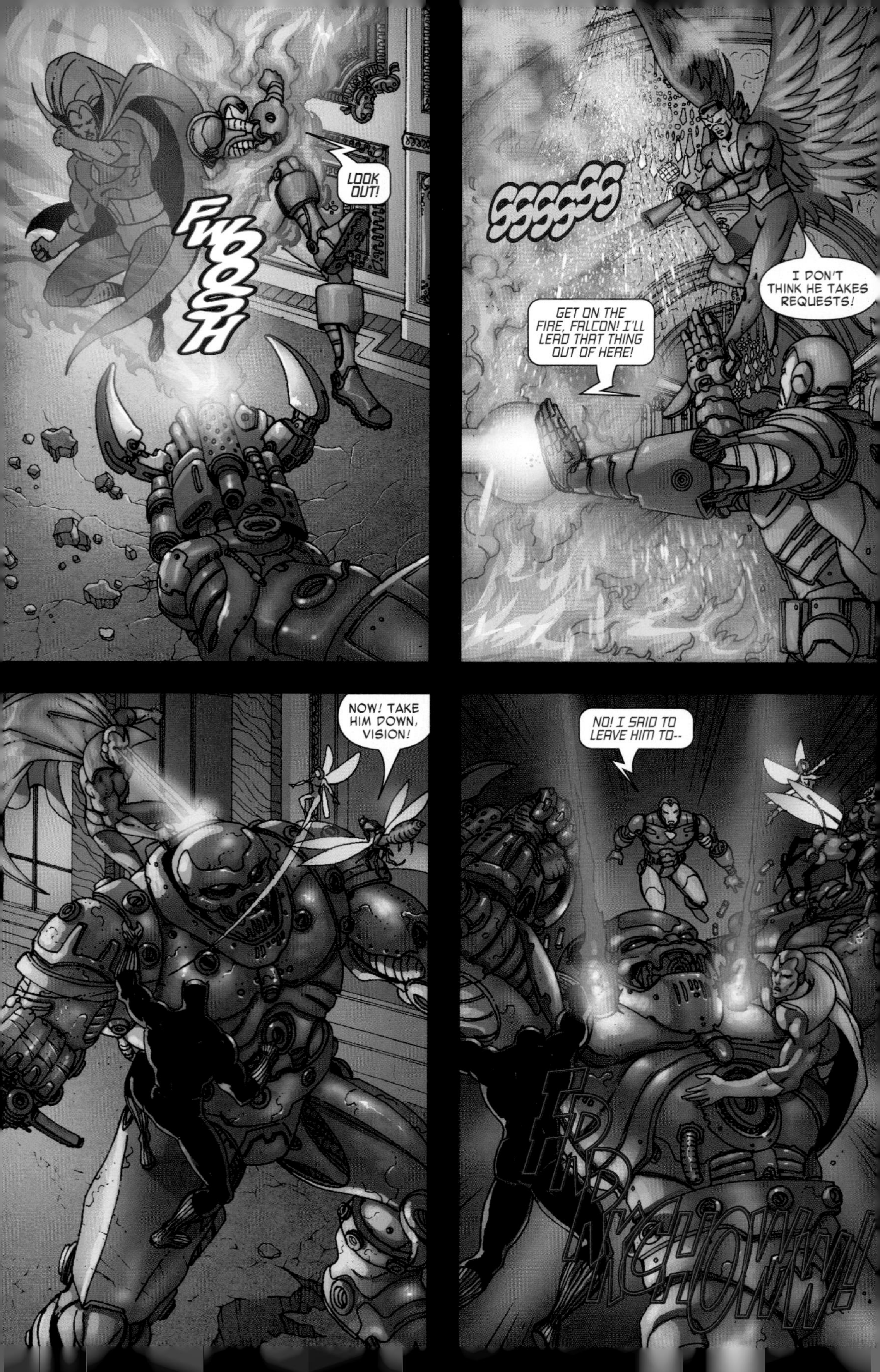
LOOK OUT!
FWOOSH
SSSSSS
GET ON THE FIRE, FALCON! I'LL LEAD THAT THING OUT OF HERE!
I DON'T THINK HE TAKES REQUESTS!
NOW! TAKE HIM DOWN, VISION!
NO! I SAID TO LEAVE HIM TO--

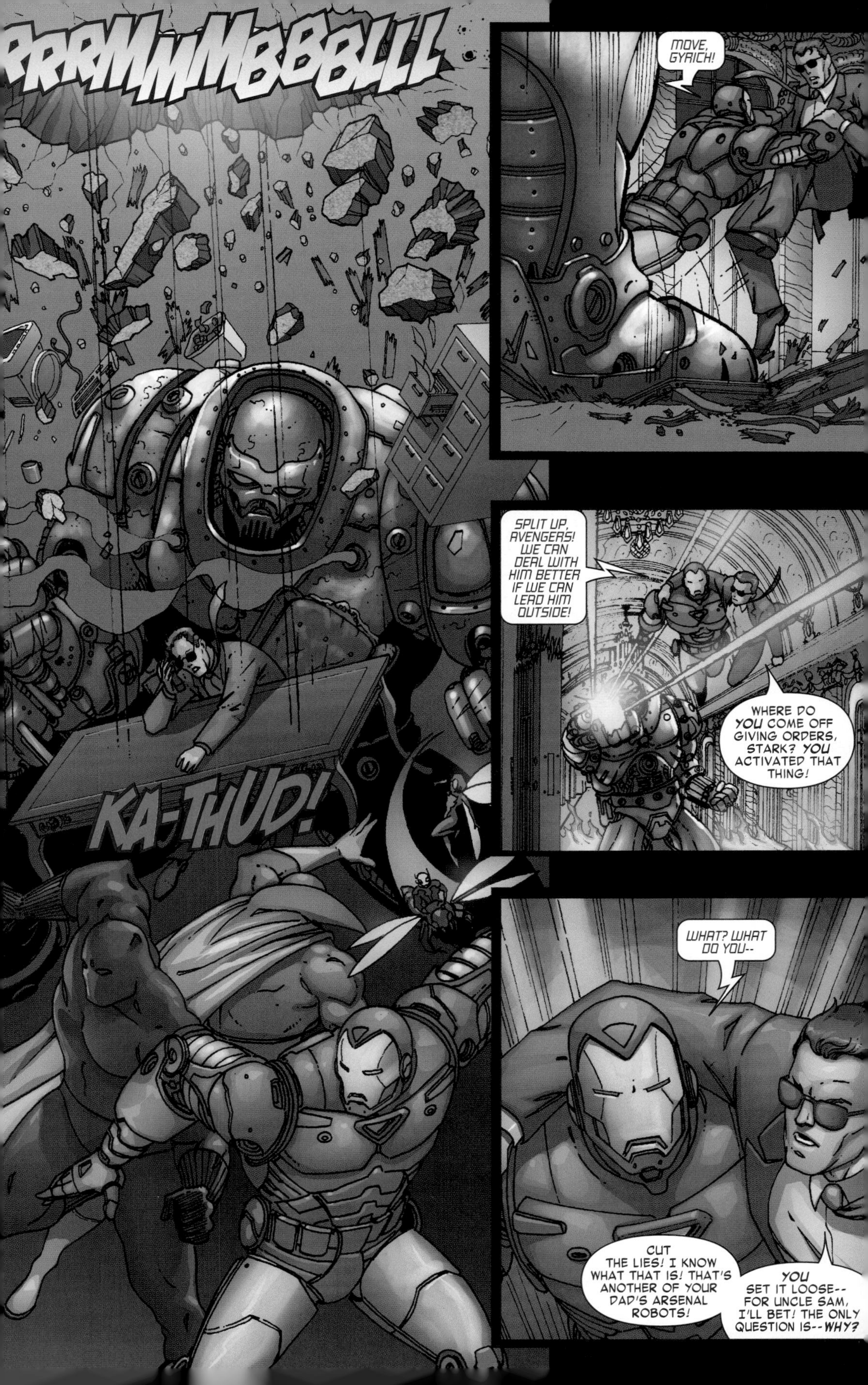
RRRMMMBBBLLL
KA-THUD!
MOVE, GYRICH!
SPLIT UP, AVENGERS! WE CAN DEAL WITH HIM BETTER IF WE CAN LEAD HIM OUTSIDE!
WHERE DO YOU COME OFF GIVING ORDERS, STARK? YOU ACTIVATED THAT THING!
WHAT? WHAT DO YOU--
CUT THE LIES! I KNOW WHAT THAT IS! THAT'S ANOTHER OF YOUR DAD'S ARSENAL ROBOTS!
YOU SET IT LOOSE-- FOR UNCLE SAM, I'LL BET! THE ONLY QUESTION IS--WHY?

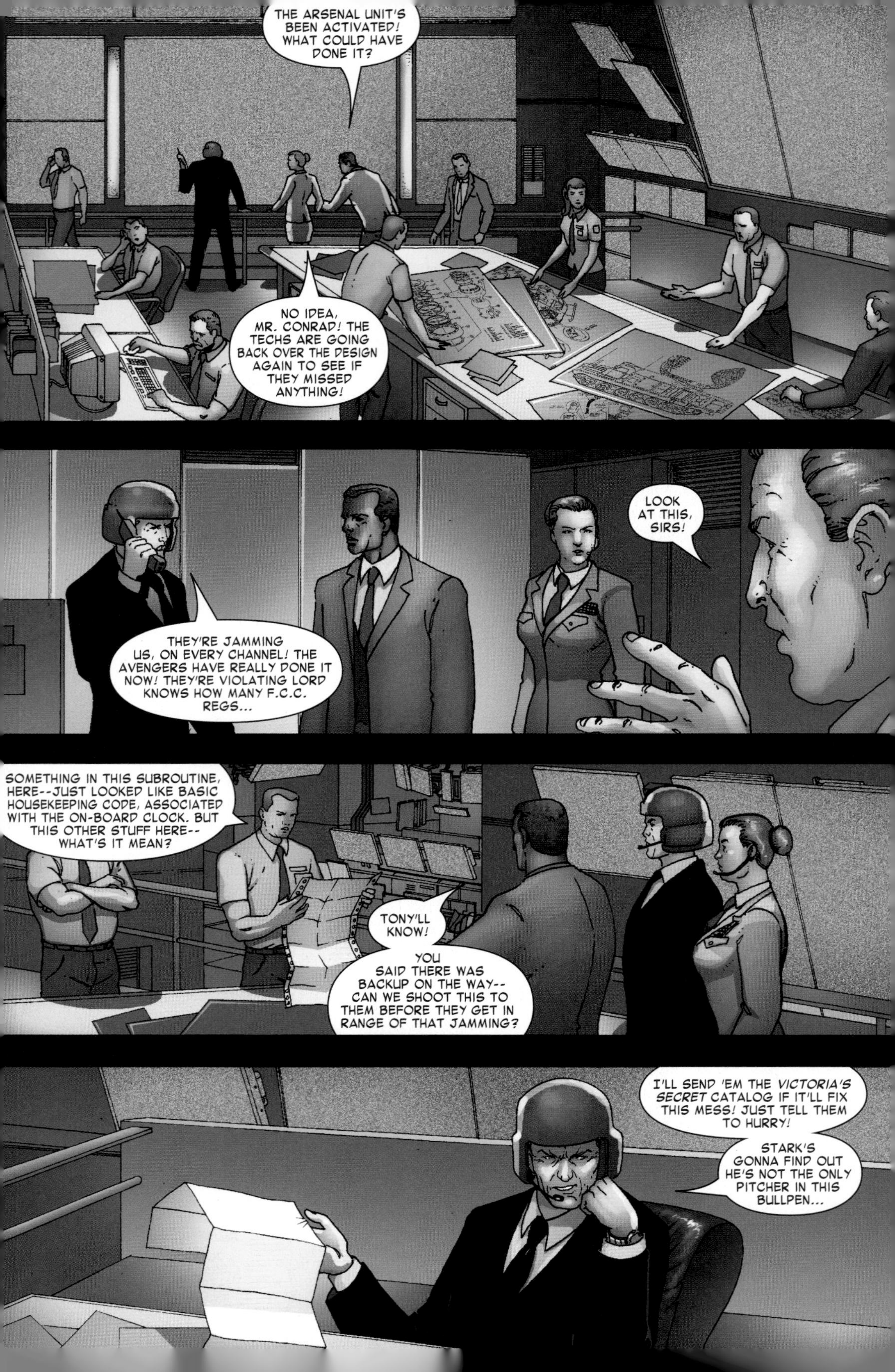
THE ARSENAL UNIT'S BEEN ACTIVATED! WHAT COULD HAVE DONE IT?
NO IDEA, MR. CONRAD! THE TECHS ARE GOING BACK OVER THE DESIGN AGAIN TO SEE IF THEY MISSED ANYTHING!
THEY'RE JAMMING US, ON EVERY CHANNEL! THE AVENGERS HAVE REALLY DONE IT NOW! THEY'RE VIOLATING LORD KNOWS HOW MANY F.C.C. REGS...
LOOK AT THIS, SIRS!
SOMETHING IN THIS SUBROUTINE, HERE--JUST LOOKED LIKE BASIC HOUSEKEEPING CODE, ASSOCIATED WITH THE ON-BOARD CLOCK. BUT THIS OTHER STUFF HERE--WHAT'S IT MEAN?
TONY'LL KNOW!
YOU SAID THERE WAS BACKUP ON THE WAY--CAN WE SHOOT THIS TO THEM BEFORE THEY GET IN RANGE OF THAT JAMMING?
I'LL SEND 'EM THE *VICTORIA'S SECRET* CATALOG IF IT'LL FIX THIS MESS! JUST TELL THEM TO HURRY!
STARK'S GONNA FIND OUT HE'S NOT THE ONLY PITCHER IN THIS BULLPEN...

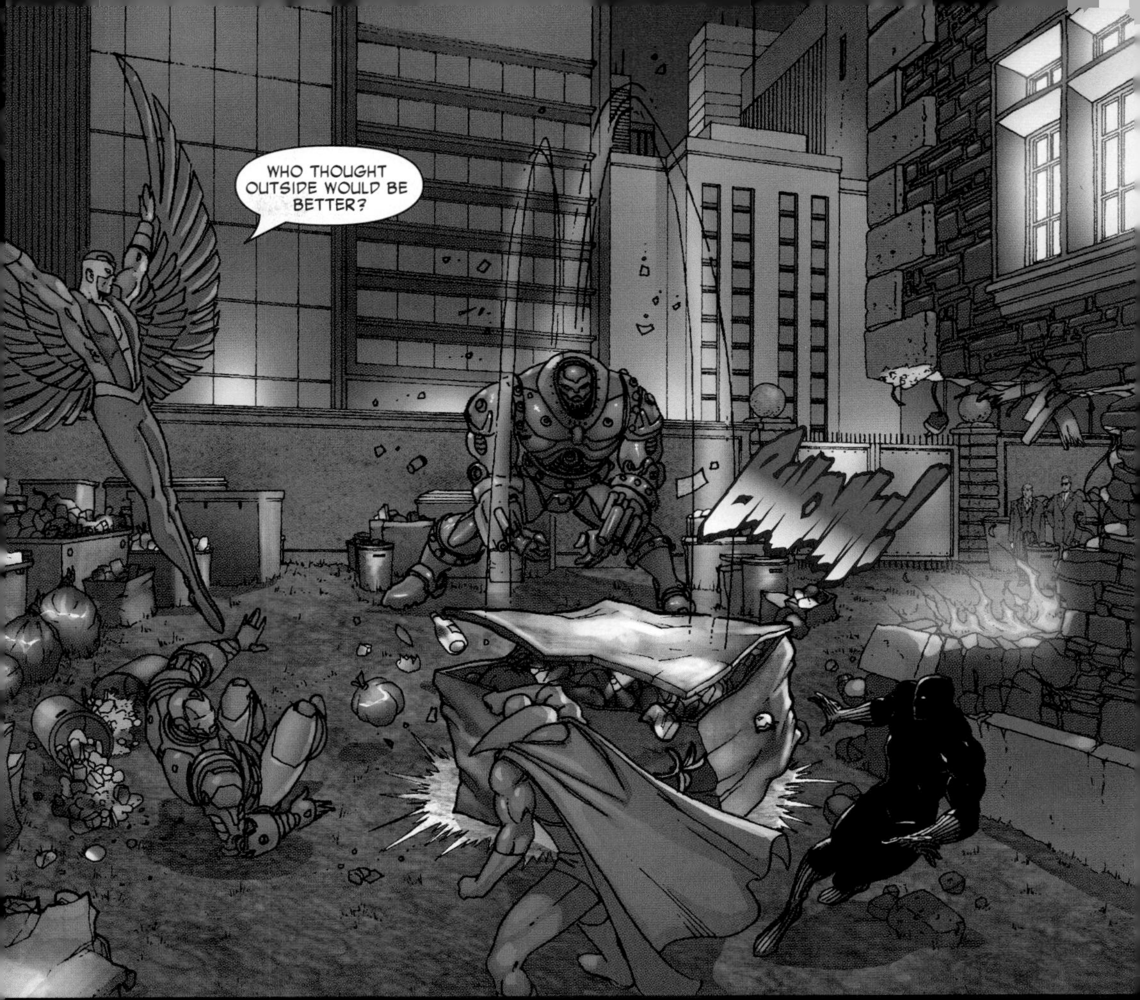
WHO THOUGHT OUTSIDE WOULD BE BETTER?

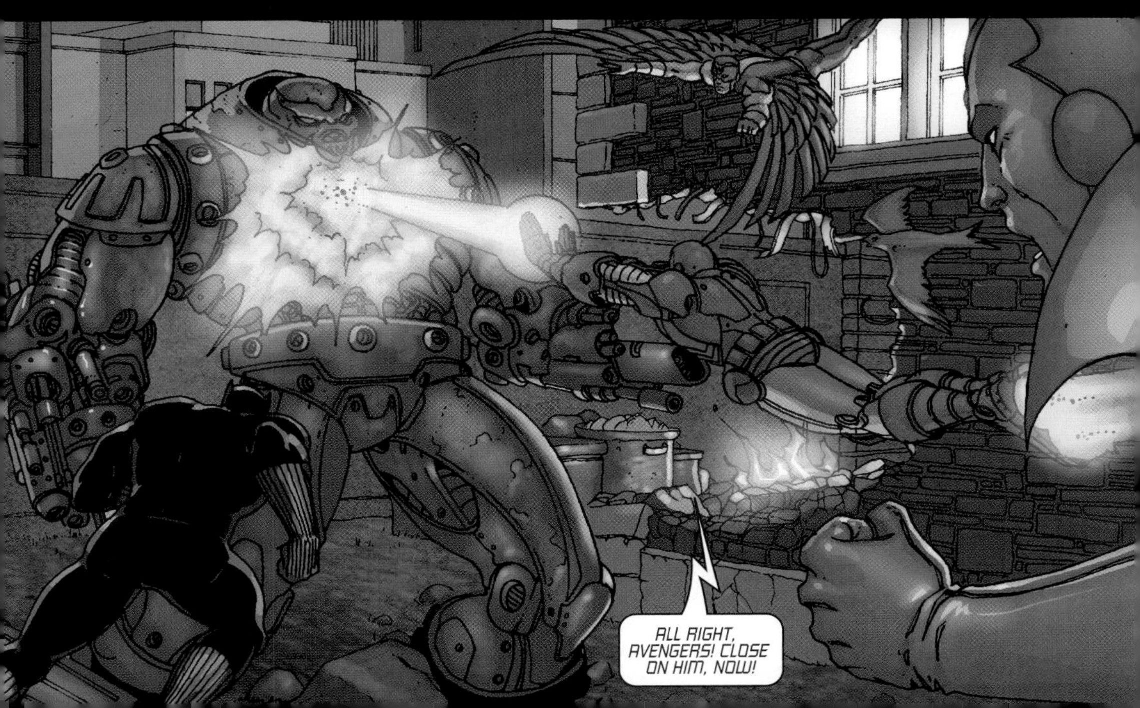
ALL RIGHT, AVENGERS! CLOSE ON HIM, NOW!

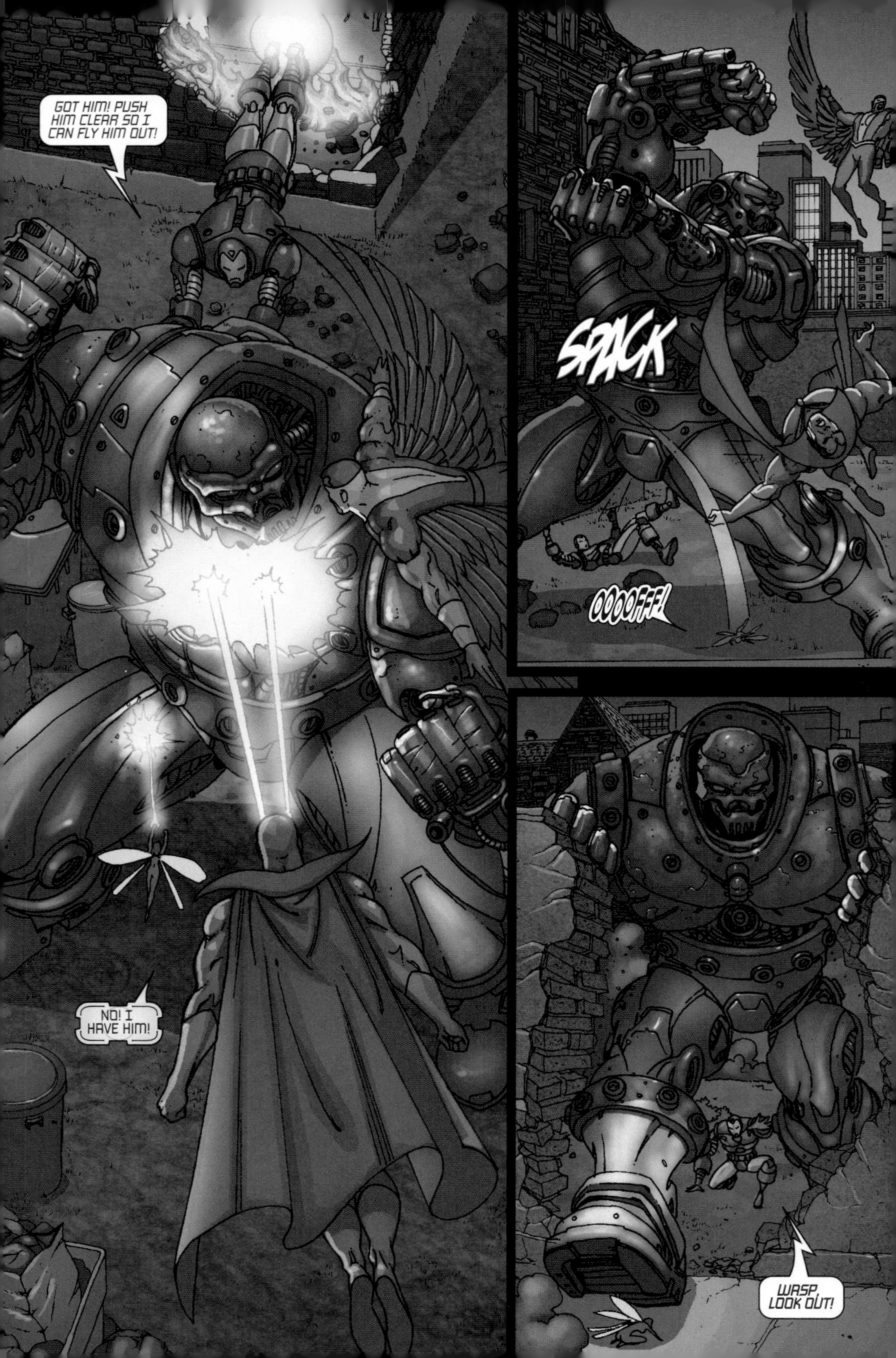
GOT HIM! PUSH HIM CLEAR SO I CAN FLY HIM OUT!
NO! I HAVE HIM!
SPACK
OOOOFFF!
WASP, LOOK OUT!

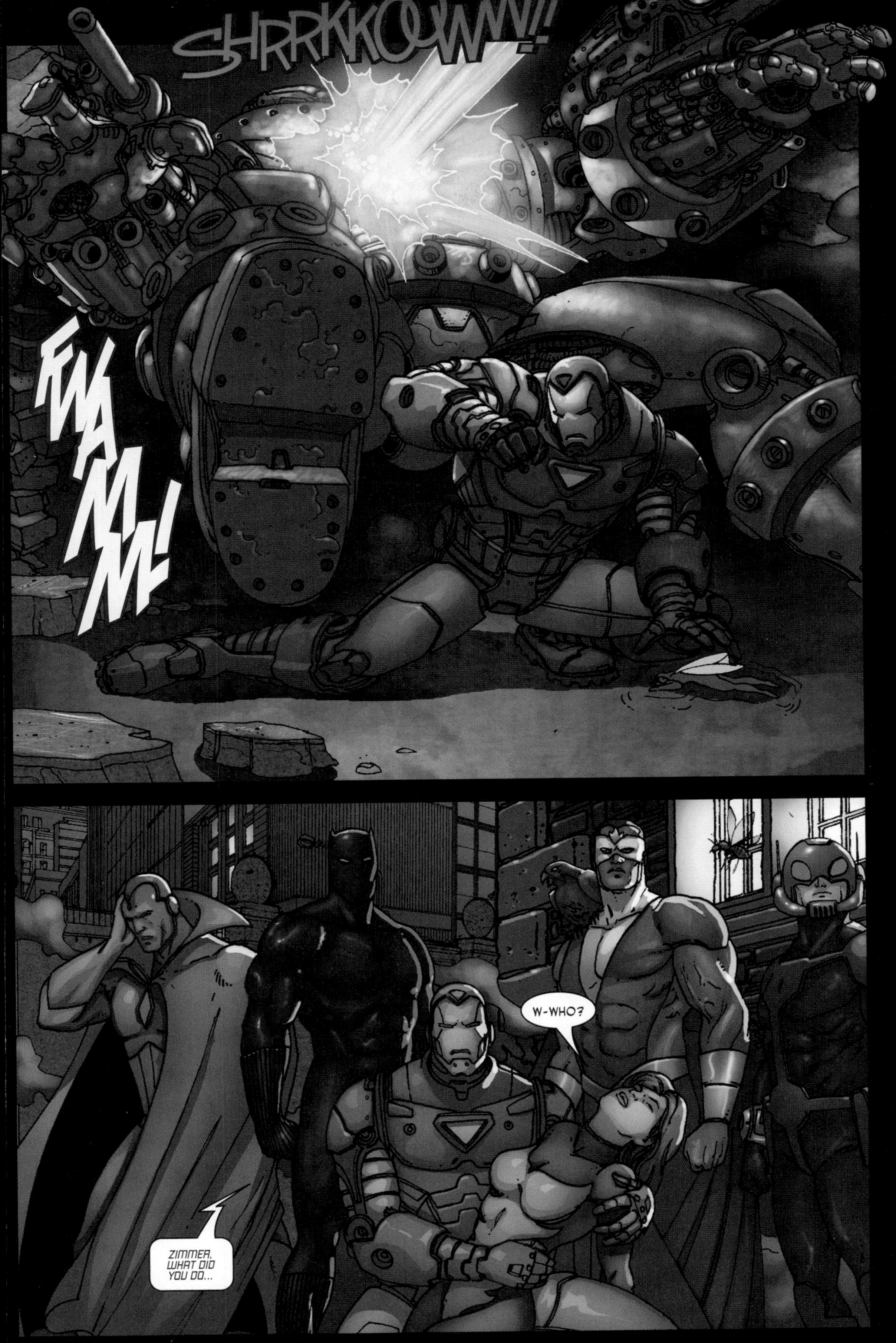
SHRRKKOOWW!!
FWANNN!
W-WHO?
ZIMMER, WHAT DID YOU DO...

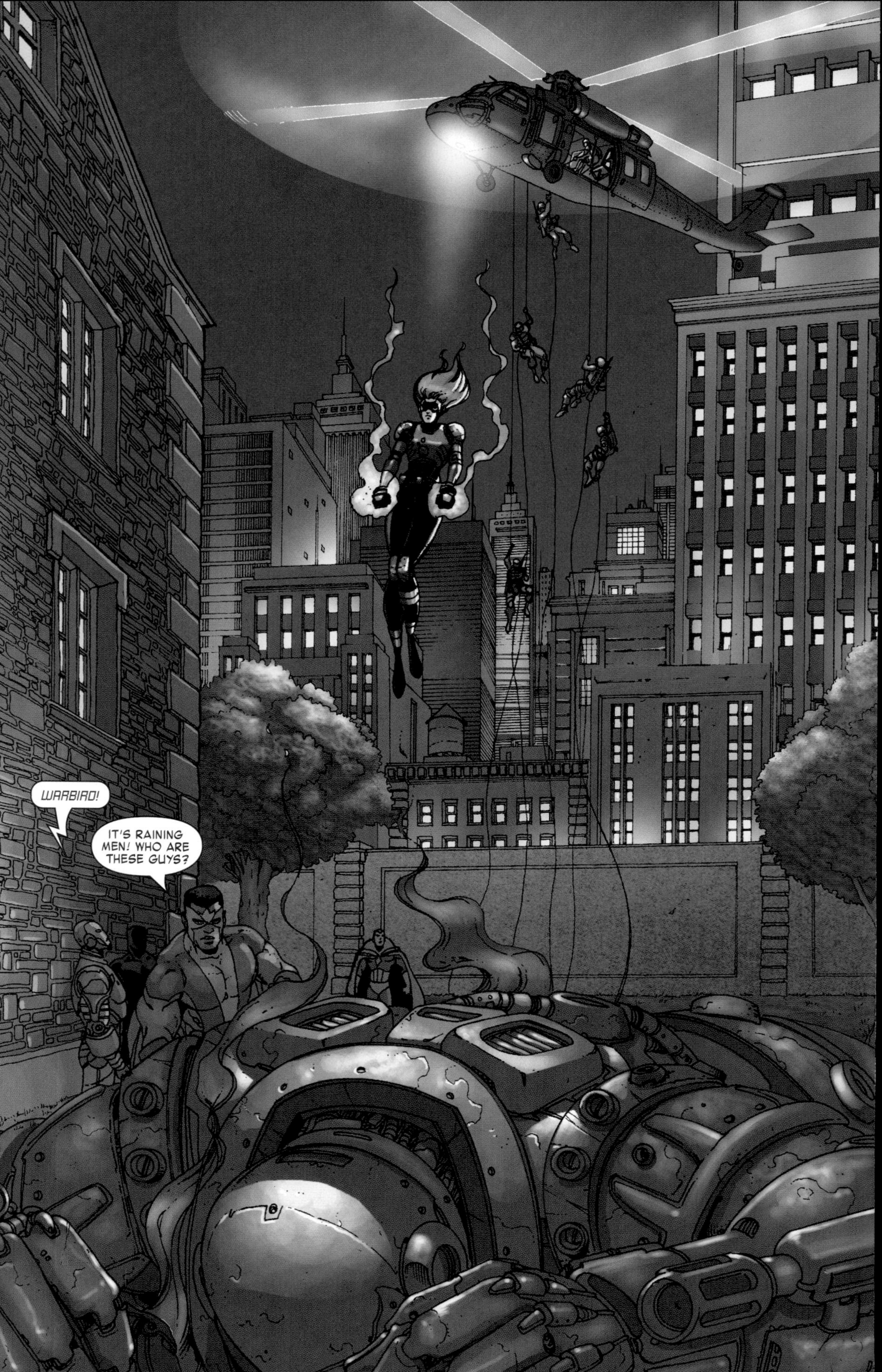
WARBIRD!
IT'S RAINING MEN! WHO ARE THESE GUYS?

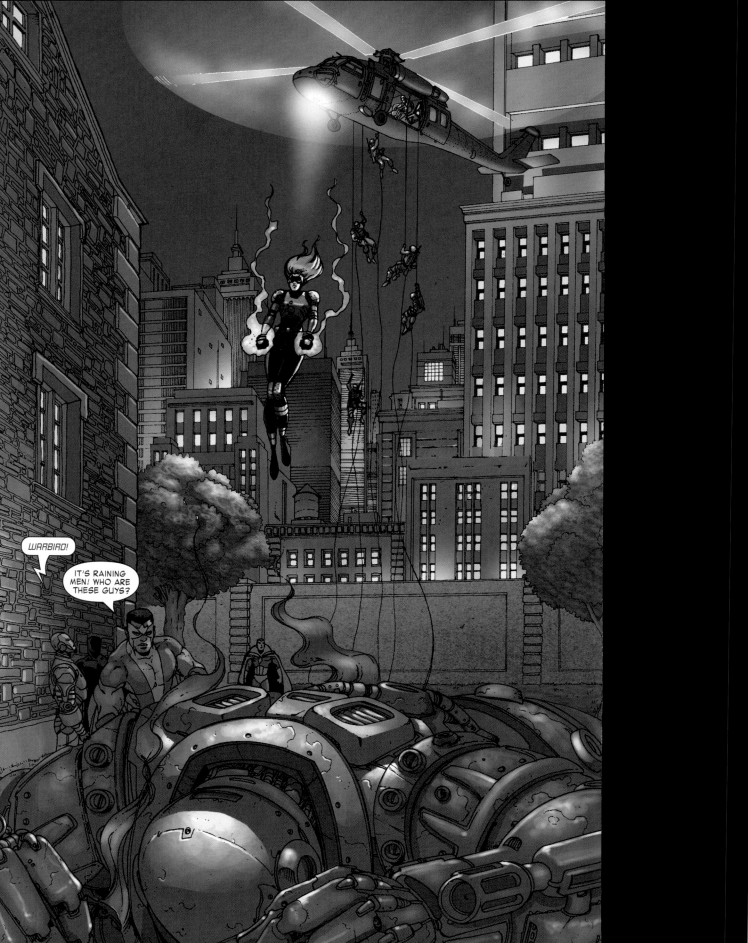

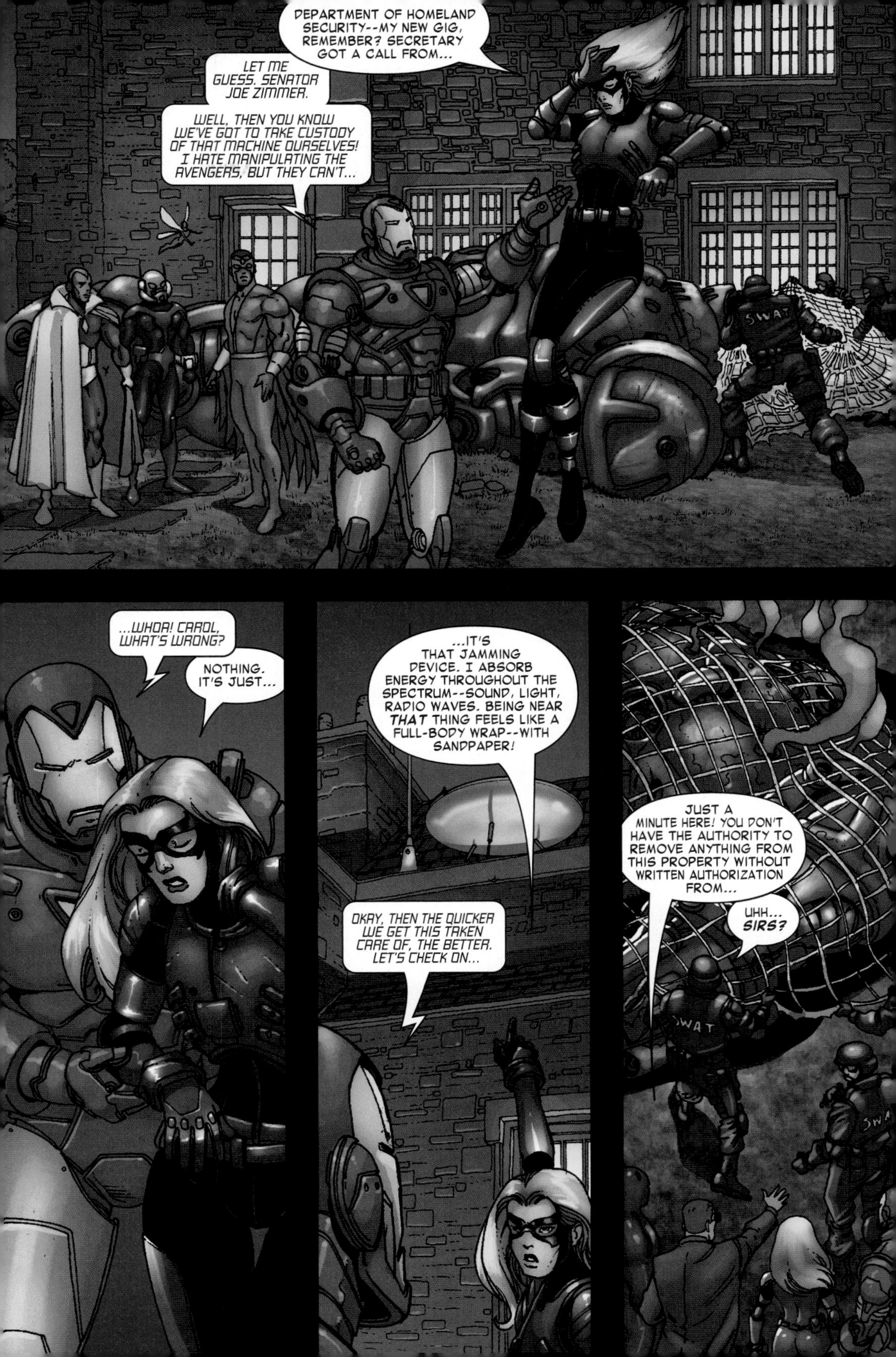
LET ME GUESS. SENATOR JOE ZIMMER.
DEPARTMENT OF HOMELAND SECURITY--MY NEW GIG, REMEMBER? SECRETARY GOT A CALL FROM...
WELL, THEN YOU KNOW WE'VE GOT TO TAKE CUSTODY OF THAT MACHINE OURSELVES! I HATE MANIPULATING THE AVENGERS, BUT THEY CAN'T...
...WHOA! CAROL, WHAT'S WRONG?
NOTHING. IT'S JUST...
...IT'S THAT JAMMING DEVICE. I ABSORB ENERGY THROUGHOUT THE SPECTRUM--SOUND, LIGHT, RADIO WAVES. BEING NEAR THAT THING FEELS LIKE A FULL-BODY WRAP--WITH SANDPAPER!
OKAY, THEN THE QUICKER WE GET THIS TAKEN CARE OF, THE BETTER. LET'S CHECK ON...
JUST A MINUTE HERE! YOU DON'T HAVE THE AUTHORITY TO REMOVE ANYTHING FROM THIS PROPERTY WITHOUT WRITTEN AUTHORIZATION FROM...
UHH... SIRS?
SWAT

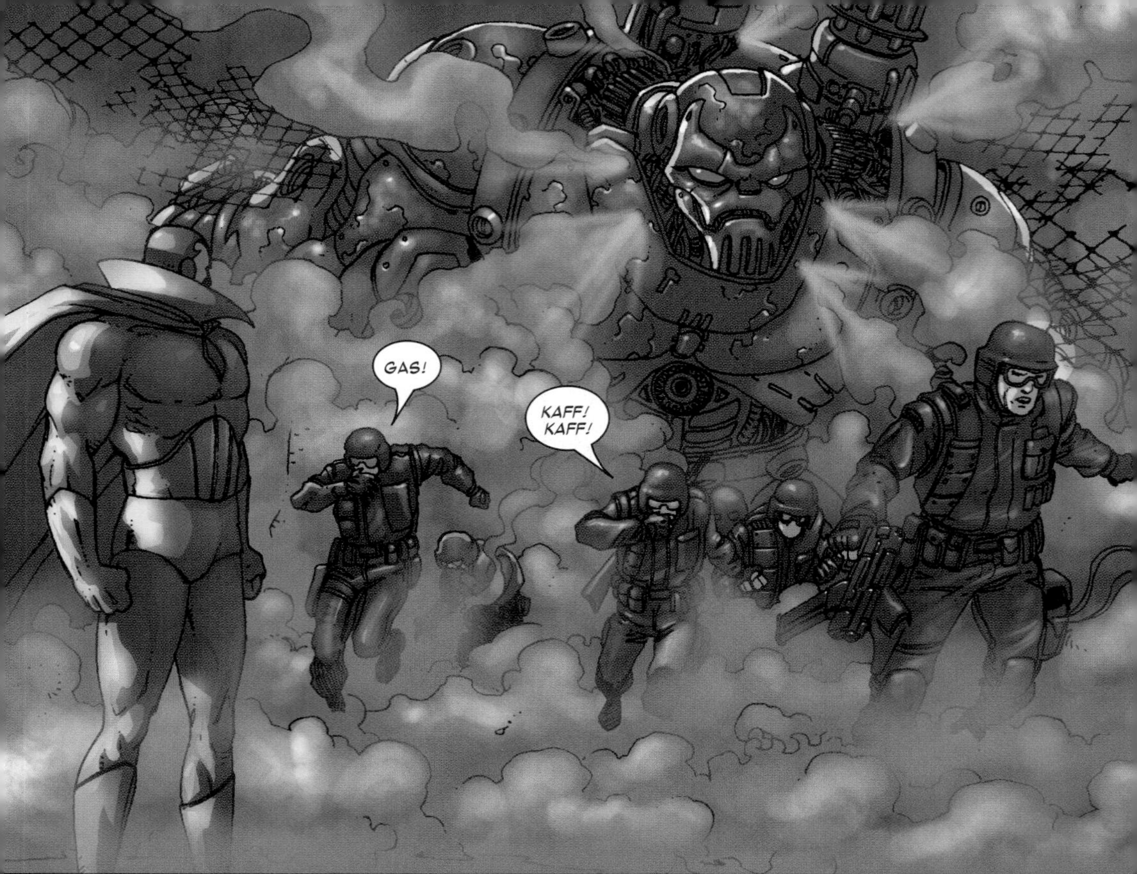
GAS!
KAFF! KAFF!

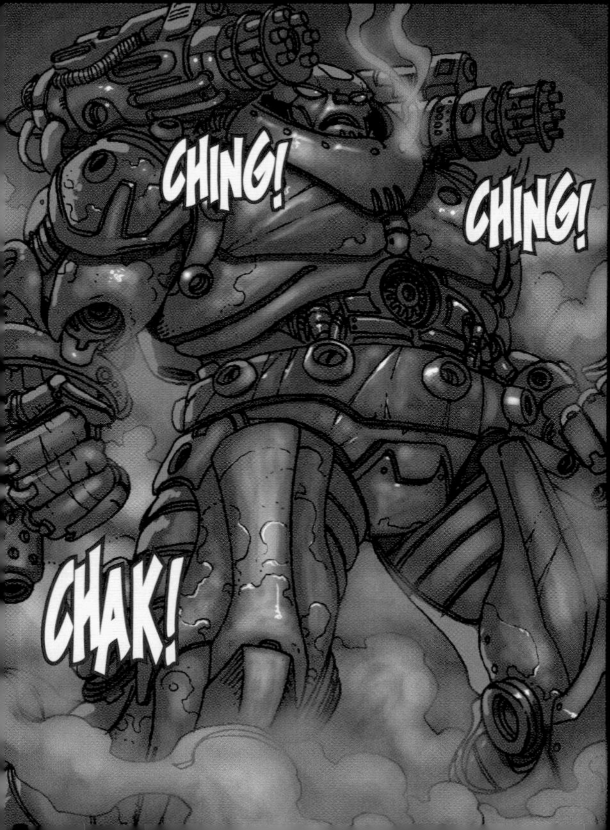
CHING!
CHING!
CHAK!

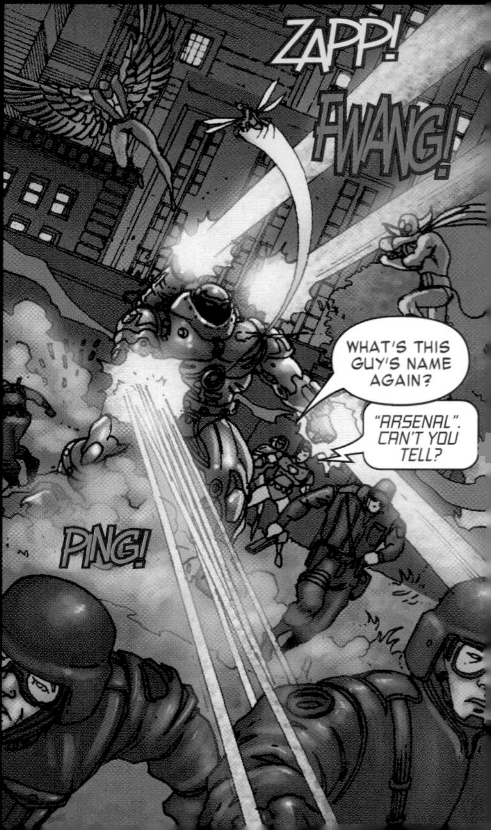
ZAPP!
FWANG!
WHAT'S THIS GUY'S NAME AGAIN?
"ARSENAL". CAN'T YOU TELL?
PING!

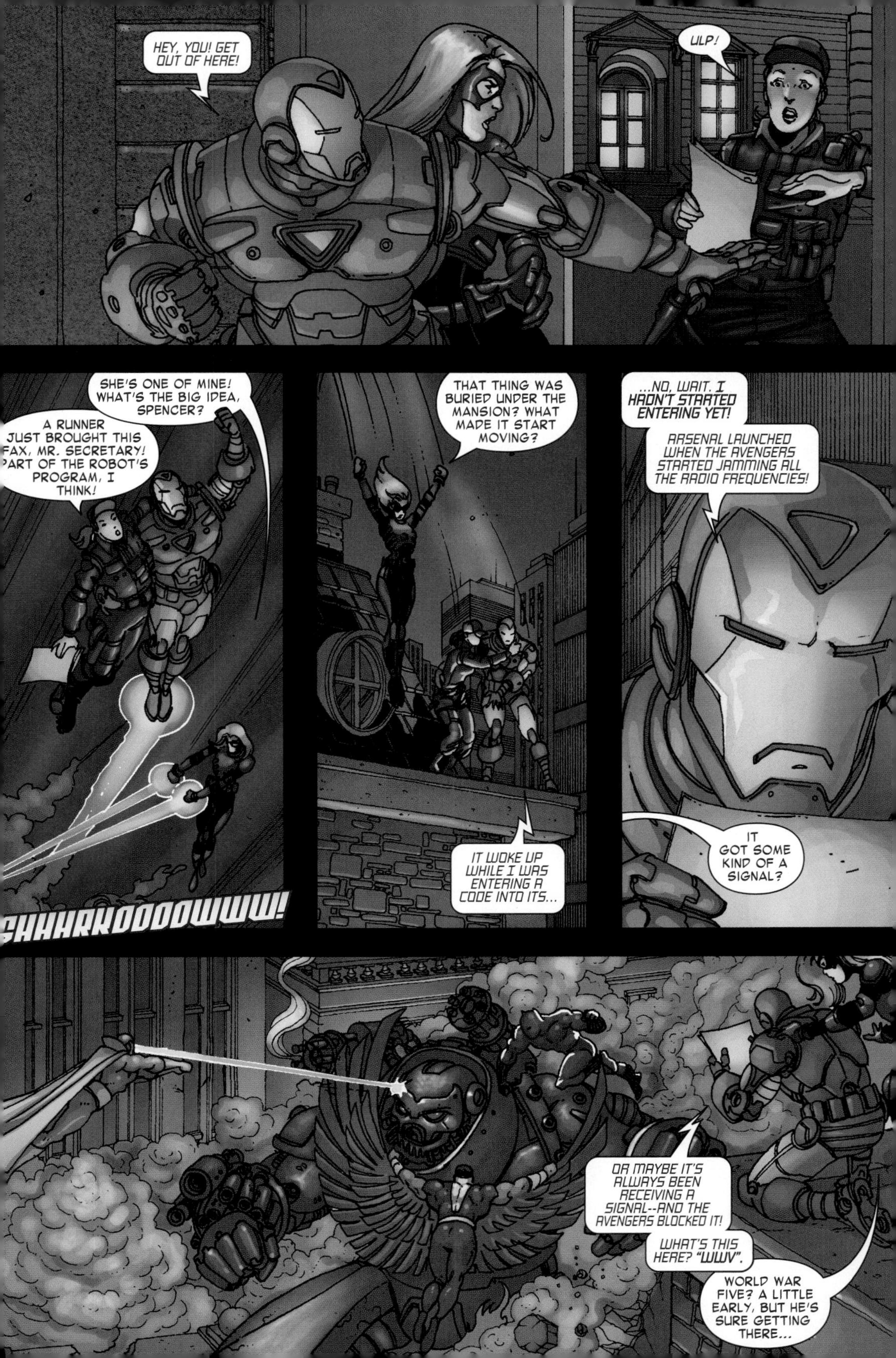
HEY, YOU! GET OUT OF HERE!
ULP!
SHE'S ONE OF MINE! WHAT'S THE BIG IDEA, SPENCER?
A RUNNER JUST BROUGHT THIS FAX, MR. SECRETARY! PART OF THE ROBOT'S PROGRAM, I THINK!
SHHHRKOOOOWWW!
THAT THING WAS BURIED UNDER THE MANSION? WHAT MADE IT START MOVING?
IT WOKE UP WHILE I WAS ENTERING A CODE INTO ITS...
...NO, WAIT. I HADN'T STARTED ENTERING YET!
ARSENAL LAUNCHED WHEN THE AVENGERS STARTED JAMMING ALL THE RADIO FREQUENCIES!
IT GOT SOME KIND OF A SIGNAL?
OR MAYBE IT'S ALWAYS BEEN RECEIVING A SIGNAL--AND THE AVENGERS BLOCKED IT!
WHAT'S THIS HERE? "WWV".
WORLD WAR FIVE? A LITTLE EARLY, BUT HE'S SURE GETTING THERE...

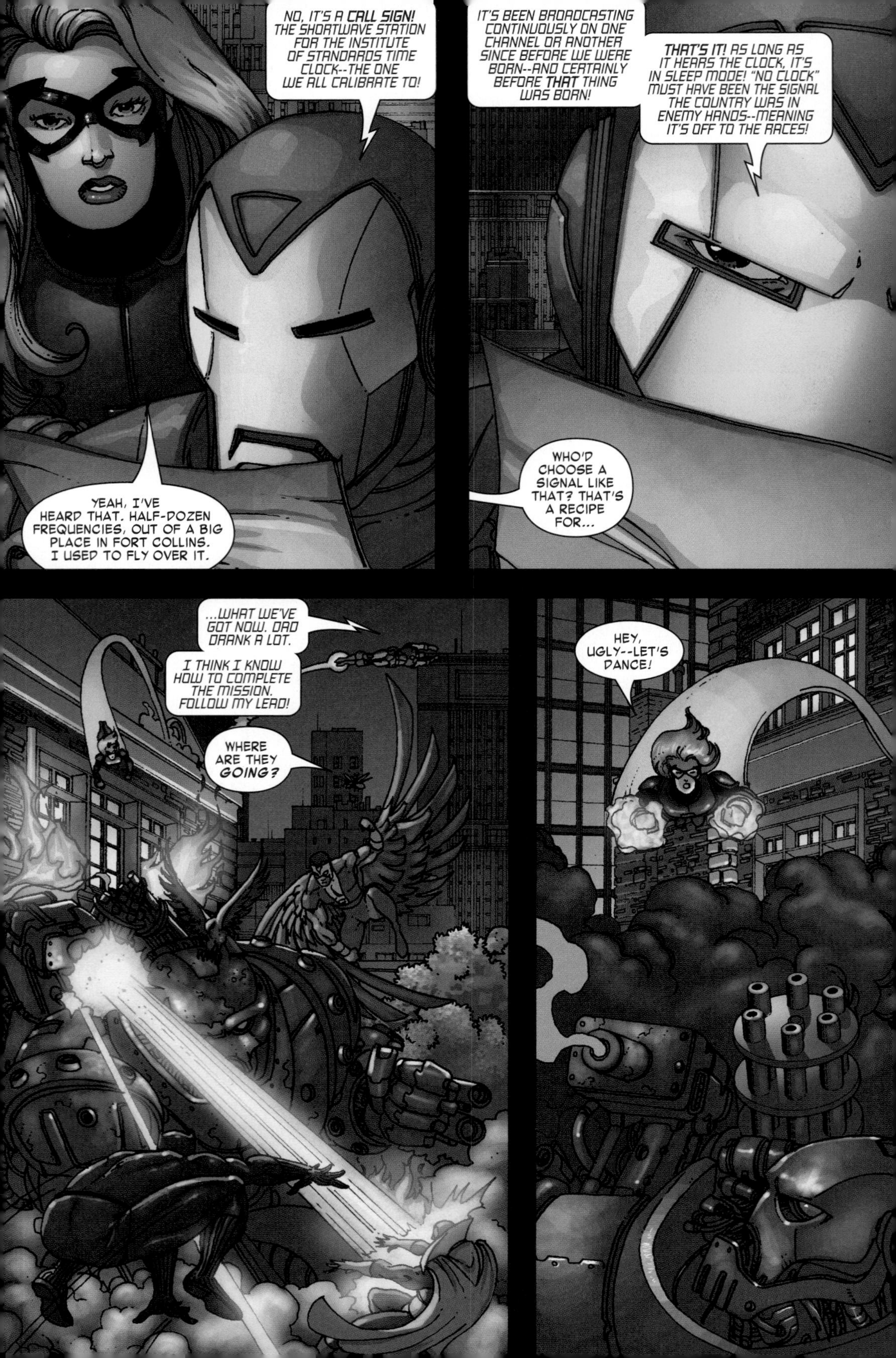
NO, IT'S A CALL SIGN! THE SHORTWAVE STATION FOR THE INSTITUTE OF STANDARDS TIME CLOCK--THE ONE WE ALL CALIBRATE TO!
YEAH, I'VE HEARD THAT. HALF-DOZEN FREQUENCIES, OUT OF A BIG PLACE IN FORT COLLINS. I USED TO FLY OVER IT.
IT'S BEEN BROADCASTING CONTINUOUSLY ON ONE CHANNEL OR ANOTHER SINCE BEFORE WE WERE BORN--AND CERTAINLY BEFORE THAT THING WAS BORN!
THAT'S IT! AS LONG AS IT HEARS THE CLOCK, IT'S IN SLEEP MODE! "NO CLOCK" MUST HAVE BEEN THE SIGNAL THE COUNTRY WAS IN ENEMY HANDS--MEANING IT'S OFF TO THE RACES!
WHO'D CHOOSE A SIGNAL LIKE THAT? THAT'S A RECIPE FOR...
...WHAT WE'VE GOT NOW. DAD DRANK A LOT.
I THINK I KNOW HOW TO COMPLETE THE MISSION. FOLLOW MY LEAD!
WHERE ARE THEY GOING?
HEY, UGLY--LET'S DANCE!

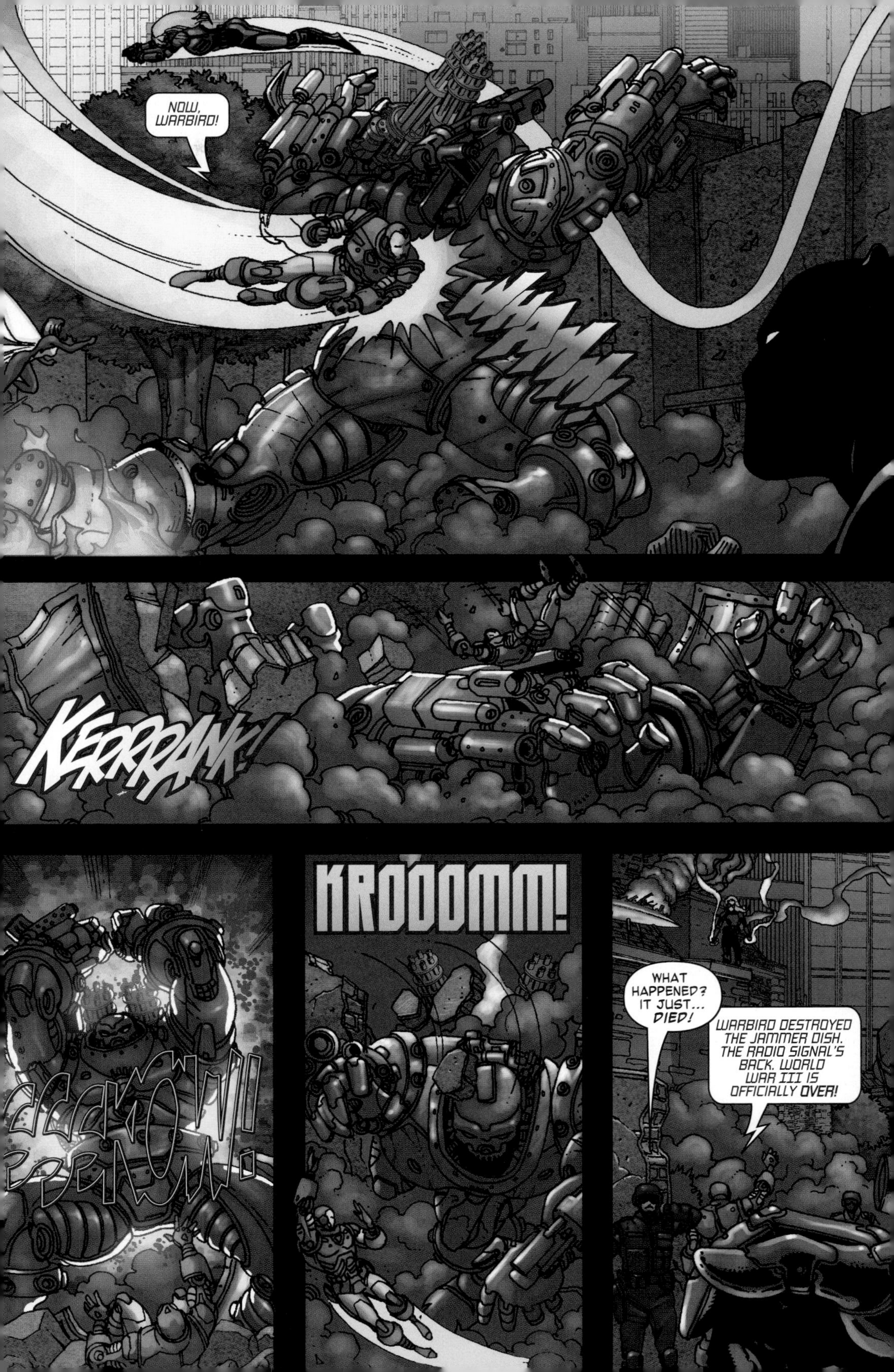
NOW, WARBIRD!
KERRRANK!
KROOOMM!
WHAT HAPPENED? IT JUST... DIED!
WARBIRD DESTROYED THE JAMMER DISH. THE RADIO SIGNAL'S BACK. WORLD WAR III IS OFFICIALLY OVER!

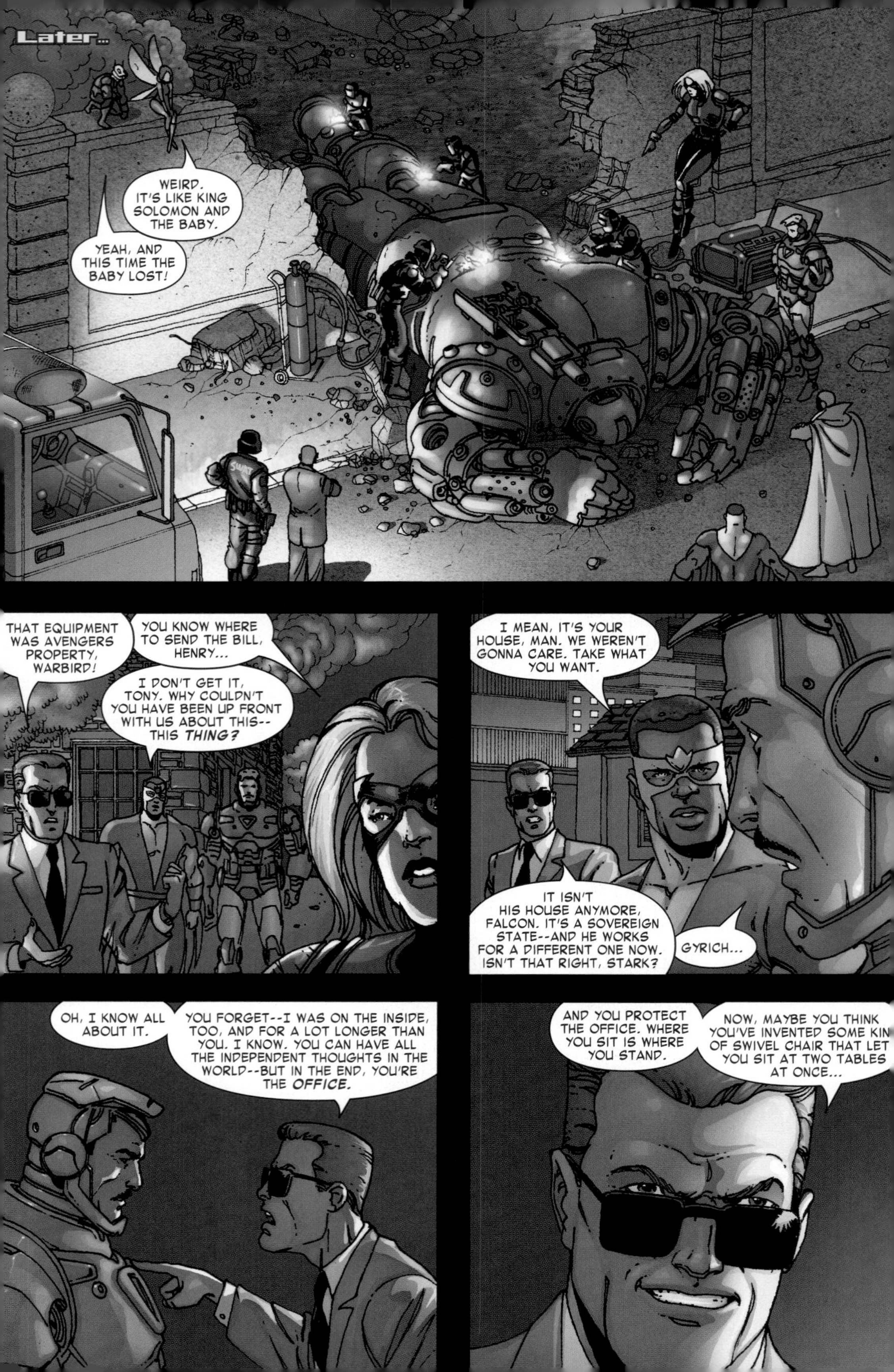
Later...
WEIRD. IT'S LIKE KING SOLOMON AND THE BABY.
YEAH, AND THIS TIME THE BABY LOST!
SWAT
THAT EQUIPMENT WAS AVENGERS PROPERTY, WARBIRD!
YOU KNOW WHERE TO SEND THE BILL, HENRY...
I DON'T GET IT, TONY. WHY COULDN'T YOU HAVE BEEN UP FRONT WITH US ABOUT THIS-- THIS THING?
I MEAN, IT'S YOUR HOUSE, MAN. WE WEREN'T GONNA CARE. TAKE WHAT YOU WANT.
IT ISN'T HIS HOUSE ANYMORE, FALCON. IT'S A SOVEREIGN STATE--AND HE WORKS FOR A DIFFERENT ONE NOW. ISN'T THAT RIGHT, STARK?
GYRICH...
OH, I KNOW ALL ABOUT IT.
YOU FORGET--I WAS ON THE INSIDE, TOO, AND FOR A LOT LONGER THAN YOU. I KNOW. YOU CAN HAVE ALL THE INDEPENDENT THOUGHTS IN THE WORLD--BUT IN THE END, YOU'RE THE OFFICE.
AND YOU PROTECT THE OFFICE. WHERE YOU SIT IS WHERE YOU STAND.
NOW, MAYBE YOU THINK YOU'VE INVENTED SOME KIN OF SWIVEL CHAIR THAT LET YOU SIT AT TWO TABLES AT ONCE...

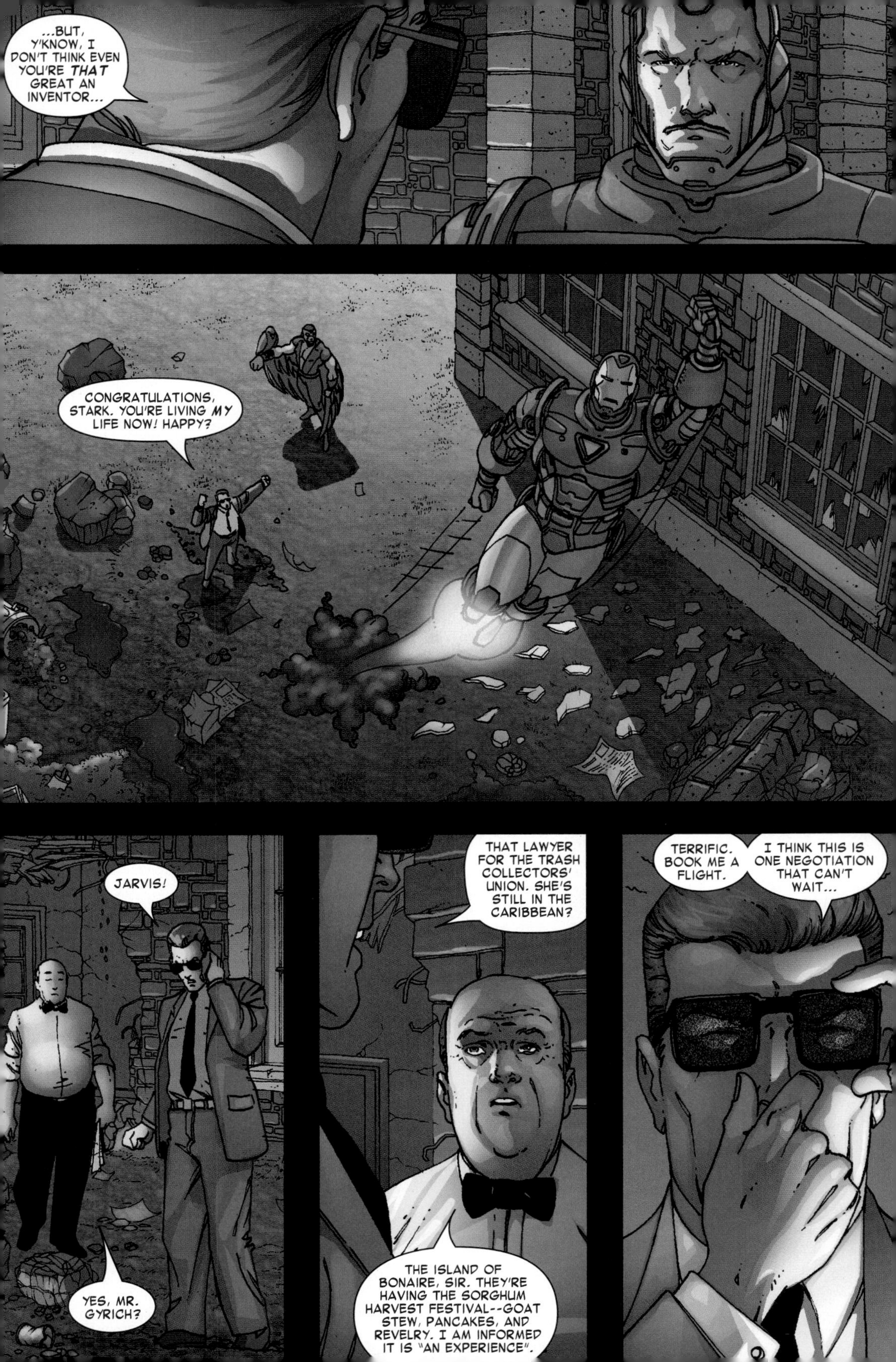
...BUT, Y'KNOW, I DON'T THINK EVEN YOU'RE *THAT* GREAT AN INVENTOR...
CONGRATULATIONS, STARK. YOU'RE LIVING *MY* LIFE NOW! HAPPY?
JARVIS!
YES, MR. GYRICH?
THAT LAWYER FOR THE TRASH COLLECTORS' UNION. SHE'S STILL IN THE CARIBBEAN?
THE ISLAND OF BONAIRE, SIR. THEY'RE HAVING THE SORGHUM HARVEST FESTIVAL--GOAT STEW, PANCAKES, AND REVELRY. I AM INFORMED IT IS "AN EXPERIENCE".
TERRIFIC. BOOK ME A FLIGHT.
I THINK THIS IS ONE NEGOTIATION THAT CAN'T WAIT...

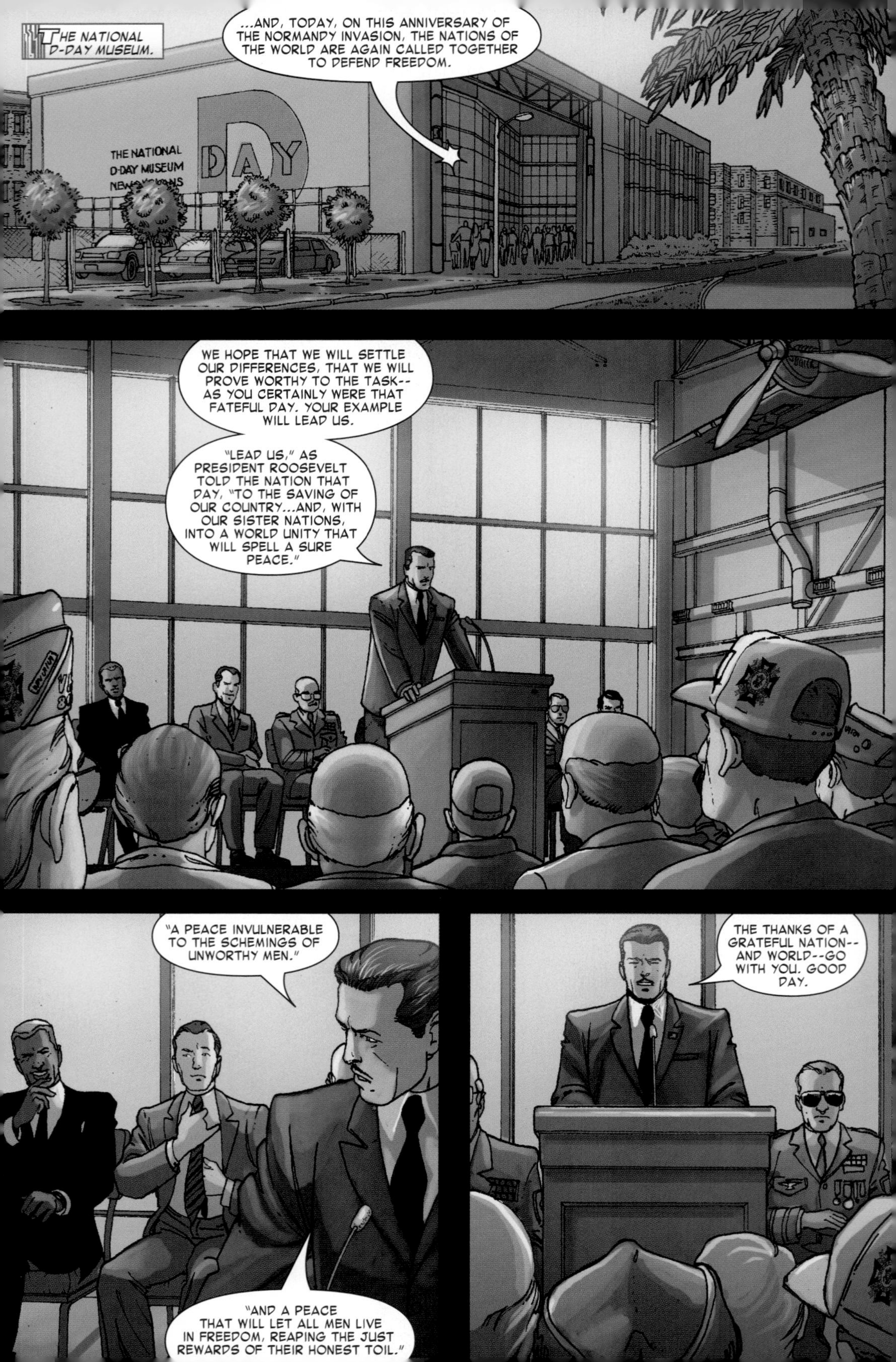
THE NATIONAL D-DAY MUSEUM.
...AND, TODAY, ON THIS ANNIVERSARY OF THE NORMANDY INVASION, THE NATIONS OF THE WORLD ARE AGAIN CALLED TOGETHER TO DEFEND FREEDOM.
THE NATIONAL D-DAY MUSEUM
D DAY
WE HOPE THAT WE WILL SETTLE OUR DIFFERENCES, THAT WE WILL PROVE WORTHY TO THE TASK-- AS YOU CERTAINLY WERE THAT FATEFUL DAY. YOUR EXAMPLE WILL LEAD US.
"LEAD US," AS PRESIDENT ROOSEVELT TOLD THE NATION THAT DAY, "TO THE SAVING OF OUR COUNTRY...AND, WITH OUR SISTER NATIONS, INTO A WORLD UNITY THAT WILL SPELL A SURE PEACE."
"A PEACE INVULNERABLE TO THE SCHEMINGS OF UNWORTHY MEN."
"AND A PEACE THAT WILL LET ALL MEN LIVE IN FREEDOM, REAPING THE JUST REWARDS OF THEIR HONEST TOIL."
THE THANKS OF A GRATEFUL NATION-- AND WORLD--GO WITH YOU. GOOD DAY.

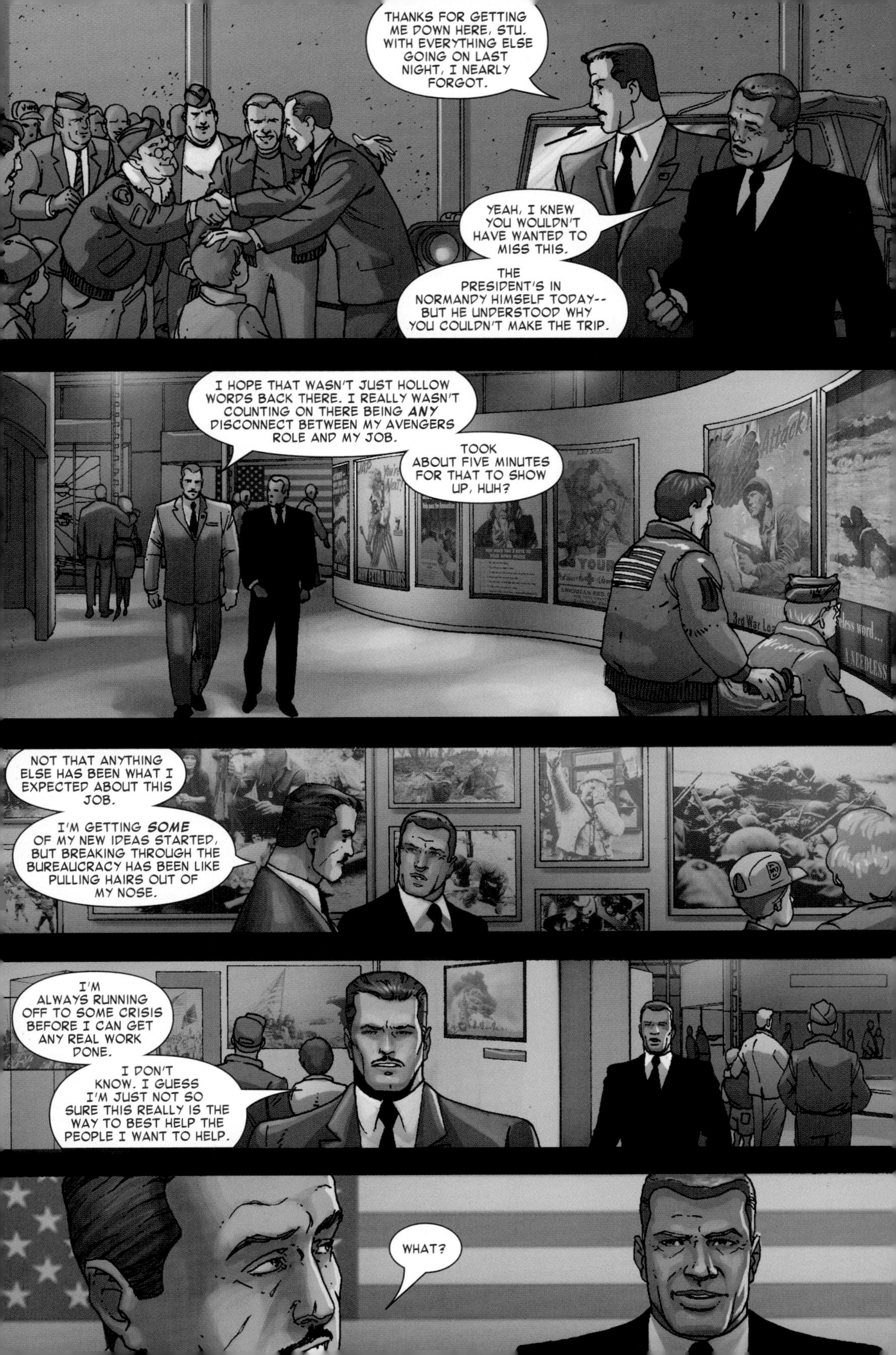
THANKS FOR GETTING ME DOWN HERE, STU. WITH EVERYTHING ELSE GOING ON LAST NIGHT, I NEARLY FORGOT.
YEAH, I KNEW YOU WOULDN'T HAVE WANTED TO MISS THIS.
THE PRESIDENT'S IN NORMANDY HIMSELF TODAY-- BUT HE UNDERSTOOD WHY YOU COULDN'T MAKE THE TRIP.
I HOPE THAT WASN'T JUST HOLLOW WORDS BACK THERE. I REALLY WASN'T COUNTING ON THERE BEING *ANY* DISCONNECT BETWEEN MY AVENGERS ROLE AND MY JOB.
TOOK ABOUT FIVE MINUTES FOR THAT TO SHOW UP, HUH?
NOT THAT ANYTHING ELSE HAS BEEN WHAT I EXPECTED ABOUT THIS JOB.
I'M GETTING **SOME** OF MY NEW IDEAS STARTED, BUT BREAKING THROUGH THE BUREAUCRACY HAS BEEN LIKE PULLING HAIRS OUT OF MY NOSE.
I'M ALWAYS RUNNING OFF TO SOME CRISIS BEFORE I CAN GET ANY REAL WORK DONE.
I DON'T KNOW. I GUESS I'M JUST NOT SO SURE THIS REALLY IS THE WAY TO BEST HELP THE PEOPLE I WANT TO HELP.
WHAT?

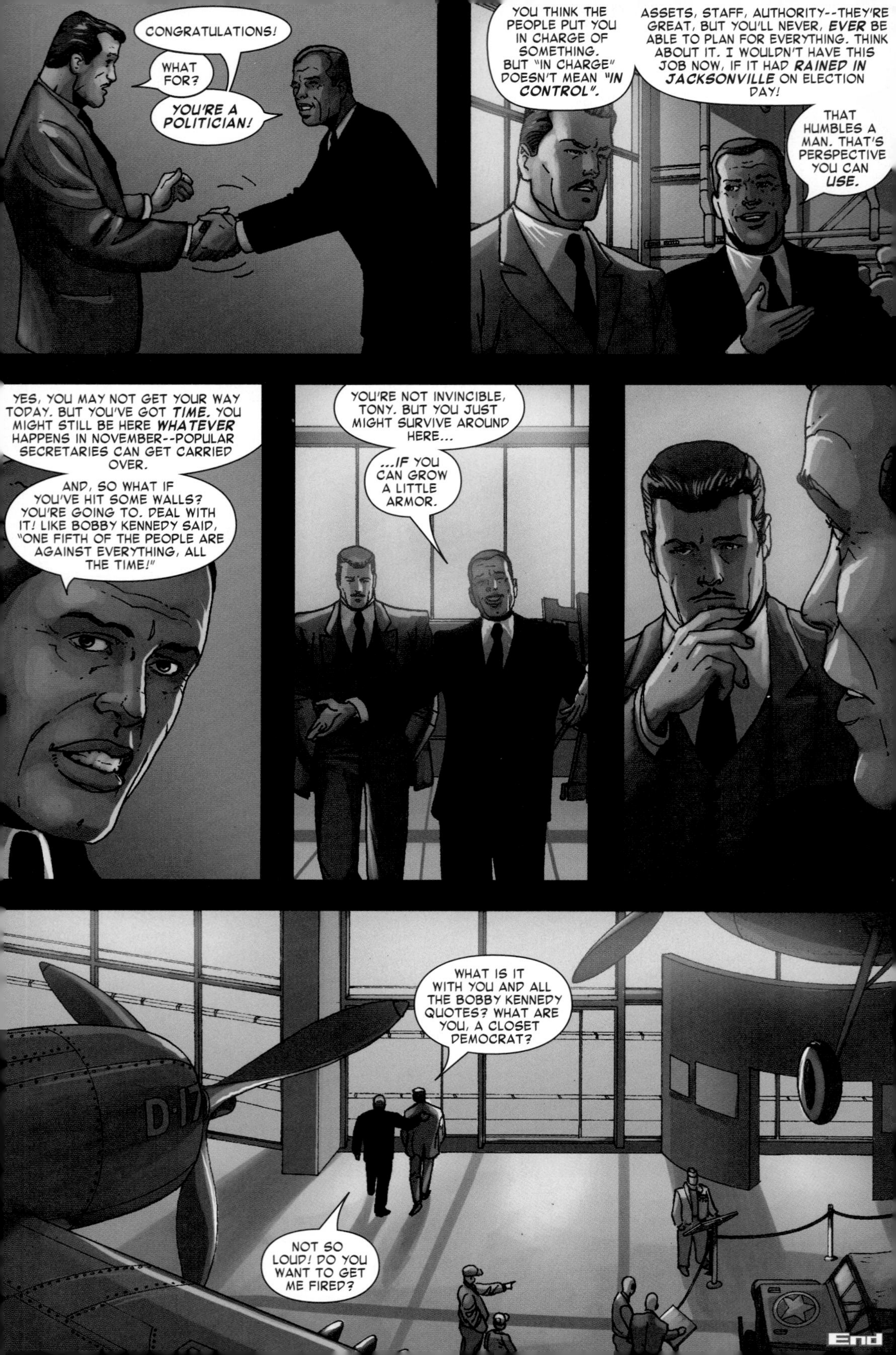
CONGRATULATIONS!
WHAT FOR?
YOU'RE A POLITICIAN!
YOU THINK THE PEOPLE PUT YOU IN CHARGE OF SOMETHING. BUT "IN CHARGE" DOESN'T MEAN "IN CONTROL".
ASSETS, STAFF, AUTHORITY--THEY'RE GREAT, BUT YOU'LL NEVER, EVER BE ABLE TO PLAN FOR EVERYTHING. THINK ABOUT IT. I WOULDN'T HAVE THIS JOB NOW, IF IT HAD RAINED IN JACKSONVILLE ON ELECTION DAY!
THAT HUMBLES A MAN. THAT'S PERSPECTIVE YOU CAN USE.
YES, YOU MAY NOT GET YOUR WAY TODAY. BUT YOU'VE GOT TIME. YOU MIGHT STILL BE HERE WHATEVER HAPPENS IN NOVEMBER--POPULAR SECRETARIES CAN GET CARRIED OVER.
AND, SO WHAT IF YOU'VE HIT SOME WALLS? YOU'RE GOING TO. DEAL WITH IT! LIKE BOBBY KENNEDY SAID, "ONE FIFTH OF THE PEOPLE ARE AGAINST EVERYTHING, ALL THE TIME!"
YOU'RE NOT INVINCIBLE, TONY. BUT YOU JUST MIGHT SURVIVE AROUND HERE...
...IF YOU CAN GROW A LITTLE ARMOR.
WHAT IS IT WITH YOU AND ALL THE BOBBY KENNEDY QUOTES? WHAT ARE YOU, A CLOSET DEMOCRAT?
NOT SO LOUD! DO YOU WANT TO GET ME FIRED?
D-17
End

MARVEL
32
.com
MS. MARVEL™
412TH TEST WING
YARDIN
1
REED
SIQUEIRA
SANTOS
SOTOMAYOR

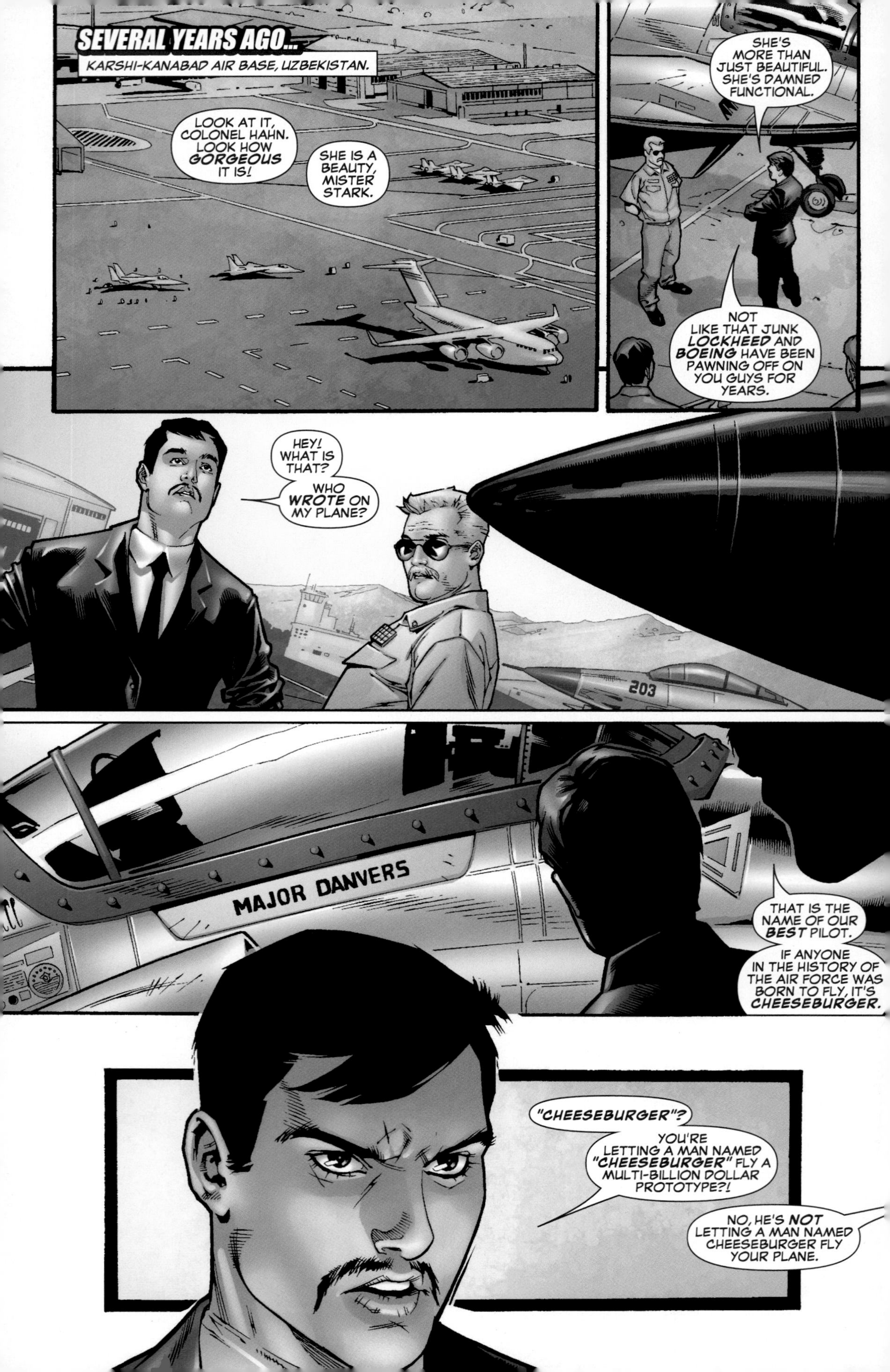
SEVERAL YEARS AGO...
KARSHI-KANABAD AIR BASE, UZBEKISTAN.
LOOK AT IT, COLONEL HAHN. LOOK HOW GORGEOUS IT IS!
SHE IS A BEAUTY, MISTER STARK.
SHE'S MORE THAN JUST BEAUTIFUL. SHE'S DAMNED FUNCTIONAL.
NOT LIKE THAT JUNK LOCKHEED AND BOEING HAVE BEEN PAWNING OFF ON YOU GUYS FOR YEARS.
HEY! WHAT IS THAT?
WHO WROTE ON MY PLANE?
203
MAJOR DANVERS
THAT IS THE NAME OF OUR BEST PILOT.
IF ANYONE IN THE HISTORY OF THE AIR FORCE WAS BORN TO FLY, IT'S CHEESEBURGER.
"CHEESEBURGER"?
YOU'RE LETTING A MAN NAMED "CHEESEBURGER" FLY A MULTI-BILLION DOLLAR PROTOTYPE?!
NO, HE'S NOT LETTING A MAN NAMED CHEESEBURGER FLY YOUR PLANE.

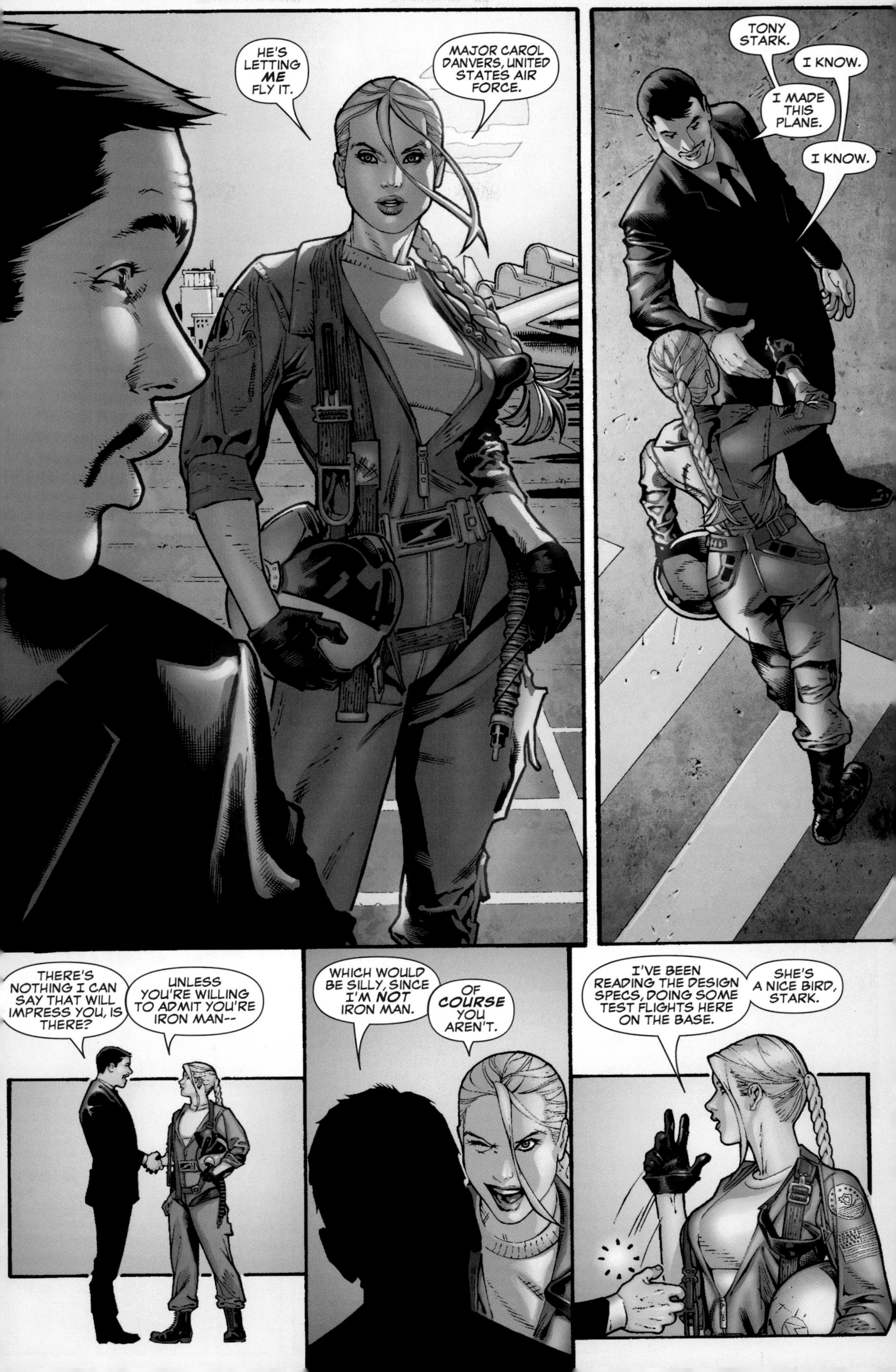
HE'S LETTING ME FLY IT.
MAJOR CAROL DANVERS, UNITED STATES AIR FORCE.
TONY STARK.
I KNOW.
I MADE THIS PLANE.
I KNOW.
THERE'S NOTHING I CAN SAY THAT WILL IMPRESS YOU, IS THERE?
UNLESS YOU'RE WILLING TO ADMIT YOU'RE IRON MAN--
WHICH WOULD BE SILLY, SINCE I'M NOT IRON MAN.
OF COURSE YOU AREN'T.
I'VE BEEN READING THE DESIGN SPECS, DOING SOME TEST FLIGHTS HERE ON THE BASE.
SHE'S A NICE BIRD, STARK.

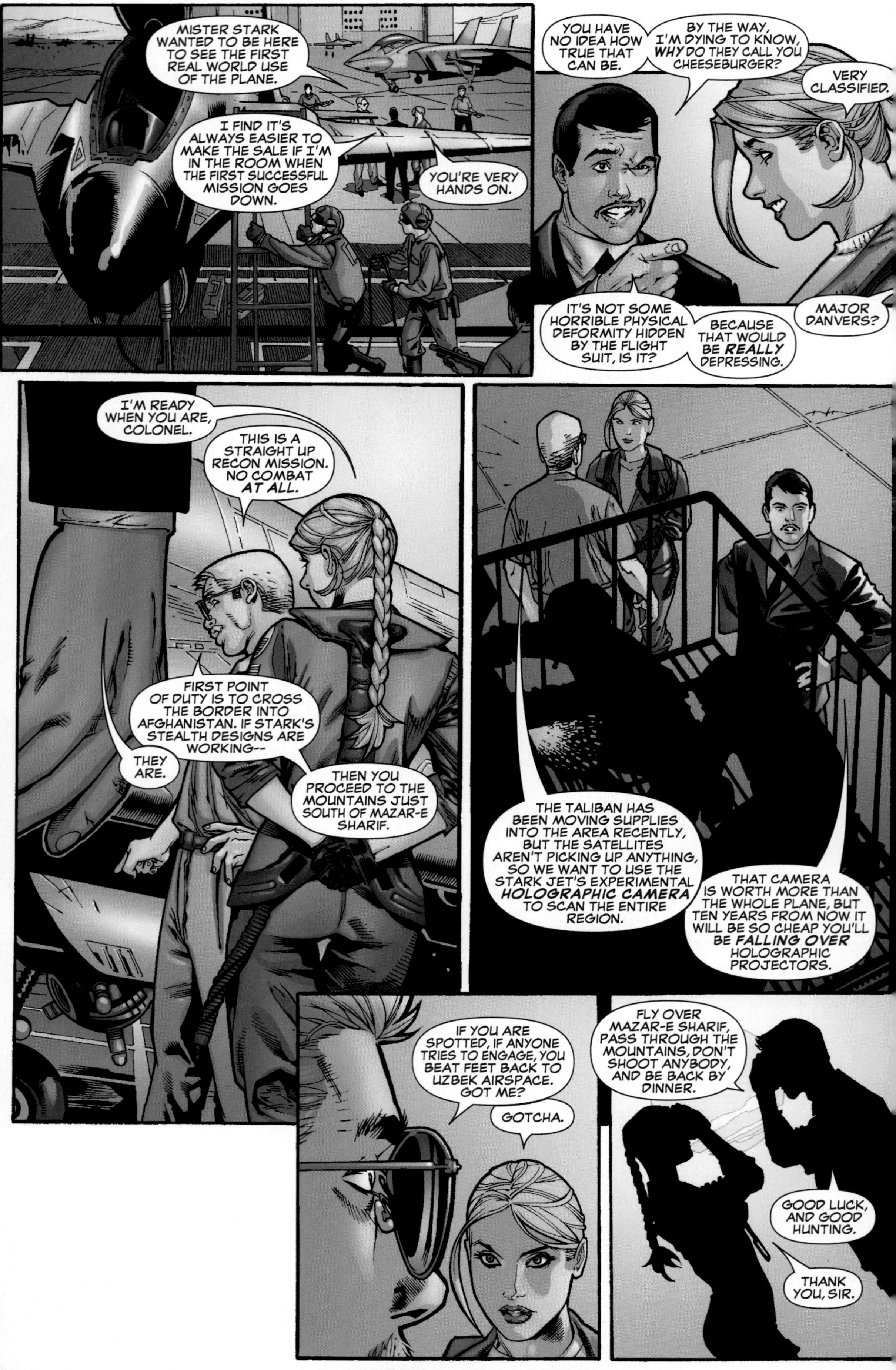
MISTER STARK WANTED TO BE HERE TO SEE THE FIRST REAL WORLD USE OF THE PLANE.
I FIND IT'S ALWAYS EASIER TO MAKE THE SALE IF I'M IN THE ROOM WHEN THE FIRST SUCCESSFUL MISSION GOES DOWN.
YOU'RE VERY HANDS ON.
YOU HAVE NO IDEA HOW TRUE THAT CAN BE.
BY THE WAY, I'M DYING TO KNOW, WHY DO THEY CALL YOU CHEESEBURGER?
VERY CLASSIFIED.
IT'S NOT SOME HORRIBLE PHYSICAL DEFORMITY HIDDEN BY THE FLIGHT SUIT, IS IT?
BECAUSE THAT WOULD BE REALLY DEPRESSING.
MAJOR DANVERS?
I'M READY WHEN YOU ARE, COLONEL.
THIS IS A STRAIGHT UP RECON MISSION. NO COMBAT AT ALL.
FIRST POINT OF DUTY IS TO CROSS THE BORDER INTO AFGHANISTAN. IF STARK'S STEALTH DESIGNS ARE WORKING--
THEY ARE.
THEN YOU PROCEED TO THE MOUNTAINS JUST SOUTH OF MAZAR-E SHARIF.
THE TALIBAN HAS BEEN MOVING SUPPLIES INTO THE AREA RECENTLY, BUT THE SATELLITES AREN'T PICKING UP ANYTHING, SO WE WANT TO USE THE STARK JET'S EXPERIMENTAL HOLOGRAPHIC CAMERA TO SCAN THE ENTIRE REGION.
THAT CAMERA IS WORTH MORE THAN THE WHOLE PLANE, BUT TEN YEARS FROM NOW IT WILL BE SO CHEAP YOU'LL BE FALLING OVER HOLOGRAPHIC PROJECTORS.
IF YOU ARE SPOTTED, IF ANYONE TRIES TO ENGAGE, YOU BEAT FEET BACK TO UZBEK AIRSPACE. GOT ME?
GOTCHA.
FLY OVER MAZAR-E SHARIF, PASS THROUGH THE MOUNTAINS, DON'T SHOOT ANYBODY, AND BE BACK BY DINNER.
GOOD LUCK, AND GOOD HUNTING.
THANK YOU, SIR.

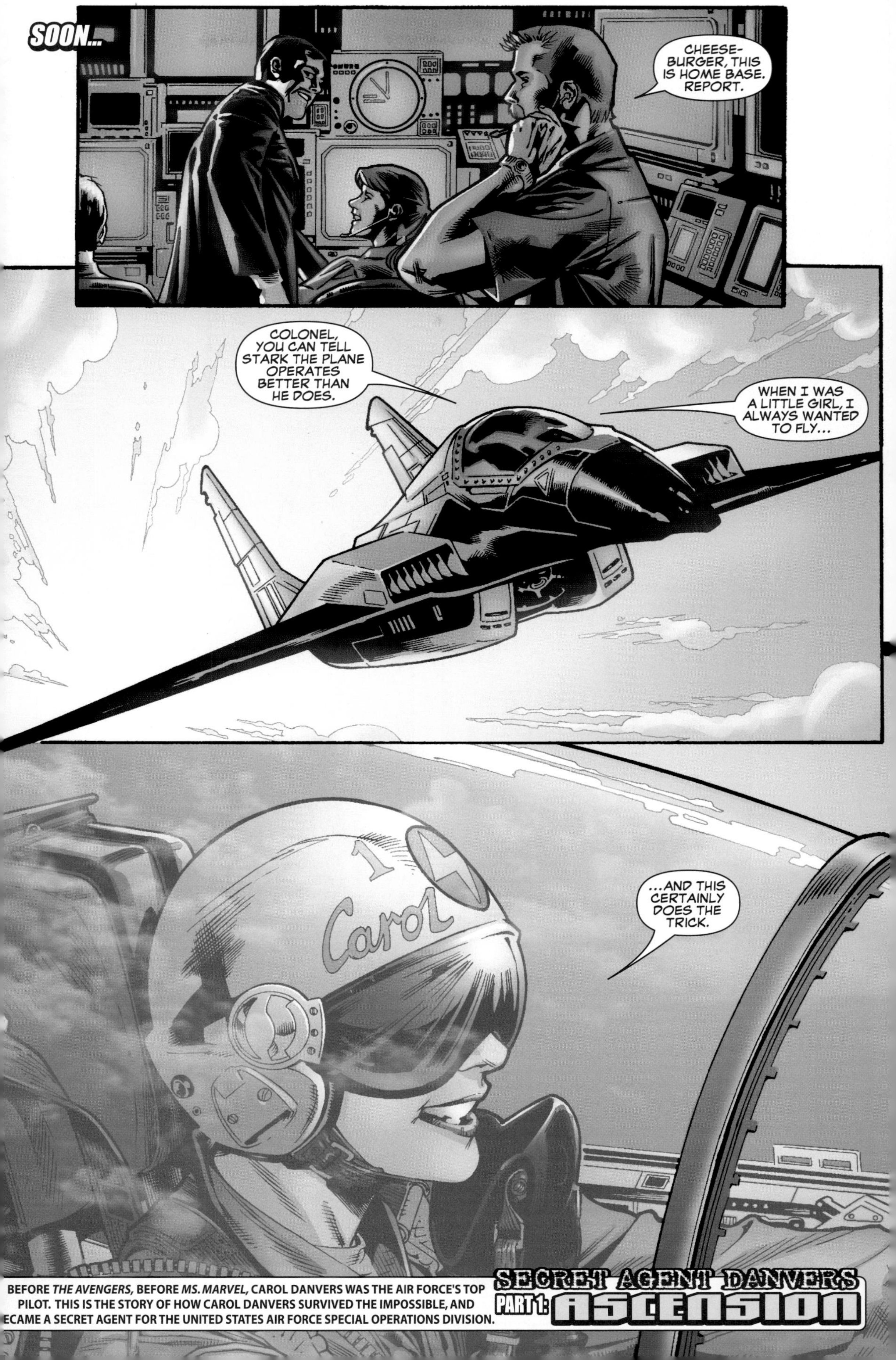
SOON...
CHEESE-BURGER, THIS IS HOME BASE. REPORT.
COLONEL, YOU CAN TELL STARK THE PLANE OPERATES BETTER THAN HE DOES.
WHEN I WAS A LITTLE GIRL, I ALWAYS WANTED TO FLY...
...AND THIS CERTAINLY DOES THE TRICK.
1
Carol
BEFORE *THE AVENGERS,* BEFORE *MS. MARVEL,* CAROL DANVERS WAS THE AIR FORCE'S TOP PILOT. THIS IS THE STORY OF HOW CAROL DANVERS SURVIVED THE IMPOSSIBLE, AND ECAME A SECRET AGENT FOR THE UNITED STATES AIR FORCE SPECIAL OPERATIONS DIVISION.
SECRET AGENT DANVERS
PART 1: ASCENSION

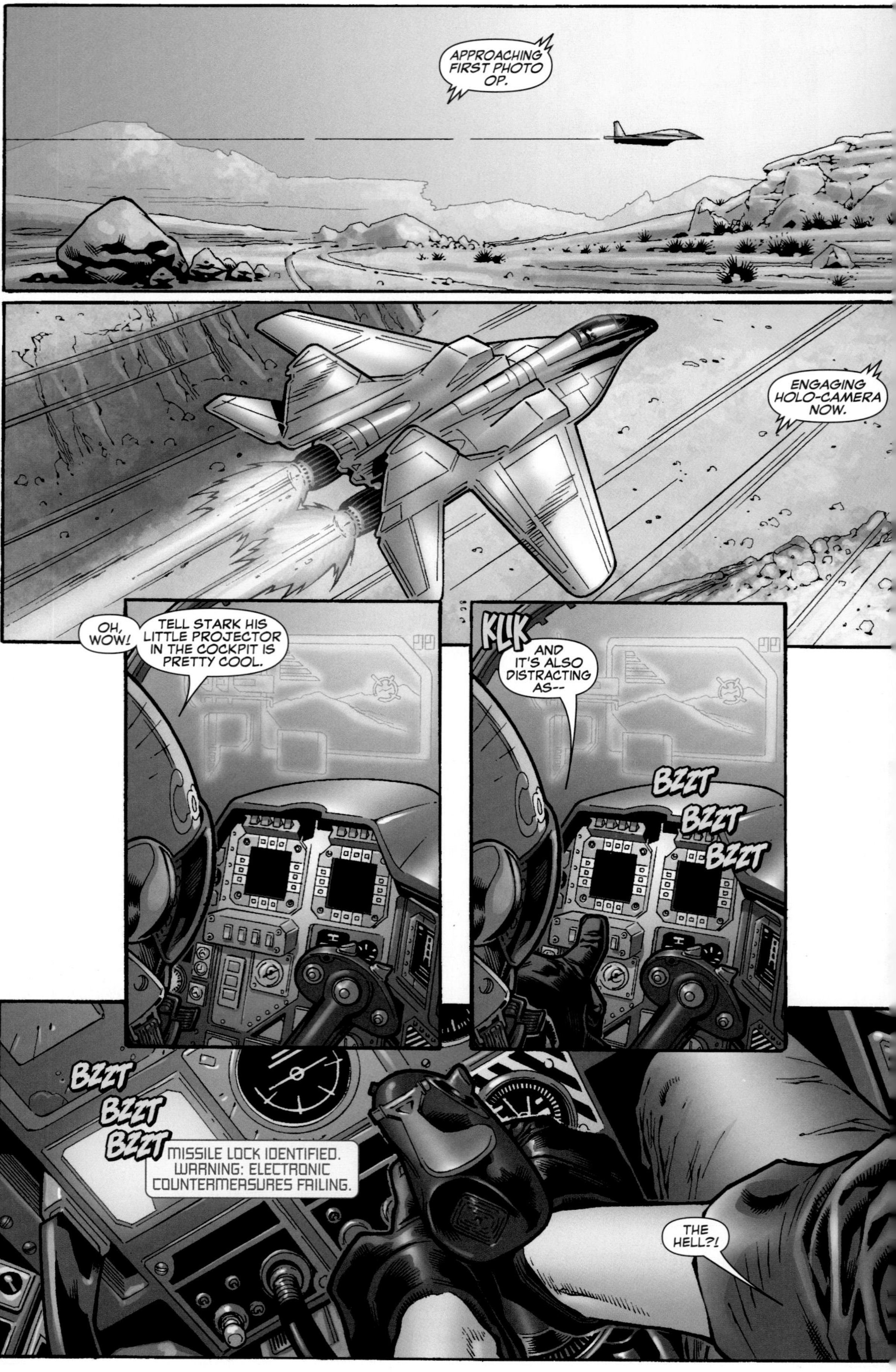
APPROACHING FIRST PHOTO OP.
ENGAGING HOLO-CAMERA NOW.
OH, WOW!
TELL STARK HIS LITTLE PROJECTOR IN THE COCKPIT IS PRETTY COOL.
KLIK
AND IT'S ALSO DISTRACTING AS--
BZZT
BZZT
BZZT
BZZT
BZZT
BZZT
MISSILE LOCK IDENTIFIED. WARNING: ELECTRONIC COUNTERMEASURES FAILING.
THE HELL?!

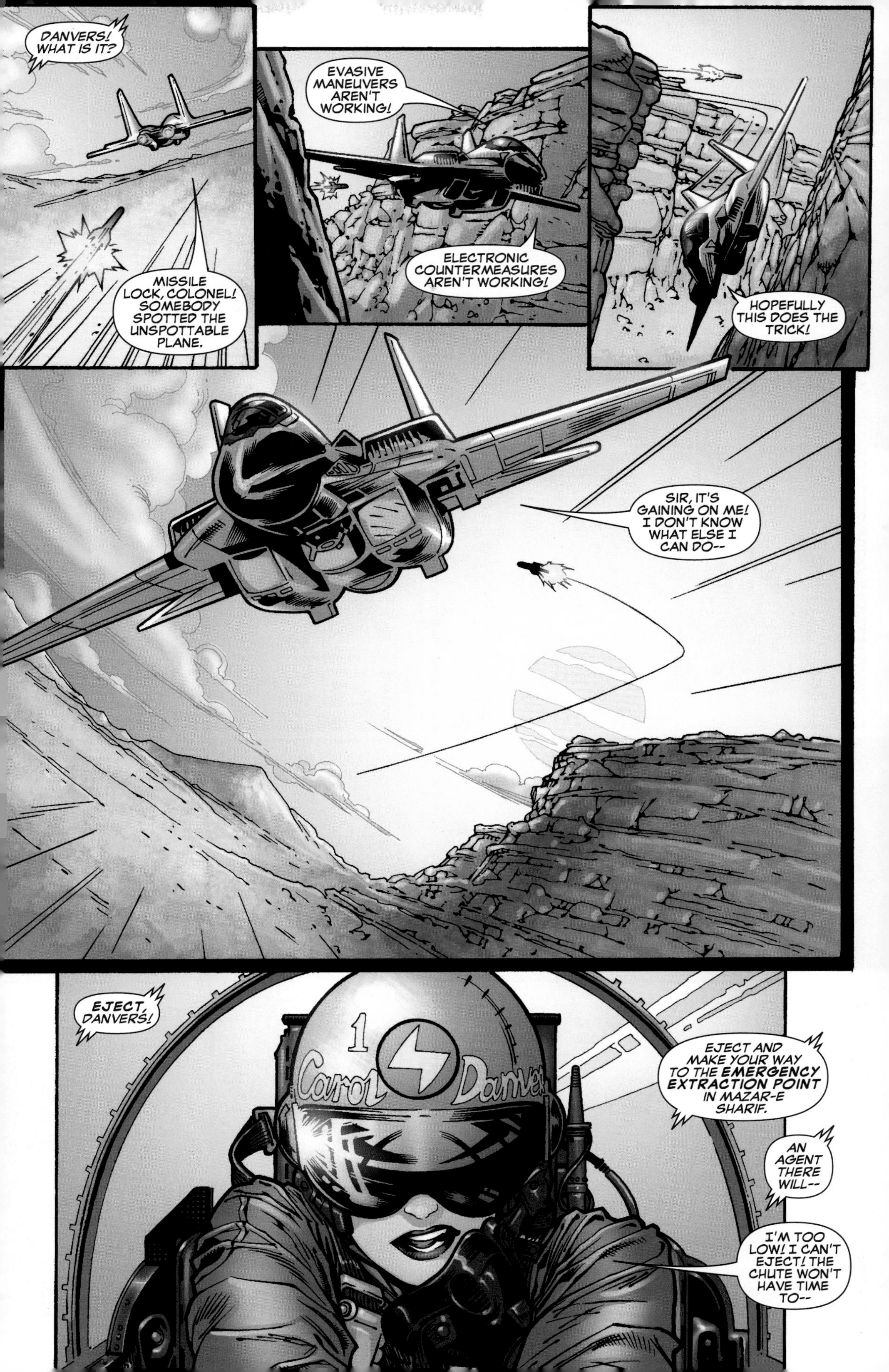
DANVERS! WHAT IS IT?
MISSILE LOCK, COLONEL! SOMEBODY SPOTTED THE UNSPOTTABLE PLANE.
EVASIVE MANEUVERS AREN'T WORKING!
ELECTRONIC COUNTERMEASURES AREN'T WORKING!
HOPEFULLY THIS DOES THE TRICK!
SIR, IT'S GAINING ON ME! I DON'T KNOW WHAT ELSE I CAN DO--
EJECT, DANVERS!
1
Carol Danvers
EJECT AND MAKE YOUR WAY TO THE EMERGENCY EXTRACTION POINT IN MAZAR-E SHARIF.
AN AGENT THERE WILL--
I'M TOO LOW! I CAN'T EJECT! THE CHUTE WON'T HAVE TIME TO--

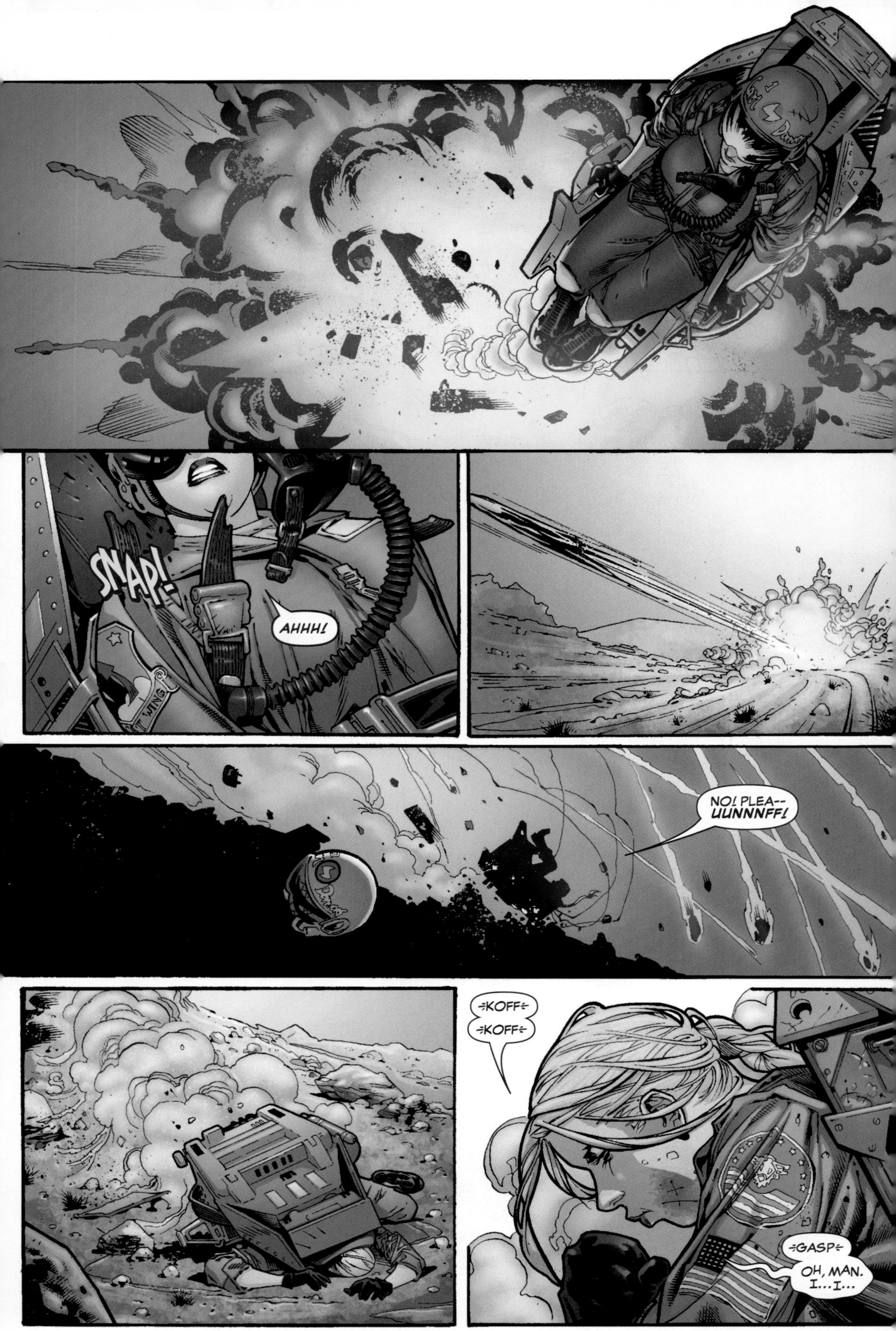
SNAP!
AHHH!
NO! PLEA--
UUNNNFF!
KOFF
KOFF
GASP
OH, MAN.
I...I...

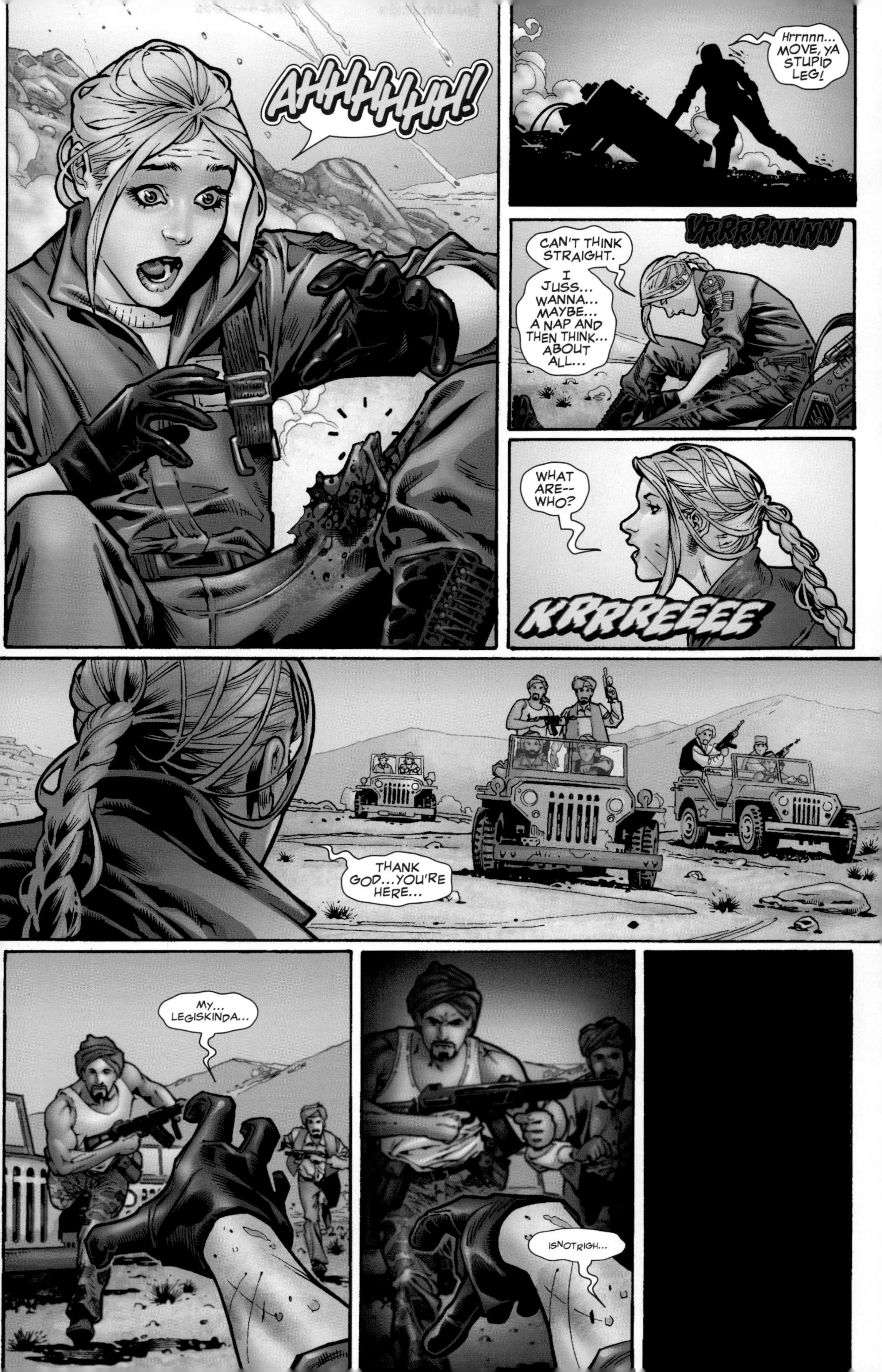
AHHHHHHH!
Hrrnnn... MOVE, YA STUPID LEG!
VRRRRNNNN
CAN'T THINK STRAIGHT.
I JUSS... WANNA... MAYBE... A NAP AND THEN THINK... ABOUT ALL...
WHAT ARE-- WHO?
KRRREEEE
THANK GOD...YOU'RE HERE...
MY... LEGISKINDA...
ISNOTRIGH...

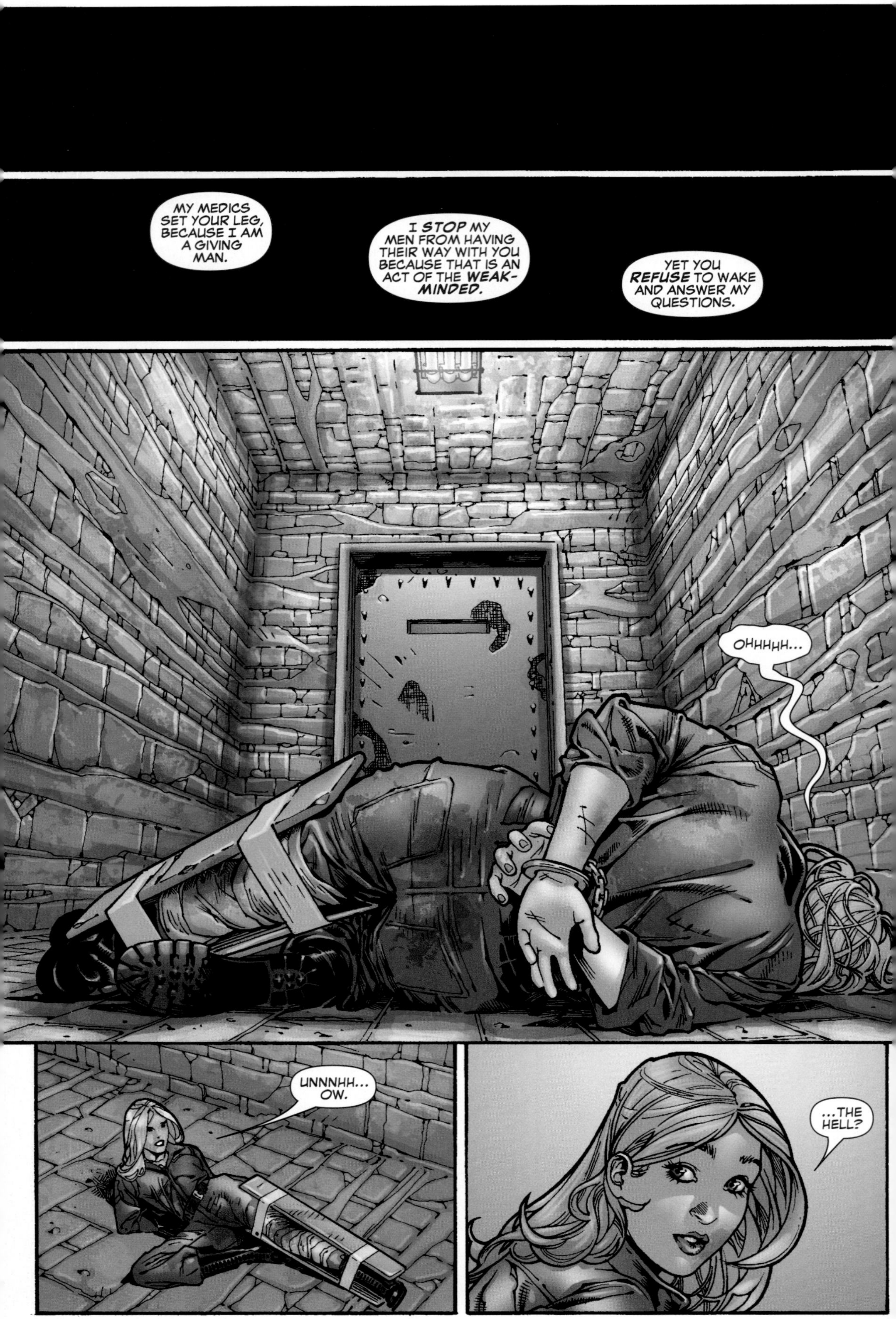
MY MEDICS SET YOUR LEG, BECAUSE I AM A GIVING MAN.
I STOP MY MEN FROM HAVING THEIR WAY WITH YOU BECAUSE THAT IS AN ACT OF THE WEAK-MINDED.
YET YOU REFUSE TO WAKE AND ANSWER MY QUESTIONS.
OHHHHH...
UNNNHH... OW.
...THE HELL?

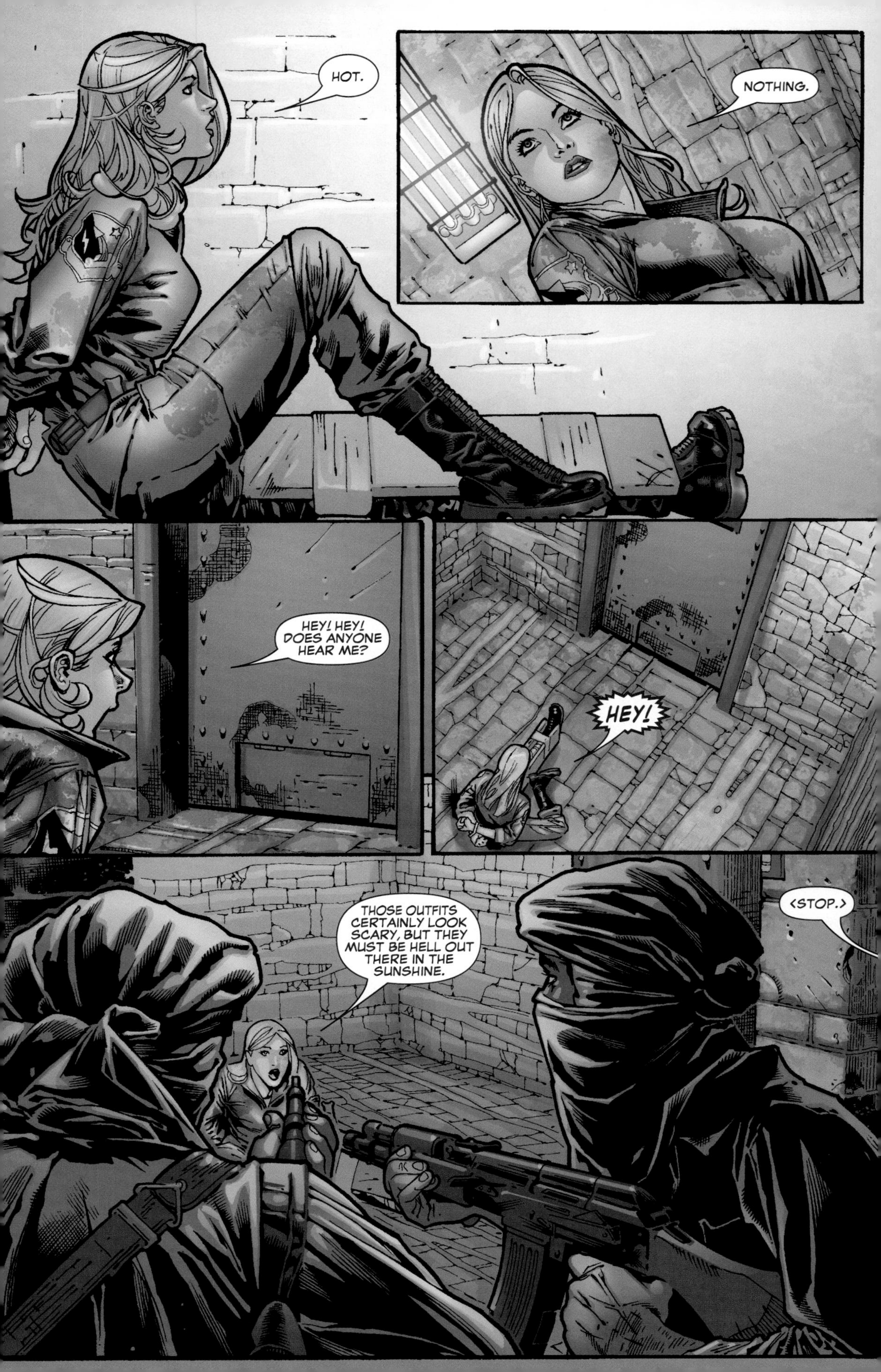
HOT.
NOTHING.
HEY! HEY! DOES ANYONE HEAR ME?
HEY!
THOSE OUTFITS CERTAINLY LOOK SCARY, BUT THEY MUST BE HELL OUT THERE IN THE SUNSHINE.
<STOP.>

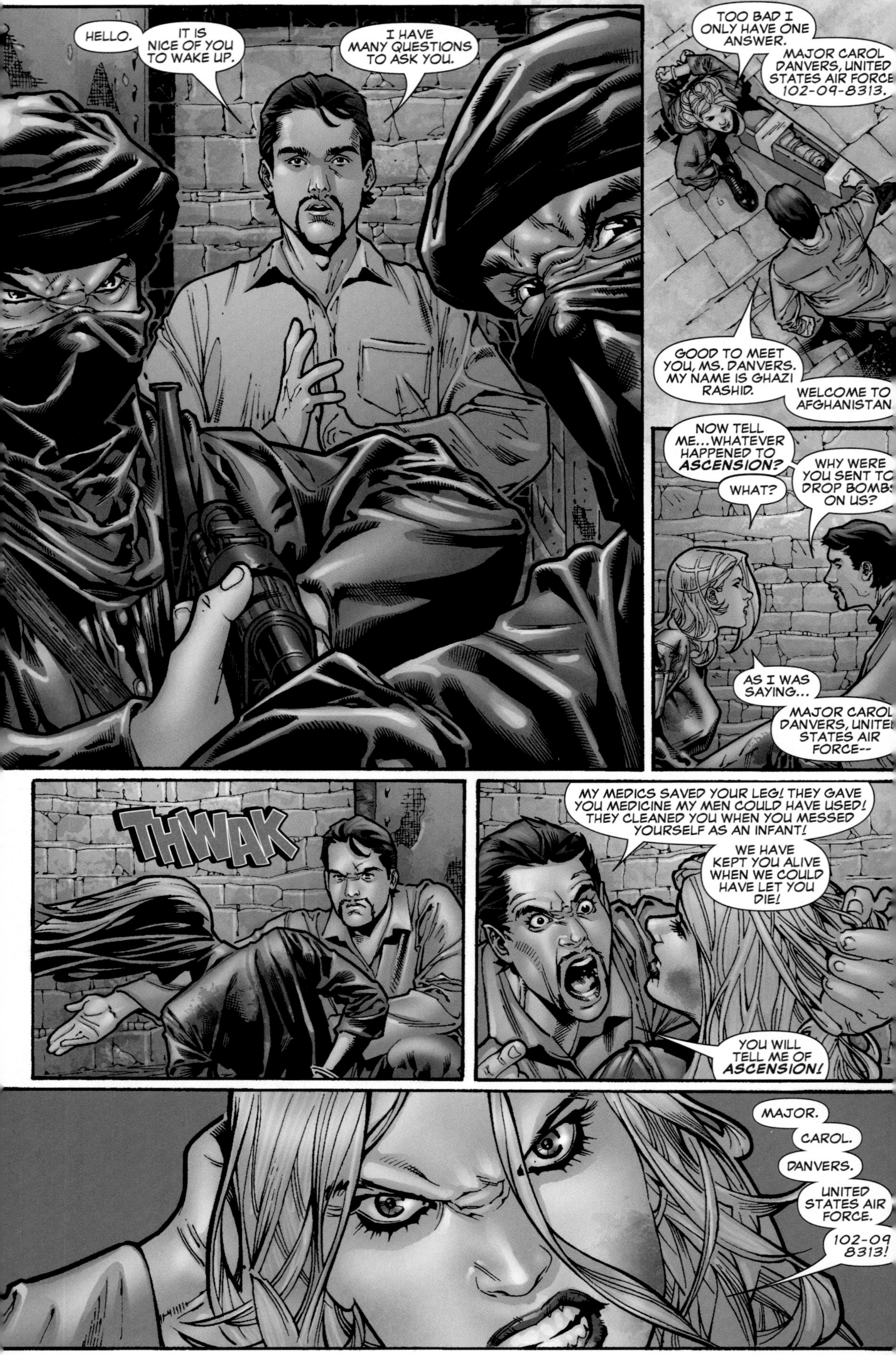
HELLO.
IT IS NICE OF YOU TO WAKE UP.
I HAVE MANY QUESTIONS TO ASK YOU.
TOO BAD I ONLY HAVE ONE ANSWER.
MAJOR CAROL DANVERS, UNITED STATES AIR FORCE 102-09-8313.
GOOD TO MEET YOU, MS. DANVERS. MY NAME IS GHAZI RASHID.
WELCOME TO AFGHANISTAN.
NOW TELL ME...WHATEVER HAPPENED TO ASCENSION?
WHAT?
WHY WERE YOU SENT TO DROP BOMBS ON US?
AS I WAS SAYING...
MAJOR CAROL DANVERS, UNITED STATES AIR FORCE--
THWAK
MY MEDICS SAVED YOUR LEG! THEY GAVE YOU MEDICINE MY MEN COULD HAVE USED! THEY CLEANED YOU WHEN YOU MESSED YOURSELF AS AN INFANT!
WE HAVE KEPT YOU ALIVE WHEN WE COULD HAVE LET YOU DIE!
YOU WILL TELL ME OF ASCENSION!
MAJOR.
CAROL.
DANVERS.
UNITED STATES AIR FORCE.
102-09 8313!

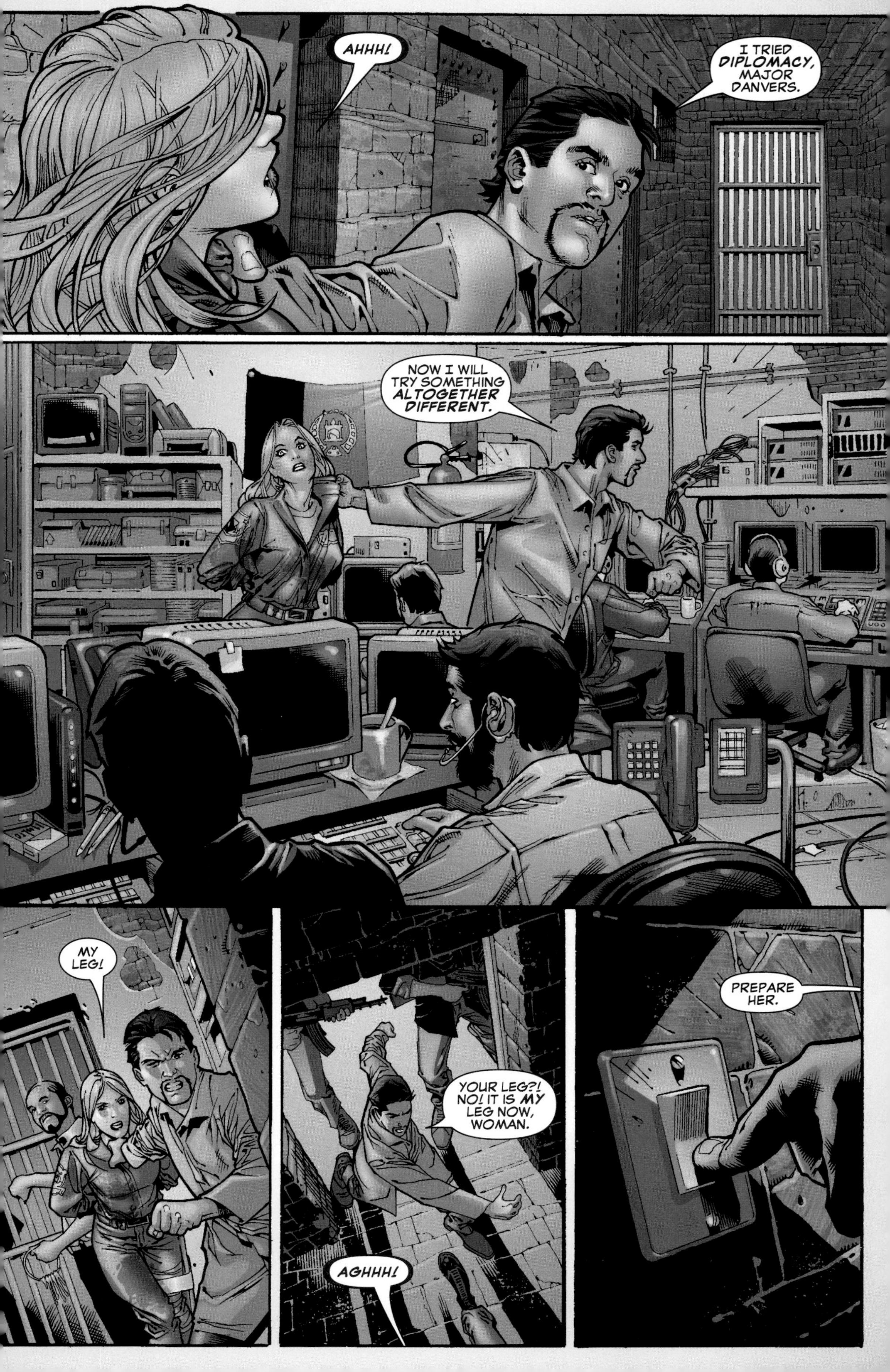
AHHH!
I TRIED DIPLOMACY, MAJOR DANVERS.
NOW I WILL TRY SOMETHING ALTOGETHER DIFFERENT.
MY LEG!
YOUR LEG?! NO! IT IS MY LEG NOW, WOMAN.
AGHHH!
PREPARE HER.

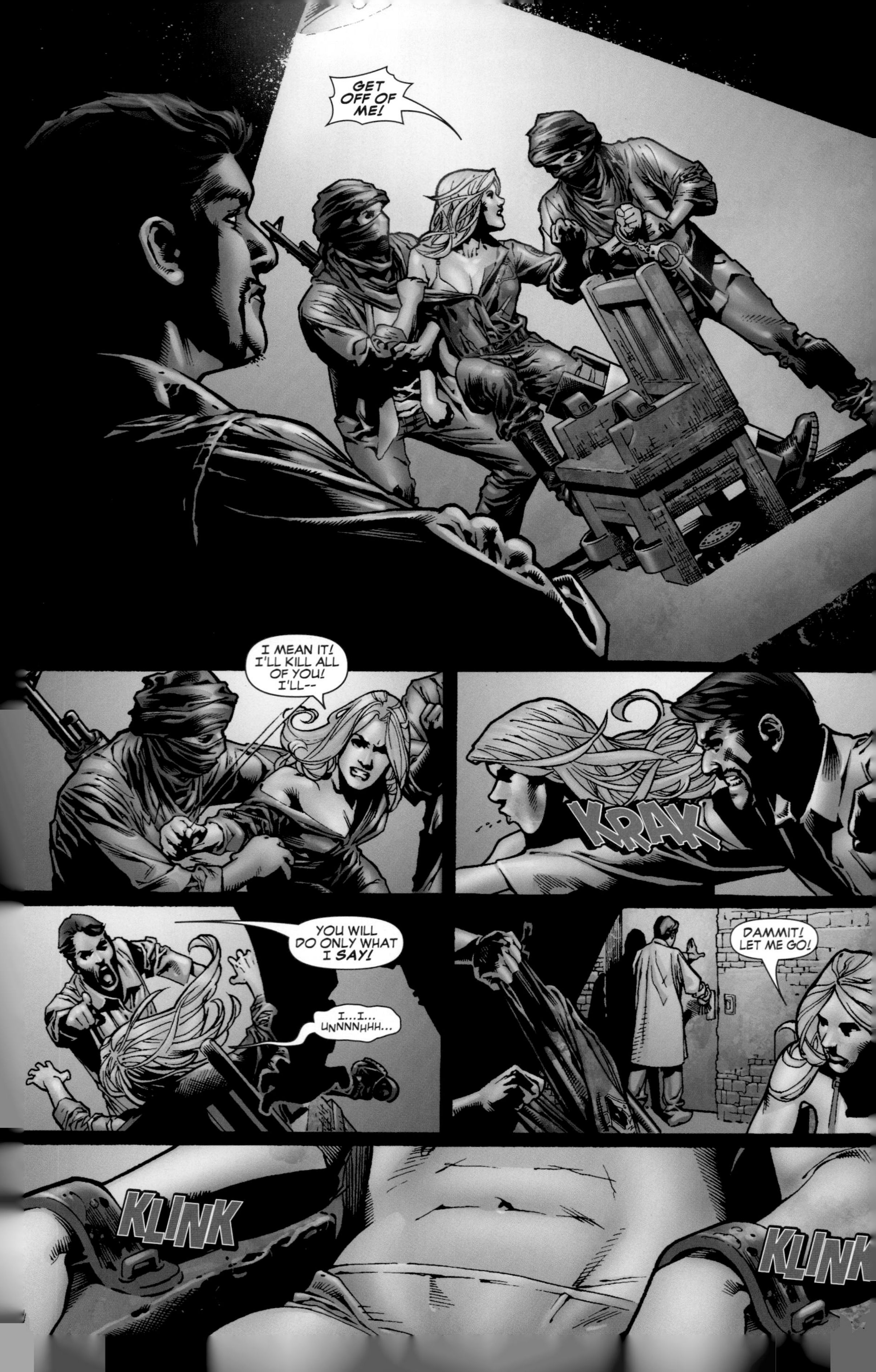
GET OFF OF ME!
I MEAN IT! I'LL KILL ALL OF YOU! I'LL--
KRAK
YOU WILL DO ONLY WHAT I SAY!
I...I... UNNNNHHH...
DAMMIT! LET ME GO!
KLINK
KLINK

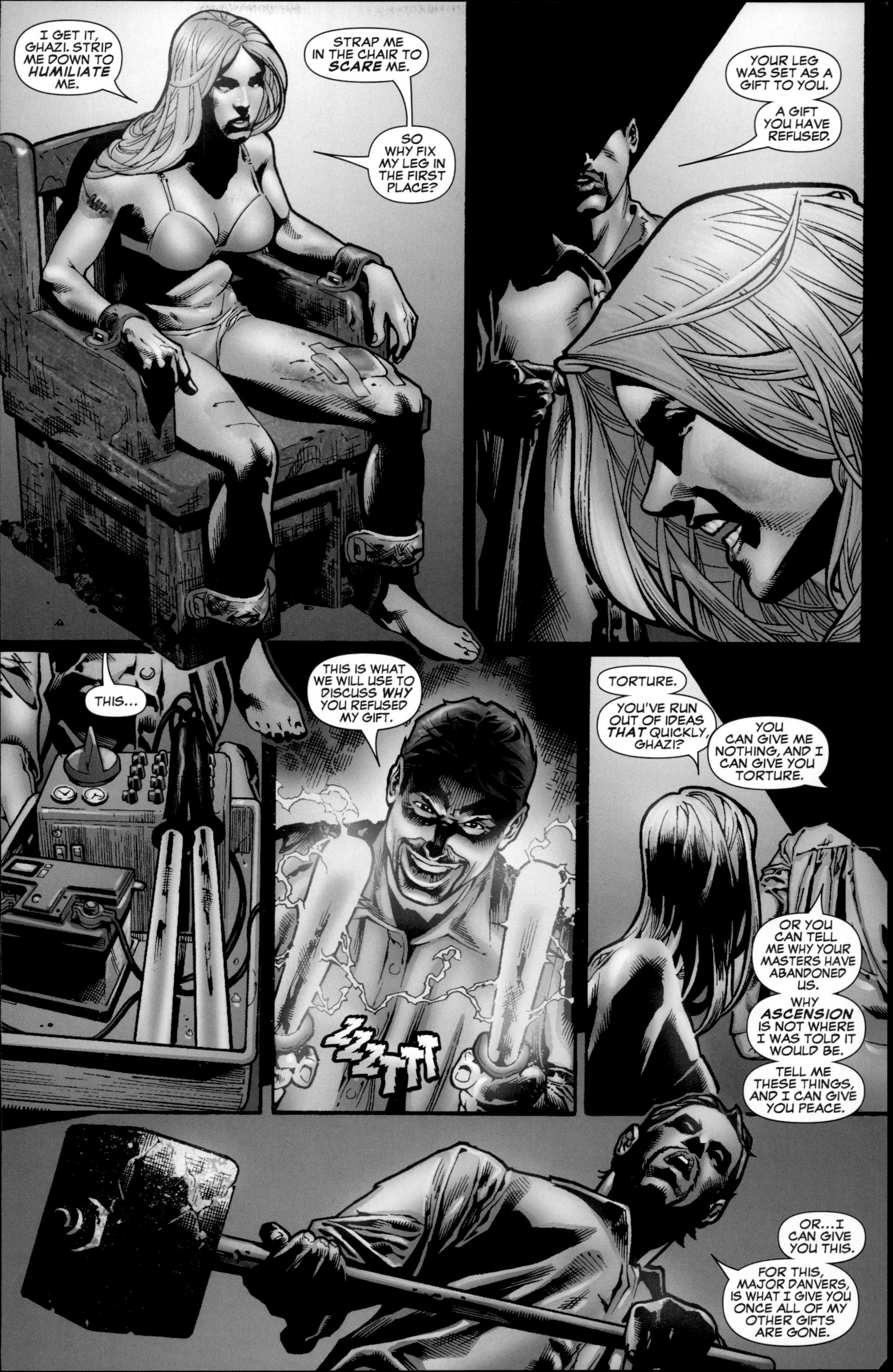
I GET IT, GHAZI. STRIP ME DOWN TO HUMILIATE ME.
STRAP ME IN THE CHAIR TO SCARE ME.
SO WHY FIX MY LEG IN THE FIRST PLACE?
YOUR LEG WAS SET AS A GIFT TO YOU.
A GIFT YOU HAVE REFUSED.
THIS...
THIS IS WHAT WE WILL USE TO DISCUSS WHY YOU REFUSED MY GIFT.
ZZZTTT
TORTURE.
YOU'VE RUN OUT OF IDEAS THAT QUICKLY, GHAZI?
YOU CAN GIVE ME NOTHING, AND I CAN GIVE YOU TORTURE.
OR YOU CAN TELL ME WHY YOUR MASTERS HAVE ABANDONED US.
WHY ASCENSION IS NOT WHERE I WAS TOLD IT WOULD BE.
TELL ME THESE THINGS, AND I CAN GIVE YOU PEACE.
OR...I CAN GIVE YOU THIS.
FOR THIS, MAJOR DANVERS, IS WHAT I GIVE YOU ONCE ALL OF MY OTHER GIFTS ARE GONE.

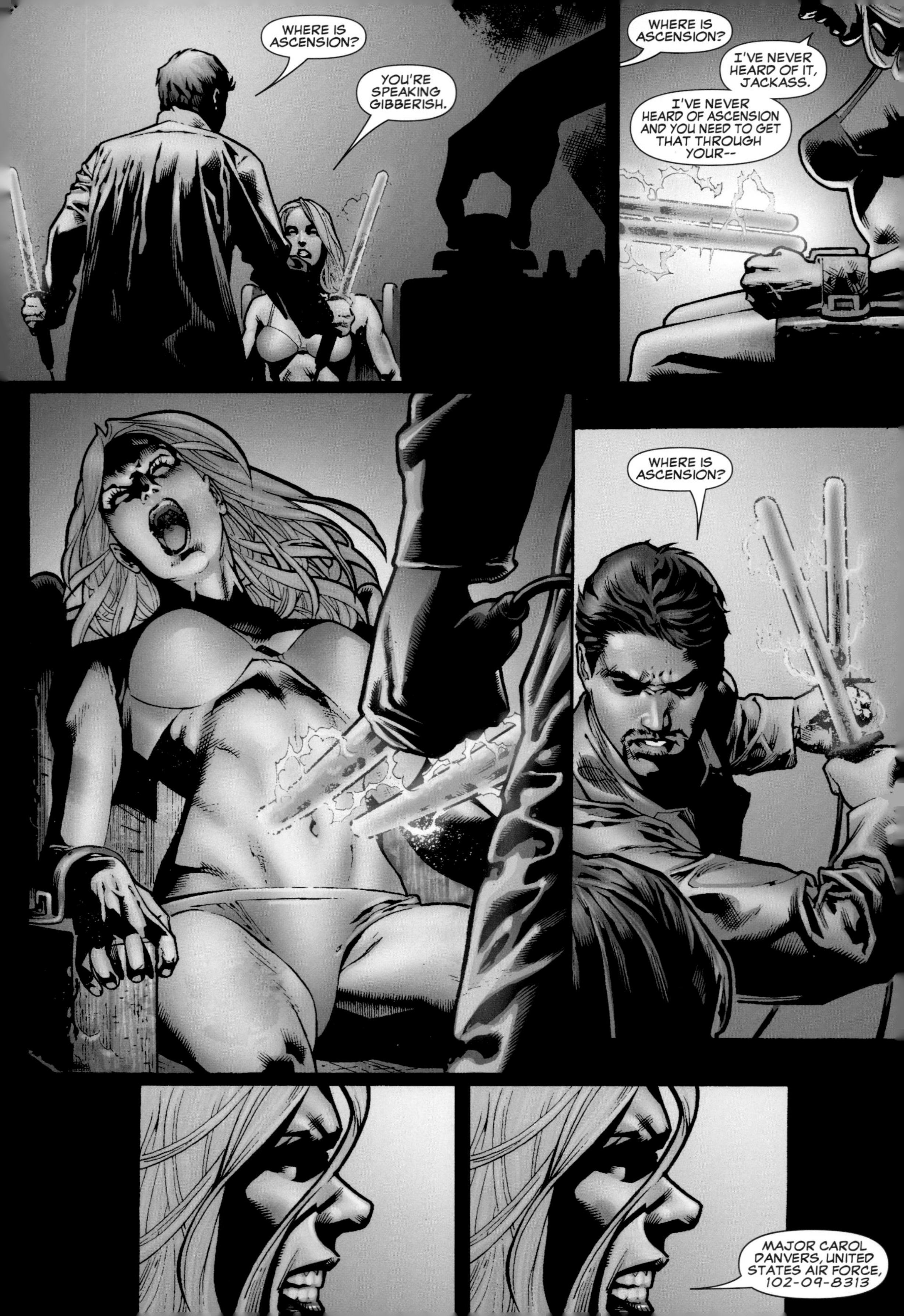
WHERE IS ASCENSION?
YOU'RE SPEAKING GIBBERISH.
WHERE IS ASCENSION?
I'VE NEVER HEARD OF IT, JACKASS.
I'VE NEVER HEARD OF ASCENSION AND YOU NEED TO GET THAT THROUGH YOUR--
WHERE IS ASCENSION?
MAJOR CAROL DANVERS, UNITED STATES AIR FORCE, 102-09-8313

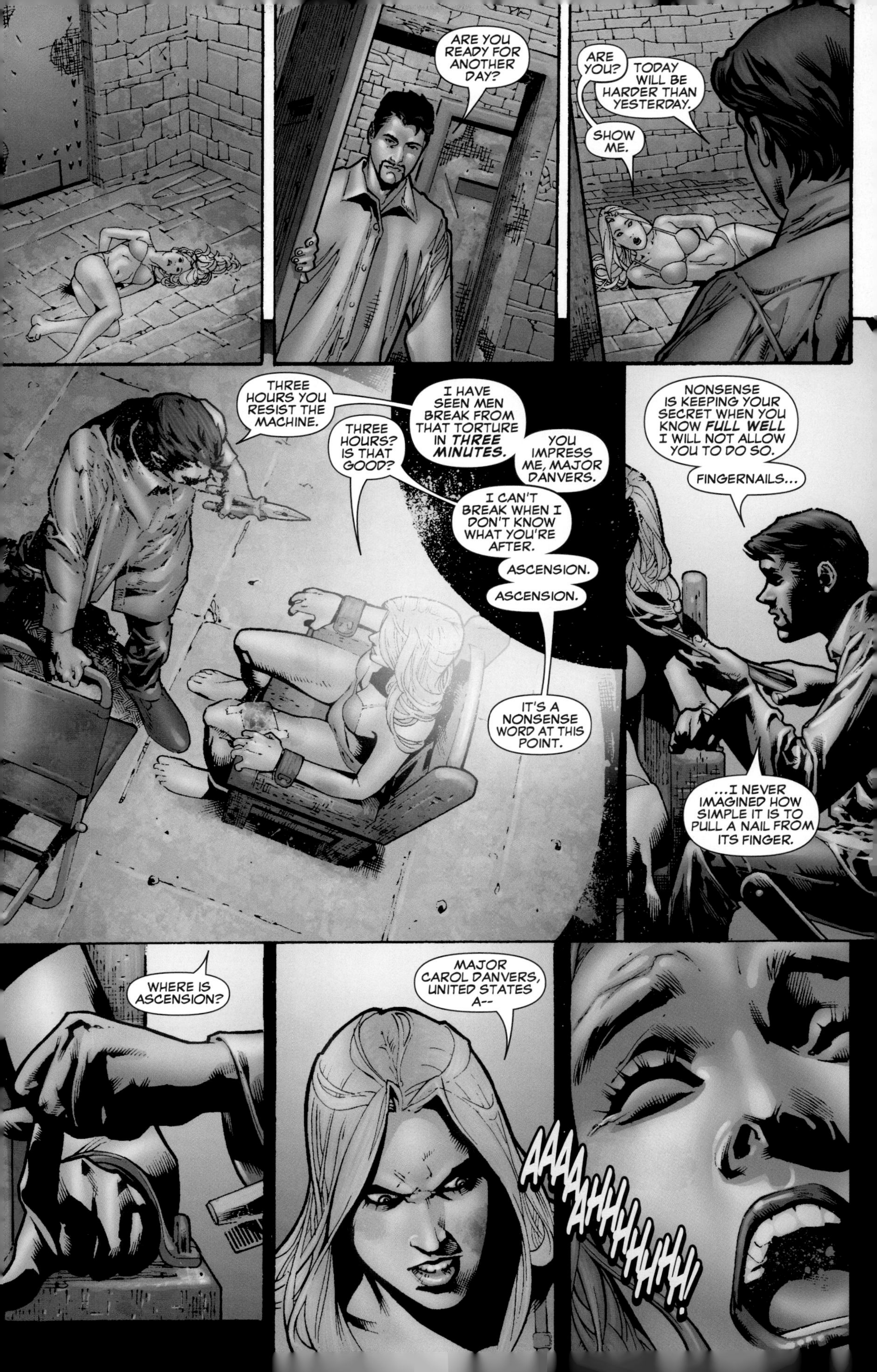
ARE YOU READY FOR ANOTHER DAY?
ARE YOU?
TODAY WILL BE HARDER THAN YESTERDAY.
SHOW ME.
THREE HOURS YOU RESIST THE MACHINE.
I HAVE SEEN MEN BREAK FROM THAT TORTURE IN THREE MINUTES.
THREE HOURS? IS THAT GOOD?
YOU IMPRESS ME, MAJOR DANVERS.
I CAN'T BREAK WHEN I DON'T KNOW WHAT YOU'RE AFTER.
ASCENSION.
ASCENSION.
IT'S A NONSENSE WORD AT THIS POINT.
NONSENSE IS KEEPING YOUR SECRET WHEN YOU KNOW FULL WELL I WILL NOT ALLOW YOU TO DO SO.
FINGERNAILS...
...I NEVER IMAGINED HOW SIMPLE IT IS TO PULL A NAIL FROM ITS FINGER.
WHERE IS ASCENSION?
MAJOR CAROL DANVERS, UNITED STATES A--
AAAAAHHHHHHHH!

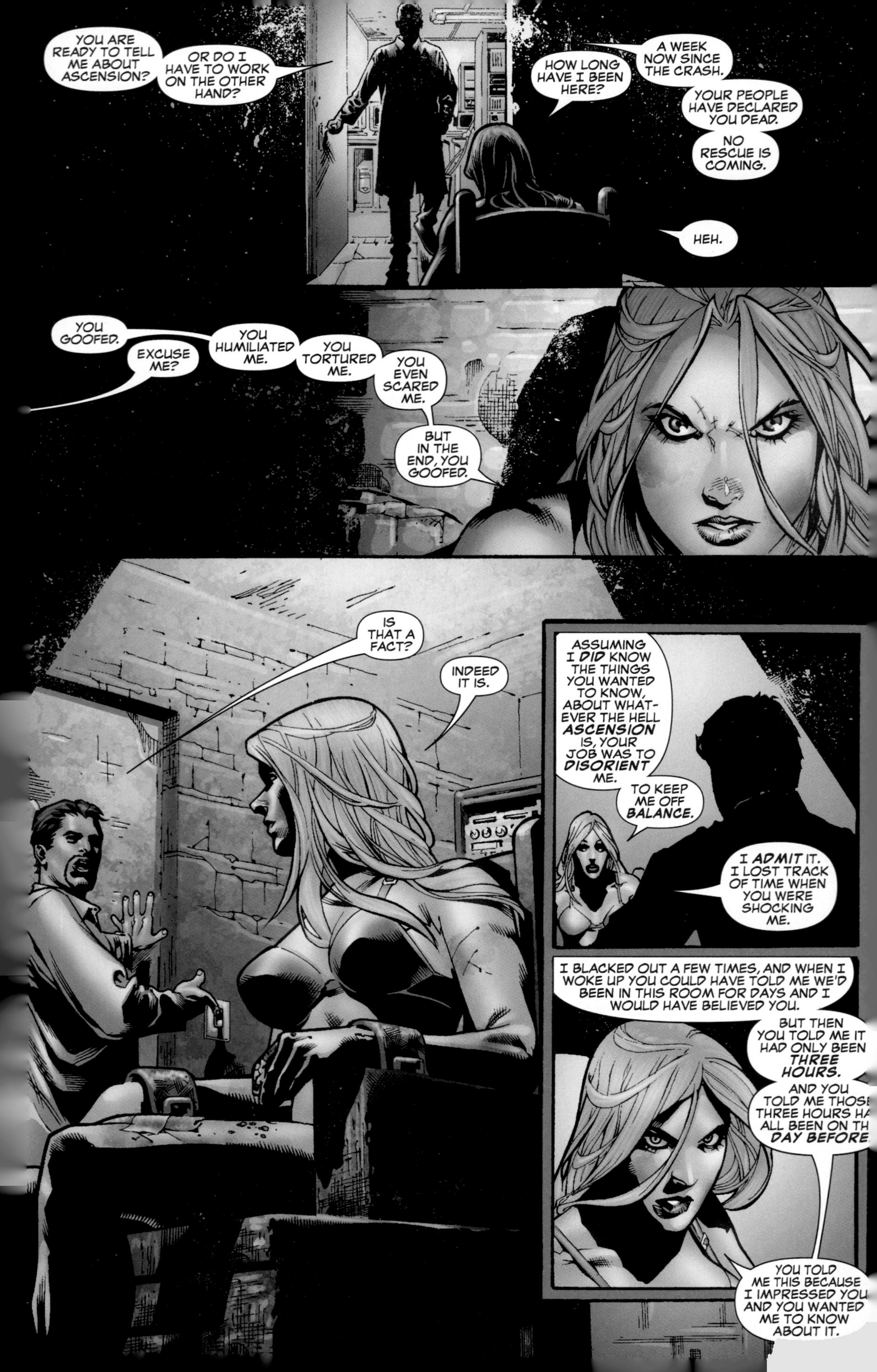
YOU ARE READY TO TELL ME ABOUT ASCENSION?
OR DO I HAVE TO WORK ON THE OTHER HAND?
HOW LONG HAVE I BEEN HERE?
A WEEK NOW SINCE THE CRASH.
YOUR PEOPLE HAVE DECLARED YOU DEAD.
NO RESCUE IS COMING.
HEH.
YOU GOOFED.
EXCUSE ME?
YOU HUMILIATED ME.
YOU TORTURED ME.
YOU EVEN SCARED ME.
BUT IN THE END, YOU GOOFED.
IS THAT A FACT?
INDEED IT IS.
ASSUMING I DID KNOW THE THINGS YOU WANTED TO KNOW, ABOUT WHAT-EVER THE HELL ASCENSION IS, YOUR JOB WAS TO DISORIENT ME.
TO KEEP ME OFF BALANCE.
I ADMIT IT. I LOST TRACK OF TIME WHEN YOU WERE SHOCKING ME.
I BLACKED OUT A FEW TIMES, AND WHEN I WOKE UP YOU COULD HAVE TOLD ME WE'D BEEN IN THIS ROOM FOR DAYS AND I WOULD HAVE BELIEVED YOU.
BUT THEN YOU TOLD ME IT HAD ONLY BEEN THREE HOURS.
AND YOU TOLD ME THOSE THREE HOURS HA ALL BEEN ON TH DAY BEFORE.
YOU TOLD ME THIS BECAUSE I IMPRESSED YOU AND YOU WANTED ME TO KNOW ABOUT IT.

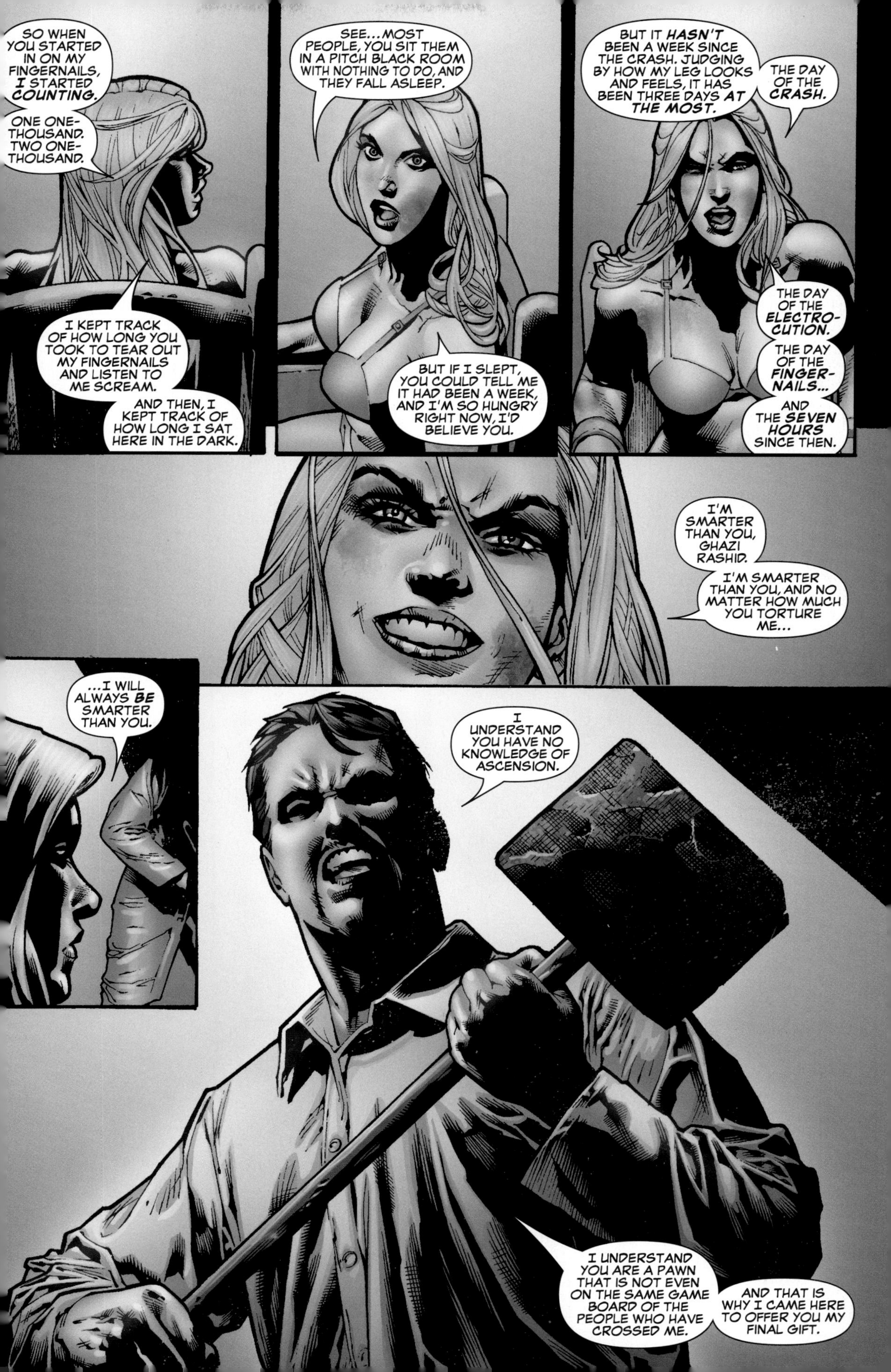
SO WHEN YOU STARTED IN ON MY FINGERNAILS, I STARTED COUNTING.
ONE ONE-THOUSAND. TWO ONE-THOUSAND.
I KEPT TRACK OF HOW LONG YOU TOOK TO TEAR OUT MY FINGERNAILS AND LISTEN TO ME SCREAM.
AND THEN, I KEPT TRACK OF HOW LONG I SAT HERE IN THE DARK.
SEE...MOST PEOPLE, YOU SIT THEM IN A PITCH BLACK ROOM WITH NOTHING TO DO, AND THEY FALL ASLEEP.
BUT IF I SLEPT, YOU COULD TELL ME IT HAD BEEN A WEEK, AND I'M SO HUNGRY RIGHT NOW, I'D BELIEVE YOU.
BUT IT HASN'T BEEN A WEEK SINCE THE CRASH. JUDGING BY HOW MY LEG LOOKS AND FEELS, IT HAS BEEN THREE DAYS AT THE MOST.
THE DAY OF THE CRASH.
THE DAY OF THE ELECTROCUTION.
THE DAY OF THE FINGERNAILS...
AND THE SEVEN HOURS SINCE THEN.
I'M SMARTER THAN YOU, GHAZI RASHID.
I'M SMARTER THAN YOU, AND NO MATTER HOW MUCH YOU TORTURE ME...
...I WILL ALWAYS BE SMARTER THAN YOU.
I UNDERSTAND YOU HAVE NO KNOWLEDGE OF ASCENSION.
I UNDERSTAND YOU ARE A PAWN THAT IS NOT EVEN ON THE SAME GAME BOARD OF THE PEOPLE WHO HAVE CROSSED ME.
AND THAT IS WHY I CAME HERE TO OFFER YOU MY FINAL GIFT.

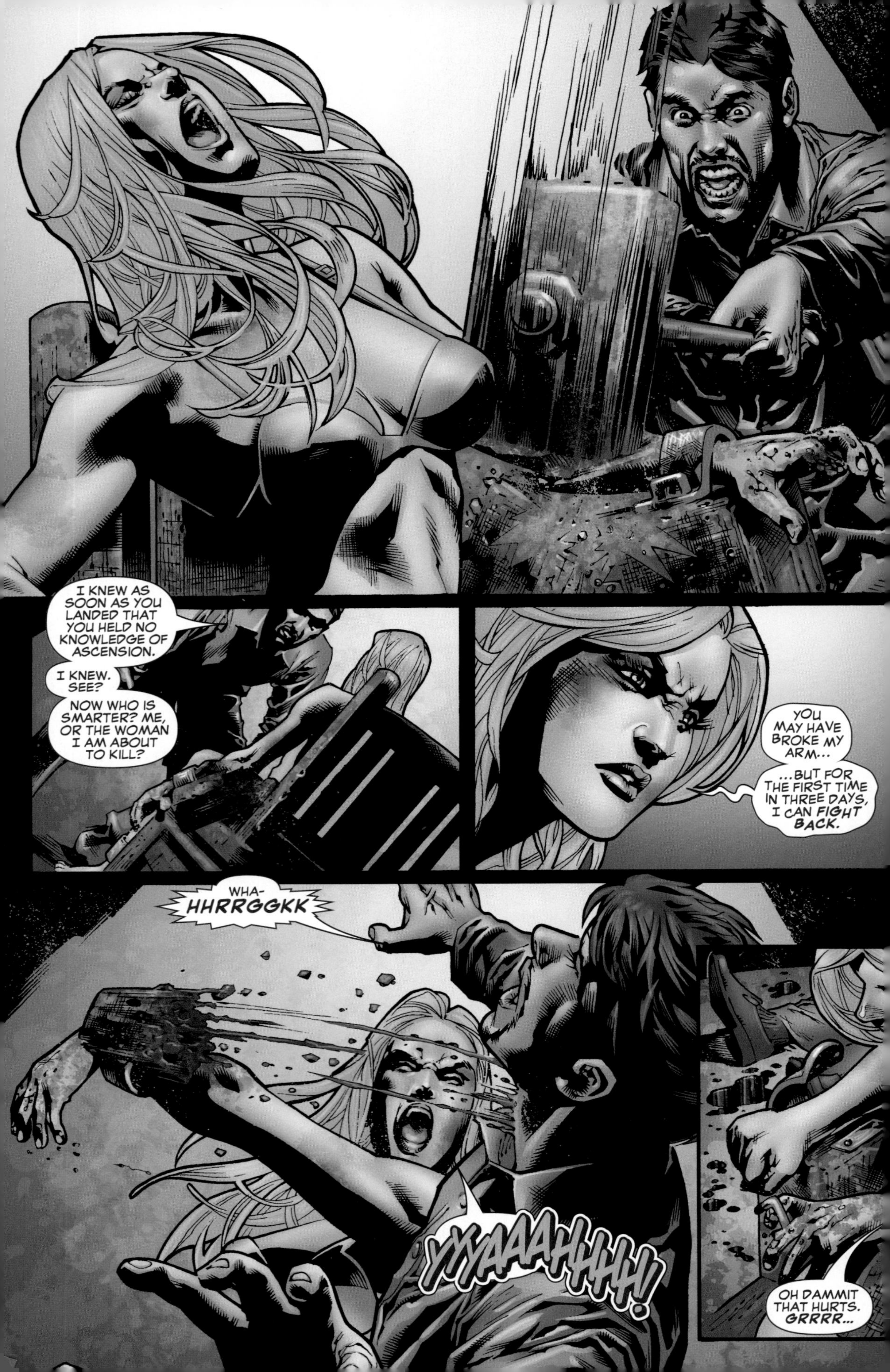
I KNEW AS SOON AS YOU LANDED THAT YOU HELD NO KNOWLEDGE OF ASCENSION.
I KNEW. SEE?
NOW WHO IS SMARTER? ME, OR THE WOMAN I AM ABOUT TO KILL?
YOU MAY HAVE BROKE MY ARM...
...BUT FOR THE FIRST TIME IN THREE DAYS, I CAN FIGHT BACK.
WHA- HHRRGGKK
YYAAAHHHH!
OH DAMMIT THAT HURTS. GRRRR...

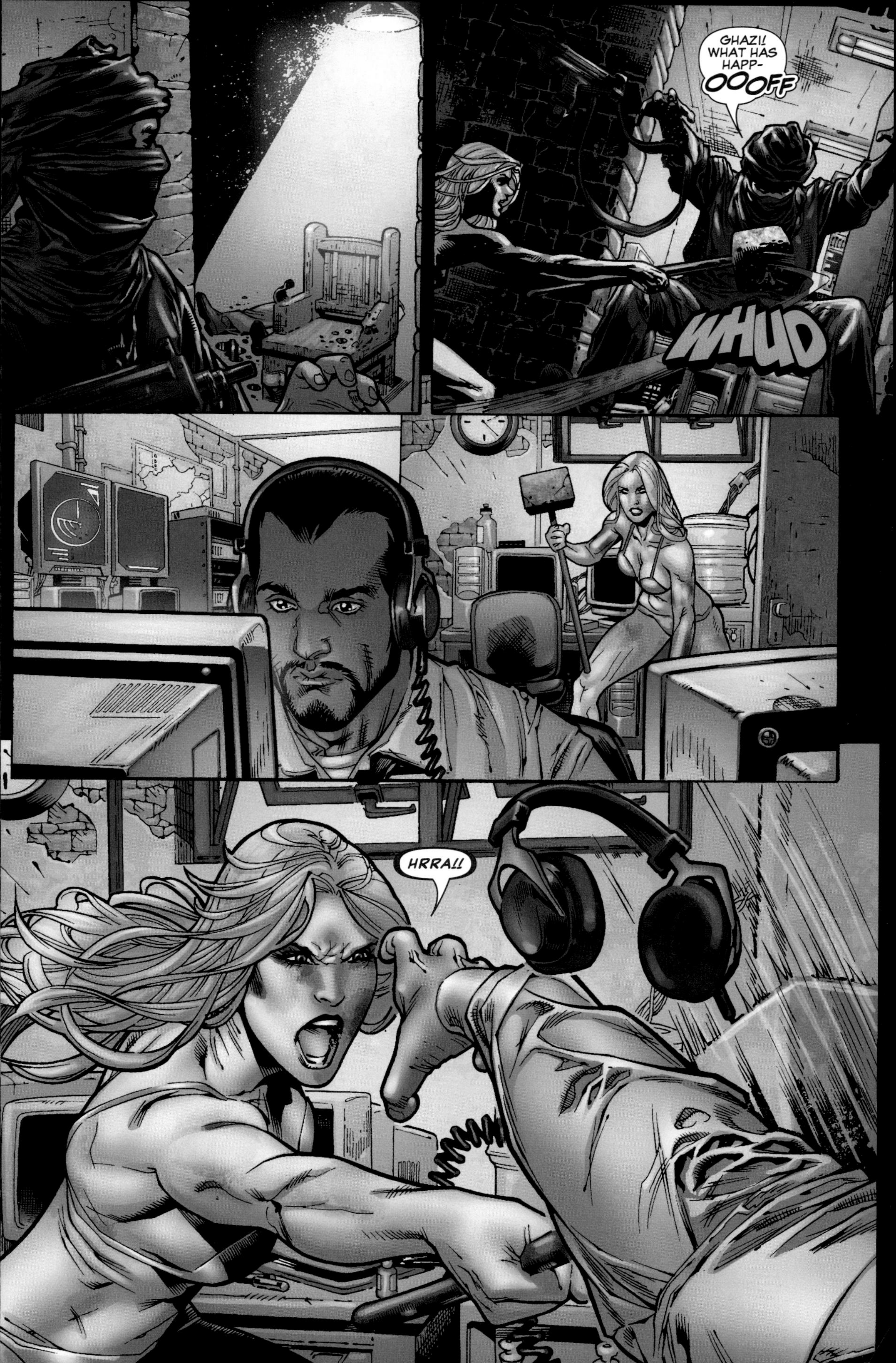
GHAZI!! WHAT HAS HAPP- OOOFF
WHUD
HRRA!!

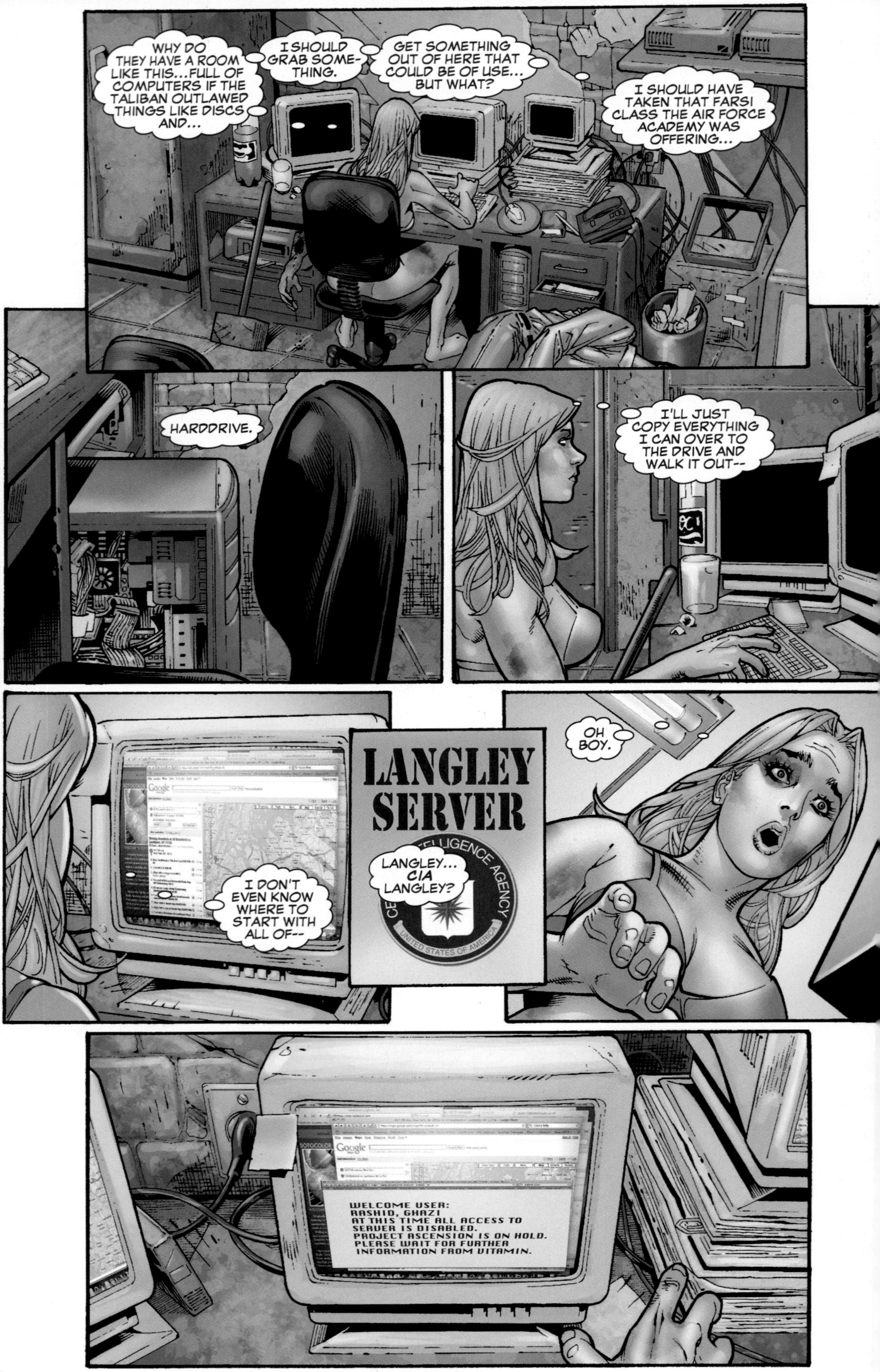
WHY DO THEY HAVE A ROOM LIKE THIS...FULL OF COMPUTERS IF THE TALIBAN OUTLAWED THINGS LIKE DISCS AND...
I SHOULD GRAB SOME-THING.
GET SOMETHING OUT OF HERE THAT COULD BE OF USE... BUT WHAT?
I SHOULD HAVE TAKEN THAT FARSI CLASS THE AIR FORCE ACADEMY WAS OFFERING...
HARDDRIVE.
I'LL JUST COPY EVERYTHING I CAN OVER TO THE DRIVE AND WALK IT OUT--
I DON'T EVEN KNOW WHERE TO START WITH ALL OF--
LANGLEY SERVER
LANGLEY... CIA LANGLEY?
UNITED STATES OF AMERICA
OH BOY.
WELCOME USER:
RASHID, GHAZI
AT THIS TIME ALL ACCESS TO
SERVER IS DISABLED.
PROJECT ASCENSION IS ON HOLD.
PLEASE WAIT FOR FURTHER
INFORMATION FROM VITAMIN.

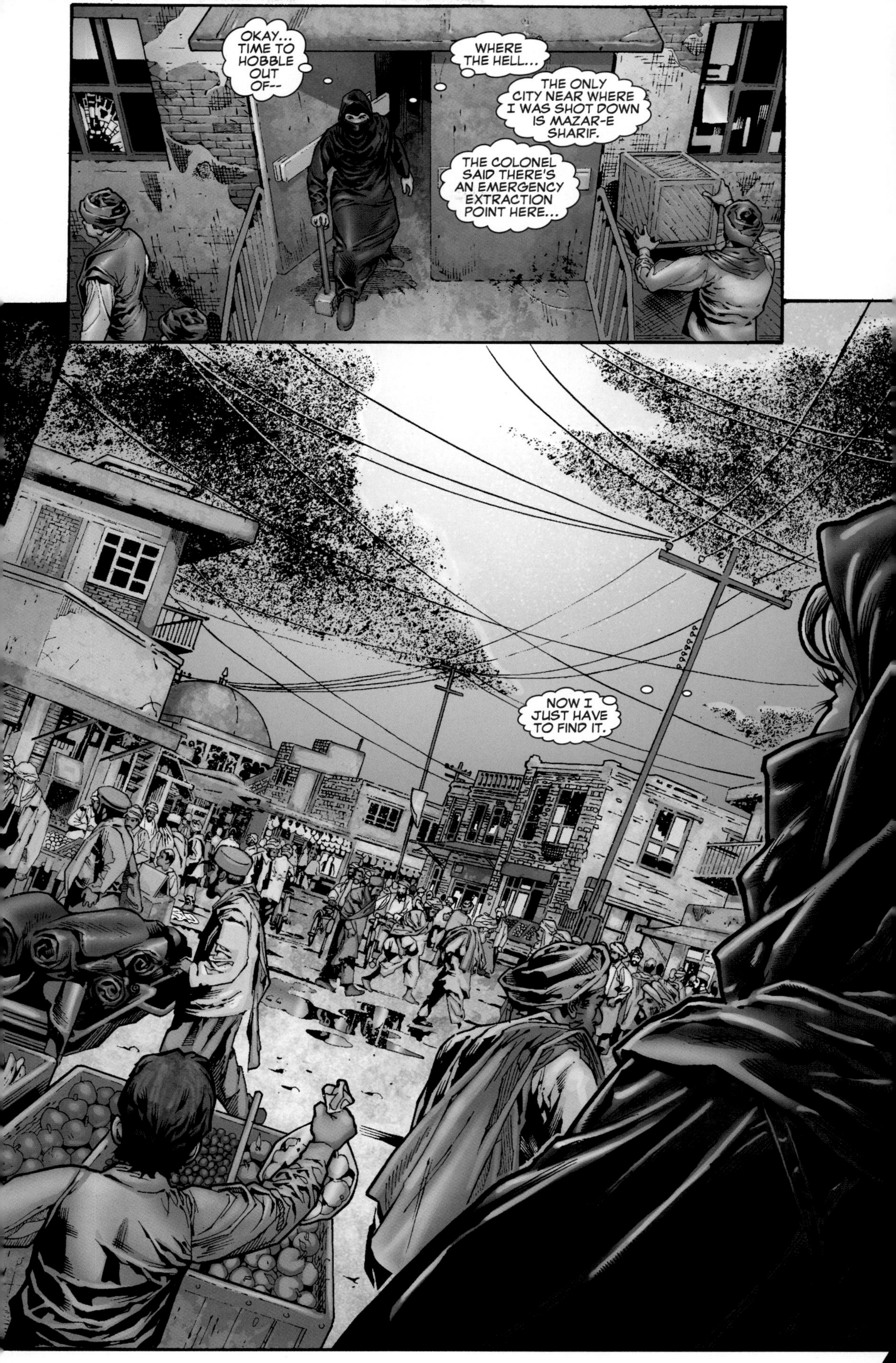
OKAY... TIME TO HOBBLE OUT OF--
WHERE THE HELL...
THE ONLY CITY NEAR WHERE I WAS SHOT DOWN IS MAZAR-E SHARIF.
THE COLONEL SAID THERE'S AN EMERGENCY EXTRACTION POINT HERE...
NOW I JUST HAVE TO FIND IT.

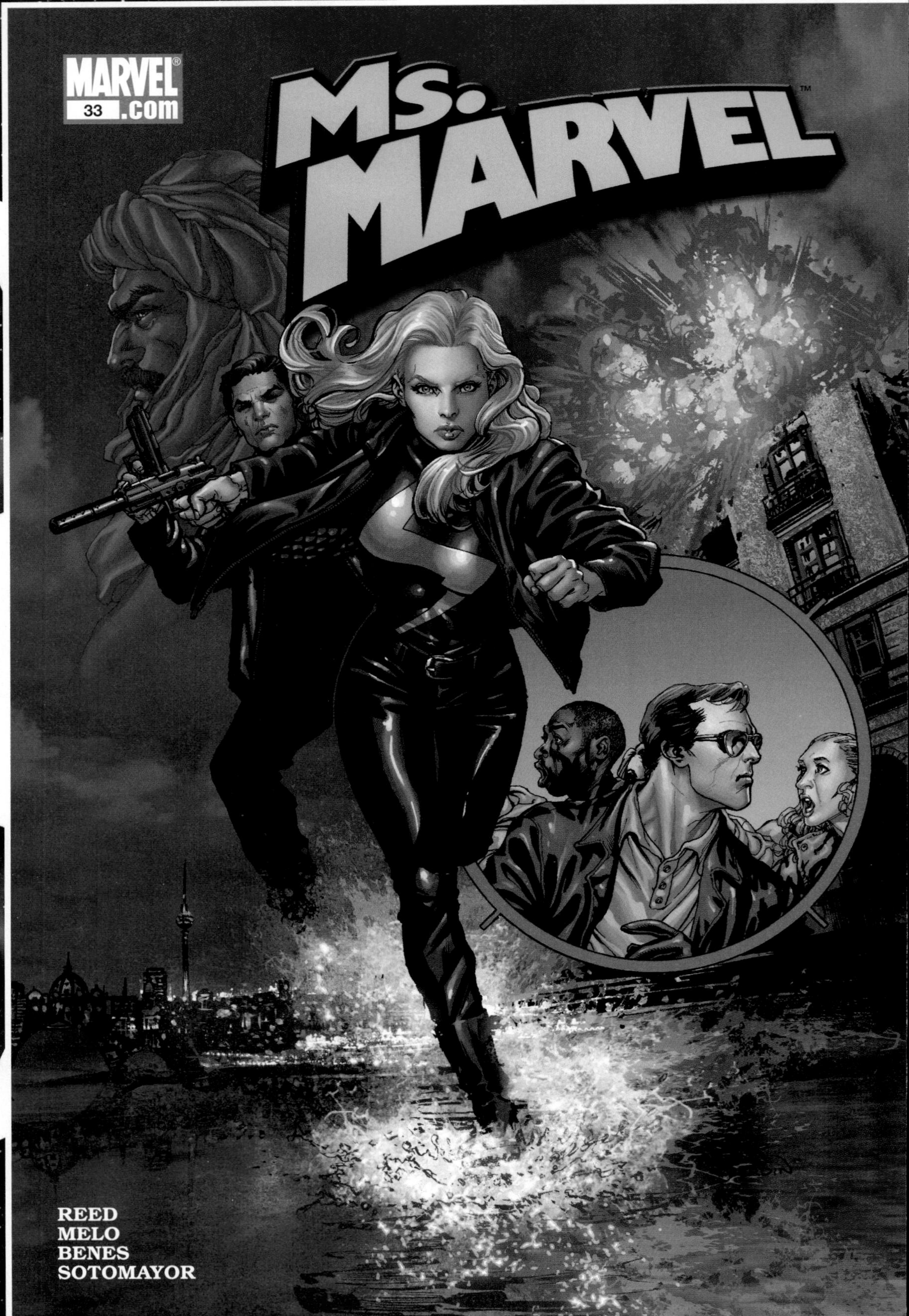
MARVEL®
33 .com
MS. MARVEL™
REED
MELO
BENES
SOTOMAYOR

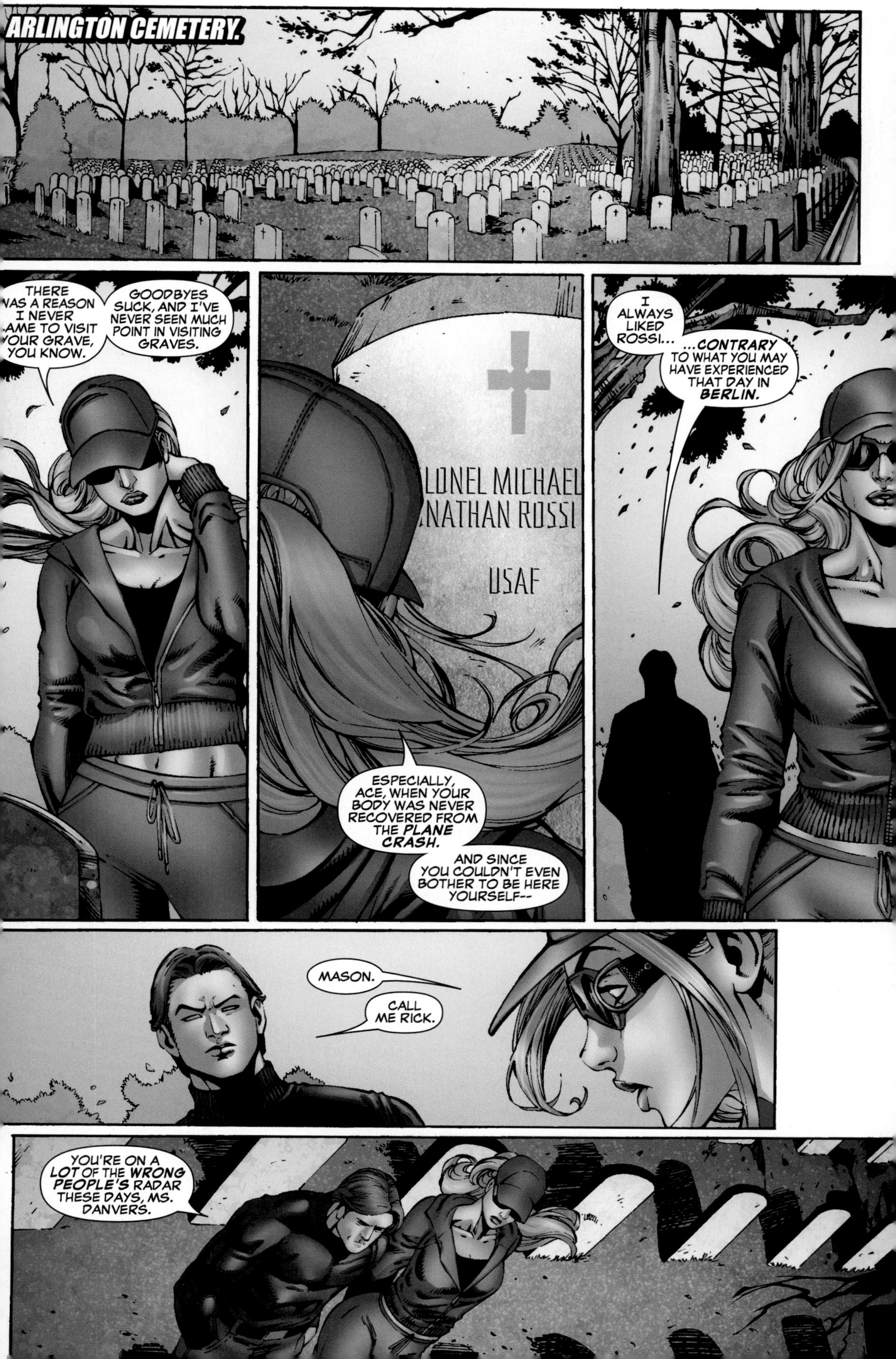
ARLINGTON CEMETERY.
THERE WAS A REASON I NEVER CAME TO VISIT YOUR GRAVE, YOU KNOW.
GOODBYES SUCK, AND I'VE NEVER SEEN MUCH POINT IN VISITING GRAVES.
LONEL MICHAEL NATHAN ROSSI
USAF
ESPECIALLY, ACE, WHEN YOUR BODY WAS NEVER RECOVERED FROM THE PLANE CRASH.
AND SINCE YOU COULDN'T EVEN BOTHER TO BE HERE YOURSELF--
I ALWAYS LIKED ROSSI...
...CONTRARY TO WHAT YOU MAY HAVE EXPERIENCED THAT DAY IN BERLIN.
MASON.
CALL ME RICK.
YOU'RE ON A LOT OF THE WRONG PEOPLE'S RADAR THESE DAYS, MS. DANVERS.

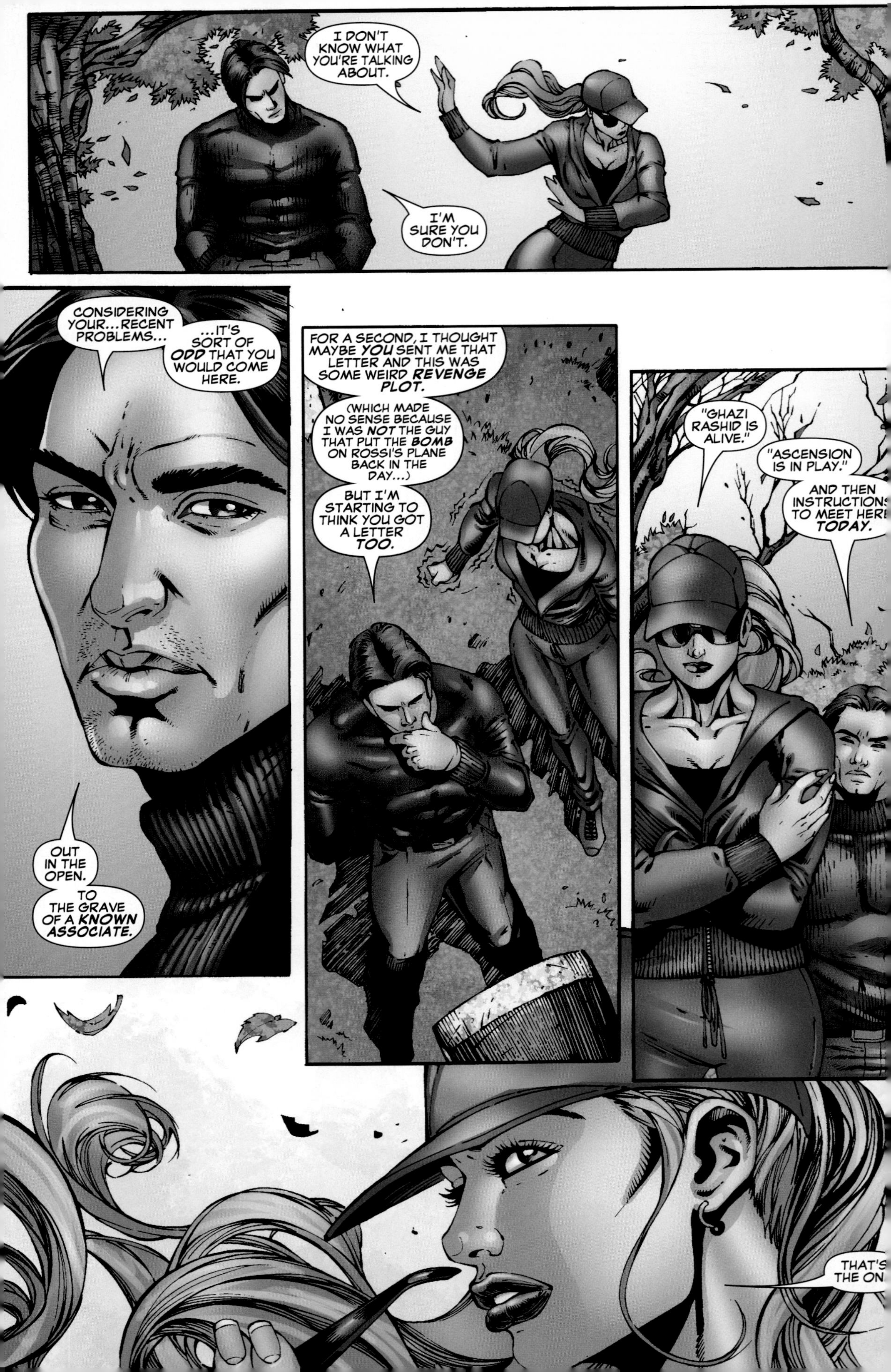
I DON'T KNOW WHAT YOU'RE TALKING ABOUT.
I'M SURE YOU DON'T.
CONSIDERING YOUR... RECENT PROBLEMS...
...IT'S SORT OF ODD THAT YOU WOULD COME HERE.
OUT IN THE OPEN.
TO THE GRAVE OF A KNOWN ASSOCIATE.
FOR A SECOND, I THOUGHT MAYBE YOU SENT ME THAT LETTER AND THIS WAS SOME WEIRD REVENGE PLOT.
(WHICH MADE NO SENSE BECAUSE I WAS NOT THE GUY THAT PUT THE BOMB ON ROSSI'S PLANE BACK IN THE DAY...)
BUT I'M STARTING TO THINK YOU GOT A LETTER TOO.
"GHAZI RASHID IS ALIVE."
"ASCENSION IS IN PLAY."
AND THEN INSTRUCTIONS TO MEET HERE TODAY.
THAT'S THE ON

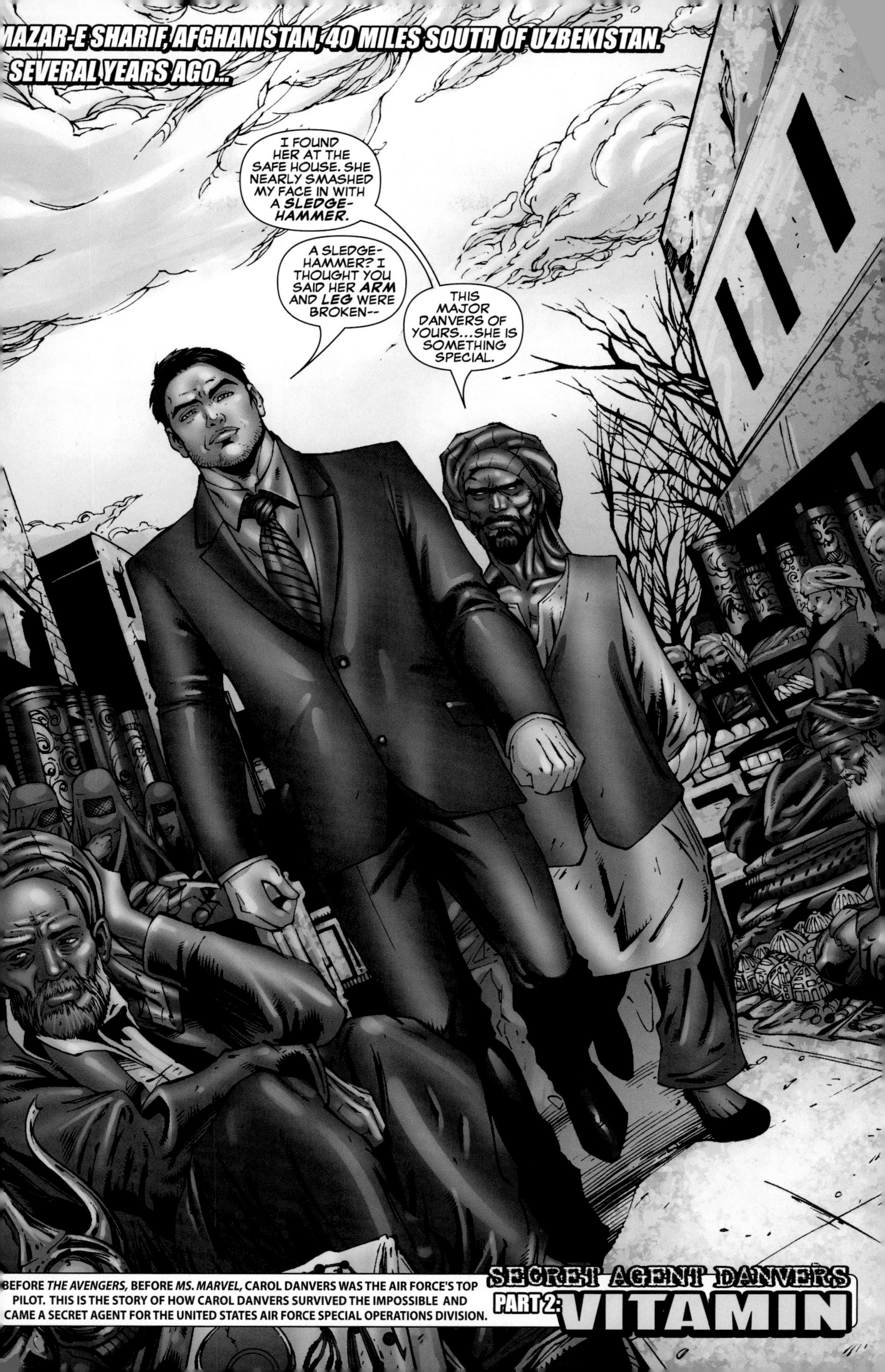

MAZAR-E SHARIF, AFGHANISTAN, 40 MILES SOUTH OF UZBEKISTAN.
SEVERAL YEARS AGO...
I FOUND HER AT THE SAFE HOUSE. SHE NEARLY SMASHED MY FACE IN WITH A *SLEDGE-HAMMER.*
A SLEDGE-HAMMER? I THOUGHT YOU SAID HER *ARM* AND *LEG* WERE BROKEN--
THIS MAJOR DANVERS OF YOURS...SHE IS SOMETHING SPECIAL.
BEFORE *THE AVENGERS*, BEFORE *MS. MARVEL*, CAROL DANVERS WAS THE AIR FORCE'S TOP PILOT. THIS IS THE STORY OF HOW CAROL DANVERS SURVIVED THE IMPOSSIBLE AND CAME A SECRET AGENT FOR THE UNITED STATES AIR FORCE SPECIAL OPERATIONS DIVISION.
SECRET AGENT DANVERS
PART 2: VITAMIN

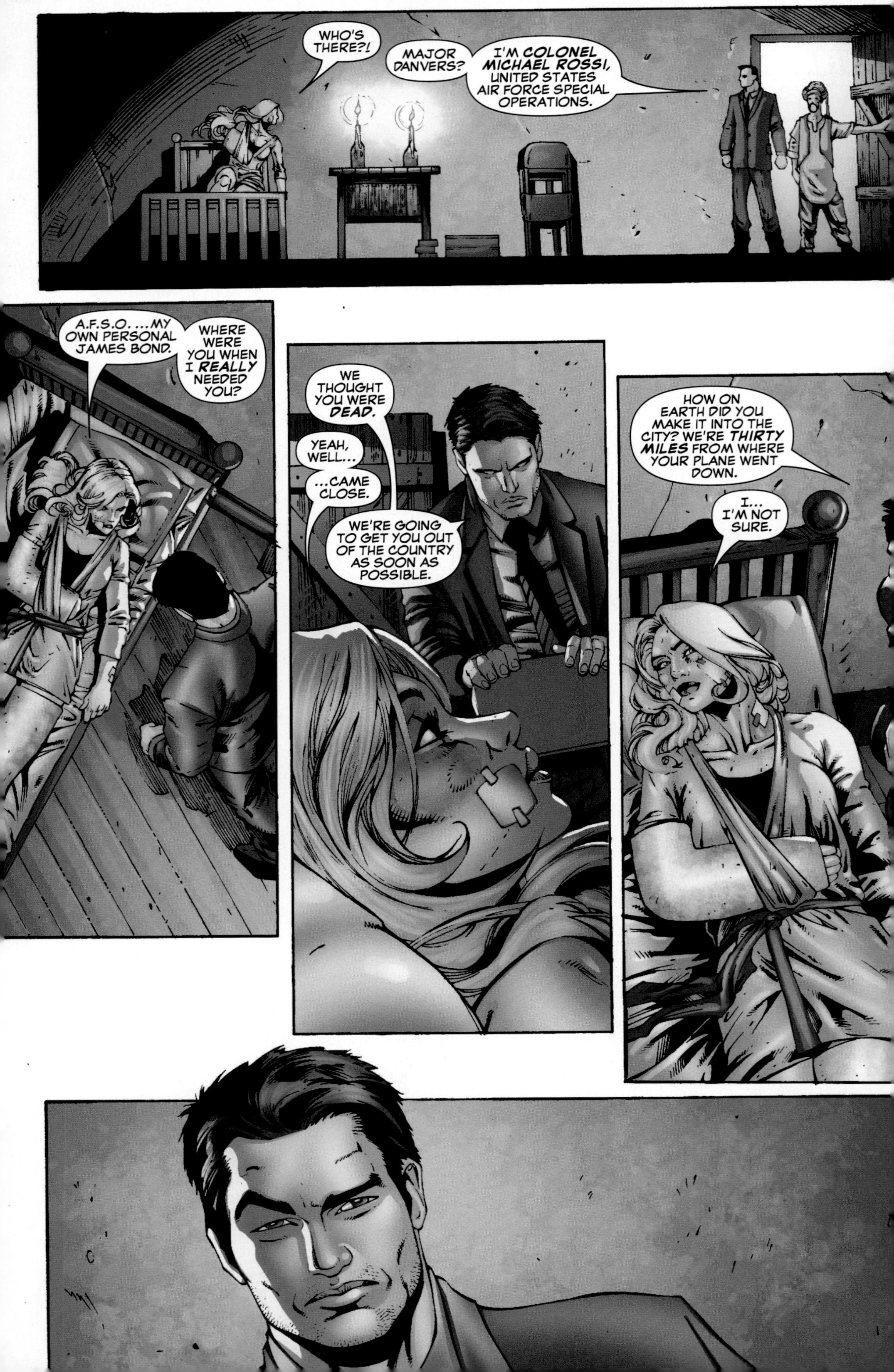
WHO'S THERE?!
MAJOR DANVERS?
I'M COLONEL MICHAEL ROSSI, UNITED STATES AIR FORCE SPECIAL OPERATIONS.
A.F.S.O. ...MY OWN PERSONAL JAMES BOND.
WHERE WERE YOU WHEN I REALLY NEEDED YOU?
WE THOUGHT YOU WERE DEAD.
YEAH, WELL...
...CAME CLOSE.
WE'RE GOING TO GET YOU OUT OF THE COUNTRY AS SOON AS POSSIBLE.
HOW ON EARTH DID YOU MAKE IT INTO THE CITY? WE'RE THIRTY MILES FROM WHERE YOUR PLANE WENT DOWN.
I... I'M NOT SURE.

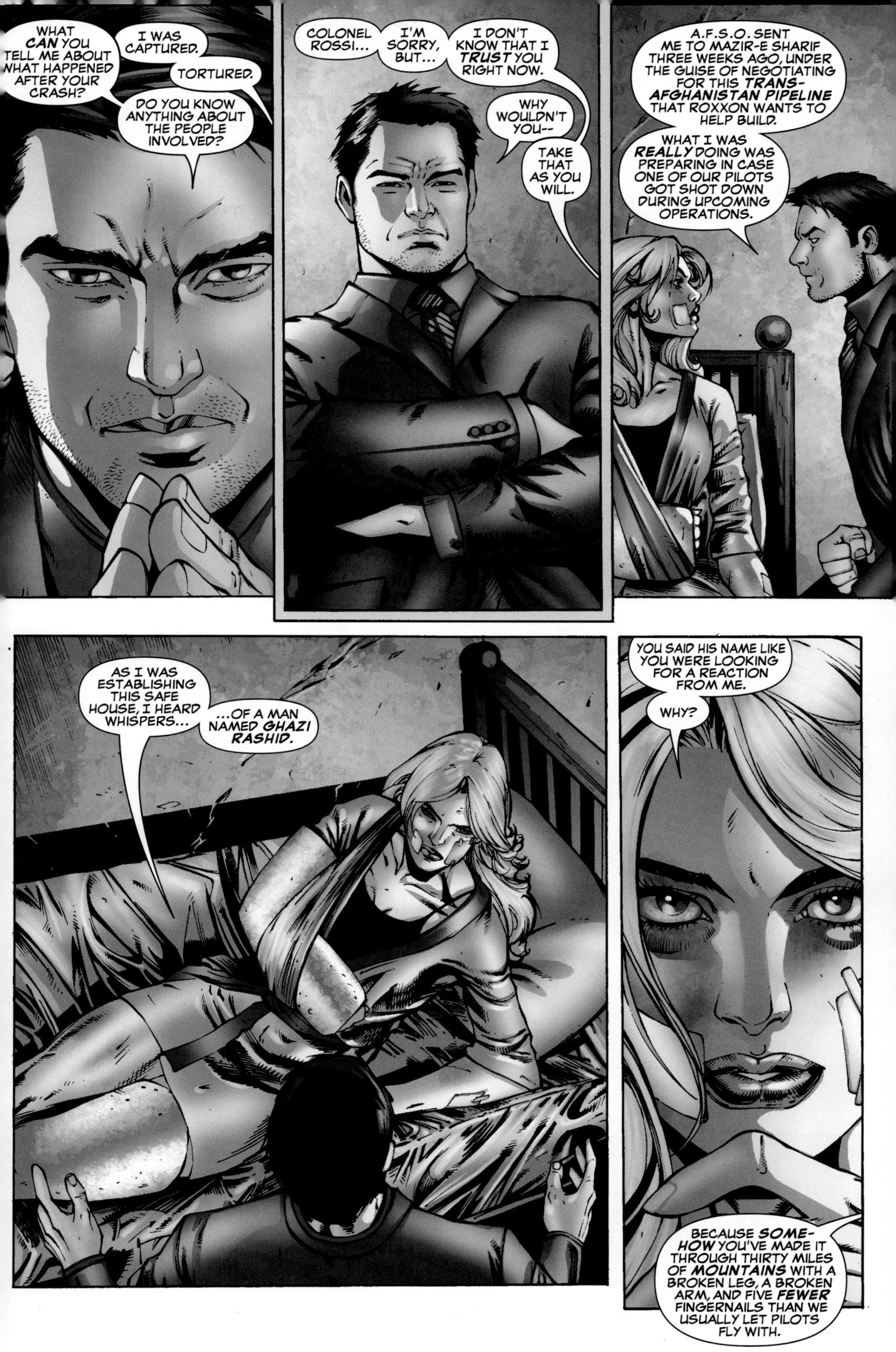
WHAT **CAN** YOU TELL ME ABOUT WHAT HAPPENED AFTER YOUR CRASH?
I WAS CAPTURED.
TORTURED.
DO YOU KNOW ANYTHING ABOUT THE PEOPLE INVOLVED?
COLONEL ROSSI...
I'M SORRY, BUT...
I DON'T KNOW THAT I **TRUST** YOU RIGHT NOW.
WHY WOULDN'T YOU--
TAKE THAT AS YOU WILL.
A.F.S.O. SENT ME TO MAZIR-E SHARIF THREE WEEKS AGO, UNDER THE GUISE OF NEGOTIATING FOR THIS **TRANS-AFGHANISTAN PIPELINE** THAT ROXXON WANTS TO HELP BUILD.
WHAT I WAS **REALLY** DOING WAS PREPARING IN CASE ONE OF OUR PILOTS GOT SHOT DOWN DURING UPCOMING OPERATIONS.
AS I WAS ESTABLISHING THIS SAFE HOUSE, I HEARD WHISPERS...
...OF A MAN NAMED **GHAZI RASHID.**
YOU SAID HIS NAME LIKE YOU WERE LOOKING FOR A REACTION FROM ME.
WHY?
BECAUSE **SOME-HOW** YOU'VE MADE IT THROUGH THIRTY MILES OF **MOUNTAINS** WITH A BROKEN LEG, A BROKEN ARM, AND FIVE **FEWER** FINGERNAILS THAN WE USUALLY LET PILOTS FLY WITH.

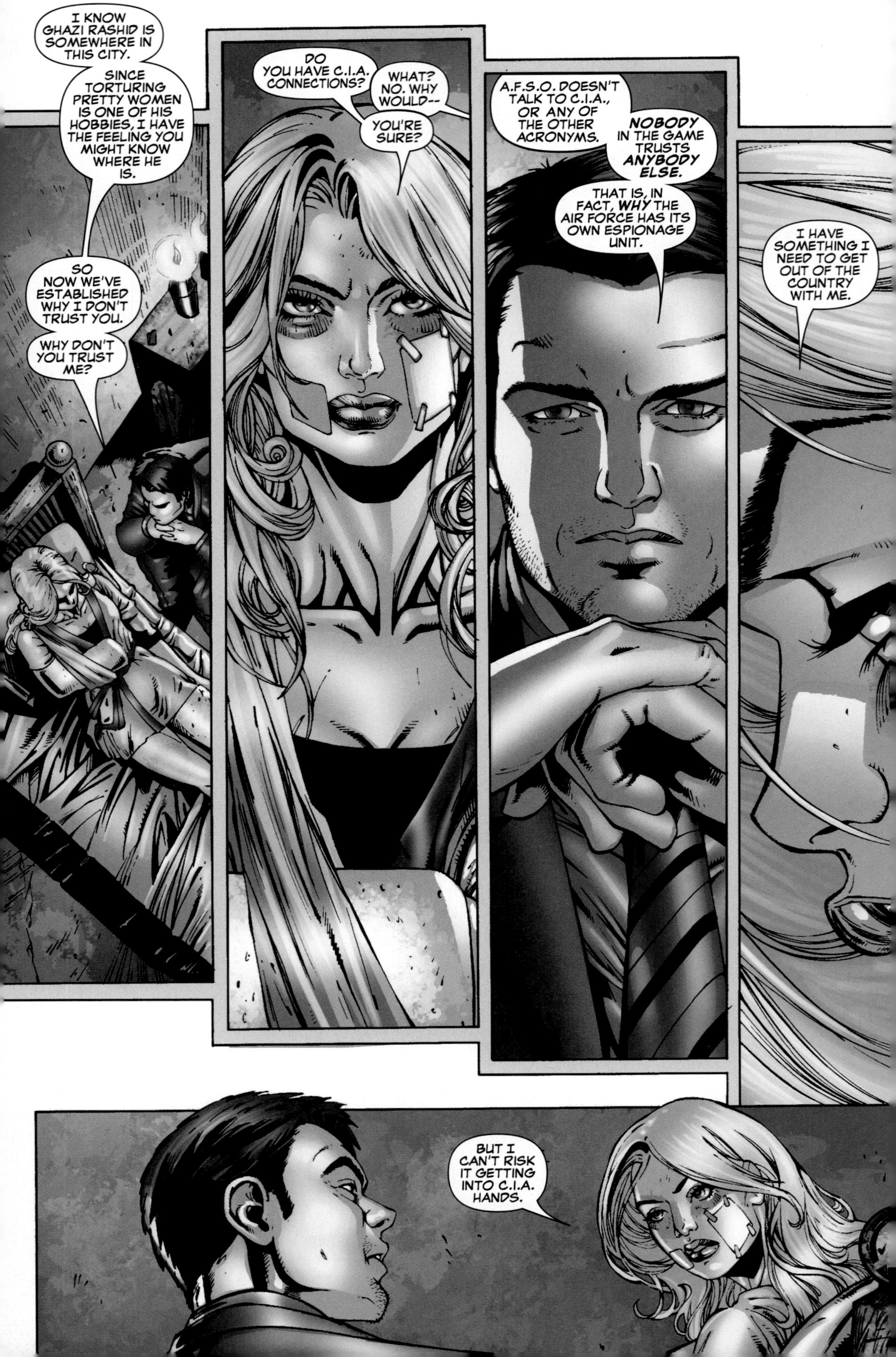
I KNOW GHAZI RASHID IS SOMEWHERE IN THIS CITY.
SINCE TORTURING PRETTY WOMEN IS ONE OF HIS HOBBIES, I HAVE THE FEELING YOU MIGHT KNOW WHERE HE IS.
SO NOW WE'VE ESTABLISHED WHY I DON'T TRUST YOU.
WHY DON'T YOU TRUST ME?
DO YOU HAVE C.I.A. CONNECTIONS?
WHAT? NO. WHY WOULD--
YOU'RE SURE?
A.F.S.O. DOESN'T TALK TO C.I.A., OR ANY OF THE OTHER ACRONYMS.
NOBODY IN THE GAME TRUSTS **ANYBODY ELSE.**
THAT IS, IN FACT, **WHY** THE AIR FORCE HAS ITS OWN ESPIONAGE UNIT.
I HAVE SOMETHING I NEED TO GET OUT OF THE COUNTRY WITH ME.
BUT I CAN'T RISK IT GETTING INTO C.I.A. HANDS.

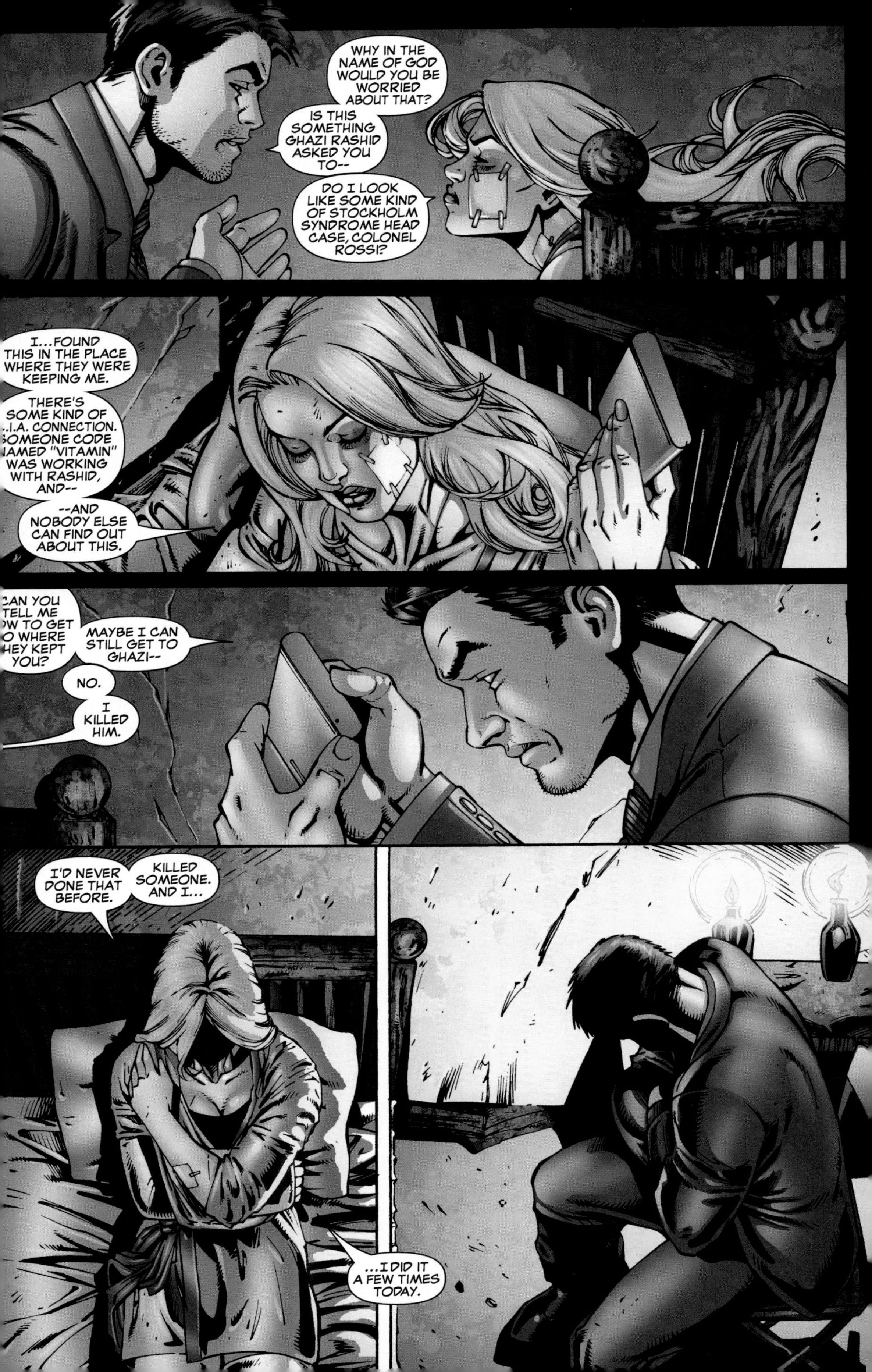
WHY IN THE NAME OF GOD WOULD YOU BE WORRIED ABOUT THAT?
IS THIS SOMETHING GHAZI RASHID ASKED YOU TO--
DO I LOOK LIKE SOME KIND OF STOCKHOLM SYNDROME HEAD CASE, COLONEL ROSSI?
I...FOUND THIS IN THE PLACE WHERE THEY WERE KEEPING ME.
THERE'S SOME KIND OF .I.A. CONNECTION. OMEONE CODE NAMED "VITAMIN" WAS WORKING WITH RASHID, AND--
--AND NOBODY ELSE CAN FIND OUT ABOUT THIS.
CAN YOU TELL ME W TO GET O WHERE HEY KEPT YOU?
MAYBE I CAN STILL GET TO GHAZI--
NO.
I KILLED HIM.
I'D NEVER DONE THAT BEFORE.
KILLED SOMEONE. AND I...
...I DID IT A FEW TIMES TODAY.

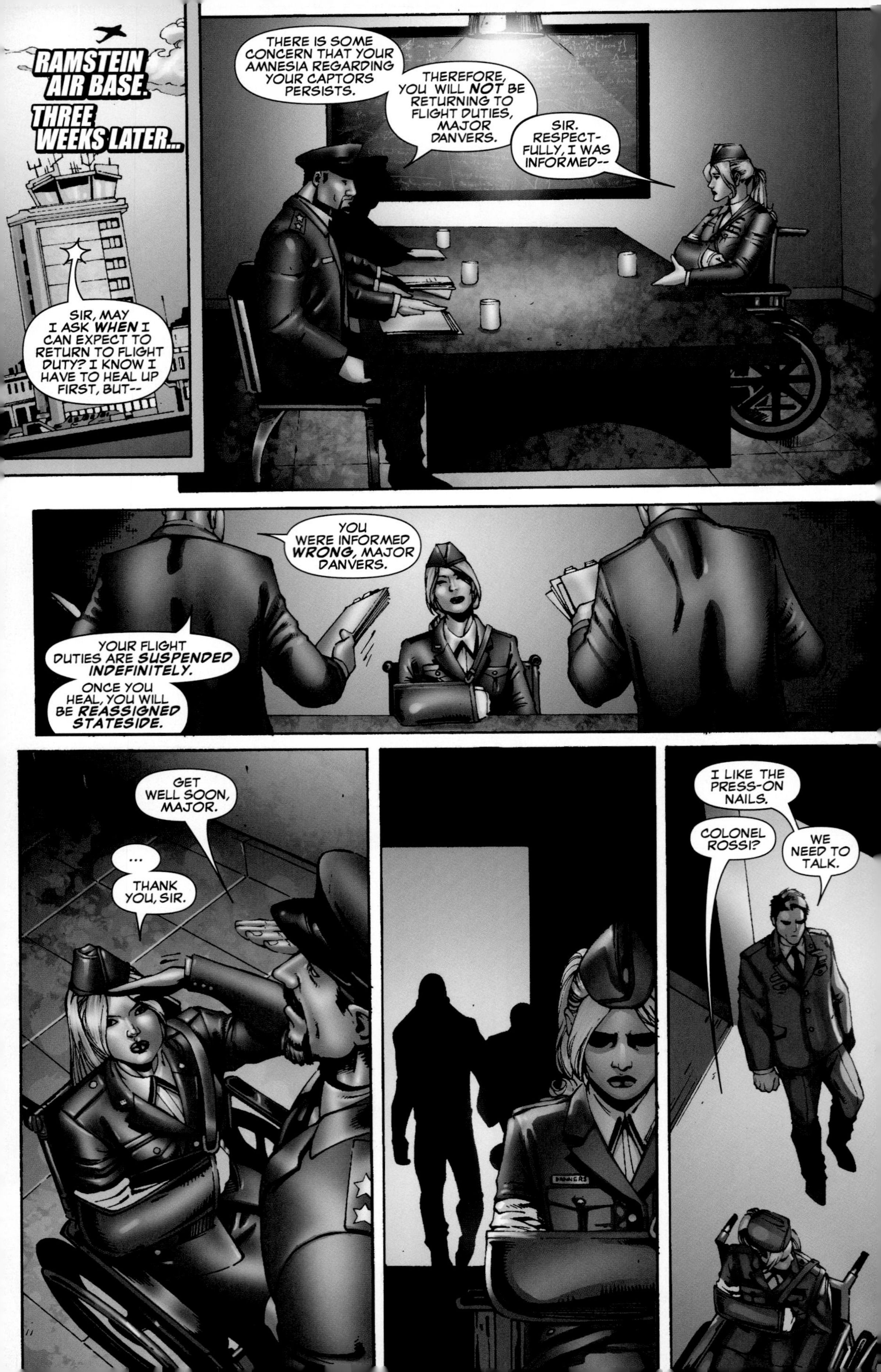
RAMSTEIN AIR BASE.
THREE WEEKS LATER...
SIR, MAY I ASK WHEN I CAN EXPECT TO RETURN TO FLIGHT DUTY? I KNOW I HAVE TO HEAL UP FIRST, BUT--
THERE IS SOME CONCERN THAT YOUR AMNESIA REGARDING YOUR CAPTORS PERSISTS.
THEREFORE, YOU WILL NOT BE RETURNING TO FLIGHT DUTIES, MAJOR DANVERS.
SIR. RESPECT-FULLY, I WAS INFORMED--
YOU WERE INFORMED WRONG, MAJOR DANVERS.
YOUR FLIGHT DUTIES ARE SUSPENDED INDEFINITELY.
ONCE YOU HEAL, YOU WILL BE REASSIGNED STATESIDE.
GET WELL SOON, MAJOR.
...
THANK YOU, SIR.
I LIKE THE PRESS-ON NAILS.
COLONEL ROSSI?
WE NEED TO TALK.

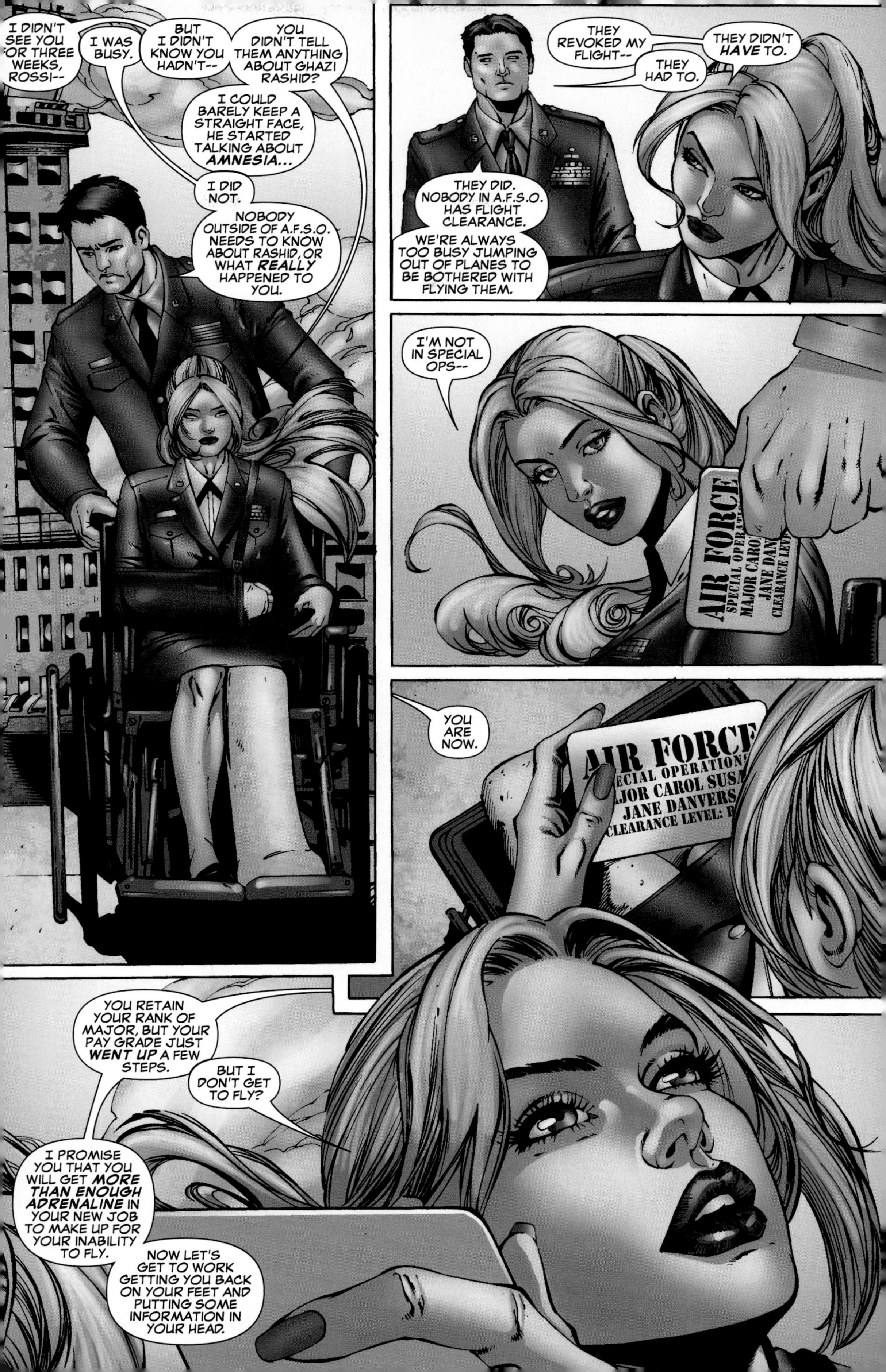

I DIDN'T SEE YOU FOR THREE WEEKS, ROSSI--
I WAS BUSY.
BUT I DIDN'T KNOW YOU HADN'T--
YOU DIDN'T TELL THEM ANYTHING ABOUT GHAZI RASHID?
I COULD BARELY KEEP A STRAIGHT FACE, HE STARTED TALKING ABOUT AMNESIA...
I DID NOT.
NOBODY OUTSIDE OF A.F.S.O. NEEDS TO KNOW ABOUT RASHID, OR WHAT REALLY HAPPENED TO YOU.
THEY REVOKED MY FLIGHT--
THEY DIDN'T HAVE TO.
THEY HAD TO.
THEY DID. NOBODY IN A.F.S.O. HAS FLIGHT CLEARANCE.
WE'RE ALWAYS TOO BUSY JUMPING OUT OF PLANES TO BE BOTHERED WITH FLYING THEM.
I'M NOT IN SPECIAL OPS--
YOU ARE NOW.
AIR FORCE
SPECIAL OPERATIONS
MAJOR CAROL SUSA
JANE DANVERS
CLEARANCE LEVEL: R
YOU RETAIN YOUR RANK OF MAJOR, BUT YOUR PAY GRADE JUST WENT UP A FEW STEPS.
BUT I DON'T GET TO FLY?
I PROMISE YOU THAT YOU WILL GET MORE THAN ENOUGH ADRENALINE IN YOUR NEW JOB TO MAKE UP FOR YOUR INABILITY TO FLY.
NOW LET'S GET TO WORK GETTING YOU BACK ON YOUR FEET AND PUTTING SOME INFORMATION IN YOUR HEAD.

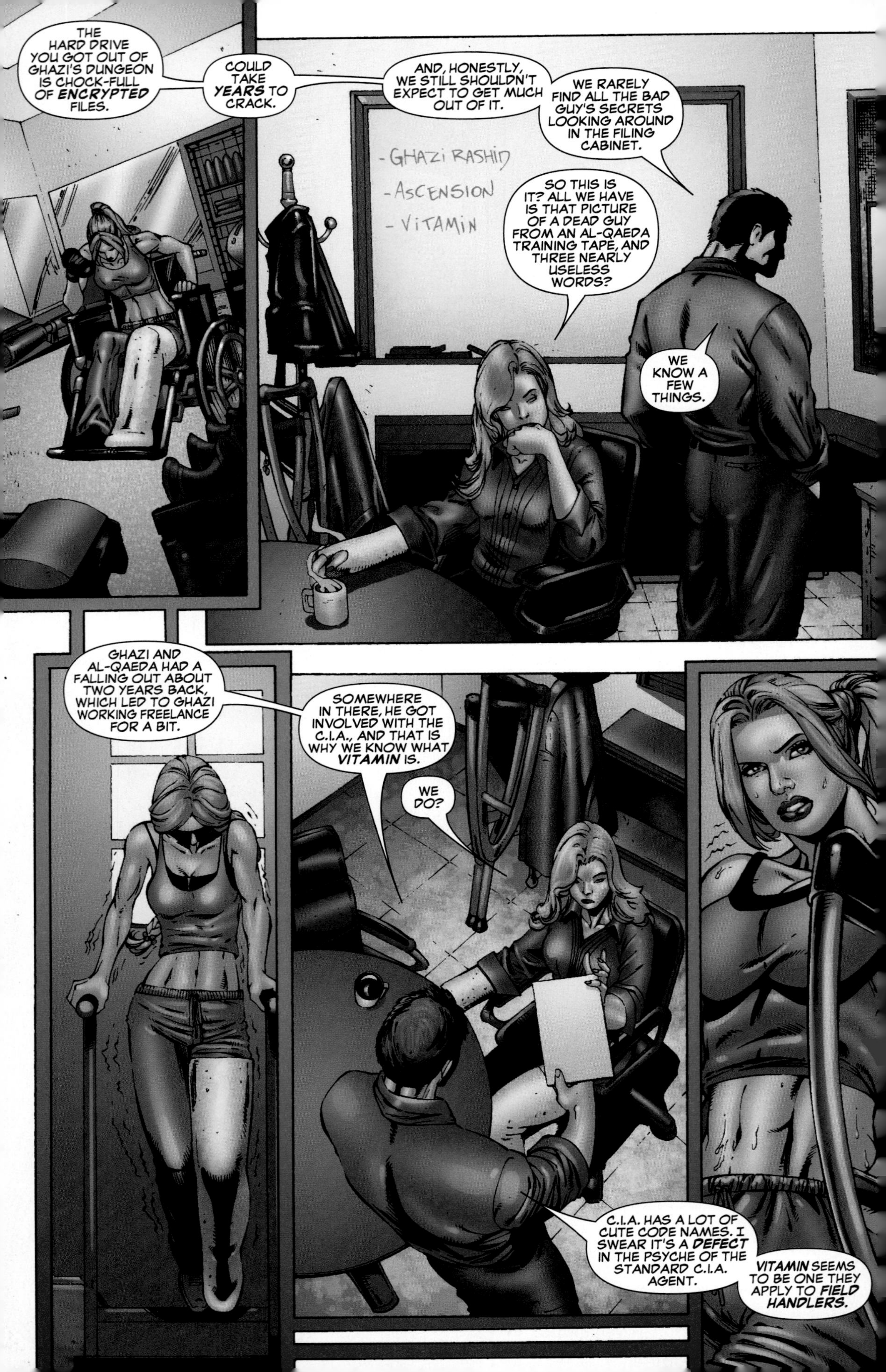

THE HARD DRIVE YOU GOT OUT OF GHAZI'S DUNGEON IS CHOCK-FULL OF ENCRYPTED FILES.
COULD TAKE YEARS TO CRACK.
AND, HONESTLY, WE STILL SHOULDN'T EXPECT TO GET MUCH OUT OF IT.
WE RARELY FIND ALL THE BAD GUY'S SECRETS LOOKING AROUND IN THE FILING CABINET.
-GHAZI RASHID
-ASCENSION
-VITAMIN
SO THIS IS IT? ALL WE HAVE IS THAT PICTURE OF A DEAD GUY FROM AN AL-QAEDA TRAINING TAPE, AND THREE NEARLY USELESS WORDS?
WE KNOW A FEW THINGS.
GHAZI AND AL-QAEDA HAD A FALLING OUT ABOUT TWO YEARS BACK, WHICH LED TO GHAZI WORKING FREELANCE FOR A BIT.
SOMEWHERE IN THERE, HE GOT INVOLVED WITH THE C.I.A., AND THAT IS WHY WE KNOW WHAT VITAMIN IS.
WE DO?
C.I.A. HAS A LOT OF CUTE CODE NAMES. I SWEAR IT'S A DEFECT IN THE PSYCHE OF THE STANDARD C.I.A. AGENT.
VITAMIN SEEMS TO BE ONE THEY APPLY TO FIELD HANDLERS.

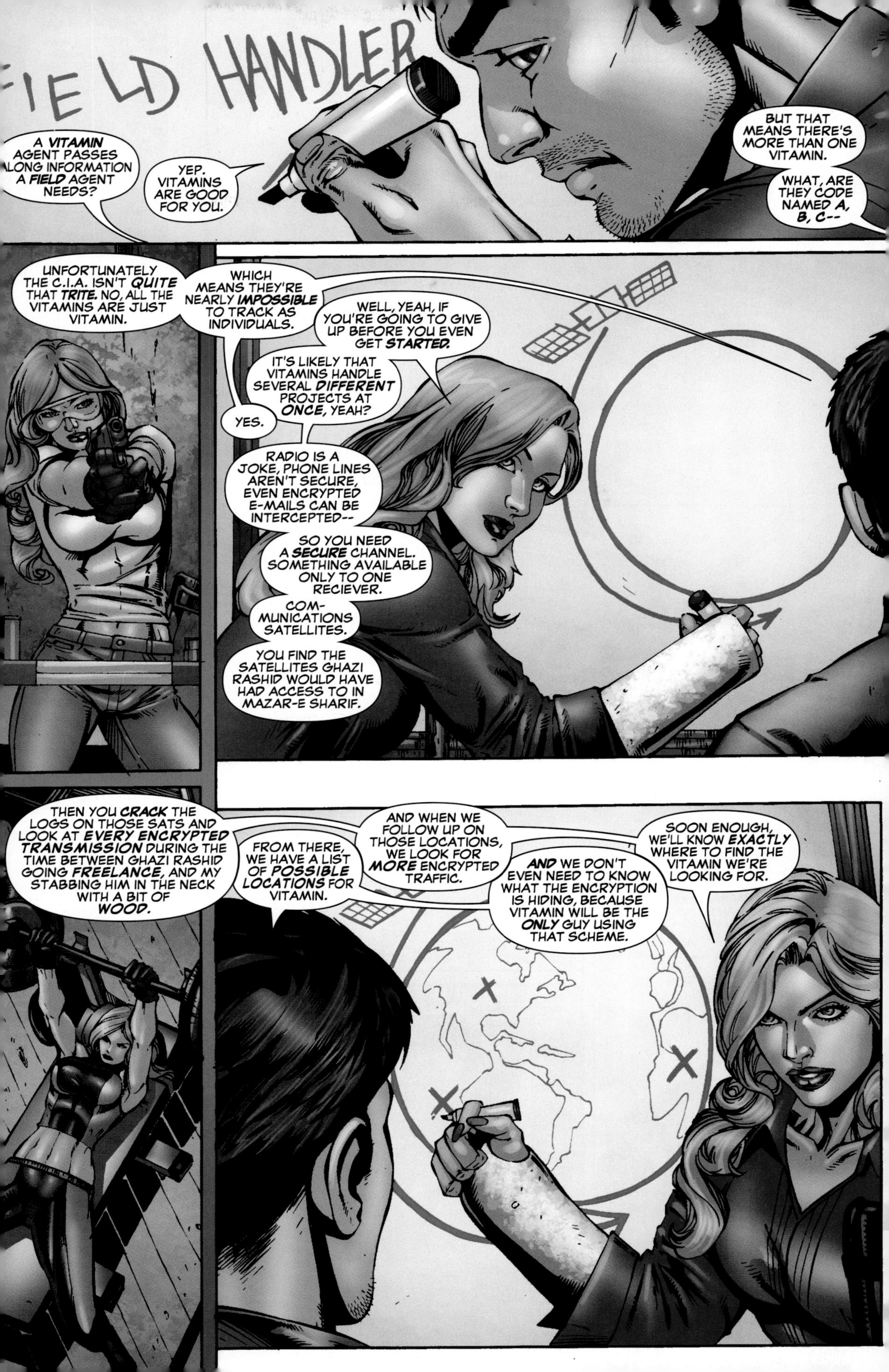
FIELD HANDLER
A VITAMIN AGENT PASSES ALONG INFORMATION A FIELD AGENT NEEDS?
YEP. VITAMINS ARE GOOD FOR YOU.
BUT THAT MEANS THERE'S MORE THAN ONE VITAMIN.
WHAT, ARE THEY CODE NAMED A, B, C--
UNFORTUNATELY THE C.I.A. ISN'T QUITE THAT TRITE. NO, ALL THE VITAMINS ARE JUST VITAMIN.
WHICH MEANS THEY'RE NEARLY IMPOSSIBLE TO TRACK AS INDIVIDUALS.
WELL, YEAH, IF YOU'RE GOING TO GIVE UP BEFORE YOU EVEN GET STARTED.
IT'S LIKELY THAT VITAMINS HANDLE SEVERAL DIFFERENT PROJECTS AT ONCE, YEAH?
YES.
RADIO IS A JOKE, PHONE LINES AREN'T SECURE, EVEN ENCRYPTED E-MAILS CAN BE INTERCEPTED--
SO YOU NEED A SECURE CHANNEL. SOMETHING AVAILABLE ONLY TO ONE RECIEVER.
COM-MUNICATIONS SATELLITES.
YOU FIND THE SATELLITES GHAZI RASHID WOULD HAVE HAD ACCESS TO IN MAZAR-E SHARIF.
THEN YOU CRACK THE LOGS ON THOSE SATS AND LOOK AT EVERY ENCRYPTED TRANSMISSION DURING THE TIME BETWEEN GHAZI RASHID GOING FREELANCE, AND MY STABBING HIM IN THE NECK WITH A BIT OF WOOD.
FROM THERE, WE HAVE A LIST OF POSSIBLE LOCATIONS FOR VITAMIN.
AND WHEN WE FOLLOW UP ON THOSE LOCATIONS, WE LOOK FOR MORE ENCRYPTED TRAFFIC.
AND WE DON'T EVEN NEED TO KNOW WHAT THE ENCRYPTION IS HIDING, BECAUSE VITAMIN WILL BE THE ONLY GUY USING THAT SCHEME.
SOON ENOUGH, WE'LL KNOW EXACTLY WHERE TO FIND THE VITAMIN WE'RE LOOKING FOR.

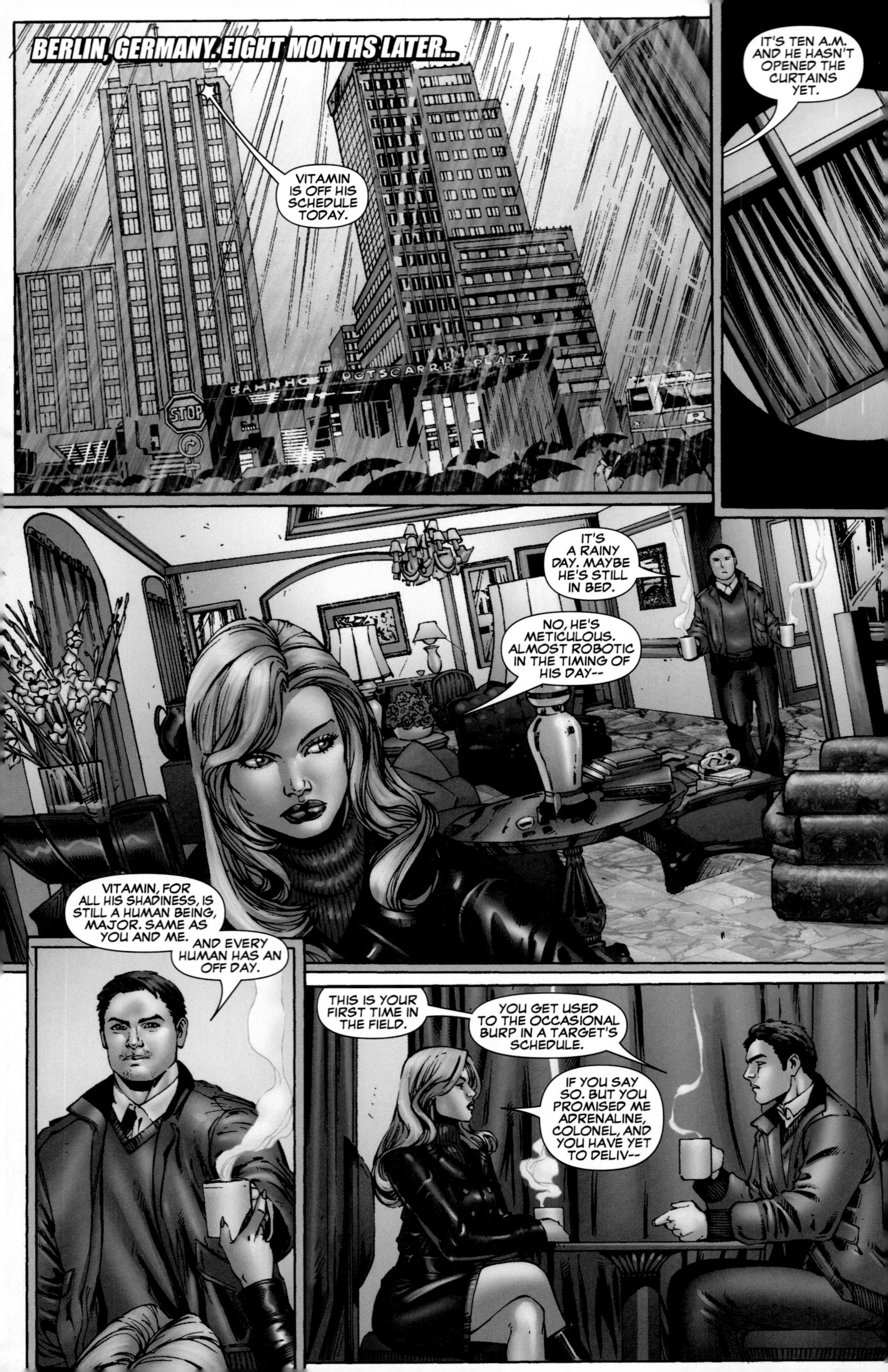
BERLIN, GERMANY. EIGHT MONTHS LATER...
VITAMIN IS OFF HIS SCHEDULE TODAY.
IT'S TEN A.M. AND HE HASN'T OPENED THE CURTAINS YET.
IT'S A RAINY DAY. MAYBE HE'S STILL IN BED.
NO, HE'S METICULOUS. ALMOST ROBOTIC IN THE TIMING OF HIS DAY--
VITAMIN, FOR ALL HIS SHADINESS, IS STILL A HUMAN BEING, MAJOR. SAME AS YOU AND ME.
AND EVERY HUMAN HAS AN OFF DAY.
THIS IS YOUR FIRST TIME IN THE FIELD.
YOU GET USED TO THE OCCASIONAL BURP IN A TARGET'S SCHEDULE.
IF YOU SAY SO. BUT YOU PROMISED ME ADRENALINE, COLONEL, AND YOU HAVE YET TO DELIV--
STOP

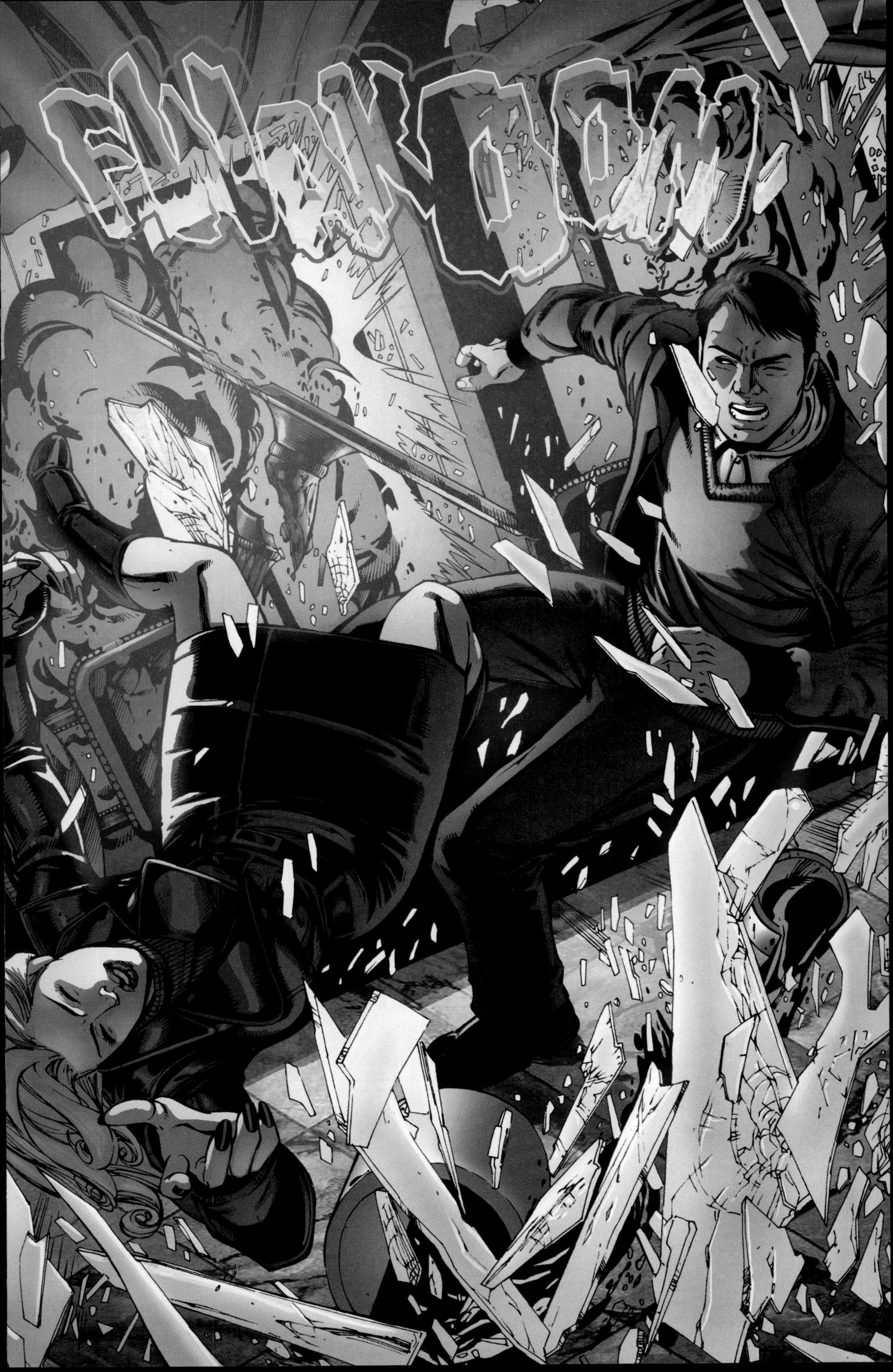
FWAKOOM

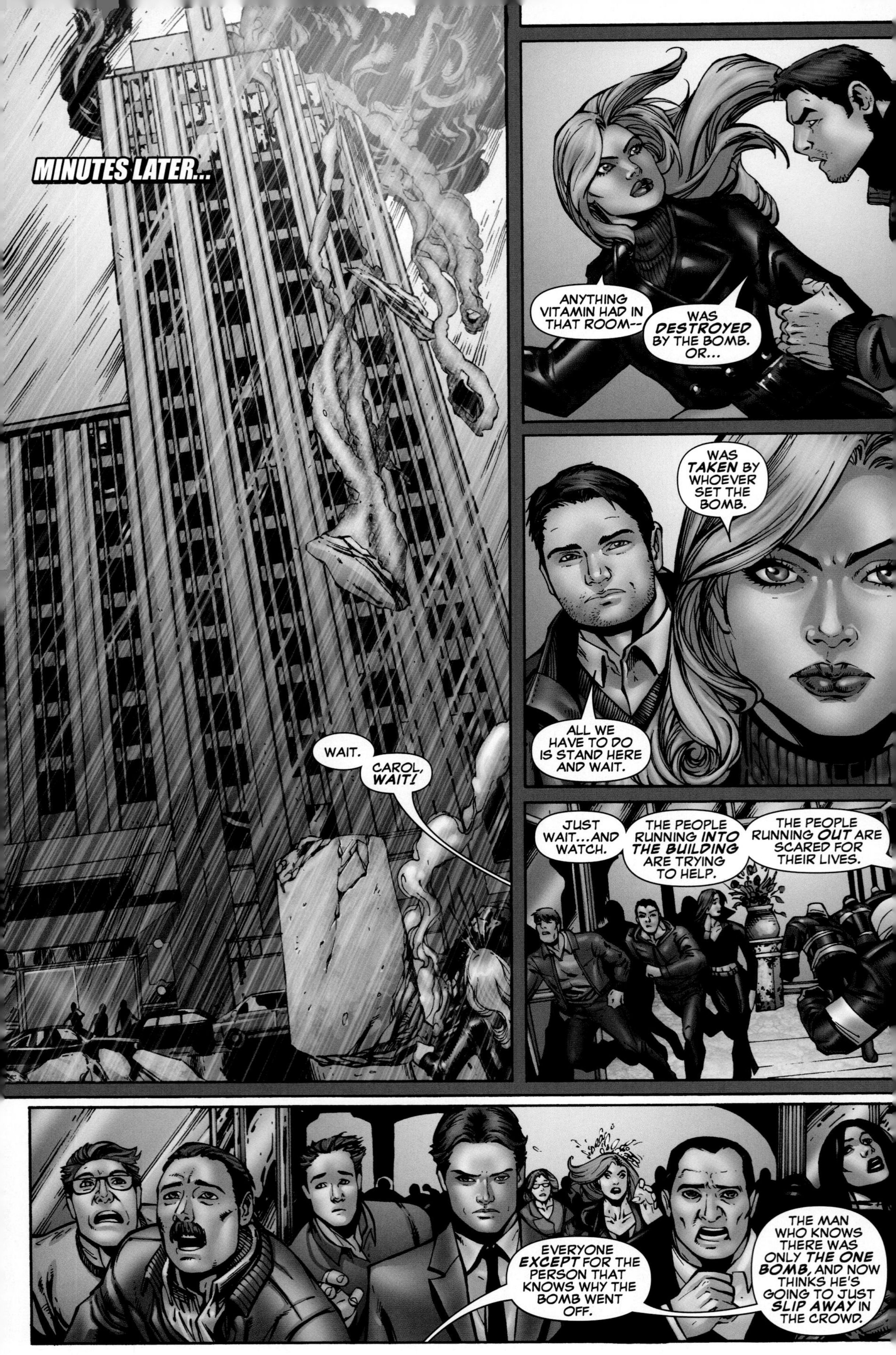
MINUTES LATER...
ANYTHING VITAMIN HAD IN THAT ROOM--
WAS DESTROYED BY THE BOMB. OR...
WAS TAKEN BY WHOEVER SET THE BOMB.
ALL WE HAVE TO DO IS STAND HERE AND WAIT.
WAIT.
CAROL, WAIT!
JUST WAIT...AND WATCH.
THE PEOPLE RUNNING INTO THE BUILDING ARE TRYING TO HELP.
THE PEOPLE RUNNING OUT ARE SCARED FOR THEIR LIVES.
EVERYONE EXCEPT FOR THE PERSON THAT KNOWS WHY THE BOMB WENT OFF.
THE MAN WHO KNOWS THERE WAS ONLY THE ONE BOMB, AND NOW THINKS HE'S GOING TO JUST SLIP AWAY IN THE CROWD.

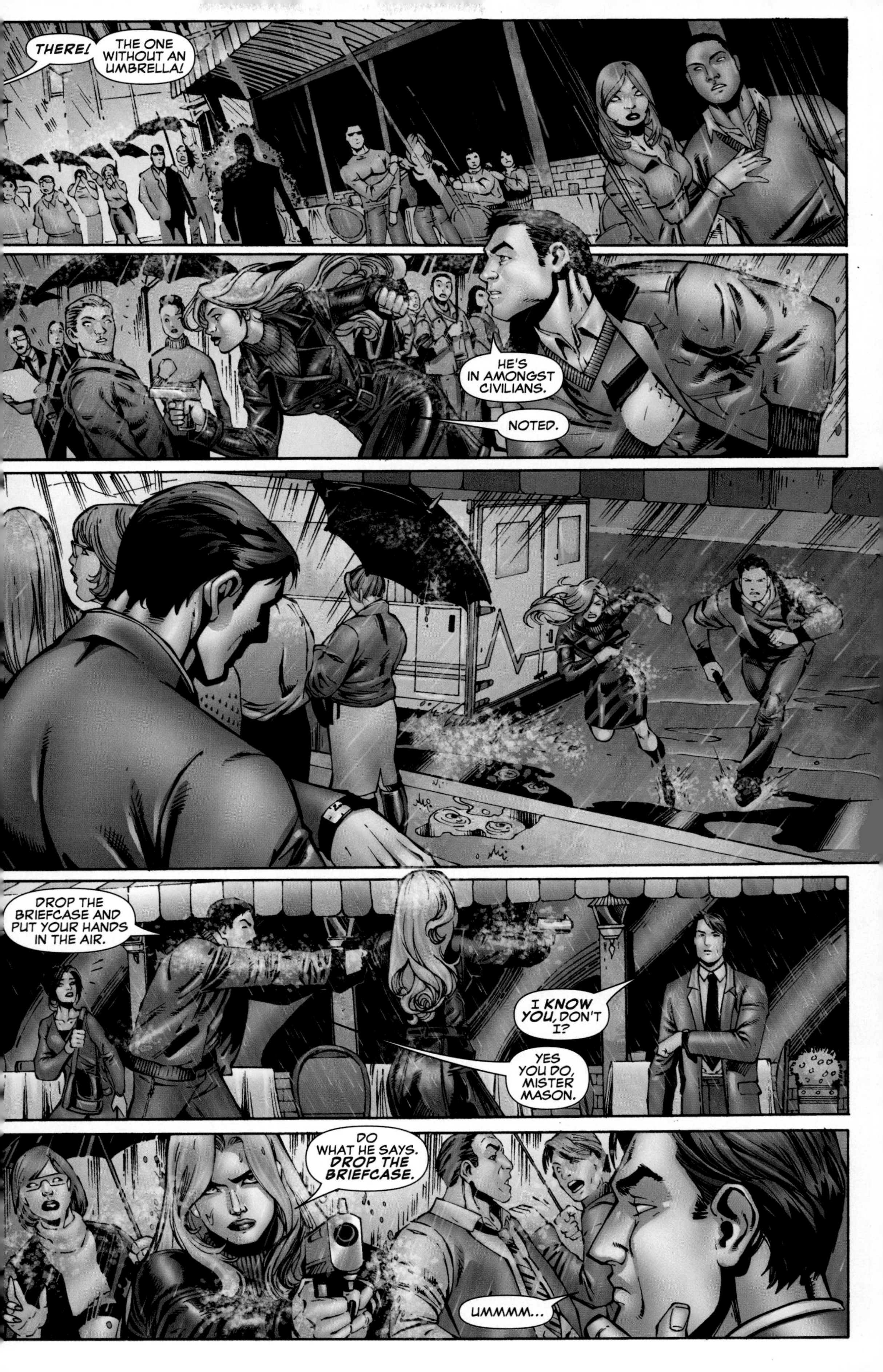
THERE!
THE ONE WITHOUT AN UMBRELLA!
HE'S IN AMONGST CIVILIANS.
NOTED.
DROP THE BRIEFCASE AND PUT YOUR HANDS IN THE AIR.
I KNOW YOU, DON'T I?
YES YOU DO, MISTER MASON.
DO WHAT HE SAYS. DROP THE BRIEFCASE.
UMMMM...

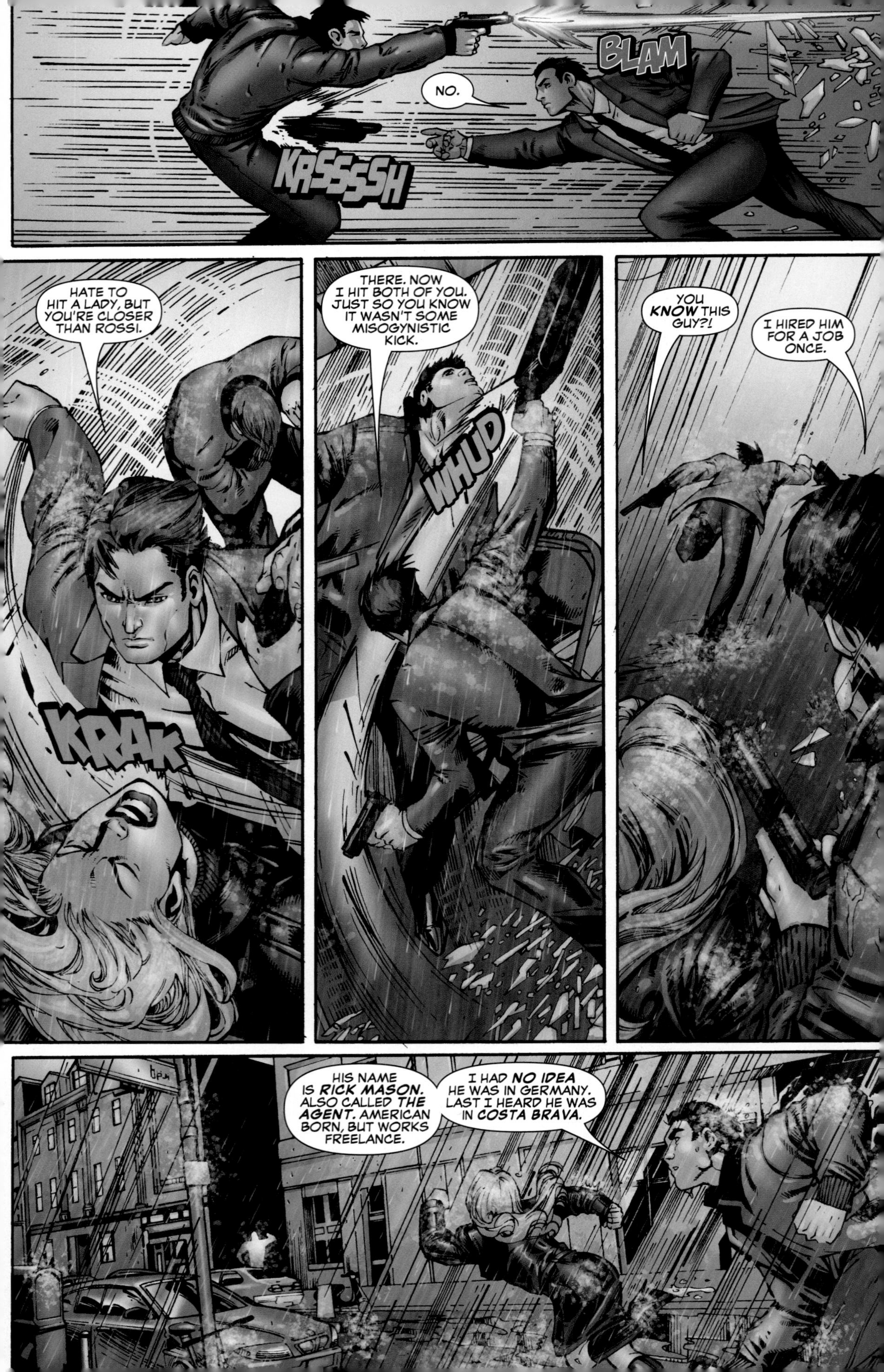
BLAM
NO.
KRSSSSSH
HATE TO HIT A LADY, BUT YOU'RE CLOSER THAN ROSSI.
KRAK
THERE. NOW I HIT BOTH OF YOU. JUST SO YOU KNOW IT WASN'T SOME MISOGYNISTIC KICK.
WHUD
YOU **KNOW** THIS GUY?!
I HIRED HIM FOR A JOB ONCE.
HIS NAME IS ***RICK MASON.*** ALSO CALLED ***THE AGENT.*** AMERICAN BORN, BUT WORKS FREELANCE.
I HAD ***NO IDEA*** HE WAS IN GERMANY. LAST I HEARD HE WAS IN ***COSTA BRAVA.***

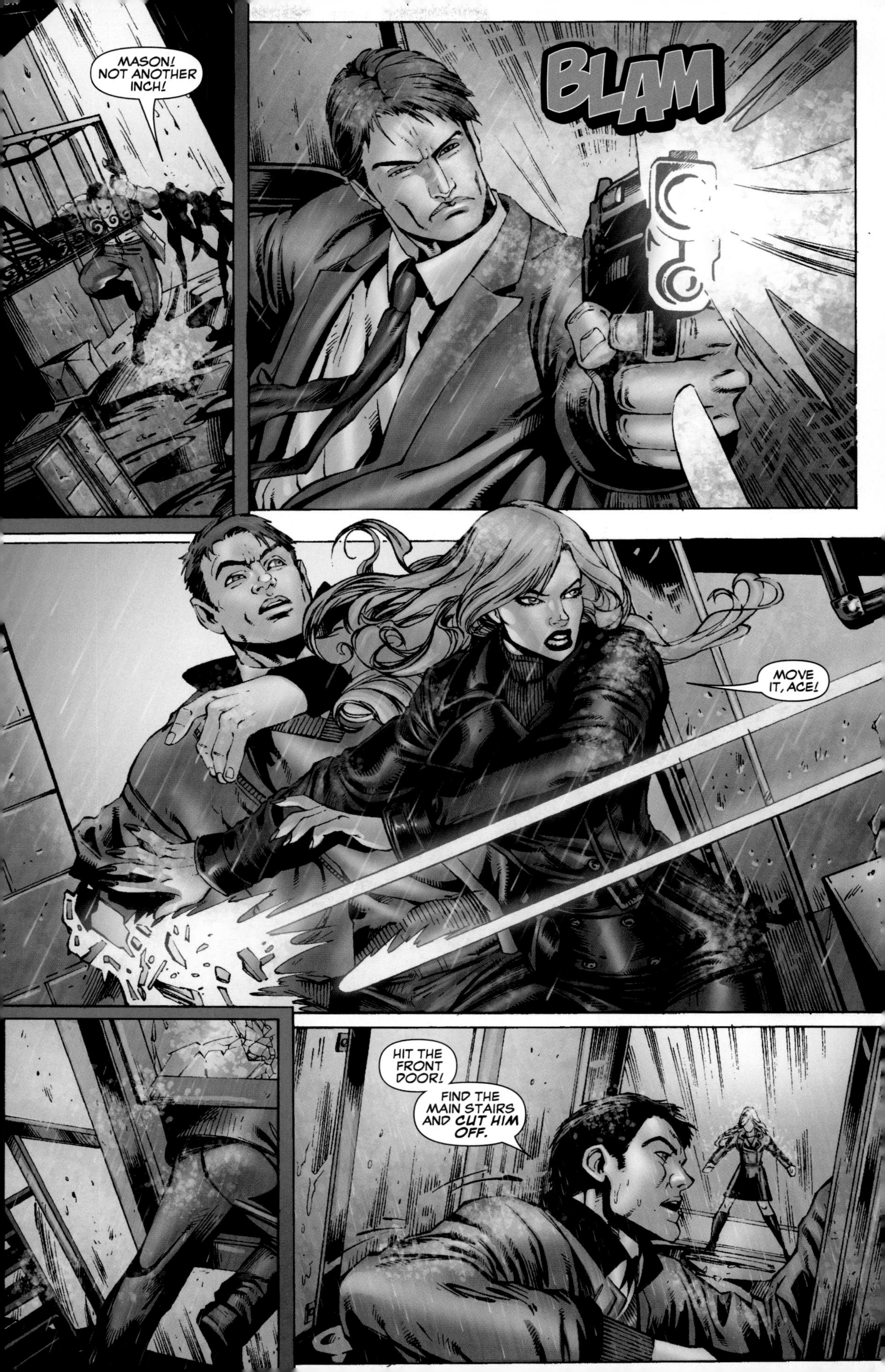
MASON! NOT ANOTHER INCH!
BLAM
MOVE IT, ACE!
HIT THE FRONT DOOR!
FIND THE MAIN STAIRS AND CUT HIM OFF.

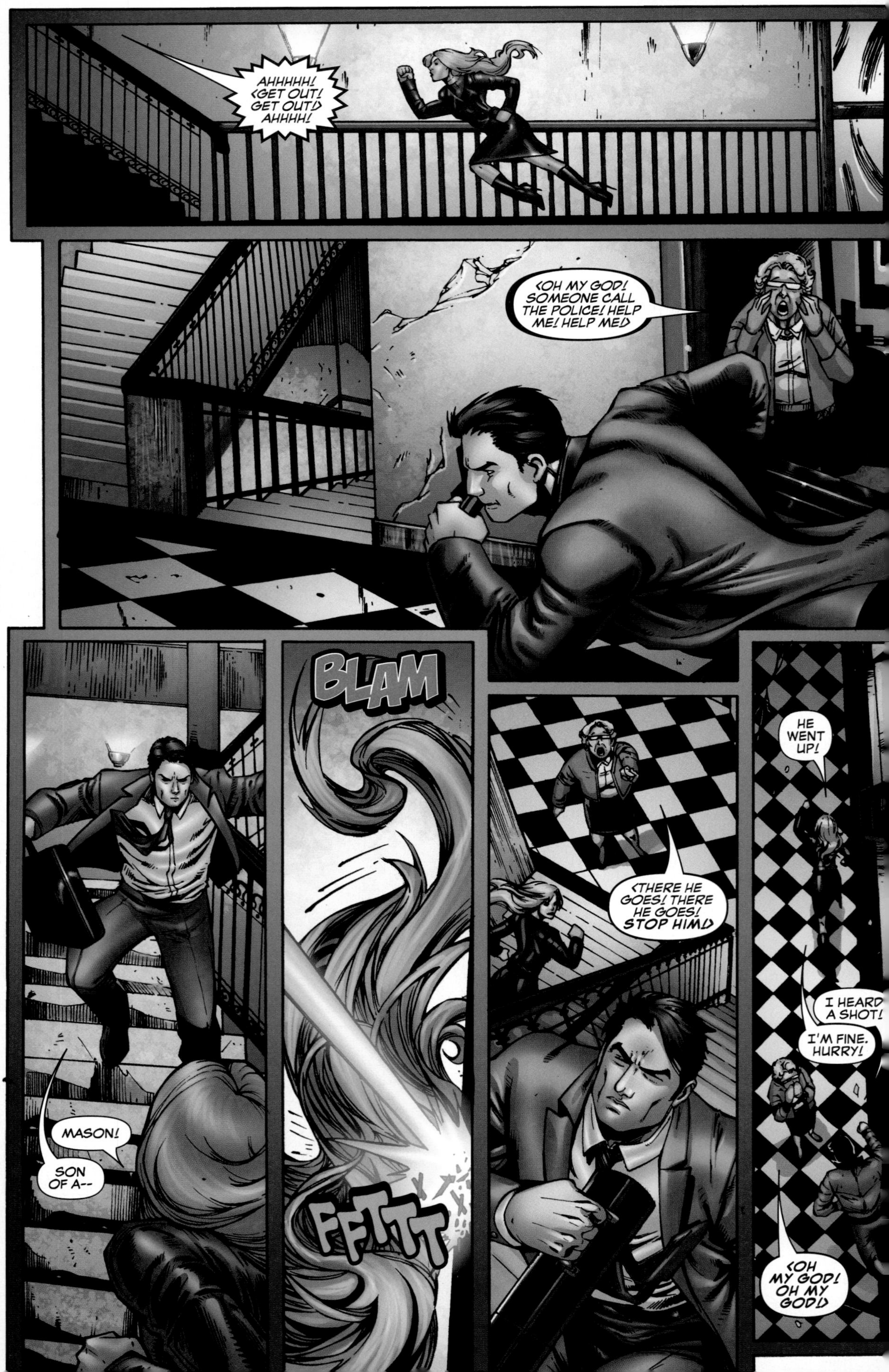
AHHHHH! <GET OUT! GET OUT!> AHHHH!
<OH MY GOD! SOMEONE CALL THE POLICE! HELP ME! HELP ME!>
MASON!
SON OF A--
BLAM
FFTTT
<THERE HE GOES! THERE HE GOES! STOP HIM!>
HE WENT UP!
I HEARD A SHOT!
I'M FINE. HURRY!
<OH MY GOD! OH MY GOD!>

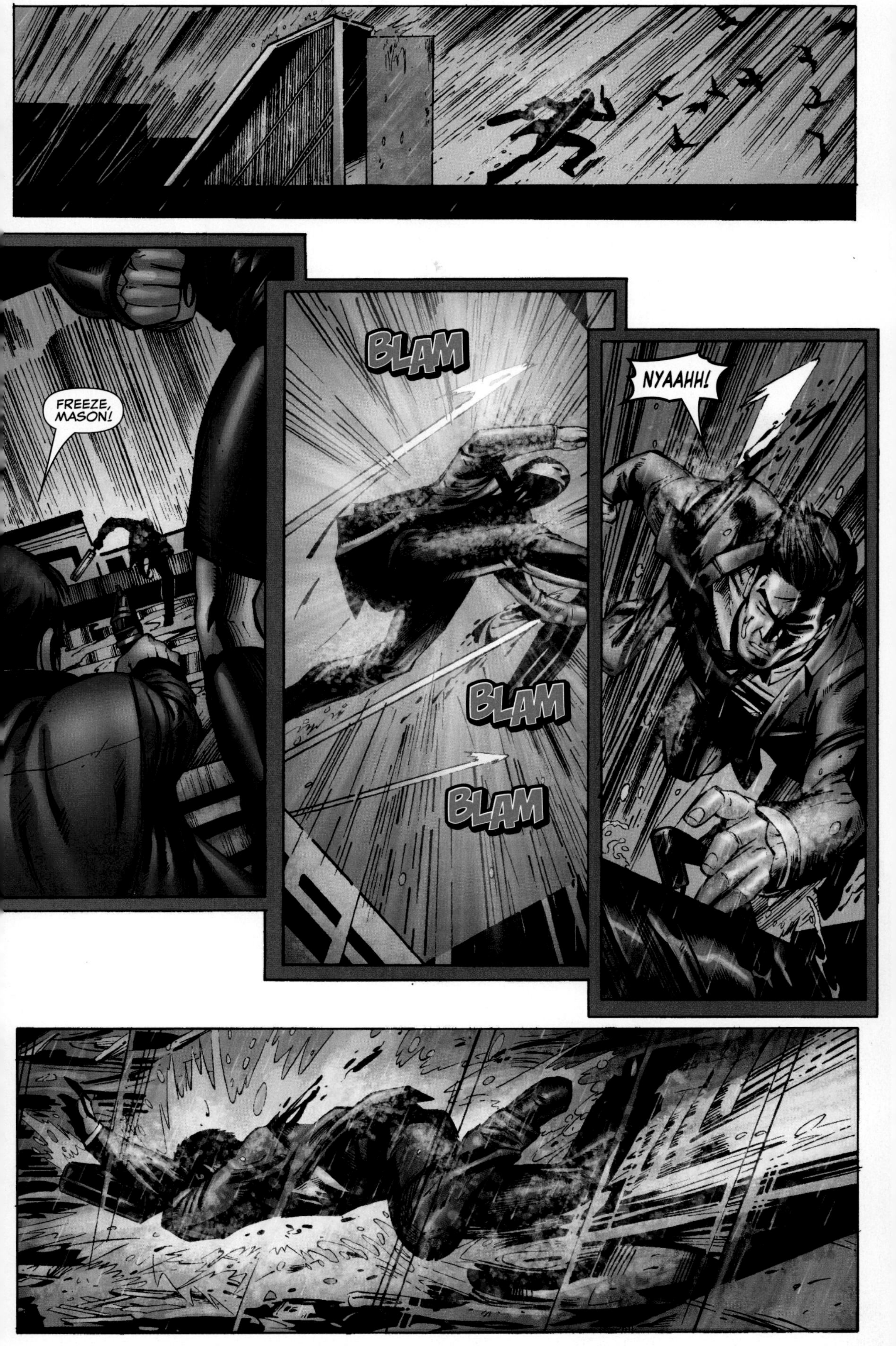
FREEZE, MASON!
BLAM
BLAM
BLAM
NYAAHH!

ALL RIGHT, DAD. WHERE'S YOUR LITTLE TOY?

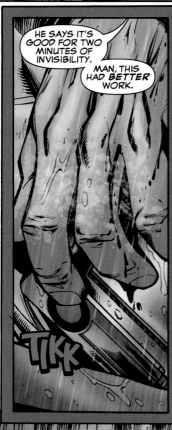

HE SAYS IT'S GOOD FOR TWO MINUTES OF INVISIBILITY.

MAN, THIS HAD BETTER WORK.

TIKK

DAD, I'LL NEVER DOUBT YOU AGAIN.

SON OF A--

HE'S GONE!

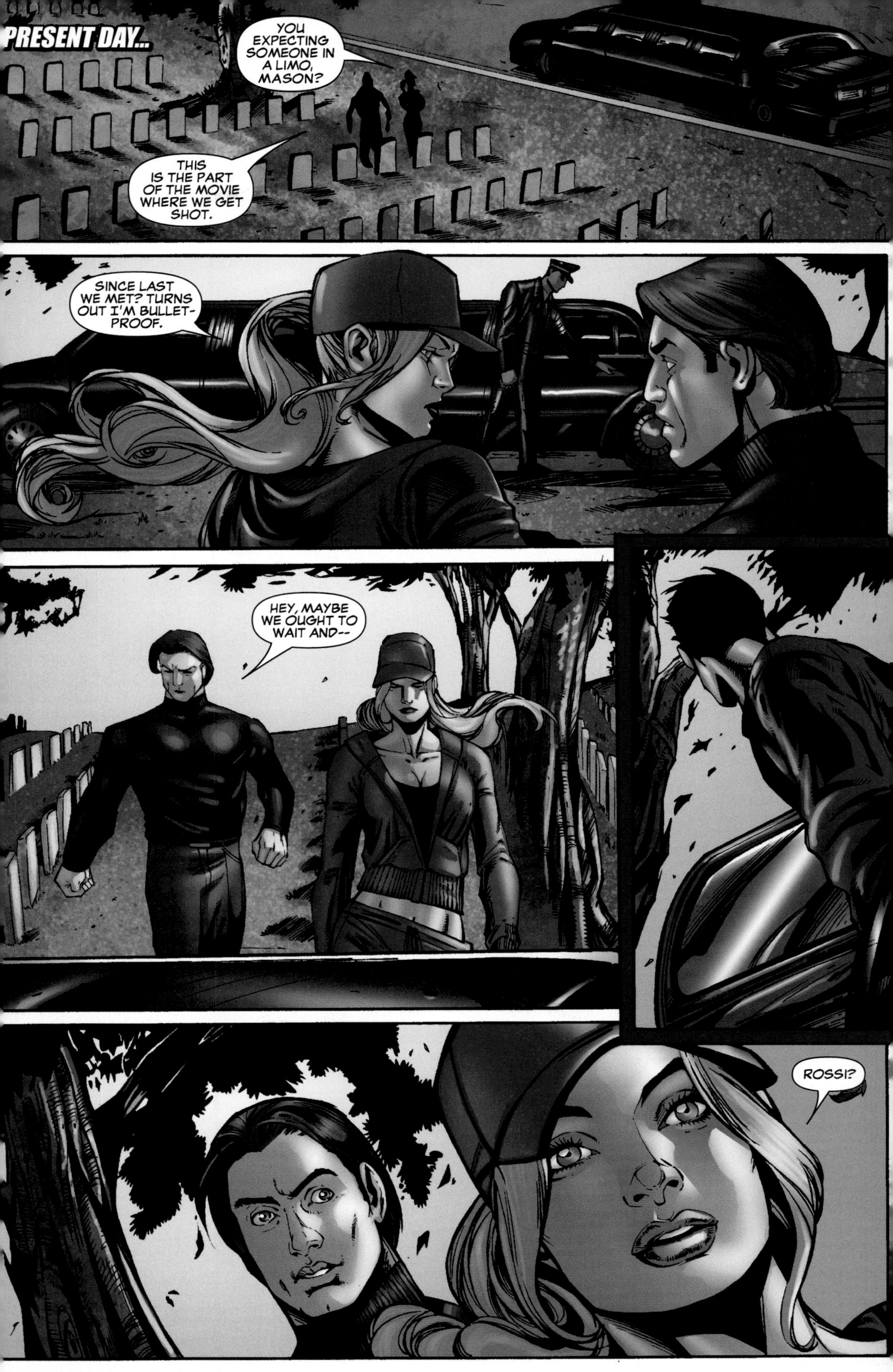
PRESENT DAY...
YOU EXPECTING SOMEONE IN A LIMO, MASON?
THIS IS THE PART OF THE MOVIE WHERE WE GET SHOT.
SINCE LAST WE MET? TURNS OUT I'M BULLET-PROOF.
HEY, MAYBE WE OUGHT TO WAIT AND--
ROSSI?

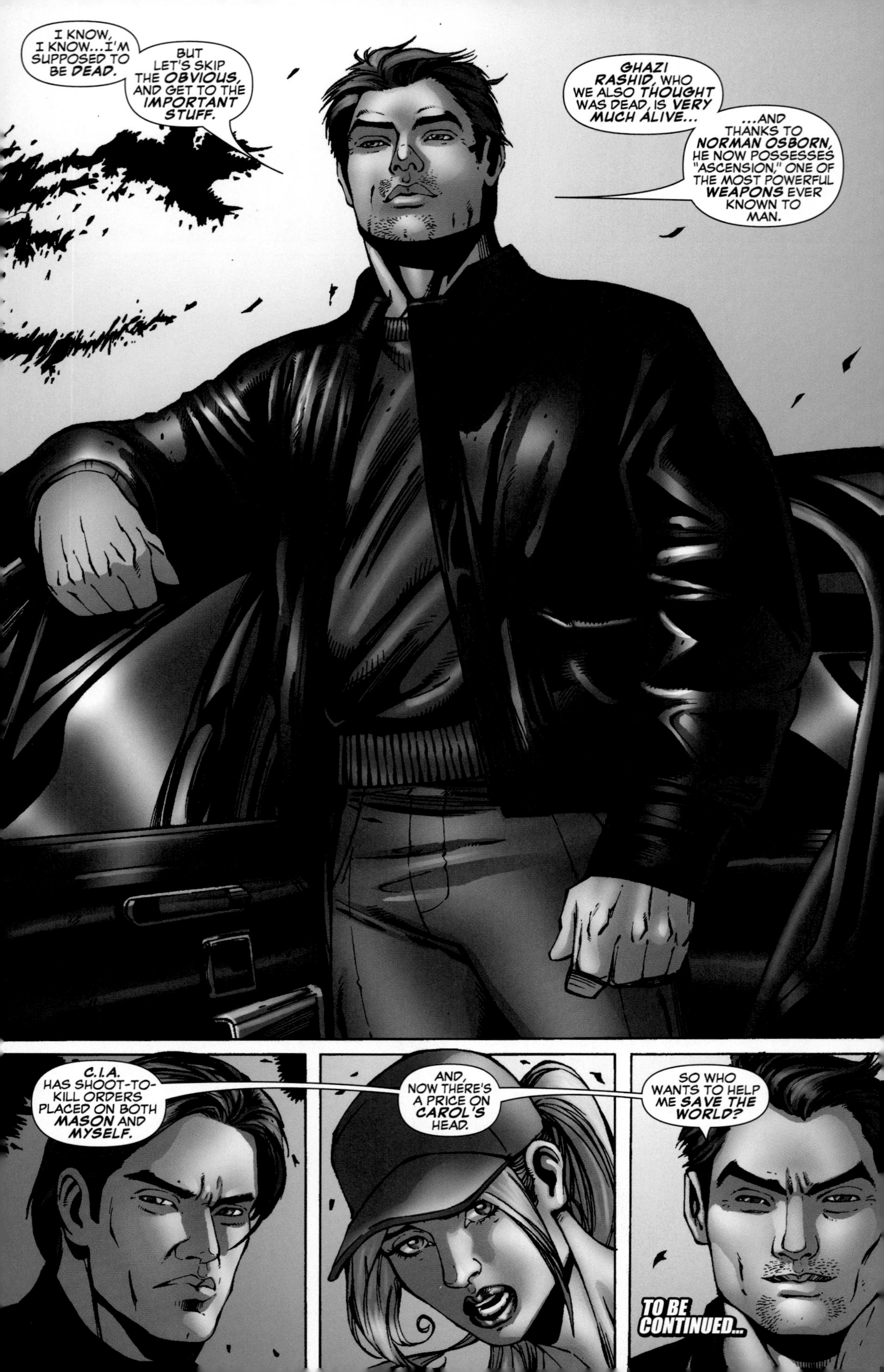
I KNOW, I KNOW...I'M SUPPOSED TO BE DEAD.
BUT LET'S SKIP THE OBVIOUS, AND GET TO THE IMPORTANT STUFF.
GHAZI RASHID, WHO WE ALSO THOUGHT WAS DEAD, IS VERY MUCH ALIVE...
...AND THANKS TO NORMAN OSBORN, HE NOW POSSESSES "ASCENSION," ONE OF THE MOST POWERFUL WEAPONS EVER KNOWN TO MAN.
C.I.A. HAS SHOOT-TO-KILL ORDERS PLACED ON BOTH MASON AND MYSELF.
AND, NOW THERE'S A PRICE ON CAROL'S HEAD.
SO WHO WANTS TO HELP ME SAVE THE WORLD?
TO BE CONTINUED...

EARTH'S MIGHTIEST HERO
MARVEL
CAPTAIN
MARVEL
#1
DECONNICK
SOY

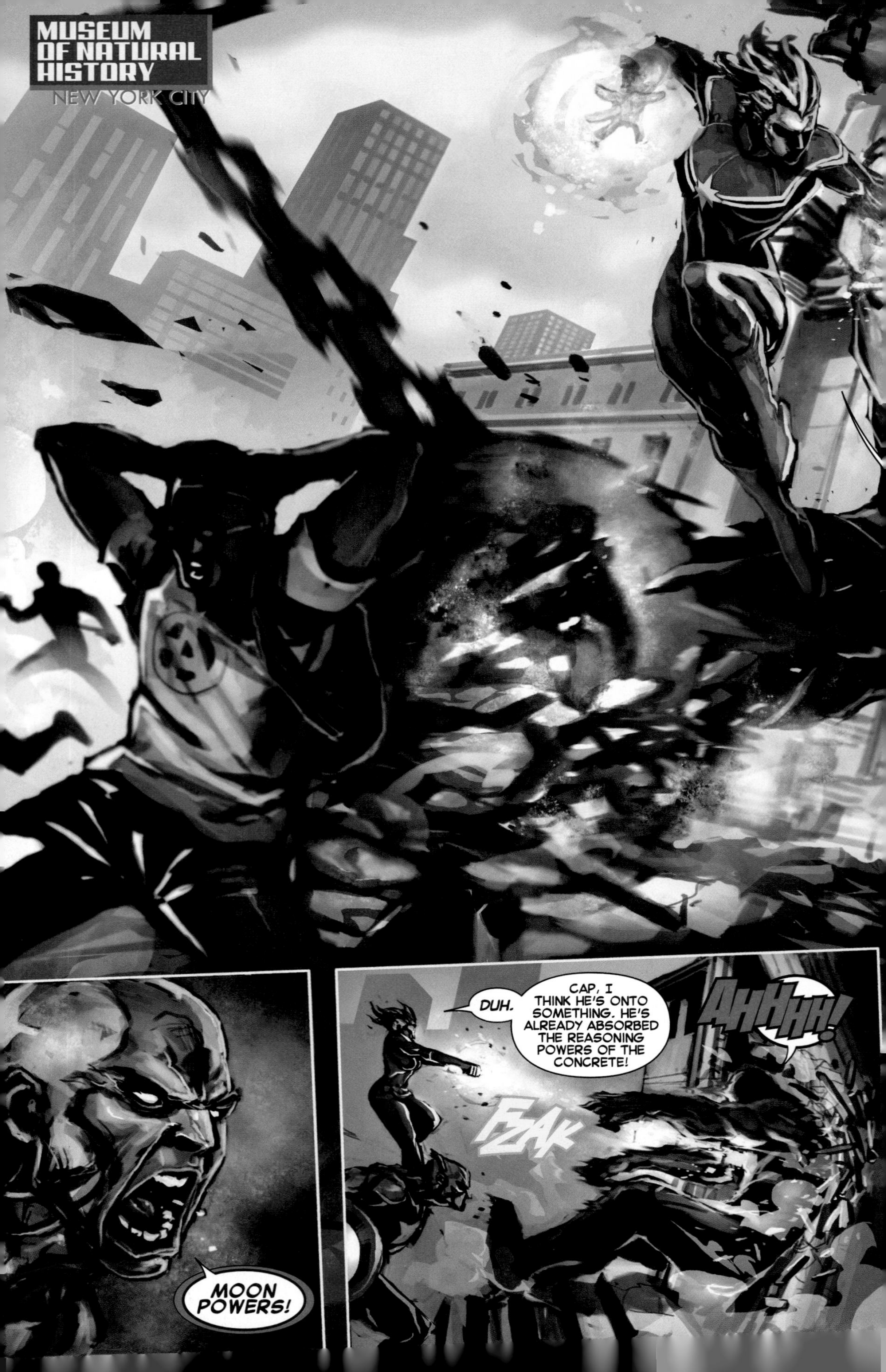
MUSEUM OF NATURAL HISTORY
NEW YORK CITY
MOON POWERS!
DUH.
CAP, I THINK HE'S ONTO SOMETHING. HE'S ALREADY ABSORBED THE REASONING POWERS OF THE CONCRETE!
AHHHH!
FZAK

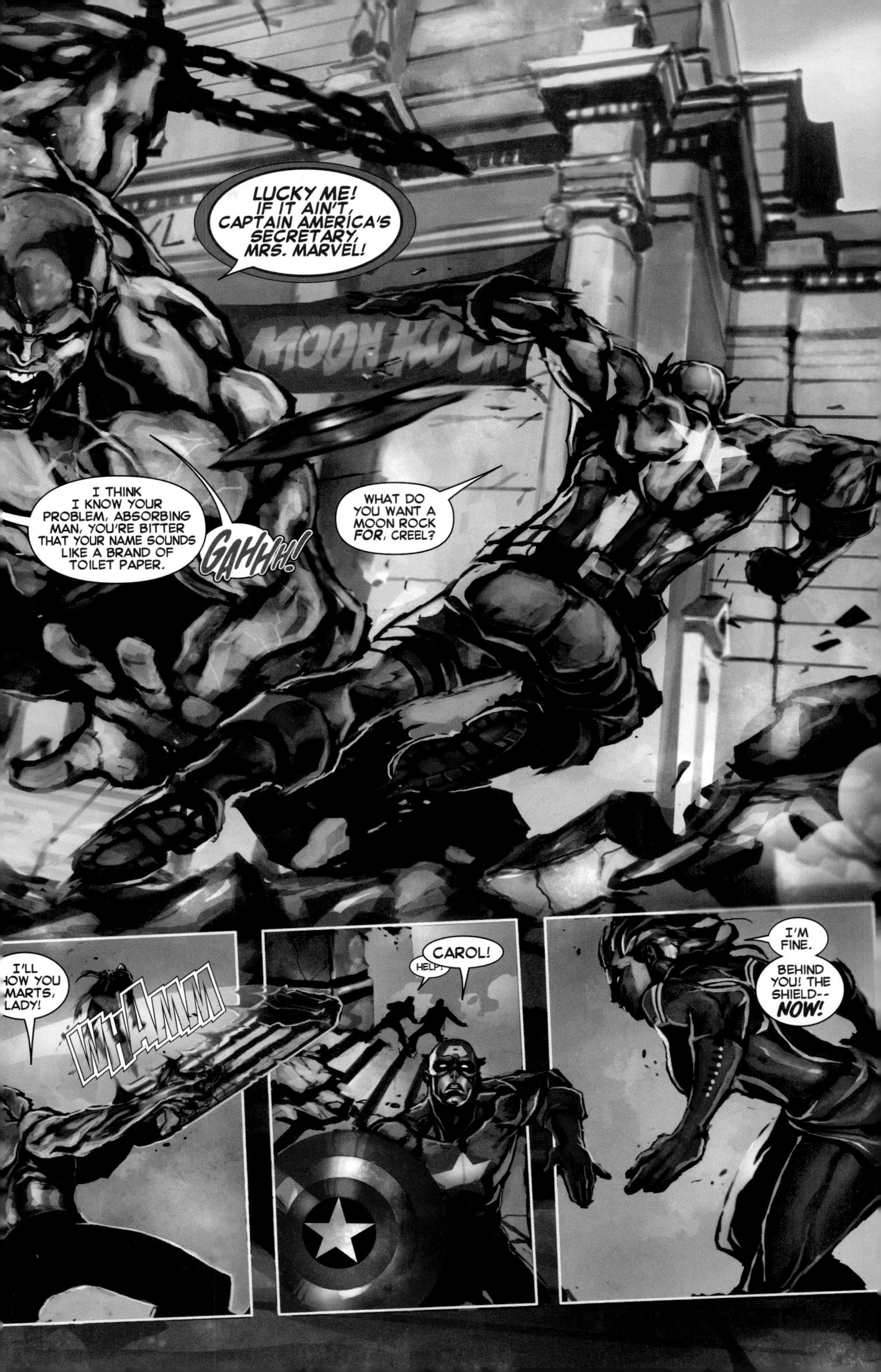
LUCKY ME! IF IT AIN'T, CAPTAIN AMERICA'S SECRETARY, MRS. MARVEL!
MOON ROCK
I THINK I KNOW YOUR PROBLEM, ABSORBING MAN, YOU'RE BITTER THAT YOUR NAME SOUNDS LIKE A BRAND OF TOILET PAPER.
GAHHH!
WHAT DO YOU WANT A MOON ROCK FOR, CREEL?
I'LL HOW YOU MARTS, LADY!
WHAMM
HELP!
CAROL!
I'M FINE.
BEHIND YOU! THE SHIELD-- NOW!

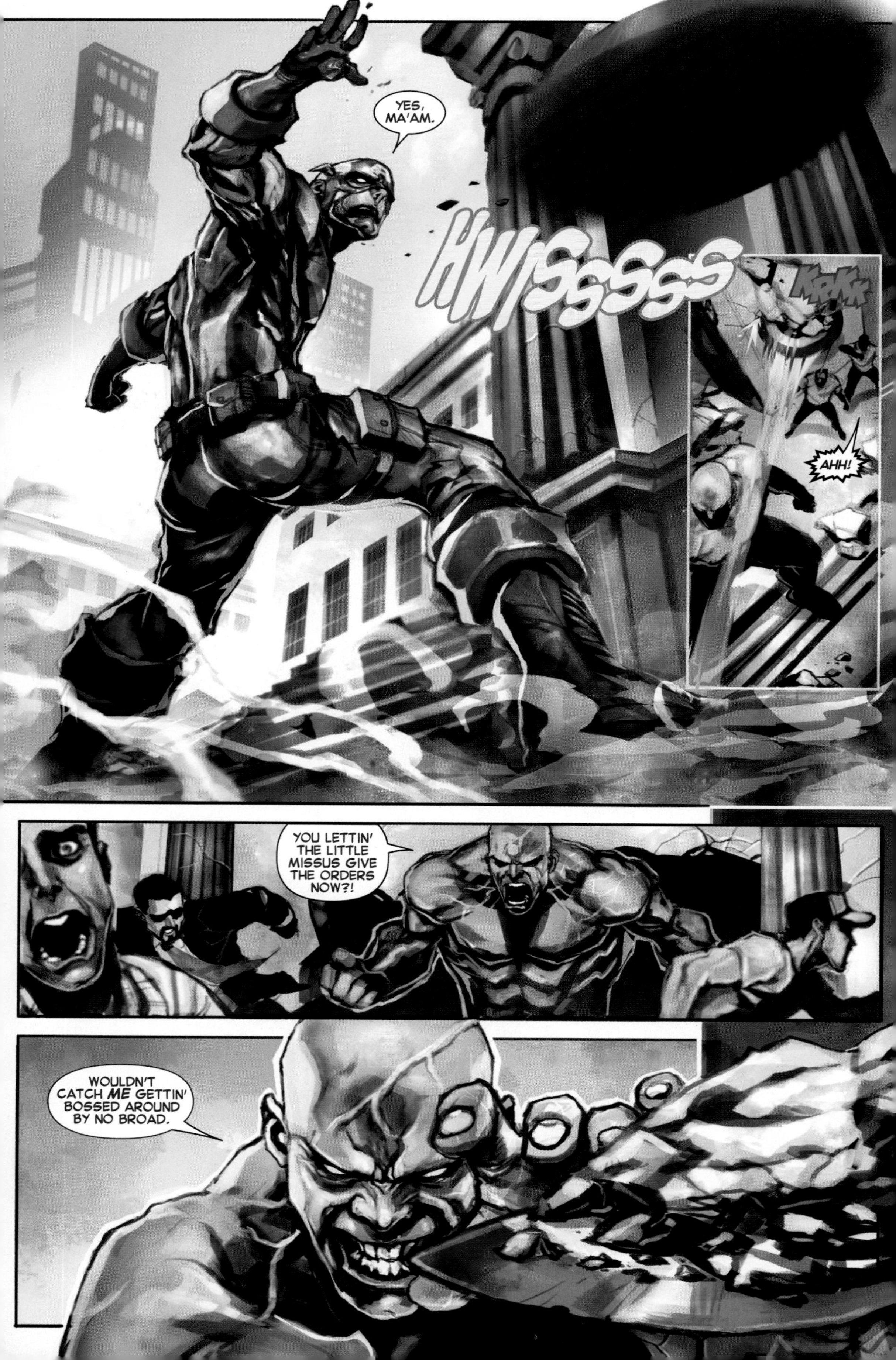
YES, MA'AM.
HWISSSSS
KRAKK
AHH!
YOU LETTIN' THE LITTLE MISSUS GIVE THE ORDERS NOW?!
WOULDN'T CATCH *ME* GETTIN' BOSSED AROUND BY NO BROAD.

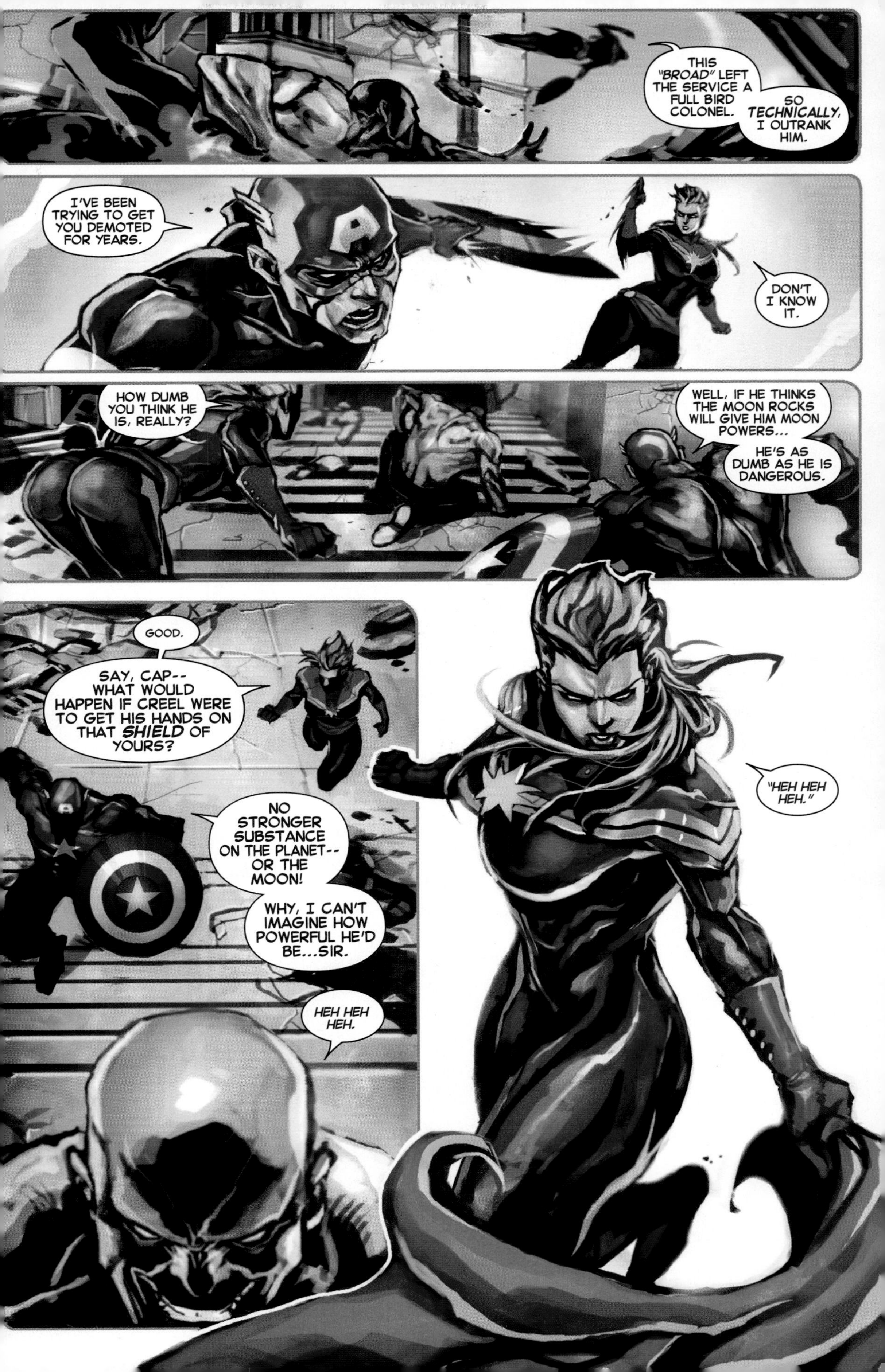
THIS "BROAD" LEFT THE SERVICE A FULL BIRD COLONEL.
SO TECHNICALLY, I OUTRANK HIM.
I'VE BEEN TRYING TO GET YOU DEMOTED FOR YEARS.
DON'T I KNOW IT.
HOW DUMB YOU THINK HE IS, REALLY?
WELL, IF HE THINKS THE MOON ROCKS WILL GIVE HIM MOON POWERS...
HE'S AS DUMB AS HE IS DANGEROUS.
GOOD.
SAY, CAP-- WHAT WOULD HAPPEN IF CREEL WERE TO GET HIS HANDS ON THAT SHIELD OF YOURS?
NO STRONGER SUBSTANCE ON THE PLANET-- OR THE MOON!
WHY, I CAN'T IMAGINE HOW POWERFUL HE'D BE...SIR.
HEH HEH HEH.
"HEH HEH HEH."

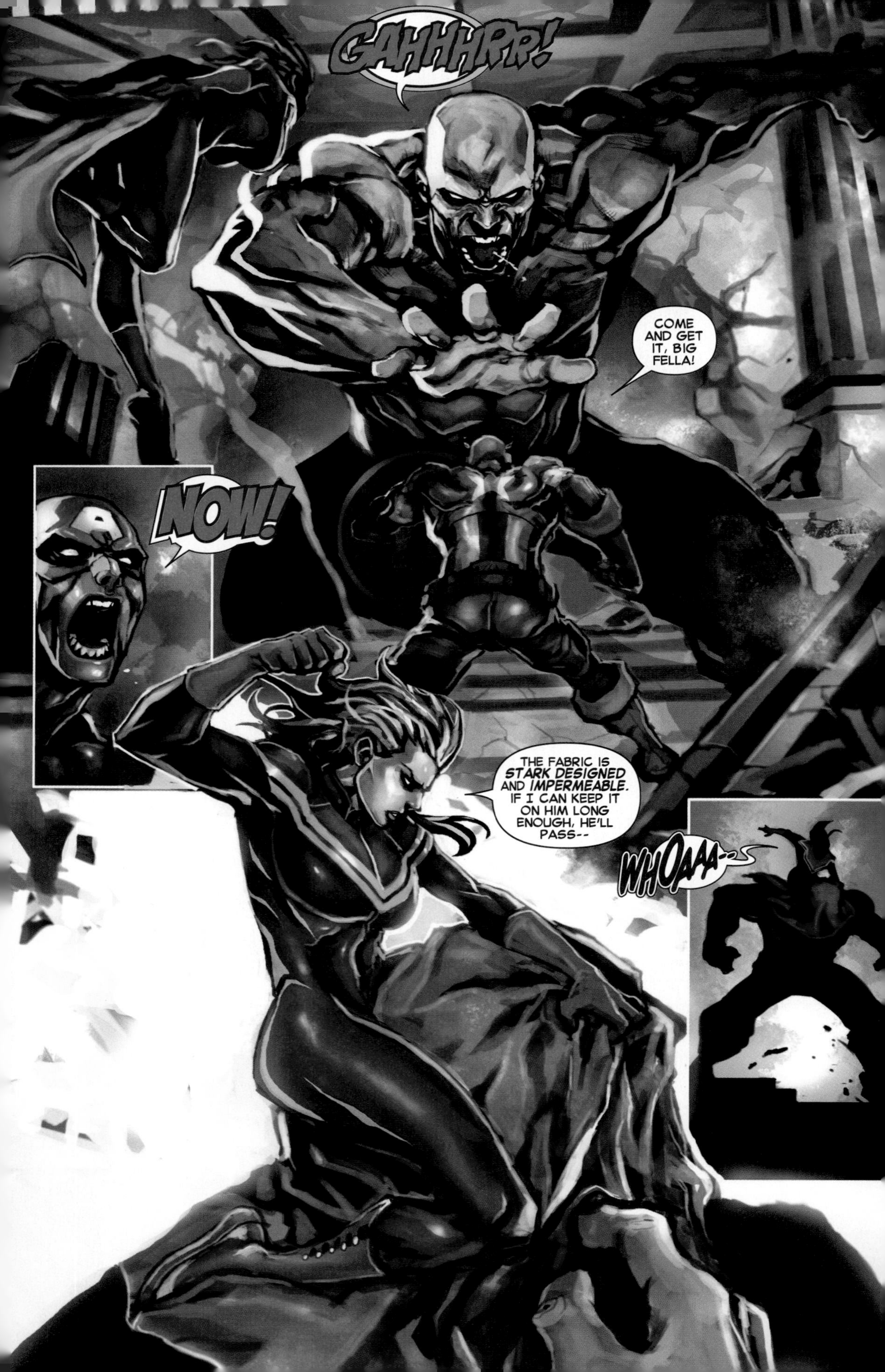
GAHHHRR!
COME AND GET IT, BIG FELLA!
NOW!
THE FABRIC IS STARK DESIGNED AND IMPERMEABLE. IF I CAN KEEP IT ON HIM LONG ENOUGH, HE'LL PASS--
WHOAAA--

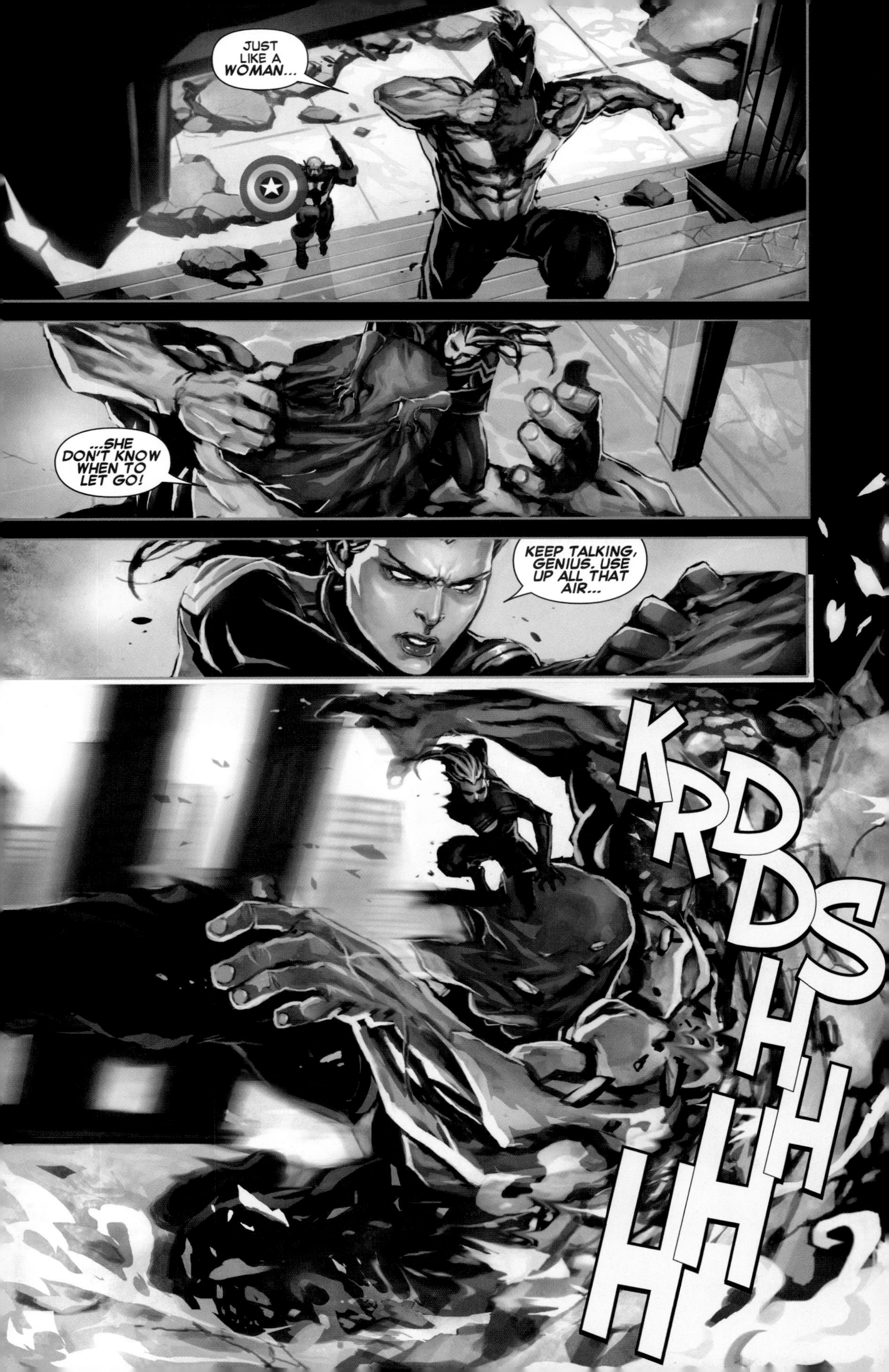
JUST LIKE A WOMAN...
...SHE DON'T KNOW WHEN TO LET GO!
KEEP TALKING, GENIUS. USE UP ALL THAT AIR...
KRDDSHHHHH

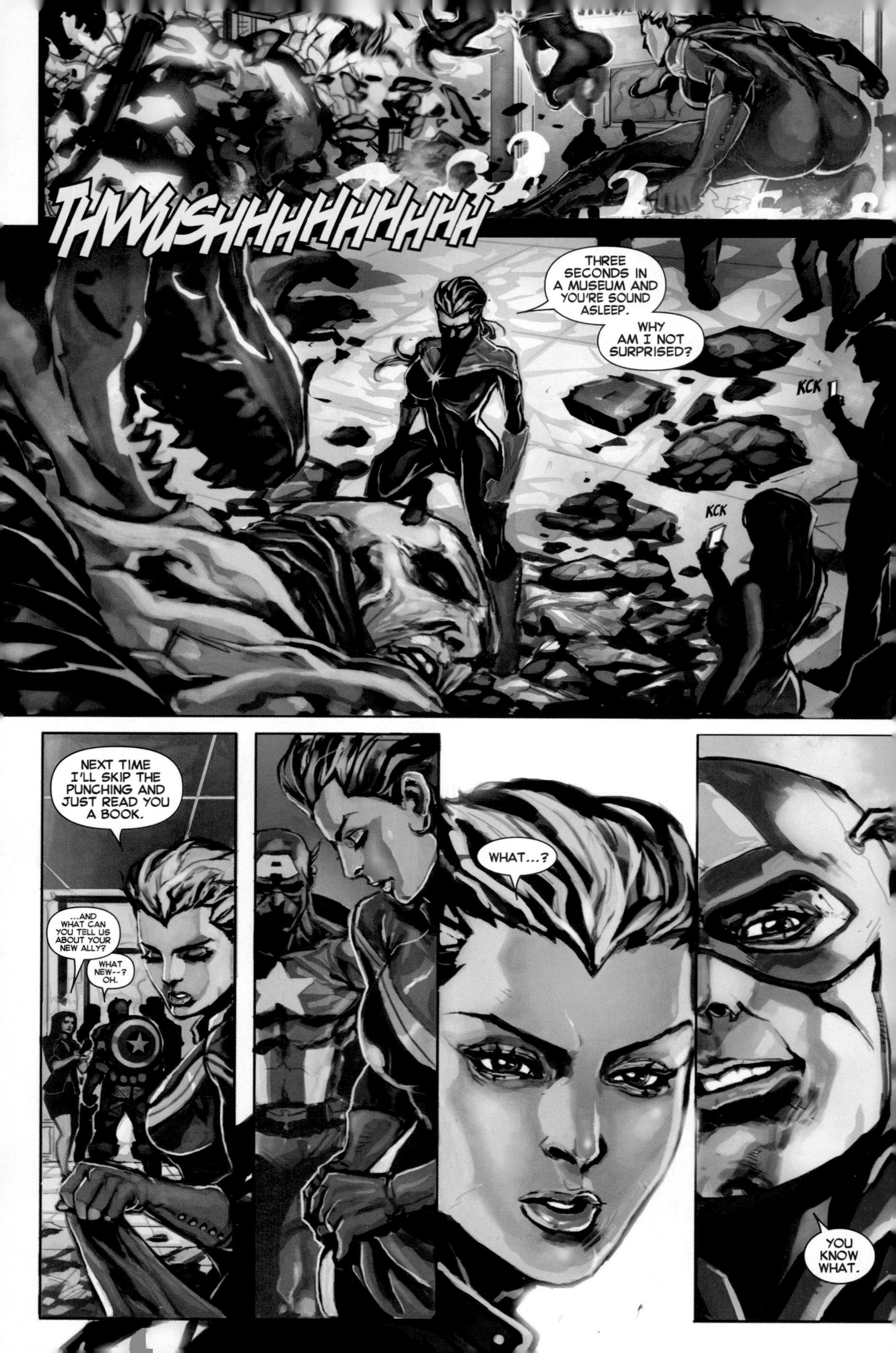
THWUSHHHHHHHHH
THREE SECONDS IN A MUSEUM AND YOU'RE SOUND ASLEEP.
WHY AM I NOT SURPRISED?
KCK
KCK
NEXT TIME I'LL SKIP THE PUNCHING AND JUST READ YOU A BOOK.
...AND WHAT CAN YOU TELL US ABOUT YOUR NEW ALLY?
WHAT NEW--? OH.
WHAT...?
YOU KNOW WHAT.

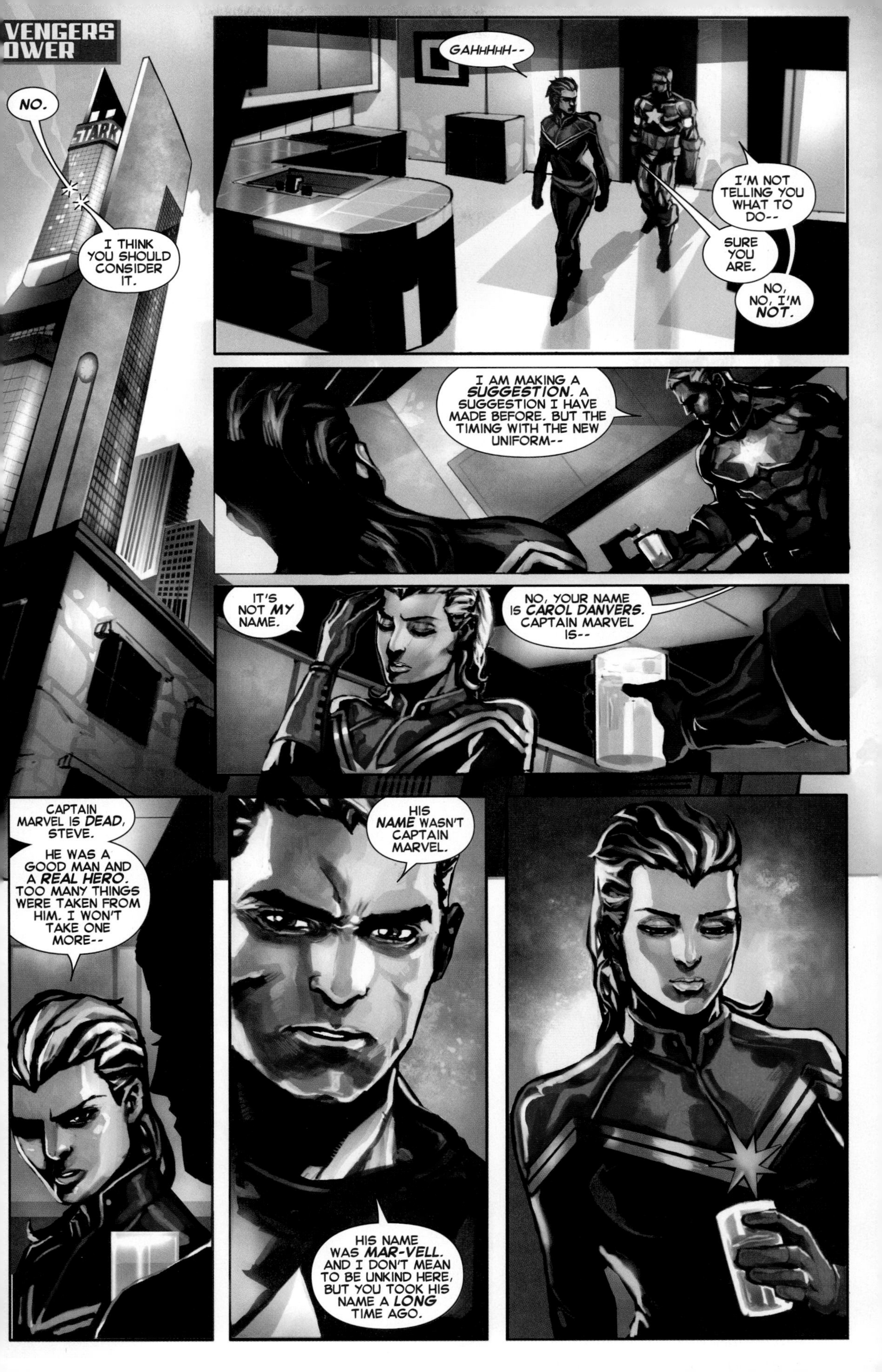
VENGERS
OWER
NO.
I THINK YOU SHOULD CONSIDER IT.
STARK
GAHHHHH--
I'M NOT TELLING YOU WHAT TO DO--
SURE YOU ARE.
NO, NO, I'M NOT.
I AM MAKING A SUGGESTION. A SUGGESTION I HAVE MADE BEFORE. BUT THE TIMING WITH THE NEW UNIFORM--
IT'S NOT MY NAME.
NO, YOUR NAME IS CAROL DANVERS. CAPTAIN MARVEL IS--
CAPTAIN MARVEL IS DEAD, STEVE.
HE WAS A GOOD MAN AND A REAL HERO. TOO MANY THINGS WERE TAKEN FROM HIM. I WON'T TAKE ONE MORE--
HIS NAME WASN'T CAPTAIN MARVEL.
HIS NAME WAS MAR-VELL. AND I DON'T MEAN TO BE UNKIND HERE, BUT YOU TOOK HIS NAME A LONG TIME AGO.

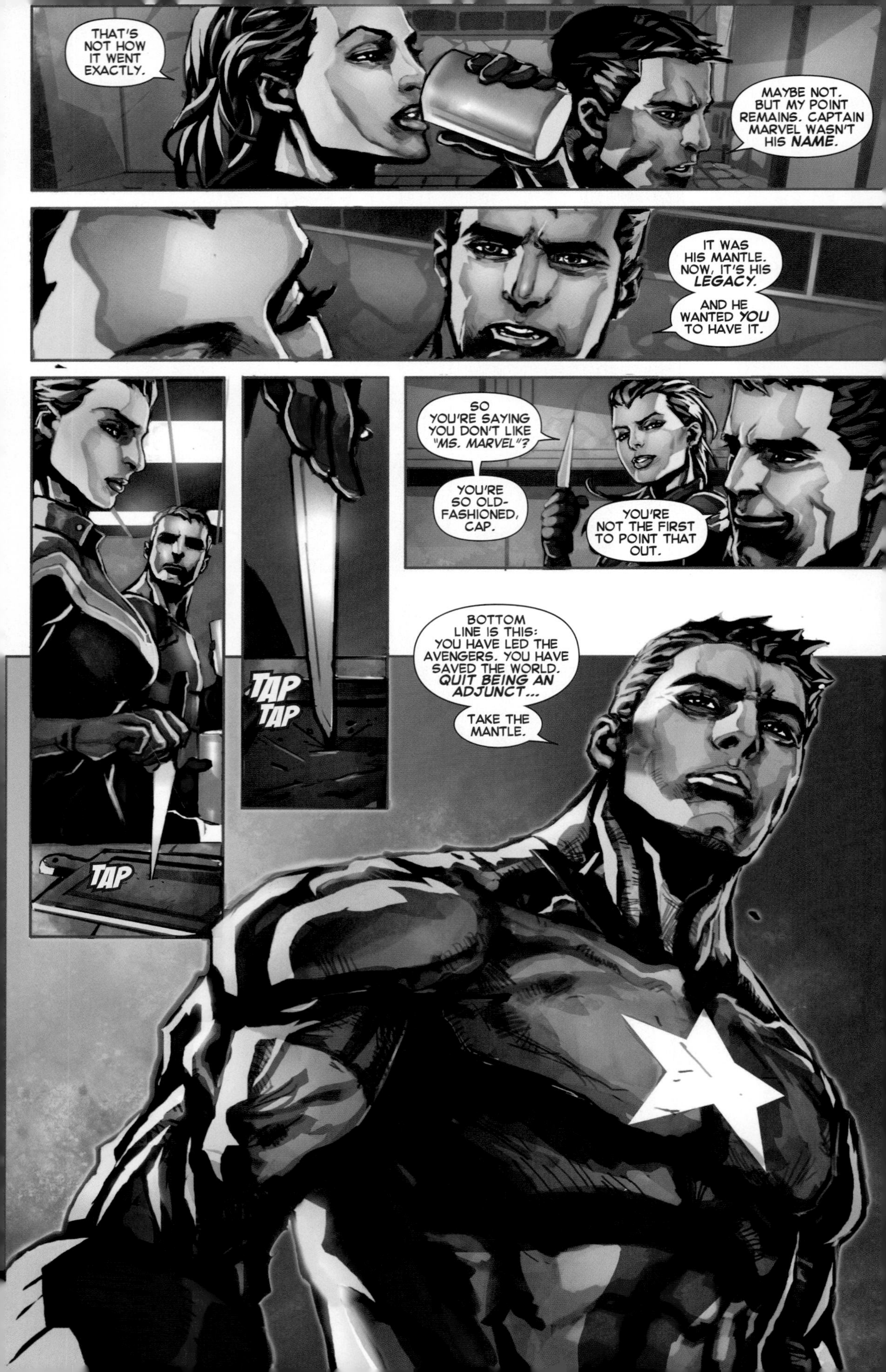
THAT'S NOT HOW IT WENT EXACTLY.
MAYBE NOT. BUT MY POINT REMAINS. CAPTAIN MARVEL WASN'T HIS NAME.
IT WAS HIS MANTLE. NOW, IT'S HIS LEGACY.
AND HE WANTED YOU TO HAVE IT.
TAP
TAP TAP
SO YOU'RE SAYING YOU DON'T LIKE "MS. MARVEL"?
YOU'RE SO OLD-FASHIONED, CAP.
YOU'RE NOT THE FIRST TO POINT THAT OUT.
BOTTOM LINE IS THIS: YOU HAVE LED THE AVENGERS. YOU HAVE SAVED THE WORLD. QUIT BEING AN ADJUNCT...
TAKE THE MANTLE.

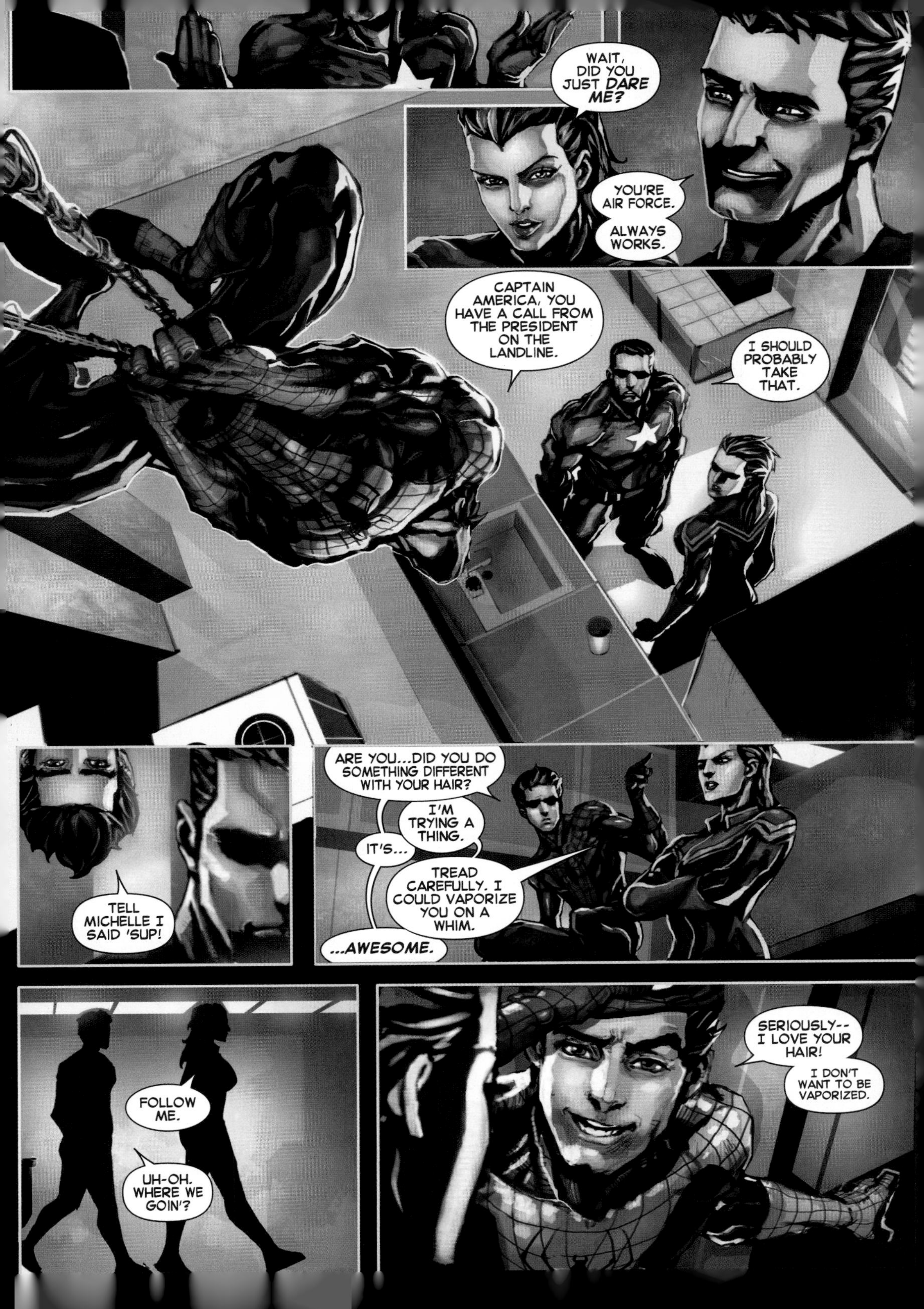

WAIT, DID YOU JUST DARE ME?
YOU'RE AIR FORCE.
ALWAYS WORKS.
CAPTAIN AMERICA, YOU HAVE A CALL FROM THE PRESIDENT ON THE LANDLINE.
I SHOULD PROBABLY TAKE THAT.
TELL MICHELLE I SAID 'SUP!
ARE YOU...DID YOU DO SOMETHING DIFFERENT WITH YOUR HAIR?
I'M TRYING A THING.
IT'S...
TREAD CAREFULLY. I COULD VAPORIZE YOU ON A WHIM.
...AWESOME.
FOLLOW ME.
UH-OH. WHERE WE GOIN'?
SERIOUSLY-- I LOVE YOUR HAIR!
I DON'T WANT TO BE VAPORIZED.

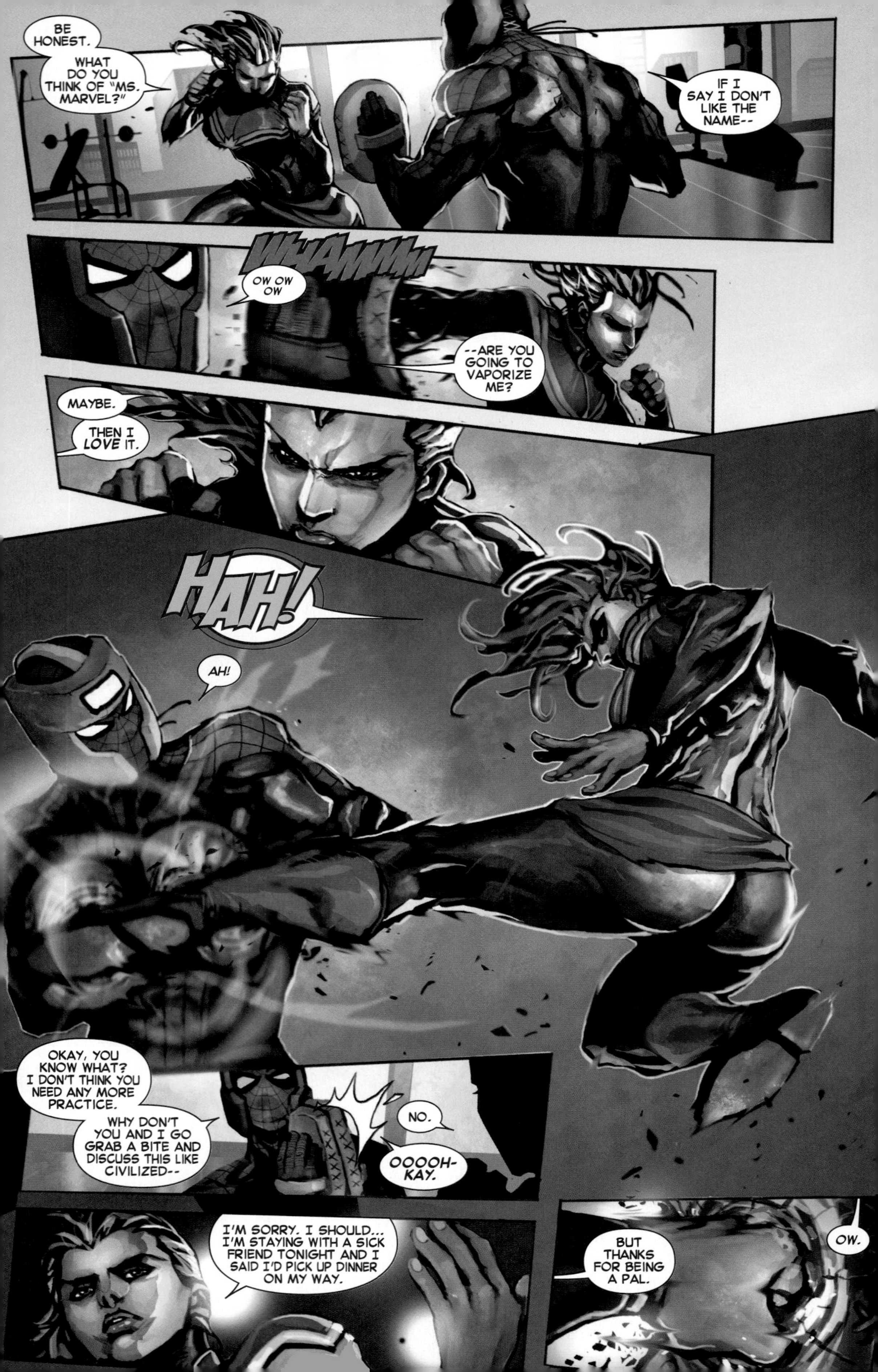
BE HONEST.
WHAT DO YOU THINK OF "MS. MARVEL?"
IF I SAY I DON'T LIKE THE NAME--
WHAAMM
OW OW OW
--ARE YOU GOING TO VAPORIZE ME?
MAYBE.
THEN I LOVE IT.
HAH!
AH!
OKAY, YOU KNOW WHAT? I DON'T THINK YOU NEED ANY MORE PRACTICE.
WHY DON'T YOU AND I GO GRAB A BITE AND DISCUSS THIS LIKE CIVILIZED--
NO.
OOOOH-KAY.
I'M SORRY. I SHOULD... I'M STAYING WITH A SICK FRIEND TONIGHT AND I SAID I'D PICK UP DINNER ON MY WAY.
BUT THANKS FOR BEING A PAL.
OW.

I WAS A LUCKY KID BECAUSE I HAD TWO HEROES--MY DAD AND A PILOT NAMED HELEN COBB.

HELEN HELD FIFTEEN SPEED RECORDS WHEN SHE RETIRED.

FIFTEEN.

I'M NOT PRONE TO ENVY. BUT THOSE RECORDS...

I *ENVY* THOSE RECORDS.

I CAN FLY. *FAST.*

REAL FAST.

BUT THESE *"ABILITIES"* COME AT A COST. FOR ONE THING, I'LL NEVER BE ALLOWED TO HOLD A RECORD LIKE HELEN'S.

I CAN'T EVEN COMPETE. WOULDN'T BE A FAIR FIGHT.

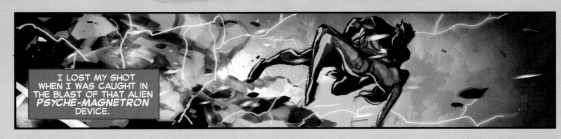

I LOST MY SHOT WHEN I WAS CAUGHT IN THE BLAST OF THAT ALIEN *PSYCHE-MAGNETRON* DEVICE.

THE PARTICLE BOMBARDMENT GRAFTED THE GENETIC STRUCTURE OF THE KREE WARRIOR MAR-VELL ONTO MY OWN DNA.

IT'S A HELL OF A REWARD...BUT IT ERASED WHAT I LOVED MOST...

...THE *RISK.*

ONE MINUTE, FIFTY-EIGHT SECONDS FROM BROADWAY TO THE END OF OUR ATMOSPHERE, A NEW PERSONAL BEST.

LUCKY ME.

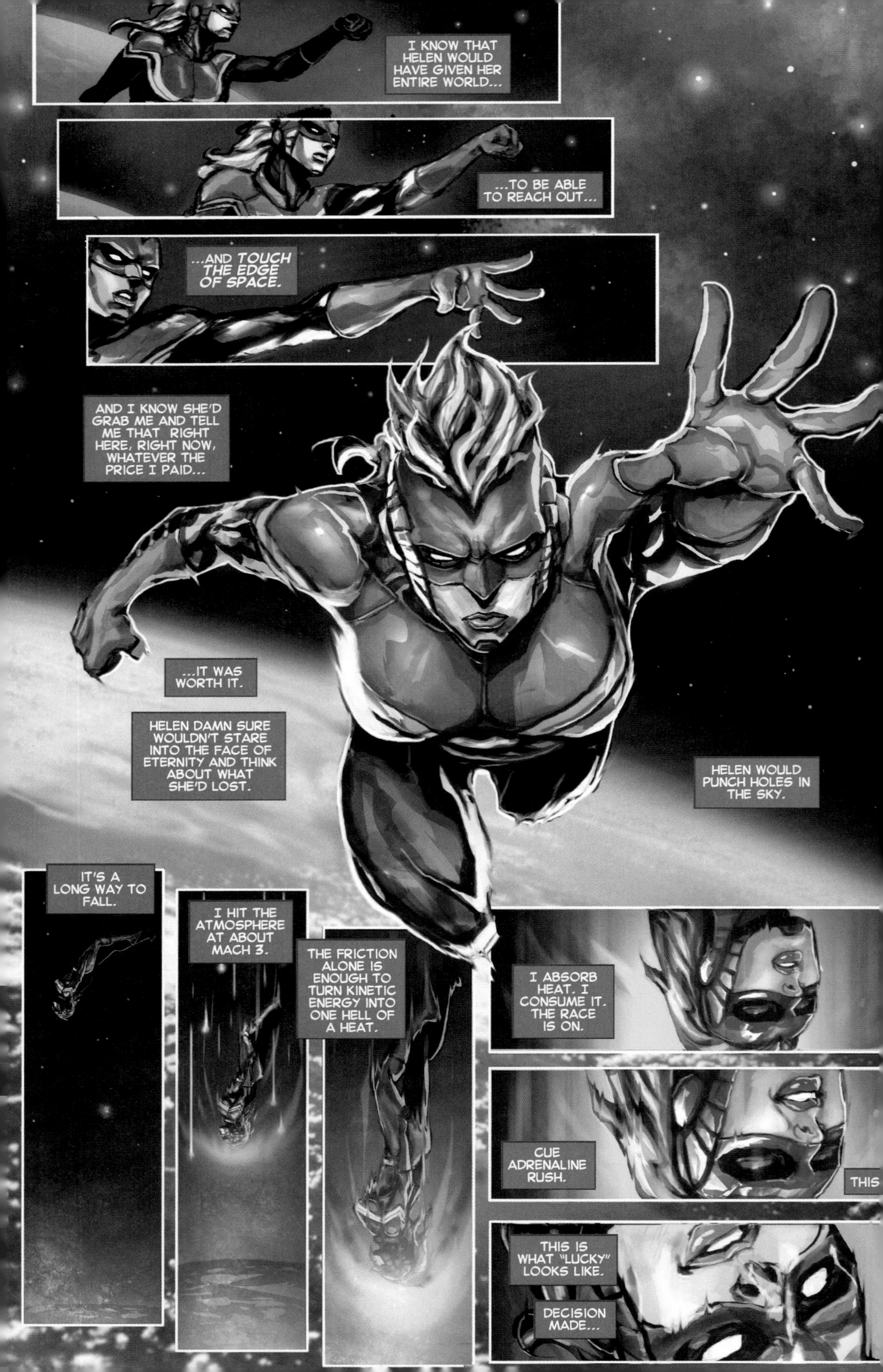
I KNOW THAT HELEN WOULD HAVE GIVEN HER ENTIRE WORLD...
...TO BE ABLE TO REACH OUT...
...AND *TOUCH THE EDGE OF SPACE.*
AND I KNOW SHE'D GRAB ME AND TELL ME THAT RIGHT HERE, RIGHT NOW, WHATEVER THE PRICE I PAID...
...IT WAS WORTH IT.
HELEN DAMN SURE WOULDN'T STARE INTO THE FACE OF ETERNITY AND THINK ABOUT WHAT SHE'D LOST.
HELEN WOULD PUNCH HOLES IN THE SKY.
IT'S A LONG WAY TO FALL.
I HIT THE ATMOSPHERE AT ABOUT MACH 3.
THE FRICTION ALONE IS ENOUGH TO TURN KINETIC ENERGY INTO ONE HELL OF A HEAT.
I ABSORB HEAT. I CONSUME IT. THE RACE IS ON.
CUE ADRENALINE RUSH.
THIS
THIS IS WHAT "LUCKY" LOOKS LIKE.
DECISION MADE...

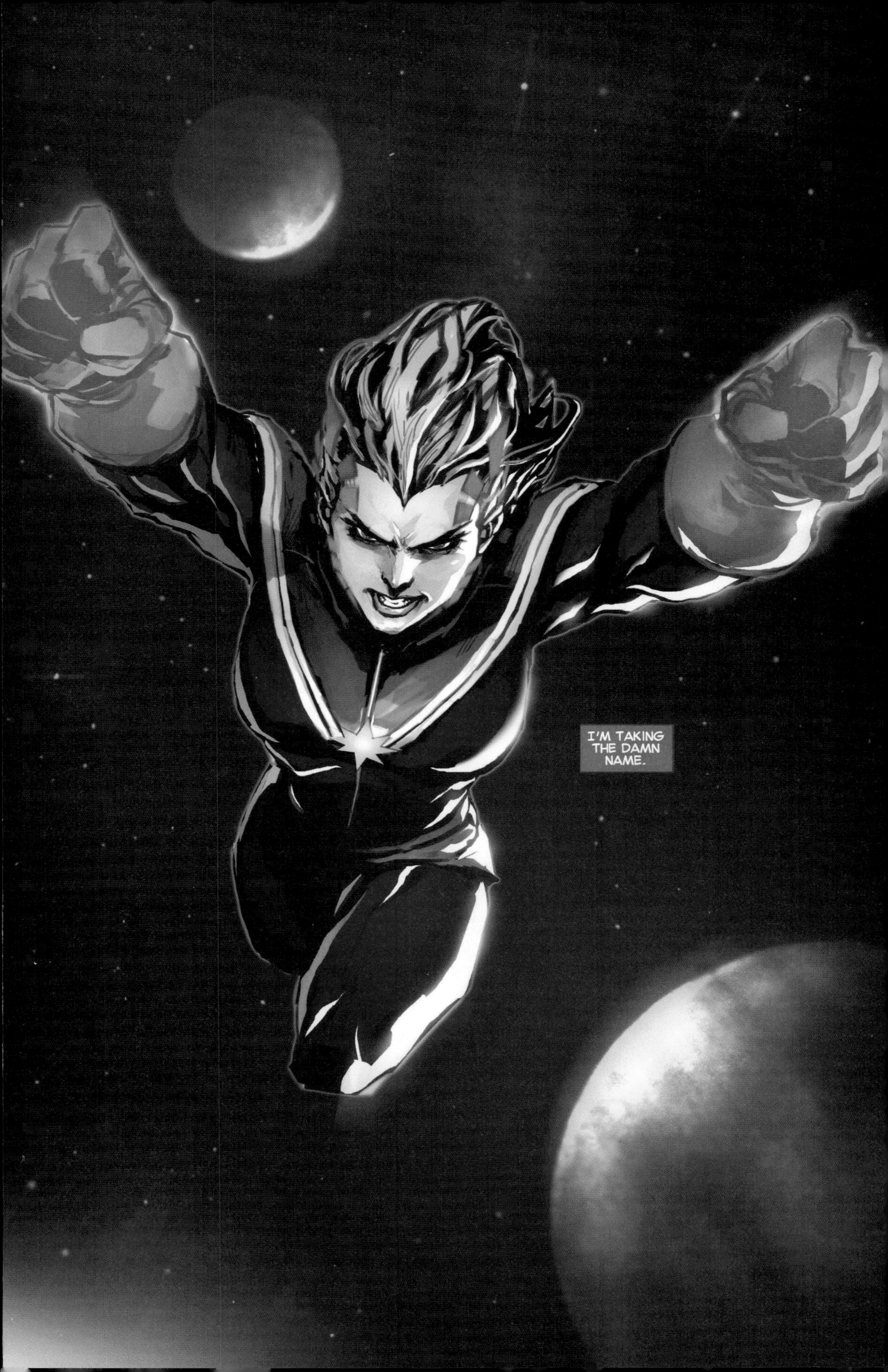
I'M TAKING THE DAMN NAME.

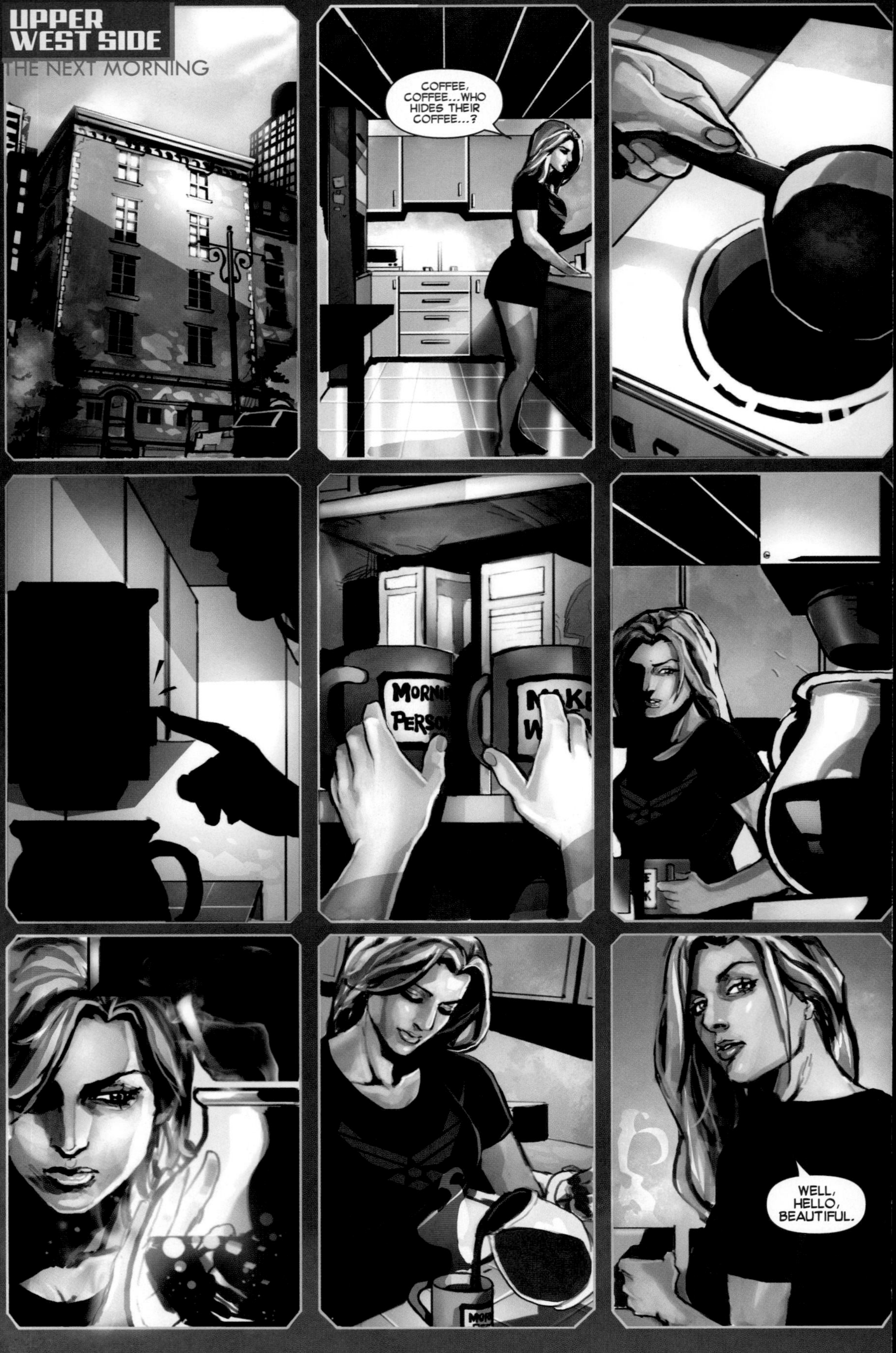
UPPER WEST SIDE
THE NEXT MORNING
COFFEE, COFFEE...WHO HIDES THEIR COFFEE...?
WELL, HELLO, BEAUTIFUL.

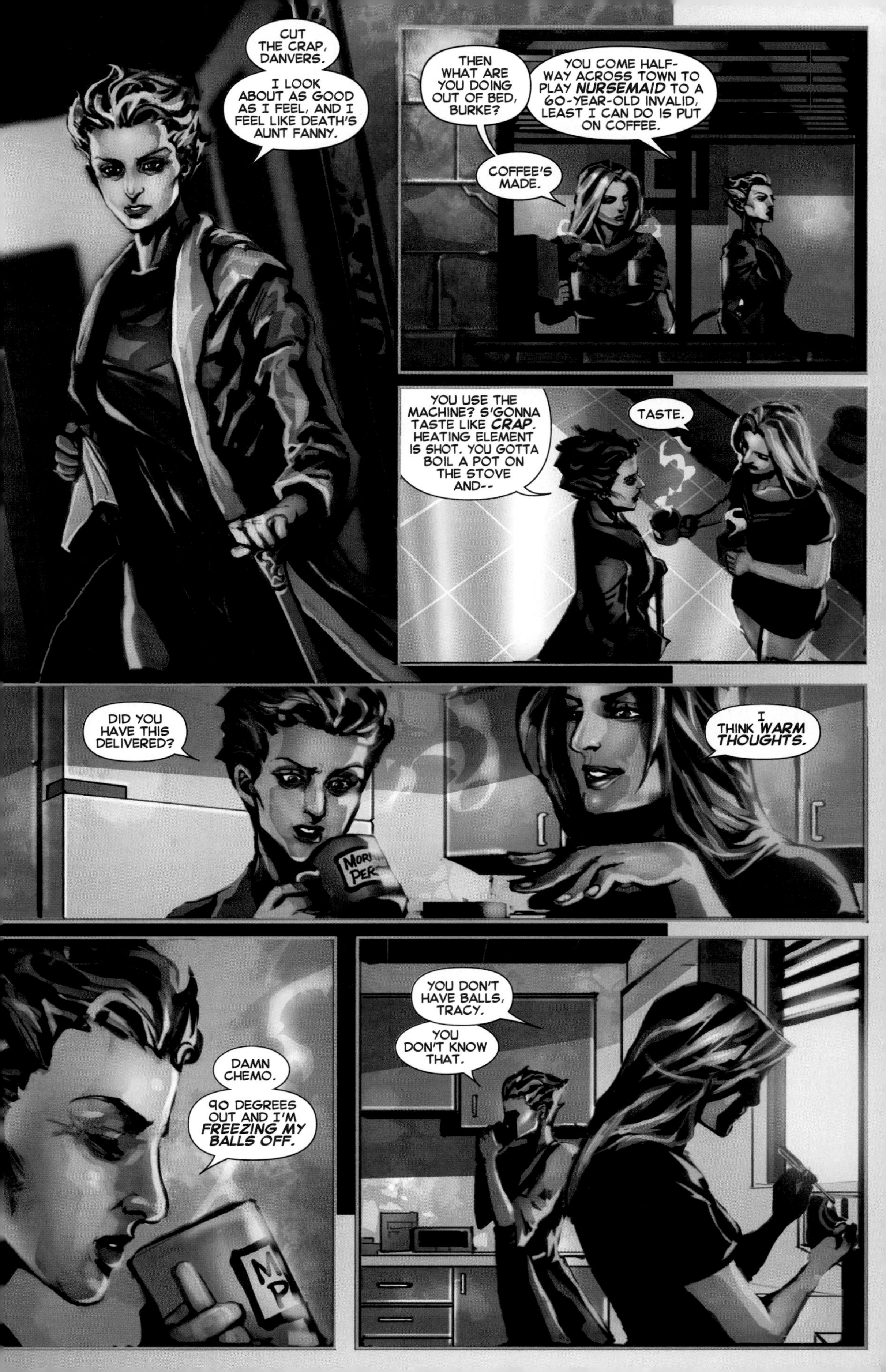
CUT THE CRAP, DANVERS.
I LOOK ABOUT AS GOOD AS I FEEL, AND I FEEL LIKE DEATH'S AUNT FANNY.
THEN WHAT ARE YOU DOING OUT OF BED, BURKE?
COFFEE'S MADE.
YOU COME HALF-WAY ACROSS TOWN TO PLAY NURSEMAID TO A 60-YEAR-OLD INVALID, LEAST I CAN DO IS PUT ON COFFEE.
YOU USE THE MACHINE? S'GONNA TASTE LIKE CRAP. HEATING ELEMENT IS SHOT. YOU GOTTA BOIL A POT ON THE STOVE AND--
TASTE.
DID YOU HAVE THIS DELIVERED?
I THINK WARM THOUGHTS.
DAMN CHEMO.
90 DEGREES OUT AND I'M FREEZING MY BALLS OFF.
YOU DON'T HAVE BALLS, TRACY.
YOU DON'T KNOW THAT.

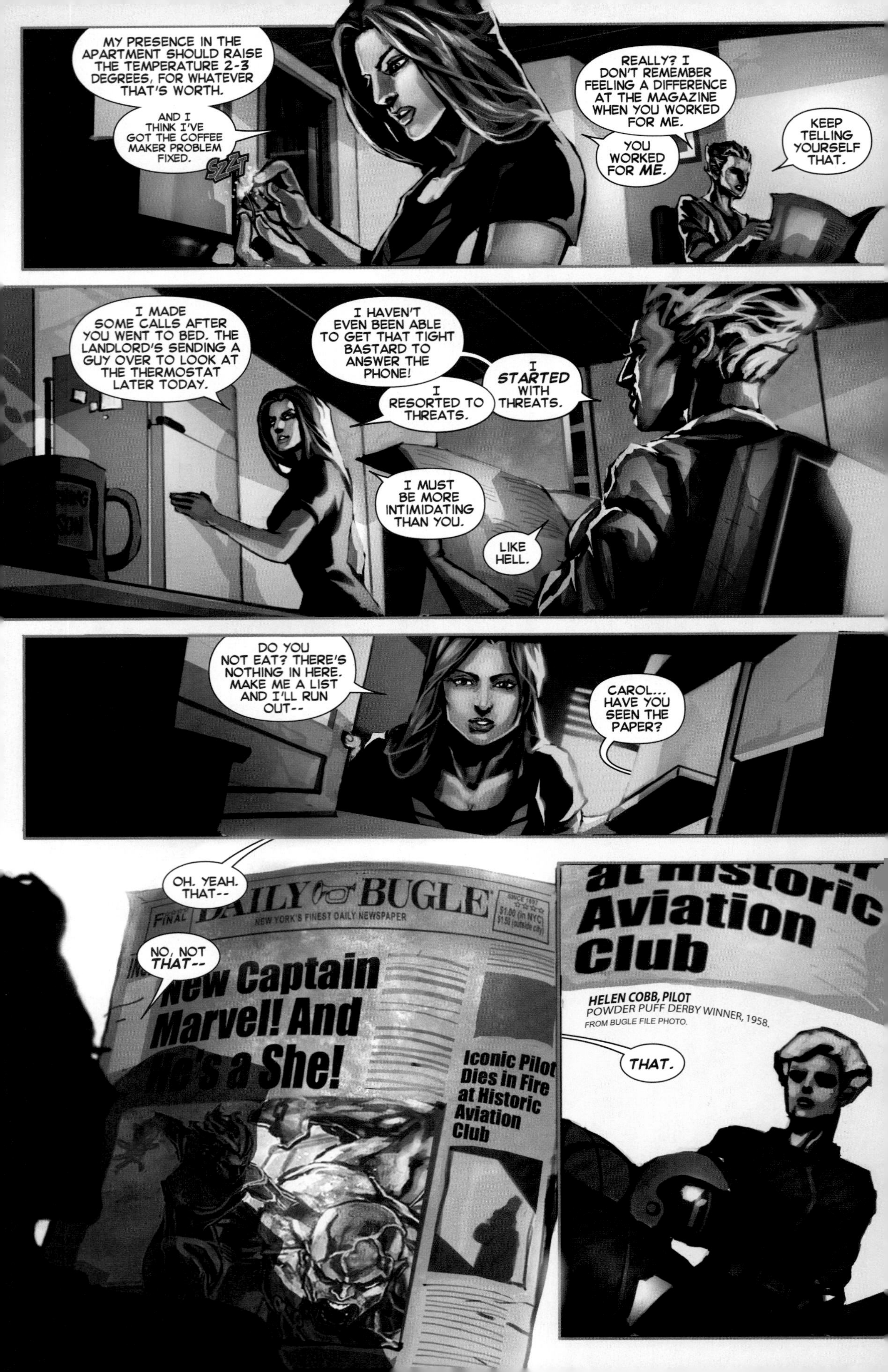
MY PRESENCE IN THE APARTMENT SHOULD RAISE THE TEMPERATURE 2-3 DEGREES, FOR WHATEVER THAT'S WORTH.
AND I THINK I'VE GOT THE COFFEE MAKER PROBLEM FIXED.
SZZT
REALLY? I DON'T REMEMBER FEELING A DIFFERENCE AT THE MAGAZINE WHEN YOU WORKED FOR ME.
YOU WORKED FOR *ME.*
KEEP TELLING YOURSELF THAT.
I MADE SOME CALLS AFTER YOU WENT TO BED. THE LANDLORD'S SENDING A GUY OVER TO LOOK AT THE THERMOSTAT LATER TODAY.
I HAVEN'T EVEN BEEN ABLE TO GET THAT TIGHT BASTARD TO ANSWER THE PHONE!
I RESORTED TO THREATS.
I *STARTED* WITH THREATS.
I MUST BE MORE INTIMIDATING THAN YOU.
LIKE HELL.
DO YOU NOT EAT? THERE'S NOTHING IN HERE. MAKE ME A LIST AND I'LL RUN OUT--
CAROL... HAVE YOU SEEN THE PAPER?
OH. YEAH. THAT--
NO, NOT *THAT*--
DAILY BUGLE
NEW YORK'S FINEST DAILY NEWSPAPER
FINAL
SINCE 1897
$1.00 (in NYC) $1.50 (outside city)
New Captain Marvel! And He's a She!
Iconic Pilot Dies in Fire at Historic Aviation Club
at Historic Aviation Club
HELEN COBB, PILOT
POWDER PUFF DERBY WINNER, 1958.
FROM BUGLE FILE PHOTO.
THAT.

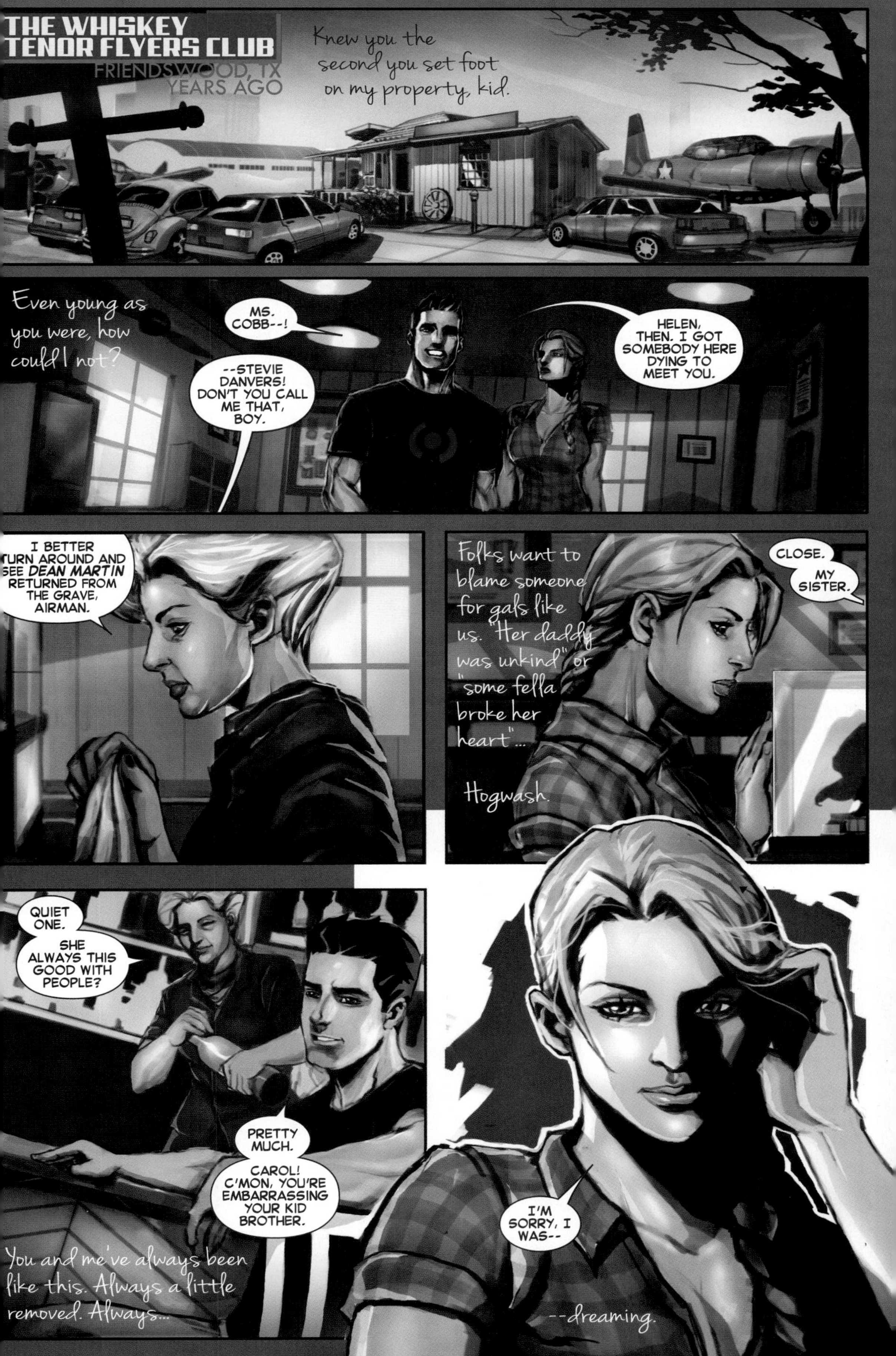
THE WHISKEY TENOR FLYERS CLUB
FRIENDSWOOD, TX
YEARS AGO
Knew you the second you set foot on my property, kid.
Even young as you were, how could I not?
MS. COBB--!
--STEVIE DANVERS! DON'T YOU CALL ME THAT, BOY.
HELEN, THEN. I GOT SOMEBODY HERE DYING TO MEET YOU.
I BETTER TURN AROUND AND SEE DEAN MARTIN RETURNED FROM THE GRAVE, AIRMAN.
Folks want to blame someone for gals like us. "Her daddy was unkind" or "some fella broke her heart"...
Hogwash.
CLOSE.
MY SISTER.
QUIET ONE.
SHE ALWAYS THIS GOOD WITH PEOPLE?
PRETTY MUCH.
CAROL! C'MON, YOU'RE EMBARRASSING YOUR KID BROTHER.
You and me've always been like this. Always a little removed. Always...
I'M SORRY, I WAS--
--dreaming.

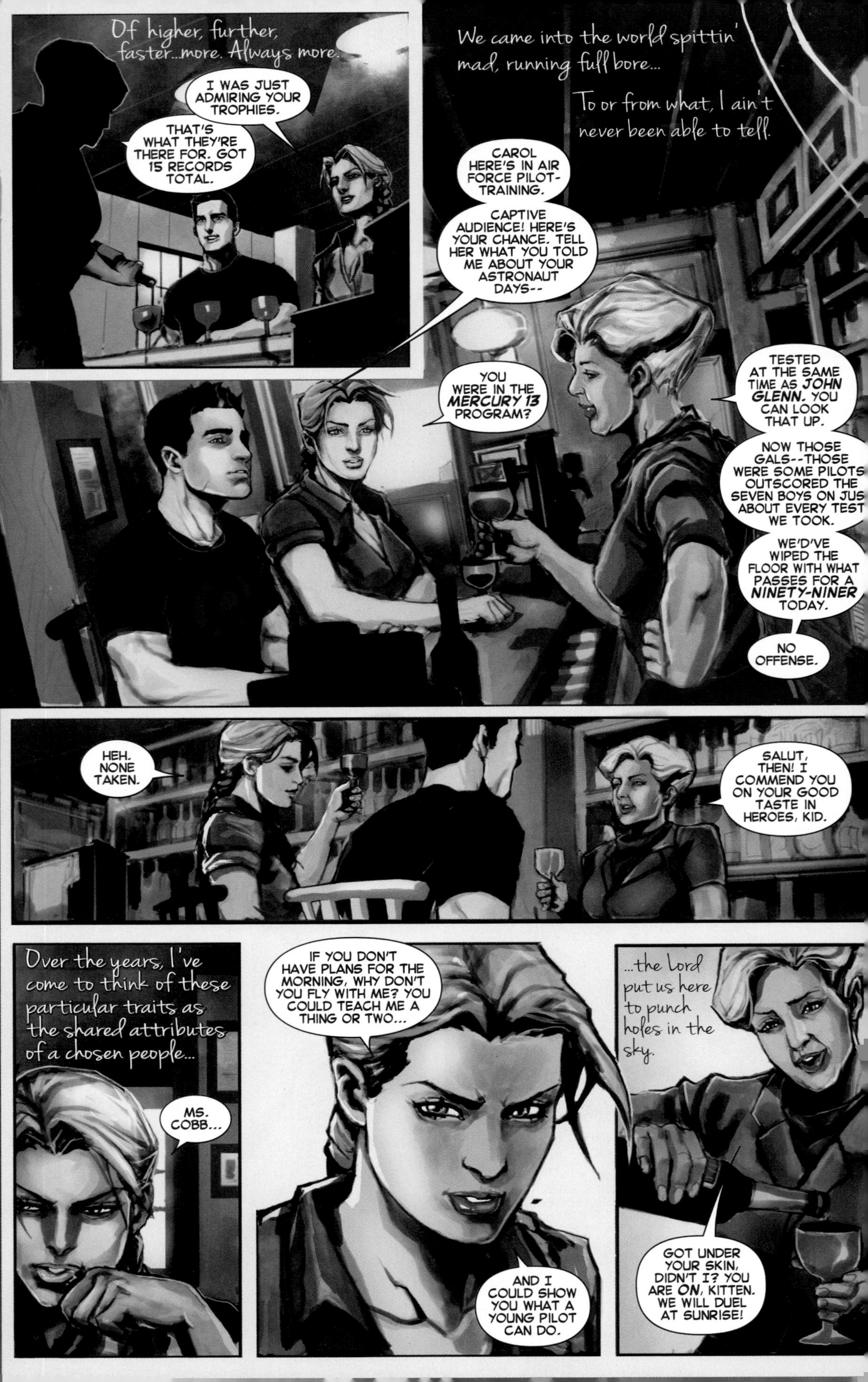

Of higher, further, faster...more. Always more.
I WAS JUST ADMIRING YOUR TROPHIES.
THAT'S WHAT THEY'RE THERE FOR. GOT 15 RECORDS TOTAL.
We came into the world spittin' mad, running full bore...
To or from what, I ain't never been able to tell.
CAROL HERE'S IN AIR FORCE PILOT-TRAINING.
CAPTIVE AUDIENCE! HERE'S YOUR CHANCE. TELL HER WHAT YOU TOLD ME ABOUT YOUR ASTRONAUT DAYS--
YOU WERE IN THE MERCURY 13 PROGRAM?
TESTED AT THE SAME TIME AS JOHN GLENN. YOU CAN LOOK THAT UP.
NOW THOSE GALS--THOSE WERE SOME PILOTS OUTSCORED THE SEVEN BOYS ON JUS ABOUT EVERY TEST WE TOOK.
WE'D'VE WIPED THE FLOOR WITH WHAT PASSES FOR A NINETY-NINER TODAY.
NO OFFENSE.
HEH. NONE TAKEN.
SALUT, THEN! I COMMEND YOU ON YOUR GOOD TASTE IN HEROES, KID.
Over the years, I've come to think of these particular traits as the shared attributes of a chosen people...
MS. COBB...
IF YOU DON'T HAVE PLANS FOR THE MORNING, WHY DON'T YOU FLY WITH ME? YOU COULD TEACH ME A THING OR TWO...
AND I COULD SHOW YOU WHAT A YOUNG PILOT CAN DO.
...the Lord put us here to punch holes in the sky.
GOT UNDER YOUR SKIN, DIDN'T I? YOU ARE ON, KITTEN. WE WILL DUEL AT SUNRISE!

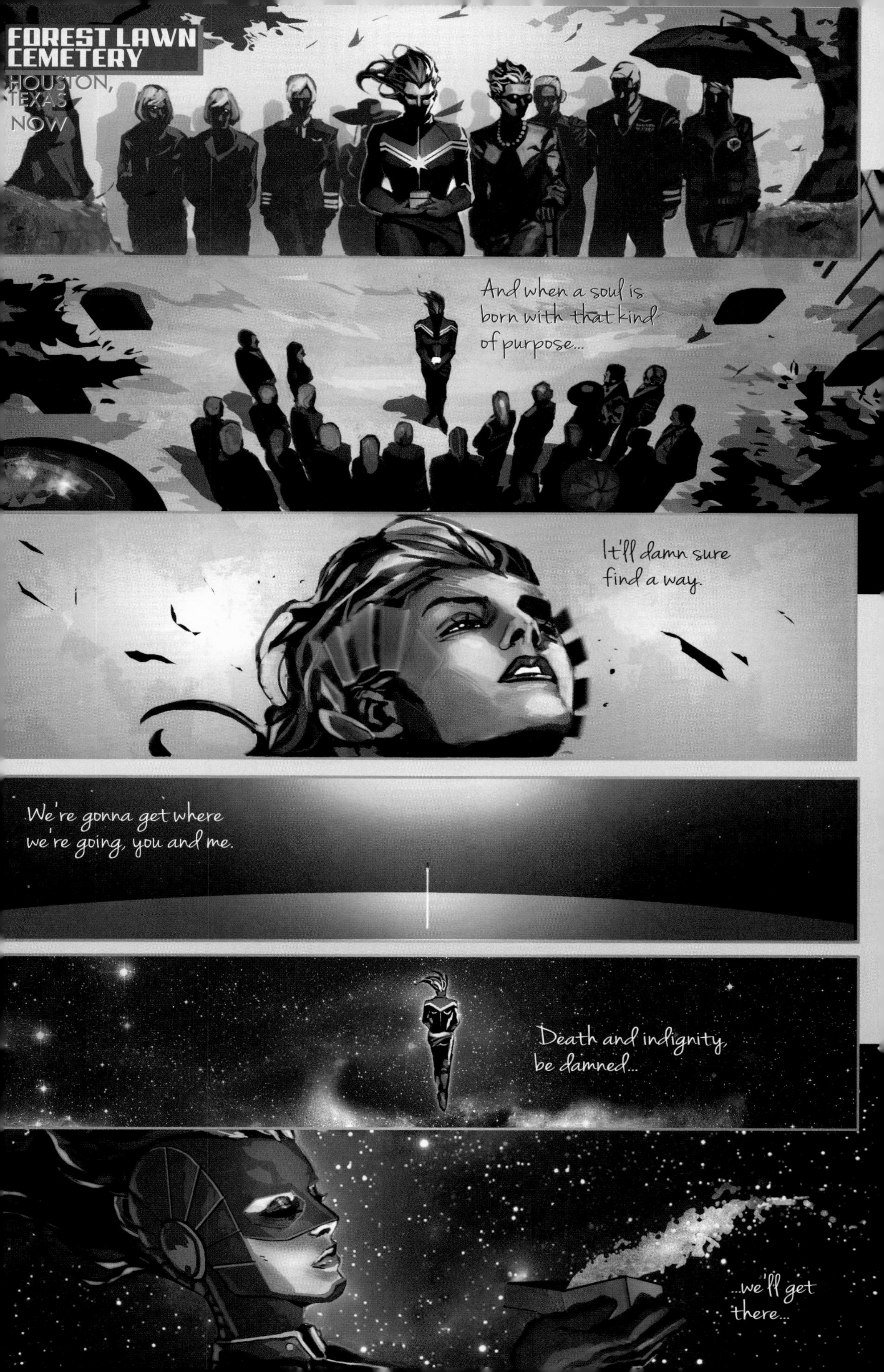
FOREST LAWN CEMETERY
HOUSTON, TEXAS
NOW
And when a soul is born with that kind of purpose...
It'll damn sure find a way.
We're gonna get where we're going, you and me.
Death and indignity, be damned...
...we'll get there...

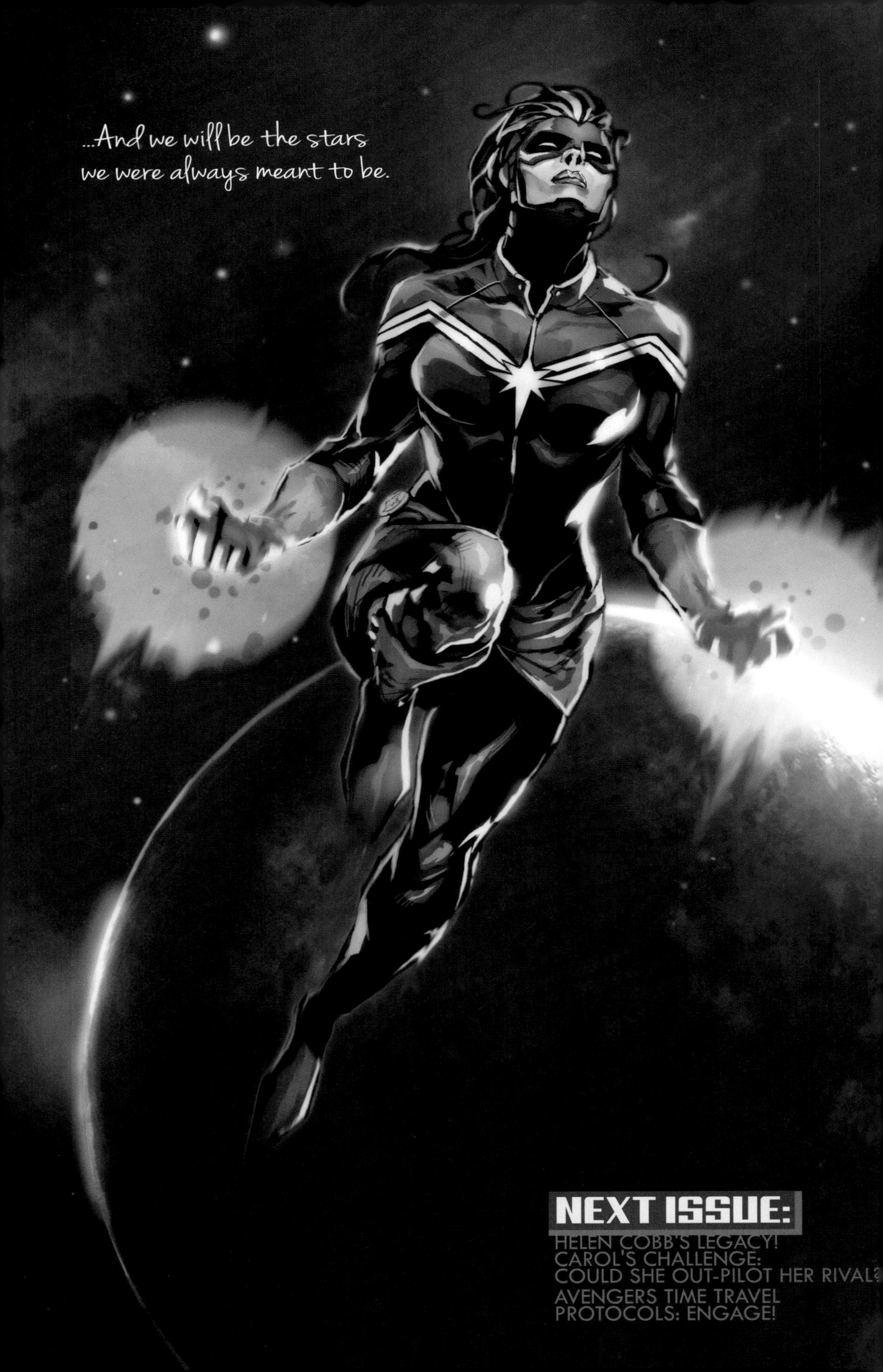
...And we will be the stars we were always meant to be.
NEXT ISSUE:
HELEN COBB'S LEGACY!
CAROL'S CHALLENGE:
COULD SHE OUT-PILOT HER RIVAL?
AVENGERS TIME TRAVEL
PROTOCOLS: ENGAGE!

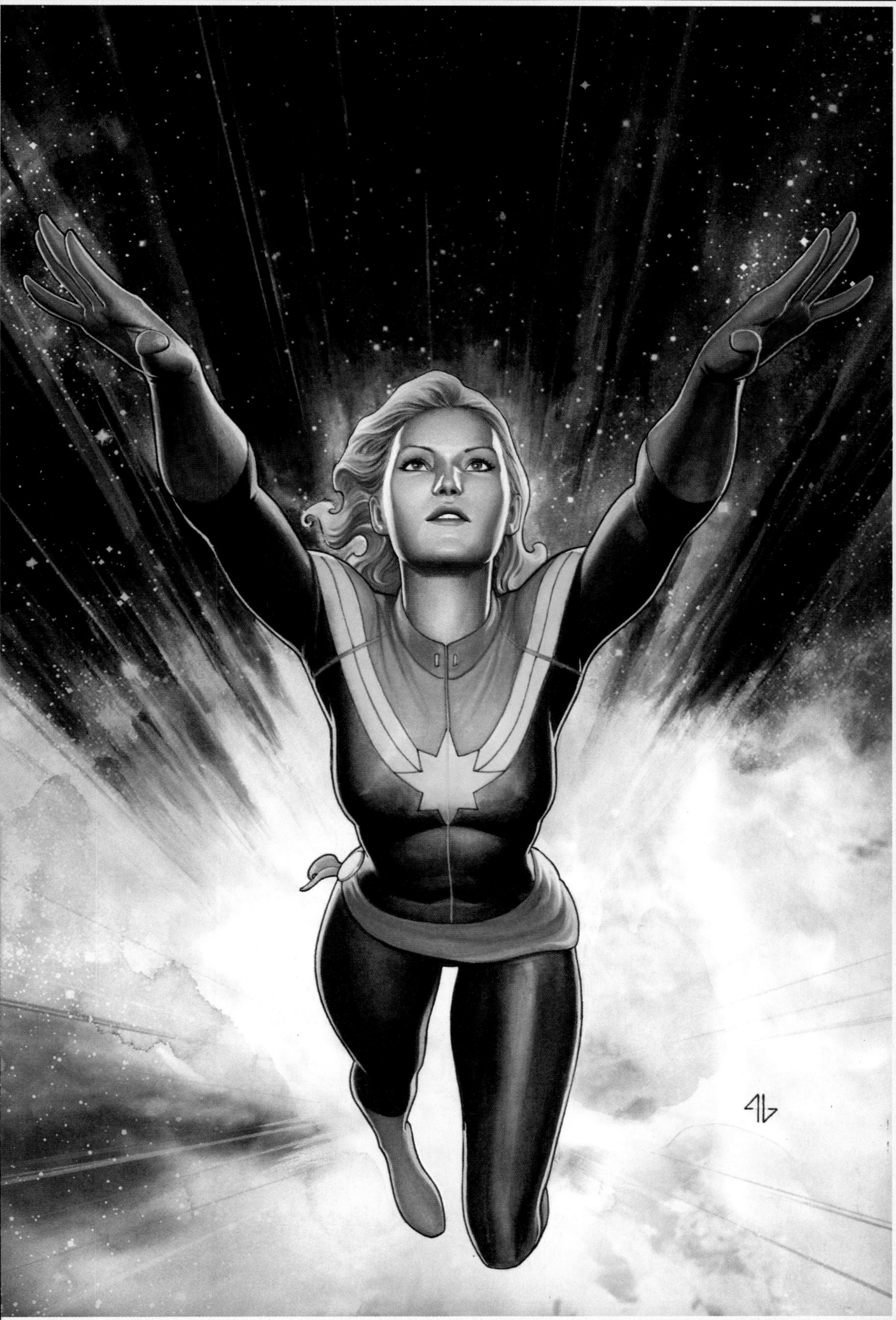

CAPTAIN MARVEL #1 VARIANT BY ADI GRANOV

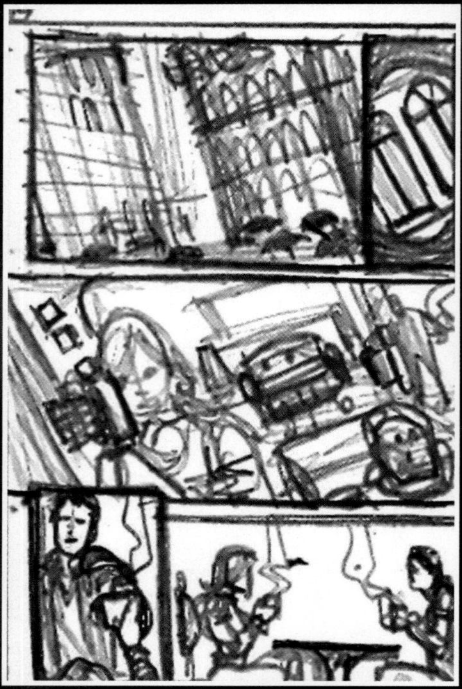

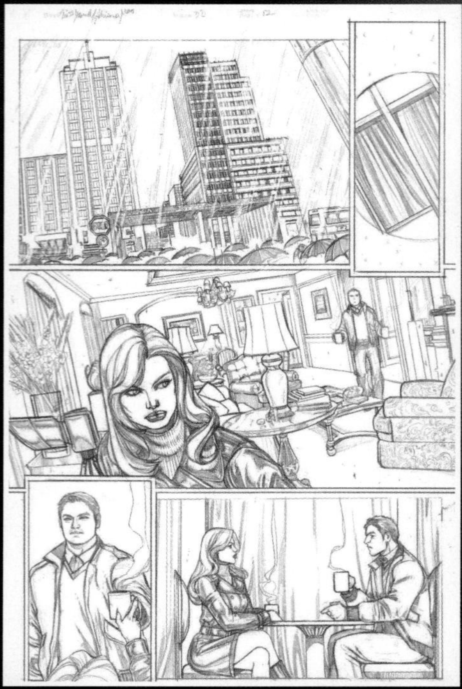

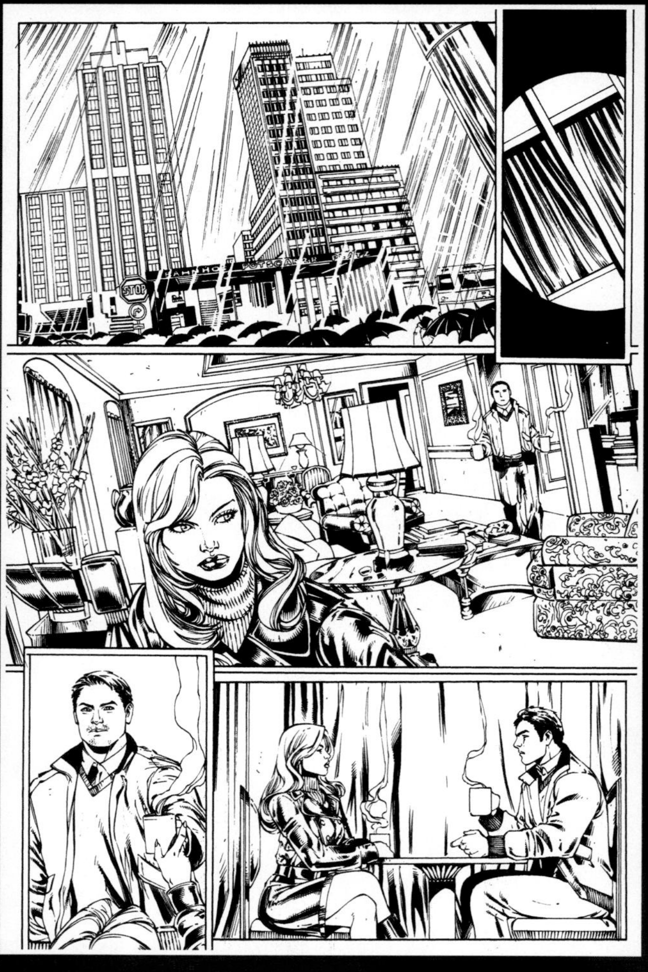
STOP

MS. MARVEL #33, PAGE 12 PROCESS
SKETCH & PENCILS BY ADRIANA MELO, INKS BY MARIAH BENES

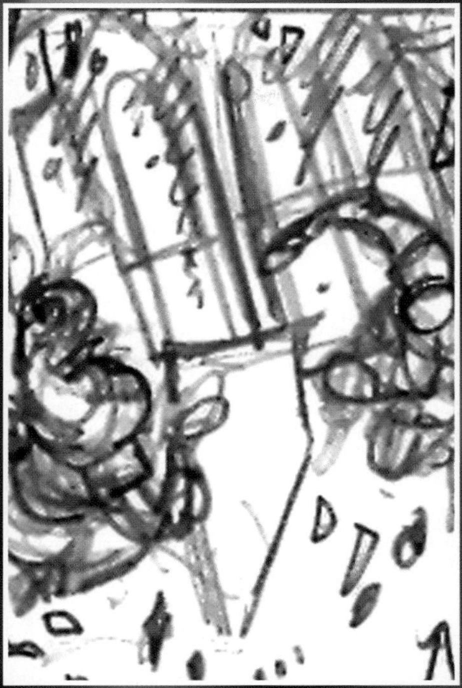

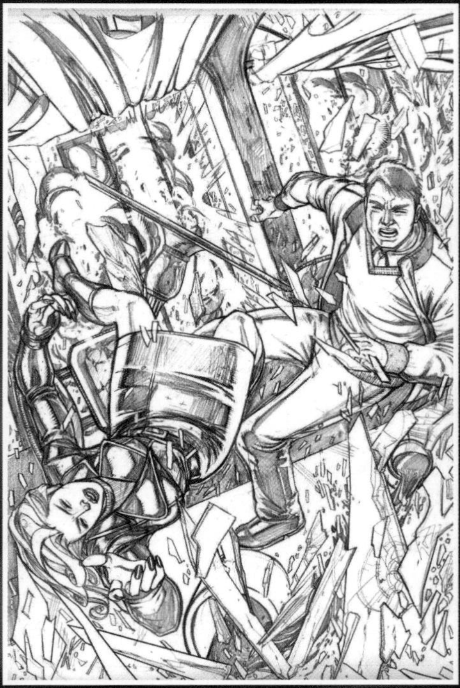

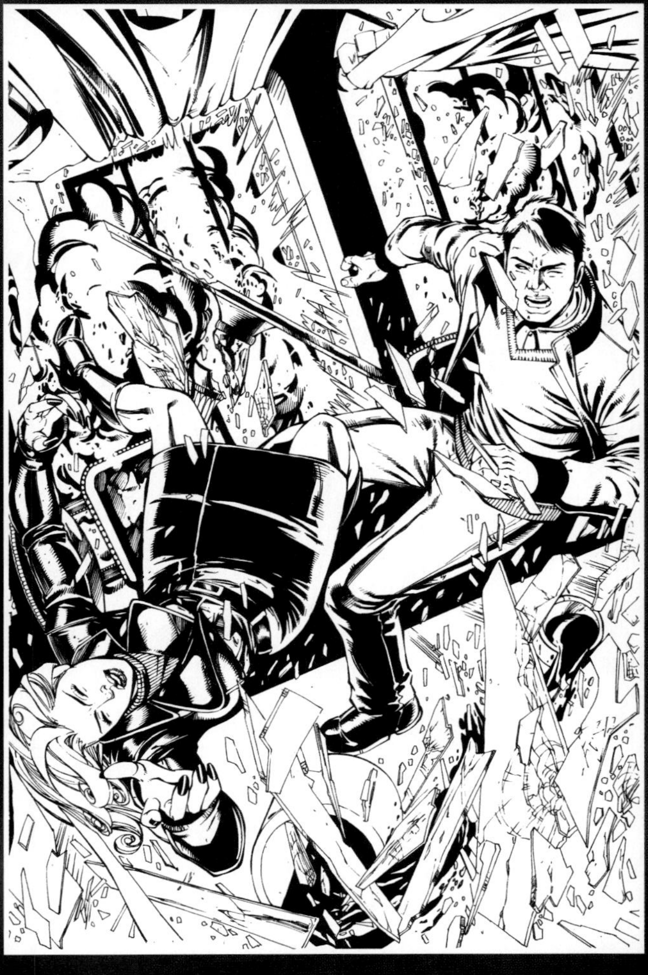

MS. MARVEL #33, PAGE 13 PROCESS
SKETCH & PENCILS BY ADRIANA MELO, INKS BY MARIAH BENES

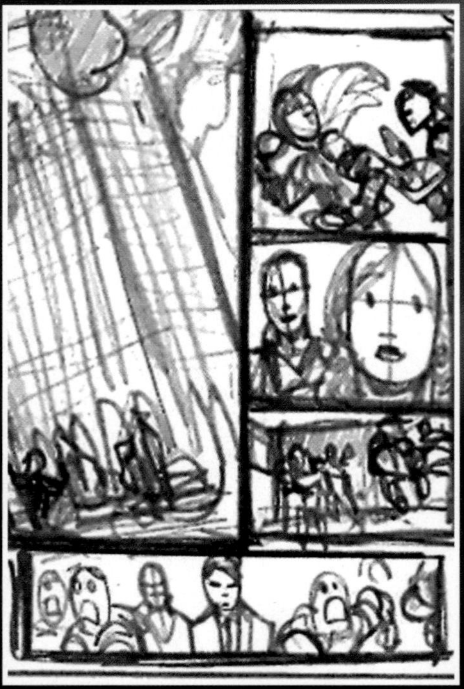

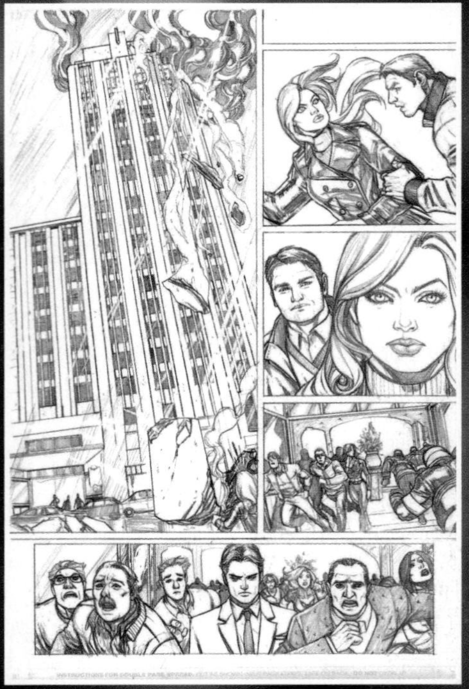

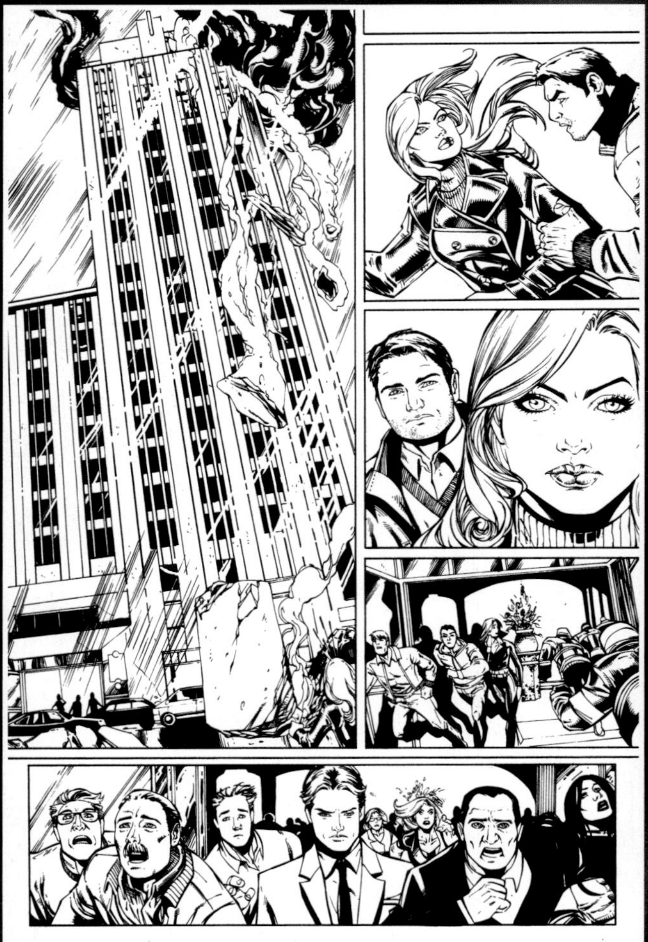